Sociology
and Social Life

Fifth Edition

Sociology
and Social Life

Fifth Edition

Raymond W. Mack
Northwestern University

John Pease
University of Maryland

 **D. Van Nostrand Company**
New York / Cincinnati / Toronto / London / Melbourne

Cartoon Credits

All cartoons reprinted by permission of Jules Feiffer.
pp. 26, 52, 234, 390 from *Hold Me!* Copyright © 1960, 1961, 1962 by Jules Feiffer. Reprinted by permission of Random House, Inc. pp. 78, 200, 474, 512 from *Feiffer's Marriage Manual.* Copyright © 1962, 1967 by Jules Feiffer. Reprinted by permission of Random House, Inc. pp. 108, 154, 180, from *Boy, Girl. Boy, Girl.* Copyright © 1959, 1960, 1961, by Jules Feiffer. Reprinted by permission of Random House, Inc. pp. 128 and 270, copyright © 1956, 1957, 1958 by Jules Feiffer. Previously printed in *Sick, Sick, Sick* (New York: McGraw-Hill, 1958). p. 308, copyright © 1960, 1961, 1962, 1963, 1964, 1965, 1966 by Jules Feiffer. Previously printed in *Feiffer on Civil Rights* (New York: Anti-Defamation League of B'nai B'rith, 1966). p. 339, copyright © 1972 by Jules Feiffer; p. 364, copyright © 1968 by Jules Feiffer; p. 414, copyright © 1962 by Jules Feiffer; p. 442, copyright © 1969 by Jules Feiffer; p. 496, copyright © 1970 by Jules Feiffer. Previously printed in *The New Republic.*

Picture Credits

p. 40 top, Kenneth Murray/Nancy Palmer Agency; p. 40 bottom, Steve Eagle/ Nancy Palmer Agency; p. 41 top, Rita Freed/Nancy Palmer Agency; p. 41 bottom, photograph by Frank Greenagel; p. 166 top and bottom, Kenneth Murray/ Nancy Palmer Agency; p. 167 top and middle, Jim Jowers/Nancy Palmer Agency; p. 167 bottom, Ron Sherman/Nancy Palmer Agency; p. 376 top and middle, photos by © Allen Green/Nancy Palmer Agency; p. 376 bottom, Ron Sherman/ Nancy Palmer Agency; p. 377, photograph by Richard Balagur/Nancy Palmer Agency.

D. Van Nostrand Company Regional Offices:
New York Cincinnati Millbrae

D. Van Nostrand Company International Offices:
London Toronto Melbourne

Copyright © 1973 by Litton Educational Publishing, Inc.

Library of Congress Catalog Card Number: 72 8604

ISBN: 0-442-23367-1

Published by D. Van Nostrand Company
450 West 33rd Street, New York, N. Y. 10001

Published simultaneously in Canada by
Van Nostrand Reinhold Ltd.

10 9 8 7 6 5 4 3

TO
KIMBALL YOUNG
1893–1972
PAST PRESIDENT OF THE AMERICAN SOCIOLOGICAL ASSOCIATION
SCHOLAR, TEACHER, FRIEND
AND SENIOR AUTHOR OF THE FIRST EDITION OF THIS BOOK

Preface

Sociology provides one way of examining social life. As an aid to this examination, sociology has developed a set of concepts making possible the ordering of the features common to a series of observations of human groups, their culture, and their interrelations.

The Fifth Edition of *Sociology and Social Life* retains the main features and the general approach of previous editions, which have proved eminently successful. It is neither an encyclopedia of sociological facts nor a cursory examination of major social problems. Our intention is to furnish the student with a systematic interpretation of the major elements of sociology.

One aim of this text is to provide the fundamentals of sociology for the student who wishes to pursue advanced work in the field. A second aim is to give the student who will take only one sociology course the familiarity with sociology that any liberally educated person should have. It will furnish him a body of knowledge as well as the major conceptual tools of sociological analysis.

This new, revised edition incorporates new photographs, new illustrative data from research literature, bibliographic references to new books, and charts, graphs, and tables reflecting the most recent data available. We have added a chapter on bureaucracy and large-scale organization and a chapter on collective behavior. We have incorporated new textual material in every chapter. In the chapter on population, for example, we have included a section that deals with the demographic transition. We have changed the organization and the order of presentation. The chapters on economics and politics now precede rather than follow the material on family, religion, and education. Chapters 3 and 4, which dealt with culture and the normative structure, have been combined into a single chapter. The separate chapters on class and mobility have also been combined into a single chapter.

We wish to thank Barbara Hetrick and Helen McInnis who contributed a great deal to this edition of the book. We would also like to thank Jules Feiffer for permission to reprint his material. We are deeply appreciative of the many students and teachers who used earlier editions of this book and who were kind enough to send us their evaluations and suggestions for improvement. We hope this book is worthy of their contributions.

Contents

2/Social Organization   153

Sociology
and Social Life

Fifth Edition

1/The Study of
Social Life

1
The
Study of
Sociology

Sociology is the scientific study of the social aspects of human life. It is a body of knowledge, compiled through the use of the scientific method, about the structure and content of social life, that is, the organization of human interaction. Sociologists study the behavior of people in a group context.

"No man is an island, entire of itself." People everywhere deal with other human beings as members of groups. Only in the most exceptional cases do individuals live in isolation, and such isolation is never absolute. Even being a hermit presupposes some social experience; a person needs to learn many things from other human beings before deciding to be a hermit. The decision to be a hermit is a socially induced decision; a person has to participate in a human group to be able to decide to participate no longer.

Every human being is born into a group and spends a lifetime in patterned social relations. Everything we do—crossing the street, naming a boat, choosing a mate, throwing a spear, buying new underwear—is closely bound up with what we expect from others and with what others expect and accept from us. How we act under various circumstances is largely a consequence of the expectations created by interaction with others. Each of us expects certain behaviors from our relatives, friends, and even people we see only casually at a traffic intersection, a bookstore, or the coffee shop between classes, and we are aware that others expect certain behavior from us in such situations. Thus group life is patterned. If we are to understand and explain the actions of people, then we must devote considerable study to the ways in which groups are organized and function. Such a study of social life is the subject matter of sociology.

THE SOCIOLOGICAL PERSPECTIVE

The primary focus of the sociological perspective is the fact that human behavior is social. People do not live separate from one another, each seeking a personal and unique solution to life's problems. People live together sharing a common way of life that patterns and organizes their group existence. People live collectively as well as individually.

Any phenomenon can be viewed from more than one perspective and what we see depends, of course, upon the perspective we assume. One need only recall the variety of ways in which sex is viewed to appreciate the difference perspective makes. For example, the sexual behavior of human beings from the perspective of the so-called swinger is "fun and games," a form of play as natural as breathing. From the perspective of those who write marriage manuals, however, it is "hard work," requiring much effort, study, and preparation. From still other perspectives, sex is seen as "sin" or "love" and so on.

The basic premise of the sociological perspective—and a basic premise of all social science—is that the behavior of people is a consequence of the social situations in which they live. "There is no private life," George Eliot wrote, "that has not been determined by a wider public life."[1] It follows that we come to know ourselves and others by knowing the places we occupy in the social world. The social world of the aristocrat is not the same as that of the agricultural migrant worker; the social organization of the metropolis is different from that of the small town and the social structure of the prison makes for very different patterns of behavior than does the social structure of the commune. The point is that

> The facts of contemporary society are also facts about the success and failure of individual men and women. When a society is industrialized, a peasant becomes a worker; a feudal lord becomes a businessman or

---

[1]George Eliot, *Felix Holt, The Radical,* 3 vols. (Edinburgh: William Blackwell and Sons, 1866), I, 88.

he is liquidated. When classes rise or fall, a man is employed or unemployed. When wars happen, an insurance salesman becomes a rocket launcher; a store clerk becomes a radar expert; a wife lives alone; a child grows up without a father.[2]

Sociology is a disciplined study of the social world; how it is organized and how it changes; how it varies from time to time and from place to place; how it remains the same and how it is interrelated and how it is not.

THE METHOD OF SCIENCE

Sociology is a relatively new social science; to understand the material that sociology covers and what sociologists do and how they do it, it is necessary to have some understanding of what is meant by science. When a student speaks of "taking science this semester," he or she usually means that he or she is learning some of the content of a body of knowledge. The body of knowledge may be labeled physics, or chemistry, or biology. A science, then, is a body of knowledge. But although this definition is correct, it is an inadequate definition because it does not distinguish science from non-science. English literature, philosophy, and eighteenth-century art are bodies of knowledge, too, but we do not consider them sciences. We need a more precise definition.

People often think of science as a laboratory pursuit, and often it is. Sociologists, for example, conduct some studies of small group behavior in highly controlled laboratory settings. But scientific knowledge need not be compiled through the use of test tubes and Bunsen burners. Volcanoes and protest demonstrations, for instance, cannot be adequately studied in a laboratory, let alone a test tube. Most of the data of political science and anthropology are not gathered in laboratories, but they are sciences nonetheless.

Articles and advertisements in popular periodicals tempt one to equate science with control. The Sunday supplement often has a feature telling the reader how to make other people do what he or she wishes by "using psychology" on them. Other columns assure us that scientists have made it possible to control the environment in myriad ways: we can drive to town on tires that will not endanger life by blowing out; power steering allows us to steer an automobile comfortably with one hand so that, with the other, we can light a cigarette from which scientists have removed the ingredient that used to stain teeth; and finally, having arrived at the drugstore, we can purchase a scientifically compounded toothpaste

[2]C. Wright Mills, *The Sociological Imagination* (New York: Oxford University Press, 1959), p. 3. Reprinted by permission.

that will prevent tooth decay. But there are sciences that do not offer us control of either our social or our physical environment. Astronomy, for example, is a body of knowledge which we classify as a science; but the astronomer does not exercise any control over the courses or rates of movement of the heavenly bodies.

What, then, is the common factor that leads us to classify certain bodies of knowledge as science? It is the way in which the knowledge is obtained. The identification of a field of knowledge as a science rests on the method used to acquire that knowledge. Knowledge obtained by what we call the *scientific method* is referred to as *scientific*; those who utilize this method to add to a body of knowledge we call *scientists*; and a body of related knowledge compiled by the method is designated a *science*.

THE CHARACTER OF SCIENCE

Three of the most essential characteristics of science, characteristics which go far toward explaining the scientific method and the activity of scientists, are empiricism, theory, and public verifiability.

Empiricism is the method or practice of obtaining knowledge from observation, experience, or experiment. A valid method of gaining knowledge is through the senses: sight, hearing, taste, smell, and touch. When a person "just has the feeling, deep inside him," that the Chicago Cubs will win the World Series, he is not basing his conclusion on empirical evidence gained through the senses. When Aristotle assumed that a horse had a certain number of teeth because that seemed a reasonable number of teeth for a horse to have, he was not proceeding empirically. Had he looked inside the mouths of a number of horses to find out how many teeth were there, or reached inside to touch and count them, he would have had empirical evidence—straight, indeed, from the horse's mouth!

Sociologists listen to people talking in small groups. They try to hear the difference in the tone of a murmuring crowd during a theater intermission, a cheering crowd at a ball game, and a roaring mob at a lynching. They taste the food which one group selects for picnics and another group defines as ceremonially unclean. They smell the perfume that is said to make a woman attractive, and they observe the smoke from chemical plants that influence people to sell their houses and move. They touch and compare what factory workers describe as a good and a bad welding job, and they watch the facial expressions of teachers supervising poor students. By no means least importantly, they observe the discrepancies between what people say and what they do. They use their senses to gather data about the behavior of human groups.

To be sure, scientists often use instruments in gathering data,

ILLUSTRATIVE DATA 1–1   VERBAL ATTITUDES AND OVERT BEHAVIOR

Three social scientists studied the difference between what people say and what they do in an exclusive suburb in northeastern United States. As part of this study, two young white women entered a fashionable restaurant and were seated. A young Negro woman then came into the restaurant, asked for her party, and was seated with the two whites. They were served courteously and without incident. The three young women went through this procedure in eleven different restaurants. In only two of the restaurants did the mixed group seem to attract any attention. They were served without protest in all eleven dining rooms.

The social scientists waited two weeks, then sent a letter to the manager of each of the eleven restaurants requesting a reservation for a table for an interracial party. Seventeen days later, not one of the letters had been answered.

They then called the managers on the telephone and inquired about the request they had mailed for a reservation. Eight of the managers denied having ever received the letter. Of the eleven, five finally approved the request for a reservation, although each of the five approvals was tentative or qualified in some way.

The next day, each of the restaurants was called again on the telephone, and a reservation was requested, but without any mention of race. Ten accepted the reservation without qualification; the eleventh stated that no reservation was necessary.

The responses to serving an interracial group of customers ranged from avoidance (to the letter) through reluctance and evasion (to the phone call) to acceptance (in the face-to-face situation). All of these responses constitute human interaction, and so are of interest to sociologists. A person's response to a letter or to a phone call (or to a questionnaire or an interview) is behavior. As human behavior, such responses merit interpretation; they are raw material from which one constructs a theory. But we should note that responses to questionnaires, interviewers, letters, and phone calls are not necessarily straightforward predictions of what interaction patterns will be, or what social behavior will be in a face-to-face situation.

Source: Bernard Kutner, Carol Wilkins, and P. R. Yarrow, "Verbal Attitudes and Overt Behavior Involving Racial Prejudice," *The Journal of Abnormal and Social Psychology,* XLVII (July, 1952), 649–652.

but these are devices that serve to extend the senses in much the same way that a magnifying glass extends the eyesight. The most refined gauge must be read by a competent person if it is to contribute to the accumulation of knowledge. The thermometer does not feel temperature; the ruler does not measure distance; the stethoscope does not hear a heartbeat. These are only auxiliary to the human senses; it is the eye and ear of the person using the devices that make of their sensitive indications a scientific observation.

Parenthetically, method should not be confused with technique. Administering a questionnaire is a technique which sociologists use, just as making a microscopic slide is a technique which biologists use. A technique is a tool for gathering or analyzing data. So too, interviewing is a technique; but science is an overall method of gaining knowledge.

Another characteristic of science is theory. A valid method of organizing knowledge is through the use of reason. We organize knowledge by making statements which relate one fact to other facts—that is, by formulating a theory. A scientific theory is a set of logically related propositions based on empirical data.

There is a widespread belief that scientists are persons who "let the facts speak for themselves." Facts never speak for themselves. Facts have no meaning unless they are seen in relationship to other facts. During our lives we all acquire a considerable amount of information which we may bring to bear upon each new fact we learn. We tend to be unaware that our brains are cataloging the newly presented information by reference to other knowledge which we already possess.

If, for example, a friend tells us that the temperature outside today is 74, we are inclined to think that this fact is meaningful by itself. Actually, it would take pages to list all the facts to which we relate this one. Here are a few. Obviously, each word in our friend's sentence has a meaning for us because we were reared in a society where English is the standard language. Then too, we are familiar with a Fahrenheit scale for measuring temperatures and know that in ordinary conversation we refer to this scale rather than to the centigrade scale. We know that water boils at 212, that it freezes at 32, that normal room temperature in our society is about 70, etc. Our conclusion—that it is unseasonably warm or cool today, or about what one would expect—indicates a knowledge of the time of year, the geographic location, and some information about temperatures in this area at this season in previous years. This simple illustration points up what we mean when we refer to a science as a body of knowledge: it is a body of knowledge because it consists of facts which have been organized with relation to one another by reason.

When we can put in order a set of related propositions—for example, what variations in temperature have to do with variations in air pressure and volume—this set of related statements constitutes a theory.

Another characteristic of scientific data is that it is publicly verifiable. A valid method of checking knowledge is through the independent conclusions of a number of competent observers. One of the reasons we sometimes have to wait so long to gain access to a scientific discovery is that a relationship between facts which seems apparent to one competent observer has not been validated by others, and hence is not yet accepted by scientists as part of scientific knowledge. It is not unknown in human experience for one observer to see small winged beings descending from the clouds, to hear them speak to him, and even to touch them. But because other competent observers cannot see, hear, or touch them, their existence is not accepted as scientific fact. Scientists sometimes agree on the data they observe, but they may disagree on what the data actually mean.[3]

THE VALUES OF SCIENCE

The scientific method is an attempt to be completely objective. The scientist tries to separate his own wishes and values from the process of observation. His own conditioning influences his choice of problems to study, of course, but he tries not to let categories of perception that he has acquired in the normal process of living influence his observation or interpretation of what he actually does find. He has absorbed from his society its values, its norms, and its way of thinking. That is exactly why he utilizes the scientific method: to attempt to get outside himself and his milieu in order to see his physical and social environment as he would if he had not acquired a whole set of notions concerning the way it seems to be. There are many jokes that illustrate the scientist's attempt to be completely objective, such as the story of the man on the train who commented to his seatmate, a scientist, "The sheep in that field have just been sheared," and the scientist replied, "They seem to have been, on this side."

This reluctance to overcommit oneself is the caution of a person who does not want to let preconceived ideas bias his or her observations. The stereotype of the absent-minded professor is perhaps not so derogatory as we sometimes assume; it is a portrait of a person who removes himself or herself from the ordinary human world of prejudice and emotion, who strives as a scientist to be an objective, unbiased, rational person.

---

[3]For a list of facts in social science which have been validated by agreement among observers and a study of the nature of such facts, see Robert C. Hanson, "Evidence and Procedure Characteristics of 'Reliable' Propositions in Social Science," *The American Journal of Sociology*, 1958, 63: 357–370. In addition, more than one thousand propositions about human behavior, with the supporting evidence, are reported in Bernard Berelson and Gary A. Steiner, *Human Behavior: An Inventory of Scientific Findings* (New York: Harcourt, Brace, and World, Inc., 1964).

In the world of science knowledge is only true until further notice. There is no theory so sacred nor any fact so absolute that it is beyond question and further study. Science as a body of knowledge is continually changing, more often because of new discoveries than because of the disproval of previous "facts." When what is learned today is added to what was known yesterday, our total understanding is often altered. Scientific knowledge is cumulative. Einstein's theory of relativity does not show that Newton's scientific facts were wrong; it only explains more about particular phenomena.

Finally, scientists generally assume that knowledge per se is worthwhile. The scientist does not assume that only facts about people are important and that facts about animals are not; or that only facts about economics are worth gathering and that information about religion is not; or that only data for which some immediate practical use can be found is worth pursuing and that study in other areas is useless. If the last assumption were held, for example, we would not be able to generate power to heat, light, and operate large factories with atomic energy; for when Einstein worked out the formula which led eventually to the splitting of the atom, his research had no immediate practical use. He was pursuing knowledge for its own sake; as a scientist, he valued the idea of giving humankind more knowledge than it previously possessed.

THE EXPERIMENTAL MODEL

The ideal model for scientific research is the classical experimental design (the controlled experiment).[4] This is a research design that requires the comparison of two groups (the experimental group and the control group) at two different points in time (before and after). The two groups must be identical at the beginning of the experiment (the "before" stage). A change (the experimental variable) is then induced in the experimental group but no change is effected in the control group. The control group is used to determine what change takes place "normally" with the passage of time and without the introduction of the experimental variable. The effect of the experiment is measured by looking at the change in both groups, and then subtracting the change (if any) in the control

---

[4]See Samuel A. Stouffer, "Some Observations on Study Design," *The American Journal of Sociology*, LV (January, 1955), 355–361. See also F. Stuart Chapin, *Experimental Designs in Sociological Research* (New York: Harper and Brothers, 1947); Ernest Greenwood, *Experimental Sociology* (New York: King's Crown Press, 1945); and John Stuart Mill, *A System of Logic* (London: Longmans, Green, Reader, and Dyer, 1872), Vol. I, Bk. III, Chap. viii, pp. 448–471.

Figure 1-1   Classical Experimental Design

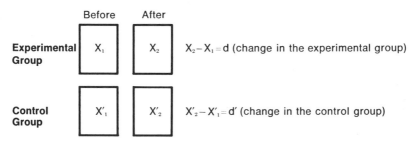

$X_2 - X_1 = d$ (change in the experimental group)

$X'_2 - X'_1 = d'$ (change in the control group)

$d - d' =$ the difference due to the experimental variable

group from the change (if any) in the experimental group. (See Figure 1-1.)

Scientists are not always able to follow the classical experimental design in their research. Sometimes they research or describe only one part of the situation (x_2 of Figure 1-1, for example). Sometimes the research involves a before and after comparison of an experimental group (x_1 and x_2) without comparable data for a control group. Research sometimes constitutes a comparison of two matched groups at one point in time (x_2 and x'_2). And some research is based on observations of one group at one time and a different group at another time (x_1 and x'_2).

The difficulties of doing research that meets the standards of the classical experimental design is one reason that statistical analysis is widely used in sociology. Probability statistics, for example, are used to estimate the "missing data" in situations where the data are not otherwise available. Although it is not always possible to meet the ideal model of a controlled experiment, one must be aware of the goal and keep it constantly in mind when evaluating research studies.

It should be emphasized that not everything that gets called science is science. Just as there was alchemy before there was a science of chemistry, so there were political philosophers who attempted to convert the lead of their opinions into the gold of facts before there were political scientists willing to employ the scientific method to learn about human political behavior. Even today one finds people who call themselves economists, sociologists, and political scientists whose primary concern is to reform the world in line with their own values or to gain recognition as experts by speculating about the course which society is taking, and who have no intention of risking their pet notions by subjecting them to empirical tests. During the past half-century, however, a larger and larger proportion of people have been interested in utilizing the scientific method to learn more about the various forms of behavior of human beings in social groups.

SOCIOLOGY AND SOCIAL SCIENCE

By *social science* we mean those bodies of knowledge compiled through the scientific method which deal with the forms and contents of human interaction. To be social is to interact, to participate in group life.

Social Environment

All human beings are social. People have to interact with other people in order to survive. Since all human beings live in a society —which is to say that every person is a member of some human group—it is just as reasonable to speak of social environment as to speak, as people more often do, of physical environment. People are profoundly influenced by their social as well as their physical surroundings. The three-year-old son of a steel mill laborer in Pittsburgh who is taken from his home and reared by foster parents in a steel mill laborer's family in Birmingham, England, not only will talk and act differently than if he had remained in Pittsburgh, but will think differently as well. The change in his physical environment will have been minimal; the alteration in his behavior will be traceable to the difference in the two social environments. As the physicist, the chemist, the astronomer, and the biologist study the universe in which we live and the elements of which it is composed in an attempt to understand our physical environment and to predict what will happen in any given set of circumstances, so the social scientist studies the social environment in which we live in an attempt to understand human society and to predict how people will interact in different sets of circumstances.

Some social scientists concentrate their study on a single aspect of the social environment. Political scientists utilize the scientific method to compile information about the interaction which occurs as people attempt to maintain order in their societies. Economists assemble knowledge about what takes place in the production and distribution of goods and services. Cultural anthropologists seek to ascertain the relationships between the political, economic, religious, and familial behavior of persons within a given society, or to contrast the ways in which people in different societies come to fulfill the same needs.

Other social scientists are concerned primarily with social phenomena that are relatively unique; they observe, record, and attempt to interpret interactions that are not recurrent. Historians

The Christian religion was launched by poor people. The Apostles were poor people with little secular power, mostly laboring folk, at the bottom of the political and economic order. Jesus himself, short of being born a slave, could hardly have been of humbler origins in a world of Roman hegemony.

As the Christian faith became organized into a church, with a hierarchy, rules, and traditions (or as sociologists say, became institutionalized), who became its most revered members? Two scholars have analyzed data concerning 2,489 saints whom they were able to catalogue by the century in which they died and by the social class into which they were born.

Their principal source of data for the study was The Lives of the Saints *by Alban Butler, a set of volumes compiled by an English Catholic priest over a period of thirty years and first published in the eighteenth century. (Herbert Thurston et al., eds.,* Butler's Lives of the Saints, *rev. ed., 12 volumes, New York: P. J. Kennedy and Sons, 1926–1938.)*

Of the 2,489 saints, 78 per cent were born into the upper class. The middle class accounted for 17 per cent. Only 5 per cent were members of the lower class. In addition, a high proportion of the saints from lower- and middle-class backgrounds lived during the first four centuries of the Church's existence. Of all the saints from lower-class origins, for example, nearly half lived in the first five centuries. Between the fifth and fifteenth centuries, virtually all of the saints were from upper-class backgrounds.

This set of figures illustrates a problem which faces all scientists: what do the data mean? Compiling the data is one thing; interpreting them is another. A militant anticlerical scholar and a devout churchman might agree on the numbers they see and the categories under which they are listed, but they might also invoke quite different theories to explain them.

Sociologists know that power gives one access to privilege, that prestige can be a potent bargaining agent for gaining esteem. Many students of power and stratification would view the social class distribution of the saints as a typical example of the workings of a system of rank, popularly phrased as "Them as has gits." An industrial sociologist or a student of bureaucracy and large-scale organization could point to parallels: awards for distinguished service in a corporation are more likely to go to vice-presidents than to laborers. The authors of the study conclude that "The value systems of stratified societies, particularly in their more extreme and exacting aspects, are typically encapsulated in and radiated by privileged and ruling groups. It is to be expected that individual members of these groups will be the ones most frequently and most adequately to embody and express these values in their lives."

Source: Katherine George and Charles H. George, "Roman Catholic Sainthood and Social Status," in Reinhard Bendix and Seymour Martin Lipset, *Class, Status, and Power: Social Stratification in Comparative Perspective,* 2nd edition, New York: The Free Press, 1966, pp. 394–401.

may draw parallels between the French Revolution and happenings
in other times and places, but their primary concern is the unique-
ness of human events; that is why a historian is more likely to be
known as an authority on eighteenth-century France than as an expert on revolutions. The field of sociology is different from history
in this respect. Its major concern is not with the unique in human
events but with the similarities among social structures and the recurring nature of patterns of social interaction.

THE FIELD OF SOCIOLOGY

The difference between the generalizing focus of sociology and
the more specialized focus in fields such as economics and political
science is well stated by Pitirim A. Sorokin.[5] Sorokin suggests that
the interactions which the economist studies be represented by letters, a, b, c, n, m, and f. The human behavior of interest to the political scientist can be called a, b, c, h, d, and j. Another social
science might have as its subject matter those interactions represented by the letters a, h, c, g, i, and q. The first concern of the sociologist would be those social elements and relationships found
among human beings whether they are acting as familial groups, say,
or as political groups, or in economic pursuits: a, b, and c. Sociologists, then, study human interaction as such. They try to learn the
likenesses among people in groups, no matter what the particular
orientation of the group may be.

Specialities Within Sociology

The general sociologist devotes himself to understanding universal social structures, such as groups and publics, and universal social
processes, such as competition and cooperation. Much of what is
synthesized into general sociological principles, however, is learned
from research carried out in specialized areas of sociology such as
the sociology of the family, of law, of the city, of education. Scholars work in these more restricted areas in order to narrow their
field of observation. They attempt to gain new insights by exploring
one area of interaction intensively instead of making a broad survey
of all human groups. This gives them an opportunity to make certain kinds of contributions to general sociology. First, they may un-
cover previously unnoted social phenomena of the type represented
by a, b, and c in the Sorokin formula. For example, a specialist

[5]Pitirim A. Sorokin, *Society, Culture, and Personality* (New York: Harper &
Brothers, 1947), pp. 6–18.

studying family organization may note that, as the family loses some of its functions to schools, public recreational facilities, and government agencies, it becomes less stable. Second, they may add to the body of knowledge about such interactions. Other sociologists may conclude from the findings of the family specialist that as any group loses functions, it loses stability. Third, specialization permits sociologists to note cases where some variation, say, in h, d, or f is accompanied by variation in g, i, or q. Thus the sociologist doing research in family organization may find that wherever families are decreasing in size, the literacy level of the population is increasing. This poses the question of whether one of the happenings is causing the other, or whether both are traceable to a third factor or variable.

Just as the delimitation of the scientist's field of observation through specialization has proved a fruitful procedure in the development of many disciplines, such as physics, chemistry, biology, and psychology, a number of the best-established principles in sociology have been derived from research in the fields of population, criminology, industry, the family, and so on.

HANDICAPS TO SOCIOLOGY

Science is the most fruitful way of observing, classifying, and interpreting physical and social environments. We are all aware of the great strides in the physical and biological sciences which have made possible modern industry and agriculture, rapid transportation and communication, and the control of disease. Yet we find people are often loath to take an objective viewpoint and apply the empirical method of science to personal and social problems. We would ridicule a person who, if an automobile did not start, would say that the engine was evil or curse the steel from which it was made. We consider ignorant, at best, the person who attempts to set a broken leg with magic incantations. Many people, however, who consider the scientific method a useful device for establishing the principles on which an automobile is built or a leg is set nevertheless resist with great emotion the suggestion that the same method might reveal knowledge and understanding about how people select mates or why some persons in a society become criminals. There are at least five reasons why such negative attitudes exist.

Resistance to Social Change

The ways of humans are hedged in by inertia. People stubbornly resist innovations which exert pressure on them to alter their socially shared values and beliefs. We need not go back to Galileo or other medieval examples; it was less than fifty years ago that a schoolteacher in Tennessee was tried in court for teaching his students about the theory of evolution.

Social facts are considerably more emotion-laden, of course, than physical facts. When physicists announce that they have learned something new about the way atoms behave, few people are excited about the discovery. They are not personally acquainted with any atoms; their parents did not teach them that good, moral atoms behave in a certain way; and they feel no obligation to revise their day-to-day thinking or behavior because of the physicists' discovery. But when sociologists announce that they have learned something new about how human groups behave, many people are likely to be agitated. They feel that their own observations of their acquaintances are just as valid as the studies of social scientists. Since their parents have taught them that good, moral people behave in a certain way, scientific knowledge about human behavior may threaten to make them feel obligated to revise their own day-to-day thinking and behavior. It takes a considerable amount of conscious effort to abandon ways of thinking to which one has become accustomed, and most people resist new knowledge, even though rationally arrived at, in favor of old superstitions or prejudices. If we have long believed that people who live in the country are happier than those who live in the city, or that white people are more intelligent than blacks, or that contact between groups of persons who resent and distrust each other will get rid of their hostility, then it is easier to reject the evidence of social scientists who inform us that these beliefs are prejudices and superstitions than it is to abandon our beliefs because the scientific evidence runs counter to them.

That people do resist facts which will force them to alter their thinking can be observed in most college classrooms where knowledge about social life is being presented. The phenomenon has been called the "my Aunt Emma" response: the demonstration of a preference for one's personal experience over observations from scientific research whenever the two are in disagreement. The instructor in a sociology class, for example, reads from a United States Census report, "On the basis of interviews with millions of people, we conclude that the average high-school teacher has a larger annual income than the average factory laborer." A student replies, "Well, I don't think that's true, because my Aunt Emma is a teacher and her husband works in a factory and his income is higher than hers." That his personal observation may be perfectly accurate without disproving the census-based generalization may not occur to Aunt Emma's nephew.

Common Sense

People everywhere develop certain standardized answers to questions about people and society that come to be accepted more or less uncritically. One of the difficulties that many of us experience is learning that some of the facts about which we are most certain are false. Because sociology (and the other social sciences) so often deals with matters about which we all have some knowledge, sociology sometimes confronts people with knowledge that is contrary to their "common sense." But common sense is often vague and contradictory. Suppose, for example, that you were to undertake a research study to determine if the statement "persons who work alone are more efficient than persons who work in groups of two or more" is true or false. If, on the basis of your research you learn that the statement is true, you may be certain that someone will tell you that what you learned is only common sense: "Everyone knows that too many cooks spoil the broth." If you find the statement to be false, you may also be certain that someone will tell you that what you learned is only common sense: "Everyone knows that two heads are better than one." The point is that common sense is usually vague and often contradictory. On the one hand we are told to "look before you leap" while on the other hand we are told that "he who hesitates is lost." Common sense is like calling a spade a spade, all the while confusing cards with shovels.

Not only is common sense sometimes vague and contradictory, it is often false and always socially relative. What is common and sensible to the very poor in the United States, for example, is often surprising and fascinating to the middle classes. What is common sense to the Amish of Pennsylvania may not be common or sensible to social workers in San Francisco. All this is not meant to denigrate common sense. On the contrary, the more common the sense, the better it is. Just remember that "common sense" is often neither common nor sensible.

Ethnocentrism

Throughout history, people everywhere have displayed an interest in themselves and other members of their own group. Enthusiasm for observing human behavior is, of course, a long first step toward social science. This enthusiasm is usually accompanied, however, by an attitude that is a serious deterrent to the development of social science. Members of any society tend to believe that their way of thinking and doing things is not only the best way but the only right way. This belief that the ways of one's own group are superior

---

ILLUSTRATIVE DATA 1–3   ETHNOCENTRISM

The following is the reply received by the 1744 Virginia Commission when it offered to educate six Indian youths at the College of William and Mary:

Several of our young people were formerly brought up at Colleges of the Northern Provinces; they were instructed in all your sciences; but when they came back to us, they were bad runners, ignorant of every means of living in the woods, unable to bear either cold or hunger, knew neither how to build a cabin, take a deer, or kill an enemy, spoke our language imperfectly, were therefore neither fit for hunters, warriors, or counsellors; they were totally good for nothing. We are, however, not the less obliged by your kind offer, though we decline accepting it; and to show our grateful Sense of it, if the Gentlemen of Virginia will send us a Dozen of their Sons we will take great care of their education, instruct them in all we know, and make Men of them.

Source: Quoted in T. Walter Wallbank and Alastair M. Taylor, *Civilization: Past and Present*, rev. ed. (Chicago: Scott, Foresman and Company, 1949), Vol. I, pp. 559–560.

to all others is called *ethnocentrism*. The Navaho of the southwestern United States refer to themselves as "Dineh"—"The People." Germans speak of *das Ausland*, collecting all countries outside Germany into a single noun. The ancient Jews classified themselves as "the Chosen People"; in ancient Greece there were only Greeks and barbarians. When the Greenland Eskimos first had white visitors, the highest compliment they could pay a white man was to say that he was, or soon would be, as good as a Greenlander. We in America have long had a tendency to lump all persons who are not members of our own society into one inferior category: foreigners.

It is easy usually for us to see ethnocentrism among foreigners. But when we read in the newspapers that free enterprise is the best possible economic system, most of us do not recognize this statement as probably an illustration of ethnocentrism. We are usually ethnocentric, too, in the way we accept the statement as "true." It may indeed be true, but we accept it not because of the evidence—which most of us don't know—but because we are ethnocentric. No category of persons, not even scientists, is free from ethnocentrism. That is why it is so difficult for an American scientist to evaluate objectively an experiment contrasting democratic and authoritarian leadership.

Science as a way to knowledge does not serve the purposes of one political group better than those of another. There is no such thing, scientifically speaking, as Methodist sociology, or Italian physics, or what the leaders of the Soviet Union call "bourgeois genetics." Until people free themselves from this mode of thinking, ethnocentrism will be an obstacle to the development of science.

Closely linked to ethnocentrism is the widespread tendency to see personal and social problems and their possible solutions as either good or bad, or right or wrong. We assign facts, situations, and people that we fear or do not like or understand to the category of the evil or dangerous. That with which we agree or with which we feel comfortable is, we say, "all right."

Confusion of Science and Engineering

Scientists assume that any knowledge, whether or not it is "practical," is worthwhile. There is a crucial difference between the scientist, who discovers knowledge, and the engineer, who applies it. The physicist discovers the laws of mass and volume; the engineer applies these laws in constructing a bridge. Sir Alexander Fleming, a bacteriologist, discovered penicillin; the physician who injects penicillin into a patient is acting, not as a scientist, but as an engineer applying knowledge discovered by a scientist. The social worker does not test hypotheses in order to evaluate a scientific theory; he applies the knowledge furnished him by sociologists and other social scientists. In other words, he is a social engineer. No invidious comparison between scientists and those who apply scientific knowledge is implied. It is important, however, to understand the differences in what they are attempting to do and how they are attempting to do it. Much of the contemporary criticism of the social sciences stems from the fact that some (amateur?) social engineers try to apply knowledge that social scientists have not yet validated.

The goal of the engineer forces him to be concerned with what will work, with principles that are immediately applicable. The goal of the scientist is to pursue with equal concern projects which have no obvious applicability as well as those that do. If there is a possibility that observations of two sets of physical or social phenomena may lead to the understanding of some significant relationship between them, the scientist is interested in those observations, whether or not they seem to offer a way to control disease, build bridges, or make money. He is aware that much of the most valuable information in the storehouse of science, such as that about atomic structures cited earlier in this chapter, had no immediate or obvious applicability at the time research leading to it was initiated. Pressures on scholars to engage only in "useful" research can do much to deter the development of science.

Inefficiency of Terminology

Words are the essential tools of thought, scientific and otherwise. All sciences require a clear and unambiguous terminology. The physical and biological scientists have solved this problem by creating complex technical vocabularies, as any freshman struggling to memorize biological terms well knows. In most of the social sciences however, the answer has not been so simple. First, many of the terms of the social sciences are words also found in everyday speech, and words in general usage are notoriously vague. Thus the word "instinct" once had a rather technical meaning in psychology and biology but, because of its literary and everyday meaning as any more or less learned but automatic response, it has been abandoned by scientists. Second, the language of sociology and psychology, because it is also the language of everyday speech, tends to be emotionally charged. Thus, if a sociologist asks on a questionnaire, "Are you a political conservative?" he may get a stream of disgust or affirmation instead of an answer, and even if the interviewee tries to answer honestly, there is no assurance that he and the scientist will be using the term *conservative* in the same way. Thus the sociologist must constantly try to prune his speech of even remotely emotionally charged words and to guard against his own human reaction to connotative language.

Science and Religion

In addition to the five roadblocks to sociology which we have discussed—resistance to social change, common sense, ethnocentrism, the confusion of engineering with science, and the terminological inefficiency—there is a traditional block for some persons to the acceptance of the scientific study of society: the notion that science is opposed to religion.

Science and religion have come into conflict in the past over matters of dogma, not ethics. The famous religion-versus-science dramas of history have occurred when scientists turned up evidence which made some theological dogma seem extremely unlikely—for example, the refusal of ecclesiastical authorities in the time of Copernicus and Galileo to consider the evidence that the earth moved around the sun. Science does not challenge the rules of morality of any religion, because such guides for living are outside the province of science.

The dogma that all species of life were created in their present form and have not changed since, scientists can disprove; but they can neither prove nor disprove the moral principle expounded in the Golden Rule, which is a statement of what one *should* do. There is no way for science to determine what one should or should not do; science at its most sophisticated stage can only predict what will happen if one does or does not do a certain thing. A scientific theory is composed of empirically testable statements of relationship: "If *a* occurs, then *b* will result." Scientific theories never contain such propositions as: "*A should* occur, because that will be better for most people."

Some people object to social science on the ground that God did not intend us to understand man and that it is therefore evil to attempt to do so. Science does not offer a method for proving that there is or is not a God, much less for fathoming His wishes or intentions. Social scientists simply proceed on the premise stated by Alexander Pope: "The proper study of mankind is man."

BASIC MODES OF ANALYSIS

In the study of social life, sociologists build their analysis around four concepts which are shared by all contemporary sciences: structure, function, pattern, and process. All modern sciences, whether physical, biological, anthropological, or whatever, use these four abstractions as their basic framework for describing their data.

By *structure* we mean the way in which the thing we are analyzing is organized, the relationship of its parts to one another. A botanist will describe the structure of a leaf, the way it is put together. A chemist is concerned with the structure of a compound, the relationship of the elements in the compound to one another. The sociologist examines the structure of human society, the relationship of the positions in a human group to one another: of husband to wife, of employee to employer, of white to Oriental, and so on.

A *function* is the consequence of a structure. If we change the way in which a thing is put together, we get different functions. Contemporary American society is so structured that most people between the ages of six and sixteen years attend school. One function of our social structure is that most young adults are literate; another function of this structure is that relatively few people under sixteen years of age are in the labor force. If we lived in a social structure which provided no schools, one function of this structure would be to put most of the burden of education on the family, religion, or some other agency in the society.

It would not be possible to generalize in any science if the structures and functions being studied were not shared and repeated over and over in an orderly fashion. This repetitiveness which allows us to make predictions is called *patterning*. In sociology, patterns of behavior are those characteristics of life in a society which regularly recur and which are shared by many members of the society.

Process is a series of changes taking place in a definite manner. When we speak of the structure of a group, we are describing it as though we had taken a flash picture of it, had stopped it at a point in time. When we speak of the functions of that structure, we are describing the consequences of the way it is put together at a given moment. When we refer to a pattern of behavior, we sound as if its recurrence in its present form and meaning were permanent. Actually, we are aware that the phenomena included under these three concepts—structure, function, and pattern—are in a constant state of flux. It is the concept of process that helps us to maintain a dynamic view of society. Social life, like all other life, is constantly undergoing modification. Terms such as *cooperation, differentiation,* or *conflict,* which describe social processes, allow us to summarize in a word certain patterns of change in social structures and their functions.

INTERPRETIVE SUMMARY

Sociology is the scientific study of human group life. Science is distinguished from other fields of learning by its commitment to the scientific method, its insistence upon objectivity, and its interest in knowledge *per se.* Social science applies the scientific method to the study of human interaction. The social scientist wants to form accurate generalizations about how people behave in groups.

The scientific method seeks knowledge on the basis of three assumptions. The scientist assumes that the most valid way of getting, organizing, and testing the reliability of knowledge is through (1) the use of man's sensory-perceptual experience, aided by instruments, to gather data, (2) the use of logic, or human reasoning, to interpret the data theoretically, and (3) agreement among a number of independent observers concerning the reliability of theoretical propositions.

The social sciences are divided into academic disciplines, some scholars studying certain important systems which appear, with variations, almost universally, others concerning themselves with the more specific event or system. Sociology is the social science dealing with human interaction as such. General sociologists attempt to find generalizations about human groups in interaction. Many sociologists specialize, dealing with particular institutions and phenomena existing at particular times and places.

Sociology is a science, embracing scientific objectives and employing scientific techniques. Sociology also shares, to some extent, scientific terminology; for example, the terms *structure, function, pattern,* and *process* are used by all sciences as a framework for the analysis of data.

The study of sociology has been handicapped in several ways, not the least of which has been the fact that people tend to think that their own ethnocentric knowledge is necessarily true. Additional handicaps to the unhampered pursuit of sociology are: (1) the tendency of people to fear and resist new ideas; and (2) the fact that the terminology of sociology, which should be as precise as that of any other science, is too often vague and emotionally charged.

SUGGESTIONS FOR FURTHER READING

Bates, Alan P. *The Sociological Enterprise.* Boston, Mass.: Houghton Mifflin Company, 1967. Several chapters with practical information for those contemplating a career in sociology are included in this volume.

Berger, Peter L. *An Invitation to Sociology.* Garden City, N.Y.: Doubleday and Company, Inc., 1963. This is a highly readable and humanistic account of what sociology is all about.

Cicourel, Aaron V. *Method and Measurement in Sociology.* New York: The Free Press of Glencoe, 1964. Assumptions in social research are critically examined with special attention focused upon the problem of social norms and what language and beliefs have to do with the structure of social meanings in a situation.

Evans, Bergen. *The Natural History of Nonsense.* New York: Alfred A. Knopf, Inc., 1946. This little book is a witty and learned demonstration that a considerable part of common sense is more common than sense and much is nonsense.

Faris, Robert E. L., ed. *The Handbook of Modern Sociology.* Chicago: Rand McNally, 1966. The current state of knowledge in each of the major subfields of sociology is assessed by a distinguished set of sociologists.

Friedrichs, Robert W. *A Sociology of Sociology.* New York: The Free Press, 1970. This book presents a detailed examination of the social production of American sociology.

Gouldner, Alvin W. and Miller, S. M., eds. *Applied Sociology: Opportunities and Problems.* New York: The Free Press, 1965. This volume is a collection of thirty-five articles on the problems and prospects of the practical uses of sociology prepared for the Society for the Study of Social Problems.

Kaplan, Abraham. *The Conduct of Inquiry.* San Francisco: Chandler Publishing Company, 1964. The author analyzes the philosophy of science as applied to the values, concepts, laws, measurement, and method of the social sciences.

Lazarsfeld, Paul F.; Sewell, William H.; and Wilensky, Harold L., eds. *The Uses of Sociology.* New York: Basic Books, Inc., 1967. Several noted sociologists explain the practical applications of sociological knowledge in a collection of essays.

Lynd, Robert S. *Knowledge for What?* Princeton, N.J.: Princeton University Press, 1939. This is Lynd's classic essay in defense of the idea that social science should give more aid in the solution of contemporary social problems. The conflict of values in the United States is noted.

Madge, John H. *The Origins of Scientific Sociology.* New York: The Free Press, 1962. This book presents a description and analysis of some of the most famous empirical studies in the annals of sociology.

Mills, C. Wright. *The Sociological Imagination.* New York: Oxford University Press, 1959. This influential and provocative essay concerns the promise of sociology and its cultural role in the modern world.

Processes –
series of changes

2
Social
Structure
and Social
Groups

When an architect speaks of the "structure" of a building, she is usually referring to three things: (1) the materials of which it is composed (brick siding, asphalt shingle roof); (2) the relationship between the parts (the porch floor that rests on a foundation, the pillars that support the porch roof); and (3) the building as a unit or whole (a split-level house, a Southern colonial dwelling). When a sociologist speaks of social structure, he or she is talking about the same three sets of features that concern the architect in describing a house: (1) the "building materials" (the number of males and females, adults and children, social positions); (2) the interrelationship of the parts (what wives expect from husbands, how employees interact with employers, how parents and children treat one another); and (3) the nature of the society as a whole—that is, the result of the materials of which it is built and the way they are put together.

BASIC UNITS OF SOCIAL STRUCTURE

The building blocks of which a social structure is composed are called *statuses.* A status is a position in a social structure. Whenever we describe a social position without regard to the individual who is occupying it, we are talking about a status. A status (or social position) is analytically distinct from the particular individual who occupies it.

Status

An infantryman is issued one winter uniform, one summer uniform, and a rifle. He must be between certain age limits. He must have an I.Q. score of 70 or above. He has authority over enemy civilians. Commissioned officers and military police have authority over him. Note that these sentences describe the *status* of infantryman; they do not describe a specific person. It does not matter whether the infantryman is dull, jolly, or morose: the personality of the individual occupying the status is quite another variable. When Willard Pack is discharged and Tom Norton is drafted to replace him, the status of infantryman remains unchanged. A status is an abstraction, a description of one's place in a social group relative to other positions in the group.

Role

A *role* is the function of a status. When an individual occupies a given position, the placement of that position above some others and below still others will have consequences for his interaction in the group. The consequences of occupying that status are called his role. We can speak, then, of the status of foreman, which is a position in a work group above that of laborer and below that of shop superintendent. The role of the foreman is the result of his status in the group: he is expected to give orders to laborers and to take orders from the shop superintendent. Like status, role io an abotruction; it remains the same even if the expectations are being met by different individuals. Retiring one foreman and hiring a replacement does not usually alter either the position (the status) or its consequences (the role).

Role Behavior

The component of the social situation that *can* be altered is the *role behavior*, or the way a particular individual fulfills the expectations of the role. The status of surgeon ranks above that of nurse; the surgeon's role includes the expectation that he will tell the nurse what to do. But the role behavior of surgeons varies considerably. Dr. Form gives specific orders in a pleasant voice, whereas Dr. Huber gives very general instructions in a harsh tone. The contrast between them stems from neither status nor role, but from role behavior.

Every person occupies many statuses. A man may be at one and the same time a citizen of the United States, an attorney, a member of the Episcopal Church, a Post Commander in the American Legion, a male, an adult, a husband, a father, an uncle, a son, a nephew, and a member of the local Board of Education. Each of these is one of his statuses. With each is associated a role, a set of expectations he is supposed to fulfill with respect to people in other related statuses, such as minister, wife, Chair of the Board of Education, and so on. To each of these roles he brings his personality, which influences some of the patterns of his role behavior. Since, fundamentally, each role and status is derived from social norms, or group-shared expectations of what ought to be, people in the society will evaluate his role behaviors and pass judgment on how well he meets the expectations of each of his roles.

Prestige and Esteem

Each status in a social structure has attached to it an evaluation. It is considered "good" or "important" or "difficult" or "routine" or "criminal" or "dirty." There is always some judgment in the norms of a society about how desirable a status is. This evaluation of the status is called its _prestige_. The evaluation of an individual's role behavior in a status which he occupies is called _esteem_. This is the judgment by one's fellows of how well he fulfills the expectations of his role. Most people in the United States believe that vice-president of a large corporation is a more desirable status than street sweeper. Thus, no matter who is occupying the status or how well he is doing, it is proper to say that the status of corporation executive has higher prestige than the status of street sweeper. However, people may notice that Jay Hendricks does an excellent job of sweeping the street, while Dick Mathers does not take his work seriously and leaves trash piled up at the curb. Hendricks then, has high esteem because of his role behavior, while Mathers has low esteem, despite the fact that the two occupy the same status.

A person may be in a status which has high prestige and earn high esteem by his role behavior there, but prestige does not ensure esteem. The alcoholic attorney has low esteem even though he is in a status which has high prestige; the best cleaning woman in an office bulding occupies a status with low prestige but earns high esteem. The esteem accruing collectively to individuals in a status can in time alter the prestige of that status. If, over a period of years, only incompetent persons were made deans of colleges, the prestige of deanship would suffer. Each of us is usually proud to point to highly esteemed persons who occupy the same status as we, because we feel (perhaps without being aware of it) that their presence raises the prestige of our position.

The Reciprocity of Roles

Since a role is a set of expectations, it is impossible to define one role without referring to another. There cannot be a parent role without a child, or an employer role without an employee. There must be another role doing the expecting. In this sense, roles are a series of rights and duties—that is, they represent certain reciprocal relations among individuals. To understand this interplay, we must define *right* and *duty*. A right is a privilege to act which is reciprocal to another's duty to permit the act. Of course, a duty is not always passive: a duty may sometimes be an obligation to act, reciprocal to another's right to expect the act. The rights of one are always qualified and limited by the obligations of another.

All societies reveal a wide range of such reciprocal relations. The economic structure *is* a structure precisely because the interactions of people in the market express more or less widely accepted rights and duties. A legal contract to work or to deliver a product at a specified time and place is a pattern of reciprocal rights and duties supported by the law of contracts. In family life the interplay of sympathetic identification of parent and child is counterpoised by obligations to provide on the part of the former and by duties of obedience on the part of the latter. Power relations in the operations of government reveal the same pattern. The king and his subjects, the judge and the accused, the police and the citizen, the elected official and the constituency, all have reciprocal rights and duties.

Of the many patterns of such reciprocities, some operate quite independently of others. Some come into conflict with each other. Many rights and duties associated with family life or religion have little or nothing to do with those outside the home or the church. In contrast, a man's ethical code about killing may cause inner conflict regarding his rights and duties as citizen-soldier when he is called on to engage in war. Or the widely accepted relations of competitive business may, in time, come into conflict with one's humanitarian feelings.

Every person occupies both ascribed statuses and achieved statuses. By *ascribed statuses* we mean those positions which are assigned to an individual regardless of his or her own abilities or performance. "Princess" is an ascribed status; where there is a hereditary royalty, a girl does not work her way up to being princess. She is *born* a princess, and whether she is pretty or ugly, tall or short, intelligent or stupid, a princess she remains. _Achieved statuses_, on the other hand, are not assigned at birth, but are left open to be filled by the persons who compete most successfully for them. Being male is an ascribed status. It is determined at birth; either you are male or you are not. Being a husband is an achieved status, it does not result automatically from one's being born a male but depends on a male's own behavior. One's racial status is ascribed. One cannot usually change one's race within one's own lifetime.

ASCRIBED STATUSES AND ROLES

In many societies most statuses are ascribed. This was true of the ancient Incan Empire, where the newborn male infant was classified as "babe in arms," later as "able to stand," and still later as "under six." Then from six to eight years he was termed a "bread receiver," and so on, until at twenty years he became "almost a man," at twenty-five "able-bodied," at fifty "half an old man," and after sixty years "an old man asleep."[1] While no modern society draws such sharp distinctions as these, highly authoritarian cultures, both contemporary and ancient, often fix statuses rather rigidly. This was true in feudal Japan, for example, where individual and family status was regulated by minute rules. In contrast one of the distinguishing features of democratic societies is the relative opportunity of individual choice and freedom. While ascription of certain statuses remains, in a wide range of activities status is acquired, not ascribed or fixed in advance.

In highly stable and rigid societies the individual usually does not experience fear and worry over roles and statuses as one does in societies demanding continual struggle for role and status. In the latter, anxiety and a heavy sense of inferiority and guilt often follow if one fails to "make good."

Age

All societies recognize differences in role and status related to age. Adults have more physical strength and more experience than children. In old age, there is some decline of physical capabilities and sometimes mental faculties, and dependence on others tends to limit the range of thought and action. Yet variations in age are defined much more by custom than by physiology. As Ralph Linton

---

[1]A. M. Tozzer, _Social Origins and Social Continuities_ (New York: The Macmillan Company, 1925), p. 208.

puts it, "In the case of age, as in that of sex, biological factors involved appear to be secondary to the cultural ones in determining the content of status."[2]

In most societies, however, there are four major categories of age differences as related to role and status: infancy and childhood, youth, maturity or adulthood, and old age.

The Ascribed Status of Child

The role and status of infant and child are always related to dependency on and guardianship by adults. Yet how societies regard babies varies among both small nonliterate societies and large industrial ones. In ancient Sparta, where there was heavy stress on the need for a strong body as well as a normal mind, sickly or deformed infants were done away with, usually by being abandoned in the hills. Among some nonliterate tribes, twins were thought to be a bad omen, and they were disposed of lest some evil descend upon the family and the tribe. In other societies, as in the United States, babies are generally idolized and made much of by adults.

Among some peoples the child is regarded as a miniature adult, and is expected to act like "a little man" or "a little woman." Among others there is firm demand for silent conformity—children are expected "to be seen but not heard" when in the presence of their "elders and betters." In still other societies a child may be given a very high status. This is the situation among the Marquesans, where the eldest son is considered the head of the family, regardless of his age. Ralph Linton reports seeing a nine-year-old Marquesan boy, son of a chieftain, drive all the adults out of the family house when he became angry over what seemed a trivial matter.[3] Sometimes there is little or no formal direction or discipline of the children until they are ready to pass into adult status.

In Western societies, it is clear that the culturally defined period of dependency and immaturity has been markedly lengthened, largely as a result of these societies' complexity, their emphasis on occupational specialization, and their high standards of living. Indeed, this prolongation of the occupancy of the ascribed status of child is one measure of the complexity of a culture.

Since each role is defined by reference to another, there are certain reciprocal relations between parent and child. The major rights and duties in this relationship tend to take shape as social norms. Obviously, the duties of the parent to the child cannot usually be

---

[2]Ralph Linton, *The Study of Man* (New York: Appleton-Century-Crofts, 1936), p. 119.
[3]*Ibid.*, p. 119.

enforced by the latter. But failure to provide for the child's care and training according to the group norms may be punished by the group. Failure of parents to live up to the norms of child care laid down by the culture usually results in some other group's taking over this obligation. In small, intimate communities, serious neglect of children by their parents usually leads to gossip as a device to stimulate the parents to do their duty, or neighbors may help the children. In large urbanized societies there are a large number of formal agencies, both privately and publicly supported, which concern themselves with child welfare. In a society which places a high value on children, failure on the part of the parents to fulfill their duties leads to their punishment by sanctions decreed in the law and to the rise of substitute means replacing parental care.

The Ascribed Status of Youth

The break between various "age" periods is largely determined by culture. While some societies recognize changes from childhood to sexual maturity by special ceremonials and overt changes in social status and role, other societies make no such sharp division. Americans for instance, recognize a certain age gradation in the division of schooling into elementary, secondary, and college. Confirmation ceremonies and high-school graduation symbolize a passage of the growing person into a new role and status. The long period of permissive and accepted preparation for adulthood is restricted, for the most part, to the urban, literate societies, largely as a result of their complexity, specialization, and high standards of living.

This transition from childhood to youth is associated with the development of full sexual capacity and the appearance of secondary sex characteristics which further distinguish the male from the female. There are also changes in height and weight, and other physical characteristics which mark the shift toward adulthood. Since there are variations in the age at which the individual passes through puberty, the culture usually provides a certain latitude for fulfillment of the expected roles and statuses related to this phase.

A major expectation of the ascribed role of youth is that one learn the essential skills that prepare one for the adult role and status. In Western societies there is a tendency to prolong this period of preparation, just as there is a tendency to prolong the period of childhood. In the United States, this fact is reflected in the law. Added protection is given to young people by increasing the years of compulsory education, by prohibiting child labor, and by restricting early marriages.

The United States has, however, a curious inconsistency in the treatment of youth. True, the continued emotional and financial dependence of children on parents is evident. Nowhere else in the world is youth given such leisure and opportunity for education. In other societies individuals in this chronological age group have ascribed adult roles. Yet American youth have greater freedom from parental control than formerly. Adolescent boys and girls are more sophisticated and mature in many ways than their parents were in their youth. Opportunities for escaping from family, neighborhood, and community controls afford young people forms of experience which their fathers and mothers often do not understand or approve of. Various factors have created a situation in which the role and status of youth, their rights and duties, and the responsibility of their elders for their future welfare are not always clearly defined. This very confusion reflects changing patterns of differentiation in the society.

The Ascribed Status of Adult

In every society the adult assumes rights and duties not expected of children, youth, or old people. The age at which the individual comes to maturity will be determined by elements in the particular culture. Thus, among the American Plains Indians, acceptance as a member of a war party marked arrival at adulthood. In our society political adulthood is assumed when the person acquires voting privileges. The capacity to hold office, too, is assumed to be related to age. In the United States, while most local and state offices are open to any qualified voter 21 years or over, the holding of federal offices is restricted to narrower age limits. A person under 25 years of age cannot hold office as a Representative in the national Congress. One must be 30 years old to be eligible for the United States Senate and 35 years to be eligible for the Presidency.

Voting privileges and eligibility to hold office and perform jury service are basic marks of adult political responsibility in a democratic country. With these, of course, go all the obligations of citizenship, which are stipulated, at least on the negative side, by legal codes regarding both private and public conduct. Under a dictatorship the adult may be accorded no voting or discussion privileges but is usually ascribed specific public roles as party member, worker, taxpayer, or soldier—roles assigned only to those considered in this society as adults.

The Ascribed Status of the Aged

Old age is determined not solely by the physiological condition of muscles, glands, and brain, but also by the culture. In most nonliterate societies old age carries with it a real distinction in prestige. In many tribes the elders are the most powerful and revered members of the group. In a society like ancient China, where ancestor worship dominated family and community life for centuries, the power of old age over the social order was everywhere apparent. Deference to old age, to the patriarch of the family, and the desire for sons to carry on ancestor worship long retarded the rise of new ideas and new ways of life.

Throughout the history of European culture, old age has retained great power. In the patriarchal family order, as in ancient Rome, the oldest male in the family retained control over all other members. It is so even today in the peasant areas of Europe. Where urbanization has taken place and industry has developed, this reverence for old age has been modified.[4]

A large percentage of our old people become dependent on others for economic support. Until recently, in our individualistic society practically all provision for old age rested on the efforts of the individual and his or her family. Only gradually are we assigning some responsibility to the community and state to provide for the aged through pensions and insurance.

Age statuses are ascribed; they are fixed for the individual at birth, regardless of his efforts in later years. No matter how hard one works at it, an eight-year-old child cannot occupy adult status. And a thirty-year-old man, whether he works at it or not, whether he wants to be or not, is considered an adult. He is an adult because the norms of the society decree that he is; the status is assigned him, not achieved.

Sex

Perhaps because it is a visible, unchangeable physical characteristic, sex also constitutes a basis for ascribed status. All societies have a dual set of roles associated with the two sexes. The first set is related to biological facts: the male and the female have different roles in the reproduction of children. But there are many other statuses ascribed on the basis of sex. Sex is a basic variable, for example in the division of labor. Occupations, religious roles, intellectual pursuits, political responsibilities, and many other activities are differentiated according to sex. The important social fact about sexually ascribed statuses, however, is the wide range of variation from society to society in the assignment of sex roles.

---

[4] A recently published set of studies detailing the family structure of older people, their social activities, reactions to retirement, and personal perspectives is Ida Harper Simpson and John C. McKinney, *Social Aspects of Aging* (Durham: Duke University Press, 1966).

Sex and Culture

People have often assumed that all male statuses and female statuses are so ascribed because of innate differences between the sexes. Women are described as having more musical ability than men, or less business sense, or as being physically weaker or more religious.

The notion that a division of labor with statuses ascribed on the basis of sex is rooted in biological differences simply does not make sense, for variations occur not only between societies but also within societies. For example, in the Midwest, women were ordinarily assigned the job of husking corn, while men were trimmers. In the Far West, the arrangement was reversed: men were huskers and women were trimmers.

The ancient myth that women are innately the weaker sex is not true. In fact, there is a mass of evidence that females withstand the hazards of life better than males. The most obvious illustration can be seen in the differences in life expectancy. As Table 2-1 shows, at birth the life expectancy of females is nearly seven and one-half years greater than that of males. More remarkable is the fact that the difference between the sexes has increased in the very period when life expectancy has been lengthened for both sexes. The same kind of difference obtains in infant mortality figures. Although infant mortality in the United States has decreased about two-thirds since 1900, the ratio of male to female deaths has actually risen.[5]

The fact that the roles most directly related to childbearing and child rearing tend to be ascribed on the basis of sex has an effect on the whole set of economic statuses. Even where economic statuses are, within sexual categories, achieved statuses, differences

Table 2-1   Life Expectancy at Birth for Males and Females
in the United States, 1900–1968

Year	Males	Females
1900	46.3	48.3
1920	53.6	64.6
1940	60.8	65.2
1960	66.6	73.1
1968	66.6	74.0

SOURCE: U.S. Bureau of the Census, *Statistical Abstract of the United States 1971* (Washington, D.C.: U.S. Government Printing Office, 1971), p. 53; and U.S. Bureau of the Census, *Historical Statistics of the United States* (Washington, D.C.: U.S. Government Printing Office, 1960).

---

[5]Amram Scheinfeld, *Women and Men* (New York: Harcourt, Brace & Co., 1944), p. 32.

ILLUSTRATIVE DATA 2-1   THE ASCRIPTION OF SEX STATUSES AND ROLES

The division and ascription of statuses with relation to sex seems to be basic in all social systems. All societies prescribe different attitudes and activities to men and to women. Most of them try to rationalize these prescriptions in terms of the physiological differences between the sexes or their different roles in reproduction. However, a comparative study of the statuses ascribed to women and men in different cultures seems to show that while such factors may have served as a starting point for the development of a division the actual ascriptions are almost entirely determined by culture. Even the psychological characteristics ascribed to men and women in different societies vary so much that they can have little physiological basis. Our own idea of women as ministering angels contrasts sharply with the ingenuity of women as torturers among the Iroquois and the sadistic delight they took in the process. Even the last two generations have seen a sharp change in the psychological patterns for women in our own society. The delicate, fainting lady of the middle eighteen-hundreds is as extinct as the dodo.

When it comes to the ascription of occupations, which is after all an integral part of status, we find the differences in various societies even more marked. Arapesh women regularly carry heavier loads than men "because their heads are so much harder and stronger." In some societies women do most of the manual labor; in others, as in the Marquesas, even cooking, housekeeping, and baby-tending are proper male occupations, and women spend most of their time primping. Even the general rule that women's handicap through pregnancy and nursing indicates the more active occupations as male and the less active ones as female has many exceptions. Thus among the Tasmanians seal-hunting was women's work. They swam out to the seal rocks, stalked the animals, and clubbed them. Tasmanian women also hunted opossums, which required the climbing of large trees.

Although the actual ascription of occupations along sex lines is highly variable, the pattern of sex division is constant. There are very few societies in which every important activity has not been definitely assigned to men or to women. Even when the two sexes cooperate in a particular occupation, the field of each is usually clearly delimited. Thus in Madagascar rice culture the men make the seed beds and terraces and prepare the fields for transplanting. The women weed the crop, but the men harvest it. The women then carry it to the threshing floors, where the men thresh it while the women winnow it. Lastly, the women pound the grain in mortars and cook it.

Source: Ralph Linton, *The Study of Man* (New York: Appleton-Century-Crofts, 1936); pp. 116–117. By permission.

exist between the roles of males and females in those ascribed according to sex. While there are some variations, warfare and the chase seem the more usual activities of the male, while sedentary occupations are more often assigned to the female, who must remain near home in order to attend to the young children. An elaborate cross-comparison of occupations and sex among nonliterate peoples showed that males are concerned either "exclusively" or "predominantly" with such matters as pursuit of sea mammals, hunting, trapping, and fishing. In contrast, females are "predominantly" or "exclusively" occupied with such activities as gathering fruit and nuts, preserving meat and fish, gathering herbs, roots, and seeds, and cooking.[6]

Contemporary peasant and farm households, until the introduction of industrial devices, were not greatly different from those of nonliterate societies. It was not until the commercial and industrial changes of the modern world took women out of the home that their economic functions changed. The emancipation of women from the household economics illustrates again how culture patterns give the direction to social processes.

Women in increasing numbers have gone into vocations outside the home, gaining money wages of their own and freedom of residence, and experiencing changes in their personalities which influence other relations of the sexes as well. Yet, in spite of great changes, there remain many inequalities between the sexes in rates of pay, hours of labor, control of working conditions, and types of work. Table 2-2 shows that women usually earn less than men even when they have the same occupational statuses.

On the whole, public reaction to the newer economic role of women is a curious paradox. On the one hand, much so-called "social legislation" aimed at control of hours, wages, working conditions, and kinds of work for women rests on the ancient attitude toward women as the "weaker sex." On the other hand, many advocates of women's equality, especially in economics and politics, demand that they be given the freedom allowed men to enter any vocation and receive equal wages, and that they have complete equality before the law.

Race

Since an entire chapter is devoted to racial inequality, we shall note here only that in the United States and some other societies, race is an ascribed status. Like age and sex, race has a modifying effect on the prestige of an achieved status and often affects the esteem one receives for the performance of achieved roles.

---

[6]See G. P. Murdock, "Comparative Data on Division of Labor by Sex," *Social Forces*, 1937, 15: 551–553.

Table 2-2   Median Annual Earnings of Male and Female Workers, 1969

Occupational Category	Males	Females	Female earnings as a percentage of male earnings 1969	1958
Professional, technical, and kindred workers	$10,516	$5,244	49.9	50.8
Elementary and secondary teachers only	9,415	5,812	61.7	66.4
Managers, officials, and proprietors (except farm)	10,300	4,766	46.3	43.9
Farmers and farm managers	3,007	1,371	45.6	*
Clerical and kindred workers	6,804	3,603	52.3	61.8
Salesworkers	6,829	1,241	18.2	22.2
Craftsmen, foremen, and kindred workers	7,944	4,004	50.4	*
Operatives and kindred workers	6,248	3,054	48.9	48.0
Service workers (except private household)	3,684	1,497	40.6	32.1
Laborers, (except farm and mine)	2,483	1,755	70.7	*

*Data not available.
SOURCE: U.S. Bureau of the Census, *Statistical Abstract of the United States 1971* (Washington, D.C.: U.S. Government Printing Office, 1971), p. 229.

ACHIEVED STATUSES AND ROLES

All societies have some ascribed statuses, though some use ascription more than others. Age and sex are universally used in human societies as a basis for ascription. All societies also have some achieved statuses. Again, the proportion of statuses which are open to achievement varies widely around the world. In the modern world, one significant mark of a free society is the relative number of statuses and roles that are open to achievement.

The more complex a society is—the more specialized its division of labor—the higher the proportion of achieved statuses it is likely to have. An elaborate division of labor offers the individual who is extremely talented a competitive advantage. If every male in a society does his own hunting, his own house-building, and his own toolmaking, a talent for toolmaking in one man or house-building in another is of little importance. But once the society is so structured

Ascribed and Achieved Statuses

The distinction between ascription and achievement is one of the most important and widely used analytical tools in sociology, but it is not always clear and unambiguous. It is difficult at times to differentiate between the two because the opportunity to *achieve* tends to be *ascribed*. There is no status in any society that is always equally open to achievement to all members of the society. Societies assign some statuses on the basis of such categories as sex and age. In addition, in many societies race, nationality, residence, social class, lineage, and religion limit one's opportunity to achieve.

that one man specializes in house-building and another in tool-making, allowing these statuses to be achieved offers dividends both for the specialists and for the society. More and better houses can be built, and more and better tools can be made if each man is encouraged to perform the task at which he excels instead of being assigned a status because his father held it before him.

In a society such as ours, most occupational statuses are open to achievement for at least some members of the society. The proliferation of secondary groups means that most organizational memberships also are achieved statuses. Many primary group roles are achieved as well; that is what we are referring to when we say that one is free to choose his friends. They are not, in other words, assigned to him by something like clan membership. We are even allowed, in our society, to treat church membership as an achieved status, which makes our social structure unusual indeed, from either the historical or cross-cultural point of view. In most societies, one is born into his religious group; it is just as much an ascribed status as his family membership. To leave it is to be excommunicated from the tribe. But in the United States, religion, like occupation, education, marital status, and many other statuses, is left to the discretion of the individual.

In a society in which almost all occupational statuses are achieved, individuals are largely interdependent. The very specialization which leads to a system of achieved statuses produces bonds of essential interaction. The woodworker is dependent on the tool-maker, the weaver is dependent on the shepherd, the grocer on the farmer, and the entrepreneur on the banker. A structure characterized by achieved statuses enhances competition for those statuses, but the specialization of roles also necessitates cooperation.

THE INTERRELATIONSHIP OF ASCRIBED AND ACHIEVED STATUSES

All societies ascribe some statuses and the assignment of each individual to some ascribed statuses provides a certain stability and security; one does not have to face a life in which all one's associates are potential competitors for every bit of prestige and esteem that one may strive for and attain. The existence of some statuses for which one is eligible to compete, on the other hand, accomplishes two things. It permits the individual some latitude in picking what he wants to do and is good at doing, and it contributes to the survival of the social structure by motivating people to seek statuses and ultimately fulfill their duties.

The distinction between ascription and achievement is one of the most important and widely used analytical tools in sociology, but the distinction between ascribed and achieved is not always clear and unambiguous. It is difficult at times to differentiate between the two because the opportunity to achieve tends to be ascribed. For example, in the United States, rich parents' children, even if they are not very bright, are much more likely to go to college than the children of the poor even if they are quite intelligent and have received good grades in high school. There is no status in any society that is always equally open to achievement to all members of the society. The presidency of the United States is an achieved status, constitutionally open to any citizen over the age of 35, but the opportunity to achieve the status is not the same for males and females, whites and blacks, the poor and the affluent.

SOCIAL GROUPS

Human life is social life. Social life becomes organized when there are established ways of interacting. We indicate these ways of interacting by such relational terms as status and role. When there is persistent interaction among the same people, there emerge social collectivities, both large and small, which we call groups. Analytically, a group is not the same as a social structure. Groups exist through the coming together of a number of identifiable people who build and develop their social relations over time into a relatively stable pattern—a social structure—and who identify to some extent with the others with whom they share this particular social structure (i.e., pattern of social interaction). Thus, groups have a social structure. A social group is defined as a plurality of people "involved in a pattern of social interaction, conscious of sharing common membership, of sharing some common understanding, and of accepting some rights and obligations that accrue only to members."[7]

This definition makes it clear that not every classification of people is a social group. Sociologists make a sharp distinction between social groups and social categories. A social category is a classification of persons who share a common characteristic but who have no social interaction, no common understanding of membership, and no consciousness of kind. Examples of social categories are all seven-year-old girls, all right-handed people, all owners of a new automobile, all bald-headed men, all high school graduates, all people born on November 10, and all widowed people. Obviously, persons who share a common characteristic have the potential of becoming a social group. For example, many people have charac-

---

[7]James B. McKee, *Introduction to Sociology* (New York: Holt, Rinehart and Winston, Inc., 1969), p. 124.

terized the activity of black Americans during the past generation as a movement from a social category to a social group.

Consciousness of Kind

Membership in a group relates people to one another in a way that is different from how they are related to others not in the group. Common membership subjects them to the expectations governing action in the group—its social norms—and to the culture that emerges from the interactions shared among the members. Members of a group, then, share a common set of cultural understandings about the meaning of membership in the group that emerges from their consensus about the purpose of the group—its functions and objectives.

This sharing of membership in a group, and a sharing of its common experiences, develops a sense of group unity that is important for the effectiveness of the group's collective activities. Franklin Henry Giddings, one of the first American sociologists, spoke of "consciousness of kind" to designate this sense of unity that common membership and common experience brings.[8] The intensity of the consciousness of kind varies from group to group, however. Many large groups suffer an attenuated sense of belonging for their members place only limited value on membership and the heterogeneity of members tends to reduce consciousness of kind. Also, the members of one group have membership in other groups, so that no one group may claim a total loyalty or a full commitment from the individual. Limited though it may be, however, membership in a group does bring some degree of consciousness of kind and some recognition of sharing with others the obligations that participation in a group requires. Without some consensus among its members as to its norms and its expectations of behavior—its definitions of its roles—there cannot be a group. Thus, a group is not merely a system of interaction; it also involves a sharing of membership among those who interact in this way.

People in social groups are not only conscious of belonging together in common memberships, but they also possess some mechanism to determine who belongs and who does not. In formally organized groups, membership qualifications may be spelled out and who belongs may be formally recognized by such means as membership rosters, membership insignia, and access to privileges that go with membership. Even in groups that are not formally organized, the recognition of who belongs and who does

---

[8]Franklin Henry Giddings, *Principles of Sociology* (New York: The Macmillan Company, 1896).

not is crucial to the group's sense of its own existence. In small and informal groups, the conferring of recognition upon a person as belonging and another as an outsider may be carried out by forms of address and by obvious ways of inclusion and exclusion in the activities of the group. No human group has any particular difficulty in making an individual feel that he or she is not wanted, that he or she is not "one of the group."

The Diversity of Groups

Social groups are not always and everywhere the same. Like other aspects of reality, groups may be classified in a great number of different ways, and the difficult task of the classification of groups is a problem of considerable magnitude. One needs only to ponder the extraordinary variety of groups and the fact that there are probably more groups than there are people in American society to appreciate the dimension of the problem. Without exception, all human beings belong to groups at some time, and most of us belong to many groups all of the time. The maze and multiplicity of groups are among the most pervasive of all social phenomena and are universally characteristic of every complex society.

Each of us is a member of many groups. With parents and brothers and sisters we make up one kind of group, a family. Many of us are tied also to a wider kinship group of aunts, uncles, and cousins. Most young people belong to school groups; many belong to social, athletic, and other special-interest groups. More than half the people in the United States belong to church groups; many are affiliated with lodges; others are members of occupational organizations. In addition to such regularized associations, we interact from time to time as members of shopping crowds, concert audiences, or other temporary collectivities. Whenever a collectivity of people interact, whether in the intimacy of a family discussion or in the roar of a bargain sale, they constitute a group. If we attempted to list all of the specific groups in American society the list would be virtually inexhaustible.

In the effort to fully understand the form and content of social groups and to chart their similarities and differences, sociologists have concentrated their study on a multitude of group characteristics. Among the more important characteristics of social groups are (1) the size of the group, (2) the degree of "consciousness of kind," (3) the patterns of interaction among the members, (4) the permanence of membership in the group, (5) the permanence of the group, (6) the nature and specificity of group goals, (7) the basis of membership, (8) the formality of the organization of the group, (9) the degree and intensity of involvement of members, (10) the social similarity of the members, (11) the form of social control within the group, and (12) the extent to which the group is dependent upon or independent of other groups.

Typologies

On the basis of these salient group characteristics sociologists have created numerous typologies to facilitate the analysis and description of social groups (and other social phenomena). Typologies are descriptions of two opposite extremes (with a range of possible types between the poles) called "ideal-types" that are used to make comparisons of two or more social phenomena. "Ideal-types" are not "ideal" in the sense of being desired or preferred but in the sense that they constitute pure types, models for measurement even though they are constructs that accentuate and even exaggerate reality. A typology, then, is a classificatory scheme used for comparisons. The most common group typologies are:

closed groups and open groups
dependent groups and independent groups
formal groups and informal groups
horizontal groups and vertical groups
in-groups and out-groups
involuntary groups and voluntary groups
large groups and small groups
majority groups and minority groups
organized groups and unorganized groups
permanent groups and temporary groups
primary groups and secondary groups

Primary and Secondary Groups

One of the most commonly used of these typologies is that of primary and secondary groups.[9] The primary group is characterized by intimate face-to-face contacts and direct interaction made possible by common locality. Social interaction is distinctly personal. Primary groups are the first groups into which the individual is inducted. With few exceptions, the *family* is the first group into which the infant is introduced. In the family the child acquires all his fundamental habits—those of bodily care, speech, morals, obedience, and so forth. He or she learns submission to authority and practices rivalry and cooperation with his or her brothers and

---

[9]The original discussion of primary groups can be found in C. H. Cooley, *Social Organization* (New York: Charles Scribner's Sons, 1909), pp. 23–31.

sisters. Affections and dislikes are deep within the family. The family is thus *primary* not only in form but also in time, since it is the first group to which the child is exposed and the one in which he or she gets his or her fundamental training.

The *play group* arises out of contact between children of the same family or neighborhood. It is more or less spontaneous in its formation, developing out of new situations not necessarily found in the family. The children in the play group meet other children of like age. Parental authority is often not present. In these associations the child learns to give and take. There may be quarrels and division, but there is also cooperation, teamwork. When the child enters the group, play habits are often influenced by home training. The child's aggressiveness or docility may be habits learned at home. The play group gives the child early training in how to meet his or her peers, how to cooperate and compete, and how to express his or her own self—things not always fully expressed or permitted within the family.

Another primary group is the *neighborhood*, where there is also a direct, face-to-face relationship. Neighborhoods are characterized by such things as borrowing and lending, social control through gossip, and communal recreational activities. Neighborhood gangs, such as the Norton gang (see Figure 2–1) in the famous study of *Street Corner Society*, are also primary groups. The gang is based upon friendship that arises out of repeated association and shared interests or experiences. Such groups lack formal organization, rules, charters, or officers; they proceed on informal common agreement. Gang members ordinarily share social activities: attend the movies, play cards, discuss politics, bowl together, and so on. Such a group is characterized by interaction of fairly high intensity, frequent contacts, and a broad general focus resting on sympathetic, affectionate relationships and persisting only so long as the members are in direct contact with one another.

Secondary groups are characterized by much more deliberate and conscious formation than primary groups. Almost always they represent partial and specialized interests. In fact, they are sometimes called "special-interest" groups. They do not necessarily depend on face-to-face contacts. A scientific association may exist for years without the members ever meeting one another. Secondary associations include the nation, the political party, the professional society, the religious body, the employers' association, and the international labor union.

Another feature of secondary groups is that they often outlast any given generation. Because the particular interests or needs they represent may persist through time, more organization is required than is found in primary groups. There develop traditions, codes,

Figure 2-1   The Social Structure of the Norton Gang

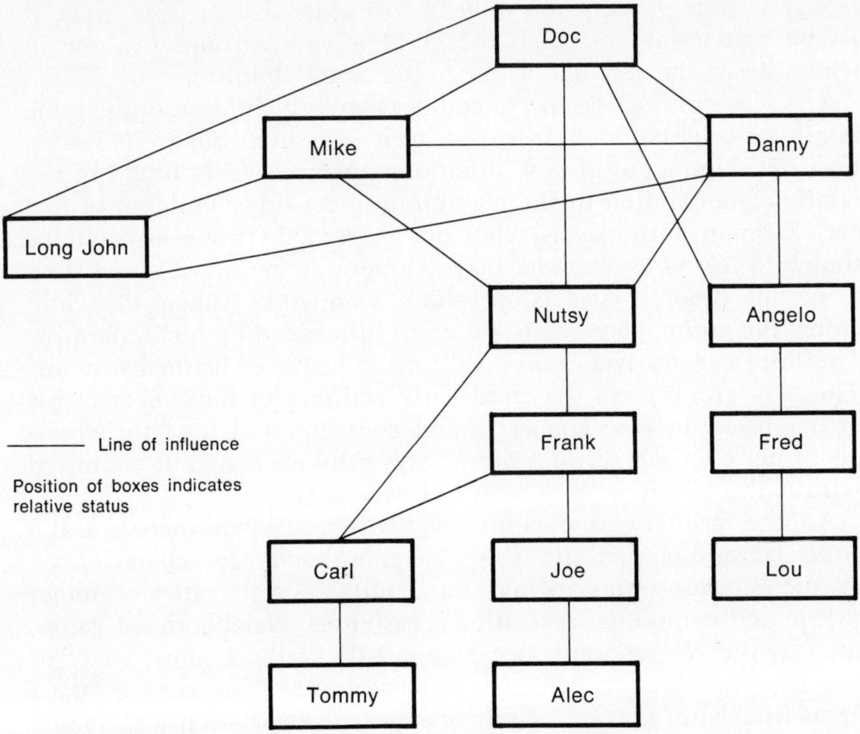

```
                            ┌──────────┐
                            │   Doc    │
                            └──────────┘
              ┌──────────┐              ┌──────────┐
              │   Mike   │──────────────│  Danny   │
              └──────────┘              └──────────┘
  ┌──────────┐
  │ Long John│
  └──────────┘
                        ┌──────────┐    ┌──────────┐
                        │  Nutsy   │    │  Angelo  │
                        └──────────┘    └──────────┘

  ───────── Line of influence   ┌──────────┐    ┌──────────┐
                                │  Frank   │    │   Fred   │
  Position of boxes indicates   └──────────┘    └──────────┘
  relative status

        ┌──────────┐    ┌──────────┐    ┌──────────┐
        │   Carl   │    │   Joe    │    │   Lou    │
        └──────────┘    └──────────┘    └──────────┘

        ┌──────────┐    ┌──────────┐
        │  Tommy   │    │   Alec   │
        └──────────┘    └──────────┘
```

Source: William Foote Whyte, Street Corner Society: The Social Structure of an Italian Slum, 2nd ed. (Chicago: The University of Chicago Press, 1955), p. 13. Reprinted by permission.

special offices, and fixed methods of carrying out the group's activities.

In-Groups and Out-Groups

The primary and secondary associations represent a basic structural and functional classification. Another important and much used typology is that of in-group and out-group. This distinction is found in all societies.

The *in-group* is any association—either primary or secondary—in which there is a sense of solidarity, loyalty, friendliness, and cooperation. It is characterized by a "we" feeling. There is a definite feeling of obligation toward the other members of the group which is especially prominent in critical situations threatening the group. It is in the in-group that we express our deepest sentiments of love and sympathy. We feel at home with those around us. We are familiar with their manner of acting and thinking, and they with ours. We understand their gestures and their words are our words. Often the vocabulary and accent are unique, and are themselves a badge of common membership. Lives center largely around the in-groups to which one belongs.

The _out-group_ consists of those persons, whether formally organized or not, toward whom we feel a sense of indifference, avoidance, disgust, competition, or outright conflict. We have no feeling of loyalty, sympathy, or cooperation toward such persons. Rather, we are often prejudiced against the members of the out-group. We may think the family on the next street is inferior to our own, or that our neighborhood is better than the one "across the tracks," or that our race or religion is much superior to another's. One's antagonisms, prejudices, and hatreds usually focus on out-groups. The trade union, for example, opposes the employers' association. Toward other members of the union the individuals feel a sense of solidarity, loyalty, helpfulness, and cooperation. Toward the employer and (especially) toward the strikebreakers, there is intense bitterness.

INTERPRETIVE SUMMARY

Status, prestige, and role are abstractions dealing with society's tendency to differentiate, to evaluate the positions it thus creates as "high" or "low," and to demand certain behavior from individuals occupying the positions. Each individual occupies many statuses. To a certain extent, a person may "coast" on the prestige of a status he occupies; but his role behavior will always be watched by society, and he will lose esteem if he does not conform to expected patterns.

All societies assign some statuses on the basis of such natural categories as sex and age; in fact, all share this age breakdown: childhood, or the period of virtual dependence; youth, the time of increasing sexual maturity and of preparation for adult responsibility; adulthood, the time of broadest rights and full responsibility; and old age, the time of declining powers. The exact age at which an individual is considered an adult, the reverence or lack of it which children or old people receive, the tasks youth is required to do vary among societies, but each society ascribes some statuses on the basis of age. Similarly, though physiological differences between the sexes are actually minimal, all societies ascribe some statuses, especially those involved with division of labor, on the basis of sex. Some societies tend to ascribe many statuses on the bases of age and sex, while other societies leave many statuses open to achievement. In the United States and in some other societies, race is also used as a basis for ascribed status.

The implications of status and role are important psychologically as well as sociologically. For example, while the reciprocal nature of roles gives the individual a certain security, role conflict may prove overwhelming. The

competition for coveted statuses is particularly intense in complex, achieve-
ment-oriented societies.

Sociologists distinguish between groups and categories. They further
classify groups according to the frequency, intensity, duration, and focus
of the interaction involved. Among groups that are relatively persistent
in time—families and close friendship groups—there are, obviously, highly
intense interactions, though they have a broad focus and an informal structure. Secondary groups typically have formalized structures, while their
members usually interact with low intensity. A social category simply refers
to all persons with a particular characteristic in common, such as all females,
all bald-headed men, or all seven-year-old girls.

SUGGESTIONS FOR FURTHER READING

Caplow, Theodore. *Principles of Organization.* New York: Harcourt, Brace,
and World, 1964. This is an insightful description and analysis of the nature
and characteristics of formal organizations.

Cooley, C. H. *Social Organization: A Study of the Larger Mind.* New York:
Charles Scribner's Sons, 1909. A classic study of the major forms of group
life, this book is oriented almost completely to Euro-American societies and
their cultures.

Davis, Kingsley. *Human Society.* New York: The Macmillan Company,
1949. This is a general treatise on social structure and normative systems
from a functional perspective.

Greer, Scott A. *Social Organization.* New York: Random House, 1955. A
brief and highly competent analysis, this volume includes a model of the
social group from the point of view of the functional interdependence of
its members.

Hare, A. Paul; Borgatta, Edgar F.; and Bales, Robert F. *Small Groups: Studies
in Social Interaction.* 2nd ed. New York; Alfred A Knopf, 1966. A wide
range of papers on both theory and research and an extensive annotated
bibliography are presented.

Homans, George C. *The Human Group.* New York: Harcourt, Brace, and
World, 1964. This book deals almost entirely with various forms of human
primary groups. The author reviews critically and systematically some of
the important research in this field.

Levy, Marion. *The Structure of Society.* Princeton, N. J.: Princeton University Press, 1952. Society is analyzed from a structural-functional perspective.

Lowie, Robert H. *Social Organization.* New York: Holt, Rinehart and
Winston, Inc., 1948. A fine examination of the organization of society, considerable data on nonliterate societies are offered.

Murdock, George Peter. *Social Structure.* New York: The Macmillan Company, 1949. This book contains the results of Murdock's study of family and kinship systems in 250 societies.

Shepard, Clovis R. *Small Groups: Some Sociological Perspectives.* San Francisco, Cal.: Chandler Publishing Company, 1964. The volume presents a review and assessment of research on small group dynamics.

Tönnies, Ferdinand. *Community and Society.* Translated by Charles P. Loomis. East Lansing, Mich.: Michigan State University Press, 1957. This is the classic study of societal typologies.

Vidich, Arthur J., and Bensman, Joseph. *Small Town in Mass Society.* Princeton, N. J.: Princeton University Press, 1958. This is an excellent study of the erosion of the communal and autonomous character of the small town in mass society.

I'VE QUIT GOING OUT.

WHAT IS THIS YOU'VE QUIT GOING OUT BIT? HOW CAN YOU QUIT GOING OUT?

I'VE JUST **QUIT**, THAT'S ALL. IT'S DISHONEST AND I'M THROUGH. **THE HELL** WITH IT!

DIS**HONEST**? WHAT DO YOU MEAN DIS**HONEST**?

ALRIGHT. A WEEK AGO I'M ASLEEP IN BED- TWO IN THE MORNING - AND THE **PHONE** RINGS - THE **SEXIEST** VOICE I'VE EVER HEARD!

SHE SAYS HER NAME IS **DARLENE** AND SHE JUST FLEW IN FROM THE COAST AND SHE'S A FRIEND OF A FRIEND AND SHE HAS NO PLACE TO STAY AND CAN I PUT HER UP FOR THE NIGHT.

ALRIGHT. I KNOW **SOMETHING** MUST BE WRONG - BUT I TELL HER TO COME OVER. AN HOUR LATER SHE ARRIVES. **THE MOST BEAUTIFUL GIRL I HAVE EVER SEEN!** AND IN SHE COMES WITH TWO BOTTLES OF BRANDY AND A DOZEN EGGS.

SHE WHIPS UP THE MOST **FABULOUS** BREAKFAST I'VE EVER TASTED. WE SIT AND TALK FOR **HOURS**. SHE'S READ **ALL** THE BOOKS I'VE READ- LOVES **ALL** THE MUSIC I LOVE - THE **BRIGHTEST**, MOST **SENSITIVE** GIRL I'VE EVER KNOWN!

ALONG TOWARD DAWN WE BEGIN TO NUZZLE A LITTLE. I BUILD A FIRE. SUDDENLY WE'RE **GRABBING** EACH OTHER! WARM? YOU WOULDN'T BELIEVE IT! AFFECTIONATE? YOU HAVE **NO** CONCEPTION!

IT WAS THE LOVELIEST, PUREST EXPERIENCE I EVER HOPE TO HAVE - A FANTASY COME **TRUE** - ME WITH THE MOST BEAUTIFUL, DELIGHTFUL GIRL IN THE WORLD - AND SHE **LOVES** ME! SHE LOVES ME!

AND ALL THAT TIME DO YOU KNOW WHAT I WAS THINKING?

WHAT?

"WAIT TILL I TELL THE FELLAS."

3
Social
Interaction
and Social
Processes

SOCIAL INTERACTION

Social interaction is the key element in all of human life and the concept is crucial to any study of the dynamics of society. Without social interaction there would be no group life. The mere placing of individuals in physical proximity, while usually resulting in a modicum of interaction, does not weld them into a social unit or group. It is when people work or play or talk together with a common end, or when they compete or quarrel with one another that associative life, properly speaking, exists. Social interaction is the basic social process, the broadest term for describing dynamic social relationships.

Basic to human survival is the struggle for material goods and other rewards culturally defined as desirable. The chief forms of such struggle or opposition are competition and conflict. Yet not all life consists of one individual striving against another individual. People also combine to gain goals and rewards. This mutual aid is called cooperation. Then too, the individual learns a variety of distinguishing behaviors that set him or her off from others according to age, sex, occupation, and class. This is the process of differentiation. Opposition, cooperation, and differentiation constitute a base line from which still other more specialized forms of interaction arise, such as accommodation, stratification, and assimilation. We shall examine first the universal processes of opposition, cooperation, and differentiation, and then we shall turn to the processes derived from them.

OPPOSITIONAL PROCESSES

Opposition, as well as cooperation, occurs in every society, although its form and direction are modified by the culture of the time and place. Opposition may be defined as a struggle *against* one or more others for a good, goal, or value; cooperation is the joint striving *with* one or more others for a good, goal, or value. A *felt scarcity* or desire for a good or value—money, power, affection, and so on—is basic to both opposition and cooperation. What people fight over, or cooperate together for, is determined in large measure by their culture.

For analytical purposes, opposition may be divided into competition and conflict. *Competition* is a form of opposition in which two or more persons or groups struggle for some need or goal but in the course of which attention is focused chiefly on the reward rather than on the competitor. In *conflict* the person or group thwarts, injures, or destroys the opponent in order to secure a goal or reward. That is, in conflict, interest is often directed initially toward frustrating the opposing individual or group and then toward the ultimate end. It is a two-step process. It is assumed or expected that once the opponent is *hors de combat*, the reward will fall to the victor.

Obviously, in real life, competition and conflict sometimes shade into one another. For example, rivals for the hand of a woman may resort to fisticuffs in their efforts to secure the maiden's favor, and for the moment they are more interested in knocking each other about than in courting. Or a business firm unable to compete with another under the usual "rules of the game" may employ gangsters to beat up the competitor's workmen or to destroy his goods with a view to forcing the opposing firm to withdraw from the struggle.

The source of competition and conflict is often the frustration which comes into play when quick attainment of a goal or reward is denied. Not only is such activity accompanied by emotions, but the blocking of the movement from desire to consummation sets up intense emotional states that serve to stimulate further the individual's striving toward his goal. Rage, fear, and love are emotions that are particularly linked to ones' efforts to get what one wants.

If a man is blocked in his efforts to secure the desired goal, he

ILLUSTRATIVE DATA 3-1   VIOLENCE AND THE POLICE

The policeman uses violence illegally because such usage is seen as just, acceptable, and, at times, expected by his colleague group and because it constitutes an effective means for solving problems in obtaining status and self-esteem which policemen as policemen have in common. Since the ends for which violence is illegally used are conceived to be both just and important, they function to justify, to the policeman, the illegal use of violence as a general means. Since "brutality" is strongly criticized by the larger community, the policeman must devise a defense of his brutality to himself and the community, and the defense in turn gives a deeper and more lasting justification to the "misuse of violence." This process then results in a transfer in property from the state to the colleague group. The means of violence which were originally a property of the state, in loan to its law-enforcement agent, the police, are in a psychological sense confiscated by the police, to be conceived of as a personal property to be used at their discretion. This, then, is the explanation of the illegal use of violence by the police which results from viewing it in terms of the police as an occupational group.

Source: William A. Westley, "Violence and the Police," *The American Journal of Sociology,* LIX (July, 1953), 41.

may proceed in various ways to avoid, offset, overcome, or get around the interference. He may make a highly emotionalized direct attack on the object or situation which blocks the way. If this fails, he may set about acquiring the skill and knowledge needed to attain the goal. And in this learning he may seek and obtain help from others. If he fails to learn the requisite techniques or does not try to acquire them, he may find a substitute for the original goal. This is well illustrated in compensation, which may be expressed in overt behavior or in daydream or fantasy. The man may, of course, give up the effort either to reach the original reward or to secure a substitute. Rather, he may regress to an earlier state or avoid the situation. When confronted by a serious or prolonged crisis, some people make no effort to adapt themselves to the situation. Perhaps the most striking illustrations occur among persons who are mentally ill and especially in severe cases of schizophrenia.

Among human beings, opposition is shaped at most points by cultural learning. For example, a child who in his earliest months was deprived of either sustenance or affection or both might well develop patterns of reactions to, say, parental authority, or to situations offering the alternative between dominance and submission—might become a little "tiger" or little "mouse." When he becomes an adult, the way he handles competition and conflict will be culturally determined in the broad sense, in that he will follow his society's rules governing these processes, and in the narrower sense in that he will always be something of the "tiger" or "mouse" he learned to be in his early social relationships.

Culture and Competition

While culture itself is rooted in man's basic drives and personal interactions, the particular goods—material or nonmaterial—for which he strives vary greatly because of historical factors, accidents or circumstance of the time and place as well as local adaptation to resources. In the United States, people take competition and conflict so much for granted that it is difficult for many Americans to understand that a tribe or nation can have little of them.

In fact, however, an examination of the far-ranging variabilities of culture makes it clear that whether whole societies become generally conditioned to competitive or to cooperative forms of economic and community life depends on the value system of the society. An excellent illustration of such variability is found in the survey of the cultures of thirteen widely separated native tribes, prepared under the direction of Margaret Mead.[1] On the basis of these surveys, Mead concluded that "no society is exclusively competitive or exclusively cooperative. The very existence of highly competitive groups implies cooperation within the groups. Both competitive and cooperative habits must exist within the society."[2] Her analysis is also helpful in indicating the relation of these two basic processes to the tribal structure and to the life organization of the individuals within these societies. Among other significant findings of Mead's survey are the following:

(1) No matter what the nature of the cultural system, strong self-esteem and a sense of power can be found in some members of the society. (2) There is no relationship between the form of the culture and the local problems of sustenance and material resources. For example, there is no reason to assume that lack of food necessarily makes for either competition or cooperation. (3) The concept and valuation of personal success are determined more by the broad and general group emphasis on either competition or cooperation

---

[1]See *Co-operation and Competition Among Primitive Peoples*, Margaret Mead, ed. (New York: McGraw-Hill Book Co., 1937). For a critical review of the psychological, and anthropological treatment of opposition and co-operation, see M. A. May and L. W. Doob, "Competition and Co-operation," *Bulletin*, No. 25 (New York: Social Science Research Council, 1937). The latter, however, fails to obtain adequate distinction between competition and conflict.
[2]*Ibid.*, p. 360.

than by the degree of technology or the plenitude of food. (4) "There is a correspondence between: a major emphasis on competition, a social structure which depends upon the initiative of the individual, a valuation of property for individual ends, a single scale of success, and a strong development of the ego" [social self].[3] This is the sort of pattern that characterizes our own society. (5) "There is a correspondence between: a major emphasis upon cooperation, a social structure which does not depend upon individual initiative or the exercise of power over persons, a faith in an ordered universe, weak emphasis upon rising in status, and a high degree of security for the individual."[4]

It must be emphasized that in none of these tribes is either competition or cooperation wholly lacking. Such fundamental processes are correlative to each other. As economists long ago pointed out, competition itself rests on certain implicit agreements to follow certain rules in the oppositional relations. Yet when a society tends to stress one process, the other process may be found to be less institutionalized and hence less recognized.

Ralph Linton and Abram Kardiner cite a striking example of the effects of a basic change in economy on social organization and individual traits.[5] Among the Tanala of Madagascar, the Betsileo tribe found it necessary, because of soil erosion and other changes, to shift from the cultivation of dry rice to that of wet rice. The system of dry-rice farming was marked by communal ownership of land, a high degree of cooperation, and equal distribution of produce under an extremely authoritarian rule of the fathers. Under this somewhat rigid but paternalistic control, the individual, though passive and obedient to authority, was well-adjusted.

The shift to an economy of wet-rice farming brought in its wake some startling changes. Communal ownership gave way to individual ownership. There was a mad rush for fertile acres in nearby valleys. The individual became important, and he soon began to feel in sharp competition with others over rights, as well as duties. The former family organization broke down, and there was a sharp increase in such deviant conduct as crime, homosexuality, black magic, and neuroticism. In time a whole new social organization emerged, including a rigid class structure of king, nobles, commoners, and slaves. This rapid shift in a basic feature of the culture illustrates clearly how much institutions influence the life organization of individuals.

[3]Mead, *Co-operation and Competition*, p. 511. This and the following quotation by permission of McGraw-Hill Book Company.
[4]*Ibid.*
[5]See Abram Kardiner, *The Individual and His Society*, Chapters 7, 8 (New York: Columbia University Press, 1939).

ILLUSTRATIVE DATA 3-2   THE POSITIVE FUNCTIONS OF SOCIAL CONFLICT

What is important for us is the idea that conflict . . . prevents the ossification of the social system by exerting pressure for innovation and creativity . . . . Conflict within and between groups in a society can prevent accommodations and habitual relations from progressively impoverishing creativity. The clash of values and interests, the tension between what is and what some groups feel ought to be, the conflict between vested interests and new strata and groups demanding their share of power, wealth and status, have been productive of vitality; note for example the contrast between the "frozen" world of the Middle Ages and the burst of creativity that accompanied the thaw that set in with Renaissance civilization.

This is, in effect, the application of John Dewey's theory of consciousness and thought as arising in the wake of obstacles to the interaction of groups. . . .

Conflict not only generates new norms, new institutions . . . it may be said to be stimulating directly in the economic and technological realm. Economic historians often have pointed out that much technological improvement has resulted from the conflict activity of trade unions through the raising of wage levels. A rise in wages usually has led to a substitution of capital investment for labour and hence to an increase in the volume of investment. Thus the extreme mechanization of coalmining in the United States has been partly explained by the existence of militant unionism in the American coalfields. . . .

. . . [A] successful reduction of industrial conflict may have unanticipated dysfunctional consequences for it may destroy an important stimulus for technological innovation.

Source: Lewis A. Coser. "Social Conflict and the Theory of Social Change," *The British Journal of Sociology*, VIII (September, 1957), 197–198. Reprinted by permission of Routledge & Kegan Paul Ltd.

It is clear, then, that competition may take a wide variety of forms. It may be central to some aspects of a cultural system and not to others. Moreover, under the impact of invention, political revolution, or shifts in the resource base of an economy, striking changes may occur in the interrelations of competition and other social processes.

Conflict

Conflict is characterized by emotionalized and violent opposition, in which the major concern is to overcome the opponent as a means of securing a goal or reward. It is direct and openly antagonistic struggle of persons or groups for the same object or end. The aim of conflict is the defeat, subjugation, or annihiliation of the other person or group as a means of obtaining the goal.

ILLUSTRATIVE DATA 3-3   CONFLICT BINDS ANTAGONISTS

If . . . a fight simply aims at annihilation, it does approach the marginal case of assassination in which the admixture of unifying elements is almost zero. If, however, there is any consideration, any limit to violence, there already exists a socializing factor, even though only as the qualification of violence. Kant said that every war in which the belligerents do not impose some restrictions in the use of possible means upon one another, necessarily . . . becomes a war of extermination. It is almost inevitable that an element of commonness injects itself into . . . enmity once the stage of open violence yields to another relationship, even though this new relation may contain a completely undiminished sum of animosity between the two parties.

One unites in order to fight, and one fights under the mutually recognized control of norms and rules.

Source: Georg Simmel, *Conflict*, trans. Kurt H. Wolff (Glencoe, Illinois: The Free Press, 1955), pp. 26, 35.

In the struggle to overcome the other person or group, the goal is often temporarily relegated to a level of secondary importance. In contrast to competition, which, at least in its stricter impersonal aspects, is more or less continuous and unconscious, conflict is an intermittent but highly conscious process. Of course, in many situations competition and conflict are interrelated, the conflict often arising at critical points in the more prolonged competitive process.

Conflict is affected by the nature of the group and its particular culture. The objects of conflict may be property, power and status, freedom of action and thought, or any other desired value. When economic interests loom large and there are many individuals or groups striving for material gain and power, conflict of economic interests may supplement the competitive process. If sectarianism is rife, we can expect conflict to occur in religion. In other words, the culturally determined values of a society will set the stage for its struggles.

Not only is the form of conflict modified by the particular societal order and its culture, but everywhere there arise regulations to govern it. In feuds, for example, there are certain accepted methods of killing the other fellow. Lynching follows a certain tradition. When the conflict is infrequent and when no adequate techniques have been worked out, more violent and unpredictable sorts of conflict arise, such as race riots. In war, of course, there are all sorts of rules more or less agreed upon by the belligerents during the interludes of peace.

At its most rudimentary level, conflict results in the removal or annihilation of the opponent. In human society, however, most conflict ends in some sort of agreement, or accommodation, or in the fusion of the two opposing elements. The essential nature of social conflict can be summarized in terms of the following five propositions:[6]

(1) Conflict requires at least two parties (groups, individuals, organizations, etc.) since it is by definition an interaction relationship.

(2) Conflict arises from some kind of "scarcity," of desired but limited resources, activities, positions, or goals.

(3) Conflict actions are designed to limit, thwart, destroy, control, or otherwise influence another party (person, group, etc.) and a conflict relationship is one in which the conflicting parties can gain only at each other's relative expense.

(4) Conflict requires interaction among parties in which their actions and counteractions are mutually opposed.

(5) Conflict relations always involve attempts to acquire or exercise social power.

COOPERATION

Cooperation, like opposition, is a basic feature of human interaction. These ambivalent patterns, we have noted, appear to underlie all other more specialized social processes. As Albion W. Small (one of the founders of sociology in America) put it, "Struggle and co-operation are correlates in every situation"—that is, there is either "conjunction" or "conflict" of interests.[7] Yet the interplay of these two processes is not always understood. Some writers consider opposition the fundamental form of interaction; others believe that cooperation is the basic social process. For example, some use the term *cooperation* as a synonym for almost all social contact, holding that opponents in fighting must "cooperate" in order to exchange blows, or that traders "cooperate" in their market relations, or that the compromise of disputes between laborers and employers represents a form of cooperation. Such broad and loose use of the term makes it practically identical with the term *social interaction* and thus too vague for effective description and analysis. We shall limit the term *cooperation* to a more specific aspect of human intercourse, one having to do with mutual aid or an alliance of persons or groups seeking some common goal or reward—in short, as some kind of conjoint rather than opposing action.

Patterns of mutual aid are found among all human groups. Such habits and attitudes begin in infancy and childhood within the

---

[6]These propositions are paraphrased from Raymond W. Mack and Richard C. Snyder, "The Analysis of Social Conflict—Toward an Overview and Synthesis," *Journal of Conflict Resolution,* I (June, 1957), 212–248.

[7]Albion W. Small, *General Sociology* (Chicago: University of Chicago Press, 1905), pp. 357, 203.

ILLUSTRATIVE DATA 3-4   CONFLICT AND SOCIAL SOLIDARITY

The group in a state of peace can permit antagonistic members within it to live with one another in an undecided situation because each of them can go his own way and can avoid collisions. A state of conflict, however, pulls the members so tightly together and subjects them to such uniform impulse that they either must get completely along with, or completely repel, one another. This is the reason why war with the outside is sometimes the last chance for a state ridden with inner antagonisms to overcome these antagonisms or else to break up definitely.

The fighter must "pull himself together." That is, all his energies must be, as it were, concentrated in one point so that they can be employed at any moment in any required direction.

The well-known reciprocal relation between a despotic orientation and the warlike tendencies of a group rests on this informal basis: war needs a centralistic intensification of the group form, and this is guaranteed best by despotism.

Source: Georg Simmel, *Conflict*, trans. Kurt H. Wolff (Glencoe, Illinois: The Free Press, 1955), pp. 87, 88, 92, 93.

family and the congeniality group. Upon the basis acquired in these primary groups, the individual develops cooperative behavior patterns as an adult. In order for rudimentary mutual helpfulness to develop into more deliberate form, people must first be directly motivated to seek a goal that may be shared. Second, they must acquire some knowledge of the benefits of such activity—hence the need for education to foster cooperation. Third, they must acquire a favorable attitude toward sharing both the work and the rewards involved. And finally, they need to equip themselves with the skills necessary to make the cooperative plan work.[8]

Like opposition, cooperation arises from the orientation of the individual to the in-group and the out-group. While competition, rivalry, and conflict may arise in the in-group, it is evident that an in-group could not persist were it not for cooperation. The solidarity of the in-group is expressed most strongly in mutual aid, helpfulness, and loyalty to the group-accepted symbols. Such cooperation is most in evidence when the in-group stands in sharp opposition to some other body of persons, an out-group. The very strength of the in-group feeling of solidarity rests in part on the fact that hostile feelings are directed toward some out-group. The intensity of the in-group feelings seems correlated, indeed, with the intensity of antagonism toward the out-group.

---

[8]See M. A. May and L. W. Doob, "Competition and Co-operation."

Cooperation imposes various forms of restraint on the participant. The individual cannot have his or her way entirely if he or she is to work cooperatively with another.

If a self-assertive trend becomes too strong, cooperation will be replaced by struggle. Cooperation always implies inhibition of certain ego-centered tendencies. A child in team play cannot always assume the chief role. The more conscious and complex the form of cooperation, the more evident this fact becomes. From the restraint so imposed there arises a moral control which stands in contrast with the impulsiveness and lack of self-control found in uninhibited conflict. In the struggle of one group against another, this moral order is highly important, as it is also in controlling the relations of persons to one another within the group itself. The function of cooperation is well summarized in the following words of C. H. Cooley:

> Co-operation . . . arises when men see that they have a common interest and have, at the same time, sufficient intelligence and self-control to seek this interest through united action: perceived unity of interest and the faculty of organization are the essential facts in intelligent combination.[9]

Culture and Cooperation

It is not necessary to posit an instinct of sociability or gregariousness in order to explain cooperation. The instances of interaction simply within the family would furnish sufficient ground upon which to construct the cooperative social order which we find everywhere. Beyond the family the neighborhood, the play group, and the whole set of secondary groups call for cooperation. If we say that human cooperation is a form of interaction between two or more persons or groups striving toward some goal or reward which may be shared in material goods, in prestige and power, or in some other accepted satisfaction, we can also say that *culture is what gives cooperation pitch and direction*.

In the United States there appears to be far more teaching of the child, youth, and adult in competitive and conflictive attitudes, habits, and ideas than in those involving cooperation. Yet the society is not given entirely to conflict or to competitive individualism. Within the social class, the team, the trade union, the employers' association, the religious confraternity, interdependence and mutual aid are absolutely essential. Nevertheless, in all these

---

[9]C. H. Cooley, *Sociological Theory and Social Research* (New York: Henry Holt & Co., 1930), p. 176. By permission.

ILLUSTRATIVE DATA 3-5   COOPERATION AMONG THE ZUÑI

In addition to obligations between kinsmen that are established at birth, the Zuñi have institutionalized a ceremonial friendship built around economic cooperation. Such friends are under obligation to lend assistance in all large undertakings. . . .

Strikingly characteristic of all social relations in Zuni is the relative lack of emphasis upon wealth. Property does not figure in marriage. Individuals do not compete for a fixed supply, and in terms of the prestige an individual may achieve, property in itself is not the determining factor. . . .

Wealth circulates freely, and property rights are neither clearly defined nor strictly enforced. . . . The property that is really valued . . . is the nonmaterial property such as songs, prayers, rituals. . . .

The principles of land tenure reveal further the basic noncompetitive and nonindividualistic property patterns in Zuni. Most of the reservation consists of land unsuitable, at present, for cultivation. These uncultivated areas belong communally to the tribe and any man may stake out new fields wherever he wishes. Such fields, in contrast to those held by the female line of a household, belong to him individually and may be disposed of by him at his pleasure. But so long as he remains associated with a household either by blood or by marriage he cultivates the field for a communal end, the products that he raises becoming the collective property of the women of the household. It is even possible to appropriate land, the title of which is held by another family, providing that it is not in use. For although distinctions are made between ownership and use of a field, these are by no means clear, and it is difficult to dispossess a family that has taken possession.

It is significant, too, that litigations over the ownership of land are rare and in most cases quickly settled. One might expect that disputes would arise frequently among a people whose concepts of ownership are so vaguely defined that boundaries between fields are marked only in one dimension, in width facing the road and not in depth.

The problem of sheep ownership. . . . Here evidently a new individualistic pattern seems to have developed under stimulation of white contact. Yet it is interesting to note that, although the ownership of sheep is individualistic, few Zuñi know how many sheep they own. Nor, in spite of the great value in which sheep are held, do men compete against one another for sheep. Rather, a young man is assisted in developing a flock of his own. A boy who offers to herd for a group of his male kinsmen receives from them at the shearing season a number of sheep as gifts. These belong to him and form the nucleus of his own herd. Next season in addition to the lambs that have been born he is given more sheep by his association until after a few seasons he has accumulated sixty sheep—a sack of wool. At this point he becomes a full-fledged member of the group and he is given no more assistance. Thus instead of attempting to acquire a monopoly, a group of men cooperate to "set up" a young relative, though this is not essential in herding. . . .

Food is shared by all in the household and is based entirely on need, with no account taken of the field it has been grown in or of who has been responsible in producing it. If, for example, A should bring in some especially choice melon from his field, his wife does not feel that she has any more claim to it than her sister. A man may, however, take food from his own field to his female relatives, his mother, his sister, or a niece, providing he has not yet brought the food into the house. For then it falls entirely under the jurisdiction of the women in the house.

Source: Irving Goldman, "The Zuñi Indians of New Mexico," *Cooperation and Competition among Primitive Peoples,* ed. Margaret Mead (New York: McGraw-Hill, 1937), pp. 326–329. Reprinted by permission.

the fundamental and persisting values are frequently those of the <u>competitive-conflictive</u> *ethos.*

An illustration of a different cultural attitude toward cooperation will illustrate this point. S. D. Porteus, a psychologist, tells of his difficulty in getting certain natives of Australia to work individually and competitively on intelligence tests. The natives turned to him for help to do the task and were clearly upset when he refused. Porteus had earlier been adopted as a tribal brother, and the natives simply could not understand how a person in such a relationship to them could refuse to cooperate in a task put before them.[10]

From an ethnocentric standpoint, forms of cooperation found in other societies may strike us as being absurd and the individuals therein as lacking in ambition and initiative. Some societies, like the one just mentioned, emphasize cooperation as a cultural value much more than Americans while other societies set less value on cooperation than we. But cooperation, like competition and conflict, is a universal characteristic of human societies; in no society is it completely lacking. Among people, as among animals, there is a good deal of nondeliberate mutual aid, especially in time of grave danger. Even in our highly individualistic, competitive world, people have also learned, especially in primary-group situations, interdependence and mutual aid in times of stress. Certainly such patterns are distinctly culturized through the Judeo-Christian religion. Again, it must be recalled that cooperation and conflict are closely related. For example, members of a group may be highly cooperative with one another and conflictive toward other groups. The ethos of the culture will define the nature and degree of such cooperation and conflict.

---

[10]See S. D. Porteus, *The Psychology of a Primitive People* (New York: Longmans, Green & Co., 1931), pp. 308–309.

DIFFERENTIATION

Some type of specialization or differentiation of role is found in every society. Such differentiation is clearly related to the division of labor. In the industrial economic order, for example, there are the different roles of entrepreneur, manager, and skilled and unskilled laborers. In the political order it is seen in the varying roles of public administrators, and in religion, in the distinctive roles of prophet, seer, and priest. Some form of specialization of role is found in every association of people and, moreover, where such differentiation is linked to basic needs and goals it takes on the permanence and persistence of institutions.

Certainly all societies show variations in social conduct, especially in role and status. However, some universals exist. All societies give a place to childhood different from the one they give to maturity or old age. Everywhere one finds some individuals who dominate others in varying social situations. Even in the most rudimentary societies, there is always some division of labor.

Differences in age and sex are obvious foundations of specialization although how the varied roles are defined depends, of course, on the particular culture. So too, different occupations create conditions for variation in roles and statuses while at the same time fostering interdependence. As the British economist Henry Clay once put it, "From the point of view of the individual, division of labor means *specialization*; from the point of view of society, it means *co-operation*."[11]

While some specialization is found in tribal societies, highly integrated specialization is associated with extensive agriculture, handicrafts, the marketplace, writing, the political state, and other aspects of a more complex culture. The ancient world, even before the rise of Greece and Rome, witnessed differentiation in economic, political, military, religious, and other areas of human association. Professions and techniques evolved, with their particular knowledge, skills, language, and status. In fact, their development illustrates the emergence of variations in group participation called "specialties."

Economic Division of Labor

The division of labor does not go very far in any society until people begin to produce goods or services in such quantity that the surplus can be exchanged for the goods or services of others. But specialization of economic roles depends not only on the level of

---

[11]Henry Clay, *Economics for the General Reader* (New York: The Macmillan Co., 1918), p. 21.

technology and the needs of the tribe or society but also on the degree of sophistication in the marketing process. People learned only gradually that division of labor benefits oneself as well as others.

While there was considerable specialization in the ancient world, it was the coming of the factory system that marked the great expansion in division of labor. The modern machine makes it possible to produce small parts that can be combined into a total product. This, of course, involves standardization and further simplification in the making of a particular part. Mechanization also makes for efficient production and fosters the development of large-scale corporate ownership and control. Finance capitalism and machine-dominated division of labor emerged at the same historical time.

Some of the functions or consequences of a highly differentiated economic structure are the following: (1) Specialization makes it possible to select workers according to their capacity to do a particular job. Both intelligence and temperament may be important. (2) It facilitates the acquisition of high skill in some one craft or phase of an operation. The "Jack-of-all-trades" is displaced by one who can learn the needed skill quickly and accurately. (3) It increases efficiency because it makes for concentration of attention and skill on single items of work, and this, in turn, is associated with (4) standardization of product, which makes mass production possible and often—though not always—results in a better product. (5) It saves time and human energy. This is the virtue of automation. (6) It permits classification of skills and products, making in turn for effective management.[12] And (7), to repeat, it promotes the factory system and the organization of large-scale units of production. This means the assembly of workers and many machines under one management, making supervision simpler, allowing concentration of raw materials at convenient points, and permitting urbanization with its more advantageous marketing.

Some of the alleged negative consequences of division of labor, especially in the machine age, are the following: (1) Factory work and machine production involve safety hazards and may produce ill-health if not properly regulated. (2) Overspecialization may so concentrate attention and skill on simple muscular responses as to make for monotony and fatigue, destroying incentive and creative interest in one's job. Critics of the modern factory system often

---

[12]The extent of specialization is indicated in the listing of over 40,000 titles of particular jobs in the *Dictionary of Occupational Titles*, 2 vols., 2nd ed. (Washington, D.C.: U.S. Government Printing Office, 1949). Of this number approximately 9,000 are coded titles—that is, they fall into a number of more-or-less established job categories. The rest are uncoded but usually are related to some recognized job classification. Supplement 1 (published in 1955) contains 2,260 new and revised definitions and 1,322 new code numbers.

contend that such work is unpleasant and disheartening and lowers the morale of the workers. They say that the artisan who made a total product—chair, house, pair of boots, piece of cloth—understood every step in the process, enjoyed putting the material together, and had genuine satisfaction in seeing the finished product. They argue that *the machine dominates the personality*. These critics tend to agree with Karl Marx, who defended the thesis that the machine—an objective, impersonal thing—controlled the spirit, initiative, and freedom of the operator. Instead of being the end or aim of the economic process, the individual, Marx said, becomes merely the means to production, an appendage to a system of machines that reduces him to a nonentity. The impersonality which characterizes much of modern life would thus be traceable not merely to the operations of the market and the wage system, but to the factory system itself. (3) The modern machine tends to destroy the skilled trades and to substitute semiautomatic and automatic machines, leaving the operator only simple movements to perform. (4) In a capitalistic society, such high specialization tends to make the worker increasingly dependent on the owner-manager. Moreover, the business cycle subjects the worker to seasonal and long-term periods of unemployment.

The features which we have just described are, of course, familiar. Efficient and advantageous as the factory system is for our economic welfare, it has not contributed to the larger society and culture without some human costs. Yet man's ability to make new adjustments is great; and when there is good health, adequate income with steady employment, and retirement benefits, many of the negative effects of overspecialization tend to disappear. In general, highly industrialized societies make possible a higher level of living than mankind ever experienced in the past.

Social Implications of Specialization

In the study of the division of labor, one is concerned not only with differentiation of activities but also with how the various activities mesh or are interdependent. It is interesting that the individualism associated with a laissez-faire philosophy should produce a social structure so interdependent that the dislocation of any considerable section of it—say a key industry like steel-making or transportation—threatens the whole society. In other words, specialization promotes not only separateness but also the integration of group life. In this way, specialization fosters cooperation. The weaver is dependent on the sheep raiser for his wool, and both need a merchant or middleman to market their goods; the entrepreneur is dependent on the banker for capital; and so on. In fact, the

---

ILLUSTRATIVE DATA 3-6   INTERGROUP CONFLICT

A general principle of approach is that, except in acute crisis situations, problems of group conflict are usually most readily resolved by indirection than by frontal assault.

Changing the attitudes of groups rather than isolated individuals is the more effective approach for breaking up intergroup stereotypes and prejudices.

Hostility is decreased by any activity which leads members of conflicting groups to identify their own values and life-activities in individuals of the other group.

Conflict and hostility are rendered less probable by any activity which leads individuals to take for granted the other group (e.g., moving pictures which show Negroes as members of various kinds of groups, where the emphasis of presentation is upon what the group is doing).

Lessened hostility will result from arranging intergroup collaboration, on the basis of personal association of individuals as functional equals, on a common task jointly accepted as worthwhile.

Personal association of members of different groups is most effective in reducing hostility and increasing understanding when the focus of interaction is upon a common interest, goal, or task rather than upon intergroup association as such.

A general expectation of authoritative intervention and the possibility of punishment for acts of violence, whether in group conflict or in individual incidents, will decrease the probability of open conflict.

Source: Robin M. Williams, Jr., *The Reduction of Intergroup Tensions* (New York: Social Science Research Council, 1947), pp. 63, 66, 68, 69, 71, and 74. Reprinted by permission. The seven propositions above are taken from Williams' list of 101 propositions on intergroup conflict.

economic order consists of a vast network of competition, cooperation, and differentiation.

In societies where all women garden and cook and all men hunt and fish, the total content of the culture is little more than the combined knowledge of any two adults of opposite sex. A second consequence of elaborate occupational specialization, then, is an increase in the content of culture. Bushmen do not have much more to transmit to the next generation than any one Bushman can know. Americans have so much more to transit than any one American could possibly know that the concept of the content of culture becomes staggering.

DERIVED SOCIAL PROCESSES

From opposition, cooperation, and differentiation emerge several other social processes. These *derived* processes are also universal in human societies. Out of differentiation grows *social ranking*. Cooperation among varied groups often leads to *assimilation*. Since conflict is not usually continuous between groups, some working arrangement, or *accommodation,* arises. This section describes these processes derived from opposition, cooperation, and differentiation.

Accommodation

The word *accommodation* has been used in two related senses—to indicate a condition of institutional arrangement, and to indicate a process. As a *condition,* accommodation is the fact of equilibrium between individuals and groups and the "rules of the game" which have been developed. Etiquette, or the "proper" way of acting socially, the "agreements" developed between conflicting economic groups, treaties between nations, and the techniques, traditions, and arrangements which define the relations of persons and groups are forms of accomodation. As a *process,* accommodation has to do with the conscious efforts of people to develop such working arrangements among themselves as will suspend conflict and so make their relations more tolerable and less wasteful of energy. It concerns the movement toward the accommodated state. It is a means of resolving conflict without the complete destruction or absorption of the opponent—that is, without either party's entirely losing its identity. It takes place at a conscious—though not necessarily rational—level, and for the most part is in the nature of formal and external regulations or arrangements.

The effects of accommodation may vary somewhat with the circumstances. Accommodation may act to reduce the conflict between persons or groups as an initial step to synthesis of differences into a new pattern—in other words, it may lead to assimilation. It may serve to postpone outright conflict for a specific period of time, as in a treaty between nations or a labor-management agreement. It may permit groups separated by sharp social-psychological distance to get along together. In this function it is closely related to stratification as seen in class or caste systems. It may prevent what the culture considers an undesirable amalgamation or biological inbreeding of two groups and their subsequent assimilation. Sometimes the accommodation is viewed by the parties involved as mutually beneficial. In other instances the arrangements are imposed on one group by another with superior power and prestige.

Forms of Accommodation

Accommodative arrangements between groups or individuals take a variety of forms, from coercion through compromise and conciliation to toleration. *Coercion* is a type of accommodation in which action and thought in social relationships are determined by constraint, compulsion, or force. Coercion implies the existence of the weak and the strong in any conflict. It takes two forms—physical or direct application of force; and psychological, or indirect application of force. For example, slavery is an arrangement in which the basic social interaction is one of domination by master and subjection of slave. Slavery involves absence of political rights for the slave, compulsory labor, and property rights of the master with regard to the slave as an individual.

Various political dictatorships are coercive accommodations in which a strongly disciplined minority seizes power and inflicts its control on whole populations. It is a mistake to assume that such despotism is never welcome as a means of settling conflicts. When older values and practices are lost and a struggle rages between multiple warring interests, the masses come in time to look for a strong person who will bring peace and order. Such a person was Napoleon Bonaparte, who stabilized France after its bloody revolution. Benito Mussolini did something of this sort for Italy after World War I. It was the case with Adolf Hitler and the rise of Nazism in Germany. And under Nikolai Lenin, Joseph Stalin, and others, the Communist Party unified a discordant Soviet Union and in time welded it into a powerful nation-state.

Coercion is not confined, of course, to slavery, conquest, revolution, and international relations; it also occurs in situations involving racial, religious, industrial, and other conflicts.

Compromise, unlike coercive accommodation, implies a fair degree of equality in bargaining power of two contestants or willingness of the stronger party to substitute justice for strength as the basis for agreement. Compromise may be defined as a conscious method of settling a conflict in which all parties agree to renounce or reduce some of their demands in the interest of peace. Readiness to compromise means that groups and individuals are able to view themselves somewhat objectively, and to see themselves as others see them. Intransigent attitudes generated in the heat of conflict give way to more moderate positions. Certain international agreements and management-labor agreements on wages, hours of work, and other conditions of employment are examples of compromise. In a political democracy, too, parties or factions resolve their differences by compromise. This is especially true when they are about evenly matched in social power.

Arbitration is a special device for bringing about compromise when the contending parties themselves are unable to resolve their differences. Disputes are settled by a third party, who may be chosen by the opposing sides or appointed by some larger agency of power, as in legalized compulsory arbitration of labor disputes. _Mediation_, which is closely akin to arbitration, is the introduction into a conflict of a neutral agent whose efforts are directed toward bringing about a peaceful settlement. The mediator has no power to settle the conflict; his function is advisory only. The use of arbitrators or mediators is common in industrial and religious disputes in the United States.

Closely related to compromise and sometimes involving compromise is _conciliation_, which is an attempt to reconcile disputants as a means of bringing about an agreement. In modern industrial systems certain forms of conciliation have developed as a permanent program for settling disputes between owners and workers. Such organizations, called "works councils" or "shop committees," may or may not exist independently of trade unions. In these organizations representatives of the owners and workers set up institutional devices for handling disputes over wages, hours, and working conditions. Conciliation has also been used in racial and religious struggles. Conciliation always connotes a milder response to an opponent than coercion. In the end conciliation, like toleration, opens the door to assimilation.

While some strain may remain after an accommodative arrangement has been made, and while neither party ever gets everything it wanted, the art of accommodation is important in a world of temporizing. In our earliest social relations, all of us learn to get along with half measures. To operate in the social world on an all-or-none principle is extremely difficult, if not impossible. We soon discover that doing so will not get us the things we want. In a world of contending wishes and interests and a limited supply of goods, material or otherwise, accommodation seems inevitable.

In any case, discussion between the parties to a conflict is an essential aspect of accommodation as it is expressed in compromise, arbitration, mediation, and conciliation. Deliberation as a means of settling differences is linked to the culture patterns of democracy, individualism, liberalism, and the scientific attitude. It means that conflict is reduced in intensity from overt force to the level of verbal give-and-take. Since deliberation permits an objective consideration of many phases of a struggle, in the end it lays the foundation for a consensus of attitudes and opinions essential to any effective agreement.

One of the problems of international relations is the continuing difficulty of reducing coercion to some milder form of accommodation.

Another form of accommodation is _toleration_, or _tolerant participation_. It is an outgrowth of the live-and-let-live policy just noted. It is a form of accommodation without formal agreement. Sometimes it is not entirely deliberate and conscious, but grows up from long-continuing avoidances developed to soften hostilities. There have been many instances of this type of arrangement, such as among various language and nationality groupings in central Europe and among the Navajo and Pueblo Indians.

Social Ranking

Differentiation takes place universally on the basis of age, sex, and other factors. Out of differentiation emerges a division of labor, or assignment of various tasks to categories of people sharing different characteristics. Another process that is derived from differentiation is the ranking of social categories. Social ranking includes both the process of ranking differentiated categories and the resultant hierarchy. As a process, ranking has to do with the forms of interaction involved in the process; for example, ranking wealthy people above poor people, or people who abide by the norms of society above deviants, or people whose tasks are considered important for the welfare of society above those whose work is less highly valued.

Assimilation

If person-to-person, person-to-group, or group-to-group relations remained at the level of accommodation, there would occur no fusion of groups and their cultures. _Assimilation_ is the fusion or blending of two previously distinct groups into one. Obviously, assimilation requires more fundamental changes than the "antagonistic cooperation" which we call accommodation. When the process of assimilation takes place, the people in two distinct groups do not just compromise or otherwise agree to get along with each other; they become so much like each other that they are no longer distinguishable as separate groups.

Assimilation occurs only when there is relatively continuous and direct contact. It is a comparatively slow process, though the history of human societies is full of examples of such merging of groups and their cultures. Among the more striking cases was the assimilation of the Anglo-Saxon and Norman societies in Britain in the two centuries after 1066, when the Normans invaded England. The so-called American "melting pot" is a recent and partial instance of assimilation. It is not usually possible today to tell the descendants of Englishmen or Germans who came here in the eighteenth century from the descendants of Scotsmen who emigrated at about the same time. Previously distinct groups have become fused into one, or assimilated. A factor which helps complete the process of assimilation is amalgamation, which is the intermarriage of members of different groups.

Amalgamation

One sometimes hears that a group is partially assimilated, or that Italian-Americans, for example, are not as fully assimilated as Irish-Americans. The fact that assimilation is not an all-or-nothing condition but rather a matter of degree is simply an indication that it is a process that occurs through time. Complete assimilation always implies amalgamation—that is, accepted intermarriage between the originally divergent groups. Without biological amalgamation, complete assimilation is not possible. If the two groups are still differentiated by the provision that their members shall not intermarry, then they are, *ipso facto*, not fully assimilated.

Mere intermixture of groups to a limited degree does not guarantee assimilation. Amalgamation must be socially accepted; it must become a part of the institutional structure before assimilation exists. For instance, in the United States there has been considerable racial crossing between whites and blacks, but there has been little amalgamation, despite the fact of a common culture. No observer of the contemporary American scene would contend that blacks and whites have become fused into one indistinguishable whole. For purposes of most interaction, accommodation and ranking rather than assimilation have been the rule. On the other hand, the rate of intermarriage among European immigrant groups is a definite indication of the fusion of persons from many societies into one new one. The United States is a case study of a society composed, through assimilation and amalgamation, of a variety of social and biological elements.

Acculturation

When two or more cultures come into contact, the subsequent intermixture of shared, learned behavior patterns is called *acculturation*. This process may involve the almost complete absorption of one culture by another, or a relatively equal merging of traits and patterns from both cultures. Acculturation can occur with or without assimilation. The accommodative relations of Christian and Moslem societies through the centuries have resulted in acculturation. Christians have adopted some of the behavior patterns of Moslems, and Moslems have adopted some of the behavior patterns of Christians; but the members of the two societies have not assimilated.

The blending of Oriental and Occidental elements in contemporary Japanese culture is another instance of acculturation without assimilation of two groups. The Japanese way of life has changed considerably in a relatively short time under the impact of Western culture. Not only is there more Western-style clothing in Japan, as well as other evidences of acculturation, such as increased use of telephones, television, and subways, but there are alterations in such basic culture patterns as food consumption and formal education.

Again, the hybrid patterns of Latin-American societies have sprung from the acculturation of Spanish and Indian American cultures, characterized by a degree of both assimilation and amalgamation. Large portions of Greek and Roman culture have become acculturated with Hebraic and Germanic patterns, and have, in turn, contributed to our own culture.

The whole question of the degree of acculturation and the interplay of accommodation and assimilation is crucial in the contemporary world, not only in the relations of nation-states with one another in peace and war but in the relations of social classes to one another within societies. It is often noted that the social distance between the most privileged classes and the least educated, lowest-paid classes in our society is considerably narrower than it was a generation or two ago. When one speaks of the existence of "mass society," he or she is referring to the fact that Mrs. Astorbilt and Joe Doakes saw the same television program last night, that both are members of the Book-of-the-Month Club, and that their sons at the Old English Finishing School and Corner High, respectively, are dressed in remarkably similar clothes. We are referring, in other words, to acculturation between classes within a society.

Socialization

Socialization is interaction by means of which the individual learns the social and cultural requirements that make the individual a functioning member of society. This interaction teaches one habits, ideas, attitudes, and values. The person learns to conform to the cultural expectations, traditions, and sanctions, develops a sense of self, and learns to identify with culturally defined in-groups. One acquires the in-group's attitudes toward out-groups—attitudes of opposition, avoidance, or indifference. The initial socialization occurs in the child's contacts with parents, siblings, and playmates, but all through life the individual continues to feel the impact of society.

INTERPRETIVE SUMMARY

The word *process* describes people interacting: fighting, helping one another, teaching their young, and so on. Like structures and functions, certain processes are universal. One such process is opposition, or struggle over a goal which cannot be shared or which the antagonists refuse to share. They may calmly concentrate on attaining the goal, they may see destruction of their enemy as absolutely essential to their own success, they may be able to "see his side" and be willing to give up part of their demands so that he will not suffer, or they may not even be conscious that a struggle is going on in the first place. The form of the struggle will also be dependent on how each antagonist assesses his relative strength; a powerful force may insist on having all its demands met, while equal sides will probably settle for some sort of compromise.

Cooperation, the process of working together for a common goal, is the opposite of competition and conflict. Cooperation leads to acculturation, in which cultures or subcultures adopt behavior patterns from one another, and finally to assimilation, the state in which two groups actually blend into one.

All societies condone both opposition and cooperation under some circumstances. However, a given society may stress one more than the other, depending on the ethos of the society. Furthermore, goals themselves and the rules concerning how one may go about attaining them will differ from society to society.

Two intra-society processes are differentiation and socialization. In assigning specialities, or differentiating, a culture must take into account certain broad biological limitations which members of all societies have in common; beyond this, the culture may follow its own course in dividing necessary labor and deciding how groups should be ranked socially. Socialization is the process in which an individual is taught the ways of his culture, including its ways of carrying out the other processes.

SUGGESTIONS FOR FURTHER READING

Chase, Stuart. *Roads to Agreement: Successful Methods in the Science of Human Relations.* New York: Harper and Brothers, 1951. This is a survey of various means of accommodating conflict, such as "worker-participation" in industrial relations, the Quaker meeting, and group dynamics.

Coser, Lewis A. *Continuities in the Study of Social Conflict.* New York: The Free Press, 1968. The author discusses the positive values of conflict.

Frazier, E. Franklin. *Race and Culture Contacts in the Modern World.* New York: Alfred A. Knopf, 1957. Racial and cultural conflict, its accommodation, and the assimilation process in the world during the past two centuries are summarized.

Gordon, Milton M. *Assimilation in American Life.* New York: Oxford University Press, 1964. This is an excellent analysis of the process of assimilation of racial and national minorities and of the pressures for and against assimilation in an urban industrial society.

Hertzler, Joyce O. *Society in Action: A Study of Basic Social Processes.* New York: The Dryden Press, 1954. Chapter One contains a good discussion of the significance of the idea of process. The book has an extensive bibliography.

Kornhuser, Arthur; Dubin, Robert; and Ross, Arthur M., eds. *Industrial Conflict.* New York: McGraw-Hill Book Co., 1954. This book contains forty papers on industrial conflict, including two on its origins and several on its control and accommodation.

Lewin, Kurt. *Resolving Social Conflicts.* New York: Harper and Row, 1948. This is a discussion of the nature and causes of social conflict containing considerable material on cultural variations.

Mead, Margaret, ed. *Cooperation and Competition in Primitive Peoples.* New York: McGraw-Hill Book Company, 1936. Although prepared more than a quarter century ago, this is still an interesting and informative collection.

Montagu, Ashley F. *On Being Human.* New York: Henry Schuman, 1950. Scientific data is convincingly presented to support the thesis that cooperation, not conflict, is the "natural law of life."

Myrdal, Alva, and Klein, Viola. *Women's Two Roles: Home and Work.* New York: Humanities Press, 1956. This is a fine cross-cultural analysis on the conflict between family and work roles among American, British, French, and Swedish women.

Park, Robert E., and Burgess, E. W. *Introduction to the Science of Sociology.* 2nd ed. Chicago: The University of Chicago Press, 1924. Chapters 4-6 and 8-11 contain pertinent source materials and good theoretical discussions. This is still the classic discussion of social processes.

Williams, Robin M., Jr. *The Reduction of Intergroup Tensions.* New York: Social Science Research Council, 1947. Numerous propositions about the nature and resolution of social conflict are contained in this famous monograph.

4
Culture
and
Society

CULTURE

In every human collectivity, whether a family or a national society, there are certain recurrent, accepted, and expected ways of thinking and acting. Such patterns of behavior common to a society or other social group we call culture. Culture is that part of the human environment that people have created themselves. The classic definition of culture was written by E. B. Tylor in 1871: "Culture . . . is that complex whole which includes knowledge, belief, art, morals, law, custom, and any other capabilities and habits acquired by man as a member of society."[1] Culture is the social heritage of a people. It consists of commonly accepted and expected ideas, attitudes, values, and behavior which people learn in connection with social living. For the individual, culture is an enormous aid in learning to get on effectively in the world. The members of each new generation do not have to begin "from scratch," but benefit from the earlier generations around them, who, in turn, learned how to adjust to the physical and social world largely from their progenitors. Later, this new generation passes on

---

[1]Edward B. Tylor, *Primitive Culture* (New York: Brentano's, 1924), p. 1.

79

to the next generation what it has learned from the previous generations and what it has added to the cultural whole.

The concept of culture always refers to behavior that is shared and transmitted through learning. Behavior in this context refers to thinking and feeling as well as overt actions. Any behavior is part of a culture only when it is shared by most members, or by specifically designated members, of the group. If you are the only person who parts his hair with a wire brush, then this behavior is not part of American culture. If most Americans arrange their hair with a wire brush after they get up in the morning, then this behavior is shared; it is part of American culture. Most Americans share the belief that the United States is the best place in the world to live. This belief is part of the American culture.

By learned behavior we mean more than attitudes and ways of acting that are formally and consciously taught. Any behavior which is socially acquired (that is, which comes through participation in a human group) is learned. Some aspects of individual behavior are determined, of course, by heredity; such behavior is not cultural. If a stone is thrown in a person's face, the person will blink. This is shared behavior, but it is not learned; it is inherited. Therefore, blinking in this instance is not part of the culture. Hunger pangs are not culturally learned, but the thought of fried chicken as satisfying or of fried beetles as repulsive is learned and hence is cultural.

It is difficult to exaggerate the importance of culture as a determinant of human behavior. One way to try and grasp the significance of culture is to imagine the human condition without it. Fifty years ago Graham Wallas visualized modern urban people without culture and concluded:

> If the earth were struck by one of Mr. [H. G.] Wells' comets, and if, in consequence, every human being now alive were to lose all the knowledge and habits which he had acquired from preceding generations (though retaining unchanged all his own powers of invention, and memory, and habituation), nine-tenths of the inhabitants of London or New York would be dead in a month, and 99 per cent of the remaining tenth would be dead in six months. They would have no language to express their thoughts, and no thoughts but their revery. They could not read notices, or drive motors or horses. They would wander about, led by the inarticulate cries of a few . . . individuals drowning themselves, as thirst came on, in hundreds at the riverside landing places, looting those shops where the smell of decaying food attracted them, and perhaps at the end stumbling on the expedient of cannibalism. Even in the country districts men could not invent, in time to preserve their lives, methods of growing food, or taming animals, or making fire, or so clothing themselves as to endure the

northern winter. An attack of constipation or measles would be invariably fatal. After a few years mankind would almost certainly disappear from the northern and temperate zones. The white races would probably become extinct everywhere. A few primitive races might live on fruit and small animals in those fertile tropical regions where the human species was originally evolved until they had slowly accumulated a new social heritage.[2]

The Importance of Language

Language makes culture possible. Without the ability to communicate ideas people could not have developed the patterns of behavior which we call culture. Some animals have a very limited social heredity, but they lack the language needed to develop a culture. One ape, for example, may imitate another in using a stick to knock down a stem of bananas that is out of reach, but, unlike a human being, he cannot tell his offspring about it. Ants and bees interact but they have no language and therefore no culture. Only human beings possess culture. Language enables man to transmit ideas about situations which are not present. Further, it allows him to communicate judgments concerning the proper behavior in such situations.

Most persons in our society, on entering a hotel for the first time, would not go directly to a room without stopping at the desk, nor would they go behind the desk and pick out a room key. They would not do such things because the patterns of behavior expected under such circumstances have been communicated to them by someone else in their generation or a preceding one who knew the proper procedure. The information, attitudes, ideas, and values of each generation can be passed on to the succeeding generation by means of language, and individuals can be prepared for unusual as well as ordinary events.

Language is so vital a characteristic of any culture that a difference in language between groups is one of the more reliable means of differentiating between cultures—for example, between the cultures of France and Britain. One of the most obvious things an observer will notice as he moves from one society to another is the change in language, although other differences are also soon discernible.

To a considerable degree, language both shapes and reflects the rest of the culture. An extreme example will make this clear. There are tribes which have no word for the color gray and, since people think with words, members of such a society are unable to think of gray. It is often noted that the English and American cultures

---

[2]Graham Wallas, *Our Social Heritage* (New Haven, Conn.: Yale University Press, 1921), p. 16.

are quite similar, though by no means identical. The languages spoken in the United States and in England differ somewhat, in content as well as pronunciation. Both are very different, however, from the language spoken in Japan, and the cultures show a similarly marked difference. While this does not imply a direct cause-effect relationship, it does indicate that linguistic similarities are found between cultures which share many other patterns, and radical differences in language tend to accompany radical differences in other aspects of culture.

THE FORM AND CONTENT OF CULTURE

Culture refers to the total social inheritance of a people. In this sense, the term designates all human behavior which is socially learned rather than biologically inherited and which is shared by most human beings or by specifically designated sets of them. In addition to this general use of the term, we use it more specifically to refer to the shared learned behaviors of a particular group of human beings.

Cultural Traits

Because of the complexity of any culture, it is often useful, for purposes of description and analysis, to examine a culture piece by piece, looking at one part, or a combination of related parts, at a time. Some anthropologists, for instance, analyze culture by breaking it down into small elements or units, called *culture traits*. These represent single combinations of acts and ideas related to a particular need or situation. For instance, fire-making may be thought of as a culture trait involving the use of certain implements and skills. For a nonliterate person this may be the device of rubbing two dry sticks together over a small pile of tinder. For contemporary people it usually means the use of matches or a mechanical lighter. So too, ways of saluting another person—such as a man's lifting his hat to greet a lady—or parts of a ritual are other illustrations of cultural traits.

An analysis of culture by traits is informative but by itself provides an inadequate understanding of culture. One must examine the interrelationships of cultural traits.

Cultural Complexes

Plow agriculture, so important a step in human history is a cultural complex consisting of many culture traits: the way the plow is made, the manner in which the animals or machines that draw it are harnessed or driven, the use of the plant that is domesticated and harvested, how the seeds are put into the ground, and so on through a wide range of activities. The belief in and worship of one god, which we call monotheism, is another cultural complex made up of a wide variety of specific ideas, emotions, and habits. In industrial societies, what the economists call the "market" is a complex and systematic patterning of a wide variety of separate acts and ideas: buying, selling, lending, transporting, and so on.

Ethos

Those patterns of culture of a particular society which most distinguish it from other societies we call the *ethos*. Sumner, a pioneer American social scientist, defined ethos as "the totality of characteristic traits by which a group [i.e., a society] is individualized and differentiated from others." Thus Sparta and Athens, Judea, India, China, and the industrialized, capitalistic United States represent distinctive patterns and values. Moreover, as Sumner wrote, "The ethos of one group furnishes the standpoint from which it criticizes the ways of any other group."[3] The ethos of a people, therefore, is a major clue to cultural change. The ethos is the heart of any culture.

Universals, Alternatives, and Specialties

An analysis of the place of a culture in the life of an individual or of a group of individuals in a given society reveals wide ranges of participation. Even in small societies, differences in thought and conduct are linked to age, sex, and occupational differences. In a complex industrialized society it is quite impossible for any one person to participate actively in all the many phases of the culture. The way in which the demands of the culture play upon an individual will vary. Three levels of participation in a culture may be distinguished.[4]

Universals are those core features of a culture which are widely accepted and required by the society. They are learned behaviors so widely shared that, without them, one is obviously "different" or an outcast. Examples of universals are the language spoken in the society, the standard patterns of social relationships (such as monogamy in our society), and the deep-seated moral values. In general, ethnocentric beliefs are universals. The term *universal*

[3]W. G. Sumner, *Folkways* (Boston: Ginn and Company, 1906), pp. 70, 73.
[4]Ralph Linton, *The Study of Man* (New York: Appleton-Century-Crofts, 1936), pp. 272–274.

refers to behaviors associated with a particular culture; a pattern may be universal within one culture and unheard of in another. For example, in some Arab societies, men wear robes, and the wearing of trousers is confined to women and serves as a mark of femininity.

Alternatives are activities in which individuals are allowed a choice. For instance, a universal in our culture demands legalized marriage for couples who wish to live together with the approval of the community; however, they are offered certain alternatives: they may be married at home, in a church, or at the city hall, by a minister, priest, rabbi, or justice of the peace. Alternatives are different activities allowed and accepted for achieving the same end.

Specialties are learned behaviors shared by the members of certain social categories but not by most people in the society. The physician, for example, knows things most of us do not know and performs certain activities in which most of us do not participate. In general, specialties are very often a consequence of the division of labor, and are shared according to sex, age, class, or occupation.

Subcultures

The place of culture in the life of particular groups and individuals in any given society reveals some range of variation. Even in small societies, some differences in thought and conduct are specific to age and sex. In large and complex industrial societies, it is quite impossible for any one person or group to participate actively in all the many phases of the culture. American society, for example, includes thousands of different occupations and no one person can be a part of all of them. Anyone who has listened to a discussion among a group of medical students knows that they have a special language and a set of values of their own. Such shared, learned behavior that is common to a specific group is called a subculture. Railroaders, for further example, share in the general values of the society but they also have a special language, place a special value on time, and know things and have ideas that are not shared among most members of the society. In other words, people who share distinctive occupational specialities can be said to participate in the same occupational subculture.[5] Other subcul-

---

[5]See Howard S. Becker, *Outsiders: Studies in the Sociology of Deviance* (New York: Free Press of Glencoe, 1963). For other examples of research on occupational subcultures, see W. F. Cottrell, *The Railroader* (Stanford, California: Stanford University Press, 1940); S. Kirson Weinberg and Henry Arond, "The Occupational Culture of the Boxer," *American Journal of Sociology*, 1952, 57: 460–469; William Bruce Cameron, "Sociological Notes on the Jam Session," *Social Forces*, 1954, 33: 177–182; and Raymond W. Mack, "Occupational Ideology and the Determinate Role," *Social Forces*, 1957, 36: 37–44.

tures revolve around religion, race, ethnicity, etc., and variously exhibit special modes of dress, food, language, beliefs, and so on that are shared within the group but do not characterize the society as a whole.

CULTURAL DIVERSITY

The uniformities of culture are more easily explained than the variations in time and place. The elements common to cultures everywhere stem, in part, from the fact that all human beings are basically the same biologically, so that their need for survival leads to certain commonalities in behavior. For example, all human beings must eat a certain amount of nourishing food, and a group must reproduce in order to survive as a society. But the patterns of acquiring and consuming food vary greatly from place to place, and the rules regarding who is supposed to have children, how often, and under what circumstances may differ from culture to culture.

Geography and Culture

One explanation for the range of variation among cultures is the diversity of materials provided by the physical environment, by the effect of climate and landscape on the inhabitants. Certain effects of the physical environment on people are readily identifiable. The rigors of winter demand more clothes and warmer houses. To build shelters, people ordinarily have had to use materials near at hand: mud for huts in some places, stone in others, and ice or snow in still others. So too, living in places of rich soil and adequate rainfall produces social arrangements different from those produced by living on a rainless and windy desert or in the hot and humid regions of the tropics.

These daily and seasonal effects of the weather, water supply, and soil are obvious enough. Out of such repeated experiences arose popular and often erroneous notions about the impact of geography on human thought and action. For example, one sometimes hears people argue that the Latins, living in warm climates as they do, have "hot blood" and are given to quick anger and impetuous behavior. In contrast, the Finns and Swedes, who live in cold latitudes, are said to be stolid in temperament and slow to action. The fallacy of these and similar views must not mislead us. Geographic factors *do* play an important part in individual and group living. While there is no evidence that, unaided by culture, the desert makes for the invention of religious mysticism or the tropics for an inferiority of racial stocks, we cannot ignore the influence of climate, topography, and natural resources on human existence. This is especially true of elements of material culture, such as food-getting, housing, manufacturing, and transport. *Yet even in these matters the geographic factors are chiefly limiting rather than directly causative.* The following illustrations bring out the manner in which cultures vary even when the geographic conditions are the same.

Consider, for example, the fact of *cultural differences within similar geographic environments.* The Eskimo represents a remarkable adaptation to a highly unfavorable environment; and if his were the only arctic culture we knew, we might assume that all arctic inhabitants followed much the same pattern. Take housing: is anything more natural than that the arctic dweller should build huts from the bountiful supply of snow at hand? Yet if we look across the Bering Sea to the Chuckchee of northeastern Siberia, in a similar climate, we find these people in winter months living not in snow houses but in large, "clumsy" tents of hide stretched over heavy supports. Furthermore, the Chuckchee use the domesticated reindeer for draft purposes, while the Eskimos use dogs to draw their sleds. The Chuckchee apparently borrowed the use of the domesticated reindeer from their neighbors, the Tungus, living to the south of them. The Eskimos domesticated this convenient animal themselves only recently.

Or since the Pacific Northwest Indians have developed woodworking into a high art, why haven't the northern California tribes, with equally ample woodlands, done so? The answer, it seems, lies not in the natural environment but in cultural divergences.

The American Southwest offers another striking contrast. The Hopi are intensive farmers; the Navahos do little farming, living a pastoral life. The Hopi live in terraced sandstone or adobe houses; the Navahos live in conical earth huts. The Hopi possess high art in pottery making; the Navahos show very crude ceramics workmanship. The Hopi men do the weaving; the Navaho women handle the loom. The Hopi are strictly monogamous; the Navahos permit polygyny. The family organization of the Hopi has strong mother-in-law taboos and gives the maternal uncles great power over their sisters' sons, whereas the Navahos have no such rigid taboos and have a different form of family organization. There are also marked differences in religious and magical practices. Finally, the Navahos, like the Plains tribes, have been warlike, while the Hopi have a relatively peaceful history.

The Negroid African Bushmen are seed-gathers and hunters, live in crude windbreaks or caves, and use the bow and arrow. In contrast, their neighbors in the same sections of South Africa, the Hottentots, are a pastoral people, living in mat-covered portable huts and using the spear as their principal weapon, although they have the bow and arrow. While these tribes have many myths and other features of culture in common, the differences in material traits are striking. Once more we must seek the explanation largely in the history of their cultures and not in the physical environment.

The Paiutes, or "Digger Indians," living on the edge of the Great American Desert, considered the Rocky Mountain locust a particular delicacy. The locusts infested these areas periodically in great numbers, and the Indians drove them into brush enclosures to roast and eat them. When the Mormon colonists settled the Great Basin, beginning in 1847, they were greatly troubled during the first decade by plagues of these insects, which devoured every blade of grass, wheat, or corn. The Mormons did what they could to destroy the pests, but were unable to bridge the cultural chasm between themselves and their Indian friends and bring themselves to take up a new dietary habit. Had their own food taboos been less severe they, like the Indians, might have made something of a blessing out of what was to them a curse.

These examples show that culture is perhaps the crucial determinant of social behavior. Yet the effects of natural environment, though often indirect and secondary, are nonetheless ever-present and consequential. Even with modern technology, agriculture is limited by soil, climate, and topography. If one wishes to grow bananas, he has his best chance of success in the rainy tropics. If he tries it in a semiarid section of the tropics, he will find it economically impractical. And in a humid, continental temperate zone one simply could not raise bananas at all, because killing frosts would destroy the crop. Similarly, coal miners are found in western Pennsylvania, with steel workers near by, but no such division of labor is found in central Texas. So too, in the developing air age, air currents and degrees of cloudiness and storminess in various regions will affect air transportation and, as a result, the location and function of certain cities.

As man has advanced to more complex forms of culture, he has overcome some of the handicaps of the "natural landscape." Not only has he changed the face of the earth and devised new and more rapid means of communication and transportation, but he has partially overcome poor soil by fertilization, provided more adequate water supply for crops by irrigation, insured himself against some changes in temperature and humidity and, by the use of refrigeration in transporting and storing foodstuffs, removed earlier restrictions on the use of seasonal foods. In brief, cultural history runs a course from the most rudimentary societies, isolated and tied rather closely to their immediate physical environment, to technologically advanced societies in which there is little left in the physical environment of the ordinary person that has not been altered by culture, including the quantity of clean air and water.

Race and Culture

Some people believe that race, rather than geography holds the key to cultural variation. The belief, however, is false. For instance, there persists a widespread belief that nonliterate peoples have powers of sight, hearing, smell, taste, and touch that far exceed those of other people. There is a concomitant belief that nonliterates lack the capacity to reason clearly and logically. The first notion has been thoroughly disproved by a long series of studies by psychologists who measured the sensory and motor capacities of nonliterates. Interestingly enough, it has also been shown that, even in these apparently simple psychological processes, cultural training influences the responses. What members of a race or group see, hear, or otherwise sense is determined not by their physiological capacities but by what they have been taught by others in their group and culture.

Nevertheless, the recognition that these mental and motor responses of nonliterates and "modern" people do not differ has not destroyed the conviction that in the higher mental functions there are sharp differences. This latter belief has been expressed by many writers who take the position that the "high civilization" of present-day European and American peoples rests on an inherent intellectual superiority of members of the white race. It is often asked for example, why, if the colored races are equal in ability to the whites, the African tribes did not develop a high culture such as that which emerged in the Fertile Crescent and later in Greece, Rome, and modern Europe. Or why, if the Mongolians are as intelligent as the whites, the inventions that make modern technology possible did not occur in the Far East. Questions such as these are both ethnocentric and naïve. They are ethnocentric because they assume that the best culture is Western culture and that the ways of life in other times and places are to be judged in terms of Western standards. Social scientists, however, long ago demonstrated the emptiness of ethnocentrism as an avenue to understanding human conduct and replaced it with the doctrine of cultural relativism. Briefly, the doctrine of cultural relativism holds that the meaning of any expression of social behavior is relative to its cultural setting and that patterns of human conduct are valid only in relation to the particular time and place in which they occur. Every culture is to be evaluated on its own terms.

Questions that make invidious comparisons between fundamentally different cultures are naïve because they ignore the fact

ILLUSTRATIVE DATA 4-1   100 PER CENT AMERICAN

Our solid American citizen awakens in a bed built on a pattern which originated in the Near East but which was modified in Northern Europe before it was transmitted to America. He throws back the covers made from cotton, domesticated in India, or linen, domesticated in the Near East, or wool from sheep, also domesticated in the Near East, or silk, the use of which was discovered in China. All of these materials have been spun and woven by processes invented in the Near East. He slips into his moccasins, invented by the Indians of the Eastern woodlands, and goes to the bathroom, whose fixtures are a mixture of European and American inventions, both of recent date. He takes off his pajamas, a garment invented in India, and washes with soap invented by the ancient Gauls. He then shaves, a masochistic rite which seems to have been derived from either Sumer or ancient Egypt.

Returning to the bedroom, he removes his clothes from a chair of southern European type and proceeds to dress. He puts on garments whose form originally derived from the skin clothing of the nomads of the Asiatic steppes, puts on shoes made from skins tanned by a process invented in ancient Egypt, and cut to a pattern derived from the classical civilizations of the Mediterranean, and ties around his neck a strip of bright-colored cloth which is a vestigial survival of the shoulder shawls worn by the seventeenth-century Croatians. Before going out for breakfast he glances through the window, made of glass invented in Egypt, and if it is raining, puts on overshoes made of rubber discovered by the Central American Indians and takes an umbrella, invented in southeastern Asia. Upon his head he puts a hat made of felt, a material invented in the Asiatic steppes.

On his way to breakfast he stops to buy a paper, paying for it with coins, an ancient Lydian invention. At the restaurant a whole new series of borrowed elements confronts him. His plate is made of a form of pottery invented in China. His knife is of steel, an alloy first made in southern India, his fork, a medieval Italian invention, and his spoon a derivative of a Roman original. He begins breakfast with an orange, from the eastern Mediterranean, a cantaloupe from Persia, or perhaps a piece of African watermelon. With this he has coffee, an Abyssinian plant, with cream and sugar. Both the domestication of cows and the idea of milking them originated in the Near East, while sugar was first made in India. After his fruit and first coffee he goes on to waffles, cakes made by a Scandinavian technique from wheat domesticated in Asia Minor. Over these he pours maple syrup, invented by the Indians of the Eastern woodlands. As a side dish he may have the eggs of a species of bird domesticated in Indo-China, or thin strips of the flesh of an animal domesticated in Eastern Asia, which have been salted and smoked by a process developed in northern Europe.

When our friend has finished eating, he settles back to smoke, an American Indian habit, consuming a plant domesticated in Brazil in either a pipe, derived from the Indians of Virginia, or a cigarette, derived from Mexico. If he is hardy enough he may even attempt a cigar,

transmitted to us from the Antilles by way of Spain. While smoking
he reads the news of the day, imprinted in characters invented in
Germany. As he absorbs the accounts of foreign troubles he will, if he
is a good conservative citizen, thank a Hebrew deity in an Indo-
European language that he is 100 per cent American.

Source: From: *The Study of Man: An Introduction,* by Ralph Linton. Copyright 1936 and 1964. By permission of Appleton-Century-Crofts, Educational Division, Meredith Corporation.

of the slow cumulation of the important elements in a culture. Many fundamental features of a culture, such as the use of fire, making of tools, development of language, weaving, art, and religion were initiated by races of people now extinct. According to Ralph Linton, "there is probably no culture extant to-day which owes more than 10 per cent of its total elements to inventions made by members of its own society."[6] It is true that the use of metals, the wheel, written language, etc., were developed largely by certain ancestors of the present Mediterranean people, but even in this instance it is clear that other races of people played a part in their development.

Take, for example, the case of social inventions. There is no scientific evidence that any category of people is more inventive than any other. However, desert dwellers are not likely to invent a winning fishhook, let alone an outboard motor. Every invention is dependent upon previous inventions. Until someone discovered the principle of the wheel, no one could invent the pulley, much less the modern steam shovel. Until a way of striking fire was found, the idea of smelting iron was out of the question. Nowhere is the fact of the cumulative nature of culture made more dramatic than in the history of invention, reflected in Newton's statement, "if I have seen farther [than other men], it is by standing on the shoulders of giants." Try to imagine the hundreds of human beings through the centuries who had to contribute original ideas, or shape several already created implements into new combinations, before one could produce a modern automobile, with its springs, combination air- and water-cooled engine, upholstery made of synthetic fibers, chromium plating, sprayed-on paint, and countless other features far removed from the invention of the piston.

Isolation and Culture Contact

The content of a culture and the character of its change is not a matter of race. Every culture, however, reflects its relative social isolation. The barriers of the sea, for example, long insulated the

---

[6]Ralph Linton, *The Study of Man* (New York: Appleton-Century-Crofts, Inc., 1936), p. 325.

Figure 4-1   Mechanical Invention as a Combination of Known Elements

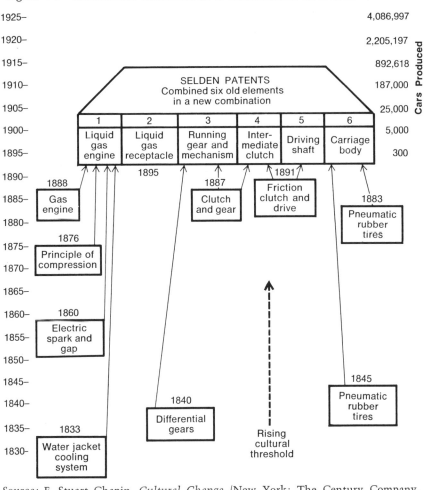

Source: F. Stuart Chapin, Cultural Change (New York: The Century Company, 1928). Courtesy of Appleton-Century-Crofts, Educational Division, Meredith Corporation.

Australians from the mainstreams of Asiatic culture. So, too, during the period of "high" Mediterranean culture, sub-Saharan Africa was socially isolated. Although they had learned the art of metallurgy, developed a complex social organization, created distinctive art forms, etc., their isolation precluded their participation in European culture until relatively recently.

Moreover, since inventions are essentially recombinations of existing elements of culture, the opportunity for invention is a consequence of the number of cultural elements available for invention. Two items can be combined in only one way, but the number of combinations possible for 10 items is 1,013; for 15 items, 32,744 combinations are possible; and for 20 items, more than a million combinations are possible.

Another persuasive indication of the extent to which invention is dependent upon the accumulated cultural heritage of a particular time and place is the fact that many inventions and discoveries have been made simultaneously by two or more people working completely independently of one another. Fifty years ago, two sociologists, William F. Ogburn and Dorothy Swaine Thomas, catalogued 148 of these simultaneous innovations and since then many others have been added to the list. Some of the more notable of these simultaneous and independent discoveries and inventions are:

Calculus: Newton (1671); Leibnitz (1676)
Logarithms: Napier (1614); Burgi (1620)
Nitrogen: Rutherford (1772); Scheele (1773)
Pendulum clock: Burgi (1575); Galileo (1582); Huygens (1656)
Phonograph: Cros (1876); Edison (1876)
Photography: Daguerre-Niepce (1839); Talbot (1839)
Reapers: Hussey (1833); McCormick (1834)
Telegraph: Henry (1831); Cooke-Wheatstone (1837); Morse (1837); Steinheil (1837)
Telephone: Bell (1876); Gray (1876)
Telescope: Porta (1558); Digger (1571); Johannides, Metius (1608); Drebbel, Fontana, Janssen (1608); Galileo (1609)
Theory of mutations: Korschinsky (1899); DeVries (1900)
Theory of natural selection: Darwin (1858); Wallace (1858)

If a major invention is announced in England tomorrow morning, Americans will hear of it on newcasts and read about it in the papers tomorrow evening. The rapid and extensive contact between these two societies makes it likely that they will become more and more similar as time goes by. It is as difficult to find an Italian town where one cannot buy Coca-Cola as it is to locate an American town where no restaurant serves spaghetti. Culture contact makes for uniformities in behavior. This fact provides a clue for explaining the wide variation among cultures. Throughout most of human history, most societies have had no contact with outside societies other than their immediate neighbors. Only in the past few thousand years have people gained extended contact with cultures markedly different from their own.

Just as interaction between people who participate in different cultures makes for similarities between the cultures through the exchange of traits and patterns, so does a long period of isolation contribute to cultural variability. Since there are virtually infinite possibilities for variation in the ways man is capable of meeting his needs, the longer two societies are isolated from each other, the more likely they are to display different patterns of behavior. In one society, an inventive female will put a metal ring around her neck, and others will copy the fashion. Women with more leisure to make necklaces or more wealth to buy them will wear more than one. Eventually, the number of necklaces a woman wears will become such a standard way of indicating her wealth and position in the society that families will invest as much wealth as they can spare in metal rings to place around the necks of their daughters. Indeed, this can reach the point where the attractiveness of a female is judged partly by the length of her neck, with the result that parents place metal hoops around the necks of their young daughters to stretch them.

In ancient China, tiny feet were looked on as a mark of daintiness and femininity. Parents bound the feet of their girl children so tightly that the feet could not grow normally. This resulted, from the point of view of our culture, in young women who were crippled and deformed; but from the viewpoint of the other culture, the result was lovely, attractive, small-footed ladies. In fact, small feet became a mark of upper-class standing in China because, much as they may have admired small feet, poorer families recognized that tiny feet meant less ability to work, and girls were needed to aid in the family labors.

So long as there is no contact between the society where a long neck is a criterion of femininity and position and the society where tiny feet are a similar indication, there will be no opportunity for the values of the one culture to have any impact on the values of the other. The tendency will be for them to continue to develop along different lines. Female deities in one will have long necks; in the other, they will have small feet.

This is only one small example of cultural variability: differences in patterns of behavior aiming at artificial beautification. When one considers that there are opportunities for different lines of cultural development in every area of human behavior, it becomes apparent that variation between cultures, far from being just a quaint possibility, is virtually inevitable. Given the range of available choices, it is hardly possible that two societies isolated from each other would make the same selections. Furthermore, as cultures develop in relative isolation from one another they are likely to become more and more divergent, each new trait and complex having to fit in with those previously developed, as well as with the general value system. For example, a certain culture, esteeming men more than women, may provide that men should be the property owners and that no woman can hold land. Because of this the culture cannot develop an inheritance system which provides for daughters to

ILLUSTRATIVE DATA 4-2   WARFARE AND CULTURAL DIVERSITY

Warfare is another social theme that may or may not be used in any culture. Where war is made much of, it may be with contrasting objectives, with contrasting organization in relation to the state, and with contrasting sanctions. War may be, as it was among the Aztecs, a way of getting captives for the religious sacrifices. Since the Spaniards fought to kill, according to Aztec standards they broke the rules of the game. The Aztecs fell back in dismay and Cortez walked as victor into the capital.

There are even quainter notions, from our standpoint, associated with warfare in different parts of the world. For our purposes it is sufficient to notice those regions where organized resort to mutual slaughter never occurs between social groups. Only our familiarity with war makes it intelligible that a state of warfare should alternate with a state of peace in one tribe's dealings with another. The idea is quite common over the world, of course. But on the one hand it is impossible for certain peoples to conceive the possibility of a state of peace, which in their notion would be equivalent to admitting enemy tribes to the category of human beings, which by definition they are not even though the excluded tribe may be of their own race and culture.

On the other hand, it may be just as impossible for a people to conceive of the possibility of a state of war. Rasmussen tells of the blankness with which the Eskimo met his exposition of our custom. Eskimos very well understand the act of killing a man. If he is in your way, you cast up your estimate of your own strength, and if you are ready to take it upon yourself, you kill him. If you are strong, there is no social retribution. But the idea of an Eskimo village going out against another Eskimo village in battle array or a tribe against tribe, or even of another village being fair game in ambush warfare, is alien to them. All killing comes under one head, and is not separated, as ours is, into categories, the one meritorious, the other a capital offence.

I myself tried to talk of warfare to the Mission Indians of California, but it was impossible. Their misunderstanding of warfare was abysmal. They did not have the basis in their own culture upon which the idea could exist, and their attempts to reason it out reduced the great wars to which we are able to dedicate ourselves with moral fervour to the level of alley brawls. They did not happen to have a cultural pattern that distinguished between them.

War is, we have been forced to admit even in the face of its huge place in our own civilization, an <u>asocial trait</u>. In the chaos following the World War [I] all the wartime arguments that expounded its fostering of courage, of altruism, of spiritual values, gave out a false and offensive ring. War in our own civilization is as good an illustration as one can take of the destructive lengths to which the development of a culturally selected trait may go. If we justify war, it is because all peoples always justify the traits of which they find themselves possessed, not because war will bear an objective examination of its merits.

Source: Ruth Benedict, *Patterns of Culture* (New York: The New American Library, 1946), pp. 27–29. First published by Houghton Mifflin Co., in 1934. By permission.

inherit property or which prohibits sons from inheriting anything from their fathers. In other words, a culture has some internal consistency.

Cultural History

The history of a people provides another important clue to their culture and the way it changes. In the Western world, concern with physical welfare led to an increasing body of skills and knowledge centering on mechanical and scientific inventions and discoveries. Such a cultural base has in turn largely determined the interests— the "run of attention"—of those who are its beneficiaries. Modern Euro-American culture is heavily loaded on the side of science, technology, and activities involving material goods and services. In contrast, the Oriental peoples followed philosophic and artistic lines. Only in relatively recent times have they begun to show an interest in technology. Yet there is no evidence that the Mongoloid peoples are *innately* more given to mystic philosophy or moral searching than members of the white or Negro race.

When it comes to matters of human conduct, the key is culture, not race. Clyde Kluckhohn states the heart of the issue this way:

> Why do the Chinese dislike milk and milk products? Why would the Japanese die willingly in a Banzai charge that seemed senseless to Americans? Why do some nations trace descent through the father, others through the mother, still others through both parents? Not because different peoples have different instincts, not because they were destined by God or Fate to different habits, not because the weather is different in China and Japan and the United States. Sometimes shrewd common sense has an answer that is close to that of [social science]: "because they were brought up that way." By "culture" [one] means the total life way of a people, the social legacy the individual acquires from his group. Or culture can be regarded as that part of the environment that is the creation of man.[7]

Every society operates under some set of rules. Every group has certain regulations which its members learn. On the basis of what they learn, individuals are usually able to predict the behavior of others. Most people learn the basic rules so well that, under ordinary circumstances, they are not even aware of them. One example of a relatively minor set of expectations will serve to illustrate the fact that societies could not operate if their cultures did not provide grounds for anticipating the behavior of the members in specific circumstances. When a person approaches a traffic light that is green,

---

[7]Clyde Kluckhohn, *Mirror for Man* (New York: McGraw-Hill Book Company, Inc., 1949), p. 17.

he or she proceeds confident that people traveling at right angles are facing a red light and will stop. The driver does not *know* that the light in other directions is red at this place and at this time; it is *assumed*. One is not acquainted with the people approaching at ninety-degree angles; one has never personally made arrangements with them to assure that they will stop at red traffic signals. But one has learned that one has a right to expect the city street department to keep the light in proper repair, to wire it so that when it is red in one direction it will be green at right angles to that direction. One has learned that one has a right to expect people to stop when the signal is red in their direction, that one has an obligation to stop when it is red in his or her direction and that people who violate these expectations will be punished.

VALUES

Values are assumptions, both conscious and unconscious, of what is good, right and important. Values concern standards of desirability. Some set of values forms the core of every culture. The ethos—that is, the fundamental characteristics—of any culture is a reflection of its basic values. During the tremendous industrial and population growth from 1870 to the present American society, for example, became characterized by a number of culture features, including (1) belief in individual material success and general national progress; (2) faith in universal literacy and education as a means of solving social and personal problems; (3) belief in the virtue of sheer size, witnessed in ever-larger skyscrapers, schools, industrial plants, and corporations; (4) rapid movement through space, seen in increased mobility of population and improved means of communication and transportation; (5) love of novelty—constant change to something new and more exciting, as in sensational news, exciting drama, speed racing, crazes, and fads; and (6) the craving for domination—the booster and the "bigger and better" spirit in almost every important aspect of public life.

In contrast to this, in the Orient during the nineteenth century (before Western civilization and its values reached there), human thinking and acting took quite different patterns. There was no belief in the American value of progress. Mere physical size had no special merit. Certainly no virtue inhered in rapid movement. Instead, the ideal was the calm deliberation of the scholar or sage. In India, among large numbers of the population, instead of desire for personal material success and continued identification of the self with individual striving and "getting ahead," the fundamental desire expressed in religious life was renunciation of self, the abandoning of personal desire, and the elimination of the ambition to be important. Such radical differences in cultural values result, of course, in widely divergent social structures and patterns of expectations in social interaction.

SOCIAL NORMS   *most are informal not written down*

Social norms are group-shared expectations. A set of expected behaviors can be associated either with a certain situation or with a given position in the social structure. Examples of the former are "Who ever heard of eating peas with honey?" "A Scout is courteous," "A gentleman pays his debts," or, more generally, "You shouldn't have done that." One is supposed to be quiet, respectful, and not to interrupt others in a house of worship. On the other hand, one's trust that his lawyer need not and thus will not give the court damaging evidence against him is an expectation associated with the lawyer's position in the social structure.

Of course, not everyone in any society abides by all the norms all the time, and no norm is always obeyed. Moreover, not all norms—or even most of them—are written or legalized. Most of the understandings we share with other members of society are informal. There is no law saying that one should not eat peas with a knife, that one should lend money only to friends, or that one shakes hands when introduced. Yet these are shared and learned expectations; they are part of our culture, and most of us conform to them most of the time.

Sociologists differentiate norms, according to the degree of importance attached to the rules by the society, into folkways and mores.[8]

Folkways — *imp determined by punishment given when broken*

The most obvious way to determine the importance of a norm for the members of a society is to observe how severely they punish those who violate it. Norms which are not looked on as extremely important—or, to state it another way, norms which can be violated

---

[8]William Graham Sumner introduced the concepts of folkways and mores in *Folkways* (Boston: Ginn and Company, 1906), pp. 78–108. In his writing, *folkways* is the more general term; *mores* are folkways deemed especially important by the society. We believe that greater clarity can be maintained by reserving the term *folkways* for the less crucial norms, violations of which are not severely punished, and separating these from the morally judged norms, or mores, violations of which bring more stringent penalties. Useful discussions of the use of the idea of norms by contemporary sociologists can be found in Richard T. Morris, "A Typology of Norms," *American Sociological Review*, 1956, 21: 610, and in Jack P. Gibbs, "Norms: The Problem of Definition and Classification," *American Journal of Sociology*, 1965, 70: 586–594.

ILLUSTRATIVE DATA 4-3   THE CENTRAL IDEAS OF BOHEMIANISM

The idea of salvation by the child. *Each of us at birth has special potentialities which are slowly crushed and destroyed by a standardized society and mechanical modes of teaching.*

The idea of self-expression. *Each man's, each woman's purpose in life is to express himself, to realize his full individuality through creative work and beautiful living in beautiful surroundings.*

The idea of paganism. *The body is a temple in which there is nothing unclean, a shrine to be adorned for the ritual of love.*

The idea of living for the moment. *It is stupid to pile up treasures that we can enjoy only in old age.... Better to seize the moment as it comes.*

The idea of liberty. *Every law ... that prevents self-expression or the full enjoyment of the moment should be shattered and abolished.*

The idea of female equality. *Women should be the economic and moral equals of men ... same pay ... same working conditions, the same opportunity for drinking, smoking, taking or dismissing lovers.*

The idea of psychological adjustment. *We are unhappy because ... we are repressed.*

The idea of changing place. *"They do things better in...."*

Source: Malcolm Cowley, *Exile's Return* as quoted in Bennett M. Berger, "Hippie Morality—More Old than New," *Trans-action*, V (December, 1967), 19–20.

without severe punishment—are called folkways. Adult males should wear a coat and tie to church. People should arrive on time for appointments. Professors should not serve whiskey in their offices. People should not park their automobiles in zones labeled "No Parking." School children should not call teachers by their first names. One should not persistently make loud noises late at night in a residential area. People should not smoke in a chapel. One should bathe frequently enough so that others are not conscious of his bodily odors. People should eat three meals a day. A person should respect his parents.

Each of the sentences in the preceding paragraph is a statement of a group-shared expectation, or norm, in contemporary American society. Some norms are covered by formal laws; others are not. Violations of some would be met by fines, imprisonment, or dismissal from one's job; failure to abide by others would be punished only by verbal statements of disapproval or by ostracism. Each of these norms have one thing in common, however: the fact that they are not regarded by most people as moral matters. People who smoke in chapel are regarded as crude, but not as immoral. People who are persistently late for appointments are considered thoughtless; they are not viewed as sinners. People who disturb the peace are a nuisance, not lost souls. We may avoid people who do not bathe frequently, but we do not judge them wicked. You may get fined for leaving your car in a no-parking area, but nobody will think the Devil inspired you to park there.

Folkways are rules which most people in the society expect most other people in the society to obey most of the time. They are deemed the "right" way, and "normal" people accept most of them unquestioningly. One can, however, challenge a folkway and suggest that it would not really hurt anything to alter it, without being judged a menace to his society. Herein lies the difference between folkways and mores.

Mores

The mores are not open to question. The individual so thoroughly internalizes the mores that he or she seldom thinks of them consciously as rules. The professor may be so irked at her warm academic robes that she toys with the idea of going to commencement in a T-shirt, but it will not occur to her to go in the nude. Law enforcement agencies might take seriously a suggestion from a traffic authority for a set of graduated penalties for parking offenses: only a warning the first time, a small fine the second, a larger fine for the third violation, and suspension of the driver's license for the fourth offense. No one would take seriously a similar plan for dealing with wanton murderers: let them off the first time and gradually "crack down" on them. Murder is a violation of the mores, and there is no disposition either to treat it lightly or, for that matter, to discuss whether or not it should be considered a violation of the mores.

Probably the best evidence of how thoroughly we internalize the mores is the difficulty most people would have in thinking of examples. Many generalized maxims that spring to mind are not mores. Taking a human life, for instance, is not necessarily a violation of the mores—it depends on who does it and under what circumstances. On some occasions our society gives medals, rewards, and public acclaim to those who take human life. In wartime, we decorate the man who has shot down more enemy planes than any other flier, and parades are given in honor of the soldier who single-handedly has slain a number of enemy soldiers. A hero's treatment is accorded the policeman who kills a dangerous criminal in a gun battle. A sizable portion of our movies have heroes who, in the course of the story, violate the injunction "Thou shalt not kill." A storekeeper often will not be punished for shooting a burglar in his store. Neither the law nor the mores prohibit killing in self-defense. Unintentional killing is not criminal unless it is the result of negligence on the part of the killer.

While there are laws to deal with wanton murder, some mores are assumed to be so well learned that no law is needed to enforce them. The rare violations are met by community rejection and expressions of loathing of the participants and, if legally cataloged at all, are treated as "indecency" or "disturbance of the peace." Moral imperatives of this magnitude are so deeply impressed upon the members of society that the average person cannot remember when or how he came to learn that certain behavior is wrong. Incest is such a prohibition. Most of us do not know when or from whom we learned that incest is morally wrong, but a father who has sexual relations with his own daughter arouses feelings of revulsion and contempt.

Law

In most relatively complex societies, some kind of political order serves as an overall seat of authority in which law becomes an important norm of control. Laws are laid down to establish or maintain the rights, duties, and liberties of the members of the state. Rights imply a two-sided relationship, in which one person owes the other a duty and the other person benefits thereby. A person has rights only insofar as others have duties toward him. One's rights set limits on other people's liberties. Freedom and responsibility always go together. In complex societies, the law represents the most certain of all the social norms.

In modern democracies, the law usually falls into three categories: constitutional, statutory, and judge-made. The first sets out the basic features of the political order. The second is the product of legislative bodies and covers a wide range of individual and group activities. The third is the product of the courts—it consists of judicial decisions which are used as the basis of adjudication of subsequent cases.

To adjudicate cases involving legal disputes, courts are established. The judicial system usually has two levels: courts of original jurisdiction and those for appeal. In addition, most courts fall into two legal categories: criminal law and civil law. *Criminal law* deals with such offenses against the public peace, morality, and order as misdemeanors and the more serious offenses, such as murder, treason, rape, housebreaking, and arson. *Civil* cases are suits at law between persons or between duly constituted associations, such as corporations. These relate to such matters as enforcement of contract, titles to property, collections of debts, torts (which have to do with injuries of person to person that may lead to recovery of damages), guardianship of children, marriage and divorce, and many other matters not strictly related to the public peace. The definition of what constitutes a criminal and what a civil case depends on the culture. In many primary-group communities, homicide and feuding, for example, are treated as private, not public, matters. In urban societies these are considered crimes.

SANCTIONS – *rewards or punishments*

Sanctions are the rewards or punishments used to establish *social control*—that is, to enforce the norms in a society. Sanctions may be applied in various ways, ranging from the use of physical force to symbolic means, such as flattery. Sanctions are the normative means that are used to force or persuade an individual or group to conform to social expectations.

Informal and Formal Sanctions

Sanctions may be either informal or formal. Informal sanctions are illustrated by customs, the mores, and public opinion. The formal sanctions are those worked out by the state through law and administrative devices, those consciously developed within organizations for their own regulation, or those developed between or among organizations to regulate their relations. Sanctions are formalized as standardized codes of conduct, are set down and managed by special groups and passed on from generation to generation by special agencies. In the rise of the political state, formal lawmaking and the invention of writing, which made possible the keeping of records and the preservation of codes, were especially important. The modern, complex, industrial society is dependent upon formal sanctions, upon impersonal and indirect contacts. In nearly all situations, the formal and informal aspects of control are intertwined, and in many instances of community life, the informal tends to outweigh the formal. But in the more highly institutionalized groups, although the informal is not unimportant, the major controls flow through formal channels.

Purpose of Sanctions

The basic purpose of sanctions is to bring about conformity, solidarity, and continuity of a particular group, community, or larger society. Sanctions may be used to achieve a balance of power among contending social units, or to deal with the threatened exploitation of one group by another. Sanctions are also used to exact conformity from individuals whose behavior is thought to endanger the solidarity of the group.[9]

To control behavior means to bring about regular and recurrent sanctions. Such regulation makes possible the prediction of behavior. We can usually anticipate what an individual will do or what his punishment will be if he fails to act. For example, a contract usually enables the parties involved to know in advance what to expect and what each party will do. There is no changing of intention from day to day, and the obligation is binding for some specified period of time. Furthermore, control, especially by some overall power, makes for equilibrium between warring factions or groups by obliging them to accommodate themselves to one another and to the needs and values of the larger society. Sanctions thus foster solidarity and integration. So too, sanctions make possible continuity. They form a part of the culture that is passed along from generation to generation. Thus each generation gets a pattern of control which keeps the social order running smoothly. If each generation had to develop its own code, there obviously would be waste of effort.

Yet, in a rapidly changing society, this continuity is disturbed, with the result that new codes have to be developed, often coming into conflict with old ones. New conditions demand new definitions, and behavior often far outruns the forms of control. For example, the present growing sense of insecurity, anonymity, impersonality, and dissociation in the individual in mass society is definitely related to the breakdown of the codes and rules of the more traditional social order.

Types of Sanctions

Individuals invoking both formal and informal sanctions may employ a wide variety of means, ranging from linguistic and gestural to those which consist of overt force. A consideration of symbolic sanctions begins with the observation that the bulk of all social interaction takes the form of words and gestures rather than bodily contact. One can push and shove another or withdraw from him; or strike, bite, punch, or kick him; or fondle, caress, and make love. But the range of interaction possible through talk and writing is enormous. The child soon learns that words are a substitute for overt sanctions. Children and adults also learn that verbal communication often will turn the trick of group regulation without

---

[9]See Eugene Litwak, "Three Ways in Which Law Acts as a Means of Social Control: Punishment, Therapy, and Education," *Social Forces*, 1956, 34: 217–223; and Bernard Beck, "Welfare as a Moral Category," *Social Problems*, 1967, 14: 258–277.

recourse to more direct coercive measures. In most cases it is easy enough to bring about a desired result in behavior by the verbal approach. Overt bodily action is usually reserved for extreme cases. The sophistication of either an individual or a society is indicated in part by the degree to which it substitutes symbolic for overt sanctions.

So far as results go, the verbal method may be either negative or positive. That is, some language appeals may be directed toward stopping oncoming or anticipated behavior; other language stimuli may impel action in the desired direction. From the standpoint of the recipient, pleasant and positive verbal methods are chiefly praise, flattery, suggestion and persuasion, some forms of education, slogans, and propaganda. Negative means are gossip, satire, name-calling, threats, and commands.

Praise is a reward in words, especially from someone in a higher social position. It induces social amenability and conformity. *Flattery* is exaggerated and somewhat false praise, often used for ulterior purposes in dealing with others, especially those in superior social position. Flattery is often a particularly effective weapon in a society dominated by individualism and desire for material goods, though it can be effective in any society where prestige plays a part in control. *Indoctrination advertising,* and *propaganda,* though often different in motive, all condition persons to act along lines which they like or imagine they like. Individuals come to want to do the things suggested to them. *Persuasion* as a form of suggestion plays a part in all three of the above, as well as in less formal situations. *Slogans* help define situations and direct behavior along desired lines. They are the verbal signposts which guide a group toward its objectives.

Closely associated with praise and flattery are rewards, badges, or other tangible objects drawn from a limited supply. *Rewards* are often unexpected benefits—for example, a reward for returning a purse one has found. *Badges* are external symbols conferred on officials or on members of a group to designate honor and authority. *Medals* granted for meritorious action not only confer prestige but have a valuable control effect on the recipient and, vicariously, on others. Other material symbols are *uniforms* and *insignia.*

While some *gossip* may be innocuous, that related to social control is largely critical in tone. Gossip helps make myths and legends and is effective in formulating public opinion.

Satire, a combination of humor and critical logic put in a sarcastic way, is a highly intellectual and hence distinctly limited means of control. It is a method of exposing the foibles and weaknesses of persons and making them squirm under the verbal lash. It is unpleasant, though the more genial satire may not sting deeply.

Laughing at others is doubtless one of the oldest sanctions. It bespeaks superiority and is highly effective, since it tends to mark off and isolate its target from his fellows, a very effective punishment. If a person loses his sense of belonging to a group, of participating in common enterprises, even though he is not bodily removed, he feels lonesome, unattached, and insecure.

Commands are a direct verbal form of ordering and forbidding— the oldest means of negative control through words. The command may be a positive order to do something or an inhibitory statement forbidding an action. Commands represent direct power. They have much more the sense of exterior authority than do satire, laughter at others, or calling names. In our society the most effective commands in secondary groups are those issued by the government, the military, industry, and the church.

Threats are the most severe form of verbal sanctions. Yet to be fully effective they must be backed by physical force or the appearance of power to deny action. If the threat does not inhibit, then the person threatened must be made to suffer injury, pain, or punishment. Threats are distinctive carriers of emotion and accordingly have great potential power. A threat puts but two alternatives before the person threatened: there are only two ways out of the dilemma, and he must choose between them.

Closely related to commands and threats is *censorship,* which is also complementary to propaganda. It is a restraint on the expression of opinion, whereas propaganda guides opinion and action along predetermined lines. Censorship is usually a command of someone in authority, often a representative of the government or the church, to stop an expression of fact or opinion. It is often physical, as in burning tabooed books, in which sense it becomes an overt sanction. In fact, it may be considered a combination of the use of external force and symbolic controls.

The method of overt action is the final sanction when no other way remains open. This means of control has historically been largely negative and restrictive. It includes fines, imprisonment, whipping, mutilation, torture, banishment, and death. Commands and threats indicate that overt action is imminent, and that is why they are uniquely powerful when they are believed. Control by gross overt action appears in both primary and secondary groups, though in more sophisticated societies the right to inflict severe punishment on the individual is usually reserved by the state.

INTERPRETIVE SUMMARY

Culture is shared, learned behavior that is created by people and transmitted from generation to generation. Humanity's basic tool for transmitting culture is language. A culture is the common way of life among a people.

The variability of culture is partly related to the physical environment; people develop different cultures as they attempt to survive in their particular environments. Geography limits rather than determines the course a culture will take. Geographically similar cultures frequently find different ways of adjusting to their environments and hold different values. Race *per se* is not a factor in cultural variability. No race is inherently superior to any other.

The written and the tacit rules of a society are called norms. A society's most important rules, such as those governing morality, are called mores. Mores may not be challenged, and defiance of them will elicit severe punishment. Folkways are less important, more flexible norms. An institution is a set of mores and folkways having the common goal of facilitating a particular function of a society.

Sanctions are the rewards and punishments employed to enforce a society's norms. Sanctions may be informally invoked or codified by law, may be physical or social, positive or negative. Sanctions themselves become norms when a society decides that a much-used manner of teaching a norm is the "right" way.

SUGGESTIONS FOR FURTHER READING

Cohen, Albert K. *Delinquent Boys: The Culture of the Gang.* New York: The Free Press of Glencoe, 1955. A brilliant attempt to understand the behavior of juvenile delinquents through sociological analysis, this book demonstrates that boys from different classes get different kinds of social rewards from participation in gang life.

Dobzhansky, Theodosius. *Evolution, Genetics, and Man.* New York: John Wiley and Sons, 1955. The topic of man's evolution is approached from the standpoint of genetics.

Keesing, Felix M. *Cultural Anthropology.* New York: Rinehart and Company, 1958. This is a general introductory text with a good balance between factual materials and theoretical interpretations.

Kluckhohn, Florence R., and Strodtbeck, Fred R. *Variations in Value Orientations.* New York: Harper and Row, 1961. This is a cross-cultural study of values and norms in five communities in the Southwest.

Kroeber, A. L., ed. *Anthropology Today: An Encyclopedic Inventory.* Chicago: The University of Chicago Press, 1953. A collection of papers summarize and interpret data from both physical and cultural anthropology.

Lewis, Oscar. *The Children of Sanchez.* New York: Random House, 1961. An intimate and powerful account of a family living in the slums of Mexico City, the story is told in their own words.

Linton, Ralph. *The Tree of Culture.* New York: Alfred A. Knopf, 1955. This volume contains chapters on cultural origins, cultural changes, and various aspects of culture in all the major regions of the world.

Murdock, George Peter. "The Common Denominator of Cultures." *The Science of Man in the World Crisis*. Edited by Ralph Linton. New York: Columbia University Press, 1945, pp. 123–142. Murdock attempts to explain cultural universals by referring to the ways in which people learn.

Roszak, Theodore. *The Making of a Counter Culture*. Garden City, N.Y.: Doubleday and Company, Inc., 1969. The current efforts to find alternative cultural patterns in a technological society are analyzed.

Simpson, George Gaylord. *The Meaning of Evolution*. Rev. ed. New York: The New American Library, 1952. The author makes an incisive analysis of present interpretations of evolution with special emphasis on the modern theory of genetics.

Sumner, William Graham. *Folkways*. Boston, Mass.: Ginn and Company, 1906. This is the classic discussion of mores and folkways.

Whyte, William F. *Street Corner Society: The Social Structure of an Italian Slum*. Rev. ed. Chicago: The University of Chicago Press, 1955. An excellent description and analysis of the behavior of youth in a slum community during the depression of the 1930s, this book includes good discussions of norms and their supporting sanctions.

WE WERE
PAYING $65
FOR FIVE ROOMS.
ALL RIGHT IT
WAS A **SLUM**.
I CALL A SPADE
A SPADE. BUT I
DON'T ASK FOR
MUCH. I WAS
MODERATELY
HAPPY.

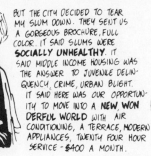

BUT THE CITY DECIDED TO TEAR
MY SLUM DOWN. THEY SENT US
A GORGEOUS BROCHURE, FULL
COLOR. IT SAID SLUMS WERE
SOCIALLY UNHEALTHY. IT
SAID MIDDLE INCOME HOUSING WAS
THE ANSWER TO JUVENILE DELIN-
QUENCY, CRIME, URBAN BLIGHT.
IT SAID HERE WAS OUR OPPORTUN-
ITY TO MOVE INTO A **NEW, WON
DERFUL WORLD** WITH AIR
CONDITIONING, A TERRACE, MODERN
APPLIANCES, TWENTY FOUR HOUR
SERVICE – $400 A MONTH.

WELL, **WE'RE** MIDDLE INCOME.
AND WE FIGURED **BUYING** A
HOUSE WOULD BE **JUST** AS
EXPENSIVE AND **WITHOUT** THE
SERVICE. AND **LOOK** WHAT
WE'D SAVE ON **COMMUTATION**.
SO, IN TWO YEARS, WE
MOVED INTO OUR **NEW,
SOCIALLY HEALTHY**,
MIDDLE INCOME HOUSING.

I DON'T ASK FOR MUCH. TRUE, THE ROOMS WERE
A LITTLE SMALLER, BUT THEY DIDN'T LOOK IT
BECAUSE THE CEILINGS WERE A LITTLE LOWER.
THE TERRACE WAS WHERE OUR OLD FIRE-
ESCAPE USED TO BE EXCEPT YOU COULDN'T
SIT ON IT WITH THE SOOT BLOWING UP
FROM THE MIDDLE INCOME INCINERATOR
WHICH ELIMINATED THE NEED FOR
NOISY AND CUMBERSOME GARBAGE
COLLECTION.

EVERYTIME WE TURNED ON A
FAUCET THE WALL BEHIND
IT GOT A **WET** STAIN. THE
PLUMBING IN THE NEXT
APARTMENT WAS **ALMOST**
AS LOUD AS THE AIR
CONDITIONER IN **OURS**.
SOMETIMES THE APPLIANCES
WORKED. THE TWENTY FOUR
HOUR SERVICE **DIDN'T**.

WITHIN A YEAR **EVERYTHING**
WAS BREAKING DOWN THE
BUILDERS HAD BEEN IN
COURT SIX TIMES OVER
AND NOTHING WAS
HAPPENING. WE WROTE
TO THE CITY TELLING
THEM OUR MIDDLE
INCOME HOUSING
WAS IN DANGER OF
BECOMING A **SLUM**.

THE CITY SENT US BACK A GORGEOUS BROCHURE
FULL COLOR. IT SAID SOCIOLOGISTS WERE NOW
COMING TO BELIEVE THAT SOMETHING **IMPORT-
ANT** HAD BEEN LOST IN THE AREA OF NEIGH-
BORHOOD INTER-FAMILY GROUP RELATIONS
WITH THE BREAKING UP OF SLUMS. IT SAID
MIDDLE INCOME HOUSING **LACKED** NEIGHBOR-
HOOD INTER-FAMILY GROUP RELATIONS. IT
SAID NEIGHBORHOOD INTER-FAMILY GROUP
RELATIONS MAY WELL BE THE ANSWER TO
JUVENILE DELINQUENCY, CRIME, URBAN BLIGHT.

SO FOR **NO**
SERVICE AND
$335 **EXTRA**
A MONTH
I'M
NOW
LIVING IN
A SOCIAL
EXPERIMENT.

5
Social
Functions
and Social
Institutions

Every society in some way is like no other society, like some other society, like all other societies. That the cultures of the world are so numerous and so diverse (as described in Chapter 4, Culture and Society) should not obscure the fact that there are many universal features of social life. Anthropologist George Peter Murdock and his associates have studied more than a thousand cultures, past and present, and have assembled a list of the uniformities of culture, which Murdock calls the "common denominators of culture" (see Table 5-1). Some of the similarity Murdock has recorded derives in part from the fact that humans everywhere have certain minimum basic needs; the ways in which they organize their patterns of social interaction must satisfy these minimum requirements if the society is to survive. All societies must perform certain basic functions for survival. Every society must have social arrangements to meet these basic needs, but the form and content of the specific social structures may vary from society to society.[1]

---

[1] There are several good discussions of universal structures and functions. Two of the best are from Davis, who calls them "societal necessities," and Bennett and Tumin, who refer to them as "functional prerequisites of continuous social life." See Kingsley Davis, *Human Society* (New York: The Macmillan Company, 1949), pp. 28–31; and John W. Bennett and Melvin M. Tumin, *Social Life* (New York: Alfred A. Knopf, 1949), pp. 41–59.

Table 5-1   Common Characteristics of All Cultures

Age grading	Joking
Athletic sports	Kin-groups
Bodily adornment	Kinship nomenclature
Calendar	Language
Cleanliness training	Law
Community organization	Luck superstitions
Cooking	Magic
Cooperative labor	Marriage
Cosmology	Mealtimes
Courtship	Medicine
Dancing	Modesty concerning natural
Decorative art	functions
Divination	Mourning
Division of labor	Music
Dream interpretation	Mythology
Education	Numerals
Eschatology	Obstetrics
Ethics	Penal sanctions
Ethnobotany	Personal names
Etiquette	Population policy
Faith healing	Postnatal care
Family	Pregnancy usages
Feasting	Property rights
Fire making	Propitiation of supernatural
Folklore	beings
Food taboos	Puberty customs
Funeral rites	Religious ritual
Games	Residence rules
Gestures	Sexual restrictions
Gift giving	Soul concepts
Government	Status differentiation
Greetings	Surgery
Hair styles	Tool making
Hospitality	Trade
Housing	Visiting
Hygiene	Weaning
Incest taboos	Weather control
Inheritance rules	

SOURCE: George P. Murdock, "The Common Denominator in Cultures," *The Science of Man in the World Crisis*, ed. Ralph Linton (New York: Columbia University Press, 1945), pp. 123–125.

UNIVERSAL SOCIAL FUNCTIONS

Every human society must have some social arrangement to provide five basic functions necessary for survival: (1) replacement of population, (2) socialization of new population, (3) maintenance of a sense of purpose, (4) production and distribution of goods and services, and (5) preservation of order. Some sociologists consider as basic functions also such things as provision of nutriment or maintenance of biologic adequacy, but since these matters are not strictly *social* in the same sense as the functions listed above, we shall not consider them here.

Replacement of Population

Sexual reproduction is not, it is true, the only method of bringing new members into a society. Annexation, the acquisition of slaves, and immigration are means of recruiting people. (Each of these three modes of population expansion has occurred in the United States during its history.) Theoretically, it would be possible for society to fill the positions of its dying members by recruiting replacements in one or more of these three ways from people born into other societies. The practical difficulty lies less in the recruitment than in the knowledge and loyalty required to maintain the social order. Teaching new members the basic cultural values and norms of a society is a task most readily accomplished when those new members are born into the society. Being entirely dependent for their survival on the adults in their primary group, small children are much more easily socialized into the accepted behaviors and attitudes than are adult immigrants or captives. American Indians, aware of this fact, in the days of frontier warfare ordinarily took captive for induction into their society only young children, seldom adults. For the bulk of its new members, therefore, generation after generation, a society depends primarily on sexual reproduction.

Many people believe that reproductive behavior is merely a natural biological phenomenon. Actually, the behavior patterns of human beings as they propagate their kind, like their behavior in any other area of social life, are shaped and modified by the culture through which they have been socialized. The basic act of procreation is influenced by the norms of the society concerning size of family, form of marriage, whether the sex act itself is considered exalted or shameful, age at which people marry, and economic obligations parents are expected to fulfill toward their children. There is no society which does not have a set of norms governing reproduction. Every culture contains some set of prohibitions, expectations, and rewards having to do with who should have children and the circumstances under which reproduction should occur. The cultural values patterned around reproduction are enforced by both positive and negative sanctions.

Socialization

In any on-going society there must be some structure which has as its function or consequence the teaching of new members. A society would cease to be, and its culture would be lost, if some social organization did not perform the function of socializing its new members. Merely having replacements is not sufficient; the replacements must learn the culture of the society. They must be taught the basic values, or ethos, around which the normative system is organized. They must learn all the thousands of little behavior patterns that are accepted as normal in the society where they are born: what to eat, how to eat it, where to eat it, when to eat it; what to wear, how to wear it, where to wear it, when to wear it; what to say, how to say it; and so on. Each new member must develop, sooner or later, a sense of self.

It would be difficult to overstress how essential this function of socialization is to the continuity of society, or what an enormous task it is. Bennett and Tumin put it well:

> . . . The newborn has no values or norms of right and wrong, nor any developed techniques. He may reasonably be conceived of as a self-seeking biologic organism whose drives and needs have to be socially channeled if they are to be satisfied with what the society has to offer. He must, moreover, learn to discriminate, in the pursuit of his needs, that point at which any further pursuit will generate opposition which may undermine his later capacity to satisfy his own needs.[2]

Socialization is carried on both formally and informally. Going to school is part of the socialization process, but so is going to the movies, or overhearing a conversation in which someone is criticized and hence learning that one can avoid criticism by avoiding the behavior of the person under discussion. Socialization is a continuous process; when, at the age of eighty-two, a person learns something new about getting along in society, he is still being socialized. Socialization is cumulative: learning to recognize the letters of the alphabet lays the groundwork for learning to comprehend written words, and reading written words enables one to learn still other things. Whenever we ask someone to give us new information in terms with which we are familiar—what a thing tastes like, what it feels like, what it is similar to—we are demonstrating the cumulative nature of socialization.

---

[2]Bennett and Tumin, *Social Life*, p. 51. By permission.

A Sense of Purpose

A major portion of the time and effort expended in socialization, especially of the young, is devoted to teaching the beliefs and goals of society, including the idea that these are good and worthy of practice and defense. But there is a further function which must be universally met. Societies must in some way motivate their members to *maintain* the conviction that life is good and worthwhile. In other words, people must be imbued with a sense of meaning. They must be convinced that fitting into the social structure as they have been taught to do—that meeting the expectations of the culture—is worth the effort.

Obviously, a society could not continue to exist if everyone decided that it was better to quit than to go on. A French sociologist, Emile Durkheim, made a fascinating study[3] of one category of people who decide to quit, in which he concluded that what he called "anomic suicide" occurs most frequently in situations of *anomie,* a French word best translated as "normlessness" (or "without rules.)" A society lacking definite norms to regulate morals and social conduct is an anomic society. In an anomic situation, such as a sudden economic depression, when the old rules no longer seem to apply and no new ones are immediately forthcoming and when people do not know what is right and wrong or what the social expectations are, they lose their sense of purpose. At such a time, suicide rates increase.

Production and Distribution of Goods and Services

A society without a social arrangement for the division of labor does not exist. The fact that new members born into a society are at first unable to provide for their own needs in itself requires such an arrangement if the society is to survive. Actually, of course, the division of labor extends far beyond what is necessitated by differences in age. The cumulative nature of culture results in the assignment of certain socially specific tasks to particular segments of society. In time, this process becomes institutionalized. It is not biologically necessary, for example, that men work as hunters or

---

[3]Emile Durkheim, *Le Suicide, trans.* John A. Spaulding and George Simpson (Glencoe, Ill.: The Free Press, 1951). Originally published in France in 1897. For other studies of suicide see Barbara G. Cashion, "Durkheim's Concept of Anomie and its Relationship to Divorce," *Sociology and Social Research,* LV (October, 1970), 72–81; Ruth S. Cavan, *Suicide* (Chicago: University of Chicago Press, 1928); Louis I. Dublin and Bessie Bunzel, *To Be or Not To Be, A Study of Suicide* (New York: Harrison Smith and Robert Haas, 1933); Andrew F. Henry and James F. Short, Jr., *Suicide and Homicide* (Glencoe, Ill.: The Free Press, 1954); Paul J. Bohannan, ed., *African Homicide and Suicide* (Princeton, N. J.: Princeton University Press, 1960).

that women work as construction laborers, although there are times and places where they do.

The economic structure and the set of values governing it differ radically from society to society, but everywhere people have some set of norms ordering their activities so that the function of producing and distributing goods and services is performed. In even the most favorable environment, some such social arrangements are necessary: even where socially defined needs are minimal and natural resources are abundant, someone has to be assigned the responsibility of picking the coconuts or berries for those unable to pick their own.

Preservation of Order

We have seen that if a society is to survive, it must reproduce new members, socialize them, provide them with a continuing sense of purpose, and insure their biological well-being by arranging for the production and distribution of goods and services. Finally, some structure within the society must result in the preservation of order. Two facets of order are essential if the society is to survive: the society must not destroy itself from within, and it must not allow itself to be destroyed from the outside by some other society.

The values and norms that serve to order a society internally are enforced through formal and informal sanctions. Some amount of obedience is essential to the continuity of a society. If a society were to reach the stage where most of its members failed to abide by the basic rules, it would be doomed. If people killed each other wantonly, refused to honor agreements, failed to fulfill social responsibilities, and meted out no punishment to those who ignored the social norms, the society would soon cease to exist. Anarchy may be a fit topic for philosophical speculation but it is not a basis for continued social life for any extended period of time.

It is equally necessary that a society protect itself from outside attack. This is hardly debatable: there are historical instances of societies which have perished through inability to maintain an order capable of resisting external pressures or attacks. Ancient Carthage was destroyed by the Romans and the Tasmanian aborigines were annihilated by an English onslaught.

In small, nonliterate tribal societies, internal order is almost entirely the result of folkways and mores. That is, order is not formalized, but is ordinarily maintained by such informal sanctions as gossip, ridicule, and ostracism. This is possible because such societies are virtually primary groups. In large urbanized societies which are spread over thousands of miles and are composed of millions of people, most of whom never see or interact directly with each other, formal sanctions are necessary to maintain order. There are elaborate bodies of written laws and regulations, and impersonal systems of police and courts to enforce the rules.

Similarly, the function of handling external relations in complex societies involves intricate webs of formal relations with representatives of other societies through full-time officials in a Department of State, the United Nations, and other bureaucratized agencies devoted to the function of preserving the society.

The Web of Social Functions

Reproduction, learning the culture - protecting, providing goods & services - laws

Each of these five major and universal social functions is closely interrelated with the others. Each is by no means separate from the others. If any one of these functions is not performed, the society and hence all the other functions come to an end. The functions are an interlocking system which makes the maintenance, stability, and continuity of social life possible. Because of this interrelationship, a change in any one of them is certain to have repercussions in the others.

SOCIAL INSTITUTIONS

The ways in which a society meets the challenges to its social order posed by these universal social functions vary substantially from time to time and from place to place. But in every human society there is some set of social structures and related norms—called social institutions—for fulfilling these basic functions. A social institution, then, is a structure of social interaction and the accompanying folkways and mores that are integrated around a principal function of the society. "We deal with institutions, then, where distinctive value-orientations and interests centering upon large and important social concerns (e.g., education, marriage, property), generate or are accompanied by distinctive modes of social interaction."[4] There are five basic social institutions that can be identified in all societies—the familial, political, educational, economic, and religious institutions. Most modern societies have many more (e.g., scientific, military, etc.).

The Family

Throughout human history, the family has been the group primarily responsible for most of these functions. Even today, in

---

[4]Louis Schneider, "Institution," *A Dictionary of the Social Sciences*, ed. by Julius Gould and William L. Kolb (New York: The Free Press, 1964), p. 339.

small, relatively isolated societies, the family is the basic primary group around which the major tasks of social life are organized.

In all societies, ancient or modern, small or large, the family is the structure which provides for the reproduction of new members for the society. Families may be organized with one husband, one wife, and their children; one husband, multiple wives, and their children; one wife, multiple husbands, and their children. Or they may consist of great-grandparents plus all their male children and spouses for four generations. And so on. Regardless of the concrete form of family organization, all societies have some form of family, and it is that institution that results in the function of reproduction.

Education

The family always participates in socialization as well, but the extent varies considerably from society to society. In the United States, for example, many Indian children are taken from their parents at a very early age and sent to boarding schools hundreds of miles from their homes.[5] In very small, nonindustrial societies, the family may serve the function of the "school," having almost the entire responsibility for inducting the child into the ways of the society.

People are socialized as a result of participation in many social structures. One learns something about one's society by interacting with others in religious groups, whether Sunday School classes or tribal ceremonies. Membership in a peer group of playmates is also a source of socialization; the child here comes in contact with the values of the culture that surround him or her and learns to conform to group expectations. In the twentieth century public schools have been assuming an important part of the socialization process. Some societies do not have "schools," but all societies have an educational institution—some set of social structures and accompanying folkways and mores that performs the function of socialization.

Religion

As in the case of socialization, the sense of purpose is taught to people and maintained in them through a variety of social structures. Because of the range of cultural variability, sociologists use the word *religion* in a considerably broader sense than that in which it is ordinarily defined. For one person, a belief that the scientific method offers the possibility for a better life in this world may serve this function; for another person, the belief that service to a

---

[5]Sar A. Levitan and Barbara Hetrick, *Big Brother's Indian Programs—with Reservations* (New York: McGraw-Hill Book Company, 1971), pp. 36–41.

supernatural being promises a blissful and eternal afterlife may serve the same function.

Some structures in all societies have as a secondary or even latent function the fostering of a sense of purpose. Groups such as Senior Citizens' Clubs, community centers, and Marine Corps platoons are not religious structures, but are similar to religious structures insofar as they offer the individual something to participate in and believe in, and allow him to convince himself that his behavior is purposive, that his efforts are not in vain.

The Economy

In the days of the frontier in the United States, the family was the basic economic unit. Father, mother, and children worked the fields together, producing most of what they consumed. Now father may work for one company, mother for another, and brother and sister for a third and fourth. The corporation has become the major economic organization in our economy, as secondary groups perform the functions of producing goods and services formerly carried out by primary groups.

Whatever the economic organization of a society—corporate and industrial or primary and agricultural—some groups exist which produce and distribute goods and services. They may specialize in economic activity, as does a steel company, or they may meet this need in addition to others, as does a family. But in all societies there are structures that carry out this function.

The Polity

Like other social structures, those which preserve the domestic order vary greatly in their complexity, depending in general on the size and complexity of the rest of the society. A tribe may be composed of half a dozen families, with the head of one serving as chief, settling disputes within the group and/or leading warriors in battle. At the other extreme are the large nation-states of the mid-twentieth century, each of which has an enormous formal governmental structure with a military branch, a foreign relations branch, a taxation branch, and police and courts at various levels to maintain order within the society. In every state in the United States, for example, there is (1) a legislature (2) chosen by the residents of that state (3) on a competitive basis (4) with each adult citizen having one vote (5) which he is not required to cast but can use or not as he sees fit. Each legislator (6) serves for a specified period of time, after which he must vacate his status or again compete for it, and (7) the legislature has certain specific powers and is denied certain others. Through this set of related norms, and many others

Figure 5-1   The Interrelationships of Social Structures and Social Functions

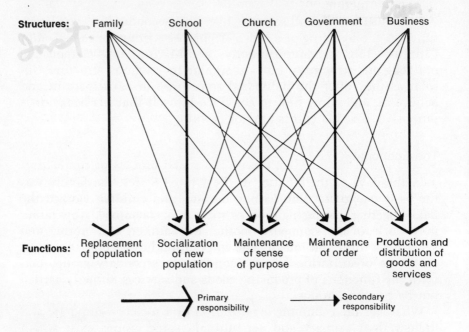

specifying the roles of federal, state, and local executives, judges, policemen, and people in related statuses, the function of maintaining order in the society is carried out.

It is necessary only to note that, as in the cases or reproduction, socialization, and so on, all societies must have some particular structures which ensure social control or norm-enforcing functions.

The Web of Social Institutions

Each social institution is integrated around a major societal function but each invariably performs supplementary functions. Conversely, a function may derive from more than one structure. This is graphically shown in Figure 5-1. "Every institution centers around a fundamental need, permanently unites a group of people in a cooperative task, and has its particular doctrine and its technique or craft. Institutions are not correlated simply and directly to their function; one need does not receive one satisfaction in one institution."[6] The crucial nature of these institutions is indicated by the relatively tight balance which obtains among them. A change in the economy, for example, from a homestead agricultural system

---

[6]Bronislaw Malinowski, "Culture," *Encyclopedia of the Social Sciences* (New York: The Macmillan Company, 1931), Vol. 4, p. 626.

to a mass-production factory system necessitates a change from an all-relatives-under-one-roof familial group to an immediate family. This, in turn, will alter the early socialization of the child, and so on. Social functions and social structures are so closely interrelated that an alteration in one has repercussions throughout the social system. The integration of social institutions is never perfect, however. It is in a constant state of readjustment as the operation of social processes causes alteration in the social structure. However, there must be some degree of integration of institutions or the society will collapse.

An instance of integration among the institutions of our own society will illustrate this point. The social process of competition is stressed as a positive cultural value in the American economic institution. "Free enterprise" is spoken of favorably; people are urged to strive to "get ahead"; competitive examinations are held for promotion in many jobs; we admire the poor boy who works harder than his fellows and becomes a "success"; we pass legislation to prevent monopoly because "competition is good for the market." The political and educational institutions are integrated with our economic institution: people compete for high political office; children are taught to compete for grades, for athletic honors, for fraternity bids, for scholastic prizes. While there is not a perfect meshing of values (it is sometimes bad taste to compete, as for the last piece of candy in the box), our institutions, in general, like those of any other going society, are so integrated that the norms of one institution support those of another.

Institutional Structures

Every institution, in order for its functions to be performed, has a division of labor among its participants. Among the many norms making up the institution are those defining the various roles necessary to the performance of the institutional function. The familial institution, for instance, is responsible for the reproduction of new members for the society; it will therefore specify role behavior appropriate to the statuses of father, mother, son, daughter, suitor, husband, wife, and any other statuses, such as obstetrician or midwife, which are related to the reproductive function in the society.

Of course, not every person who participates in a given institutional structure has exactly the same behavior as every other person in the same role. For one thing, the expectations of one institutional role may interfere with those of another. The expectations of career woman *vs.* those of mother, for example, create role conflict for a person who tries to work and rear children at the same time. Trying to balance the requirements of sometimes conflicting roles, then, can lead individuals to behave differently within the same institutional framework. In addition, each of us brings our own personality to any group in which we participate; we may all conform to its major norms, but our behavior will vary in many small ways. It is obvious that two women who may be described as mothers may behave differently within this role. There are, however, certain major expectations laid down within the familial institutions which lead to a set of similarities in their behavior: the institutionalized role of mother.

Sociologists are especially concerned with the place of each institution in any society; indeed, an emphasis on any one institution or number of institutions is a good indication of the ethics of a culture. A society which demands that its members spend half their time in worship and contemplation leaves them less time for family life, business, and other pursuits than a society with religious requirements that are not so stringent. The dominance of a single institutional structure is less likely for most persons in an urban society, because the urban way of life requires specialization, and each of one's roles tends to be but a segment of his total social life. As Arnold M. Rose says,

> Institutions vary in the degree of specialization expected of persons, and this is often related to the degree of control the institution has over the life of its members. The more specialized and segmentalized the relation of a given member to an institution, the less is its control over him. The teacher is associated with the school only in his occupational life, whereas the nun is associated with the church in most aspects of her life. Even within the same institution this holds true: the religious leader (rabbi, priest, minister) has a less specialized relation to his church than does the average member, and his life is much more controlled by the institution. To the extent that an individual's life is controlled by one institution, he must have fewer relationships to other institutions. A priest, for example, must even withdraw from family life.[7]

INSTITUTIONAL CHANGE

Like any other part of the social order, social institutions change through time; and alterations in one institution invariably reverberate throughout the structure of society. In the industrialized countries of the twentieth century, institutional change is both constant and complex. One attempt to detail institutional change

---

[7]Arnold M. Rose, *Sociology: The Study of Human Relations* (New York: Alfred A. Knopf, 1956), p. 131. By permission.

Figure 5-2   The Relative Influence of Social Institutions in America, 1900 and 1960/1965

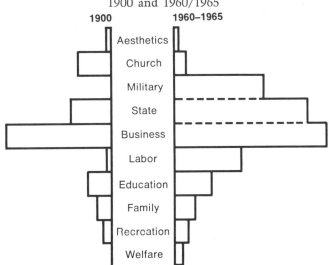

Source: (Figures 19.2 and 19.3) from Delbert C. Miller and William H. Form, *Industrial Sociology*, 2nd Edition (Harper & Row Publishers, Inc., 1964, pp. 827–828). Reprinted by permission.

in the United States has been made by Miller and Form (see Figure 5-2). On the basis of their investigation, Miller and Form suggest that the major institutional change in America since 1900 has been "the prominent rise of the political state into a new level of power."[8]

> In 1900 private business was relatively free from political regulation. Businessmen made the important decisions affecting the economy and the society. They became the established social leaders and set the values in most American communities. The school, state, church, recreational and aesthetic institutions were largely controlled by boards of businessmen or lived by their philanthropy. The family was drawn ever more tightly into the orbit of the business institutions as economic self-sufficiency was replaced with an economic dependence upon those who owned factories, offices, and stores.[9]

The last half-century has also witnessed a relative decline of religion, the institutionalization of welfare and recreation, and an increase in the salience of labor and education. But the most important change has been the position of the political institution. By the mid-1960s, the political institution had so increased its relative

[8]Delbert C. Miller and William H. Form, *Industrial Sociology*, 2nd ed. (New York: Harper and Row, 1964), p. 827.
[9]*Ibid.*

position that "it now threatens to rival the long-established dominance of business institutions."[10] The size of the federal budget and the growth and size of the military organization are two major components of this institutional change.

One of the institutional changes in American society that has received considerable attention is the pattern of courtship. Here is an example of a relatively gradual change reflecting the interdependence of social institutions. The change in our cultural patterns of courtship and the norms governing the selection of a spouse is variously related to changes in religion, the economy, urbanization, and the mass media.

Courtship Patterns

Our present concepts of courtship and marriage derive mainly from the belief that romantic love is the true foundation of happy marriage. The sentiment involves several ideas, most of them mystical: the idea that one can tell when he or she is "in love," that such love is abiding, that it involves mutual sacrifices as well as satisfactions, that the prospective mate will fulfill an ideal, that sexual passion is beautiful when it is an expression of love, and so on.

The cultural root of Western ideas about romantic love is to be found in the latter Middle Ages, in the so-called Age of Chivalry. The notion of romantic love arose among the nobility and their literary protégès. Gallant knights and troubadours carried romantic love to great heights, in poetry and perhaps in life. However, the "amorous cravings," the romanticism, and the sentimentalism about women were expressed" outside the bonds of matrimony,"[11] marriage being arranged by parents, who kept in mind matters of status and wealth. Ideally, at least, true love was chaste, the idea that sexual fulfillment is all right for those "in love" developing later. The rationale of medieval romanticism is described thus by Taylor:

> Love, with the Troubadours and their ladies, was a source of joy. Its commands and exigencies made life's supreme law. Love was knighthood's service; it was loyalty and devotion; it was the noblest human giving. It was also the spring of excellence, the inspiration of high deeds. This love was courteous, delicately ceremonial, precise, and on the lady's part exacting and whimsical . . .[12]

---

[10]*Ibid.*
[11]For an account of medieval romantic love, see Henry Osborn Taylor, *The Mediaeval Mind*, 4th ed., Vol. I (New York: The Macmillan Co., 1925), pp. 586–602. Quotation from p. 587.
[12]*Ibid.*, pp. 588–589. By permission of The Macmillan Company, publishers.

While such high-flown and extreme expressions of romantic love disappeared with the decay of feudalism, the ideas and practices were carried down in the courts of kings and nobles. Finally, in the last three centuries, the rich bourgeois class everywhere has imitated the nobility; and since the eighteenth century the petty bourgeoisie has taken over many romantic ideas from these other classes.

The idea of romantic love has conflicted somewhat with traditional religious doctrines which deny the flesh and emphasize the life to come. However, since the idea of romantic love is pleasant and moreover is compatible with the stress on individualism which accompanied the rise of Protestantism and capitalism, it has flourished. What has emerged is a combination of features of both the romantic and Judeo-Christian ideals: stress on free choice of mate, constancy in love and stability of the family, disapproval but some sympathy for the wayward.

In colonial America, although the father continued to have chief control over the marriage of children, young people were allowed some freedom in the choice of a spouse. The colonies safeguarded marriage by requiring that the consent of the parents be clearly expressed and that the marriage be recorded. On the frontier and in rural America during the nineteenth century there was considerable freedom in the choice of mates. "Keeping company" was a folkway, though courtships tended to be brief. Romance in the rural community was usually but a prelude to a marriage and family life in which a wife and children were useful as economic assets, in addition to any affectional needs they might satisfy. Courtship in the town life of the nineteenth century tended to be somewhat more prolonged. It was a period of testing and trying, in which "spooning" was tolerated but sex relations were tabooed.

Rapid urbanization since the turn of the century brought further changes in courtship patterns. The high mobility of the population, the decline of some primary-group controls, the increasing degree of specialization, the impersonal nature of many contacts, and other aspects of mass society have profoundly influenced courtship practices. For example, the sexual element in love-making has become openly recognized, both in communication and in overt conduct. Young people talk more freely about the biological foundations of mating. Advertisements carry material dealing with personal hygiene which would not have been tolerated a few decades ago. The automobile has permitted freedom of movement and thus helped do away with the former rigid control of love-making through community gossip. Young people are now able to escape the eyes and ears of parents and neighbors. The motion picture, television, and other media of mass communication have also helped alter the older family controls, as well as providing new romantic imagery. One indication of the extent of this change is shown in a 1966 study contrasting the attitudes of 217 co-eds with the beliefs held by their mothers which revealed considerable differences between the generations.[13] Asked about the value of preserving their virginity until marriage, 13 per cent of the daughters said that was "not important"; not a single one of their mothers agreed. Virginity was rated "very important" by 88 per cent of the mothers, but by only 55 per cent of the daughters. The middling position that virginity is "generally important" accounted for 12 per cent of the mothers' responses, but for a third of the daughters'. When they were asked their attitudes toward engaged couples having sexual intercourse, 83 per cent of the mothers said it was "very wrong," but only 35 per cent of their daughters agreed. While 17 per cent of the daughters thought it was "right in many situations," only 2 per cent of the mothers shared this view.

The Family in China

The change in the norms governing courtship and marriage in American society illustrates institutional dynamics over a considerable period of time. An example of rapid institutional change can be seen in the Chinese family.[14]

For centuries, Chinese culture was characterized by a familial structure based on filial piety and extensive obligations to relatives. An individual's marriage was therefore a matter of great concern to his whole family, since it constituted a contract of mutual obligations among all those related to both spouses. Among the upper classes, the choice of a husband or wife lay with the parents and grandparents, since marriage was defined as an alliance between households. The most important criterion in the selection of a mate was the wealth and prestige of the family. Through shrewd marriage contracts a number of families of high status could be combined into a powerful group. Among the peasants, the principal factor to bear in mind in selecting a wife was her working ability. Her phys-

---

[13]Robert R. Bell, "Parent Conflict in Sexual Values," *Journal of Social Issues*, 1966, XXII: 34–44.

[14]Hsaio-Tung Fei and C. Chang, *Earthbound China: A Study of Rural Economy in Yunnan* (Chicago: University of Chicago Press, 1945); M. H. Fried, *Fabric of Chinese Society: A Study of the Social Life of a Chinese County Seat* (New York: Frederick A. Praeger, 1953); Francis L. K. Hsu, "The Family in China," *The Family: Its Function and Destiny*, ed. Ruth N. Anshen (New York: Harper & Brothers, 1949), pp. 73–92; Francis L. K. Hsu, *Under the Ancestor's Shadow: Chinese Culture and Personality* (New York: Columbia University Press, 1948); Francis L. K. Hsu and J. H. Hu, "Guild and Kinship Among the Butchers in West Town," *American Sociological Review*, 1945, 10: 317–364; Rose Hum Lee, "Research on the Chinese Family," *American Journal of Sociology*, 1949, 54: 497–504; Marion J. Levy, Jr., *The Family Revolution in Modern China* (Cambridge: Harvard University Press, 1949).

ical attractiveness or ability to inspire romantic inclinations was of no importance compared with her potential productivity as a field laborer.[15]

Even before the Communists achieved political dominance in China, the beginnings of "Westernization" of the family could be seen.[16] The traditional patriarchal, extended family was giving way to a smaller, husband-wife-and-child family unit, and mutual affection rather than family obligation was the rationale for mate selection. This change in familial institutions was still in process at the time of the Chinese revolution in 1949.

Since the revolution, the norms governing familial social relations have undergone another radical change. The government is making a concerted attempt to use the familial institution for the benefit of political solidarity. The state urges young Chinese to select spouses with a view to founding a family that will contribute to the new order.

> Marriage is no longer taken as a matter involving two families as in traditional China, nor between two individuals as in the Western world, but a spiritual union of two comrades of different sexes; and the first task of the couple is to strengthen and cherish their commonly shared belief of communism, and then to engage in production to build a new society.[17]

Contemporary China illustrates a deliberate attempt at institutional change. The family was long the dominant institution in Chinese society. Authorities are now trying to make the political institution dominant.

INTERPRETIVE SUMMARY

Several universal social functions may be pinpointed, since all societies must perform certain basic tasks in order to survive. Each society must replenish its population, must produce and distribute food and other necessities, and must guard against destruction from within or without. Furthermore, each society must teach new members the values, knowledge, and skills of the society, and must convince each individual that life on his society's terms is worthwhile.

Each society must develop some institutionalized means for renewing itself, for distributing goods and services, and so on. Specific structures of social institutions vary with the society. More complex cultures, for instance,

---

[15]Hsaio-Tung Fei, "Peasantry and Gentry: An Interpretation of Chinese Social Structure and its Changes," *American Journal of Sociology*, 1946, 52: 1–17.
[16]Olga Lang, *Chinese Family and Society* (New Haven: Yale University Press, 1946).
[17]Shu-Ching Lee, "China's Traditional Family, its Characteristics and Disintegration," *American Sociological Review*, 1953, 18: 280.

have many specific social structures, each having a basic function, each having secondary functions which reinforce the work of other structures.

While each institution has at least one avowed function, many have one or more functions which are unrecognized by some or even all participants. Finally, institutions are dynamic. They may change gradually or rapidly, as a result of conscious effort of participants or outsiders, or by the gradual falling off of outworn norms. The way in which the United States has modified and blended traditional standards concerning love and marriage is a good example of gradual, cumulative change in an institution. The change in China from the patriarchal, extended family unit to the westernized husband-wife-and-child pattern was also gradual and not conscious, while the later attempt by political authorities to change the pattern was deliberate. A change in one institution will cause changes in other institutions and functions throughout the society.

SUGGESTIONS FOR FURTHER READING

Drake, Joseph T. *The Aged in American Society*. New York: The Ronald Press Company, 1958. Part one contrasts the status of the aged in agrarian and in urban industrial societies.

Friedenberg, Edgar Z. *Coming of Age in America*. Vintage Books. New York: Random House, 1967. The author provides a provocative critique of American education and describes a clash in values between the schools, which are oriented to adult values, and their clientele, whose adolescent values reflect their status.

Gross, Neal; Mason, Ward S.; and McEachen, Alexander W. *Explorations in Role Analysis: Studies in the School Superintendency Role*. New York: John Wiley and Sons, 1958. Supported by an emprical study of formal educational roles, the authors attempt to develop a cluster of role concepts for the social sciences.

Habenstein, Robert W., and Christ, Edwin A. *Professionalizer, Traditionalizer, and Utilizer.* Columbia, Missouri: The Institute for Research in the Social Sciences, 1955. This is an interpretative study of the work of the general-duty nurse in nonmetropolitan general hospitals in central Missouri. Chapters five and seven are particularly pertinent, since they deal with role and status in relation to the three sociological types of nurses that provide the title for this monograph.

Hughes, Everett C. "Dilemmas and Contradictions of Status," *The American Journal of Sociology*, L (March, 1945), 352–359. The article briefly describes the problems stemming from situations in which people are faced with socially incompatible roles.

Janowitz, Morris. *The Professional Soldier*. New York: The Free Press, 1964. This is an excellent presentation of status and role in the military establishment.

Klapp, Orrin E. *Heroes, Villians, and Fools.* Englewood Cliffs, N. J.: Prentice-Hall, Inc., 1962. This book explores the major social types in American culture.

Komarovsky, Mirra. "Cultural Contradictions and Sex Roles," *The American Journal of Sociology,* LII (November, 1946), 184–189. The role conflicts of college-educated women in America are analyzed.

Linton, Ralph. *The Study of Man.* New York: Appleton-Century-Crofts, 1936. Chapter eight is the classic statement on status and role.

Mead, Margaret. *Male and Female: A Study of the Sexes in a Changing World.* New York: William Morrow and Company, 1949. This book is the product of many years of field research and solid thinking on the relations of men and women in various societies.

Parsons, Talcott. *The Social System.* New York: The Free Press of Glencoe, 1951. Institutional structures and their functions are systematically treated.

Williams, Robin M., Jr. *American Society, A Sociological Interpretation.* 2nd ed. New York: Alfred A. Knopf, 1961. Williams examines the institutional structure of contemporary United States from a functional point of view.

IT STARTED WITH MY MOTHER.

SHE SAID: "YOU **ALWAYS** HAVE TO BE **DIFFERENT** WHY DON'T YOU GO OUT AND PLAY LIKE EVERYONE ELSE?"

SO I DID. AND I MADE FRIENDS. AND MY FRIENDS SAID:

"YOU **ALWAYS** HAVE TO BE **DIFFERENT.** WHY DON'T YOU JOIN **GANGS** LIKE EVERYONE ELSE?"

SO I DID. AND THINGS WERE GOING ALONG **FINE.**

UNTIL COLLEGE WHEN MY ADVISER SAID: "DON'T BE **SOCIALLY HOSTILE.** JOIN A FRAT LIKE EVERYONE ELSE."

SO I DID. AND I BOUGHT A PIPE — AND I STARTED BOOZING — AND SOON YOU COULDN'T TELL ME FROM EVERYONE ELSE.

SO WHEN I GOT OUT, I JOINED MADISON AVENUE.

NOW THEY TELL ME I'M A CONFORMIST.

6
The
Person
and Society

There are few questions in all of Western thought that have received as much consideration as the question of the relationship of the individual to society. Much of the discussion has focused around the idea that there is an inevitable conflict between the individual and the groups of which he or she is a member. For many sociologists, however, the question of the person versus society is a false question in the sense that it asserts an autonomy of each which does not exist. As Charles Horton Cooley once wrote, "a separate individual is an abstraction unknown to experience, and so likewise is society when regarded as something apart from individuals."[1] The person is shaped and developed within the context of society, not prior to or outside of it. The human being becomes human and social only through participation in the society. The anthropologist Ruth Benedict also argued that there is "no proper antagonism between the role of society and that of the individual."[2] "Most people," she wrote, "are shaped to the form of their culture

---

[1]Charles Horton Cooley, *Human Nature and the Social Order* (New York: Charles Scribner's Sons, 1902), p. 84.
[2]Ruth Benedict, *Patterns of Culture* (Baltimore,: Penguin Books, 1946), p. 232.

because of the enormous malleability of their original endowment. They are plastic to the moulding force of the society into which they are born."[3]

A long-standing discussion concerns the relative importance of heredity and environment in shaping human behavior. At one extreme are those who attribute almost all variation among human personalities to differential heredity. At the other extreme are those who assume that hereditary differences are so negative that any variations in behavior observed among people can only be accounted for as resulting from different social environments. Actually, the evidence does not support either one of these extreme positions.

PERSONALITY: HEREDITY AND ENVIRONMENT

Heredity is the transmission of genetic characteristics from parents to their offspring. Hereditary traits, then, are innate; they are present at birth. By *environment* people usually mean those forces, situations, and so on that affect the individual from outside. Environment includes the *physical* world external to the individual: the constant threat of starvation facing someone in an arctic setting might contribute to a personality organization different from that likely on a lush tropical island. The *social* environment also molds the personality: a child reared by loving, indulgent, and permissive parents will have a personality different from that of a child with similar inherited characteristics reared by unloving, unconcerned, and restrictive parents.

Heredity

The essential characteristics inherited by all human beings can be classified as follows:

(1) physical structure (how tall or short one is, whether one has a long or short nose, large or small feet—briefly, how one is put together)
(2) reflexes (direct responses to stimuli, such as withdrawing from a pinprick, blinking when something approaches the eye)
(3) innate drives (impulses to act based on physiological tensions; but these must be linked through learning with activities which will reduce the tensions)
(4) intelligence (the capacity to learn, to modify responses)
(5) temperament (patterned and recurrent responses associated with basic emotional make-up—for example, imperturbability, excitability, or lethargy)

---

[3]*Ibid.*, p. 235.

Of the categories above, that of innate drives is probably subject to the greatest misunderstanding. The source of the confusion is the tendency to equate the drive with the activity that reduces the tension. Activity that will reduce tension must be learned. It stems, in other words, from environment. The innate drive does not need to be learned; one is born with it. The walls of the stomach will contract in a newborn baby; the hunger drive is present. What to do about hunger must be learned, and is hence subject to a certain degree of cultural control. Whether one learns to relish fried chicken or fried crickets depends on the society in which he is reared; either can reduce the hunger drive. Human beings do have socially acquired drives, but these are rooted in social learning, not in heredity. Desires for a college education or for a communal existence are tensions as real and as definite as innate drives, but they are a product of social life, not genes.

Heredity has a limiting influence on personality development. A person can be born severely mentally retarded and therefore so restricted as to make it impossible for him to become as fully a participating member of society as one who is born with the mental capabilities of a "genius" even if they both receive the same social opportunities. The limiting nature of heredity is nowhere more dramatically illustrated than in the observations which were made of an ape and a child reared in an American home as if they were brother and sister.

The Story of Gua and Donald

In June, 1931, Professor and Ms. W. N. Kellogg, then at Indiana University, brought into their home a female chimpanzee 7½ months old, which they named Gua. Their plan was to rear this ape in company with their own 10-month-old son, Donald. (Had the ape and the child been reared together from birth, the procedure would have more closely approximated the ideal design for a controlled experiment we discussed in Chapter 1.) The ape and the child lived in the same household and were exposed to more or less the same daily training and kindly care until March, 1932. The regimen included training in postural and body habits, in walking and feeding, play, and all the other habits which a young child in our American society acquires. There was little punishment in connection with their training, but a persistent effort was made by word and deed on the part of the adults to facilitate development. In connection with the daily routine, the Kelloggs made systematic tests, observations, and comparison of Gua's and Donald's capacities, traits, and activities. They measured their physical growth and strength, their hearing, seeing, and other senses, and their social-emotional development; and they put them through a number of critical learning tests involving manual skill, memory, recognition, and language.[4]

While Gua and Donald had similar reflex organization, the ape was more mature than the child in a number of items, such as strength of the grasping and rejecting responses. In motor dexterity the ape was in many ways far superior to the child, especially in climbing, in pulling open drawers, and in escaping danger. At 7½ months the ape easily climbed into a high chair; the child was 18½ months before he could do so. Gua learned to walk erect on her hind feet some time before Donald managed walking alone; she learned early to run and to skip, whereas Donald did not learn to skip during this period.

In our society, the fundamental training in habits of elimination ordinarily begins toward the end of the first year, and both ape and child were put on regular schedules shortly after Gua's arrival. From the outset the child was superior to the ape in bladder control (the water intake of the ape was much larger, so that her frequency of urination was about one-third greater than the child's). In bowel control the child was at first superior to the ape, but after four months there was no difference (even though the ape eliminated from four to seven times in 24 hours, whereas the child's usual reaction was but twice in the same span).

In a number of sensory-perceptual responses, also, the ape and the child were much alike. Both reacted vigorously to tickling, and the observers reported not only smiling on the part of the ape but a whimpering sound which they termed laughter. Gua, however, disliked too-bright illumination, had remarkable visual acuity, and was much more responsive to noises—slight or loud—than the boy.

At play the ape and child were much alike in handling, biting, and exploring their toys. From the outset, however, Donald showed more interest in examining and manipulating things in the environment. At first their play was of the solitary sort, but later simple social games and mutual examination and exploration began. Both were intrigued by the face; they tried kissing and tactile interplay. They became quite protective of each other, holding on to each other, for instance, while riding in a play wagon.

Yet significant differences were early apparent. Gua never got accustomed to older children or to strange adults. In contrast, as Donald grew older he showed increased concern with both children and grownups in the neighborhood. One of the most telling reactions was the growing intensity of the emotional dependence of the

---

[4]See W. N. Kellogg and L. A. Kellogg, *The Ape and the Child* (New York: McGraw-Hill Book Co., 1933).

ape on Professor and Ms. Kellogg. She ran to them when frightened, and from the beginning showed much stronger fear responses than the child. As time passed, Gua revealed increasing anxiety whenever they left the house without her. Jealousy also was more evident in Gua than in Donald. Her craving for affection and attention from others was much stronger. Donald at 15 months showed distinct bashfulness—an evidence of emerging sense of self. Gua never did reveal such an attitude.

To test their intelligence, a large number of (Gesell) infant tests were used. In many of these the ape showed a more rapid rate of learning. In many rudimentary memory tests the ape was superior to the child, but in matters requiring minute manual dexterity, the ape was inferior. In age of walking erect and alone and in showing interest in its own reflection in the mirror, the ape was more advanced. Gua learned to eat with a spoon at 13 months, a habit Donald did not acquire until he was 17½ months old. The ape also managed to drink from a glass at an earlier age, and she was more successful in using a toy to get at objects placed behind an obstruction. Yet, taking all the Gesell tests together, the learning of the two was closely parallel.

In vocal communication and the beginning of higher mental powers as seen in the beginnings of language, the child was clearly superior. Both soon learned to follow correctly all sorts of vocal commands to perform simple motor tasks, and Gua early showed great sensitiveness to vocal indications of approval or disapproval from adults. The ape was at first more correctly responsive to human commands than was the child. She learned to comprehend simple verbal responses by pointing to a picture of a dog on the command "show me a bow-wow," and she learned to utter certain distinctive bark-like sounds to indicate "Yes" when asked "Do you want an orange?" Later the child surpassed the ape in verbal comprehension.

However, in spite of nine months of living with human beings and being exposed to kindly and patient teaching, *Gua never acquired a single human word.* That is, she could not use names for objects. Donald, on the contrary, before the first year began using words for objects. He called Gua "Gya" and acquired the usual vocabulary and simple sentences for a child of his age. There is little doubt that, had the ape remained in the Kellogg home, her human companion would soon have outstripped her in acquiring the essential habits of communication and conduct which so sharply distinguish the *Homo sapiens* from the anthropoid. These involve such characteristics as language and the use of concepts, memory expressed in symbolic form, the skilled use of tools and other material objects, and, above all else, the self-image which plays such an important part in human personality.

ILLUSTRATIVE DATA 6-1   CULTURE AND PERSONALITY

The case of adolescence . . . is in the limelight in our own civilization and . . . a whole library of psychological studies has emphasized the inevitable unrest of the period of puberty. It is in our tradition a physiological state as definitely characterized by domestic explosions and rebellion as typhoid is marked by fever. There is no question of the facts. They are common in America. The question is rather of their inevitability.

The most casual survey of the ways in which different societies have handled adolescence makes one fact inescapable: even in those cultures which have made most of the trait, the age upon which they focus their atention varies over a great range of years. At the outset, therefore, it is clear that the so-called puberty institutions are a misnomer if we continue to think of biological puberty. The puberty they recognize is social, and the ceremonies are a recognition in some fashion or other of the child's new status of adulthood. This investiture with new occupations and obligations is in consequence as various and as culturally conditioned as the occupations and obligations themselves. . . . In ordei to understand puberty institutions . . . we need . . . to know what is identified in different cultures with the beginning of adulthood and their methods of admitting to the new status. Not biological puberty, but what adulthood means in that culture conditions the puberty ceremony.

Adulthood in central North America means warfare. Honour in it is the great goal of all men. The constantly recurring theme of the youth's coming-of-age, as also of preparation for the warpath at any age, is a magic ritual for success in war. They torture not one another, but themselves: they cut strips of skin from their arms and legs, they strike off their fingers, they drag heavy weights pinned to their chest or leg muscles. Their reward is enhanced prowess in deeds of warfare.

In Australia, on the other hand, adulthood means participation in an exclusively male cult whose fundamental trait is the exclusion of women. Any woman is put to death if she so much as hears the sound of the bull-roarer at the ceremonies, and she must never know of the rites. Puberty ceremonies are elaborate and symbolic repudiations of the bonds with the female sex; the men are symbolically made self-sufficient and the wholly responsible element of the community. To attain this end they use drastic sexual rites and bestow supernatural guaranties.

Puberty rites may also be built upon the facts of girls' puberty and admit of no extension to boys. One of the most naïve of these is the institution of the fatting-house for girls in Central Africa. In the region where feminine beauty is all but identified with obesity, the girl at puberty is segregated, sometimes for years, fed with sweet and fatty foods, allowed no activity, and her body rubbed assiduously with oils. She is taught during this time her future duties, and her seclusion ends with a parade of her corpulence that is followed by her marriage to her proud bridegroom. It is not regarded as necessary for the man to achieve pulchritude before marriage in a similar fashion.

The usual ideas around which girls' puberty institutions are centered, and which are not readily extended to boys', are those concerned with menstruation. The uncleanness of the menstruating woman is a very widespread idea, and in a few regions first menstruation has been made the focus of all the associated attitudes. Puberty rites in these cases are of a thoroughly different character from any of which we have spoken. Among the Carrier Indians of British Columbia, the fear and horror of a girl's puberty was at its height. Her three or four years of seclusion was called "the burying alive," and she lived for all that time alone in the wilderness, in a hut of branches far from all beaten trails. She was a threat to any person who might so much as catch a glimpse of her, and her mere footstep defiled a path or a river. She was covered with a great headdress of tanned skin that shrouded her face and breasts and fell to the ground behind. Her arms and legs were loaded with sinew bands to protect her from the evil spirit with which she was filled. She was herself in danger and she was a source of danger to everybody else.

Girls' puberty ceremonies built upon ideas associated with the menses are readily convertible into what is, from the point of view of the individual concerned, exactly opposite behaviour. There are always two possible aspects to the sacred: it may be a source of peril or it may be a source of blessing. In some tribes the first menses of girls are a potent supernatural blessing. Among the Apaches I have seen the priests themselves pass on their knees before the row of solemn little girls to receive from them the blessing of their touch. All the babies and the old people come also of necessity to have illness removed from them. The adolescent girls are not segregated as sources of danger, but court is paid to them as to direct sources of supernatural blessing. Since the ideas that underlie puberty rites for girls, both among the Carrier and among the Apache, are founded on beliefs concerning menstruation, they are not extended to boys, and boys' puberty is marked instead, and lightly, with simple tests and proofs of manhood.

The adolescent behaviour, therefore, even of girls was not dictated by some physiological characteristic of the period itself, but rather by marital or magic requirements socially connected with it. These beliefs made adolescence in one tribe serenely religious and beneficent, and in another so dangerously unclean that the child had to cry out in warning that others might avoid her in the woods. The adolescence of girls may equally, as we have seen, be a theme which a culture does not institutionalize. Even where, as in most of Australia, boys' adolescence is given elaborate treatment, it may be that the rites are an induction into the status of manhood and male participation in tribal matters, and female adolescence passes without any kind of formal recognition.

These facts, however, still leave the fundamental question unanswered. Do not all cultures have to cope with the natural turbulence *of this period, even though it may not be given institutional expression? Dr. Mead has studied this question in Samoa. There the girl's life passes through well-marked periods. Her first years out of babyhood are passed in small neighbourhood gangs of age mates from which the little boys are strictly excluded. The corner of the village to which she belongs is all-important, and the little boys are traditional enemies. She has one duty, that of baby-tending, but she takes the baby with her rather than stays home to mind it, and her play is not seriously hampered. A couple of years before puberty, when she grows strong enough to have more difficult tasks required of her and old enough to learn more skilled techniques, the little girls' play group in which she grew up ceases to exist. She assumes woman's dress and must contribute to the work of the household. It is an uninteresting period of life to her and quite without turmoil. Puberty brings no change at all.*

A few years after she has come of age, she will begin the pleasant years of casual and irresponsible love affairs that she will prolong as far as possible into the period when marriage is already considered fitting. Puberty itself is marked by no social recognition, no change of attitude or of expectancy. Her pre-adolescent shyness is supposed to remain unchanged for a couple of years. The girl's life in Samoa is blocked out by other considerations than those of physiological sex maturity, and puberty falls in a particularly unstressed and peaceful period during which no adolescent conflicts manifest themselves. Adolescence, therefore, may not only be culturally passed over without ceremonial; it may also be without importance in the emotional life of the child and in the attitude of the village toward her.

Source: Ruth Benedict, *Patterns of Culture* (New York: The New American Library, 1946), pp. 22–29. First published by Houghton Mifflin Co., 1934. By permission.

PERSONALITY AND SOCIETY

The comparison of Gua with Donald exemplifies how no amount of training can overcome the limitations imposed by heredity on mental capacity. We know too, however, that inherited capacity alone cannot produce a human personality. No matter how impressive the capacities an individual may inherit, he or she becomes a person only through interaction with others. Without society, the individual personality does not and cannot come into being. An individual deprived of all communication with other humans from birth would never become human in any conventional sense of the word. Such an individual would possess no language, and his or her thinking would extend very little beyond momentary recall of sense impressions. Such an individual would have no social status, no loyalties, no beliefs, no love of country, no concept of mother, and no worship of God. In this sense, to be human is to be social. Just how essential the social environment is to the development of personality can be seen in the records of children kept in almost total isolation. In the words of one writer, these cases show "what happens when the social environment of a child approaches zero."[5]

Feral Children

There are a number of folks tales and semi-scientific accounts which tell of humans who allegedly were raised by nonhuman animals. Zeus and Tarzan are probably the two most legendary heroes who were supposedly raised without the benefit of human association. There are also tales that the alleged founders of Rome, Romulus and Remus, were raised by animals. But not all of those who have presumably benefited from such an upbringing have been persons of such high repute; there have also been a large number of lesser mortals who were supposedly raised by animals. In fact, Bergen Evans has learned of accounts of a fish girl of Holland, a swine girl of Bavaria, a bear boy of Lithuania, a chicken boy of Ireland, a badger boy of Winnipeg, a sheep boy of Ireland, baboon boys of South Africa, and a very large number of "wolf-children," the most notable of whom are probably Amala and Kamala.[6]

These tales of feral (meaning wild, existing in a state of nature, or undomesticated) people are sometimes amusing, but none is authenticated. The best *guess* about their authenticity is that some are total fabrications, a couple proven hoaxes, and the rest probably cases of socially unwanted children (possibly mentally retarded or otherwise congenitally deficient) who were mistreated by their families and left in some uninhabited place to die. Bruno Bettleheim is very likely correct when he suggests that the reported behavior of so-called feral children is produced not when wolves behave like human mothers, but vice-versa. "The conclusion tentatively forced on us is that while there are no feral children, there are some very rare examples of feral mothers, of human beings who become feral to one of their children."[7]

The data regarding the "feral" children are so speculative and insufficient that they are of no value for sociology. There is no creditable case of a person being reared from infancy without human

[5]Francis N. Maxfield, "What Happens When the Social Environment of a Child Approaches Zero," unpublished manuscript, quoted in Kingsley Davis, *Human Society* (New York: The Macmillan Company, 1948), p. 206.
[6]For a summary account of feral people, see J. A. L. Singh and R. M. Zingg, *Wolf Children and Feral Man* (New York: Harper and Brothers, 1942). For a brilliant critique of the nonsense of these reports, see Bergen Evans, "Wolf, Wolf," *The Natural History of Nonsense* (New York: Vintage Books, 1946), pp. 85–97.
[7]Bruno Bettleheim, "Feral Children and Autistic Children," *The American Journal of Sociology*, LXIV (March, 1959), 467.

influence. There are, however, a few moderately well documented cases of social isolates—persons who had very limited social contact for an extended period of time—which dramatically illustrate much of what is known about the relationship between the individual and society, about the socialization process of preadolescents, and about the extent to which the person is a product of society.

Social Isolation

Two examples of social isolation are the cases of Anna and Isabelle, reported by Kingsley Davis.[8] In the late 1930s and within the span of nine months, in separate states and separate incidents, these two girls were "discovered" by authorities to have been virtually socially isolated for the first six years of their lives.

The Story of Anna

On February 6, 1938, the New York Times carried a story about a six-year old child who had been found "tied to an old chair" in an attic room of a farmhouse in Pennsylvania. The child, Anna, had apparently suffered from extreme malnutrition and social isolation and had lived nearly all of her life with only a minimum of human care. When Anna came to the attention of the authorities, she was removed to a county home and then to a foster home. Later she was placed in a private school for the mentally retarded where she died on August 6, 1942.

Anna was an "illegitimate" child whose grandfather, a widowed farmer in whose house the mother lived, strongly disapproved of the child. Consequently, Anna was shifted from place to place for the first six months of her life. For a short period of time, she was placed in a children's home and various foster homes. But for some reason, Anna was returned to her mother at the age of six months after having lived in ten different places.

Because of the anger and aversion of the maternal grandfather, Anna was hidden in an attic-like room. She received only enough care to keep her alive. Anna was kept in a crib almost constantly until she was "discovered" at six years of age. She appeared to have

[8]The following descriptions follow closely the reports by Kingsley Davis, "Extreme Isolation of a Child," The American Journal of Sociology, XLV (1940), 554–565; Kingsley Davis, "Final Note on a Case of Extreme Isolation," The American Journal of Sociology, LII (1947), 432–437; and Marie K. Mason, "Learning to Speak after Six and One-half Years of Silence," Journal of Speech Disorders, VII (1942), 295–304. See also Bruno Bettleheim, "Feral Children and Autistic Children, The American Journal of Sociology, LXIV (March, 1959), 455–467; and William F. Ogburn, "The Wolf Boy of Agra," The American Journal of Sociology, LXIV (March, 1959), 449–454.

been moved from one position to another seldomly; she had no toys, no instruction, and no friendly attention. She was almost always alone. Her only contacts were with her mother and occasionally with her step-brother, who reportedly teased and taunted her. She was fed on virtually nothing except cow's milk during all of the time she was in her mother's care. She was seldom if ever bathed, caressed, or in any way socialized.

When Anna was discovered after five and one-half years of isolation, she was extremely undernourished and had skelton-like legs, a bloated belly, and very little clothing. She could neither walk, talk, nor do anything that remotely showed intelligence. She remained in a supine position, immobile and indifferent to those around her. She appeared to be totally deaf and her interaction with people was either perfunctory or "openly antagonistic."

As a result of a new diet and massages, her physical condition improved rapidly. Gradually she began to develop some mental and social traits normal for children her age. She acquired visual discrimination as to color and improved in posture and motor coordination, including the ability to chew food. Yet after four months she had not learned to speak. By the end of six months, however, she began to walk. In time she learned to control her elimination. She also gradually showed interest in the people around her. Approximately two years after being discovered, Anna could walk, could feed herself, was fairly neat, and could recall people and understand simple commands, but she could not speak. She had, in general, the mental and behavioral characteristics of a child under two years of age.

In April, 1940, at the age of eight, a clinical psychologist reported that she was large for her age, normal in hearing and vision, now able to climb stairs, and had reached the "babbling stage" of speech reactions, with some promise of further linguistic development. At this time it was estimated that Anna had a mental age of 19-23 months.

On July 1, 1941, the school reported that she had grown in height and weight, could bounce and catch a ball, and had made progress in adjustment to group life with other children. Finally, she had begun to talk. The report concluded that there was nothing peculiar about her except that she was mentally retarded. Two months before her death, another report indicated that she could talk, mainly in phrases, and would repeat words and try to carry on a conversation. She was tidy in her personal habits; walked and ran fairly well; and, while somewhat excitable, was good-natured. At the time of her death, Anna's chronological age was ten and one-half years and her estimated mental age was two and one-half years.

It seems evident that Anna's social isolation prevented a considerable amount of the mental and physical development that was part of her capacity. While we cannot know her exact capacity, it is clear that Anna would have never realized the capabilities she actually did develop after her period of confinement if she had remained in isolation.

The Story of Isabelle

The second child, Isabelle, was discovered in Ohio under conditions very similar to Anna's. She was born in 1932 and discovered in November, 1938, nine months after the discovery of Anna. Like Anna, Isabelle was an "illegitimate" child and had been secluded at least partly for that reason. Her mother was a deaf-mute, and the best evidence is that she and Isabelle spent most of their time together in a dark room, shut off from the rest of the mother's family. Isabelle had no opportunity to develop speech although she communicated with her mother by means of gestures. Her diet was inadequate and she saw virtually no sunlight during her period of isolation.

At the time of her discovery, Isabelle was unable to walk; her legs were so bowed that when she was put in a standing position, the soles of her shoes came together. At first it was difficult to tell whether or not she could hear, and her estimated mental age was approximately two years.

Unlike Anna, Isabelle was placed in a skilled, systematic program of intensive training immediately following her discovery. At the end of one month she attempted speech, and at the end of one year she had acquired the fundamentals of speech and a moderate vocabulary. At the end of two and one-half years of training she reached the normal level of an eight year old child. In other words, she accomplished in two and one-half years what ordinarily requires six years. In 1947, at the age of 14, Isabelle was in the seventh grade of public school and was reportedly doing well both in her school work and in her social-emotional adjustment to her classmates.

The question arises, "Why did Isabelle make a more complete recovery than Anna?" Although no clear answer is available, the differential post-isolation recovery of Anna and Isabelle is probably due to some combination of three factors: (1) The innate ability of the two girls may have been different. Perhaps Anna was mentally retarded at birth while Isabelle was not. (2) It may be that the different social treatment received by the two girls following their discovery explains all or part of their differential recovery. Isabelle received prolonged and expert training immediately upon her removal from isolation, while Anna did not. (3) It may be that while both girls were extremely isolated, Anna was more socially isolated

---

ILLUSTRATIVE DATA 6-2   EMPEROR FREDERICK II CONTRA SOCIOLOGY

[In the thirteenth century Emperor Frederick conducted an experiment to determine] . . . what kind of speech and what manner of speech children would have when they grew up, if they spoke to no one beforehand. So he bade foster mothers and nurses to suckle the children, to bathe and wash them, but in no way to prattle with them or to speak to them, for he wanted to learn whether they would speak the Hebrew language, which was the oldest, or Greek, or Latin, or Arabic, or perhaps the language of their parents, of whom they had been born. But he laboured in vain, because the children all died. For they could not live without the petting and the joyful faces and loving words of their foster mothers. And so the songs are called "swaddling songs," which a woman sings while she is rocking the cradle, to put a child to sleep, and without them a child sleeps badly and has no rest.

Source: James B. Ross and Mary M. McLaughlin (eds.), *The Portable Medieval Reader* (New York: Viking Press, 1949), pp. 366–367.

than Isabelle. Anna had no human contact other than during indifferent feedings; Isabelle spent most of her time with her deaf mother and communicated with her, if only through simple nonverbal gestures.

Another study that indicates the importance of society for personal development is one by Rene A. Spitz.[9] The Spitz study is different from the cases of Anna and Isabelle in that the persons studied had more social contact than either of the girls. The major hypothesis of this study was that prolonged social isolation results in general retardation of such a nature that the subject can never realize his or her full (before) potential. In other words, social isolation results in irreparable mental and physical damage.

"Moderate" Social Isolation

Spitz compared four groups of infants in different social situations. One group consisted of infants from urban professional families. All of these children lived at home in a "normal" family situation. A second group of children were from a fishing village of approximately 500 inhabitants which was relatively isolated from other communities and where physical conditions were difficult. These village children also lived with their families. A third group consisted of children born in prison to women who were pregnant at the time of their arrest. The children lived in a nursery annexed

---

[9]Rene A. Spitz, "Hospitalism," *The Psychoanalytic Study of the Child* (New York: International Universities Press, 1945), I, 53–72.

Table 6-1   Developmental Quotients of Infants in Different Social
Situations During the Early and Late Periods
of their First Year

Type of Environment	Social Situation	Developmental Quotient		Differ-ence
		Average of First Four Months	Average of Last Four Months	
Parental Home	Professional	133	131	−2
	Fishing Village	107	108	+1
Institution	Prison Nursery	102	105	+3
	Foundling Home	124	72	−52

SOURCE: Rene A. Spitz, "Hospitalism," *The Psychoanalytic Study of the Child*
(New York: International Universities Press, 1945), I, 53–72.

to the prison until they were about a year old. The fourth group
were children from urban backgrounds who had been placed in a
foundling home for orphans when they were just a few days old.

To compare the development of the infants in these four social
environments, a series of tests and observations were made for each
of the four groups and combined into a "developmental quotient"
(roughly analogous to an I.Q.) based upon what might be expected of
"average" infants and calculated for three different periods of the
first year of life. In this way, Spitz hoped to obtain a "before-and-
after" test of the effects of social environment upon the development of the infants. The average developmental quotient for the
first four months and the last four months of each group is shown
in Table 6-1.

Spitz found that the development of children in the first three
social situations was the same at the end of a year as it was during
the infants' first four months of life but that the average developmental quotient of the infants in the fourth group had dropped by
fifty per cent!

The Foundling Home

Why did the developmental quotient for the infants in the foundling home group drop so dramatically while it remained relatively
constant for the other three groups? Why did three groups continue

to develop "normally" when the fourth did not? To learn the answers to these questions, Spitz made a detailed comparison of the conditions in the prison nursery with the conditions in the foundling home. He found that both institutions were the same in many ways. Both provided excellent facilities, medical care, clothing, housing, food, and other items of physical comfort. However, the two facilities were markedly different in four significant ways that offered a clue to the lack of development among the children of the foundling home.

(1) Toys. While the infants in the prison nursery regularly played with one or more toys, the infants in the foundling home rarely had any toys to play with.

(2) Visual radius. Trees, landscape, and sky were visible to the infants in the nursery. There was also a bustling activity of mothers carrying, tending, feeding, and playing with their infants as well as chatting with each other. The cribs permitted the infants to see everything that was going on around them. They could see into the corridors, look out of the windows, and see infants in other cubicles. In the foundling home, however, the infants' visual field was severely limited except when five to eight nurses came into the room to feed the children. Most of the time there was no activity to attract the infants' attention. Moreover, the foundling home routinely placed bed sheets over the foot and the sides of the railings of each crib. Thus, the child lying in the cot was effectively screened from viewing anything but the interior of the crib and the bare ceiling. The result was that each infant lived in virtual solitary confinement most of the time.

(3) Radius of locomotion. The radius of locomotion in the nursery was limited to the space available in the crib; this provides a fairly satisfactory range until the child is about six months old. Theoretically the same situation would have obtained in the foundling home. But because the infants also lacked stimulation, they lay listlessly in their cribs for so many weeks that a hollow was worn into their mattresses. Consequently, this hollow effectively prevented the infants from turning in any direction when they reached an age when they might have turned from back to side (approximately six months). As a result, most foundling home infants were still lying listlessly on their backs at ten and twelve months of age.

(4) Personnel. The nursery was run by a head nurse and three assistants whose only duties were to provide medical treatment and to instruct the mothers in child care. The infants were nursed, fed, and cared for by their mothers. Thus, in the nursery each infant had the full-time care and attention of an adult. In the foundling home, the infants were cared for only by nurses, each of whom was responsible for seven to twelve infants. These nurses generally

appeared only at feeding and bathing times and did not fondle or play with their charges.

The Follow-Up Study

At the time of this study there were 91 children in the foundling home. Two years later only twenty-one of the original children were still in residence.[10] (Thirty-seven per cent of the original 91 had died, despite the excellent medical care.) Of the remaining twenty-one children, between two and four years of age at the time of the follow-up study, only five could walk unassisted; one could dress himself; and one could speak in sentences (see Table 6-2).

These data regarding the consequences of relative social isolation emphasize that individuals who are denied group participation during most of their early years will fail to develop language and other basic features associated with being a person, with having personality. The data also indicate that prolonged and severe isolation from human groups tends to hinder or prevent the development of human potential. Human life is group life. People do not live apart, each seeking a private solution to the problems of sur-

Table 6-2   Level of Development of Twenty-one Children Two to Four Years of Age in Foundling Home

Bodily development		Ability to handle material objects		Speech development	
Num-ber		Num-ber		Num-ber	
5	Incapable of locomation	12	Cannot eat alone with spoon	6	Cannot talk at all
3	Sit up alone but not walk	9	Can eat alone with spoon	5	2-word vocabulary
8	Walk with assistance	21	Total	8	3–5-word vocabulary
5	Walk without assistance	20	Cannot dress alone	1	About 12 words
		1	Can dress alone	1	Uses sentences
21	Total	21	Total	21	Total

SOURCE: Rene A. Spitz, "Hospitalism: A Follow-up Report," *The Psychoanalytic Study of the Child* (New York: International Universities Press, 1946), II, 113–117.

[10]Rene A. Spitz, "Hospitalism: A Follow-up Report," *The Psychoanalytic Study of the Child* (New York: International Universities Press, 1946), II, 113–117.

vival. They live together and share a common way of life that regulates their collective existence and provides methods for adapting to the world around them. The data also suggests that it is the influence of society that really makes individuals different from one another and that contact with other human beings increases the differences between individuals.

If the "true individual" is defined as a person whose behavior is free of the influences of society, past or present, then it must be said that such a person does not exist. The isolated individual is either a philosopher's fiction or a tragic accident.

Heredity and Environment

The cases of Anna, Isabelle, and the infants also make clear that the question of heredity *or* environment is an unproductive question because it presents a false dichotomy, that is, a false choice between one or the other, when in fact both heredity *and* environment have some part in the final process. Heredity is not a factor that acts independently of the social environment. Rather, it helps determine the way an individual reacts in various environments. Inherited capacity is clearly important in the development of the individual, but learning always occurs within a social context. No matter how impressive the capacities an individual may inherit, he or she can become a person only through interaction with others.

SOCIALIZATION

Each human being at birth is totally helpless and dependent upon others. Everything he or she eventually will know and be able to do must be learned. Each individual must acquire his or her social nature. The process by which he or she does so is called *socialization*. It consists of teaching the person the culture which he must acquire and share, of making him a participating member in society and its various groups, and of persuading him to accept the norms of his society. Socialization is a matter of learning, not of biological inheritance. In the socialization process the individual learns the folkways, mores, sanctions, and other patterns of the culture, as well as the skills, ranging from language to manual dexterity, which will enable him to become a participating member of society.

All that the individual must learn is learned from other members of the society: consciously, from being told what to do by parents, brothers and sisters, friends, or teachers; or unconsciously, by picking up incidental information while observing other people, reading books, watching television, hearing people discuss the behavior of others, and imitating the behavior of others. In all these situations, the learning is social. The whole process of socialization falls within the scope of interaction. It is within the structure of the human group that the individual acquires culture.

The Social Self

The case histories of Anna and Isabelle show that, with virtually no socialization, "personality" does not develop. For the infant at birth there is no distinction between self and not-self. This distinction has to be learned. The individual has no self-concept (no concept of oneself as a unique individual) prior to interaction with others. The self is social, and arises out of interaction with an awareness of others.

To develop a sense of self, the individual must learn to view himself or herself as an object. A person must, in popular parlance, "see himself as others see him." For example, learning to conform to the demands of others involves learning the distinction between those others, or potential need-satisfiers, and the self, whose needs must be met. From such beginnings, the sense of selfhood emerges. Shortly after birth, an infant is aware only of innate drives. The stomach contracts; the baby cries. The skin is pierced by a sharp object on the edge of his bed; the baby withdraws. Soon he or she learns to notice other people, and to expect certain things from them. The approach of someone to the bed may mean the disturbing process of diaper-changing, and the infant cries.

It is only when the individual perceives that others expect certain behaviors from him or her and learns to act as he or she thinks they want him or her to act that the person develops a social self. When a boy knocks over a vase and has learned to say to himself something like, "Mother will think I should be sorry; I'll apologize," he is developing a social self. This is the major process in the emergence of human personality.[11] The development of the sense of self enables one to take a place in a social structure, to learn cultural behaviors, to expect positive sanctions when one conforms and negative ones when one deviates, to become a socialized, fully participating member of society.

The child's learning to act as others anticipate he or she will act is the process of socialization. The process is mostly unconscious for the child.

---

[11]It is this interactional component that Baldwin was alluding to in his reference to the development of self-feeling as the "dialectic of personal growth." See J. M. Baldwin, *Mental Development in the Child and Race*, 1895, rev. ed., 1906 (New York: The Macmillan Company) and *Social and Ethical Interpretations in Mental Development*, 1897, rev ed., 1906 (New York: The Macmillan Company).

Role-Taking

One of the fundamental processes that come into play during socialization is identification. As part of the learning process, identification makes it possible for one person to "take over" or accept ideas, attitudes, or habits of another. Psychologically this mechanism depends on imagination—on the capacity to develop within the internal subjective world the image of another. Identification is the key process in imitation. It is the basis of sympathy, and mixed in it are large elements of the emotion of love.

The process of identification or imitation may be regarded as a form of role-taking or "role practice," as R. R. Sears calls it.[12] The mother or some other adult serves as a model whom the child imitates. Thus he or she may play the role of the mother, assuming her voice, gestures, attitudes, and actions. At another time he or she may identify with a father, an aunt, or a neighbor. Moreover, in this process of interaction the mother or others come to expect or anticipate the child's taking certain roles and not others.

"Looking-Glass" Self

The child associates his or her own actions with the demands or responses of others, thereby building up habits and attitudes or roles concerning what he or she should do in their presence. The self arises when the individual takes the view and action toward his or her own act and thoughts which he or she learns or infers that others take toward them, that is, the sense of selfhood develops out of social interaction at that point where the individual is capable of considering his or her whole set of habits, thoughts, feelings, and emotions as an object to himself or herself. But the individual can view the self as an object only to the extent that he or she can "take the role of the other," can stand in another's position, seeing and evaluating himself or herself as the other person does. Because this process of realizing one's self requires the ability to see one's self reflected in another's eyes, Cooley used the phrase, the "looking-glass self."

In a very large and interesting class of cases the social reference takes the form of a somewhat definite imagination of how one's self . . . appears in a particular mind, and the kind of self-feeling one has is determined by the attitude toward this, attributed to that other mind. A social self of this sort might be called the reflected or looking-glass self:

---

[12]R. R. Sears, Eleanor E. Maccoby, and Harry Levin, *Patterns of Child Rearing* (Evanston, Ill.: Row, Peterson & Company, 1957), pp. 369–376.

> Each to each a looking-glass
> Reflects the other that doth pass.

A self idea of this sort seems to have three principal elements: the imagination of our appearance to the other person; the imagination of his judgment of that appearance; and some sort of self-feeling, such as pride or mortification.[13]

The generalized sense of self is really the organization of generalized attitudes, traits, and ideas which become coordinated into the total sense of selfhood. In time the various specific roles of the child begin to get organized or integrated into larger patterns of response. That is, out of a wide range of specific roles of "others" which he or she has played, there emerges a generalized and more or less total role of the child. The child assumes this role in all areas of life—play, school, family. Later he or she will be pupil, comrade, industrial worker, religious participant, voter, and the like, carrying into new roles certain elements of the first roles.

The Generalized Other

The individual, however, internalizes not only a set of specific roles of others, he or she also incorporates into the self-concept a role image of entire social collectivites. George Herbert Mead called this internalized conception of social groups the "generalized other." According to Mead,

> The organized community or social group which gives the individual his unity of self may be called "the generalized other." The attitude of the generalized other is the attitude of the whole community. Thus, for example, in the case of such a social group as a ball team, the team is the generalized other in so far as it enters—as an organized process or social activity—into the experience of any one of the individual members of it.
>
> If the given human individual is to develop a self in the fullest sense, it is not sufficient for him merely to take the attitudes of other human individuals toward himself and toward one another within the human social process, and to bring that social process as a whole into his individual experience merely in these terms; he must also . . . take their attitudes toward the various phases or aspects of the common social activity or set of social undertakings in which as members of an organized society or social group they are all engaged; and he must then, by generalizing these individual attitudes of that organized society or social group itself, as a whole, act toward different social projects

---

[13]Charles Horton Cooley, *Human Nature and the Social Order* (New York: Charles Scribner's Sons, 1902), pp. 151–152.

which at any given time it is carrying out, or toward the various larger phases of the general social process which constitutes its life and of which these projects are specific manifestations.[14]

Most people have a more or less integrated central self and a series of partially diviant selves that serve them in adapting to varied situations.[15] In any case, it is the generalized self that makes possible

Figure 6-1 Social Groups, Social Processes, and Personality Integration

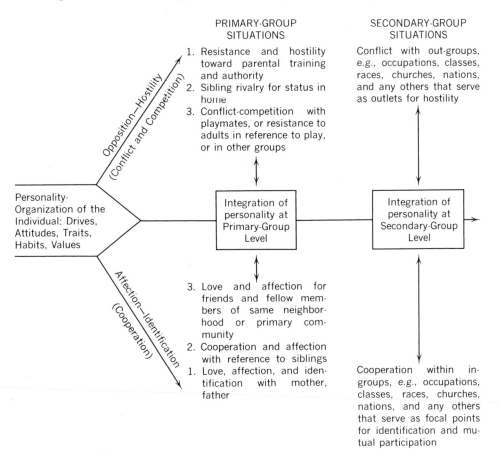

---

[14]George Herbert Mead, *Mind, Self, and Society* (Chicago: University of Chicago Press, 1934), pp. 154–155.

[15]On the whole topic of the rise of the self, see G. H. Mead, *Mind, Self, and Society* (Chicago: University of Chicago Press, 1934). The literature on dissociated personalities is enlightening, since it gives us some clue to the wide range of potential self-organization. Most of us probably possess potentialities for quite different selves from those we expose to our fellows under ordinary circumstances. On this topic consult Kimball Young, *Personality and Problems of Adjustment,* 2nd ed. (New York: Appleton-Century-Crofts, Inc., 1952), pp. 174–178.

consistency, continuity, and hence predictability of behavior in an individual. The uniformities of needs, situations, and cultural expectancies all operate together to produce some sort of unity in the personality. What the moralists call "character" illustrates the matter. Honesty, truthfulness, integrity, dependability, fidelity, and all the other virtues are but traits of a certain ideal person who is consistent and predictable in his interactions with his fellows. The integration of the personality is made possible by the relation of the individual to persons and symbols of the in-group and the out-group. We can love our fellow members of the in-group and cooperate with them, and at the same time despise and be hostile toward members of the out-group. Figure 6-1 shows how an individual can indulge conflicting impulses in primary and secondary groups and still maintain a reasonably integrated, efficiently functioning personality.

To the extent that the individual apes the behavior of those around him and incorporates into his own belief system the beliefs and values of those around him, he experiences the consequences of socialization—social control. Indeed, one cannot fully comprehend the significance of socialization without realizing the extent to which an ostensibly external process becomes internalized. According to Peter Berger,

> What happens in socialization is that the social world is internalized within the child. The same process, though perhaps weaker in quality, occurs every time the adult is initiated into a new social context or a new social group. Society, then, is not only something "out there," . . . but is also "in here," part of our innermost being. Only an understanding of internalization makes sense of the incredible fact that most external controls work most of the time for most of the people in a society. Society not only controls our movements, but shapes our identity, our thought and our emotions. The structures of society become the structures of our own consciousness. Society does not stop at the surface of our skin. Society penetrates us as much as it envelops us.[16]

INTERPRETIVE SUMMARY

Numerous studies have shown that personality is a product of both heredity and environment. Studies of individuals with widely different heredities who were reared together or in similar environments and studies of individuals with similar hereditary make-up who were reared in different environments both indicate that heredity and environment together have a limiting effect on intelligence, temperament, and physical condition.

Personality is developed through the process of socialization. In the early months of life, the maturing child learns that he is an entity. From this point

---

[16]Peter L. Berger, *Invitation to Sociology: A Humanistic Perspective* (Garden City, N. Y.: Doubleday and Company, Inc., 1963), p. 121.

on he learns the attitudes and skills he will need in order to exist in his society. To this extent his personality will be similar to everyone else's. At the same time, however, his social experiences will lead him to develop certain opinions and patterns of behavior which set him off from other individuals. He will undoubtedly experiment with entire roles, discarding parts of roles as inimical to his idea of self and retaining others. Desires which conflict with his self-image and with what he thinks others expect of him will be inhibited or channeled into socially acceptable outlets; his personality will be integrated. The entire process of developing an integrated personality will be largely unconscious.

SUGGESTIONS FOR FURTHER READING

Duncan, Hugh Dalziel. *Symbols in Society.* New York: Oxford University Press, 1969. This book investigates the relationship of various forms of communication to all basic social institutions.

Goffman, Erving. *The Presentation of Self in Everyday Life.* Garden City, N.Y.: Doubleday and Company, 1959. A provocative descriptive analysis of social interaction, this book devotes considerable attention to the function of role expectation and role performance.

Hall, Edward T. *Hidden Dimension.* New York: Doubleday and Company, 1966. An anthropologist discusses man's use of space in relation to stress, alienation, and the collapse of normal behavior and shows that cultural variation in utilization of space has its effects on human feeling and behavior.

Hall, Edward T. *The Silent Language.* Garden City, N.Y.: Doubleday and Company, Inc., 1959. This is a gem of a book on culture and language.

Homans, George C. *Social Behavior—Its Elementary Forms.* New York: Harper and Brothers, 1961. This book discusses personality and gives some attention to social and cultural factors as they bear on its development and function.

La Barre, Weston. *The Human Animal.* Chicago: University of Chicago Press, 1954. This is a witty and sound presentation of the interplay of man's biological make-up and his cultural environment.

Mead, George Herbert. *Mind, Self, and Society.* Edited by Charles W. Morris. Chicago: The University of Chicago Press, 1934. This is a seminal work on the development of the self.

Piaget, Jean. *The Moral Judgment of the Child.* Translated by Marjorie Gabain. New York: Harcourt, Brace and World, 1932. A classic volume on the personality development of children, this book emphasizes how the child's moral judgment is formed by the process of socialization.

Riesman, David; Glazer, Nathan; and Denny, Reul. *The Lonely Crowd: A Study of the Changing American Character.* New Haven, Conn.: Yale University Press, 1950. Riesman develops his now famous characterization of "tradition-directed," "inner-directed," and "other-directed" man in a discussion of the effects of modern culture upon personality.

Sears, Robert R.; Maccoby, Eleanor E.; and Levin, Harry. *Patterns of Child Rearing.* Evanston, Ill.: Row, Peterson and Company, 1957. An analysis of data collected through interviews of 379 American mothers, this study details how they reared children from birth to kindergarten age.

Wheelis, Allen. *The Quest for Identity.* New York: W. W. Norton and Company, 1958. This is an insightful discussion of the significance for personality of the technological and ideological changes in our way of life.

Whiting, John W. M., and Child, Irvin L. *Child Training and Personality: A Cross-Cultural Study.* New Haven, Conn.: Yale University Press, 1953. The authors have made comparisons among a wide range of nonliterate peoples with regard to such matters as socialization, fixation, and the origins of fear and guilt.

2/Social Organization

IT'S ALWAYS BEEN A STRUGGLE FOR ME TO FIND MY PLACE IN SOCIETY. THAT'S WHY I HAVE TO READ BOOKS.

FOR INSTANCE, IN COLLEGE I THOUGHT I WAS GETTING ON FINE, UNTIL I READ THAT MINE WAS A **SILENT GENERATION**. SO I SHUT UP.

AFTER COLLEGE I WENT INTO INDUSTRY AND THOUGHT I WAS DOING FINE, UNTIL I READ THAT I WAS REALLY A **CONFORMIST ORGANIZATION MAN**. SO I WENT OUT AND CONFORMED AND BELONGED.

WELL, I BEGAN MAKING A LOT OF MONEY AND FELT THAT I WAS DOING FINE, UNTIL I READ THAT, IN TRUTH, I WAS A MEMBER OF AN **ACQUISITIVE SOCIETY**. SO I BOUGHT THINGS.

OF COURSE, I NOW HAD A LOT OF TIME ON MY HANDS, BUT I FELT FINE, UNTIL I READ THAT MY INCOME GROUP HAD A **LEISURE PROBLEM**. SO I LEARNED HOBBIES.

NOW FOR A WHILE THERE I FELT FINE, UNTIL I READ THAT THE **ROOT** PROBLEM OF MY AFFLUENT SOCIETY WAS **STATUS SEEKING**.

WELL, IN BETWEEN BEING 'SILENT,' 'CONFORMING,' BELONGING, ACQUIRING AND TAKING CARE OF MY LEISURE PROBLEM I HAVEN'T YET HAD A CHANCE TO SEEK STATUS.

I GUESS I'LL FIT IT IN **SOMEHOW**.

7
Community
and Society

The concept of society, like that of the group, has always been a central concept in sociology; sociology is often defined as the study of society. A society is a collectivity of people who share a common culture, live in a definite geographical territory, and consider themselves a social unit. It is the broadest social group to which a people belong and encompasses all the other social groups of which they are members. A society, then, refers to the inclusive networks of social interaction among a culturally defined people that sustain a complex social structure. This social structure provides for the totality of a way of life for that people.

Such a conception of society does not dictate a size requirement. Societies are both large and small. Prior to the emergence and widespread growth of the nation-state, societies were usually smaller entities. In the modern world, however, there is a trend toward large national societies that are politically organized and controlled by a nation-state and that monopolize control over a given territory customarily inhabited by and identified with the people of that society. This transition from small-scale to large-scale forms of social organization is one of the most significant changes in the history of human life.

THE TRANSFORMATION OF SOCIETY

The systematic study of society was spurred by the recognition that human society had been radically altered by the Industrial Revolution. The great Western intellectuals of the nineteenth century realized that the Industrial Revolution involved more than the introduction of a new technology with new and different jobs. It was changing the whole social order: the older forms of social organization were "breaking down;" the social patterns of traditional society were being destroyed; and there was widespread dread of the future of society.

Prior to the Industrial Revolution, people lived in small traditional villages where everyone knew everyone else. The traditional village was more than a geographical site. It was small, personal, familiar, shared, and intergenerational, and allowed for few alternatives in behavior. People knew who they were and they knew their place in the scheme of things. The city, on the other hand, was more impersonal, more rational, nontraditional, new, and not socially integrated.

The city gradually replaced the traditional and secure village. Although it was not a new social invention, the big city loomed as a new and strange social experience. Being a stranger fast became a common experience as the transition from small-scale to large-scale social organization occurred. The city was regarded as the antithesis of the small, traditional village. People were being "torn from their roots" and the intellectuals of the time described the process as "social disorganization."

The Secular Crisis

During the "secular crisis of the 19th century" the world was reshaped. The Industrial Revolution had razed the traditional social fabric and new questions and new assumptions began to occupy the minds of Western intellectuals. Much of their concern was centered on the issues of social solidarity, size (i.e., bigness), and social control. In the transition from the small-scale traditional village to the large-scale diversified city, how can 30,000 strangers move to one restricted place and so coordinate their activities that meaningful social relations will result? How does social solidarity come about? How will people hold themselves together? What unites people? What new social order, if any, will come to exist?

The focal point of concern was the recognition that the Industrial Revolution was a genuine social revolution that totally changed people's lives. There were unanticipated consequences in the alteration of the social world in this transition from an agricultural village society to an industrial society. The urban experience fast became the common denominator with a new and complex division of labor. People became involved in a large pattern of activity for which they had no sense of belonging.

Nowhere was this change more evident than in the change of the character of the family. In the traditional world, work and home life were one and the family was both an economic and a social unit. Furthermore, the family was the setting for almost all of the other social functions as well—welfare, recreation, education, religious instruction, and so on. With industrialization the family, as an institution, became separated from most of these functions. Education is now performed almost entirely by schools; recreation is largely handled by commerical enterprises; and welfare is the responsibility of government. The family today is now chiefly charged with fulfilling psychological and emotional needs, and many people say that it is not even performing this function very well.

The Industrial Revolution

Industrialization has altered drastically the structure of human societies. In societies which are highly industrialized, most people no longer directly produce the materials for their own food, clothing, and shelter; the bulk of the labor force is engaged in service occupations. Almost everyone is literate. This combination of education and release from much menial toil promotes a rapid rate of discovery and invention. Industrial societies export their knowledge, and change the faces of nonindustrial societies. Modern techniques of sanitation and medical care reduce infant mortality and maternal mortality, for example, thus creating the population explosion.

Throughout most of human history, most people secured their own raw materials and owned their own tools. They worked under their own roofs on their own time, and themselves gauged their market—that is, they made the decisions as to both the quality and the quantity of what they should produce and sold the finished product to a consumer. Before the Industrial Revolution, a guildsman, say, in medieval Europe, who lived in a commercial town and made linen secured his own raw materials, grew flax on the land adjacent to his cottage, spun the flax into thread on his own spinning wheel and wove the thread into linen cloth on his own loom, under his own roof; he gauged his own market, deciding whether it was better to establish a reputation as a man who made the best linen and got a good price for it but sold only a little or a man from whom you could get linen tomorrow if you needed it at once.

Within limits, he set his own pace; when he was through making his linen, he sold it. Some people came to his shop for purchases. Occasionally he went around the countryside to trade fairs, set up a stand, and marketed his product. He took the money he made, spent it for food and his other needs, grew more flax, spun more thread, wove more linen, and sold it.

This social structure began to change when the entrepreneur, an individual capitalist, took over some of these operations. What such a man did was to acquire a good deal of raw materials, more than he himself could work on. Instead of growing flax outside his house and owning his own spinning wheel and loom, for example, he purchased more flax than he could possibly process by himself. He then made agreements with a number of cottagers around the countryside, took the flax around and deposited a certain amount of it with each of them, picked up linen they had finished, took it to town, and sold it. And he came back the next week, having taken the proceeds, the money from selling his linen, and bought more flax; he passed this out to his cottagers and picked up what linen they had finished that week, took it to town, and sold it. In other words, the entrepreneur greatly altered what had been the system of human work. Now it was the entrepreneur, not the worker, who secured the raw materials, gauged the market, determined the quality and the quantity of the product. It was he who brought the flax, took the linen, and paid off the workers. He told them whether to produce a great deal of cheap linen or a little excellent linen. And he sold the finished product.

Mass Production

The domestic system under which goods were made in the home did not last long as the production of goods was moved from home to factory. This change had certain advantages for the entrepreneur: he could keep his eye on the worker, he could put pressure on him, and he could see that a little more was produced when he needed a little more. Eventually, as the system prospered, the entrepreneur bought some spinning wheels, put the spinning wheels in the factory, and went out into the country to get more cottagers. They didn't even have to have their own spinning wheels.

Here are many of the essentials of mass production. There are factories, with all the people in one building. A capitalist owns the tools they work with, the roof they work under, and the raw materials. He takes the product and sells it. A labor force in the modern sense of the term has been created. This is what Karl Marx referred to as "the separation of the worker from the means of production."

As a result of this economic revolution, several important alterations occurred in the social structure. People were aggregated for the sake of efficency. This was the beginning of modern urbanism. Then, with fixed capital, the entrepreneur had money tied up in one place. This cut down his mobility in a way that the domestic system did not. Formerly, if it was not a good year for linen, the entrepreneur who had been running around the countryside picking up his linen and leaving his flax with a cottager had only to take what capital he had accumulated and go into something else. But as soon as he bought the building in town and filled it with spinning wheels, the entrepreneur of the eighteenth century may not have had a great deal of fixed capital by the standards of General Motors, but he had a great deal for those days. He had the beginning of the kind of fixed capital we know today.

With the factory system and fixed capital came another crucial change in the social structure: free labor. Back in the guildsman's day, most of the people in medieval Europe were not free. True, they were not slaves in the sense that we use the term, but they lived under a system of mutual obligation. Serfs belonged to a manor; they had rights in the land. Everybody lived under this obligation system. The baron could not drive the serfs from the land, because they had always lived there. The serfs had to give a certain portion of their labor or produce to the baron because they were allowed to live on the land and received protection from him.

This kind of social order was foreign to a mass-production, fixed-capital economy. In a mass-production economy, people must be able, when the linen business gets bad, to move somewhere else. When there are too many people working in one place and not enough in another, they must be able to go elsewhere. A free laborer is free to work for an employer of his choice. When another entrepreneur offers him more money, he is free to move; he is free to quit—and he is free to starve. This is an essential part of free labor, because the entrepreneur has his money tied up in fixed capital. With money tied up in fixed capital, the easiest cost to reduce is labor cost. The employer can lay off people until he needs more productivity, and then he can hire them again. Factory production, fixed capital, and free labor—all are characteristics of the industrial revolution; all have consequences in an industrial social order.

Education and Economy

In a large-scale economy, as in a small one, early socialization, crucial to the development of a sense of purpose, is a function primarily of the family.[1] Young people learn what is right and

---

[1] An earlier form of this section appeared in an article by Raymond W. Mack, "Social Consequences of Occupational Specialization," in *The National Elementary Principal*, May 1961, 40: 10–13. The material was first used as part of a speech.

wrong, what the social expectations are, and a large share of this socialization occurs in the family. But one consequence of the Industrial Revolution is that, while mothers and fathers still provide models for much behavior, children no longer learn the norms of work in the family. The separation of place of work from place of residence (a consequence of the requirements of a mass production line, with the resulting fixed capital) removed working fathers from the view of their children. In the English textile mills in the very early days of the Industrial Revolution, when workers and their families lived beneath the factory roof, children learned to spin and weave from their parents. But the boy who helped his father homestead a farm now has a grandson majoring in soil chemistry at the state university.

In most societies throughout most of human history, the father did not go to work, because work was right there in and around the home. The reason he goes to work now is that he is a specialist who contributes his knowledge or his acquired skill to making one part of one part of a product. Few people in the labor force can point to a finished product and say, "I made that." A person's skill is used only on an assembly line, whether it is a production or an intellectual staff line, and he has to go join other men and women in a work environment separated from their places of residence where they can pool their skills. Most children do not see their fathers earning a living, because in an industrial society he goes out to work.

Contrast this with a nonindustrial society, where the men get up every morning and go out to fish and the women get up and garden. What happens to little boys or little girls in such a society? They play until they are four or five years old. When a boy is about six years old, he starts going out on the boat with his father and his uncles as a general handyman. He gets in the way, but he helps a little, too. He can hand them this or that, and he watches what is going on. By the time he is eight years old he knows enough to help mend nets. By the time he is ten years old, he is beginning to learn where the good fishing spots are and to be able to tell what kind of weather is good for fishing. At twelve he not only knows how to repair his father's boat, but he has worked on it enough to know how to build one himself. At about fourteen he goes through a ceremony at the end of which he is told, "You are now a man!" He is ready to get on the boat the next morning and go to work with the other adults. He doesn't have to be sent to a naval college; he doesn't take any courses in bait-cutting. He already knows the job. He has been living with it for years.

His sister, meanwhile, is helping sweep the hearth when she is seven. She helps grind the maize by the time she is nine and prepare food by the time she is twelve. She knows about planting seasons and harvesting seasons. By the time she is fourteen and old enough to get married, she is long past the need for a course in home economics. She has had that course at home.

These things do not happen in contemporary industrial society. Most children in our society have very little idea of what their parents do when they go to work. They just know that they go and they come back. As a matter of fact, not only do most children not know what their fathers do, but neither do many wives know exactly. When sociological research involves interviews in a district where factory workers live, it is not at all unusual to have something like the following conversation between interviewer and housewife:

"What does your husband do?"

"He's at the Ford plant."

"What does he do there?"

"He works over at the Ford plant—you know."

"Is he on the assembly line, is he a machine operator, is he a supply man?"

"I don't know. He's worked over at the Ford plant for ten years now."

Under such circumstances, one can hardly expect the youth in a specialized economy to be able to walk out of adolescence into an adult occupational role; they have had no chance to learn how to be adult members of the labor force in practice or in imitation.

Similar, if less striking, is the impact of occupational specialization on educational institutions, particularly on the functions of formal educational structures. The same thing is happening in the school that has happened in the family. The school is an important factor in socialization, of course, but there seems to be a trend away from, rather than toward, its being a finishing school in *occupational* socialization. Lawyers often state that they *really* learned their profession in their post-graduate stints as clerks in law firms. What happens to the person who graduates from the shop curriculum in a technical high school? He or she becomes, not a welder, but a welder's *apprentice* on a construction gang. Often we praise corporations that encourage students to get a broad general educational base and let the company teach them the details of the job. We laud such firms for their enlightened dedication to the liberal arts, when what they are really dedicated to is the quite rational assumption that, given the complicated network of social expectations engendered by pooling the skills of specialists in a complex organization, the agency best equipped to socialize one into that network is that organization.

To the extent that one gains a sense of purpose from one's work, then the family and the school in an industrial society have lost much of the function of providing a sense of purpose. The large organizations which provide "on the job" socialization are now responsible for that function to some extent.

Segmental Roles

To what extent *does* one rely on his work to give him a sense of purpose? The answer is that occupational specialization contributes a good share to what we call the impersonality of urban life. People in urban-industrial societies have segmentalized roles. One may be an assembly-line worker, a Methodist, a Grand Vizier at the lodge, a father, a member of the bowling team. No one of these bears the same necessary relationship to another that the roles filled by a tribesman in an unspecialized society do. In a society which has not felt the impact of technology, one need only know a man's clan membership to predict his occupation, his religion, or his educational attainment. Among the roles which a person plays in an urban-industrial society, occupation is crucial. It is more specialized than most roles; one has an enormous investment in it. An adult male in our labor force spends more of his waking hours at work than at home; his work is likely to be a powerful factor in shaping his view of the world. Moreover, his community judges him largely according to the prestige of his occupation; he *is* what he *does*.

TYPES OF SOCIETIES

The challenge to explain and understand the "new kind of society" which was emerging from the apparent dissolution of the older, traditional ways of living has led a number of sociologists to develop a mode of social analysis—a typological analysis—that contrasts the basic characteristics of two radically different social structures. With seemingly endless variety, sociologists have compared and contrasted two ideal-types of societies: (1) that which characterized most of Europe prior to the Industrial Revolution and much of the nonindustrial world today and (2) that typified by the society produced by the Industrial Revolution.

Some of the more prominent of these typologies of society are:

Robert Redfield—folk society and urban society
Howard Becker—sacred society and secular society
Charles Horton Cooley—primary society and secondary society
Robert MacIver—communal society and associational society
Pitirim Sorokin—familistic society and contractual society
Carle Zimmerman—localistic society and cosmopolitan society

Henry Maine—status society and contract society

Ferdinand Tonnies—gemeinschaft society and gesellschaft go-
ciety

Emile Durkheim—mechanical society and organic society

Although there are some differences between these typologies,
each is primarily concerned with describing and understanding the
same social phenomena; each calls attention in different ways and
with varying degrees of emphasis to approximately the same social
facts. Each is an attempt to analyze the great social transformation
wrought largely by the Industrial Revolution. These ideal-types of
folk society and urban society are analytical tools designed to bring
into relief the essential features of two polar opposite types of
societies.

THE FOLK SOCIETY

The family, band, clan, tribe, and small village long antedate
urban society. The very first forms of human society, however, can
only be inferred. We know, of course, that the primary forms of
human grouping are far older than the secondary. Earliest people
apparently lived in relatively small groups formed on the basis of
family and blood ties. Their economy consisted of seed and root
gathering, and hunting and fishing. Their social organization must
have been relatively delimited.[2]

The culture of present-day primary communities stems from the
Neolithic Revolution. The domestication of plants and animals and
the development of agriculture made possible more permanent
settlement. This in turn brought changes in social organization and
division of labor, and laid the foundations of rural culture patterns
which have come down into our own time.

Even today, from two-thirds to three-fourths of the world's people
live in what may be called folk societies with a strong solidarity of
family life, importance of religion, and forms of moral control.
The two outstanding characteristics of the social structure of folk
society are small size and social isolation. "There are no more
people in it than can come to know each other well, and they
remain in long association with each other."[3] There are no strangers
in a folk society. These structural features clearly have consequences for social life. The social isolation means a limitation of the
opportunities for stimulus and response. Our chief concern here is

---

[2]For a very readable and extended reconstruction of the life of early man, see
George R. Stewart, *Man: An Autobiography* (New York: Random House, 1946).
[3]Robert Redfield, "The Folk Society," *American Journal of Sociology*, 1947, 52:
293–308.

the effects on the primary community of spatial or geographical isolation, effects which in reality are largely cultural.

Social Isolation

Cultural isolation induces variability in life patterns. If the segregation continues over long periods, certain distinctions may arise which mark off one society sharply from another. On a smaller scale, the Southern mountain whites of the United States illustrate some of the effects of isolation. Living for generations relatively undistributed by changes going on around them, these people have continued a culture which still reflects many aspects of the seventeenth and early eighteenth centuries. Their habits, attitudes, and ideas are similar to those of the colonist and pioneer, and they are generally suspicious of the outside world.[4]

Among the most interesting forms of isolation are the "cultural islands" of distinct groups that have persisted in the midst of highly secularized and technologically developed areas. The Amish, Mennonites, Dunkers, and other "plain people" who migrated from Europe have maintained certain cultural traits for generations. Their clothing, agricultural practices, vehicles, and certain social institutions have been carried down with little change from the time of the Protestant Reformation. These groups have regarded the "simple life" as the "good life," and have fought doggedly to keep from becoming "worldly." The more conservative sects, particularly the House Amish, shun all technological innovations except those absolutely necessary to their survival. Similarly, "agricultural islands," in which distinct occupational practices of bygone days have been retained, are found in several places in America.

The folk society is typically small, with a minimal division of labor and consequently only a limited differentiation of social roles. The role of the male among many nonliterate societies is roughly the same for almost all adult men, with some differences only in terms of age and marital status.

The only important economic differentiation is in terms of sex and age. There are few specialized roles pertaining to religion and leadership. There is no formal structure of political roles. Families and other primary groups make up the important units within the

---

[4]See J. C. Campbell, *The Southern Highlander and His Homeland* (New York: Russell Sage Foundation, 1921); M. T. Matthews, *Experience-Worlds of Mountain People*, Teachers College Contributions to Education, no. 700 (New York: Teachers College, Columbia University, 1937). For comparison, see O. W. Junek, *Isolated Communities: A Study of a Labrador Fishing Village* (New York: American Book Company, 1937). Peter A. Munch, *Sociology of Tristan da Cunha* (Oslo, Norway: I Kommisjon hos Jacob Dybwad, 1945) is an invaluable study of community isolation on an inaccessible island in the south Atlantic.

society as a whole. One result of the small population size, the social isolation, and the lack of occupational specialization and social differentiation is the social homogeneity of the population. The different physical types, interests, occupational roles, values, religious groupings, and ideologies so obvious in the urban society are absent from the folk community. While the family and community are the most primary of all associations, even folk societies have some delimited groups which serve the more special interests of their members. Tribal councils, secret societies, and formalized age and sex groups sometimes appear. Nevertheless, in primary communities the number of such organizations is relatively small, and among those which do exist the social contacts tend to be very informal.

Social roles are, therefore, inclusive rather than segmental; they include many aspects of behavior rather than merely some limited segment of an individual's activities. Since members of a folk society perform inclusive rather than segmental roles, they necessarily interact with one another in a wide variety of contexts. Social relationships are, therefore, long-lasting, inclusive, intimate, and personal. Social relationships have intrinsic significance; they are valued (positively or negatively) for themselves rather than as means to other ends. The reciprocal expectations of persons involved in these primary relationships are diffuse and generalized. One must live up to standards of respect, loyalty, or affection, for example, rather than merely fulfilling specifically defined obligations.

Homogeneity

The absence of secondary groups and the homogeneity of values and behavior patterns produces a powerful sense of unity binding the people together. The members of a folk society exhibit a strong in-group feeling. Since the whole of their social lives is wrapped up in a society which is essentially a primary group, they are inclined to view the entire outside world as an out-group.

In the folk society, behavior is regulated largely by custom; the many aspects of everyday life are governed by a complex array of rules and regulations regarding the activities of eating, sleeping, hunting, fishing, praying, dancing, and love-making. Behavior flows fairly smoothly through conventional grooves. With the informal norms exercising a strong hold upon behavior, there is little need for formal sanctions. Social control is part of tradition; it is not codified or rationalized, not enacted or dictated. Instead, it emerges from the traditional experience of the society. It is incorporated in the folkways and mores known and accepted by its members. There

Folk Society/Urban Society

Comparisons of rural life and city life often tend to emphasize the positive features of the small community and the negative features of the large metropolis. The folk community is built upon primary relationships and has a homogeneity of values and behavior patterns which produces its sense of unity. In such a community, however, behavior is regulated largely by custom, and the opportunities for individual choice and freedom are relatively limited. On the other hand, as Louis Wirth noted, "The city is not only the point at which great numbers are concentrated into limited space, but it is also a complex of human beings exhibiting the most extraordinary heterogeneity in almost every characteristic in which human beings can differ from one another."

is a strong feeling that what the culture moves one to do is well worth doing.

Folk societies are also notable for the extent to which social control is informal. Sanctions are imposed through gossip, ridicule, or ostracism. Behavior is governed by folkways and mores; there is little formal law. Where everyone knows everyone else intimately, the informal pressures of the community are sufficient to enforce the norms.

In the folk society social roles are inclusive rather than segmental; social relationships are personal and intimate; and there are comparatively few subgroups other than family and kinship units. In this typically small, isolated, nonliterate, and homogeneous society, tradition permeates all aspects of life and the range of alternative patterns of behavior open to individuals is inevitably restricted. There is resistance to change and innovation.

THE URBAN SOCIETY

The social structure and culture of urban societies differ from those of folk societies. The simplest summary of the differences between the two types of social organization is to recall that they are opposites: whereas the folk society is homogeneous, the urban is heterogeneous, and so on.

Two dominant features of the urban society are size and population density. There is, of course, no sharp dividing line for classification according to size or density of population. When a community becomes large enough that most of the residents are not able to know most of the others personally, some of the patterns of social relations typical of a folk society tend to disappear and are replaced by other forms of social interaction. One function of relatively large population size, then, is impersonality in interaction. An urban society as a whole cannot be primary when there are too many people in it for each to have personal knowledge of most of the others. In most rural communities in the United States, it is considered polite to speak to anyone you meet on the street. But if you tried to greet everyone you met as you walked across Times Square in New York City, you would find that you had set yourself an impossible task, and the people whom you addressed would be divided in their opinion as to whether you intended to fleece them of their money or were mentally unbalanced. Neither can a sharp line be drawn between folk and urban societies simply on the basis of density of population. It is obvious, however, that many of the factors associated with urbanism are closely related to the density of the population.

One characteristic of a city is that it has such a high density of population that it could not support itself by farming the land it occupies. The urban society has a complex division of labor and a proliferation of social roles. Since, unlike mines or farms, cities are usually not places where raw materials are produced, the people living in cities depend entirely on non-city dwellers for these materials. City people thus must support themselves by manufacturing finished products from raw materials, marketing these products, or supplying services, which range from dry cleaning to symphony music. Such economic organization results from specialization for efficient production and service and leads to a more elaborate stratification system than is typical of folk societies.

Heterogeneity

Urban differentiation and stratification give rise to a great heterogeneity in the population. The impersonality of urban life allows people with a different skin color or accent or religion to pass relatively unnoticed in a way that could never be possible in the primary organization of a folk community. In addition, the occupational specialities associated with the complex division of labor create differences in the population: variation in training, values, work hours, recreation patterns, and so on.

> In the city the ways of life are legion, and the diversities of its man-made scene admit extreme variations of equipment of opportunity. There is no sense of a common and vital dependence on the aspects of the seasons and the vagaries of the weather. There is no sense of a common fate. There are few common tasks, few incidents all men share. . . . There are no common hours of work and rest, no common occasions of meeting for personal gossip or public discussion.[5]

Another consequence of the size and heterogeneity of the population is the proliferation of secondary groups. Community-wide organizations to satisfy some of the needs for social contact have long been a part of urban life. Settlement houses, various youth groups, and other organizations aim to provide recreation and education for individuals. Civil Defense organizations and "drives" for the Red Cross and other organizations illustrate how a given crisis may serve to stimulate formal organizations and at least temporarily revive neighborliness in large cities. Sometimes out of these come primary-group relations which did not previously exist.

---

[5]Robert M. MacIver and Charles H. Page, *Society* (New York: Holt, Rinehart and Winston, Inc., 1949), pp. 312–313.

Urbanism as a Way of Life

The urban society also induces variability, inventiveness, and cultural change. Urban life may and does foster creativeness in basic as well as secondary situations, in personal life organization, and in social movements. Yet, on the whole, the larger the community, the more likely we are to find a sense of personal isolation, loss of intimacy with others, and similar marks of mass society. A central integrating set of values may be difficult to find. "Purchasability of services and things" tends to displace "personal relations as a basis of association."[6] The roles of the individual become so varied and so segmentalized that both competition and cooperation seldom involve the whole personality. One comes to think of oneself as a combination of bits and pieces, not an integrated participant in society. Individuals in the urban society must fit into a complex social structure in which they occupy a large number of statuses and roles which are frequently unrelated. Whether one is a Catholic, a Protestant, or a Jew is, in principle, irrelevant to the particular occupation one follows; treatment in a court of law is supposedly unaffected by one's political affilations and activities, the clubs to which one belongs, and one's economic position. A person's wage or salary is not influenced by whether he or she is single or married, childless or the parent of a large brood. The various roles people play are segmental; they are limited to specific contexts and confined to a narrow range of activities.

One example of the urban type of social relationship is the narrowly contractual relation of buyer and seller in an open market exchange transaction. In this type of social situation everything is formally irrelevant to the relation except considerations of the price, quantity, and quality of the goods being exchanged. The rights and obligations of the parties are specific and definite—neither more nor less than explicitly agreed upon for the specific occasion. The establishment of any particular urban relation does not imply any other social relations between the participants.

Social relations of this kind are essentially instrumental; they are not important in themselves but for the goals or ends which they bring closer to realization. As a result there is less of an emotional involvement with other persons than there is in the case of primary relationships. Social relationships in the urban society, therefore, tend to be transitory, superficial, and impersonal. Individuals asso-

---

[6]See Louis Wirth, "Urbanism as a Way of Life," *American Journal of Sociology*, 1938, 44: 17. This entire article is a classic statement of the social psychology of city life.

ciate with one another for limited purposes and social interaction tends to be confined to the specific interests involved.

Life in the urban society loses its unitary, cohesive character. Economics and family life are seemingly separated; religion is apt to be confined to particular times and places instead of permeating the whole of human existence. Work and leisure are sharply distinguished. As a result, the family does not occupy the same central place in the social structure of the urban society that it possesses in folk society, and people belong to many groups and many bureaucratically organized associations.

In the complex, diversified urban society with its many groups and competing interests, the pervasive hold of tradition has largely been broken. The comparative uniformity of thought has been replaced by an almost endless variety. There are relatively few universally accepted beliefs, values, and standards of behavior. The norms have been weakened and formal law has emerged to regulate behavior and govern both social and sexual intercourse. Therefore, in the urban society, change is rapid. Status is achieved rather than ascribed and there is a constant readiness for change. Indeed, innovation and invention are heavily rewarded in most areas of social life.

Urban society renders more contact between individuals, but it is less emotional contact. A superficial observer might imagine that modern cities are by all odds the most favorable places for social interaction. While it is true that city dwellers may talk to many people, it has often been said that persons may feel more lonely in large cities than anywhere else. There is a vast difference between the incidental and temporary contiguity in urban mass society and the shared experience and interstimulation of members of a small community.

In rural and small-town life, the community continues to have a definite place. It is the area of borrowing and lending, of mutual aid, and of intimate gossip. In earlier periods it seldom had any very formal organizations. Yet urban influences affect community life in rural and small-town areas. The rise of a secondary-group organization of society means the introduction of all sorts of formal associations having to do with agriculture, education, religion, and recreation where there were none before.

The urban society, as it grows larger, is characterized by a decline of neighborly interaction. A number of factors help account for the lessening of the importance of such contacts for the city-dweller. (1) There is a complex division of labor and an individualization of interest. (2) High residential mobility does not permit a sense of "settling down" in any one street or section of the city. (3) Easy

ILLUSTRATIVE DATA 7-1   MASS SOCIETY

The conception of "Mass Society" can be summarized as follows: The revolutions in transport and communications have brought men into closer contact with each other and bound them in new ways; the division of labor has made them more interdependent; tremors in one part of society affect all others. Despite this greater interdependence, however, individuals have grown more estranged from one another. The old primary group ties of family and local community have been shattered; ancient parochial faiths are questioned; few unifying values have taken their place. Most important, the critical standards of an educated elite no longer shape opinion or taste. As a result, mores and morals are in constant flux, relations between individuals are tangential or compartmentalized rather than organic. At the same time greater mobility, spatial and social, intensifies concern over status. Instead of a fixed or known status symbolized by dress or title, each person assumes a multiplicity of roles and constantly has to prove himself in a succession of new situations. Because of all this, the individual loses a coherent sense of self. His anxieties increase. There ensues a search for new faiths. The stage is thus set for the charismatic leader, the secular messiah, who, by bestowing upon each person the semblance of necessary grace, and of fullness of personality, supplies a substitute for the older unifying belief that the mass society has destroyed.

In a world of lonely crowds seeking individual distinction, where values are constantly translated into economic calculabilities, where in extreme situations shame and conscience can no longer restrain the most dreadful excesses of terror, the theory of the mass society seems a forceful, realistic description of contemporary society, an accurate reflection of the quality and feeling of modern life.

Source: Daniel, Bell, "The Theory of Mass Society," *Commentary,* 22 (July, 1956), pp. 75–76. Reprinted from *Commentary* by permission; Copyright © 1956 by the American Jewish Committee.

availability of transit facilities for reaching work or friends reduces the need to seek contacts next door. (4) A wide variety of secondary groups outside the immediate area of one's residence provides outlets for one's interests.

THE PURPOSE OF TYPOLOGIES

The descriptions of the folk and urban societies are characterizations of ideal-types; they are not descriptions of actual societies, let alone descriptions of the only two types of societies in existence. There is no society that is completely a folk society and none is a completely urban society. Every known society, for example, includes primary social relationships. The purpose of these ideal-types is to provide a benchmark, a baseline with which to (1) compare and contrast societies of different times and places; (2) specify the ways in which various aspects of a society are interrelated; and (3) interpret social change. That is, the folk-urban continuum suggests that as the population of a society increases and its relative social isolation decreases, social roles tend to become less inclusive and more segmentalized. The society tends to become less homogeneous and more heterogeneous. The relative number of secondary relationships increases while the number of primary relationships decreases. Occupational differentiation increases and the number of social contacts increases.

The usefulness of the typological approach to the study of society notwithstanding, it should be noted that these typologies tend to emphasize the positive features of the folk society and the negative features of the urban society. They underscore the personal, primary, and communal aspects of the folk existence but they do not give equal attention to the fact that life in the folk society is difficult and harsh. The descriptions of the urban society emphasize the exploitative and impersonal aspects of social relations, but they do not give equal attention to the increased opportunity for individual choice and freedom. In the folk community, one's life situation is largely ascribed from birth. In the urban society, there is room for individual choice and achievement. Literacy, social change, and innovation are encouraged in the urban society while they are discouraged in the folk society. For instance, students at large universities often complain of the impersonal, cold, and bureaucratic aspects of multiversity life, while students at small colleges in small towns complain of being "cut-off" from the world, of the lack of variety, and of the absence of recreational alternatives.

THE EFFECTS OF URBANIZATION ON FOLK SOCIETY

In our time, rural culture is being influenced more and more by that of the urban, industrial world. The farmer typically produces surplus goods for a wider market, makes use of the money economy of urban society, and takes part in a larger political order by paying taxes, voting, and sending his children to intercommunity or consolidated schools.

The continued extension of commercial farming with an eye to profits, along with the introduction of machinery, has greatly influenced the social organization of rural communities. In those countries where agriculture has come to operate within the framework of a money and marketing economy, the self-sufficient farmstead, which still characterizes much of the world's agriculture, is disappearing. The introduction of commercialization and mechanization into agriculture has meant that the urban ways of life—level of living, secularization, and so forth—have infiltrated rural culture more and more.

Until rapid means of transportation and communication were introduced, with the consequent intrusion of urban culture into these rural and village areas, the small town and village communities were not very different from the farming regions around them. Contact for the most part was face-to-face. There was a strong sense of independence, on the one hand, and a kind of rural solidarity, on the other. There was a strong conservatism and prejudice against new ideas and practices, except perhaps those bearing directly on economic techniques. The range of interaction was limited largely to the primary community. Contacts with the outside came through some reading of newspapers and through such institutions as the school, the political forum, and the church, although even these reflected the rural culture for the most part.

However, it was the towns in the farming areas which experienced the first breakdowns of primary-group organization. The initial impact was usually on their economic functions. The trend was from self-sufficiency to specialization, from a barter to a money economy, from independence to interdependence, with growing domination by the urban centers outside.

It should be remembered that in the contemporary United States most of the people who live in rural places are in general part of an urban structure, not a folk one. They are closely linked to the city by the interdependence of roles in an urban society. The greater the impact of the metropolitan centers on their rural hinterlands, the less the visible difference between the rural and urban structures in an urban society. For instance, city populations used to be markedly younger than farm populations in the United States. By 1950, however, this characteristic had largely disappeared. Similarly, there is little difference between rural and urban areas in sex composition. Most structural differences seem to decrease as the rural community is linked more closely to the urban by improved transportation and communication.

Many aspects of the transition from folk society to urban society can be seen in the changes taking place in the newly emerging nations of the non-Western world. Uganda, for example, is a nation of nearly seven million people occupying an area to the north of Lake Victoria about the size of Oregon. The country is largely rural; about 95 per cent of the people live outside of the towns, while the other 5 per cent at the time of the last census in 1959 lived in aggregations of 500 or larger. The two largest urban centers are the capital city, Kampala (together with adjacent Mengo Municipality, Kawempe, and Nakawa), and the industrial town of

Jinja. The Kampala urban complex totals some 130,000, while Jinja in 1959 was nearly 30,000 in total population. On the surface this is hardly a picture of pressing urbanization; rather, it is comparable to America at the time of the Revolution, when the population was five million and only 5 per cent urban.

The urban population of Uganda is centralized around the capital city. In the 1959 census this urban area, composed of four adjacent urban authorities (Kampala, Mengo, Nakawa, and Kawempe), accounted for two-fifths of the nation's urban population. The next most populous town is Jinja, which accounted for 9 per cent of the total and which had the highest growth rate for the period between 1948 and 1959. The combined populations of the next two towns, Entebbe and Mbale, made up 7.5 per cent of the total urban population. Beyond these towns the remaining urban population (42.8 per cent of the total) was distributed among small places between 500 and 10,000 in size. The substantial basis for this distribution of Uganda's urban population is the division of the country into 17 districts, each with its own district headquarters. In addition to these places are numerous trading centers and a few fishing and mining villages. The district organization which distributes important government services, especially the wide distribution of schools and health facilities, and the many different linguistic and cultural divisions may produce in Uganda a somewhat more balanced urban development than has occurred in many countries, and thus a mitigation of some of the problems of overcentralization.

In 1964 a survey of Kisenyi, an area of blight, underdevelopment, and slum appearance (which had been carefully studied in a previous survey in 1954) was completed.[7] Though far from a model of law, order, and cleanliness in 1964, the area had some paved streets, policing, running water to main structures, and regular garbage collection. The improvements over 1954 were notable. Collection of taxes and law enforcement were in the hands of the Batongole Chief and his assistant—local chiefs in the traditional order, which now have been integrated into the modern governmental machinery of Mengo Municipality.

Although this area is still one of heavy transiency, the proportion has dropped in the past ten years. The age structure of the population was also changing and the proportion of young people attending schools increased notably. The number of self-employed occupations had doubled in the ten year period. In short, within the ten years' time Kisenyi had become a more complex urban area with

---

[7]Alvin H. Scaff, "Urbanization and Development in Uganda: Growth, Structure, and Change," *Sociological Quarterly*, 1967, 8: 111–121.

more variety, a more substantial economy, more secondary relation-ships, more education, more occupational specialization, and an improved physical environment.

Urbanization in Uganda has not at the present time produced the conditions of human degradation and exploitation which have given foundation to the bitterest critics of urban development. Although there is some concentration of urban population around the capital city of Kampala, there is still some 42 per cent of the urban population distributed widely among very small towns of 500 to 10,000 in size. Although there are some problem areas in the cities, especially Kampala-Mengo, these are relatively low in density (about 45 persons per acre) and show signs of improvement rather than further deterioration. There is no evidence that the towns are breeding places for political dissent and disruption. On the contrary, the towns, and especially the national capital, bring together the people of different tribal and language backgrounds and help to produce the more cosmopolitan relations necessary to support a modern nation. The present rate of urbanization, though more than twice that of the population as a whole, still does not constitute a threat to the economy. After twenty years of urban growth at the rate of 6.3 per cent per year, the urban population will amount to only 10.4 per cent of the total in Uganda.

The recent experience in Uganda, a country in the initial phase of its urban development, indicates that urbanization produces changes but not necessarily disorder. The difference is crucial, for broader and more integrated social structures than exist in tradi-tional society are essential to economic development. These neces-sary structures can evolve or be nurtured in urban centers which serve as the transforming agencies from tribal to rational society.

Integration of Cities

In spite of the dominance of secondary-group interests and of impersonal relations, many cities have community goals and com-mon values in life. Edward L. Thorndike and Robert C. Angell have both made attempts to find factors leading to unity among such people who have different backgrounds and interests.[8]

A review of Angell's study of a sample of American cities will

---

[8]See Edward L. Thorndike, *Your City* (New York: Harcourt, Brace & Co., 1939) and his *144 Smaller Cities* (New York: Harcourt, Brace & Co., 1940); Robert C. Angell, "The Social Integration of Selected American Cities," *American Journal of Sociology*, 1942, 47: 575–592; and Angell, *Integration of American Society: A Study of Groups and Institutions* (New York: McGraw-Hill Book Co., 1941). See also Angell, "The Moral Integration of American Cities," *American Journal of Sociology*, 1951, 57, Part 2: 1–140.

show a particular approach to this topic. For selected cities Angell collected sociological data on education, employment of women, ratio of native-born to foreign-born, recreation, and other items. He also set up certain indices of social integration based on such criteria as crime rates and existence of community welfare work. Angell tentatively concluded that social integration in a city tends to be higher where (1) there is a long tradition of strong support of schools, libraries, and public recreation; (2) fewer mothers are gainfully employed; (3) there is a high proportion of native-white population; and (4) there is the least disparity among incomes by class groupings.

While Angell's findings are admittedly inconclusive, they suggest some ways of measuring the emergence of culture patterns of mass society. This is a vital matter in our present-day world, where the city has come more and more to dominate the entire culture.

INTERPRETIVE SUMMARY

Sociology began in the nineteenth century as an attempt to understand the major social changes brought about by the Industrial Revolution. The Industrial Revolution had a profound effect on the nature of human society. It influenced the production and distribution of goods and services as the domestic cottage industry gave way to the entrepreneur and finally to mass production. These major changes in the economy brought about changes throughout the structure of society and the manner in which social functions were institutionalized.

Much of the sociological analysis of society has involved a comparison of two polar ideal-types of social organization—the folk society and the urban society. The folk society is characterized by small population size, relative social isolation, primary group relationships, and minimal division of labor. It is a homogeneous social order where statuses and roles are ascribed and where social control is realized by informal sanctions. The urban society is characterized by a large population, high population density, a complex division of labor, and secondary group relationships. There is substantial diversity of interests in the urban sociey and social control is formalized in law.

The main purposes of the typological study of societies are to specify the ways in which various aspects of the social structure of a society are interrelated and to provide a basis for the interpretation of social change.

SUGGESTIONS FOR FURTHER READING

Durkheim, Emile. *The Division of Labor in Society.* Translated by George Simpson. New York: Free Press, 1964. This is a classic discussion of the changes in social structure brought about by increasing population and social density. It contains Durkheim's theory of the two types of society, which he called mechanical and organic.

Geertz, Clifford. *Old Societies and New States*. New York: The Free Press of Glencoe, 1963. This is a fine theoretical analysis of the sociology of emerging nations.

Goode, William J. *World Revolution and Family Patterns*. New York: The Free Press of Glencoe, 1963. This book is an important contribution to the sociological understanding of institutional change.

Polanyi, Karl. *The Great Transformation*. Boston: Beacon Press, 1957. An analysis of the economic basis of contemporary society, this volume places considerable emphasis on conceptions of social welfare.

Redfield, Robert. *Folk Culture of Yucatan*. Chicago: University of Chicago Press, 1941. Both the theoretical framework and content of this sociological classic are excellent.

Redfield, Robert. *The Little Community*. Chicago: University of Chicago Press, 1965. This is probably the most cited volume on the study of small folk societies.

Sanders, Irwin T. *The Community: An Introduction to a Social System*. New York: The Ronald Press, 1958. This book analyzes the social and cultural characteristics common to all communities regardless of size.

Sjoberg, Gideon. *The Preindustrial City*. New York: The Free Press, 1960. This is an excellent scholarly and careful presentation of the earliest cities.

Tönnies, Ferdinand. *Community and Society*. Translated and edited by Charles P. Loomis. East Lansing: Michigan State University, 1957. Tönnies' basic distinctions of gemeinschaft and gesellschaft are translated and his essential contributions to sociology are related to those of other pioneering figures such as Durkheim and Cooley as well as to contemporary sociologists.

Vidich, Arthur, and Bensman, Joseph. *Small Town in Mass Society*. Princeton, N. J.: Princeton University Press, 1958. The primary issue in this case study of a small town is the persistence of the rural myths of "independence" that continue to prevail in a community sorely dependent upon the mass society outside its borders.

Wilensky, Harold L., and Lebeaux, Charles N. *Industrial Society and Social Welfare*. New York: Free Press, 1965. This book surveys the materials on the development of welfare services in the United States.

Williams, Robin M., Jr. *American Society: A Sociological Interpretation*, 2nd ed. New York: Alfred A. Knopf, 1960. This is a survey of the major groups and institutions of American society.

THE COMPANY'S BEEN VERY GOOD TO ME SINCE I GOT OUT OF SCHOOL.

FIRST THEY ENROLLED ME IN THEIR EXECUTIVE TRAINING SQUAD— LEARNING ALL PARTS OF THE FIELD AND GETTING PAID FOR IT AS WELL.

THEN THEY HELPED EVELYN AND ME FIND A HOUSE CONVENIENTLY LOCATED IN A SECTION WHERE **OTHER** YOUNG EXECUTIVES LIVE—

AND WHEN EVELYN BECAME ILL SMACK DAB IN THE MIDDLE OF HER TWENTY FIRST BIRTHDAY PARTY THEY ALLOWED US FULL BENEFIT OF THE COMPANY'S HOSP-ITALIZATION PLAN EVEN **THOUGH** I WAS A MONTH SHORT ON ELIGIBILITY—

AND IN SPITE OF MY LOW SCORE ON THE MONTHLY PROMOTIONAL EMOTIONAL QUIZ AND SUBSEQUENT DAILY MAKE-UP SESSIONS WITH THE MORALE DEPARTMENT'S PSYCHOANALYST.

THEN WHEN, BECAUSE OF EVELYN'S DRINKING PROBLEM, IT LOOKED LIKE I MIGHT BE CASHIERED, THE EMER-GENCY AID COMMITTEE OF THE COMPANY'S FAMILY COUNSELING PLAN PLUS THE WIVES' AUXILIARY'S "BE A PAL" SERVICE HELPED PULL US THROUGH.

NOW THE LITTLE WOMAN AND I ARE BACK IN STEP. HERE I AM ONLY TWENTY-FOUR AND ALREADY A SECOND CONSULT-ATION ASSISTANT. AND JUST YESTER-DAY EVELYN ENROLLED OUR THREE-YEAR-OLD IN THE EXECUTIVE JUNIORS TRAINING SQUAD.

I COULD DIE FOR THE COMPANY

8
Bureaucracy and Large-Scale Organization

With the increase in the size and heterogeneity of the population, the proliferation of social roles, and urbanization which resulted from the Industrial Revolution, people came to pursue their collective goals in ever-larger groups and faced new and complex problems of social structure. The Industrial Revolution brought with it a scale of social organization which has steadily increased. Large-scale organizations have become permanent features of industrial societies, commanding an ever-greater share of social resources and exercising pervasive and substantial social power. For example, when the Ford Motor Company began in 1903, it employed slightly more than 100 people and had approximately $150,000 in capital. Though not the largest organization in the country, Ford now has over 300,000 employees and well over $6 billion in assets.[1]

The traditional, face-to-face mode of primary group organization that characterizes the small folk society is inadequate to meet the collective goals of huge numbers of people in large urban areas who are engaged in very different activities, at different times, and in different locations. As the population of a society increases, the com-

---

[1]John Kenneth Galbraith, *The New Industrial State* (Boston: Houghton Mifflin Company, 1967), pp. 11–12.

plexity and the volume of activity necessary for its maintenance also increase.

How do people effectively coordinate their activities to meet common problems without knowing one another and without face-to-face interaction? How is social order possible outside the primary group? The existence of such problems and the need for organizing and coordinating the efforts of large numbers of socially heterogeneous people to meet these problems were noted centuries ago. In his discussion of the Roman Empire of the first century, the historian Dio Cassius wrote:

> The cause of our troubles is the multitude of our population and the magnitude of the business of our government; for the population embraces men of every kind, in respect both of race and endowment, and both their tempers and their desires are manifold; and the business of the state has become so vast that it can be administered only with the greatest difficulty.[2]

THE BUREAUCRATIZATION OF SOCIAL LIFE

The major response to the problems of large-scale social organization has been the development and spread of bureaucracy. Bureaucracy is defined as "a formal, rationally organized social structure [involving] clearly defined patterns of activity in which, ideally, every series of actions is functionally related to the purposes of the organization."[3] The term "bureaucracy" originally referred to the administration of government by means of bureaus, that is, special units to care for such matters as taxation, police protection, communications, foreign relations, and military defense. Today, the term is often popularly used to refer to certain negative and "unintended" but nonetheless important features of governmental administration. One such feature is the development of self-perpetuating social patterns in which the means of public service often become ends in themselves and in which administrative personnel are more concerned with their own protection than with the service of the public interest.

Bureaucratic Influence

We are now witnessing the pervasiveness of the bureaucratically structured large-scale organization that Max Weber foresaw when he

---

[2]Quoted in G. H. Stevenson, "The Imperial Administration," *The Cambridge Ancient History* (Cambridge, England: Cambridge University Press, 1934), Volume X, p. 182.
[3]Robert K. Merton, *Social Theory and Social Structure*, rev. ed. (New York: The Free Press, 1957), p. 195.

suggested that this form of the rational coordination of behavior would increasingly dominate people's lives. The pervasiveness of bureaucracy and large-scale organizations is reflected in many ways. The number of white-collar workers, many of whom are engaged in the administration of large organizations and/or the performance of routine bureaucratic tasks, has increased steadily and substantially. Millions of other workers are subject to bureaucratic controls on the job. Consumers who seek redress of their grievances about unsatisfactory consumer products are confronted by a bureaucratic maze.

> Modern man is man in organizations. If the most dramatic fact that sets our stage apart from earlier ones is that we live today under the shadow of nuclear destruction, the most pervasive feature that distinguishes contemporary life is that it is dominated by large, complex, and formal organizations. Our ability to organize thousands and even millions of men in order to accomplish large scale tasks—be they economic, political, or military—is one of our greatest strengths. The possibility that free men become mere cogs in the bureaucratic machineries set up for this purpose is one of the greatest threats to our liberty.[4]

The person in modern society is a person in organizations, so much so that Robert Presthus has dubbed the industrial world the "organizational society."[5] We live our lives in and through organizations, and we devote large amounts of time, energy, and thought to organizations. Indeed, an increasing lament of our time is that we have become organization men and women. For many persons, the sense of attachment to the organization for which they work is more real than the sense of attachment to their community, their religion, or even their extended family. In the early 1900s more than three-fourths of the population was self-employed—mostly in farming—but today less than five per cent are self-employed. On the other hand, American Telephone and Telegraph employs three-fourths of a million persons; the United States government employs over two million people in civilian jobs and over four million in the armed services.

The state, of course, is a historical product. As populations grew, increasing differentiation of roles led to a change of controls and the need for extension of regulations to new areas of conduct. This meant a shift from a family or kinship basis of social control to one founded on the larger community, with particular individuals, groups, or classes setting down the rules and putting them into effect. More integrated forms of government tended to arise as groups or

---

[4]Peter M. Blau and Richard Scott, *Formal Organizations* (San Francisco: Chandler Press, 1962), p. ix.
[5]Robert Presthus, *The Organizational Society* (New York: Alfred A. Knopf, 1965).

societies were threatened by, or fell into conflict with, other societies. This tendency was most important in the rise of more complex states: warfare between groups makes for stronger in-group solidarity. Growth of government has meant an increase in the relative importance and role of the administrative structure in comparison with the legislative and judicial branches. This shift has brought with it increased public concern over the nature of the executive structure.

The extension of governmental functions brings people into frequent contact with all sorts of governmental officials: tax collectors, draft boards, plumbing inspectors, unemployment officers, license clerks, policemen, social security representatives, and so on. In many other areas of social life people are continually confronted with large-scale, bureaucratically structured organizations that limit or direct their behavior. People who wish to enroll at a state university, to marry, divorce, vote, travel abroad, buy or repair a house, or obtain a driver's license all confront some form of bureaucracy. Registration at a state university requires the completion of many forms, compliance with a myriad of regulations, and the submission of appropriate papers in the right order and usually in duplicate, triplicate, or quadruplicate. Rules and regulations govern attendance, examinations, grades, the use of university facilities, and many other areas of collegiate life.

In some societies the political organization is such that bureaucratic controls appear to be maximized. The long reach of the state extends into areas once free from or only slightly dominated by political regulations. Bureaucracy is not confined to any one form of political organization or ideology; modern societies—communist, fascist, democratic, and socialist—make extensive use of what Max Weber called "man's greatest social invention." As Weber noted, "the great modern state is absolutely dependent upon a bureaucratic basis. The larger the state, and the more it is or the more it becomes a great power state, the more unconditionally is this the case."[6]

Bureaucracy is a form of social structure found not only in federal, state, and local governments, but throughout the institutions of society. Churches, corporations, prisons, armies, welfare agencies, universities, unions, nonprofit research foundations, banks, factories, businesses, political parties, voluntary civic associations, and even some criminal activities are bureaucratically organized.

THE SOCIAL SOURCES OF BUREAUCRACY

Full-scale bureaucracy probably emerged as an answer to the problems of political and military organization in the Roman Empire and

---

[6]Max Weber, *From Max Weber: Essays in Sociology*, edited and translated by H. H. Gerth and C. W. Mills (New York: Oxford University Press, 1946), p. 211.

in the ancient civilizations of China and Egypt. Bureaucracy was characteristic of the great empires of the past, notably the Roman, Byzantine, Ottoman, and Chinese empires. With the great transformation accompanying the Industrial Revolution, the growth of other large organizations such as the Catholic Church, international labor unions, and business associations, and the increasing size and scope of educational institutions, religious institutions, philanthropic agencies, professional groups and other associations found in industrial society, bureaucracy came more and more to typify social life.

Efficiency

Although the social conditions which give rise to bureaucracy differ somewhat from time to time and from place to place, the pervasiveness of bureaucracy, according to Weber, is due to its technical superiority.

> The decisive reason for the advance of bureaucratic organization has always been its purely technical superiority over any other form of organization. . . . Precision, speed, unambiguity, knowledge of the files, continuity, discretion, unity, strict subordination, reduction of friction and of material and personal costs—these are raised to the optimum point in the strictly bureaucratic organization.[7]

Efficiency alone does not account for the growth of bureaucracy. People must become conscious of the need for a highly rational process of ordering human conduct to recognize the technical advantages of bureaucracy and to be ready to abandon traditional ways of organizing selected aspects of social life.

The increased size, scale, and differentiation of social organization as well as the range and complexity of its activities have made traditional administrative procedures and structures inadequate. The growth of the nation-state and of large-scale economic enterprises strongly encouraged tendencies toward bureaucratic organization. A strong emphasis in Western society upon rationalism in science, philosophy, and Calvinist religion encouraged a rational approach to organization. Calvinism, which Weber demonstrated to be significant in the emergence of capitalism, encouraged hard work as a moral virtue and provided a cultural foundation for the order, the discipline, and the selfless, disinterested conduct required in a bureaucratic structure.

Weber related bureaucracy to the growth of a money economy. He demonstrated the way in which bureaucracy developed more fully when money became the conventional medium of exchange.

---

[7]*Ibid.*, p. 214.

Money possesses an abstract quality that encourages rational calculation. It permits the payment of regular salaries, a method of remuneration that facilitates the maintenance of control over officeholders. Salaried officials are more likely to depend on their earnings, to count on the security of their position, and to see the possibilities for advancement in terms of constantly increasing income. The emergence of bureaucracy has frequently been accompanied by the transformation of traditional obligations into monetary terms, thus encouraging formal and rational relations between the official and the client.

WEBER'S IDEAL-TYPE OF BUREAUCRACY

The effort to create an organization that provides an efficient coordination of diverse human behavior toward a common goal leads to the formalization of social structure. Bureaucracies differ in the details of their organization and operations, but they are sufficiently similar to construct an "ideal-type" of bureaucratic social structure. This ideal-type, derived from the work of Max Weber, is a conceptual model of a rationally ordered social structure and is useful in analyzing the character and functions of any bureaucracy.[8]

According to Weber, there are six essential characteristics of a bureaucratic social structure, each contributing to the efficient operation of the organization and each functionally related to the others. These characteristics are:

(1) The positions become clearly and explicitly defined offices.

(2) There is a formal hierarchical order with clear-cut lines of authority and responsibility.

(3) Personnel are specialized and are selected on the basis of technical and professional competence.

(4) Rules and regulations governing official action are explicit.

(5) Social relationships are inherently impersonal.

(6) There is security of tenure and the possibility of a career by promotion in the hierarchy.

Offices

Each person in a bureaucratically structured organization occupies an office—hence, is an official. The duties, competence, prerequisites, and tasks expected of the incumbent of each office, as well as the relationship of each office with other offices, are explicitly and

[8]Max Weber, "Bureaucracy," *Economy and Society: An Outline of Interpretive Sociology,* 3 vols., edited by Guenther Roth and Claus Wittich (New York: Bedminister Press, 1968), Vol. III, pp. 956–1005.

clearly prescribed. The set of formally defined offices both dictates and limits the activities of people in a bureaucracy. All offices exist independently of their incumbents and, unlike traditional social roles which can be filled only by particular persons, bureaucratic roles are formally established and can be occupied by anyone with the appropriate qualifications. In the bureaucracy there is no indispensible person; no one has a special claim on any office by virtue of family status or special privilege.

There are important consequences of the sharp separation of the office from the person who occupies it. First, this separation serves to free the organization from the power of or the dependence upon particular persons in particular positions. The separation of the office from the person applies the principle of the interchangeability of parts to human material. No person can monopolize the right to his or her office. Bureaucracy, Weber once noted, compares with any other form of organization "exactly as does the machine with the nonmechanical mode of production."[9] If an officeholder were to resign, die, or retire, the functioning of the organization would not be impaired. The organization merely secures another qualified person to assume the duties of the office. So long as the offices are filled by qualified persons, the organization continues to operate effectively.

Hierarchy

The organization of a bureaucracy takes the form of a hierarchy with a "clearly established system of super- and sub-ordination in which there is a supervision of the lower offices by the higher ones."[10] The formal organization thus tends to assume a pyramidal form with a few offices at the top, a larger number of lesser offices in the middle ranks, and most offices at the base. The prototype of this kind of social structure is probably the military organization with its ranks of commissioned and noncommissioned officers, its enforced recognition of duties and responsibilities for those with authority, and its insistence upon obedience to superiors. Bureaucracy thus makes explicit the location of authority and its limits for each office. In all large, formal organizations some form of coordination of effort is required.

The major consequence of hierarchy is that it locates responsibility in specific positions and allows for a clear-cut determination of policy. Everyone in a bureaucracy is responsible for the behavior of those under his or her authority. Establishing lines of authority facilitates the effective coordination of efforts. Moreover, this arrange-

---

[9]Weber, *From Max Weber*, p. 214.
[10]Weber, *Economy and Society*, p. 957.

ILLUSTRATIVE DATA 8-1   THE PETER PRINCIPLE
"IN A HIERARCHY, EVERY EMPLOYEE TENDS TO RISE TO HIS LEVEL OF INCOMPETENCE"

The competence of an employee is determined not *by outsiders but by his superior in the hierarchy. If the superior is still at a level of competence, he may evaluate his subordinates in terms of the performance of useful work—for example, the supplying of medical services or information, the production of sausages or table legs or the achieving of whatever are the stated aims of the hierarchy. That is to say, he evaluates output.*

But if the superior has reached his level of incompetence, he will probably rate his subordinates in terms of institutional values: he will see competence as the behavior that supports the rules, rituals, and forms of the status quo. Promptness, neatness, courtesy to superiors, internal paperwork, will be highly regarded. In short, such an official evaluates input.

"Rockman is dependable."
"Lubrik contributes to the smooth running of the office."
"Rutter is methodical."
"Miss Trudgen is a steady, consistent worker."
"Mrs. Friendly co-operates well with colleagues."
In such cases, internal consistency is valued more highly than efficient service. . . .

Source: The Peter Principle by Laurence J. Peter and Raymond Hull. New York: William Morrow and Company, Inc., 1969, p. 42.

ment sets up a line of advancement for persons seeking a career within the organization.

Technical Competence

Offices in the bureaucracy are filled by persons who are technically and/or professionally qualified and who demonstrate their technical competence. This makes important the development of tests and other measures of technical achievement by which the qualified can be certified. Examinations were employed in China before the Christian era, and it is reported that in the bureaucracy of feudal China one had to demonstrate excellence in such humanistic skills as writing poetry as part of the "civil service examination." American civil service examinations typically focus upon precise skills that reflect a high degree of specialization of functions. The selection of persons for positions in the bureaucracy on the basis of what they know rather than who they know contrasts sharply with the situation in nonbureaucratic situations in which personal loyalty, kinship, inheritance, tribal connections and such determine the appointment to positions.

The consequence of this characteristic is that trained people are more likely to do their jobs with skill, especially in the highly specialized bureaucracies of today. In addition, it facilitates the independence of the organization beyond the individual.

Rules and Regulations

In the bureaucracy the normative structure is spelled out in a written and codified form that explicitly details the rules and regulations of the organization. "The management of the modern office," wrote Weber, "is based upon written documents (the files), which are preserved in their original or draft form. . . ."[11] Oral agreements are too easily forgotten and distorted. The formal regulations dictate the appropriate behavior—the official conduct of the officeholders. The rules and regulations in a bureaucracy are specific; they impersonally apply to definite situations and circumstances. Problems are solved by the rules rather than by the personal judgment of an officeholder.

Although there are many complaints about "red tape," there would doubtless be confusion, inconsistency, and inefficiency without rules and regulations. The function of rules and regulations is to minimize the disruptive effects of personal biases and predilections and to provide for continuity and uniformity of treatment both within the organization and for the clients of the bureaucracy. The formality which is imposed by adherence to rules and regulations renders the social relations within the bureaucracy impersonal. Consequently, people can work with one another in spite of any personal frictions that might exist between them. As Merton has noted, "In this way, the subordinate is protected from the arbitrary action of his superior, since the actions of both are constrained by a mutually recognized set of rules.[12]

Impersonality

Due to the separation of person and office, the hierarchical organization, and the emphasis on technical qualifications and rules and regulations, relationships in the bureaucracy are formally prescribed relationships among offices, not among personalities. The relationships necessary to carry out the tasks of a bureaucracy are impersonal. Personal feelings are subordinated to the demands of the office

---

[11]*Ibid.*
[12]Merton, *Social Theory and Social Structure,* p. 195.

and are formally contained so as not to impede or disrupt the formally required interaction.

The spirit of impersonality is one of detachment and distance. According to Weber, the ideal-type of bureaucracy is one which "succeeds in eliminating from official business love, hatred, and all purely personal, irrational, and emotional elements which escape calculation."[13] Impersonality promotes equality of treatment, insures cooperation among persons who must interact to meet the obligations of their offices, and enhances the capacity to render rational and objective judgments, uninfluenced by likes and dislikes of particular individuals. Bureaucracy is corrupted when technical competencies are influenced by personal responses to other persons; or, as Weber observed, "Bureaucracy develops the more perfectly, the more it is 'dehumanized'. . . ."[14]

Career and Tenure

Bureaucracy also provides for careers within the organization, typically by fixed steps as in the military or civil service. Officeholders are given security of tenure (usually after a probationary period) in an effort to exact competent and unbiased performance and loyalty to the organization. Security renders bureaucrats less susceptible to outside pressures and the bureaucracy assures itself of continued efficiency by offering the possibility for advancement. Promotion, like initial appointment, is based upon demonstrated ability and/or seniority. An adequate reward system in a bureaucracy ensures continuous and competent performance as well as adequate recruitment of personnel.[15]

BUREAUCRACY'S "OTHER FACE"

Every large, formal and complex organization is more than a bureaucratic form of social structure. Bureaucracy is an internal social structure that large-scale organizations use to deal with the problem of achieving effective and efficient operation, but bureaucracy is not synonymous with the substantive organization itself. Any given organization, no matter how highly bureaucratized, is always more than a bureaucracy. Moreover, no bureaucracy conforms exactly to the "pure" type described by Weber. No large-scale organization is exclusively impersonal. Within every large-scale organization there

---

[13]Weber, *Economy and Society*, p. 975.
[14]*Ibid.*
[15]Stanley H. Udy, Jr., *Organization of Work* (New Haven, Conn.: HRAF Press, 1959).

emerges an "informal structure" of social relationships that Charles H. Page has aptly called "bureaucracy's other face."[16]

The gap which usually exists between the formal and the informal structure is aptly illustrated in the following report by Peter Blau on a state employment agency in a large Eastern city:

> The trainee learned that requests for workers, when received from employers over the telephone, must be recorded on a form, the job order. The procedure for obtaining all the information needed to fill out the twenty-five categories on this form was fully explained and exemplified. . . . The interviewer was taught the formula "What? How? Why? What is involved?" . . . Two days of training were devoted to the use of the four volume codebook which contained numerical codes for 29,000 occupations. . . .
>
> A series of demonstrations showed how to match the information on the job order with that on the application form in order to select the client best suited for a given vacancy. . . .
>
> . . . Interviewers were taught how to recognize a client's need for counseling and were told about the two types of counseling the agency offers. . . .
>
> . . . All recipients of unemployment insurance benefits . . . [were] required to report periodically to the employment agency. Interviewers . . . [were] responsible for notifying the unemployment insurance agency whenever a benefit client . . . [refused] a suitable job "without good cause."
>
> . . . In Department X, the procedures . . . were quite different from those discussed in the training course. Occupational codes were not used. The "job formula" was never mentioned. Application forms were rarely made out. Selection of candidates for jobs was not made from application files but from incoming applicants. Counseling was virtually prohibited. . . .
>
> . . . In the case of benefit clients . . . refusals [of jobs] could be discouraged by reminders that a refusal might disqualify the client for benefit payments. . . .
>
> . . . This interfered with the placement goal of the service agency, which was to help clients find jobs they wanted, not to conscript them.[17]

Anyone who has worked within a large organization knows of the development of cliques and the interplay of personal likes and dislikes. The informal structure can usurp the formal structure of authority and can efficiently block the execution of policy. Middle-level officials sometimes deviate from official policy to aid a friend,

[16]Charles H. Page, "Bureaucracy's Other Face," *Social Forces*, XXV (October, 1946), 88–94.
[17]Peter M. Blau, *The Dynamics of Bureaucracy* (Chicago: University of Chicago Press, 1955), pp. 22–23, 25–26.

to secure a favor from a superior, or to protect their own position within the bureaucracy.

The informal structure does not necessarily obstruct the purposes or weaken the efficiency of the organization. While the informal side of bureaucracy sometimes acts in opposition to officialdom, at other times it parallels and supplements official policy. The efficiency of the bureaucracy may actually be enhanced precisely because the formal requirements are ignored. For instance, intimate personal relationships among employees might deviate from official policy but also promote morale and, in turn, increase the efficiency of the employees.

Informal groups in the large-scale organization are sometimes so important that to secure maximum efficiency the bureaucrat must make use of personal relationships and sentiments. For instance, a superior may overlook minor violations of minor regulations by his or her subordinates to ensure their loyalty and/or friendship, thereby guaranteeing special efforts in their work. Completely ignoring "bureaucracy's other face" may lead to resistance to policy, blocked lines of communication, and even the deliberate sabotage of the goals of the organization.

Leadership and Group Effectiveness

The interrelations of higher and lower echelons will be qualified by the aim of the organization, its particular social structure, the already-existing patterns of control, and a variety of other factors. Numerous research studies have shown how the values, attitudes, and output of a group are affected by the nature of the relationship of the members to the leader and to one another.[18]

The dominance that an individual may exercise will vary according to cultural patterns. The leader of a group anticipates identification, obedience, and deference from the group members. However, it should not be imagined that because dominant individuals in leadership positions are not voluntarily chosen for their positions, their followers are less inclined to do as they say. Whether they are or not depends on their social-cultural training.

Studies of morale and leadership in the United States Army during World War II show that good morale among the troops was correlated with their having as officers men who were interested in them, understood their needs, recognized their abilities, were just in discipline, job assignment, and promotional policy, and kept them in-

---

[18]For a review and discussion of the literature on these topics, see Ralph M. Stogdill, *Individual Behavior and Group Achievement* (New York: Oxford University Press, 1959); and Bernard Bass, *Leadership, Psychology, and Organizational Behavior* (New York: Harper & Row, 1960).

formed—insofar as security permitted—as to the nature of particular missions. The men did not greatly resent dominance and control, but they wanted to know "what the score was," as they put it.[19]

Much the same reactions have been noted in industry and business. A wide range of studies of the interplay of productivity, supervision, and employee morale has shown the importance of a firm but understanding supervisory force. Such a force facilitates the workers' identification with their jobs and with the informal as well as formal organization in the factory or in the store. So too, as Morris S. Viteles remarks,

It appears that the supervisor who sees the problem of productivity exclusively in the technical terms of work methods and standards is less likely to motivate workers to increased production than one who sees the problem in terms of workers' status, characteristics, needs, and aspirations. The development of "employee-oriented" supervisors, adequately equipped for dealing with interpersonal relations on the job therefore represents one promising approach to the solution of problems of motivation and morale in industry.[20]

To summarize, we may say that among other things important in making a work group or any other group effective are these: the individuals want to feel secure; they want social approval when it is pertinent; they want to know what to do and what is expected of them; they want a sense of participation; they want consistent discipline; and they want to be treated fairly and justly. If appropriate relations are maintained between the workers and their managers and supervisors, even rather authoritarian headship will be effective. But as a survey of the presidents of 171 of the largest corporations in the United States shows, although 50 per cent of the top executives support an autocratic rather than a democratic management, they specify that "the autocrat must listen to the top management group he heads."[21]

Place of Informal Association

In addition to the formal organization of leadership, some kind of informal association and ordering of control often arises.

[19]See S. A. Stouffer, et al., Studies in Social Psychology in World War II, 4 vols. (Princeton, N.J.: Princeton University Press, 1949). For the discussion here, Vols. 1 and 2, The American Soldier, are the most pertinent.
[20]Morris S. Viteles, Motivation and Morale in Industry (New York: W. W. Norton & Company, Inc., 1953), pp. 161–162. This book contains a review and discussion of a wide range of studies in the United States and elsewhere dealing with individual morale.
[21]Joseph B. Marshall, "America's Best-Managed Companies," Dun's Review and Modern Industry, 1960, 75: 38–40.

Thus, in a military unit, government bureau, or factory section, voluntary leadership may grow out of the day-to-day interactions of the soldiers, the clerks, or the industrial workers. Sometimes, especially in periods of crisis, these informal leaders wield more power and influence than the formal heads of the operation. Productivity, morale, and sense of participation in the group are all greatly affected by such informal leadership.

The informal groupings that arise within the formal organization perform important functions not only in productive efficiency but in the matter of group morale. Cliques and friendships develop among the workers, and within these leaders emerge. Sometimes these groups have bearing on the work operations of the structure itself, and sometimes they deal only with recreational relationships. With regard to productivity, one important function of these informal groupings of workers is to protect themselves against practices which they consider a menace to their welfare. For example, in one plant, pressure by other employees was put on any worker who tended to exceed a certain minimum standard of output. This pressure consisted of ridicule, name-calling ("rate buster"), and even a certain amount of mild physical punishment. In this particular study, many of the men admitted to the research team that they could have turned out much more work but said they feared that if production were increased too much, the rates of pay would be cut.[22]

On the development of the informal organization, Stogdill had this to say:

> Informal organization comes about as a result of the development of discrepancies (a) between work performances and responsibilities as defined and (b) between informal interactions and formally defined interactions. Thus leadership is ever confronted with the task of reconciling discrepancies—discrepancies between what ought to be done and what is being done, between goals and achievements, between organizational needs and available resources, between the needs of individual members and the requirements of organization, between formal lines of co-operation and informal patterns of co-operation.[23]

THE CONSEQUENCES OF BUREAUCRACY

Although Weber regarded bureaucracy as an instrument for achieving maximum efficiency, Blau (among others) has questioned

---

[22]See F. J. Roethlisberger and W. J. Dickson, *Management and the Worker* (Cambridge: Harvard University Press, 1939); and their *Management and Morale* (same publisher, 1943).

[23]Ralph M. Stogdill, "Leadership, Membership and Organization," *Psychological Bulletin*, 1950, 47: 1–14. Quotation from p. 7. By permission of the author and the American Psychological Association, Inc.

whether impersonality and other characteristics of Weber's ideal-type result in maximal efficiency:

> If reserved detachment characterizes the attitudes of the members of the organization toward one another, it is unlikely that high *esprit de corps* will develop among them. The strict exercise of authority in the interest of discipline induces subordinates, anxious to be highly thought of by their superiors, to conceal defects in operations from superiors, and this obstruction of the flow of information upward in the hierarchy impedes effective management. Insistence on conformity also tends to engender rigidities in official conduct and to inhibit the rational exercise of judgment needed for efficient performance of tasks.[24]

Furthermore, Drucker has emphasized that while specialization is not inherently inefficient, the assumption that it is necessarily the most efficient form of the division of labor is questionable.

> [W]e have learned that it is neither necessary nor always efficient to organize all mass production in such a manner as to have the majority of workers confine themselves to doing one and only one of the elementary manipulations. . . . It was impossible [because of wartime shortages of skilled labor] to "lay out" the job in the usual assembly-line fashion in which one unskilled operation done by one unskilled man is followed by the next unskilled man. The operation was broken down into its unskilled components like any assembly-line job. *But then the unskilled components were put together again with the result that an unskilled worker actually performed the job of a highly skilled mechanic*—and did it as reliably and efficiently as had been done by skilled men.[25]

One bureaucratic dilemma lies in the fact that hierarchy and highly formal relationships and standardized procedures sometimes inhibit the free flow of information and obstruct effective communication throughout the organization. According to Blau and Scott,

> Studies of experimental and work groups have shown that status differences restrict the participation of low-status members, channel a disproportionate amount of communication to high-status members, discourage criticism of the suggestions of the highs, encourage rejecting the correct suggestions of the lows, and reduce the work satisfactions of the lows and their motivation to make contributions.[26]

---

[24]Peter M. Blau, *Bureaucracy in Modern Society* (New York: Random House, 1956), p. 33.

[25]Peter Drucker, *Concept of the Corporation* (New York: John Day, 1946), pp. 183–184.

[26]Peter M. Blau and W. Richard Scott, *Formal Organizations* (San Francisco: Chandler Publishing Co., 1962), p. 243.

ILLUSTRATIVE DATA 8–2   "YOU CAN'T GO WRONG
IF YOU STICK TO THE BOOK"

*According to a ruling of the department of labor, Bernt Balchen
[Admiral Bryd's pilot on his historic flight over the South Pole] . . .
cannot receive his citizenship papers. Balchen, a native of Norway,
declared his intention in 1927. It is held that he has failed to meet the
condition of five years' continuous residence in the United States. The
Byrd Antarctic voyage took him out of the country, although he was
on a ship carrying the American flag, was an invaluable member of the
Antarctic expedition, and in a region to which there is an American
claim because of the exploration and occupation of it by Americans,
this region being Little America.*

*The bureau of naturalization explains that it cannot proceed on the
assumption Little America is American soil. That would be trespassing
on international questions where it has no sanction. So far as the
bureau is concerned, Balchen was out of the country and technically
has not complied with the law of naturalization.*

Source: Chicago Tribune, June 24, 1931, p. 10.

The point is that formal regulations and procedures will not in
themselves automatically yield the desired results. As Blau noted:

> The problem of central concern is the expeditious removal of the
> obstacles to efficient operations which recurrently arise. This cannot
> be accomplished by a preconceived system of rigid procedures . . . but
> only by creating conditions favorable to continuous adjustive develop-
> ments in the organization. To establish such a pattern of self-adjust-
> ment in a bureaucracy, conditions must prevail that encourage its
> members to cope with emergent problems and to find the best method
> for producing specified results on their own initiative, and that obviate
> the need for unofficial practices which thwart the objectives of the
> organization, such as restriction of output.[27]

The structure of administrative roles—the "table of organization,"
as military parlance has it—sometimes becomes so sacred that no
deviation from it is permitted. The fixed rules designed to facilitate
decision tend to predominate at the expense of variable situations.
As bureaucratic members of the military are fond of saying, "You
can't go wrong if you stick to the book"—that is, to the rules and
procedures laid down by those in the higher echelons of authority.
Such emphasis means a tendency to view various activities as fitting
neatly into predetermined and rigid categories. Everything has to be
labeled, acted on, and reported in formalist fashion, with no devia-

---

[27]Peter M. Blau, *Bureaucracy in Modern Society* (New York: Random House, 1956),
pp. 64–66.

tions. The flow of decisions may become so intricate that the purpose or intent of the action becomes secondary to the proper fulfillment of the procedural rules. This means a high degree of impersonality in handling cases requiring administrative decision. The bureaucrat is symbolic of his organization: he has no power to make personal decisions.

Such stress on "the book" and on cautious following of the rules results in what Veblen aptly called "trained incapacity"—that is, loss of flexibility to meet new situations. Personnel are chosen by examinations to prove their preparation or competence for the job; but once past a usually short probation period, they are protected by various regulations concerning tenure, recurrent promotion, and seniority, whether their competence is maintained or not. The whole structure is a fixed and safe world, marked by rigid rules, methodical and impersonal execution of the rules, and hence a predictable outcome. Once such a scheme gets into operation, it resists modification.

Bureaucratic Personality

The regimen set down in institutions has its counterpart in the human beings who operate the system. There is no neater illustration of the interplay of culture and personality than in the field of bureaucratic administration. The competence needed for a job will vary with what is expected, and the incumbent in a given office must come up to certain standards. But once he is on the job, there is pressure to be prudent, methodical, and precise in carrying on his work. One needs little or no initiative or imagination, and one avoids responsibility by passing difficult questions on to a higher authority or by hiding behind the rules. In fact, to demonstrate such qualities will usually lead to punishment of some kind, not reward. Innovations are not welcome in a bureaucratic world. Rather, this world encourages and rewards conformity, timidity, and deference to higher authority and regulations.

Yet, living in a safe world, bureaucrats often show arrogance or indifference to their clientele. The officeholder can compensate for his enforced conformity by showing his power over others. This is a feature of bureaucracy which those conditioned to a culture of individualism, personal give-and-take, and flexible decisions find so frustrating in military service and in dealing with corporate and governmental bureaus generally. While bureaucratic features may arise in the economic order, at least under "free enterprise" individuals can "take their business elsewhere." But if you do not like the service at the United States Post Office, you cannot decide to patronize some other firm. There simply is no place else to go for most governmental services.

Some believe there is a drift toward administration by professional bureaucrats in government, just as there is in private enterprise. This drift may be even stronger in societies without representative democracy, because public service there usually is a means of rewarding party members for their political adherence. It is, in effect, a spoils system on a vast scale.

In short, once the administration of government or of business becomes encrusted with bureaucracy, the system tends to perpetuate itself, unless some devices are set up to prevent its doing so. Cautious and "safe" people pick persons like themselves for the jobs. There is a kind of empire-building of the timid to protect themselves. The bureaucrats fear any inroads on their role and status by bold and ingenious people. Officialism, like extreme ecclesiasticism in the church, means that the form of the law remains, but the "spirit," the dynamic function, disappears.

INTERPRETIVE SUMMARY

One of the most significant changes associated with the Industrial Revolution was the increasing pervasiveness of burcaucratically structured, large-scale organization. Bureaucratization has been one of the major responses to the problem of coordinating the social life of large heterogeneous, and physically dispersed collectivities of people.

People in urbanized societies spend a substantial amount of their lives in the influence of bureaucracy, either directly or indirectly. The modern person is increasingly a person in organizations. Churches, political parties, schools, prisons, voluntary associations, corporations, and much more are bureaucratically structured.

A bureaucracy is a rationally organized social structure with clearly defined patterns of activity in which each series of activity is related to the purposes of the organization. Bureaucracy, as an ideal-type, has six essential characteristics set forth by Max Weber: clearly defined offices (positions), a hierarchical chain of command, selection of personnel on the basis of technical qualifications, rules and regulations governing official action, impersonal social relationships, and security of tenure.

Large-scale organizations do not conform exactly to Weber's ideal-type. Formal regulations and procedures do not automatically yield maximum efficiency. The stress on "the book" and the cautious following of rules sometimes results in "trained incapacity" and produces a personality type which is conforming, timid, methodical, and precise. Moreover, every large organization is always more than social structure and the informal social relationships which emerge within the organization clearly effect its operation.

SUGGESTIONS FOR FURTHER READING

Barnard, Chester A. *The Functions of the Executive.* Cambridge, Mass.: Harvard University Press, 1938. This was one of the first books to emphasize the importance of informal social relationships within the large-scale organization.

Blau, Peter M. *Bureaucracy in Modern Society*. New York: Random House, 1956. This is a first-rate, brief review of the sociology of bureaucracy.

Blau, Peter M., and Scott, W. Richard. *Formal Organizations: A Comparative Approach*. San Francisco: Chandler Publishing Company, 1962. This volume is a good basic text on bureaucracy.

Crozier, Michel. *The Bureaucratic Phenomenon*. Chicago: The University of Chicago Press, 1964. A case study of a French bureaucracy, this book provides a good basis of comparison with American bureauracies.

Etzioni, Amitai. *A Comparative Analysis of Complex Organizations*. New York: The Free Press of Glencoe, 1961. This is a comparative study of the circumstances and techniques under which formal organizations secure compliance from their personnel.

Gouldner, Alvin W. *Patterns of Industrial Bureaucracy*. New York: The Free Press, 1954. This is a case study of the differential emergence of bureaucracy in two divisions of a gypsum plant.

Peter, Lawrence F., and Hull, Raymond. *The Peter Principle*. New York: William Morrow and Company, Inc., 1969. This is a humorous and interesting discussion of many "dysfunctions" of the large-scale organization.

Roethlisberger, F. J., and Dickson, William J. *Management and the Worker*. Cambridge, Mass.: Harvard University Press, 1949. A classic study, this book summarizes the research carried out on informal work groups at the Western Electric Hawthorne Works.

Selznick, Philip. *TVA and the Grass Roots*. Berkeley: The University of California Press, 1949. This is an important study of the way in which relations of an organization to outside forces affect its operation.

Tannenbaum, Arnold S. *Control in Organizations*. New York: McGraw-Hill Book Company, Inc., 1968. This is a comparative study of the problems of influence and power in organizations.

Thompson, James D. *Organizations in Action*. New York: McGraw-Hill Book Company, Inc., 1967. This is an analysis of the structure of complex organizations and what they have in common regardless of institutional or individual variation.

Whyte, William H., Jr. *The Organization Man*. New York: Simon and Schuster, 1956. This is a study of the shift in values that is accompanying the bureaucratization of American life.

DO YOU THINK IT'S MORALLY RESPONSIBLE TO BRING A CHILD INTO THIS WORLD?

ABSOLUTELY NOT. LEON AND I HAVE GIVEN IT A LOT OF DISCUSSION.

WALTER SAYS NO TOO. HE SAYS WE HAVE NO RIGHT.

LEON SAYS THE SAME THING. "WHAT KIND OF HERITAGE ARE WE LETTING THEM IN FOR?" HE ASKS ME.

BUT I SAID TO WALTER, "WALTER, WE HAVE TO GO ON LIVING."

I DON'T KNOW. WE GET MORE CONVENIENCES, BUT DOES ANYTHING REALLY EVER GET ANY BETTER?

THAT'S WHAT WALTER SAYS. BUT I SAID, "WALTER, YOU CAN'T TURN YOUR BACK ON THE WORLD."

LEON'S MOTHER SAID EXACTLY THE SAME THING.

THAT'S NOT A VERY NICE THING TO SAY TO ME, MARSHA.

BOY, WHAT A FIGHT! FINALLY LEON SAID HE WAS NOT GOING TO HAVE A CHILD SO IT COULD BE LIED TO ABOUT THE WORLD AS HE HAD BEEN.

WE WERE ALL LIED TO. THAT'S PART OF GROWING UP. AS I SAID TO WALTER," THE REAL REASON YOU DON'T WANT CHILDREN IS NOT THE LIES. THE REAL REASON IS YOU'RE AFRAID TO GROW UP."

LIES. THE BOMB. HATE ALL AROUND US. WE JUST DECIDED IT WASN'T WORTH IT, THAT'S ALL.

WELL, THE MOMENT I EXPLAINED TO WALTER THAT THE JOY OF LIVING IS TO CONQUER YOUR FEAR OF THE UNKNOWN, HE SAW THE LIGHT. SO TO HELP CONQUER IT WE'RE HAVING A BABY.

LEON AND I COMPLETELY DISAGREE WITH YOU. ONE NIGHT FIVE MONTHS AGO WE SPENT A WHOLE NIGHT TALKING IT OUT. WE DEFINITELY DECIDED AGAINST IT.

SO WHAT HAPPENED?

WE GOT DRUNK.

9
Population
and
Society

The culture patterns of a society are always influenced by the size, composition, and distribution of its population. The study of population deals directly with analyses of such topics as birth and death rates, migration, marriage, health conditions, and the interrelationship of population and social structure. The study of population also entails a consideration of the actual and potential pressures of population on such resources as food, water, timber, and minerals, the relation of population size to industrial and military manpower, and the quality of the population and the optimum population for a country in the light of problems of resources.

The study of population, therefore, deals directly with (1) trends in population size; (2) birth and death rates; (3) distribution—spatial and cultural; (4) composition and characteristics, such as age, sex, marital status, race, religion, and occupation; (5) movement—that is, in- and out-migrations; and (6) the dynamic aspects of culture and social structure which require analysis. Of central concern in the study of population are such questions as how the character of a population is influenced by fertility, mortality, and migration; how the culture of the time and place affects population

Figure 9-1   World Population Growth*

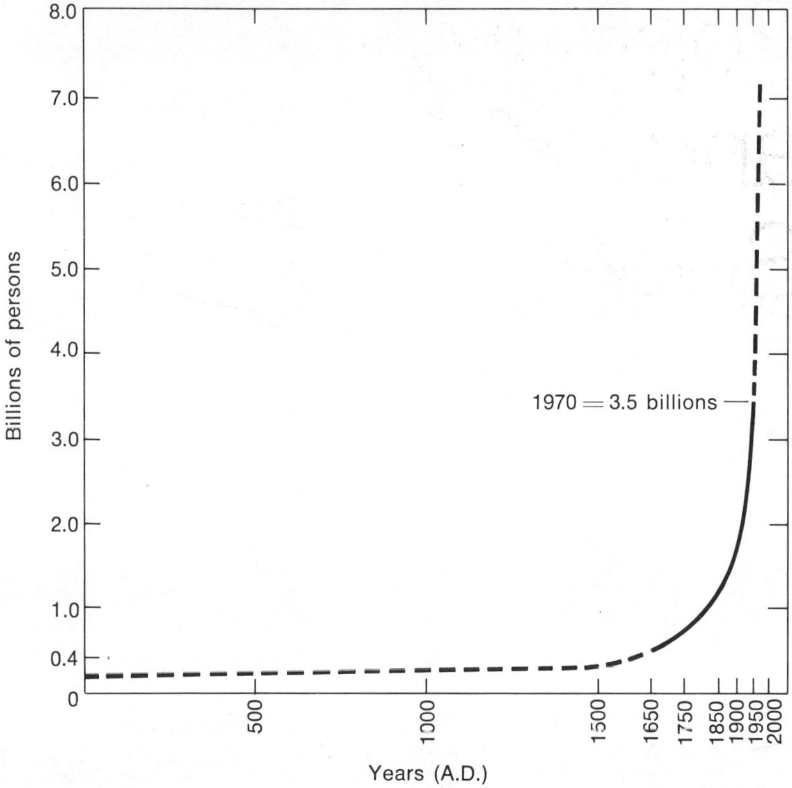

Years (A.D.)

*Estimated population of the world from 1 A.D. to 1960, and the projected population to 2000 A.D.
Source: Harold F. Dorn, "World Population Growth," The Population Dilemma, ed. Philip M. Hauser. © 1963 by the American Assembly, Columbia University, New York, N.Y. Reprinted by permission of Prentice-Hall, Inc., Englewood Cliffs, N.J.

trends; and how the values and institutional arrangements of a people influence the size and composition of the population.

WORLD POPULATION GROWTH

In the eighteenth century, after centuries of only relatively slight increase, the world experienced an enormous increase in numbers. In the nineteenth and twentieth centuries, the increase has been even greater. In 1650 the estimated population of the world was approximately 500 million. Within the next 100 years it had risen to about 700 million. By about 1830 it had reached 1 billion. Estimates for 1971 put the global population at about 3.6 billion—almost three times that of a century ago. It is worth noting, moreover, that nearly two-thirds of this latter increase has taken place

Table 9-1   Estimated World Population 10,000 B.C.–1970

Year	Population (millions)
10,000 B.C.	1–10
5,000 B.C.	5–20
50 A.D.	200–250
1300 A.D.	400
1650 A.D.	500
1750 A.D.	700
1800 A.D.	900
1850 A.D.	1200
1900 A.D.	1600
1920 A.D.	1800
1930 A.D.	2000
1940 A.D.	2200
1950 A.D.	2400
1960 A.D.	2800
1970 A.D.	3500+

since 1900. By 1970 the world had added two billion people since the turn of the century.

This growth has not occurred uniformly over the earth. Between 1850 and 1950 the population of Europe more than doubled while that of the American continents and Oceania quadrupled. At the time of the writing of the Declaration of Independence, the United States population was just under 4 million. In 1900 it was 76 million, a nearly 19-fold increase in a little more than a century.

Similar upsurges have taken place elsewhere in the world, although not at such a marked rate. In fact, as the population in many industrialized countries of the Euro-American culture tends to become more or less stationary, the growth in other regions and countries has accelerated. At the present rate of increase, India, which now has a population of over 500 million, will more than double by the turn of this century (unless limitations are imposed). Accurate figures for China are hard to obtain, but a census taken in June, 1953, showed a total population of 602 million and the estimate for 1970 was 740 million. Japan has a population of over 100 million, considerably more than twice its population in 1900. During much of the first half of this century, Japan added more than a million people a year. The Soviet Union already has a population of 241 million.

For the world as a whole, not only have the total numbers increased, but the annual rates of increase have risen steadily. It is estimated that the rate of growth in 1650 was 0.25 per cent per year. By 1800 the rate of increase had risen to 0.4 per cent per year and in 1970 it was estimated that the rate of world population growth was about 2.0 per cent per year.

Reasons for Population Growth

Almost all this tremendous increase in the world population is the result of a *reduction in the death rate*, not a rise in the birth rate. This reduction of the death rate derives from numerous causes, among the most important of which are the following: (1) Advances in modern medicine led to the reduction of infectious and contagious diseases, improvement in maternal and infant care, and the introduction of public sanitation. These advances all acted to cut the death rate. Only indirectly did they influence the birth rate. (2) The Commercial and then the Industrial Revolution increased the production of manufactured goods and their transportation and distribution. Moreover, these changes in the economic patterns of culture provided jobs for an increasing number of people. All this, in turn, made for a higher standard of living. (3) New lands in the Americas and elsewhere not only provided an outlet for the expanding populations of Europe and Asia but also, in time, furnished foodstuffs and raw materials to feed the industrial system and to provide a market for goods manufactured in Europe. (4) Because of scientific advances, plant and animal stocks have been greatly improved, while commercial fertilizers and power machinery have greatly increased the production of the world's foodstuffs and commodities useful in providing clothing and shelter, such as fibers and lumber.

Variations in Population Increase

There is considerable variation in the rates of increase by countries and world regions. The most notable differences are those between highly industralized regions and those that have not experienced an industrial revolution, the "third world" countries. Most of the countries of northwestern Europe seem to be approaching a relatively stable population. In these countries the rates of population growth are clearly associated with rapid industrialization, which began about 1760. It is the nonindustrial areas that now show the most striking increases in rates of growth.

Unlike the historical situation in northwestern Europe in the nineteenth century, when industrialization and improvement in medicine went hand in hand, many present-day "third-world" countries have been influenced dramatically by modern medical care without at the same time going through industrialization. In other words, the diffusion of one set of cultural patterns—scientific medical care—has occurred without the spread of a second set of patterns that historically had been associated with the first. In fact, the application of medicine in reducing the death rate—without, however, reducing the birth rate—has produced a decline in mortality rates "much sharper than any ever experienced in the history of the presently industrialized nations."[1] Kingsley Davis thus describes what has happened:

> The amazingly accelerated reduction of mortality has . . . been accomplished by international disease control, not by economic development in these areas themselves. It required no essential change in the customs and institutions of the people, no advance in general education, nor growth in per capita income. . . .
>
> Since disease control has not involved basic changes in social institutions, education, and real income, fertility has remained high in nonindustrial regions. . . . The industrial countries began lowering their birth rates *before* their sharpest declines in mortality, but the backward areas will do so long *after* their mortality has reached a low modern level. As a result the densely settled and impoverished countries of the world are experiencing an unprecedented population growth which does not reflect economic development but in fact creates strong impediments to it.[2]

Davis doubts that "social modernization," as he calls it, can really "match the three per cent population growth per year found in these areas, much less exceed it."[3]

Changes in commercial and economic life and the spread of political democracy in the eighteenth century sounded a note of optimism in Europe and America that found ready expression in the doctrine of inevitable social progress. This optimism found even more vehement expression in the nineteenth century. As J. J. Spengler describes it,

> The common man, once looked upon as a creature of little dignity placed in the world for the service of the master classes, was coming into his own. A beneficiary, primary and secondary, of the redistribution of economic and political power under way, he was held in greater esteem than formerly; his wants, rights, and potentialities were receiving more attention than ever, and they would receive even greater

---

[1]Kingsley Davis, "The Unpredicted Pattern of Population Change," *Annals of the American Academy of Political and Social Science*, 1956, 305: 53–59. Quotation p. 55. All quotations by permission.
[2]*Ibid.*, p. 57.
[3]*Ibid.*, p. 59.

attention as the democratic movement, and the values it stood for, gained in scope.[4]

Malthus' Theory

Such men as the idealistic Marquis de Condorcet in France and William Godwin in England expressed the growing faith of the period in the steady march of mankind toward perfection. Once poverty, misery, vice, crime, and war were removed by proper social reforms, all would be well. According to Godwin, "Make men wise, and by that very operation you make them free ... There will be no war, no crime, no administration of justice as it is called, and no government. Besides this, there will be neither disease, anguish, melancholy, nor resentment. Every man will seek with effable ardor the good of all."[5]

Others, seeing poverty and the sordid conditions of the peasants and urban masses, were not so optimistic about man's perfectibility. In 1798 a controversy broke out with the publication of one of the most famous books of all time, *An Essay on the Principle of Population as it Affects the Future Improvement of Society, with Remarks on the Speculation of Mr. Godwin, M. Condorcet, and Other Writers*, written by Thomas Robert Malthus, an English clergyman.[6] Malthus contended that Godwin and others were wrong in blaming circumstances for our social ills. It was man's original nature that was at fault. The sexual urges leading to reproduction tended to people the world more rapidly than people could increase their sustenance.

In a time when romantic reformers were preaching doctrines of unlimited human progress, Malthus had gone to work making calculations concerning the relation of food supply to population increase. He argued that there is a "constant tendency in all animated life to increase beyond the nourishment prepared for it"— that is, animal life is endowed with the capacity for constant rapid reproduction, but the food supply has definite limits.

Applying this principle to human beings, Malthus worked out the following formula: "Population, when unchecked, goes on doubling

---

[4]J. J. Spengler, "Malthus's Total Population Theory: a Restatement and Reappraisal," *Canadian Journal of Economics and Political Science*, 1945, 11: 245. All quotations by permission. This entire article is a thoughtful discussion of Malthus and his period.

[5]Quoted by J. O. Hertzler, *Social Progress* (New York: Appleton-Century-Crofts, 1928), pp. 46–47.

[6]The second edition, 1803, was called *An Essay on the Principle of Population, or a View of Its Past and Present Effects on Human Happiness with an Inquiry into Our Prospects Respecting the Future Removal or Mitigation of the Evils Which It Occasions.*

itself every twenty-five years, or increases in geometric ratio." Food supply, which he called the "means of subsistence," under circumstances the most favorable to human industry, could not possibly be made to increase faster than in arithmetical ratio.[7] In other words, a population would increase every twenty-five years in the ratio of 1, 2, 4, 8, 16, 32, 64, 128, 256, and so on, while the food supply would increase, at best, in the ratio of 1, 2, 3, 4, 5, 6, 7, 8, 9, etc. According to this computation, in three hundred years the ratio of the population to the means of subsistence would be 13 to 4,096.

Population does not increase at the highest theoretically possible level, however; and Malthus recognized that there were two kinds of checks on population increase—positive checks and preventative checks. The *positive* checks are those which increase the death rate and arise from want of adequate subsistence, poverty, disease, starvation and war. The *preventive* checks include celibacy, deferment of marriage, and moral (that is, sexual) restraint, leading to reduction in the number of births. Malthus argued that no devices of political or economic organization or of emigration would stop the positive checks from operating, but only moral restraint of the biological passions. This did not imply, so rationalized the pious Malthus, that God has not our welfare at heart, but rather that "natural and moral evil seems to be the instrument employed by the Deity in admonishing us to avoid any mode of conduct which is not suited to our being and will consequently injure our happiness."[8]

The doctrine of progress and man's perfectibility was not easily dismissed. Nineteenth-century enthusiasts arose on every hand to denounce Malthus. Significant expressions of optimism were found in the works of those who denied that population necessarily outruns the food supply. Karl Marx argued that the problem of feeding the population results from the exploitation of the masses by the ruling class. Once the injustices of faulty distribution of wealth were remedied, there would be food enough for all. Henry George, best known for his theory of the single tax on land values, argued that "nowhere can want be properly attributed to the pressure of population against the power to procure subsistence in the then existing degree of human knowledge; that everywhere the vice and misery attributed to overpopulation can be traced to warfare,

---

[7]Spengler, p. 245. Malthus confuses the reader by identifying food supply with subsistence. At times he discusses what we today call "level of living," which includes more than food. Elsewhere he uses "means of subsistence" to mean only food. For a most incisive discussion of the relation of population to food supply, see Edward S. Deevey, Jr., "The Human Population," *Scientific American*, 1960, 203: 195–198, 200, 202–204.

[8]These quotations are from the 9th edition of Malthus's *Essay*.

tyranny, and oppression, which prevent knowledge from being utilized and deny the security essential to production." He thought it was only a faulty economic and political order that "in the midst of wealth condemns men to want."[9]

Throughout the nineteenth century, while the theorists argued, population continued to increase at a rapid rate. And in spite of "free" land and increased industrial production, poverty, misery, crime, and vice persisted. With a view to improving the condition of the masses, there arose in England about 1880 a movement known as *Neo-Malthusianism*. It aimed to educate the masses consciously to reduce the number of births. The leaders, Annie Besant and Charles Bradlaugh, argued that the spread of contraceptive practices in order to reduce the birth rate would lead to an improvement in health, in family life, in the standards of living, and in morality.

But the critics of birth control were not far behind. As birth rates did decline, especially in the Western world, the cry of "race suicide" was heard. One of the most vocal exponents of large families and rapid increase of population was Theodore Roosevelt, who expressed the beliefs and attitudes of millions who saw in the declining birth rate a threat to man's very existence. Then too, many feared that the price of a Neo-Malthusian program might be loss of the white man's supremacy in the world.

The debate still goes on. Thirty years ago, the world heard such dictators as Hitler and Mussolini in Europe and the militarists of Japan calling for larger populations in their countries. Since their downfall and in the face of postwar problems, most students of the issue have stressed the dangerous implications of the continuing growth of population as it relates to food and other resources and to standard of living. In the face of some divergencies of interpretation about the seriousness of the present-day population problem, and especially in view of some of the sharp differences in rates of growth in various areas of the world, let us examine some of the facts about the relation of population to resources.[10]

Food Supply and Population

Population and food supply are related, but these are not the only factors to be taken into consideration in discussing the increase in world population. The densely crowded countries of northwestern

[9]Quoted by E. A. Ross, *Tests and Challenges in Sociology* (New York: Appleton-Century-Crofts, 1931), p. 8.
[10]See Kingsley Davis, "The Theory of Change and Response in Modern Demographic History," *Population Index*, 1963, 29: 345–366.

Europe could not possibly have supported themselves on the food raised on their own land; they furnished goods and services to other regions which, in turn, provided them with foodstuffs and raw materials. Technological advances provided work for millions in the production, manufacture, and distribution of goods and services. So long as commerce between nations of the world went on freely, large massing of population in industrial centers did not appear to be a serious problem.

Yet in spite of the tremendous improvement in agricultural production (most of which has come from mechanical devices and not from improvement in natural fertility of land), in spite of the rising consciousness of the need to conserve water and forest and mineral resources, in spite of the possibility of synthetic foods produced by applied chemistry, and in spite of increased industrialization, the population in many parts of the world is still pressing on the means of subsistence: foods, timber, coal, iron, and oil. Clearly, land and climate distinctly limit the range of man's habitation. Of the total land surface of the earth, little more than one-third is available for raising food and other necessary articles of consumption. Yet the number of people that the world will support is, of course, definitely related to the standard of living. The earth would support at a bare subsistence level a great many more people than there are now. Improved use of present arable lands and their extension—for example, the use of rich tropical lands in South America and of the semiarid regions of Asia—could add measurably to the available food supply. But whatever else happens, nearly all authorities agree that there must be a reduction in the birth rate and an increase in the practice of birth control. Those supporting the latter measure are up against formidable opposition, however.[11]

THE DEMOGRAPHIC TRANSITION

On the basis of what is known about the changes in population which accompanied the industrialization and urbanization of Western societies, students of population have developed a generalization called the demographic transition. It is a generalization that holds that societies experience similar demographic changes in birth, death, and growth rates as they become industrialized. Generally speaking, there are three major stages in the demographic transition. (See Figure 9-2.)

Societies in stage I are in a situation of "high growth potential."

---

[11]For accounts of resistance to the use of contraceptive devices, see Carl E. Taylor, John B. Wyon, and John E. Gordon, "Ecological Determinants of Population Growth," *Milbank Memorial Fund Quarterly,* 1958, 36: 107–125.

Figure 9-2   The Demographic Transition

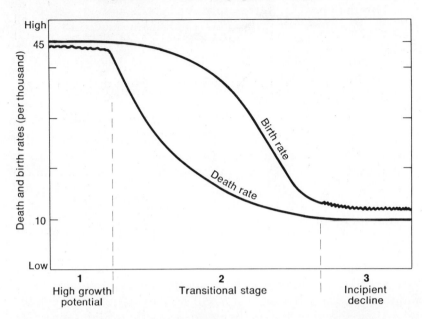

This stage characterizes the demographic balance of preindustrial societies in which there is a high birth rate and a high death rate. Consequently, the rate of population growth is quite low. Since in these societies the birth rate remains high, the rate of population growth depends upon the death rate which varies with the positive checks of droughts, natural disasters, and so on. Life expectancy in these societies is relatively low, typically less than 35 years, and the median age of the population is relatively low—approximately 15 years.

Stage II is the stage of the "demographic transition." This stage characterizes the demographic situation of societies undergoing industrialization. In the early phases of industrialization the death rate begins to fall but the birth rate remains high. As industrialization continues, the death rate plummets and the birth rate begins to fall. Since the death rate decreases first and much more rapidly than the birth rate, the rate of population growth is very high—indeed, there is a "population explosion." Life expectancy is about 45–50 years and the median age is about 21–23 years.

The third and final stage characterizes "mature" industrial societies and is called the stage of "incipient decline." Societies in this stage have relatively low birth and death rates and therefore the growth rate is low and relatively stabilized. The life expectancy in these societies is about 70 years and the median age is about 30 years.

Figure 9-3   The Demographic Transition in the West

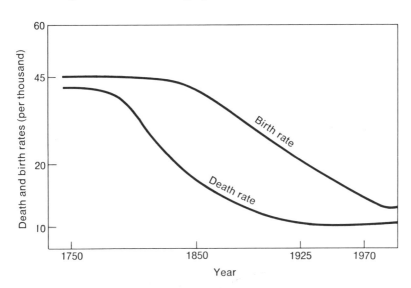

Obviously, a major question for people concerned with the population crisis is whether or not one can predict the future of population in the "third world" on the basis of the Western experience. Two-thirds of the world has not completed the demographic transition. In considering this question, a number of factors must be taken into account. First of all, as noted above, there has been a rapid increase in population in a number of countries that as yet have not become industrialized. This is the result of the diffusion of modern medical care independently of any basic change in the economy and education of these areas. Moreover, conditions in these regions are not precisely like those that existed in the nineteenth century when the cycle began in western Europe (and the United States). While far more efficient technologies for rapid industrialization are available today than in 1800, there is a dearth of resources and little new land for expanding agriculture.

As to voluntary restriction of births, the whole force of culture in some regions is contrary to such practices. It is questionable whether measures of birth control will be adopted before the industrialized culture patterns and demands for higher standards of life have become widespread in all classes and ancient and sacred folkways have largely disappeared. Moreover, the "third world" will have to make the transition in a much shorter time than Western societies did. In the West, the demographic transition took place over a period of about 125 years and many authorities argue that the world cannot now wait that long for the current population explosion to end.

Figure 9-4   The Demographic Transition in the Third World

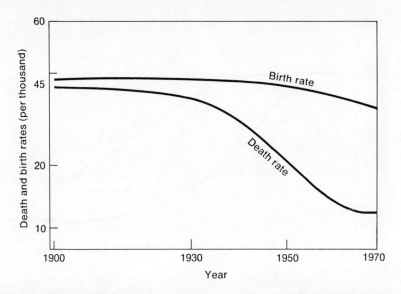

Density of Population

Population is by no means evenly distributed over the earth. Nor are all areas equally blessed with good climate, soils, and other resources that make them acceptable places to live. For example, the wide steppes, the deserts, and the extensive mountainous sections of Asia make up at least half of its land mass. These regions support very few people. In contrast, the rich valleys of India and China support millions. In other regions—the United States, Canada, and the Soviet Union in Europe—there are ample soil and other resources but relatively fewer people.

A measure frequently used in studies of population is density of persons per square mile of land area. Population density, however, must be interpreted in relation to the degree of industrialization, extent and kind of soil resources, and rates of growth. For example, Java and India are chiefly agricultural, and yet the pressure of numbers on the food supply is mounting year by year and the pressure on the arable lands is also increasing. Sumatra, an island neighbor of Java, has rich untapped soil resources, but the Javanese for the most part do not look with favor on migration to Sumatra. So too, there are some excellent unused areas in parts of southern India, but the millions in the congested sections of the country are not interested in moving to these distant areas. Australia, long a target of expanding Oriental populations, has recently been stimulating immigration from Great Britain, but so far is unwilling to accept Far Eastern people.

ILLUSTRATIVE DATA 9-1   THE POPULATION PROBLEM

Throughout most of human history, many societies have been governed by norms which encouraged people to have children. In tribal and pre-industrial societies, the idea of having too many people did not arise. With high infant and maternal mortality, the standard worry was that a society might diminish in size in a few generations and lose power. All this has changed with the advent of modern techniques of medical care and sanitation. Birth rates remain high in many societies where death rates have plummeted, and the world is faced with an accelerating rate of population growth.

World population breaks down into two well-defined categories:

(1) The low birth rate countries. These mainly comprise the industrial nations of Europe (including the U.S.S.R.), North America, Oceania, and Japan. Birth rates in these countries are under 25 births per 1,000 population per year. About a fourth of the world's people live in these relatively slow growing lands. The number of years to double their populations range from 700 years for Malta to 32 for New Zealand. In East Germany, population is actually declining at a rate of .2 percent per year. The United States is growing more rapidly than most of the industrial countries and, at the present rate, its population would double in about 40 years.

(2) The so-called "developing countries." These comprise most of the population of Asia, Africa, and Latin America. They have birth rates at traditionally high levels and declining death rates. Births range from 35 to 60 per 1,000 population per year. The increase in these countries is due to continuing traditionally high fertility rates combined with declining death rates. The rate of natural increase–being the difference between the birth rate and the death rate–ranges upwards from 2 percent to 4 percent per year, in the case of Costa Rica, where there are 5 births for every death.

The developing countries show a wide range in their rates of population increase. In a few of them, migration is a more important factor than the balance of births and deaths. In fact, the number of years to double population ranges downward from 78 in the case of Algeria, which has experienced heavy emigration, to 6 for oil-rich Kuwait, where immigration has been heavy.

A 3 percent rate of increase such as that which characterizes tropical Latin America doubles the population in 24 years. In a century of growth at this rate, a population increases 18 times. The population of Brazil, for example, now 84 million, would increase at the current rate of 3.1 percent to 1.7 billion by 2066.

In general, the countries with the most rapid population growth are least equipped to deal with it. Per capita income is distressingly low; in many countries hunger and illiteracy are endemic. Because of the high fertility and declining mortality, a large proportion of the people in these countries are children. The percentage of the population under 15 years of age in the high birth rate countries averages about 40 percent. In contrast, the low birth rate countries have less than 30 percent of their population under 15 years of age, with a correspondingly lower dependency load.

This has many important social and economic implications. Such relatively large proportions of youth in the developing countries demand heavy expenditures from an already overburdened economy for clothing, housing, feeding, and schooling. This tends to siphon off the limited capital resources urgently needed for economic development. In the United States, with a per capita income of over $3,000 and 31 percent of the population under 15, the costs of schooling absorb a major part of state and local taxes and considerable federal subsidies. The per pupil cost of education in the United States averages more than $500 per year. This is about 6 times the annual per capita income of the people in India, which is estimated to be less than $100.

The high child ratio in the developing countries has another somber aspect. Each year, on the average, an increasing number of young people will be moving into the reproductive age brackets. Barring changes in the death rate, the number of women in the high fertility age group, 20–30, will increase by approximately a half in the next 20 years. This growing "fertility potential" adds significantly to the gravity of the looming population crisis.

Source: Population Reference Bureau, "World Population Growth Accelerates." Washington, D.C.: Population Reference Bureau, January 16, 1967.

Highly industrialized countries, such as Britain and Belgium, are able to support relatively high concentrations of population. Both countries raise only a part of their own food, and export manufactured goods in exchange for a heavy amount of foods and raw materials. If they had to depend on their own farming, both these countries would probably soon feel the pinch of famine. The population density per square mile of arable land in Britain is about 2,500 persons, in Belgium about 2,200. A similar situation exists in Japan, whose growth in numbers has been possible only because it has been the only highly industrial nation of the Far East. Japan's attempt to get more and more of the trade of that region was one reason for its entry into World War II. With a density of about 3,200 persons per square mile of arable land, Japan probably could not provide its own food.

It seems clear that the matter of population density can be understood only in relation to the amount and nature of basic resources— agricultural and otherwise—and the extent of industrialization as these, in turn, are related to absolute numbers of people and rates of growth. Yet the future of many industrialized nations, especially in Europe, is not altogether certain, despite their relatively stable populations. Without external markets they may face a lowering of standards of living as other nations become industrialized and no longer import manufactured goods from Europe.

FERTILITY AND MORTALITY

The two basic determinants of population size are birth and death rates. These, together with the rates of in- and out-migration, are the only immediate determinants of population change in a society. All other factors such as wars and famines make their influence felt through one of three factors—fertility, mortality, and migration.

The size of a population at any given time can therefore be stated algebraically as:

$$\text{Population}_{t_2} = \text{Population}_{t_1} + \text{Births}_{t_1-t_2} - \text{Deaths}_{t_1-t_2}$$
$$+ \text{ or } - \text{ Net Migration}_{t_1-t_2}$$

where t_1 and t_2 refer to an earlier and a later point in time respectively, and where t_1-t_2 refers to the interval between the two times.

Birth Rates

In discussing rates of growth, it is necessary to distinguish between fecundity and fertility. *Fecundity* is the potential power of reproduction in a population—the birth rate if every woman of childbearing age bore all the children she possibly could. *Fertility* is the actual rate of reproduction. It is measured by the birth rate, but we must distinguish between the crude birth rate and the specific birth rate. The *crude birth rate* is simply the number of births per 1,000 people at a given period. The *specific birth rate* is the births per 1,000 women of childbearing age, usually considered to be from 15 to 44 years. The crude birth rate gives an estimate of the fertility of any population, but it does not take into account the age and sex distribution of the population.

For long-range comparisons of population growth or decline, the *net reproduction rate* is a better index than either crude or specific birth rates. Such a rate is based on the average number of daughters that will be born per 100 females starting life together if birth and death rates at different age levels remain constant. Thus a net reproduction rate of 1.00 means that, on the average, the survivors of a group of 100 females of the same age will give birth to 100 daughters. An index of 1.00 means that a given population is replacing itself; anything less means that it is not.

As we noted earlier, until the fourth decade of this century, there was a steady decline in the birth rate in countries of western Europe, in the British Dominions, and in the United States. In fact, in some countries the net reproduction rate fell to less than 1.00. But during World War II and subsequently, both the marriage rate and the birth rate increased for a time. As a result, the net reproduction rate in most countries of the same world areas has gone up.

Reliable data from the Soviet Union and its satellites is not easy to secure, but there are indications that birth rates in these countries also rose after World War II.

Death Rates

Mortality may be measured by the *crude death rate*, which is the ratio between the number of individuals who die in a given time and the median number of individuals alive during that interval, usually stated in thousands. Thus a death rate of 12 means 12 deaths per 1,000 of the population. Specific death rates may be computed for age, sex, and other factors.

Throughout history the births in many societies have just about balanced the deaths, so that the population size remained practically stationary for generations. This was true for long periods in the Orient and, until three centuries ago, in Europe. In fact, until recently, in all countries outside western Europe, the United States, Canada, New Zealand, Australia, and the scattered European colonies, high death rates have accompanied high birth rates. Among nonliterate peoples the birth rates and the mortality rates are both unusually high by our standards.

Recent decades have witnessed a rapid decline in the death rate. This trend has been going on in Europe for well over a century. There has been a similar decline in the death rate in the United States, where the annual average in 1906–1910 was 15 per 1,000. The death rate has fallen off considerably since then, except in 1918, when it was 18 per thousand because of an influenza epidemic. By 1920 it had dropped to 13 per thousand. Since 1950 the death rate has varied between 9.3 and 9.7 per thousand. In 1970 the death rate was 9.4 per thousand.

While the principal decline in the death rate has occurred among Western nations, the phenomenon is worldwide. Although birth rates are also falling, mortality rates in many regions are falling somewhat faster.

Medical science has dramatically influenced the death rate for the early years of life. A noteworthy decline in infant and child mortality is evident in every large country and in most small ones. The decrease in child mortality is due in large part to: (1) improvement in child care at home, especially in feeding and sanitation; (2) decrease in the number of children born to the average mother, permitting more adequate care of those who are born—studies in France, England, and the United States bear out the fact that infant mortality is much lower in small families than in large; (3) improvement in economic status of large sections of the population; and (4) control of diseases of childhood and early adult life. Additional progress in the conquest of disease the world over makes for the reduction of death in all age groups.

Reduction in infant and child deaths means an increase in life expectancy. In 1920 the life expectancy at birth in the United States was 54 years; in 1968 it was 70 years.

INTERNATIONAL RELATIONS AND POPULATION PROBLEMS

The survival of humankind has always rested on a somewhat precarious balance between the size of population and the means of subsistence. This balance is maintained largely by fluctuations in the death rate, as Malthus pointed out. It is quite clear that at least half of the world's population is living at or below a mere subsistence level. World affairs and the future of peace and welfare of the world are closely bound up with differences in rates of growth as they are related to food and other resources, health, and extent of industrialization.

Income, Food and Death Rates

While it is difficult to secure completely accurate information on the relation of death rates to standards of food consumption and income, estimates have been made. These give a rather grim picture. The countries of high mortality are also those of low income and inadequate diet. The "developed" countries of the world have about one-third of the world's population and four-fifths of the world income. The world is really separated into two great population pools: one is relatively contracting; the other is extending itself rapidly. In the one, the ratio of population to resources has been brought under control. In the other, the Malthusian factors continue to operate. The problem is how to reconcile this disparity. To meet the present difficulty a number of changes appear to be necessary.

Increase in Food

One crucial and immediate task is to increase the world production of foodstuffs to take care of the increasing and undernourished populations. Considerable advances have been made, but in India and Indonesia—to note two of the most needy regions—the race between people and production goes on apace. Only 7 per cent of the land area of the world is under cultivation and there are wide variations in the per capita density of land used for food production. In eastern and southern Asia there are, respectively, less than 0.5 and 0.8 of an acre of cultivated land per person. Yet these are the very regions where the pressure of population on food resources is becoming most severe. By way of contrast, in North America there are nearly 4 acres of cultivated land per capita. Moreover, the yield in calories per acre is much higher so that the output of food per person is vastly greater.

Industrialization

The development of industry is also thought to be an important step in relieving the pressure of population. The argument is that the cycle of growth which resulted in stabilization of population in the Western world, represents a pattern of change essential for the rest of the world. However, the inadequacy of resources for further industrialization and the constant need for new capital are two of several problems that obstruct industrialization in many countries. Moreover, the shift of large numbers of persons from peasant agriculture to skilled and semiskilled industrial occupations would not be easy. As has been demonstrated by the experience of the Soviet Union, it takes time to train the workers of a peasant economy to become factory hands and time is crucial. J. J. Spengler, studying the relation of economy to population and resources, was not optimistic about the future.

> The evidence presented . . . lends no support to the easy optimism of those who see in industrialization a simple and ready solution for the overpopulation that already affects more than half the world. Countries marked by intense overpopulation must virtually raise themselves by their own bootstraps. They lack land, capital, and the opportunity to make up this lack. They can get only limited relief through trade and capital imports.[12]

Migration

One of the oldest proposals to alleviate, if not solve, the world's population difficulties is to get people to go somewhere else. Some contend that, instead of transferring capital goods and setting up new industries, people should emigrate to other, less crowded areas. One should view with some suspicion schemes to stimulate the migration of large numbers of people from crowded to less crowded areas. It has been shown that, unless the country of origin is cutting its own birth and death rates at the time of out-migration, emigration will only temporarily relieve the pressure. The places of those

---

[12]J. J. Spengler, "Aspects of the Economics of Population Growth, Parts I and II," *Southern Economic Journal*, 1947, 14: 123–147; and 1948, 14: 233–265. Quotation from p. 265. By permission.

ILLUSTRATIVE DATA 9-2   POPULATION CHANGE IN JAPAN

Japan constitutes one case study in the demographic correlates of modernization of a predominantly industrial type, albeit a peculiarly significant one. Japan's historic culture is Eastern. Her industrial and urban transformation was thus divorced from a base in the nonmaterial culture of the West except in so far as specific elements were deliberately selected for imitation or diffused through more informal mechanisms. . . .

The population growth that accompanies indigenous and comprehensive industrial development and the slowing of that growth through a progressive limitation of childbearing are alike products of the changes in ways of living and thinking that are precondition and product of industrialization. The relations of culture and demography proceed through the intermediation of the economic process itself. Political stability, a disciplined labor force, and rapid capital accumulation are necessary aspects of substantial industrialization. Cultural factors exert a major influence on the extent and speed of the economic transformation, for there are cultural preconditions to indigenous economic transformations and cultural limitations to imposed transformations. As industrialization extends over time and expands over wider segments of a nation, the demographic transition of declining mortality and declining fertility becomes a necessary consequence of the accompanying economic pressures and cultural stimuli. But industrialization regarded as economic, political, or social process is in turn modified by the changing dynamics of population. The relationships are complex; the particular constellation of factors that produced the population growth of Imperial Japan will not be duplicated in detail elsewhere. The fundamental fact, though, is that experience within the East corroborates the hypothesis deducible from Western experience: substantial increases in the size of the total population is a correlate of industrialization, but the social and psychological transformations implicit in industrialization result eventually in a lessened rate of reproduction and a slowing growth. Given the technologies and the basic values of the twentieth century, both population growth and the ultimate slowing of the growth are predictable consequences of the industrial and urban transformation of agrarian cultures.

If the experience of the one nation in Monsoon Asia that has achieved a substantial degree of industrialization can be transferred to project the future of the other cultures, industrialization and urbanization will lead eventually to declines in fertility that will first lessen and then eliminate the growth that accompanies modernization.

Source: Irene B. Taeuber, "Population and Labor Force in the Industrialization of Japan, 1850–1950." *Economic Growth: Brazil, India, Japan,* eds. S. Kuznets, W. E. Moore, and J. J. Spengler (Durham, N. C.: Duke University Press, 1955), pp. 358–359. By permission.

who go somewhere else will be taken by the newborn of those who remain at home. As Notestein puts it, "... emigration will not check growth in the most important areas of population pressure at the present stage of their demographic evolution. It would be unfortunate to waste the open spaces of the world in a fashion that could only intensify future problems of adjustment."[13] Radhakamal Mukerjee believes that "a complementary program of birth control and 'open door'" should be undertaken. The expanding and pre-industrial countries would practice birth control, but in the meantime the industrialized countries would permit immigration to relieve the present pressures of the Orient especially.[14]

Population Pressures, War, and Peace

Although imbalances of peoples and means of livelihood have been known in history, the present problem of disproportion between population and means of survival is particularly acute. The "have-nots" are pushing on the "haves" for a redistribution of resources, a "push" which the latter resent and resist. As Thompson says,

> In order for population pressures to become dangerous to peace, the people of a given country must feel this pressure and believe (rightly or wrongly) that something can be done about acquiring larger resources by force. ... When ... a people comes to feel that it is being kept from lands and resources it really needs by peoples who are not using them or are using them in only a limited way, we have a dangerous situation.[15]

The problem is sociological, rather than strictly biological. When disease, vice, poverty, and early death are taken for granted, people are not likely to bestir themselves to raise their level of living. It is when hope, not despair, is generated that pressures arise. Individuals and nations come to feel discriminated against because they do not have free access to the world's resources. They view with envious eye the great expanses of sparsely settled lands in Australia or the Americas and they object to the laws in those countries which discriminate against the immigration of Orientals.

---

[13]Frank W. Notestein, "Problems of Policy in Relation to Areas of Heavy Population Pressure," in *Demographic Studies of Selected Areas of Rapid Growth* (New York: Milbank Memorial Fund, 1944), p. 150. By permission.
[14]See Radhakamal Mukerjee, "Population Theory and Politics," *American Sociological Review*, 1941, 6: 784–793.
[15]W. S. Thompson, *Population Problems*, 4th ed. (New York: McGraw-Hill Book Co., 1953), pp. 359–360. By permission.

Population imbalances and pressures are bound up with economic and political trends. Strong nationalist states, many with imperialist ambitions, have dominated the world's resources and industrial development for more than 300 years. It is very doubtful that the world, split into warring sovereign states which precariously fluctuate between peace and war, will realize a full and permanent peace so long as gross inequities in resources continue to increase.

POPULATION PATTERNS

Certain aspects of community life reflect or are affected by variations in the sex and age composition of the population. If, for example, there are a great many more males than females, as was true in most pioneer communities, marriage rates will be affected, and there will be a high percentage of unmarried men but few unmarried women. If the proportion of children is high, as in residential suburbs, the problem of education will certainly be different than if there are very few children, as is true of certain sections of our major cities inhabited largely by adult males. Again, when the population has a disproportionate number of people in the older age groups, a host of conditions involving the labor force and medical care will exist that are not found when the population is younger.

The importation of foreign-born adults into a community produces problems of accommodation, acculturation, and assimilation that will not be found when the population is recruited from births within the community. From about 1820 to World War I, the United States experienced an increasing influx of foreigners. Because the chief call was for a vigorous labor force, the age and sex distribution of the foreign-born tended to be skewed in the direction of the males and concentrated in the middle range of age classes. After World War I, severe restrictive laws were passed to reduce the number of immigrants to be admitted in any one year. As a result, foreign-born people have become an ever-smaller part of the American population.

Internal Migration

Throughout the history of the United States, the basic pattern of migration has been from east to west. This was true when the early colonists landed on the East coast and moved inland; it was true when the pioneers pushed West to homestead land and it is still true.

Young adults account for most of the migration in the United States.

People in early adult life constitute the most mobile segment of our civilian population. They generally migrate to take advantage of job opportunities and to provide better living conditions for their families. In recent years there has also been an increasing tendency for people at the older ages to settle in areas with mild climates, particularly southern California and Florida.[16]

The other basic pattern of internal migration has been from farm to city: the nation has become more and more urbanized. The extent of movement from farm to cities varies greatly from region to region, but in general it involves from one-fourth to one-half of all farm youth. For the country as a whole it has been estimated

Table 9-2   Selected Population Characteristics of the
United States, 1620–1970

Year	Population (in millions)	Rate of Population Increase in the Preceding Decade	Population Density*	Median Age
1620	.002			
1650	.05			
1700	.3			
1750	1			
1790	4		4.5	
1800	5	3.0˙	6.1	16
1820	10		5.6	17
1840	17	2.8	9.8	18
1860	31		10.6	19
1880	50	2.6	16.9	21
1900	76	1.9	25.6	23
1910	92		31.0	24
1920	106	1.4	35.6	25
1930	123	1.5	41.2	27
1940	132	0.7	44.2	29
1950	151	1.4	42.6	30
1960	179	1.7	50.5	30
1970	203	1.3	57.4	28

*Population per square mile of land area.
SOURCE: U.S. Bureau of the Census, *Statistical Abstract of the United States, 1971* (Washington, D.C.: U.S. Government Printing Office, 1971); and U.S. Bureau of the Census, *Historical Statistics of the United States, Colonial Times to 1957* (Washington, D.C.: U.S. Government Printing Office, 1960).

[16]From "Population Still Moving Westward," *Statistical Bulletin*, 1955, 36: 8.

that about two-fifths of all individuals between the ages of 10 and 19 years who lived on farms in 1920 had migrated from there by 1930. The cityward drift of population continues as commercialization and industrialization of agriculture expand and as contacts between cities and farms continue to grow. A particularly interesting phase of this migration has been the steady shift of blacks from the rural South to Northern industrial centers and to employment areas in the West. With further mechanization of agriculture in the South, we may expect the northward shift to continue.

Table 9-3 Population Characteristics of the World's 25 Largest Countries, 1969

Country	World Rank	Estimated Population (in millions)	Estimated Annual Per Cent Increase (1963–1969)	Estimated Population Density
China	1	740	1.5	200
India	2	537	2.8	425
U.S.S.R.	3	241	1.2	28
United States	4	203	1.2	57
Indonesia	5	116	2.7	201
Pakistan	6	112	2.2	306
Japan	7	102	1.1	716
Brazil	8	91	3.2	28
Nigeria	9	64	2.6	179
Germany, Fed. Rep. of	10	59	1.0	612
United Kingdom	11	56	0.6	591
Italy	12	53	0.8	458
France	13	50	0.9	237
Mexico	14	49	3.8	64
Philippines	15	37	3.8	321
Thailand	16	35	3.4	175
Turkey	17	34	2.7	114
Spain	18	33	1.0	169
Poland	19	33	1.0	259
United Arab Republic	20	33	2.7	84
Korea, Republic of	21	31	2.6	819
Iran	22	28	3.2	44
Burma	23	27	2.3	103
Ethiopia	24	25	2.2	52
Argentina	25	24	1.6	22
World total		3,552	2.0	68

SOURCE: U.S. Bureau of the Census, *Pocket Data Book, USA, 1971* (Washington, D.C.: U.S. Government Printing Office, 1971), p. 38.

Median Age

The populations of western Europe, the United States, and the British Dominions are growing older—that is, there is an increasingly higher ratio of individuals in the older age groups. A common measure of this shift is the increase in median age. (This is the age at which 50 per cent of the population falls above and 50 per cent below.) For the United States, to cite only one example, the median age in 1800 was 16 years; in 1860 it was 19 years; in 1900 it was 23 years; and in 1960 it was 30 years. During the last decade the median age in the United States has declined. In 1970 the median age of the U.S. population was 28.3 years.

Residence and Fertility

On the average, city families have fewer children than farm families. Such variations in fertility rates are not a recent phenomenon. They seem to have appeared as early as the eighteenth century in Europe, and they became increasingly evident as the Industrial Revolution spread, first throughout Great Britain and then on the Continent. They have been characteristic of the United States for a long time.

Religion and Fertility

Throughout Christian history, religious bodies have, on the whole, encouraged large families and opposed birth control. Now urbanization and secularization are undermining these traditional religious values. There have been a number of studies that reveal significant differences in the fertility rates of Protestants and Catholics, but for some time the true importance of the religious factor was veiled because other variables were not adequately studied.

One study of the relation of religious affiliation and fertility was made by Donald J. Bogue, who used 1957 data from the federal Bureau of the Census. Bogue found, among other things, "that no one of the religious groups is subject to uncontrolled fertility.... Although the fertility of every religious group is above the replacement level, no group is characterized by rates of children ever born that imply an average of 5 or 6 children per married woman. Thus, fertility control is a widely-accomplished fact throughout all major American religious groups."[17]

Baptists have the highest fertility, but this partly reflects the high

[17]Bogue, *The Population of the United States*, p. 696. See also Frank W. Notestein, "Class Differences in Fertility," *The Annals of the American Academy of Political and Social Science*, 1936, 188: 32.

percentage of blacks in this church, as well as the fact that a large percentage of the Baptists, both blacks and whites, were born in the rural sections of the South where birth rates are also high for non-Baptists. Among older women, the Roman Catholics are more fertile than any other group except the Baptists. But Bogue goes on to indicate that younger Catholic women have so fully accepted planned parenthood that "their age-standardized fertility measure in 1957 was only one per cent above that of the nation."[18] The lowest birth rates are found among the Jewish and Presbyterian women. Lutherans have moderately low fertility rates, and the Methodists have average fertility. It has been pointed out, however, that these differential birth rates among denominations also reflect age, color, residential, and occupational variations. Yet Bogue claims that "there is . . . unmistakable evidence that differences in religious doctrines *do* stimulate fertility differences, independent of these other traits."[19]

A study of social-psychological factors affecting fertility (of the white population of Indianapolis, Indiana) tends to confirm Bogue's views. This investigation of 6,551 completed families showed significant differences in fertility between Catholics and Protestants. Of the Protestant couples, 67 per cent had only one or two children, while of the Catholic couples only 52 per cent had this few. The average number of children in Protestant families was 2.19 and 2.74 in Catholic families. These differences were found at all economic levels except the very lowest, where the size of the Protestant families slightly exceeded the size of Catholic families.[20]

Earlier European studies showed that Catholics tend to have larger families than Protestants. Yet, because the probable effects of income, class, education, and locality were not carefully controlled, it is difficult to tell how much of the difference was due to such factors and how much to religious views alone. One cannot neglect the probability, however, that religious values do influence fertility. The high ratio of children to women in Utah, for instance, may be attributed to the emphasis the Mormon Church places on the desirability of large families.[21] It is generally assumed that as people "lose their religion" they become more inclined to use some means of restricting conception.[22]

---

[18]*Ibid.*, p. 696.
[19]*Ibid.*, p. 697.
[20]Clyde V. Kiser and P. K. Whelpton, "Social and Psychological Factors Affecting Fertility, II: Variations in the Size of Completed Families of 6,551 Native White Couples in Indianapolis," *Milbank Memorial Fund Quarterly*, 1944, 22: 72–105.
[21]See Harold T. Christensen, "Mormon Fertility: A Survey of Student Opinion," *American Journal of Sociology*, 1948, 53: 270–275.
[22]See A. C. Kinsey, *et al.*, *Sexual Behavior in the Human Male* (Philadelphia: W. B. Saunders Co., 1948), pp. 479–487.

Kinsey found some differences in degree of sexual activity—as he defined it—among religious groups. The Orthodox Jews and devout Catholics were less sexually active than those Jews and Catholics who reported little interest in their traditional religious faiths. Similarly, there was some variation among Protestants in consonance with strength of religious belief. There is obviously some correlation between frequency of sexual intercourse and likelihood of pregnancy when contraceptives are not used.

Stratification and Fertility

Differential fertility is also associated with social status. A study by Berent indicates that both social class and social mobility affect fertility. Both upper-class position and upward mobility have a marked effect on lowering the birth rate. It is highly probable that a similar pattern is found throughout the industrialized Western world. An analysis of census data shows the persistence of differentials in fertility as related to occupation, income, and education. Persons in the upper economic categories tend to postpone somewhat longer the birth of their first child and to have their last child after fewer years of marriage than persons in the lower economic categories. Beginning in the last quarter of the nineteenth century and continuing to the present, there has been a steady decline in family size in all classes in Western industrialized countries. The rate of this decrease has not been uniform by class, however, as a number of studies of differential fertility have indicated.[23]

> The classes that first gained control over fertility lived predominantly in the cities and were of better than average socioeconomic status. However, the knowledge of conception control spread gradually–first, to other urban groups of lower socioeconomic status, and later, to rural groups. As this took place fertility declined in all classes, but for some time it continued to decline more rapidly in the upper socioeconomic classes. ... Since it seems likely ... that economic considerations are going to play a more and more important role in determining the size of the family as voluntary control increases, it seems not improbable that the less favored economic groups will soon have as small families as the more favored groups, or, perhaps, even smaller.[24]

Mortality

During the past century, there has been not only a general decline in birth rates in Western countries but also a marked decrease in

---

[23]For a review of these studies, see Thompson, *Population Problems*, pp. 191–194.
[24]*Ibid.*, p. 195. By permission.

Table 9-4   Fertility Differentials in the United States, 1964
(Number of Children per 1,000 Women 15–44 Years Old)

Money Income of Family	Number of Children per Thousand
$10,000 and over	2,402
$7,500–$9,999	2,420
$5,000–$7,499	2,500
$4,000–$4,999	2,527
$3,000–$3,999	2,728
$2,000–$2,999	2,840
Below $1,999	2,877
Husband's Occupation	
Professional, technical, and kindred workers	2,227
Proprietors, managers, and officials	2,553
Clerical and kindred workers	2,085
Sales workers	2,164
Craftsmen, foremen, and kindred workers	2,583
Operatives and kindred workers	2,606
Service workers	2,436
Laborers, except farm and mine	3,170
Farmers and farm managers	3,147
Farm laborers and foremen	3,443

SOURCE: *Current Population Reports*, Series P-20, No. 147 (January 5, 1966), pp. 16 and 17.

the mortality rates. For example, the crude death rate in Sweden during 1808–1812 was 33 per 1,000, and 26 in France for the same period. In 1950 the corresponding rates were 13 and 10. In 1848–1852 the crude death rate in England and Wales was 23; in 1970 it was 12. These rates vary widely from country to country, but in some countries they are dropping quite sharply. Comparable demographic data for some sections of the world are still inadequate. This is true for most of Africa, Southeast Asia, China, and certain areas in the Near East. Nevertheless, what evidence we have seems to support the idea that in these regions, too, the death rate has been going down in recent decades. For the United States as a whole, adequate mortality statistics were not available before 1900. In that year the crude death rate was 17 per thousand. Since the end of the Second World War, the U.S. crude death rate has stabilized between 9 and 10 per thousand. In 1969 the death rate was 9.5.

Other trends in the reduction of the death rate in the United States since 1870 show these facts: (1) The mortality rate for infants (persons under one year of age) did not decline materially until after 1900, when the infant death rate was 162 per thousand. By 1968 the infant death rate had dropped to 22. The infant death rate for blacks and other nonwhites in 1968, however, was 35 per thousand, thus reflecting one major consequence of racial discrimination.[25] (2) The death rate for individuals over four years old but under middle age has moved slowly downward. And (3) the mortality rate for persons in the upper-age brackets has remained about the same.

One factor that has long influenced the death rate has been high maternal mortality. This has been drastically reduced by advances in medical science. In 1920 the maternal mortality rate was 80 per 10,000 live births and even as late as 1940 the maternal mortality rate was 32 for whites and 77 for nonwhites. In 1968 maternal mortality for whites was down to 1.7 and to 6.4 for nonwhites.

Age, Sex, and Mortality

The influence of disease on the death rate is qualified in most instances by age. Some diseases, such as diarrhea, whooping cough, mealses, diphtheria, and scarlet fever, occur chiefly in infancy and childhood. In addition, earliest infant mortality is affected by congenital defects. Other diseases, such as typhoid and pulmonary tuberculosis, attack middle life most frequently. Adults in the later years are most susceptible to pneumonia, cancer, diabetes, and to such organic breakdowns as heart and circulatory disorders, nephritis, and Bright's disease.

With the decrease in infant and childhood mortality and the aging of the population, there has been a change in the relative seriousness of acute and chronic diseases. Modern medicine and sanitation have largely eliminated the incidence of the acute diseases of childhood and have restricted the incidence and spread of typhoid, diphtheria, smallpox, and other acute disorders that formerly attacked young and old alike. In contrast, chronic diseases—that is, those that persist or recur with such virulence as to need continued medical and nursing care—have become more prevalent in the last half century.

For the younger ages, the disasters of disease and death tend to be related to poor living conditions, inadequate health care, and infectious diseases due to lack of adequate public health measures. Death in the later years seems most often related to organic breakdowns, which may have various causes—earlier infections, congenital defects, occupational hazards, poor medical care, and so on.

---

[25]Bogue, p. 177.

Changes in the causes of death are related not only to the advances of medical knowledge and skill, but also to shifts in the age distribution of the population and to improvement in levels of living. In the United States, there were more than four times as many people 65 years old or over in 1960 as there were in 1900, which means that disorders related to aging have become increasingly significant. At the beginning of the century, the leading causes of death were influenza and pneumonia, tuberculosis, and diarrhea and enteritis. In 1969 nearly 40 per cent of all deaths were due to diseases of the heart and about 17 per cent to cancer and related maligancies.[26] The fourth major cause is death by accidents.[27]

Sex, Marital Status, and Mortality

Demographic data show that women have a higher survival rate than men. Apparently a lethal selection begins almost from the start of life. More males are conceived than females, in a ratio of about 125 to 100. However, even prenatally, the death toll is higher for males than for females. At the time of birth the sex ratio is about 106 males to 100 females. But even this slight advantage does not last. Among infants under one year, death takes a higher toll of boys than girls. And right on through the age brackets, the death rate is lower among females. Up to age 65, the female rate is about half that of the male rate; at 65 years and over, the female rate is about one-third lower.

Another differential is evident when we compare the mortality of single, married, and widowed persons. Studies both in Europe and in this country reveal the general fact that married persons live longer than single persons. In general, however, single people have a lower death rate than widowed and divorced people.

Occupation and Mortality

The kind of work a person does will determine in part his exposure to various kinds of illness or accidents, and thus play a part in affecting type and time of death. Obviously, construction workers, truck drivers, and miners are more exposed to hazards of working conditions than are bookkeepers or schoolteachers. In discussing various studies of occupational mortality made in Great Britain, Thompson points out a vicious circle.

---

[26]See J. Frederic Dewhurst and Associates, *America's Needs and Resources: A New Survey* (New York: The Twentieth Century Fund, 1955), pp. 299–300. Also Bogue, pp. 197–198, and *Statistical Abstract of the United States, 1971* (Washington, D.C.: U.S. Government Printing Office, 1971), pp. 57–58.
[27]*Statistical Abstract of the United States, 1971,* p. 58.

... poor pay makes decent living impossible. The inevitable result of ... circumstance is an extremely high death rate in certain occupational groups. It is, perhaps, the living conditions enforced by poorly paid work, even more than the nature of the work itself, that cause the high death rates in many occupations.[28]

Residence and Mortality

For many decades, rural communities have had lower death rates than urban communities. In the United States the rural areas still have lower rates, but with the extension of public health facilities, sanitation, and improved medical care in the cities, the differences are lessening. An important element in the dropping of the death rate has been the sharp decline in infant mortality. One Census Bureau report notes that "Between 1915, the first year for which a comparable figure is available, and 1953, the infant mortality rate dropped 72 per cent."[29] The rural-urban differentials, however, continue. We may compare rural-urban differentials in metropolitan counties with like differences in nonmetropolitan counties. Table 9-5 presents these contrast for 1964. "The contrast in infant mortality rates between the metropolitan counties and the nonmetropolitan is greater than that between urban and rural areas. . . . The small cities show slightly lower rates than the large cities and the rural areas."[30]

Table 9-5   Rural-Urban Differentials in Infant Mortality in Metropolitan and Nonmetropolitan Counties in the United States, 1964. Deaths under One Year per 1,000 Live Births

Metropolitan Counties		Nonmetropolitan Counties	
Urban—white	21.7	Urban—white	23.0
Urban—nonwhite	38.3	Urban—nonwhite	43.6
Balance of Area—white	19.7	Balance of Area—white	22.4
Balance of Area—nonwhite	40.3	Balance of Area—nonwhite	46.9

SOURCE: *Vital Statistics of the United States, 1964.* Washington, D.C.: Department of Health, Education and Welfare. Volume II, Mortality, Table 7–2, p. 7–61.

INTERPRETIVE SUMMARY

Since the eighteenth century, and particularly in our century, the world has experienced a rapid growth in population. In industrial societies, the decline in the death rate as a result of medical progress and improved standards of living has been somewhat offset by the concomitant decline in the birth

---

[28]Thompson, p. 254. By permission.
[29]*Vital Statistics–Special Reports*, vol. 42, no. 15, January 4, 1956, p. 327.
[30]*Ibid.*, p. 329.

rate. Other societies have reaped the benefits of medical knowledge, which are relatively easy to administer as far as lowering the death rates is concerned, without managing to keep birth down.

One problem stemming from the population explosion in such countries is, of course, lack of food. Sharing knowledge about improved methods of agriculture, conservation, and birth control, and migration of people in underdeveloped countries to places with extra resources have been suggested to help solve the problem. Those who see industrialization as essential to improved standards of living would lend money and technicians to help countries to industrialize. All these suggestions have been tried and all have worked to some extent, though factors such as poor resources, cultural inertia, and widespread lack of education in the countries needing help have impeded improvement.

Western industrial societies are experiencing a long-range decline in fertility. However, rates of fertility vary among different groups and social categories. In the United States, though several interrelated factors affect birth rates, differences among groups are declining. For example, though city families on the average still have fewer children than do farm families, the differential is decreasing. Though birth rates still vary considerably among religious groups, the number of individuals of all faiths who are apparently planning family size is increasing. Again, though upper economic groups still tend to have fewer children, starting their families later and finishing earlier, this differential also has decreased markedly as contraceptive education has been made available to poor people and secularization has become widespread.

The death rate in Western countries, as well as in many non-Western countries, is also declining. The most striking decrease has come in the lower age groups, as medical science has conquered or restricted the diseases of childhood. Medical advances have also increased life expectancy. The fact that people are living longer has had consequences throughout the society.

SUGGESTIONS FOR FURTHER READING

Bogue, Donald J. *The Population of the United States*. Glencoe, Ill.: The Free Press, 1959. This is a basic reference that presents a clear and comprehensive description of the social characteristics of the population of the United States and analyzes the trends altering this composition.

Ehrlich, Paul, and Ehrlich, Anne H. *Population, Resources, Environment: Issues in Human Ecology*. San Francisco: W. H. Freeman and Company, 1970. This book is a plea for effective action to deal with the crisis in ecology.

Handlin, Oscar. *The Newcomers*. Cambridge: Harvard University Press, 1959. This book compares Puerto Rican adjustment in New York City with that of previous immigrants.

Hauser, Philip M., and Duncan, Otis Dudley, eds. *The Study of Population: An Inventory and Appraisal*. Chicago: University of Chicago Press, 1959.

The editors review the status of demography as a science and draw comparisons and interrelationships of demography with other system variables in sociology.

Hill, Reuben; Stycos, J. Mayone; and Back, Kurt W. *The Family and Population Control*. Chapel Hill: University of North Carolina Press, 1959. The Puerto Rican effort to popularize birth control is intensively analyzed.

Petersen, William. *Population*. New York: Macmillan, 1961. In addition to the usual coverage of fertility, mortality rates, and so forth, this book includes a chapter on the population of nonliterate peoples, one on pre-industrial societies, and one on population during the Industrial Revolution.

Spengler, Joseph J., and Duncan, Otis D., eds. *Demographic Analysis: Selected Readings*. Glencoe, Ill.: The Free Press, 1956. This volume presents basic demographic information and an analysis of certain concrete problems, with some attention to research methodology and techniques.

Spengler, Joseph J., and Duncan, Otis D., eds. *Population Theory and Policy: Selected Readings*. Glencoe, Ill.: The Free Press, 1956. This is a companion volume to the one above and presents papers dealing chiefly with demographic data as it relates to social structure and socioeconomic changes and demographic theory.

Thompson, W. S. *Population Problems*. 4th ed. New York: McGraw-Hill Book Company, 1953. This general text combines sociological theory and the basic facts of demography.

Westoff, Charles F., and Potvin, Raymond H. *College Women and Fertility Values*. Princeton, N. J.: Princeton University Press, 1967. A study of the attitudes of 15,000 freshmen and senior women in 45 American colleges and universities, this book examines religion, career intention, family background, and college experience as determinants of values concerning fertility.

Woytinsky, W. S., and Woytinsky, E. S. *World Population and Production: Trends and Outlook*. New York: The Twentieth Century Fund, 1953. This is a broad survey of the collective resources and of the economic performance and promise of the nations of the world.

Wrong, Dennis H. *Population*. New York: Random House, 1956. This brief introduction to demography is especially concerned with world population growth and distribution, with the continuing problems of people and food resources, and with problems of fertility, mortality, and migration.

OUR SUBJECT TODAY IS **URBAN ARCHITECTURE** OF THE NINETEENTH AND TWENTIETH CENTURIES—BASED ON EXCAVATION AND RECONSTRUCTION OF THE RUINS OF THAT PERIOD IN HISTORY.

OF COURSE, WITH THE EVIDENCE OF SO MUCH TOTAL DESTRUCTION WE ASSUMED THE RUINS WERE CREATED BY **WAR**— UNTIL A CHANCE DISCOVERY OF A HIDDEN DOCUMENT PROVED THAT IT WASN'T WAR AT ALL — IT WAS A **GUERILLA** INSURRECTION—SOMETHING CALLED "URBAN RENEWAL."

OUR FIRST SLIDE SHOWS A RECONSTRUCTION OF THE EARLIEST AND MOST **PRIMITIVE** FORM OF THAT PERIOD — THE **GLASS SLAB** — BUILT PROBABLY IN THE MIDDLE NINETEENTH CENTURY— NOTICE ITS **VACUOUSNESS** AND LACK OF SCALE.

NEXT WE HAVE A **LATER**, MORE **TRANSITIONAL** HOUSE OF THE EARLY TWENTIETH CENTURY— **STILL** RATHER MONOTONOUS BUT FEATURING GREATER SOPHISTICATION OF **DETAIL**. THE RECORDS WE FOUND PROVE THAT THESE CONSTRUCTIONS WERE AT FIRST KNOWN AS "**HOUSING PROJECTS**," A CLUMSY TERM LATER SIMPLIFIED INTO "SLUMS."

OUR **LAST** SLIDE REPRESENTS A **HIGH** POINT OF PROGRESS. BUILT IN THE LATE TWENTIETH OR EARLY TWENTY-FIRST CENTURY THIS BUILDING KNOWN AS A "BROWNSTONE" UTILIZES A TASTE AND A FLAIR FOR EXPERIMENTATION THAT SUGGEST AN ARCHITECTURAL RENAISSANCE.

ONE CAN ONLY BE LEFT BREATHLESS BY THE BRILLIANCE OF A SOCIETY THAT WAS ABLE TO MAKE SUCH GIANT STRIDES IN A MERE ONE-HUNDRED FIFTY YEARS.

10
Ecology
and
Urbanization

When a traveler arrives by bus in the center of a large American city, he or she often finds himself or herself in an area containing pawnshops, all-night theaters, and "cheap" bars, hotels, and restaurants. Bus stations are usually located in the section of the city with relatively inexpensive services for transients. If the traveler wants to find the largest theater or department store in the city, he or she can assume with confidence that it will be only a few blocks away, near the center of the city. If he or she is on the way to visit a schoolteacher who lives in a single-family house, he or she can assume that his or her destination will be a considerable distance from the bus station: middle-class single-family dwellings are ordinarily built farther away from the central business district, near the periphery of the city. The person can make all these predictions because human activities are patterned spatially as well as in other ways.

Human ecology is that part of sociology which studies the spatial distribution of human groups and social institutions. Geography is not the only factor determining spatial distribution of a population. The north side of town may not be topographically different from the south side, but if early settlers on the north side are or become wealthy and influential, certain other people will want to live near them and be associated with them, and property on the north side will become culturally desirable. Poor laborers, ethnic minorities, and other lower-status people are often not able to afford homes on this side of town. Nor will they have enough influence to keep polluting factories from being built in their neighborhood. The cultural character of the area of residence will determine social space: residence within these geographic boundaries will be taken as a status symbol and will be a factor in defining social relations.

Ecologists are interested in the spatial distribution of any social phenomenon: what part of the community has the most suicides, where the areas of high and low economic status are located, where minorities live, whether people go to church in the neighborhood where they live, and so on. The ecologist regards spatial relations as an index of social relations and thus is interested in the spatial structuring of human activities in order to learn about the social structure and social groups.

Ecologists, like other sociologists, are concerned with both structure and process.[1] Ecological structure is represented by a map showing the distribution of some social activity, such as gambling or fertility or wholesale trade. Ecological processes include changes in the ecological structure, such as the expansion of the area devoted to retail trade or the change of a Polish-American neighborhood to a Puerto Rican neighborhood.

THE ECOLOGY OF SMALL COMMUNITIES

Because small communities and rural areas emphasize primary rather than secondary group relations and because they have fewer people and are more homogeneous, the ecology of the small or rural community is less complex than the large urban metropolis. Nevertheless communities are not identical. The institutions and organizations found in small communities vary in their ecological setting and culture.

Ecology and Land Settlement

The family has traditionally been the basic social unit in all agricultural societies, but the spatial distribution of farm families has varied greatly. In some regions farm families are dispersed through-

---

[1] In a single chapter we can do no more than summarize the major findings of human ecology. For more detailed treatments of the field, see Amos H. Hawley, *Human Ecology: A Theory of Community Structure* (New York: The Ronald Press Company, 1950); and James A. Quinn, *Human Ecology* (Englewood Cliffs, N. J.: Prentice-Hall, 1950).

out the entire area. In others the population is relatively concentrated in a hamlet or village and work the adjoining land. Probably most of the world's farmers follow the latter pattern. While the concentrated village is the principal dwelling place of farmers in Europe and the Orient, exceptions are found in Great Britain, France, Germany, the Low Countries, the northern part of Scandinavia, and sporadically in southern Europe. The village is the chief pattern in India and China, but there are variations. In Latin America and Africa, rural settlements are usually of the village type.

The ecology of an area is usually influenced by historical developments and the United States is a case in point. The clustered-village type of community was brought to the colonies from England and the Continent. But local differences began to evolve as settlers moved into the interior. Individuals and single families crossed the Alleghenies and squatted on "new" lands, and their claims were later validated by legal action. In the Southern colonies the plantation system emerged out of commercial agriculture supported by slave labor. Later, federal laws influenced the form of land settlement. In 1785 the rectangular survey was established, and public lands were divided first into townships of 36 square miles each. These were then subdivided into sections of 640 acres and quarter sections of 160 acres. In 1841 the requirement was made that, to obtain title to such land, the individual had to live on it. Still later the Homestead Act (1862) provided for settlement and payment for public lands at a low cost per acre.

The rectangular division of land made for a gridiron form of farms and fostered the separation of farmsteads from each other by considerable distances. As a matter of fact, much of the best agricultural land of the United States was settled under this pattern. It is a neat illustration of how a culture trait, in this case law, may influence the ecology of a community. However, there are some variations in the types of farm settlement.

The Rural Community

Since the small, spatially isolated community is based upon face-to-face relationships, the neighborhood is probably more primary than any other group except the family. The characteristic feature is that families live near one another and that they are bound together by intimate and personal relationships. The greater the number of bonds, the more distinctive the community. Frequently neighborhoods in highly urbanized areas are built around a single interest or institution, such as a country school or a mill. In contrast, the community is formed around common interests and the means of satisfying most human needs or interests.

Historically, the community has been a very significant organization. In pre-industrial times the whole social life of open-country groups centered there. Most manufacturing was done at home, and the economic system was largely one of the direct exchange of goods and services. Today the community has declined for many people as wider ranges of interaction have developed. The traditional rural community is changing its function as the bonds of mere locality are being replaced by urban forms of social organization, such as special-interest groups. Wherever good highways and proximity to trading centers permit, urban services, such as commercial baking, laundering, dry cleaning, and the like, are affecting the patterns of both family and community life.

American rural communities, as they have related to agriculture, may be divided into four types: the open-country, the village or town-centered community, the agricultural village and the plantation community.[2]

The Open-Country Community

Ordinarily one thinks of a community as composed of more or less definite social structure and population located within some relatively defined space. Yet there are some communities where the stores, garages, schools, and churches are dispersed rather widely. The people who live in such an area and trade in these stores or send their children to the schools or attend the churches do, however, regard themselves as members of a distinct community. Though widely diffused, these communities have names and they are thought of by the inhabitants as distinct communities, within which are to be found relatively traditional patterns of social interaction. Such communities are common in the South and in some parts of the Great Plains, and are found sporadically elsewhere.

Landaff, New Hampshire, for example, is largely of this type. Landaff has a church, a garage, a school, and some scattered service agencies, but it has no nucleus, no fixed center. Yet there is no doubt that, in the thinking of its residents, Landaff is a community.[3] Like Landaff, most communities of this kind consist of farmsteads dispersed throughout the area, with various service agencies located at more or less convenient points.

However, unless they are bound together by some emotional tie,

[2]Writers on rural sociology differ as to just how to classify rural communities. But this classification, suggested by Allen D. Edwards, will serve our purposes. His inclusion of the plantation–often neglected by rural sociologists–is a helpful addition. See his "Ecological Patterns of American Rural Communities," *Rural Sociology*, 1947, 12: 150–161.

[3]See Kenneth MacLeish and Kimball Young, "Culture of a Contemporary Rural Community: Landaff, New Hampshire," *Rural Life Studies*, No. 3, Bureau of Agricultural Economics (Washington, D.C.: Department of Agriculture, 1942).

such as a common religion or a common ethnicity, many open-country communities are likely to have a limited sense of unity and less sense of belonging together than communities with more concentrated populations—especially in this time of mass community and increasing urbanization. Furthermore, most open-country communities are far from self-sufficient. As good roads have been built, people in these places go to larger localities to satisfy most of their economic and recreational needs.

There are scattered examples of open-country communities which are closely integrated by religious, kinship, linguistic, and ethnic subcultures. Such are the Amish in Lancaster County, Pennsylvania and the Amana of Iowa. Somewhat similar are certain other pietistic denominations, such as the Mennonites. But for the most part, such integrating factors are not present in the open-country communities of the United States.

Town-Centered Communities

Most rural inhabitants in the United States tend to be oriented toward a village or town. But the degree of centralization and the ratio of open-country to actual town members are highly variable. Where the gridiron land survey made for dispersal of farmsteads on rather widely scattered farms, the town may have grown up at an important railroad stop or at the junction of two important lines of traffic, rail or highway. The townspeople may be both farmers and persons concerned with providing services connected with the rural economy.

Everywhere the earlier relations of farm families to town centers have undergone many changes. The automobile and hard-surfaced roads made it possible to buy goods and services at longer distances from the farm than formerly. So, too, the development of mail-order buying enabled farm families to get goods which might not be easily available nearby.

Yet the school, the church, the grocery store, and the garage continue to provide important services within easy reach. Some believe that in time the shift to larger centers will eliminate the need for these smaller places near the farmstead. While the relative importance of the hamlet and small town is declining, these centers will probably long continue to provide many goods and services for the farm family and other rural families.

Agricultural Villages

The settlement of farmers into more or less compact villages is not as usual in most of the United States as it is in so much of the world elsewhere. Yet the main features of the agricultural village deserve brief comment. The best-known instances of agricultural villages in the United States are those established by the Mormons when they settled in the Great Basin—western Utah, southern Idaho, and parts of Nevada.

The basic pattern was developed by Joseph Smith and first used in Nauvoo, Illinois. A community was arranged on the gridiron pattern, with streets 8 rods wide at right angles and square blocks of 10 acres each, divided into half-acre lots for single dwellings. The plan was later applied when Salt Lake City was laid out by Smith's successor, Brigham Young. And as other communities were established up and down the central valleys of Utah, the same general pattern was followed, though the street widths and size of blocks were often modified.

The necessity for protection against hostile Indians and the cooperative effort to obtain water for the farms by irrigation were not the determining factors, for the farmers lived in the village or town and the farm properties which they worked were adjacent to it. Rather, this was an interesting example of deliberate community planning. Between 1847 and 1877 more than 360 such communities were established, reaching from southern Idaho through Utah into Arizona.

In keeping with the overall program for these communities, the Mormon Church set up a colonization plan to make sure that in each new community sufficient carpenters, blacksmiths, and other specialized workers would be available, as well as enough farmers. Since the entire orientation of these activities was to make the Mormons economically self-sufficient and independent of the "gentile" (non-Mormon) world outside, many communities were *instructed* to develop various industries in addition to their agriculture.[4] Iron works were built in some places, woolen mills in others, salt plants in still others—usually where the necessary raw materials were at hand. These local industries were to supplement the home manufacturing which—at least ideally—was as much a part of family life as farming itself. Actually, the Mormon communities were planned to be more than strictly agricultural villages. They were to be not only the centers of farming and local industry but the seats of all major religious, civic, and other noneconomic community affairs.

Another nucleated community widely distributed throughout the world is the "line village." This type of community is common in southern Louisiana, where French influence was great. Among the

---

[4]For a definitive study of this whole program, see Leonard J. Arrington, *Great Basin Kingdom: An Economic History of the Latter-Day Saints, 1830–1900* (Cambridge: Harvard University Press, 1958).

rivers where frontage is particularly valuable, houses occupy small areas near the river, with the accompanying farmlands extending back in narrow strips.

It is worth noting that there have been many attempts to establish agricultural villages in the course of American history. Most of them were born of the utopian socialistic or cooperative movements of the nineteenth century. Few remain.

Certainly so far as the Mormon villages are concerned, they are marked by a high degree of community solidarity and integration. Here it is not farming but religious and other cultural elements which furnish the basis for a strong sense of belonging. Of the socialistic or cooperative settlements in this country, it is worth noting that most of them failed because those who took part in them lacked or lost the moral and religious zeal that inspired the founders and leaders.[5]

The Plantation

As a system of agricultural production, the plantation is widespread. It is found in parts of Latin America—as in coffee-growing parts of Brazil—and in the production of rubber in Malaya and Africa. Allen D. Edwards defines a plantation as a "form of social organization in which labor, under unified direction and control, is engaged in the production of an agricultural staple which is usually sold on a world market."[6]

The plantation pattern was introduced into the United States from the West Indies. Before the Civil War, cotton and tobacco cultivation in the South was largely organized under this system. The center of the large holdings consisted of the master's house, houses for his supervisors, outbuildings, and huts for slaves. And the whole economy more or less revolved around this nucleus. Even at this late date, many of the earlier managerial features remain. Sometimes the plantation is organized under the sharecropper system. In other cases the work is done by hired laborers.

In the South, smaller plantations often operated as parts of a larger plantation community. But whether large or small, the plantation was the focus and center of life for many people in the South. Moreover, the influence often reached beyond the plantation itself. Writing in the middle 1930s, Woofter reported that "Plantation customs and ideology set the pattern for relationships in small farm units.... Large planters persistently emerge as the political and

---

[5]See Arthur E. Bestor, *Backwoods Utopias: the Sectarian and Owenite Phases of Communitarian Socialism in America, 1663–1829* (Philadelphia: University of Pennsylvania Press, 1950).
[6]Edwards, "Ecological Patterns," p. 158.

economic leaders of the cotton areas . . . and the plantation stands out as the basis for a hereditary oligarchy in southern community life."[7]

Modifications of the plantation system are found in some of the large-scale corporation farms of California and elsewhere. These are what Carey McWilliams has called "factories in the fields." The vast vegetable acreage of the Imperial Valley is owned largely by corporations. The farms are operated by managers and supervisors, who hire laborers at low wages to do the work. The aim is high profit, and farming is made into as efficient a business system as possible. Certainly the communal aspects of social organization tend to disappear under such circumstances, except insofar as it continues in the noneconomic aspects of the lives of workers. So too, the collective farms of the Soviet Union are adaptations of the plantation system.

WORLD URBANIZATION

The widespread and rapid urbanization of the world is one of the most significant trends of our time. Worldwide urban expansion is bringing about great changes in the major patterns of social organization. In many ways it is as revolutionary in its effects on society and institutions as the domestication of plants and animals and the emergence of village life.

The striking growth of cities in the nineteenth and twentieth centuries is a novel event in human history. Although cities existed five or six thousand years ago, the cities of the ancient world were generally small towns by modern standards. The largest of them contained only 1 or 2 per cent of the total population of their society, and it has been estimated that it took from 50 to 90 farmers to produce the surplus needed to enable one person to live in an urban center.[8] In fact, it is here, in the ratio of farmers to urban dwellers, that the explanation can be found for the recency and suddenness of urbanization. Not until the Industrial Revolution, with its factory system, improvement of farming, and tremendous speed-up in the transportation of goods, was it possible for whole societies to become urbanized. Only when one farmer can raise enough food for many people besides himself can a society exist in which the majority of the people live and work in cities.

---

[7]T. J. Woofter et al., "Landlord and Tenant on the Cotton Plantation," *Research Monograph*, 1936, Vol. 5 (Washington, D.C.: Works Progress Administration, Division of Social Research, 1936).
[8]Kingsley Davis, "The Origin and Growth of Urbanization in the World," *American Journal of Sociology*, 1955, 60: 429–437. All quotations by permission.

Only in the past century and a half has the world known truly urban *societies,* in which a high proportion of the total population lives in cities. Table 10-1 shows that as recently as 1800 only 2.4 per cent of the world's population lived in cities of 20,000 or more; today more than one-fifth of the people live in such cities. Furthermore, (see Table 10-1) the proportion of people living in large cities has risen even more dramatically. By 1950 the proportion of people in the world living in cities was higher than that in even the most urbanized country before modern times.[9] Davis describes the increase in urbanization as follows:

> In 1800 there were apparently less than 50 cities with 100,000 or more inhabitants. This was less than the number in the million [category]. . . . By 1950 there were close to 900 cities of 100,000 or more people. . . .
>
> As yet there is no indication of a slackening of the rate of urbanization in the world as a whole. If the present rate should continue, more than a fourth of the earth's people will be living in cities of 100,000 or more in the year 2000, and more than half in the year 2050. For places of 20,000 or more, the proportions at the two dates would be something like 45 per cent and 90 per cent. Whether such figures prove too low or too high, they nevertheless suggest that the human species is moving rapidly in the direction of an almost exclusively urban existence. . . . When . . . more than a third of the population of a country lives in cities of the 100,000 class (38.4 per cent in England and Wales in 1951), the country can be described as almost completely urbanized (81 per cent being designated as "urban" in the English case in 1951). We thus have today what can be called "urbanized societies," nations in which the great majority of inhabitants live in cities. The prospect is that, as time goes on, a greater and greater proportion of humanity will be members of such societies.[10]

Table 10-1   Percentage of World's Population Living in Cities 1800–1950

	Cities of 20,000 or More	*Cities of 100,000 or More*
1800	2.4	1.7
1850	4.3	2.3
1900	9.2	5.5
1950	20.9	13.1

SOURCE: Davis, "The Origin and Growth of Urbanization in the World," *American Journal of Sociology,* 1955, 60: 434.

---

[9]*Ibid.,* p. 433.
[10]*Ibid.,* p. 434.

Table 10-2   Percentage of World's Population Living in Cities

	In Cities of 20,000 Plus	In Cities of 100,000 Plus
World	21	13
Oceania	47	41
North America (Canada and U.S.A.)	42	29
Europe (except U.S.S.R.)	35	21
U.S.S.R.	31	18
South America	26	18
Middle America and Caribbean	21	12
Asia (except U.S.S.R.)	13	8
Africa	9	5

SOURCE: Davis, p. 433.

These figures are even more impressive when one realizes that urbanization is very low in Asia, Africa, and Latin America. This fact underscores the close relationship between urbanization and industrialization. The bulk of the urbanization, as Table 10-2 shows, has occurred in Oceania, Europe, and North America and the greatest amount of urbanization is still to be found in Northern Europe.

URBAN ECOLOGICAL STRUCTURE

Cities tend to locate on trade routes, and trade tends to follow the topography of least resistance. People float their goods down streams to remote markets. Land routes along valleys, over low passes in mountains, by way of a chain of oases in a desert—all represent the effort to overcome nature's obstacles with the least expenditure of energy, time, and social resources. Wherever there is a break in this flow, cities are likely to arise: where the sea trade must be transferred to river travel, or where there is a break in land travel because of topography, political barriers, or other factors. Paris, France, grew up where trade routes north and south met the Seine River. As Charles Horton Cooley phrased it, "Population and wealth tend to gather wherever there is a break in transportation." Usually the larger the tributary or supporting area, the larger the central city. But factors of topography, population density, and political and economic organization also influence the pattern of location and growth.

An examination of a large map of any city shows how its structure and growth are first of all dependent on the nature of the site itself. Richard M. Hurd remarks:

The first step in studying the ground plan of cities is to note the topographical faults which normally control the shape of cities, by interfering with their free growth in all directions from their points of origin. These are of two kinds: water surfaces, such as harbors, lakes, rivers, creeks, and swamps, or sharp variations from the normal city level, such as steep hills, deep hollows, and ravines.[11]

Where the land is flat, with no marshes or interfering contours, a city will tend to grow outward from the original center unless man-made factors, such as highways, defense walls, and railroad trackage, interfere. Topography gives the most obvious structure to a city. The towns and cities located on waterways must follow the lines of growth laid down by the water barriers. In hill-and-valley topography, the valley tends to be the seat of easiest communication and of industrial and commercial locations, while residential sections are found on higher ground. If the hills are too steep, travel between homes and work is difficult, so that even residential growth tends at the outset to follow the line of least resistance. Hurd summarizes the major influences of topography: "Level land attracts business, moderate elevations attract residences, land below the normal level attracts transportation lines, and filled-in land is generally used for warehousing, manufacturing, and cheap tenements."[12] Of course, the longer people have been settled in a locality, the less important the influence of the natural topography becomes and the more important the man-made "cultural landscape." People level or cut through hills, drain and fill swamps, build dikes, dredge river mouths and harbors, construct canals, and otherwise alter the natural landscape.

The site of a city soon develops a structure or form, with the layout of streets playing a determining part. Unless there is a definite plan, when a city is founded the streets are laid out in conformity with natural topography, and the best available land tends to be taken for retail stores and residences. The ground plan is thus settled, more or less, once and for all. Thenceforth streets tend to become obstructions to further development. Cities with narrow or winding streets, like Boston, Massachusetts, or cities with many diagonal streets, like Washington, D.C., or Madison, Wisconsin, produce unusually serious automobile traffic problems.

Unless modified by plan or unusual topography, cities tend to develop in either an axial or radial fashion. Where the streets are laid out with regularity, in squares or rectangles, the city's growth

---

[11]Richard M. Hurd, *Principles of City Land Values,* 4th ed. (New York: Real Estate Record and Guide, 1924), p. 33. By permission.
[12]*Ibid.,* p. 36. By permission. However, in Chicago, filled-in land along Lake Michigan has been used for high-rent residences, parks, and schools.

is usually restricted to the direction determined by two main intersecting streets or thoroughfares. There are some advantages and some disadvantages in the rectangular form. It allows the plotting of about equal-size blocks, makes easy the division of the city into administrative districts, and facilitates adequate police and military control. Also, with rectangular blocks there are no main thoroughfares to facilitate circulation between the center and the periphery, although within the center itself movement may not be difficult.

The radial pattern arises when there is a natural center at the end of a number of converging thoroughfares. As the city grows, it tends to follow these major traffic lanes, producing star-shaped cities like Tokyo, Nuremberg, and the older sections of London. This is perhaps the most efficient form of development.

Sometimes one finds a combination of rectangular and radial patterns. Often there were originally a number of highways leading to the village or town, and as the city grew it was laid out in regular rectangular form superimposed on this system of highways. Washington, D.C., was deliberately planned to combine the radial with the rectangular scheme.

In Europe, some streets were developed around certain sections of cities as walls were torn down, moats filled in, or parks cut up. In Paris there are at least four sets of circular streets which arose as old walls were torn down and new ones were built farther away, only to be razed and themselves turned into streets. The Ringstrasse in Vienna was cut out of a series of public parks which had replaced older fortifications.

While the streets provide the basic ground structure of a city, railroad lines also contribute to it. In Chicago, for example, rail lines have tended to break up and isolate certain districts from others, though for the most part the lines have followed either the lake shore or the Chicago River and its branches. Wholesale trade areas and, more particularly, industrial sites call for much trackage, and in these areas slums are likely to develop. Often railroad tracks located on the outskirts of a city later become a barrier to further growth. The geographical distribution of cities over the world reflects various developments in commerce, industry, transportation, government, religion, and agriculture. Those cities most fortunately located have flourished and today stand as large metropolitan centers more or less dominating a surrounding hinterland area. For the most part, such growth has been a concomitant of industrialization. The percentages of population which fall into the urban category vary widely, from Great Britain, with 80 per cent, West Germany, 72 per cent, and the United States, 74 per cent (in 1970), to countries showing little urbanization, such as Pakistan, with 11, and Thailand, with 10 per cent.[13]

Although most of us have an intuitive notion of what is rural and what is urban, the distinction of rural communities and urban communities is not always an easy one to make. The United States census classifies essentially all places with more than 2,500 residents as urban and all other places as rural.[14] In 1970, 74 per cent of the

Table 10-3   Urban Population and Population Density
in the United States, 1790 to 1970

Year	Per Cent Urban	Population Density*
1790	5	4
1800	6	6
1810	7	4
1820	7	6
1830	9	7
1840	11	10
1850	15	8
1860	20	11
1870	26	13
1880	28	17
1890	35	21
1900	40	26
1910	46	31
1920	51	36
1930	56	41
1940	59	44
1950	64	43†
1960	70	50†
1970	74	57†

*Resident population per square mile of land area.
†Includes Alaska and Hawaii.
SOURCE: U.S. Bureau of the Census, *Statistical Abstract of the United States, 1971* (Washington, D.C.: U.S. Government Printing Office, 1971), pp. 5, 17.

---

[13]Percentages for all countries except the U.S.A. are from Jack P. Gibbs and Kingsley Davis, "Conventional Versus Metropolitan Data in the International Study of Urbanization," *American Sociological Review*, 1958, 23: 504–514. For other discussions of this topic, see Jack P. Gibbs and Leo F. Schnore, "Metropolitan Growth: An International Study," *American Journal of Sociology*, 1960, 66: 160–170; and Philip M. Hauser, ed., "World Urbanism," *American Journal of Sociology*, 1955, 60: 427–503 (a special issue devoted to various aspects of urbanization).

[14]According to the 1970 census definition, "the urban population comprises all persons living in (a) places of 2,500 inhabitants or more incorporated as cities, villages, boroughs (except Alaska), and towns (except in New England, New York, and Wisconsin), but excluding persons living in the rural portions of extended cities; (b) unincorporated places of 2,500 inhabitants or more; and (c) other ter-

American population was in urban areas (compared with 51 per cent in 1920). Moreover, in 1970 the population density of the United States was 57 persons per square mile. The population density in the middle Atlantic states of New Jersey, New York, and Pennsylvania was 371; in New York City, it was 26,343; and in the Manhattan Borough alone, it was 67,808. If the entire land area of the United States had the population density of the Manhattan Borough, the U.S. population would be 240 billion!

There were 150 urbanized areas of more than 200,000 population in the United States in 1970 and 50 per cent of all Americans lived in counties which are located at least partly within 50 miles of the coasts. More than one-third of the four dozen large industrial-commercial cities are located on the coasts of the Great Lakes, a fact indicative of the importance of accessibility of water transportation to the development of cities.

A very high population density does not necessarily lead to intimate social relations. Urban life represents not only a certain massing of people but a different kind of interaction. As Louis Wirth put it, "The city is not merely the point at which great numbers are concentrated into limited space, but it is also a complex of human beings exhibiting the most extraordinary heterogeneity in almost every characteristic in which human beings can differ from one another."[15]

Centralization of Services

The concentration of services in strategic places is an important ecological asect of urban life. These services satisfy such common interests as work, education, government, religion, and recreation. Centralization is directly related to transportation and communication: service centers tend to be located where these intersect. The focal point of most cities, or of any community for that matter, is the retail shopping center. Many additional services are provided in this central area. Large cities in particular may provide centralized services for a wide hinterland. Organizational headquarters for a region, governmental offices for a state or nation, or other specialized functions may be located in a particular city.

Centralization may occur first by the sheer addition of activities

---

ritory, incorporated or unincorporated, included in urbanized areas." The remaining population is classified as rural. U.S. Bureau of the Census, *Statistical Abstract of the United States, 1971* (Washington, D.C.: U.S. Government Printing Office, 1971), p. 2.

[15]Louis Wirth, "The Urban Society and Civilization," in *Eleven Twenty-six: A Decade of Social Science Research* (Chicago: University of Chicago Press, 1940), p. 57.

in a common location, as when a rural trade center at a crossroads becomes, gradually, the locus of schools, churches, post office, garage, and bowling alley. Centralization may also take place through an increase in the number of individuals who find gratification of some interest at the same location. The foci of centralization are in constant competition for patronage, and changes in either the services or transportation facilities may upset any working balance that may have been attained.

Urban people tend to think of distance not in miles but in the amount of time required for movement. As concentrations persist along with population mobility, a kind of territorial specialization of activities follows. An urban community becomes studded with centers of varying sizes and degrees of specialization. These in turn act as magnets to attract the appropriate age, sex, economic, and class groupings. Specialization occurs in time as well as in space, as when an iceskating rink is converted to a swimming pool or meeting hall during the summer. More frequently a specialized business might find it worth its while to remain open only during certain months.

Decentralization

There is, of course, a point beyond which concentration and centralization cannot go. Competition for space in the central section of a city leads to such high land values that further expansion of business or other services becomes impractical. And while the construction of more and more skyscrapers keeps adding space for offices, there are physical limits to such facilities. The most obvious fact is that the higher the building, the more the space that must be used for elevators and other service fixtures and the less for commercial purposes. Then too, traffic congestion reduces the gains which come from concentration of goods and services. Loss in time and patience is, in the end, not offset by advantages of shopping or doing business in such centers. As a result, the process of centralization of goods and services appears in new areas. These changes, however, do not signify less urban domination, but the extension of urban culture. One of the first and most common forms of decentralization is the development of large retail stores, gas stations, and garages in or near residential areas. Large cities everywhere are characterized by such subcenters, which duplicate in many ways the structure and function of the original centralized area of the city. But there are other forms of decentralization. Industries may move out of a central position to the fringe of a city, or new industries may be set up on the urban periphery and thus foster a new subcenter.

Figure 10-1 An Ecological Pattern of Community Growth*

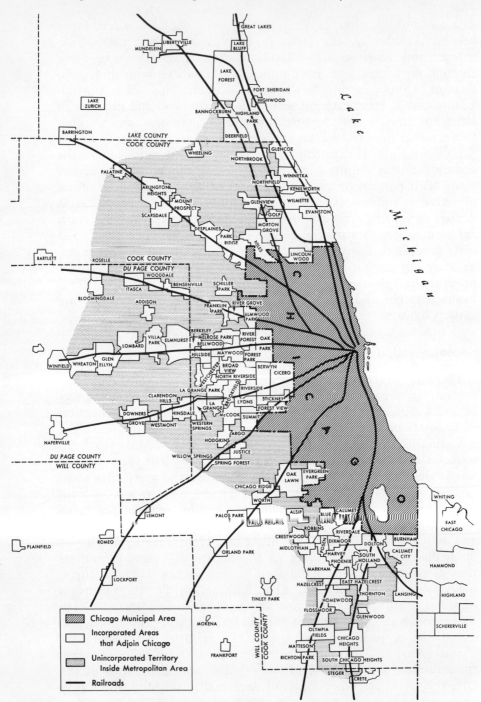

*Location of communities along railroad lines in the Chicago Metropolitan Area, 1948.

Source: The *Chicago Daily Tribune*, May 17, 1948. By permission.

Suburbs may grow up on the periphery of an expanding city as more desirable locations for families. Or as transportation lines are built nearby, smaller communities may become suburbs or satellite communities of a larger community (see Figure 10-1). Sometimes these outlying communities become a part of the larger municipality and sometimes they continue for a long time as independent political units.

Segregation

Almost every large American city has not only wealthy suburbs but settlements of minority groups as well. These areas often carry such descriptive names as Little Italy, Little Harlem, or Chinatown. Areas given over to vice or occupied by transient laborers, like Chicago's Hobohemia, also have unique features. Such segments of the urban ecological structure have been called "natural areas," to indicate that they are the outcome of competition, conflict, cooperation, and group differentiation and accommodation.[16] Similar variations are to be found in all great cities but may represent quite different culture groups: occupational, caste or class, religious bodies, or others.

Segregation is never complete as to culture group or occupation. There is usually a mixture of peoples, especially around the fringes of the area. For example, where blacks are an overwhelming majority, one finds a few scattered white families. There are also what Paul Hatt called "polyethnic" areas, which include Jews, white Christians, Chinese, Filipinos, Japanese, and blacks living in close proximity.[17] In some cities where many immigrants of like nationality reside, however, the areas tend to be more nearly homogeneous. Sometimes, as in New York City's Harlem, there is something akin to a self-contained community, with its own ecological structure along class and occupational lines.

Low income areas often encircle the center of the city. Interspersed throughout the zone are often light manufacturing and business concerns, which "invade" the area because of cheap rents and the hope of an expanding central zone. There are high ratios of poverty, delinquency, and other indices of social disadvantage, as well as many recent foreign immigrants, high birth and death rates, and a high population density.

---

[16]The term "natural area" has been variously used, but we have tried to limit it to a more specific meaning. See Paul K. Hatt, "The Concept of Natural Area," *American Sociology Review*, 1946, 11: 423–427; Hawley, *Human Ecology*, Chapter 6; and Quinn, *Human Ecology*, Chapters 12 and 18.

[17]Paul K. Hatt, "Spatial Patterns in a Polyethnic Area," *American Sociological Review*, 1945, 10: 352–356.

Assimilation and Segregation

The processes of assimilation are both helped and hindered by residental concentration of subcultures. A subcultural area often serves as a cultural island for the newcomers. It gives them a certain sense of security and so helps introduce them to the new culture. The effects of spatial segregation and retention of immigrant heritages may be characterized as follows: (1) Continuity with the old culture is maintained. (2) The immigrant sees the new country and its culture through the eyes of his own culture, especially as reflected in the ideas and attitudes of relatives and friends already settled there. The newcomer accepts the definition of the American situation offered him by his fellow countrymen already here. (3) This continuity of the old and interpretation of the new through his fellow countrymen softens the severity of the change and profoundly influences the process of assimilation itself. (4) However, it is only as the immigrant is introduced into more and more of the features of American culture, and especially as his children come into contact with the school, with agencies of recreation, with American family life, and with other patterns, that the effects of the earlier culture wear off and assimilation really gets underway.

The reactions of the established population to an immigrant are often those of avoidance and prejudice. Fear of economic competition and misunderstanding of different culture patterns were common during the period when large numbers of immigrants were coming to the United States. But in time came various accommodations which were steps to cultural assimilation and structural pluralism.

The rates of assimilation have differed. Oriental immigrants for the most part have retained considerable residential concentration, and their relations with the whites continue to be of an accommodative character. Most European immigrants, and especially their children and grandchildren, have largely broken through the barriers of discrimination and segregation and have become assimilated. Public education, improvement in economic status, intermarriage, and moving out of the immigrant area itself have been important factors in this process of change.

Invasion and Succession

Population distributions seldom remain fixed: in a highly dynamic society, invasion and succession come into play. The invasion by one group of an area occupied by another leads to segregation and finally to displacement or succession by the intruding group. In some cases lower economic classes invade an area being abandoned by the well-to-do. Sometimes the reverse is true, as when apartment houses spring up in neighborhoods which have long been occupied by families of low incomes but which afford easy access to work or have other attractive features. Good illustrations of the latter are found along the East River in mid-Manhattan or in the "near-north side" in Chicago.

Succession tends to be marked by rather sharp changes in the composition of the resident population. Not infrequently in American cities there has been a long series of intrusions and displacements. The process is accompanied by continuous competition between groups.

Migration

Residential movement follows the spatial expansion of the city toward its periphery. As one would expect, the rate of residential change is higher in hotel and rooming-house areas than in tenement sections, and higher in the latter than in districts farther out, where people own their own homes. There is a definite inverse relationship between home ownership and residential mobility. Among the many implications of high residential movement are lack of participation in community organizations, impersonal nature of human contacts, and high degree of occupational specialization, characteristics of the secondary-group organization of urban society.

The erection of skyscrapers increases congestion in movement by adding greatly to the number of persons and goods that must be moved into or out of an area and within the area itself. Some of the most striking facts about urban traffic congestion are these: (1) Between 1922 and 1944 there was an actual decline in the total passenger-carrying capacity of public utility equipment in the United States. It rose somewhat sharply in 1945 but decreased steadily through 1955. When one considers the kinds of transit equipment, there are notable changes and variations. Thus from 1935 to 1940, surface railway cars declined from 40,050 to 5,300 units, while subway and elevated cars decreased from 10,416 to 9,232. In contrast, trolley coaches increased from 578 to 6,157 and motor buses from 23,800 to 52,400. (2) With these changes has come a decrease in the use of public urban transit facilities. From 1924 through 1955, this was about one-fifth. For suburban and related areas the drop has been greater, about one-half for the same period. (3) However, the larger the city, the higher the proportion of the total population that use various means of public transportation.

In addition to public transportation, privately owned automobiles carry thousands of people over our city streets. Every major city of the United States has been harrassed by the problems of mounting

congestion and pollution from such traffic. There have been many
schemes for building multiple-deck expressways into and through
the heart of our cities, some of which work, some of which are
impractical. But even if all urban workers possessed and were to use
their own cars on fast highways, they would have to find places
to park them before they could "function at the point to which
they . . . transported themselves." Modern elevator or ramp garages
have limited possibilities. "Crediting each vehicle with the average
loading in city traffic of 1.75 persons" and assuming that a modern
office building allows an average of 150 square feet of floor space
per worker, estimates show that it would take practically as much
floor space to park a person's car as he has in which to do his work.
To provide parking space for workers, not shoppers, under the
assumptions stated, would mean doubling *"the cubage requirements
of present central area buildings."*[18]

Social Area Analysis

Several sociologists have employed a method for the analysis of
urban social structure by spatial units. Social area analysis, as the
method is called, is a technique for the study of social and economic data in the local sub-areas of a city through the use of data
collected by the United States Census Bureau on census tracts
within the city.[19]

Census tracts are combined into neighborhoods on the basis of
their similarity in three factors: social rank, urbanization, and segregation (or, as Bell prefers to call them, economic status, family
status, and ethnic status). The social rank of a neighborhood is
computed on the basis of two measures: the proportion of people
in white-collar jobs and the proportion of the population over 25
years of age with more than eight years of schooling. Social rank
therefore is based on two major stratification variables: occupation
and education. Three measures are used in calculating the index of

[18]Quotations from "Moving the Masses in Modern Cities" (New York: American
Transit Association, n.d.), pp. 24, 25 (pamphlet). By permission.
[19]See Eshref Shevky and Marilyn Williams, *The Social Areas of Los Angeles:
Analysis and Typology* (Berkeley: University of California Press, 1949); Eshref
Shevky and Wendell Bell, *Social Area Analysis: Theory, Illustrative Application
and Computational Procedures* (Stanford: Stanford University Press, 1955). See
also Maurice D. Van Arsdol, Jr., Santo F. Camilleri, and Calvin F. Schmid, "The
Generality of Urban Social Area Indexes," *American Sociological Review*, 1958,
23: 277–284. Criticism of the method can be found in Arsdol, Camilleri, and
Schmid, "An Investigation of the Utility of Urban Typology," *Pacific Sociological
Review*, 1961, 4: 26–32. For a reply, see Wendell Bell and Scott Greer, "Social
Area Analysis and Its Critics," *Pacific Sociological Review*, 1962, 5: 3–9. A cross-
cultural application of the method has been made by Dennis C. McElrath, "The
Social Areas of Rome," *American Sociological Review*, 1962, 27: 376-391.

urbanization: fertility, the proportion of adult females in the labor force, and the proportion of dwelling units which are single-family houses. Segregation is measured by the percentage of the population which is nonwhite or foreign-born from countries of eastern and southern Europe.

Social area analysis has enabled the sociologist readily to relate divorce rates, suicides, voting behavior, church attendance, or any other factor for an area to the basic structural variables of economic, family, and ethnic statuses in that area.

ECOLOGICAL STRUCTURE OF CITIES

There have been a number of attempts to discover the ecological structure of cities, but each has been only partially successful. Three of the more important theories which have been set forth are the concentric zones theory, the sector theory, and the multiple nuclei pattern.

Concentric Zones

The first and best known of these efforts, known as the pattern of concentric zones, was presented by Ernest W. Burgess in 1925. (See Figure 10-2.) According to his construct, the center of modern American cities is the point of chief concentration of specialized services. The center, Zone I, is characterized by skyscrapers, department stores, big hotels, motion-picture houses, transit lines, and daily mobility of population as it goes about its business or pleasure. In Zone II are found rooming houses, some light industry, and certain other services. In general, the second zone is characterized by rather rapid change or "transition." In Zone III are workingmen's homes, and shopping centers, schools, and occasional parks. In the fourth zone are better residences, and beyond this is Zone V, the suburban and commuter area. Typically, there is an upward gradation in such features as income and status from the center to the periphery.

Burgess developed his theoretical construct from studies of urban communities, chiefly of Chicago. The actual ecological structure of cities seldomly conforms precisely to the pattern Burgess described. Topography, waterways, lakes, harbors, and so on all influence the direction and extent of a city's development. Certainly for Chicago, Lake Michigan cuts sharply through the middle of Burgess' circles, so that there we have a series of only half-concentric rings. Moreover, the Chicago River, the railroad lines, the highways, and the desirability of lake-front residences also affect the spatial distribution. (See Figure 10-2.)

Figure 10-2   The Concentric Zones of Chicago Circa 1925

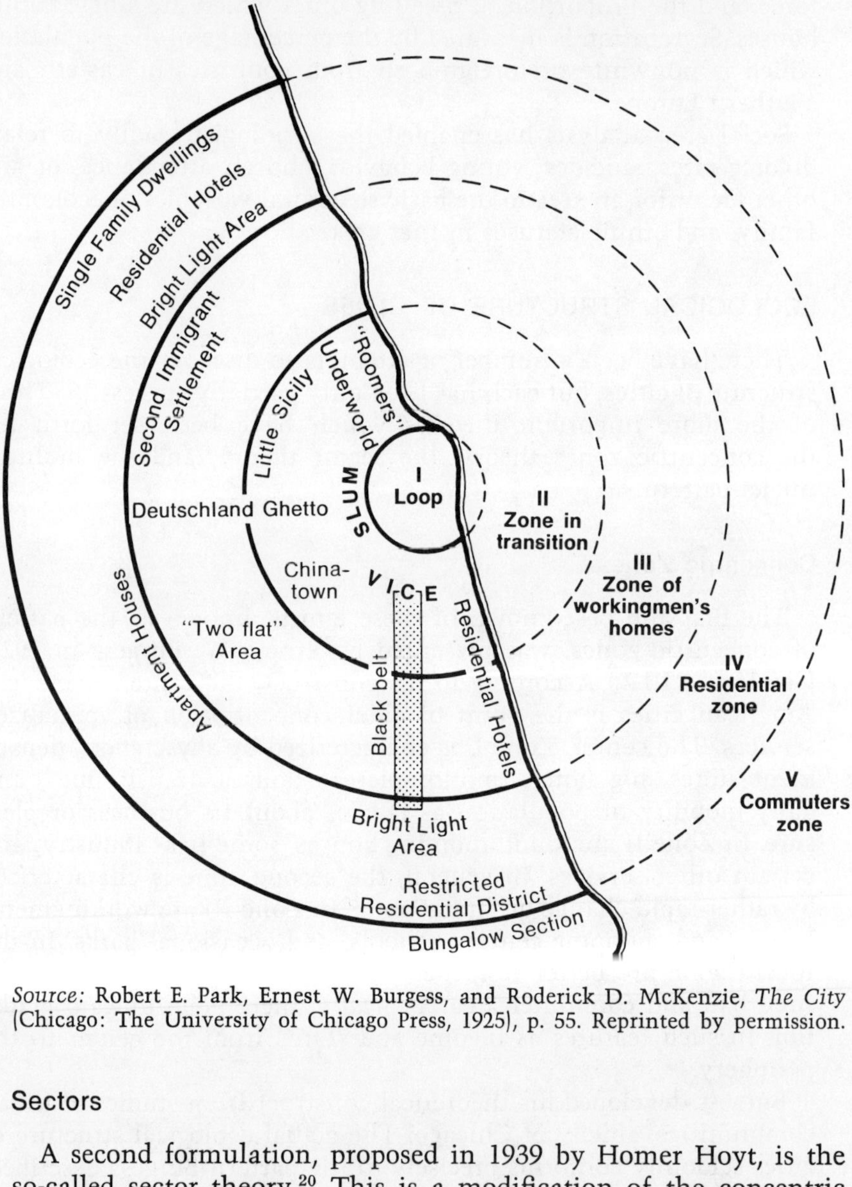

Single Family Dwellings

Residential Hotels

Bright Light Area

Second Immigrant Settlement

Little Sicily

"Roomers" Underworld

Deutschland Ghetto

I Loop

SLUM

II Zone in transition

III Zone of workingmen's homes

China-town

VICE

Residential Hotels

Black belt

"Two flat" Area

Apartment Houses

Bright Light Area

IV Residential zone

V Commuters zone

Restricted Residential District

Bungalow Section

Source: Robert E. Park, Ernest W. Burgess, and Roderick D. McKenzie, *The City* (Chicago: The University of Chicago Press, 1925), p. 55. Reprinted by permission.

Sectors

A second formulation, proposed in 1939 by Homer Hoyt, is the so-called sector theory.[20] This is a modification of the concentric zone pattern suggested by Burgess. Hoyt's proposed sector pattern gives more consideration to the influence of topographic factors and major travel arteries, sometimes producing sectors in wedge-

[20]Homer Hoyt, *The Structure and Growth of Residential Neighborhoods in American Cities* (Washington, D.C.: Federal Housing Administration, 1939).

Figure 10-3   Three Generalizations of the Internal Structure of Cities

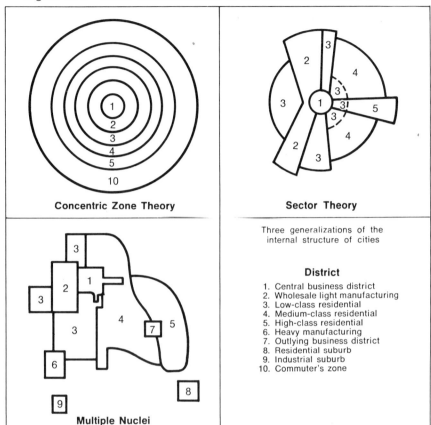

Concentric Zone Theory

Sector Theory

Multiple Nuclei

Three generalizations of the
internal structure of cities

District

1. Central business district
2. Wholesale light manufacturing
3. Low-class residential
4. Medium-class residential
5. High-class residential
6. Heavy manufacturing
7. Outlying business district
8. Residential suburb
9. Industrial suburb
10. Commuter's zone

SOURCE: Chauncey D. Harris and Edward L. Ullman, "The Nature of Cities," *The Annals of the American Academy of Political and Social Science,* CCXLII (November, 1945), 13. Reprinted by permission.

shapes extending outward from the city center. According to Hoyt, high rent and high income sections of a city tend to be on the outer fringes of one or more quadrants or sectors of the community. These areas also tend to be furthest removed from factory districts. The low rent areas sometimes extend from the very center of the city to its periphery. The growth of population is marked by an outward movement of the high rent areas along any given sector, which may be initially determined by topographic factors and travel routes. Whether a city shows a sector or concentric zone ecological structure depends in large part on the natural landscape and the initial changes made by people. Where there are no serious natural or man-made barriers as in flat terrain, cities tend to conform to the concentric zone pattern.

Multiple Nuclei

A third major generalization regarding the internal structure of the city is Harris and Ullman's multiple nuclei pattern. According to Harris and Ullman, land use within the city is organized around a number of distinct nuclei or centers, each with its own special function. Most of the nuclei were established early in the city's history. As a city increases in size, the number of nuclei also increases and each becomes more specialized in its activities.

Critique of Ecology

Some criticism of these theories has been made by a number of people. Milla A. Alihan raised significant questions about the lack of clear-cut criteria in relating the concentric zones to various gradients, measured by indices of population, crime rates, and the like.[21] Her doubts about the assumed homogeneity of population and culture within the zones may be applied equally to sectors and nuclei. On the basis of a careful review of a number of studies of American cities, Maurice R. Davie also has questioned the applicability of the concentric-zone theory. He says it "clearly does not apply to New Haven," nor to Greater Cleveland, nor to sixteen "self-contained cities." For Davie, the Burgess thesis is too simple for the complex facts of urban development. He points out that it neglects the importance of man-made topography, which follows the building of railroads and industries.[22] Both the sector and multiple nuclei were attempts to improve upon the idea of concentric zones by taking such factors into account.

Another far-reaching critique of all three generalizations has been made by Walter Firey,[23] who stresses the need to recognize the place of sentiment as it affects urban growth and functions and argues that economic competition for land is not the key variable in determining changes in business and residential locations. In his study of land use in Boston, Firey attempts to document his thesis. Actually, as John James has pointed out, his findings do not entirely refute Hoyt's thesis. And despite the topographical character of Boston, some features of population movement are not entirely incompatible with the concentric-zone theory. Certainly there are a

---

[21]Milla A. Alihan, *Social Ecology: A Critical Analysis* (New York: Columbia University Press, 1938).

[22]Maurice R. Davie, "The Pattern of Urban Growth," *Studies in the Science of Society,* ed. G. P. Murdock (New Haven: Yale University Press, 1937).

[23]Walter Firey, *Land Use in Central Boston* (Cambridge: Harvard University Press, 1947).

nucleated center and certain gradients in social-cultural features as one moves from this center to the suburban areas.[24]

On the whole, the concepts and tools of ecological research have been an aid to understanding how cities arise, grow, and change their features. The importance of cultural factors must not be so overstressed as to lead us to ignore the place of either the natural or the man-made landscape of a given locality. The ecological and the cultural are intertwined at many points. As Richard M. Hurd, one of the initiators of modern human ecology, put it, "Underneath all economic laws . . . the last stage of analysis of the problems of the structure of cities, the distribution of utilities, the earnings of the buildings which house them, and the land values resulting therefrom, turns on individual and collective taste and preference, as shown in social habits and customs."[25]

METROPOLITAN AREAS

There have been two significant changes in urban communities in the United States: first, the clustering of central cities and their suburbs, and second, their steady expansion to form what are known as metropolitan areas.

By 1910 the growth of cities beyond their legal-political boundaries led the United States Bureau of the Census to establish the category "metropolitan districts." By 1950 such a large proportion of people were part of the social structure of cities while residing outside them in suburbs that the concept of Standard Metropolitan Area (SMA) was introduced. A Standard Metropolitan Area consists of a core or central city and all of the contiguous area meeting certain Census Bureau standards of density of population, specialization of labor force, and social and economic integration with the central city. In the 1960 census these areas were officially designated as Standard Metropolitan Statistical Areas (SMSA).

In 1950 there were 162 Standard Metropolitan Areas in the United State, totaling a population of 85 million. A decade later there were 212 SMSA's with a total of 112 million people. In 1970 there were 243 such areas with a total population of 139 million. Although most of the population increase in the past twenty years has occurred in the metropolitan areas, the bulk of the increase has been in the suburbs, not in the central cities. The United States population increased 28 million from 1950 to 1960 and 89 per cent of that

---

[24]John James, "A Critique of Firey's *Land Use in Central Boston*," *American Journal of Sociology*, 1948, 54: 228–234.
[25]Hurd, *Principles of City Land Values*, 2nd ed., p. 18. By permission.

increase took place in metropolitan areas. Only 22 per cent of the increase was in the central cities. From 1960 to 1970 the population increased by 24 million and 83 per cent of that increase was in metropolitan areas and only 16 per cent in the central cities (and the white population in central cities declined by 600,000 from 1960 to 1970).

In certain sections of this country, especially along the upper Atlantic seaboard, a great many metropolitan areas overlap or adjoin each other. This is particularly evident in the 600-mile stretch from Boston, Massachusetts, to the far tip of Fairfax County, Virginia. By 1960 this section had a population of around 40 million.[26]

Suburbs

Even casual observation reveals that not all suburban communities are alike. Various attempts have been made to work out a classification.[27] One such attempt classifies suburbs of 10,000 population or more as either residential or industrial. Industrial suburbs have the following characteristics: (1) they are "employing centers" which attract workers from other sections of the metropolitan area; (2) they are concentrated in the northeastern and north-central regions of the country; (3) they tend to be older than residential suburbs; (4) while they are found throughout the entire metropolitan area, they are often located beyond the limits of the densely populated urban core; indeed, (5) they are found in greater frequency as the distance from the central city increases; and (6) they are typically known as low-rent localities.

Residential suburbs of comparable populations are found in all metropolitan areas. They differ from industrial suburbs in that (1) their chief economic activity is retail trade, usually local in scope; (2) they tend to develop with increasing frequency as the size of the central city increases; (3) they predominate among the more recently incorporated communities; (4) very few of them are found outside the densely populated urbanized area or farther than 30 miles from the central city; and (5) they have higher rents than average among suburbs.[28]

The expansion of economic and other functions depends on changes in the central city as well as the suburbs. The residential

---

[26]See Charles Grutzner, "Expansion of Cities Alters Patterns of Living in U.S.," *New York Times,* January 27, 1957.
[27]See, for example, Victor Jones, "Economic Classification of Cities and Metropolitan Areas," *The Municipal Year Book, 1953* (Chicago: International City Managers' Association, 1953), pp. 49–57.
[28]Leo F. Schnore, "The Functions of Metropolitan Suburbs," *American Journal of Sociology,* 1956, 61: 453–458.

populations of industrial suburbs grow less rapidly than those of residential suburbs, and this is directly traceable to the specialization of function in the industrial suburbs.

> Residential suburbs are growing rapidly because they are becoming even more residential in character, by means of large increments of housing construction. At the same time, employing suburbs are growing less rapidly because they are becoming more exclusively devoted to industry and other employment-providing activities. In these employing places, the net effect of this increased specialization in production and employment is (a) to drive out pre-existent residential uses of land, and (b) to discourage new construction of housing.[29]

Such differentiation and specialization of land use in suburbs is but a part of the larger changes going on throughout metropolitan areas. In time some kind of working balance will probably arise between shifts in population in the central city and the suburban fringe and changes in the socioeconomic functions.[30],

Moving to Suburbia

There are a number of social and sociological elements involved in the shifts in residence. First, a high proportion of the urban workers who live in the suburbs came originally from rural areas.[31] Suburban residents engage in more "neighboring" than their urban counterparts, and there is considerable retention of the values and attitudes of small primary communities.[32] Suburbs differ in several ways, however, from small communities of similar size which are not part of a metropolitan area. Residential suburbs tend to show higher than average incomes per family and a higher proportion of persons in white-collar occupational statuses; they spend proportionately more on schools, and in general have a higher level of living than do nonmetropolitan communities of like size.[33]

---

[29]Leo F. Schnore, "The Growth of Metropolitan Suburbs," *American Sociological Review*, 1957, 22: 165–173. Quotation from p. 171, by permission. In this article, the author uses the term "employing suburb" as practically synonymous with the "industrial suburb" of his earlier article cited above. See also Schnore's "Satellites and Suburbs," *Social Forces*, 1957, 36: 121–127.

[30]For rather exhaustive treatments of changes in metropolitan areas, see Donald J. Bogue, *Population Growth in Standard Metropolitan Areas, 1900–1950, with an Explanatory Analysis of Urbanized Areas* (Washington, D.C.: U.S. Government Printing Office, 1953); and Amos H. Hawley, *The Changing Shape of Metropolitan America: Deconcentration since 1920* (Glencoe, Ill.: The Free Press, 1956).

[31]Noel Gist, "Ecological Decentralization and Rural-Urban Relationships," *Rural Sociology*, 1952, 17: 328–335.

[32]Sylvia Fleis Fava, "Suburbanism as a Way of Life," *American Sociological Review*, 1956, 21: 34-37. This paper contains a good review of the literature on suburbia.

[33]W. F. Ogburn, *The Social Characteristics of Cities* (Chicago: International City Managers' Association, 1937), pp. 47–55.

Several studies indicate that migration to the suburbs is motivated by the desire for primary group interaction and higher level of living, while still being able to work at urban occupation and procure urban services. A sample of informants who had moved from the central city of Milwaukee to unincorparted areas outside gave as the most important reasons the following, listed in order of their importance: "better for children," "less congested," "cleaner," larger lot," "lower taxes," forced to move," and "cheaper land."[34] From interviews with suburban dwellers in the metropolitan area of Chicago, Wendell Bell concludes

> If anonymity, impersonality, defilement of air and land by industry, apartment living, crowding, and constant nervous stimulation are inherent in "urbanism as a way of life," as some writers say, then the findings of this study necessitate the conclusion that the suburbanite *is* seeking an escape from many traditional aspects of city life. The suburbanite seems to be seeking a way of life in which family, community, and immediate enjoyment through living the "good life" are dominant and interdependent ends.[35]

CONSEQUENCES OF METROPOLITAN EXPANSION

A number of serious problems result from the expansion of metropolitan areas. Some, such as those concerned with highways, streets, and parking space, are physical; some, such as those involving industrial decentralization, are economic; others are governmental—taxation and schools; and some are exclusively sociological—housing and recreation problems, for example.

Transportation Problems

The automobile played a key part in the extension of suburbia and the development of metropolitan areas. Yet the automobile has created problems of congestion and pollution. These problems are becoming steadily more serious, for both the population and the number of cars per capita are increasing. Since 1930 the number of motor vehicles has multiplied three times as fast as the number of people. The number of registered motor vehicles in the U.S. in 1950 was 49 million; in 1960, 74 million; and in 1970, 109 million.

Superhighways facilitate the flow of traffic in the open country and usually bypass the core of the larger cities. Belt routes which

---

[34]Richard Dewey, "Peripheral Expansion in Milwaukee County," *American Journal of Sociology*, 1948, 54: 118–125.
[35]Wendell Bell, "Familism and Suburbanization: One Test of the Social Choice Hypothesis," *Rural Sociology*, 1956, 21: 276–283. Quotation from p. 283. By permission.

circle downtown business districts also help reduce congestion in some areas, but the street congestion, parking problems, and pollution inside the central city are growing more serious. "The deficiency of parking space is more easily correctable than the acute highway congestion in and around urban centers. At the edge of the city limits the so-called modern highway degenerates, and the once broad expanse of adequate roadbeds narrows to nothing more than antiquated city streets."[36]

Economic Changes

Accompanying the growth of the suburbs has been the decentralization of retail business and industry. Shopping centers have spread to the fringes of larger urban communities or into the suburbs themselves. Factories, too, are rising in the suburbs of many metropolitan areas, though some localities make strenuous efforts, chiefly through zoning, to keep industrial plants out. The metropolitan fringe is particularly desirable for manufacturers who use long assembly lines since these require a great deal of space, and large tracts of low-cost land are not available in the central city.

The future advantages for industry and business in the suburbs are likely to be somewhat limited. The core cities tend to keep highly specialized service. Moreover, taxes in suburbia will rise as a result of increased demands for police and fire protection, utilities, schools, roads, hospitals, and recreational facilities. Nevertheless, a marked movement back to the central cities does not appear likely in the future.

Educational Problems

One of the strong appeals of suburbia has been the fact that, for the most part, these communities had better teachers, newer and more modern school buildings and, as a rule, higher educational standards than the central cities. But these very advantages have led to rapid growth in the suburbs, and this expansion has partially nullified the advantages. As suburban communities have mushroomed in size, school costs have risen; it has been more and more necessary to set up double sessions of classes; and there has been a mounting shortage of good teachers. In some sections of the country these difficulties have been met, in part, by consolidation of two or more school districts and by centralizing school facilities at key points. The threat of increases in taxes needed, however,

[36]From Joseph C. Ingraham, "Autos in Urban Regions Rule and Frustrate Living," *New York Times*, January 28, 1957, p. 1.

often blocks necessary programs for the extension of school facilities.

Housing Problems

As metropolitan areas have continued to increase in population and expand in space, there have been widespread efforts to clear slums, stop neighborhood deterioration, and initiate programs for orderly urban development. Within the central cities this has meant replacing slums with housing projects, both public and private, of "vertical design"—that is, multiple-storied apartments which permit a considerable density of population per unit of ground space. Such a development is the Corlears Hook section of New York. At the time this project was undertaken, the existing tenements housed 878 families. The taller apartments which replaced them provide space for almost double that number of families. The vertical design in cities, however, is not without its limitations. For one thing, such construction invariably tends to aggravate traffic congestion.

In contrast with this type of new apartment housing found in the central cities is the "horizontal design"—that is, many one- or two-story single-family dwellings—found in the suburbs. One of the most serious aspects of rapid suburban growth is the fact that cheap construction and crowding of single-family dwellings create neighborhoods which in a few years may take on the features of village slums. As one observer puts it,

> Assembly-line construction of thousands of one-family houses in a single development, smaller plots, increasing commutation rates, swamping of suburban facilities by newcomers, and poorly regulated commingling of residential and industrial use of former farmland has taken the promise out of the suburbs for many. . . ,
>
> When blight starts spawning in a suburb it may spread faster than in a central city. This is particularly true in suburbs lacking either the plan or governmental structures to support parks, transit, sanitation, and other services.[37]

Political Lag

Our governmental units are largely the products of historical factors sometimes no longer applicable to the modern metropolis, and recent cultural changes have made their inflexibility more apparent than ever. The emergence of politically independent suburbs and satellite cities has resulted in overlapping and often competing

---

[37]Charles Grutzner, "Spread of Slums Arouses U.S. Cities and Suburbs," *New York Times*, January 31, 1957, p. 16. By permission.

governmental units. More than three decades ago, a government report stated

> Overlapping . . . cities and suburbs of the metropolitan districts are several layers of different-sized, bewilderingly bounded governmental areas with separate legal and fiscal identities—counties, townships, school districts, and special districts of all kinds including sanitary, sewer, library, health, park, forest preserve, street lighting, utility, water and even mosquito abatement districts.
>
> While metropolitan life overflows the artificial network of urban boundary lines, each little bailiwick of government preserves its independent island of authority, with odd results. . . . Criminals hop over jurisdictional lines which local police dare not cross without elaborate devices for administrative coordination which are only now beginning to develop.
>
> Similarly, urban planning, highway construction, transport facilities, parks and recreational preserves too frequently must await the pleasure of minor suburbs. . . . Equally serious is the political indifference and neglect arising from the retirement into the suburbs of large blocs of urban citizenry who . . . lose all civic concern in the city governing the core of their urban community. . . .[38]

Various means have been used to eliminate at least some of the most flagrant overlapping. The interplay of state and federal rights has led to the setting up of joint boards for certain administrative functions. Such an agency is the Port of New York Authority, which has charge of the bridges and tunnels that connect New York and New Jersey. It also manages various airports, bus and motor-truck terminals, and certain shipping and storage facilities. In some instances—in Denver, Colorado, for example—city and county governments have been merged. Separate cities have been federated: the present City of New York came about from unification of the five boroughs in 1898. No doubt the coming decades will see increased coordination among governing agencies in our metropolitan areas.

In many instances the metropolitan area reaches out to include a very extensive hinterland, so that the problems of the metropolitan areas—in the narrow sense—merge into those of still larger and more extensive regions.

REGIONS

Large regional areas often possess considerable geographic and cultural unity where there is a correlation between geographic homogeneity and patterns or subculture. A region may be described in terms of the following three criteria: (1) There is a physiographic

---

[38] National Resources Committee, *Urban Government* (Washington, D.C.: U.S. Government Printing Office, 1939), p. 262

foundation in climate, topography, natural resources, and plants and animals. (2) There are always basic economic patterns linked to these "natural" environmental elements: for example, the ship-building, importing, exporting, and fishing of the New England coast, or the cotton and rice economy of the Mississippi Delta. (3) The people in a region tend in time to take on certain distinctive patterns of thinking and behaving. Because of their shared experiences and activities, they develop a set of shared, learned behaviors peculiar to their area—a regional subculture.

There may or may not be some governmental counterpart to the region. In the United States, region is recognized only informally in politics, as when the "Southern bloc" of Senators holds a policy meeting, or when the governors of the Appalachian region discuss their common problems with the President. France, in contrast, is a country where, in spite of a strong central government, regions have been linked rather closely with provincial and local administrations.[39] On the international scene, large "natural" regions have often been cut up by political states which have periodically struggled for full control of these areas. The Ruhr and Saar valleys in Europe are good examples.

Regionalism

The word *regionalism* refers sometimes to a theory of, and sometimes to an action program regarding, the place of the region in national and international affairs. Some persons concerned with national planning have characterized regionalism as "a clustering of environmental, economic, social, and governmental factors to such an extent that a distinct consciousness of separate identity within the whole, a need for autonomous planning, a manifestation of cultural peculiarities, and a desire for administrative freedom are theoretically recognized and actually put into effect."[40] Regionalism arose in France and elsewhere as a reaction to centralization of economic and political power. In the United States, on the contrary, it seems to have emerged in part from felt social differences, in part as a counteraction to the serious interstate barriers to economic and other unification of larger "natural" areas.

American Regions

Regional differences in the United States were apparent almost from the beginning of the country's history. The conflict between the

[39]See Hedwig Hintze, "Regionalism," *Encyclopedia of the Social Sciences* 13: 208–218 (New York: The Macmillan Co. 1934).
[40]National Resources Committee, *Regional Factors in National Planning and Development* (Washington, D.C.: U.S. Government Printing Office, 1935), p. 138.

South and the rest of the nation is often ascribed to political differences, notably to the degree of emphasis on states' rights, but this ignores other factors—geographic, economic, and cultural—which were correlated with political conflict. The climate which allowed a plantation economy to flourish in the South, the stratification system of slaves and an ascribed aristocracy which accompanied that plantation economy—these regional differences divided the country, and the political views of the industrial North and the plantation South were more symptom than cause of regional conflict. Important as political forces are, they do not operate independently of economic and other societal conditions.

The United States has three large physiographic regions: the rough mountains and desert of the West, the Mississippi-Missouri-Ohio drainage basin, and the lesser eastern mountains with their coastal plain. These three great regions subdivide into smaller agricultural regions determined by the length of the growing season and the amount of rainfall. The principal industrial regions are in the Northeast, in the Great Lakes states, in scattered sections of the South, and increasingly in the Pacific states. Naturally, the economic attractiveness of a region for industry depends on a number of factors: availability of raw materials and labor, sufficient power, convenience of transportation, and accessibility to markets. The extension of commercialized and mechanized farming, the decrease in proportion of the population engaged in agriculture and the concomitant increase in those employed in manufacturing and services, and the shifts of industries to new locations as new resources are found, all contribute to residential migration of the population.

INTERPRETIVE SUMMARY

The distinction between rural and urban societies made earlier is an important and useful distinction for ecologists and other students of the spatial distribution of human groups and institutions. Primary agricultural societies are classified according to the degree of centralization of residential and service areas. The plantation and its variations are distinguished from other agricultural communities by their "big business" aspects which lead to unique patterns of community contact and stratification systems.

Historically, cities have tended to locate at important trade crossroads and to develop in axial or radial fashion, following the natural topography except as people modified the pattern. Well-located, industrialized cities grow especially quickly; for example, in the United States, a relatively small number of states have a high proportion of large cities. Business and service areas in the city tend to become centralized until land in the main area becomes so expensive and access to the areas so difficult that decentralization sets in. Industries, shopping areas, and whole suburbs may move to the periphery of the city bringing the city's ways with them. Cities tend to be structured in terms of concentric zones, multiple nuclei, or sectors.

The United States is characterized by an increasing number of metropolitan areas and an increasing number of people in such areas. Most of the increase has been in suburban areas. Such areas may have an industrial, commercial, or residential orientation, but in any case the consequence is that the values and behavior patterns of city dwellers are extended to ever-widening areas.

Metropolitan expansion has been accompanied by a number of problems including traffic congestion, pollution, inadequate mass transit systems, and conflicts between the various political divisions of the city that lead to overlap and lack of effective coordination in the provision of public services.

Metropolitan areas, and indeed all areas in the United States, belong to larger areas called regions. The three major regions of the United States have distinct physical environments, economic patterns, and subcultural characteristics. In many societies, region is recognized as a basic political and administrative unit. In the United States, there have been some attempts at regional administration, but economic and other problems still tend to be treated at the local, state, or federal level.

SUGGESTIONS FOR FURTHER READING

Bogue, Donald J. *The Structure of the Metropolitan Community*. Ann Arbor: University of Michigan School of Graduate Studies, 1950. This volume describes the use of ecological techniques and theories in the study of metropolitan areas.

Duncan, Otis D., and Reiss, Albert J., Jr. *Social Characteristics of Urban and Rural Communities, 1950*. New York: John Wiley and Sons, 1956. This is an elaborate descriptive analysis that is based on census data.

Duncan, Otis Dudley; Scott, W. E.; Lieberson, Stanley; Duncan, Beverly; and Winsborough, H. H. *Metropolis and Region*. Baltimore: Johns Hopkins University Press, 1960. This is a collection of studies conducted under the sponsorship of Resources for the Future, Inc. that provide some cross-sectional data on the metropolitan areas of the United States in the mid-twentieth century.

Gist, Noel P., and Fava, Sylvia. *Urban Society*. 5th ed. New York: Thomas Y. Crowell Company, 1964. For years one of the standard books in the field, this volume presents good coverage of urban ecology.

Greer, Scott A. *Urban Renewal*. Indianapolis: Bobbs-Merrill, 1964. This is a critique of the consequences of the public policies intended to result in slum clearance.

Hawley, Amos H. *Human Ecology: A Theory of Community Structure*. New York: The Ronald Press, 1950. An elaboration of a work originally begun by McKenzie, one of the early contributors to the field of ecology, this book deals chiefly with the nature and development of community structure.

International Urban Research. *The World's Metropolitan Areas.* Berkeley and Los Angeles: University of California Press, 1959. A valuable reference work, this volume marshals data to make possible comparisons of urban phenomena across national lines.

Odum, Howard W., and Moore, Harry E. *American Regionalism.* New York: Henry Holt and Company, 1938. This is the classic statement on regionalism as a theory and of the place of the region in the social structure.

Perloff, Harvey S.; Muth, R. F.; Dunn, E. S., Jr.; and Lampard, E. E. *Regions, Resources, and Economic Growth.* Baltimore: Johns Hopkins University Press, 1960. This is a series of studies that deals with the interrelations of demographic problems, resources, and economic development.

Seeley, John R.; Sim, R. Alexander; and Loosley, Elizabeth W. *Crestwood Heights: A Study of the Culture of Suburban Life.* New York: Basic Books, 1956. This is a report of research on a suburban community in central Canada. Part I deals with structure and context; Part II discusses the family, the school, and the place of voluntary associations; and Part III concerns the normative structure.

Taeuber, Karl E., and Taueber, Alma F. *Negroes in Cities.* Chicago: Aldine Publishing Company, 1965. This is an excellent analysis of residential segregation and neighborhood change in a number of large American cities.

Weber, Max. *The City.* Translated and edited by Don Martindale and Gertrud Neuwirth. Glencoe, Ill.: The Free Press, 1958. This is a collection of Weber's historical and cross-cultural essays on the evolution of cities and city life.

I KEEP RUNNING BUT I DON'T GET ANYWHERE.

HI THERE HOWARD.

MURRAY'S A GOOD EGG. I SHOULD BE **GLAD** TO SEE HIM GET AHEAD. I WON'T BE BITTER

HELLO AND GOODBYE HOWARD.

LUCILLE HAS **LOOKS.** NO WONDER SHE GETS AHEAD. I BET SHE USES HER **BODY.** BUT I WON'T BE BITTER.

WATCH MY SPEED. HOWARD.

IRWIN IS FIVE YEARS YOUNGER THAN ME AND A NO GOOD PUNK!

I KNOW I'D DO BETTER IF NOT FOR THESE STOMACH ACHES.

11
Social
Stratification

In any human society people rarely, if ever, accept all others as social equals. In every society some people are identified as superior and others as inferior: there are aristocrats and commoners, masters and slaves, elites and masses, the privileged and the disadvantaged, the rich and the poor, the esteemed and the demeaned, and the rulers and the ruled. Social inequality is probably a universal feature of human society. In all or nearly all societies the good things in life, the things that people desire, are unequally distributed; some have more and others have less. Social stratification refers to the persistence over time of the inequality of valued rewards—as when parents pass on their wealth to their children or when children "inherit" (socially speaking) the same position as their family. When the opportunity for education and good health and social respectability is dependent upon whether or not one's parents are impoverished or affluent, social startification exists. The question which underlies and permeates the study of social stratification, therefore, is the question "who gets what and why?"

The rigidity of social stratification varies considerably from society to society. In some societies, no member can change from the class into which he is born, he must marry a person born into the same class as he, and his class position is the prime determinant of the amount of education he receives, the occupation in which he spends his life, and various other features of his social life. In other societies, one's position in the stratification structure is relatively changeable. In such a situation, it is possible for the son of an accountant to quit high school, never go to college, become a garage mechanic, and yet marry the daughter of his employer. Furthermore, there may be some disagreement among members of the society as to whether the accountant is upper class or middle class, and whether the garage mechanic is middle class or lower class.

 The more complex the division of labor becomes the more opportunity there is for a class structure to develop; therefore, settled communities are likely to have more complex stratification systems than nomadic tribes, and all urban industrial societies invariably have some form of class stratification. The degree of social inequality in any society is also dependent upon the level of technology and the amount of economic surplus (the goods and services over and above the minimum required to keep producers alive and productive) of the society. According to Lenski, the amount of societal inequality increases as the surplus of a society increases.[1] Since social stratification is related to the distribution of the scarce and valued resources in society, those societies with a very small amount of economic surplus have little inequality. As techonolgy improves and agricultural techniques are developed, the economic surplus rises and inequality reaches a peak. This process is exemplified in such great agrarian societies as the ancient empires of Rome and China. According to Lenski, inequality begins to decline with industrialization because of the nature of the industrial economy: (1) workers at various levels of expertise have skill monopolies and therefore more power in industrial societies than in agrarian societies; (2) managers and other experts have considerable authority in the industrial system and thus command great economic rewards; (3) workers organized into large factories have the power to strike and slow down production; (4) industrialism requires mass distribution and consumption of its products. The industrial system, in short, simply demands more equality than the agrarian system.

The stratification system of a society is partially dependent on the normative order of the culture, since this will determine the criteria upon which statuses are ranked: the power they have, the wealth associated with them, and so on. When we speak of a stratification structure, it is easy to sound as if it were a static, permanent thing. Actually, of course, stratification, like any other feature of social organization, is constantly changing. To achieve some perspective

---

[1]Gerhard E. Lenski, *Power and Privilege* (New York: McGraw-Hill Book Company, Inc., 1966).

11-1   Economic Surplus and Societal Inequality

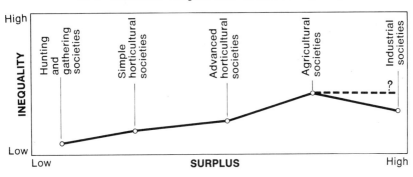

on the wide variation in social stratification and the dynamics of the stratification process, we shall look briefly at stratification in various times and places.

A CROSS–CULTURAL VIEW OF STRATIFICATION

Stratification Among Nonliterates

In North America the Kwakiutl had a rather rigid scheme, as did the warring Plains Indians. The Pueblo groups, on the other hand, had a somewhat flexible stratification structure. There were caste systems in both Peru and Mexico. In large parts of Africa, Asia, and Oceania, stratification is common. For example, in many parts of western Africa the king and his nobles make up a rigid, inheritable class rationalized as of divine sanction. Below them are various political ranks, specialized craftsmen, commoners, and slaves. There are other forms of stratification structures, as among the cattle-raising Wahuma of eastern Africa, who are the top class ruling the horticultural Bantu, whom they conquered.

In Polynesia there is an abundance of caste. The Maori nobility of New Zealand trace their descent through primogeniture back to the highest gods. Every man of distinction has to memorize his lineage so that on occasion he can recite his pedigree. There are five groups of freemen: chiefs, priests, landed gentry, large land holders, and commoners. Moreover, the gradations of rank within these castes are numerous. Complex forms of address and carefully detained rituals are worked out to control the relations of the various castes and ranks to one another. Somewhat similar caste systems exist elsewhere in the South Pacific.

Caste in India

The Hindu caste system has long been of great interest to Western peoples, and around it has grown up a host of myths and legends. In actuality it is more flexible, more dynamic, and more complex than is generally recognized. The word *caste* comes from the Portuguese *casta*, meaning lineage; and its application to the system in India shows that the first Westerners to reach the region understood the central place which kinship has in the maintenance of the gradation. The Hindu word for caste is *varna*, meaning color and there is little doubt that in India color and racial differences have had some part in setting up caste lines.

Hindu tradition relates that the major divisions were established about 600 B.C. The ancient Laws of Manu gave the four chiefs castes as follows: (1) the *Brahmans*, or priests, who were "assigned the duties of reading the Vedas [the sacred books], of teaching, of sacrificing, of assisting others to sacrifice, of giving alms if they be rich, and if indigent of receiving gifts"; (2) the military chieftains, or overlords, called the *Kshatriya*, whose duties were "to defend the people, to give alms, to sacrifice, to read the Vedas, to shun the allurements of sensual gratification"; (3) the agriculturists, herdsmen, and traders, called the *Vaisya*; and (4) the servile class of menials and industrial workers, or *Sudra*, whose duty it was "to serve the before-mentioned classes without depreciating their worth."[2]

The Laws of Manu mention 50 castes besides these major *varnas*. Outside these four orders, and outside the pale of Hinduism, is a varied mass of outcastes, the lowest of whom, the *Chandalas*, are regarded about on a par with such "unclean" animals as dogs and donkeys.[3] The four divisions, indeed, are but the skeleton of a highly complex system of castes and subcastes. The 1901 census of India listed over 800 castes and subcastes.[4] When the local differences in subcastes are taken into account, the number in fact reaches nearly 5,000. Castes and subcastes are constantly forming and reforming by division or unification. When we come to study the system closely, we find, not the static, stereotyped picture of fiction or popular legend, but a living, changing social organization. Although the Indian system of castes represents the most highly integrated system of social stratification that has arisen anywhere, its very dynamic character shows that, while the regulations are severe and of long standing, the actuality of social practice cannot be defined within narrow, unchanging limits. Moreover, caste or subcaste in India is not determined by any one standard. Castes are formed on

---

[2]Quoted material from F. Max Miller, Chapter 10, *The Laws of Manu*, Vol. 25, in *The Sacred Books of the East* (London: Oxford University Press, 1886).
[3]See L. S. S. O'Malley, *Indian Caste Customs* (London: Cambridge University Press, 1932), p. 13.
[4]After the census of 1901, the tabulation of every tribe and minor caste was abandoned as not worth the time and effort. See O'Malley, p. 3.

the basis of occupations, sectarian groups, races, tribes, or other associations of people with distinctive cultural traits or social roles.

To people of Western culture, some of the regulations of caste seem extreme indeed. For example, one may not sit down to eat with another who is not of the same caste. All meals must be prepared by one of his own caste or by a Brahman. No man of inferior caste may touch the cooked rations of one of higher caste or, for that matter, enter into the latter's culinary quarters. No water or other liquid, once contaminated by the touch of one of inferior caste, may be used. (Tanks, rivers, and other larger bodies of water, however, are not considered capable of defilement.) Articles of dry food—for instance, rice, wheat, or millet—are not made impure by passing through the hands of a man of lower caste, but they cannot be used if they become moistened or greased. Among the peoples of southern India, where the unclean castes are peculiarly offensive to the higher ranks, pollution may occur even without touching. For example, a Kaniyan pollutes a Brahman if he comes within 32 feet of him, and a Niar pollutes him at a distance of 24 feet.

The severity of social pressure on the man who has been put out of his caste is striking. When a Hindu is expelled from his caste, his friends, relatives, and fellow townspeople refuse to accept his hospitality; he is not invited to their houses; he cannot secure brides or bridegrooms for his children; his own married daughters scarcely dare visit him lest they also lose caste. His priest, barber, and washerman will not serve him. Fellow members of his caste even decline to assist at a funeral of one of his household. With group codes felt so strongly by the individual, it is no wonder that such a system persists even in the face of many forces that tend to disintegrate it.

Although the caste system remains dominant in most of rural India, many changes have weakened its hold on the urban population. The urbanization of population affords the person who has lost caste a chance to change his identity in a great city, to take up another occupation, and perhaps to marry outside his caste. Travel and mobility throw the castes together in situations that were not likely to arise before the coming of the railroad and the crowded conditions of large cities. Schooling has helped alter the attitude toward caste, especially among those with a higher education. Christianity and other foreign religions have gradually had some effect on attitudes toward caste. The spread of nationalistic and democratic ideas has had a powerful influence on the attitudes toward some features of the caste structure. In fact, in the very first years of Indian independence, measures were introduced in the national legislature to abolish many features of the caste system, including a 1955 law which made discrimination against untouchables (the lowest caste) a crime and a 1956 law which permitted inter-caste marriage. Yet the inertia of custom and tradition is powerful.[5] The village, the heart of Hindu social organization, is the seat of caste at its strongest. Family life, religion, and occupation still provide powerful support for the system.

Class and Caste in Mediterranean Societies

The class structures of Babylonia, Egypt, Persia, Greece, and Rome were often rigid, though not as elaborate as that which developed in India. In Egypt there were two upper classes—warriors and priests. Besides these there were various lesser classes of professionals and artisans, all relatively fixed. Babylonia, as early as the time of Hammurabi (ca. 1950 B.C.), had a hierarchical feudal order in which class lines were strictly drawn.

Mesopotamia was apparently fairly free from anything approaching caste, but ancient Iran, or Persia, from which the Aryan conquerors of India are thought to have come, had, according to legend, four castes—priests, warriors, agriculturists, and artificers. In Greece we find variation. Sparta long retained what was in effect a caste system, with a division of the population into spartiates, or full citizens; perioeci, those engaged in husbandry or trade; helots or serfs; and slaves. On the other hand, as Athens developed into a complex and cosmopolitan state, the ancient class structure there was greatly modified.

In Rome the story is an interesting one of relatively definite classes constantly being dissolved by changes in economic and political power and then re-established, until we get to the Empire, with its final crystallization of Roman society. With the gradual disappearance of the middle classes, the patricians formed a closed class, and the masses were rather thoroughly subjugated under a severe economic and political regime from which the individual could not escape.

Estates of Feudal Europe

With the breakup of the Roman Empire following the "barbarian" invasions, society in western Europe was refashioned along somewhat different lines. The feudal order which emerged was a more or less legally fixed system of classes, sometimes called *estates*. There were various gradations: overlords, lesser lords, knights, burghers, guild members, freemen, and serfs. A shift from one level to another

---

[5]See Fred Greene, *The Far East* (New York: Rinehart & Company, Inc., 1957), p. 376; and Gerald D. Berreman, "Caste in India and the United States," *American Journal of Sociology*, 1960, 66: 120–127.

was difficult. Gradually economic and political changes came about, and the seeds were sown for the disintegration of the old order and the rise of a more flexible class system.[6]

Classes in Modern Europe

The commercial and industrial revolutions disrupted the feudal order and set in motion cultural and social changes that not only produced a shift from primary to secondary organization of society but influenced Western class structure. While the landed aristocracy, the military class, and the ecclesiastical hierarchy remained in the upper brackets, new classes emerged: first, from the large industrial entrepreneurs, bankers, and merchants; second, from the petty business groups; and third, from the rapidly growing urban industrial masses. The last became increasingly numerous and socially more powerful than the peasant and gradually declining serf classes. The shift in the strength of the lowest class was slow. Serfdom did not disappear in France until shortly before the French Revolution, until Napoleon's time in Germany, and in Russia not until after the middle of the nineteenth century.

The most important elements in the modern world which tended to alter the class system were (1) the capitalistic business enterprise and its close associate, the factory system; (2) the political order, which stressed nationalism and, later, democracy; (3) the coming of religious tolerance and freedom following the Protestant Reformation; and (4) the expanding spirit and practice of free inquiry, which led to modern science and technology and had a marked effect on political democracy, business, and even religion.

The liquidation of former social classes following a great political-economic revolution is well documented in history. For example, in contrast to Czarist days, the present pyramid of power in Soviet Russia follows the pattern of a dominant-party elite: a vast range of administrative officials at the top and below this the masses, within which there are recognized gradations.[7] Wars, like revolutions, often bring about considerable shift in the class organization; World War I induced many such alterations in Europe, and World War II resulted in even more drastic changes.

Since the end of the Middle Ages—say from the fifteenth century to the present—there has been a gradual loosening of old patterns of

---

[6]For an excellent discussion of the estate system of medieval Europe, see Kurt B. Mayer, *Class and Society* (New York: Random House, 1955), pp. 16–21.
[7]For diagrams showing the shift in class structure in Russia, see David Dallin, *The Real Soviet Russia* (New Haven: Yale University, 1944), p. 97. See also Alex Inkeles, "Social Stratification and Mobility in the Soviet Union: 1940–1950," *American Sociological Review*, 1950, 15: 465–470.

class rule in political affairs. The emergence of nationalism led within two centuries to the beginnings of democratic control. The movement of persons up and down the political ladder—like the movement in occupations or wealth—is accelerated in periods of rapid social change or revolution. During the last century, political changes in Great Britain and western Europe brought political power into the hands of the middle classes. In the present century there have been still further shifts toward parliamentary democracy, as in the Weimar Republic of Germany and in Czechoslovakia, and a shift toward fascist revolution, as under Hitler and Mussolini. In all these cases the class system was modified. After World War II, Russian influence on central Europe fostered imitation of the Soviet pattern. Elsewhere in Europe, liberal democratic forces often found themselves in conflict with conservative elements.

In religious activity, much the same thing had taken place. Although during the history of the Roman Catholic Church certain families sometimes dominated the highest position, it is nevertheless true that the Church always provided a modicum of opportunity for people of ability to move upward from the lower social classes. The Protestant Reformation especially made it more possible for persons of lower status to rise in importance. Moreover, the individualism stimulated by Protestantism has had an effect on political, economic, and intellectual life. Hence achieved status became an important factor in the class structure.

CLASS STRUCTURE IN THE UNITED STATES

The United States is one example of a relatively open-class system in which birth or lineage is only one element in the determination of class position. Despite variations in the degree to which achieved status is overshadowed by ascribed status, the open-class system has been increasingly identified with the common man and the democratic process. Yet, social stratification persists in America. A major aspect of the American stratification structure is the fact that, along with this open-class system, there existed human slavery, which later, under military-political pressure, gave way to a caste system based on color. The persistence of the white-black caste relationship not only is an intriguing cultural paradox, but continues to present the United States with one of its most serious and pressing local and national dilemmas.[8] Similarly, opportunities for women in American society continue to be restricted in many ways, and sexism, like racism, pervades the society.

---

[8]See Gunnar Myrdal, et al., An American Dilemma: The Negro Problem and Modern Democracy, Second Edition (New York: Harper and Row, 1963.)

Social stratification is so complex and multifaceted that the criteria of class position in modern urban-industrial societies are sometimes vague and usually changing. Consequently, classes are not clearly delineated in the minds of many Americans and tend to overlap. There is, for example, general consensus in the United States that it is better to make much money than little, that it is better to be educated than ignorant, that professional occupations have higher prestige than unskilled occupations. But consensus declines when more criteria than one are involved. Who ranks higher in the class structure, the person with a moderate income and a great deal of education, or the one with a moderate amount of education and a high income?[9]

The Distribution of Wealth

Social stratification refers to the unequal distribution of the valued items of the society. In modern industrial societies few things are more valued, more consequential, and more unequally distributed than wealth. Valid and reliable data on wealth are not plentiful partly because most people, especially wealthy people, are reluctant to discuss the subject with researchers. One of the most careful and reliable studies of wealth in the United States is by Robert J. Lampman.[10] According to Lampman's estimates, persons with assets in excess of $50,000—only 2 per cent of the population—held nearly 30 per cent of all the wealth in 1953 while 50 per cent of the population held only 8 per cent of the wealth (see Table 11-1). In 1929 the richest 2 per cent of the population held 33 per cent of all privately held wealth. More current reports indicate that the distribution of wealth has not changed significantly in recent years. In 1962, for instance, the 4,132 persons who reported gross assets of

---

[9]Gerhard E. Lenski, "American Social Classes: Statistical Strata or Social Groups?" *American Journal of Sociology*, 1952, 58: 139–144; Thomas E. Lasswell, "A Study of Social Stratification Using an Area Sample of Raters," *American Sociological Review*, 1954, 19: 310–313; S. Stanfeld Sargent, "Class and Class-Consciousness in a California Town," *Social Problems*, 1953, 1: 22–27; Richard Scudder and C. Arnold Anderson, "The Relation of Being Known to Status Rating," *Sociology and Social Research*, 1954, 38: 239–241; Scudder and Anderson, "Range of Acquaintance and of Repute as Factors in Prestige Rating Methods of Studying Social Status," *Social Forces*, 1954, 32: 248–253; Werner S. Landecker, "Class Boundaries," *American Sociological Review*, 1960, 25: 868–877; and C. Arnold Anderson, "A Skeptical Note on the Relation of Vertical Mobility," *American Journal of Sociology*, 1961, 66: 560–570.

[10]Robert Lampman, "Changes in the Share of Wealth by Top Wealth-Holders 1922–1956," *Review of Economics and Statistics*, XLI (November, 1959), 379–392. Also Robert J. Lampman, "Income Distribution and Poverty," in Margaret S. Gordon, ed., *Poverty in America* (San Francisco: Chandler Publishing Co., 1965), pp. 102–114.

Table 11-1   Estimated Distribution of Wealth in the United States, 1953

Assets	Percentage of Population	Percentage of Wealth
Less than $3,500	50.0	8.3
$3,500 to $10,000	18.4	10.2
$10,000 to $20,000	21.2	29.3
$20,000 to $30,000	5.8	13.4
$30,000 to $50,000	2.7	9.5
$50,000 to $100,000	1.0	6.2
$100,000 to $1,000,000	0.9	16.6
$1,000,000 to $10,000,000	0.04	5.2
$10,000,000 and over	0.0006	1.3
Total	100.0	100.0

SOURCE: Robert J. Lampman, *The Share of Top Wealth-holders in National Wealth: 1922–1956* (Princeton, N.J.: Princeton University Press, 1962), tables 34 and 99.

$60,000 or more had a total net worth of $670 billion while 28 per cent of the population had a net worth of less than $1,000 apiece.

The Distribution of Income

Because most Americans do not have substantial wealth, they must depend upon earned income. Income is more equally distributed than wealth, but as late as 1970, when the median income for all families and unrelated individuals (persons living alone) was $8,335, nearly one-fourth of the population earned less than half

Table 11-2   Total Money Income of Families and Unrelated Individuals in the United States, 1970

Income Category	Per Cent
Less than $1,000	3.9
$1,000–$1,999	7.4
2,000– 3,999	12.6
4,000– 5,999	11.8
6,000– 7,999	12.1
8,000– 9,999	12.1
10,000–14,999	22.1
15,000–24,999	14.2
25,000 and more	3.7
Median Income	$8,335

SOURCE: U.S. Bureau of the Census, *Current Population Reports,* Series P-60, No. 80 (Washington, D.C.: U.S. Government Printing Office, 1971), p. 21.

Table 11-3   Percentage of Income Received by Each Fifth
of Families and Individuals in the United States,
1944 and 1969

Families and Individuals Ranked from Highest Income to Lowest	1944	1969
Highest Fifth	46	45*
Second Fifth	22	23
Third Fifth	16	17
Fourth Fifth	11	11
Lowest Fifth	5	4

*The lowest income included in the highest fifth in 1969 was $18,410.
SOURCE: U.S. Bureau of the Census, *Historical Statistics of the United States* (Washington, D.C.: U.S. Government Printing Office, 1960); and U.S. Bureau of the Census, *Statistical Abstract of the United States, 1971* (Washington, D.C.: U.S. Government Printing Office, 1971), p. 317.

that amount (see Table 11-2). Moreover, the distribution of income has changed very little in the last quarter century. In 1944 the 20 per cent of the population that had the highest incomes received 46 per cent of all income while the poorest 20 per cent of the population received only 5 per cent. As Table 11-3 indicates, the situation had changed very little by 1969. Taxes, it should be noted, do not have a significant effect of the equalization of income. Persons with less than $2,000 are the most heavily taxed; they pay about 44 per cent of their income in federal, state, and local taxes.[11] Persons with incomes between $2,000 and $15,000 pay about 27 per cent of their income in taxes, and persons with incomes over $15,000 pay 38 per cent in taxes.

Income and Occupation

The most frequently used measures of class are occupation, wealth, income, and education. Many other items associated with or dependent on these variables have also been used: type of home, "quality" of neighborhood, monthly rent, and the like. The two which are most often used are income and occupation.[12] Income and occupation are, of course, closely interrelated. Table 11-4 shows the relationship between wages and salary income and occupation for

[11]Joseph Pechman, "The Rich, the Poor, and the Taxes They Pay," *The Public Interest,* 17 (Fall, 1968), pp. 21–43.
[12]W. Lloyd Warner, M. Meeker, and Kenneth Eells, *Social Class in America: A Manual for Procedure for the Measurement of Social Status* (Chicago: Science Research Associates, 1949), Chaps. 8–14.

full-time, year-round male workers. Table 11-5 shows the association between education and the total money income for all year-round, full-time male workers aged 25 and older.

Furthermore, there is considerable agreement among Americans about the relative prestige of various occupations. The National Opinion Research Center conducted a public-opinion poll of people in the United States which ranked 90 different occupations on a five-point scale: excellent, good, average, below average, and poor. From two-thirds to three-fourths of all people gainfully employed in the United States were in one of the 90 occupations rated. The ratings were scored so that an occupation receiving exclusively "excellent" ratings would score 100, while one unanimously rated "poor" would score 20. Table 11-6 shows the results of this research.

CONSEQUENCES AND CORRELATES OF CLASS

Research such as the nationwide public-opinion poll on the prestige of occupations offers useful information about the existence of a status structure and the consensus among members of society about the criteria of status. Other research shows that various occupations, incomes, and amounts of education lead people to share different norms and to behave differently. In other words, the existence of a class structure leads to the development of class subcultures. And in time, the patterns fostered in the subculture themselves become criteria of placement in the class structure. Not just

Table 11-4   Occupation and Median Wage or Salary Income
of Year-Round, Full-Time Male Workers in the
United States, 1970

Occupation	*Median Wage-Salary*
White Collar Occupations:	
Managers, officials, and proprietors	$11,430
Professional, technical and kindred workers	10,722
Sales workers	7,992
Clerical workers	7,585
Blue Collar Occupations:	
Craftsmen, foremen and kindred workers	8,580
Operatives and kindred workers	6,671
Service workers (except private household)	5,027
Laborers (except farm and mine)	4,337
Farm Occupations:	
Farmers and farm managers	1,105
Farm laborers and foremen	1,911

SOURCE: *Current Population Reports,* Series P-60, No. 80, October 4, 1971, p. 129.

Table 11-5   Education and Median (Total Money) Income of
Year-Round, Full-Time Male Workers*
in the United States, 1970

Education	Median Income
Elementary	
Less than 8 years	$6,043
8 years	7,535
High School	
1–3 years	8,514
4 years	9,567
College	
1–3 years	11,183
4 years	13,264
5 years or more	14,747

*Males aged 25 and older.
SOURCE: *Current Population Reports*, Series P-60, No. 80, October 4, 1971, p. 102.

Table 11-6   Occupational Prestige Rankings in the United States,
1963 and 1947

Occupation	1963 Rank	1947 Rank
U.S. supreme court justice	1	1
Physician	2	2.5
Nuclear physicist	3.5	18
Scientist	3.5	8
Government scientist	5.5	10.5
State governor	5.5	2.5
Cabinet member in the federal government	8	4.5
College professor	8	8
U.S. representative in Congress	8	8
Chemist	11	18
Lawyer	11	18
Diplomat in the U.S. foreign service	11	4.5
Dentist	14	18
Architect	14	18
County judge	14	13
Psychologist	17.5	22
Minister	17.5	13
Member of the board of directors of a large corporation	17.5	18
Mayor of a large city	17.5	6
Priest	21.5	18
Head of a department in a state government	21.5	13
Civil engineer	21.5	23
Airline pilot	21.5	24.5

Table 11-6   Occupational Prestige Rankings in the United States, 1963 and 1947 *(Cont.)*

Occupation	1963 Rank	1947 Rank
Banker	24.5	10.5
Biologist	24.5	29
Sociologist	26.	26.5
Instructor in public schools	27.5	34
Captain in the regular army	27.5	31.5
Accountant for a large business	29.5	29
Public-school teacher	29.5	36
Owner of a factory that employs about 100 people	31.5	26.5
Building contractor	31.5	34
Artist who paints pictures that are exhibited in galleries	34.5	24.5
Musician in a symphony orchestra	34.5	29
Author of novels	34.5	31.5
Economist	34.5	34
Official of an international labor union	37	40.5
Railroad engineer	39	37.5
Electrician	39	45
County agricultural agent	39	37.5
Owner-operator of a printing shop	41.5	42.5
Trained machinist	41.5	45
Farm owner & operator	44	39
Undertaker	44	47
Welfare worker for a city government	44	45
Newspaper columnist	46	42.5
Policeman	47	55
Reporter on a daily newspaper	48	48
Radio announcer	49.5	40.5
Bookkeeper	49.5	51.5
Tenant farmer	51.5	51.5
Insurance agent	51.5	51.5
Carpenter	53	58
Manager of a small store in a city	54.5	49
A local official of a labor union	54.5	62
Mail carrier	57	57
Railroad conductor	57	55
Traveling salesman for a wholesale concern	57	51.5
Plumber	59	59.5
Automobile repairman	60	59.5
Playground director	62.5	55
Barber	62.5	66
Machine operator in a factory	62.5	64.5
Owner-operator of a lunch stand	62.5	62
Corporal in the regular army	65.5	64.5
Garage mechanic	65.5	62

Table 11-6   Occupational Prestige Rankings in the United States,
1963 and 1947 *(Cont.)*

Occupation	1963 Rank	1947 Rank
Truck driver	67	71
Fisherman who owns his own boat	68	68
Clerk in a store	70	68
Milk route man	70	71
Streetcar motorman	70	68
Lumberjack	72.5	73
Restaurant cook	72.5	71
Singer in a nightclub	74	74.5
Filling station attendant	75	74.5
Dockworker	77.5	81.5
Railroad section hand	77.5	79.5
Night watchman	77.5	81.5
Coal miner	77.5	77.5
Restaurant waiter	80.5	79.5
Taxi driver	80.5	77.5
Farm hand	83	76
Janitor	83	85.5
Bartender	83	85.5
Clothes presser in a laundry	85	83
Soda fountain clerk	86	84
Sharecropper	87	87
Garbage collector	88	88
Street sweeper	89	89
Shoe shiner	90	90
Average	71	70

SOURCE: Robert W. Hodge, Paul M. Siegel, and Peter H. Rossi, "Occupational Prestige in the United States: 1925–1963," *The American Journal of Sociology,* 70 (November, 1964), 286–302. © 1964 by The University of Chicago.

one's income, but the way he spends it; not just his occupational status, but his attitude toward it—these become factors partially determining his social status.

Style of Life

Some of the most detailed descriptions of the styles of life of people in different social classes are found in the work of W. Lloyd Warner and his associates.[13] The best known of these exhaustive in-

---

[13]W. Lloyd Warner and Paul S. Lunt, *The Social Life of a Modern Community* (New Haven: Yale University Press, 1941); W. Lloyd Warner and Paul S. Lunt, *The Status System of a Modern Community* (New Haven: Yale University Press, 1942); W. Lloyd Warner and Leo Srole, *The Social Systems of American Ethnic*

vestigations was of "Yankee City," a New England community of about 17,000. On the basis of the research, Warner identified social classes in Yankee City.

1. *Upper-upper:* the elite, based on inherited high family status and wealth, socialized in aristocratic etiquette, and comprising 1.4 per cent of the population.

2. *Lower-upper:* families with patterns of income, occupation, and participation similar to the upper-uppers, but with more recently acquired wealth and hence lacking old-family prestige; professionals and businessmen; making up 1.6 per cent of the total.

3. *Upper-middle:* moderately successful business and professional people without distinguished lineage; respected civic leaders but not "society people"; constituting 10.2 per cent.

4. *Lower-middle:* small businessmen, white-collar workers, craftsmen and foremen, living in neat houses; conservative, self-conscious about respectability; comprising 28.1 per cent.

5. *Upper-lower:* lower white-collar employees, semiskilled factory workers, and service workers; "poor but hardworking"; comprising 32.6 per cent.

6. *Lower-lower:* not "respectable" people; unskilled workers, families on relief, transients; making up 25.2 per cent.

Warner found numerous variations in style of life among the six classes. For example, some social clubs were exclusively upper-upper; upper-middle-class men belonged to luncheon clubs; fraternal lodges were primarily lower-middle; and labor unions were upper-lower. Similarly, members of the different classes attended different churches, read different magazines, and in general showed evidence of participating in a number of different aspects of community life.

There are striking similarities between the conceptions of the class structure held by the residents of Yankee City, with their assumptions of differences in morals and "respectability" between the classes, and the description of the stratification structure of Plainville, a rural community in Missouri studied by James West.[14]

An investigation of class structure in Burlington, Vermont, showed that nationality and religion in the subculture played important

---

Groups (New Haven: Yale University Press, 1945); W. Lloyd Warner and J. O. Low, *The Social System of the Modern Factory* (New Haven: Yale University Press, 1947); Allison Davis, B. B. Gardner, and M. R. Gardner, *Deep South* (Chicago: University of Chicago Press, 1941); W. Lloyd Warner et al., *Democracy in Jonesville* (New York: Harper & Brothers, 1949); A. B. Hollingshead, *Elmtown's Youth* (New York: John Wiley & Sons, 1949).
[14]James West, *Plainville, U.S.A.* (New York: Columbia University Press, 1945), p. 117.

Figure 11-2   Differential Views of the Plainville Class Structure

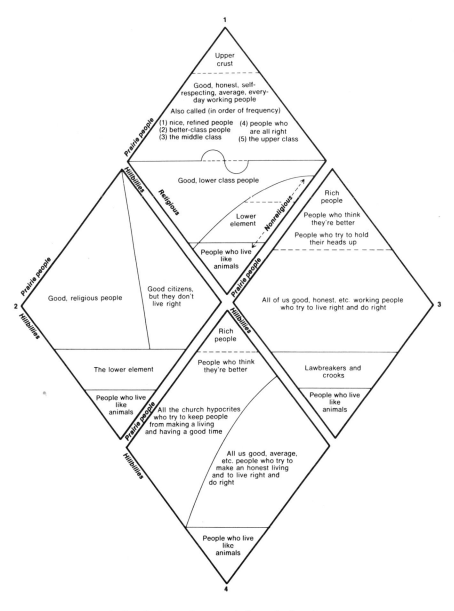

1 The Plainville class structure as seen by "upper class" people
2 The Plainville class structure as seen by "good religious" people
3 The Plainville class structure as seen by "working class" people
4 The Plainville class structure as seen by "nonreligious lower class" people

Source: James West [Carl Withers], *Plainville, U.S.A.* (New York: Columbia University Press, 1945), pp. 117 and 130. Reprinted by permission.

parts in the class system. In this community the families of old Yankee stock, although a definite numerical minority of the total population, were at the top of the stratification order. The other broad category is made up of "foreigners" and "newcomers." The "foreigners" are not necessarily individuals or families born outside the country but rather those not of the Yankee tradition. The "newcomers" are families of perhaps acceptable New England background who have not yet been thoroughly assimilated into the local community. But within this wide division there is a "maze of classes and cliques" resting, for the most part, on three kinds of distinction: (1) economic, divided between professionals and proprietary versus laboring groups; (2) religious, with Protestants considering themselves better than Catholics; and (3) "ethnic" (or nationality) differences, "which serve to enhance the divisions based on religion or economic status and also to create division within the religious worlds or the economic levels."[15]

These investigations and many others show (1) a considerable flexibility in standards, which may include income, occupation, nativity, education, religion, and length of residence; (2) a patterning, at least in regions of older settlement, which gives the residents of long standing—provided they have some wealth and education—the highest ranking; (3) only a gradual acceptance into the top class of people of recently acquired wealth; and (4) moral values and style of life as frequently important standards of judgment, though these are often linked with religious and economic distinctions.

The evidence of differences in style of life includes variations by class in sexual behavior[16] in family pattern, religious participation,[17] and many other culture patterns.

Life Chances

A person's social class, with its concomitant income, education, and style of life, affects greatly the likelihood that certain things will happen to him. As we have noted, the odds for or against one's having any given experience, as they are influenced by class, are called *life chances*. Life chances include a vast array of variables. An individual's position in the class structure alters "everything

---

[15]See E. L. Anderson, *We Americans: A Study of Cleavage in an American City* (Cambridge: Harvard University Press, 1937). Quotations from p. 125.
[16]Alfred C. Kinsey, Wardell B. Pomeroy, and Clyde E. Martin, *Sexual Behavior in the Human Male,* Chapters 10 and 11 (Philadelphia: W. B. Saunders Co., 1948); and Alfred C. Kinsey *et al., Sexual Behavior in the Human Female,* Chapters 7 and 8 (Philadelphia: W. B. Saunders Co., 1953).
[17]Liston Pope, "Religion and the Class Structure," *Annals of the American Academy of Political and Social Science,* 1948, 256: 84–91.

from the chance to stay alive during the first year after birth to the chance to view fine arts, the chance to remain healthy and grow tall, and if sick to get well again quickly, the chance to avoid becoming a juvenile delinquent—and very crucially, the chance to complete an intermediary or higher educational grade."[18]

The crucial effect of income on life chances is dramatically illustrated by the fact that the life expectancy of infants born into high-income strata is nearly ten years greater than that of children born to parents in the lowest-income class.[19] Upper-class children are larger and grow faster than lower-class children, a fact apparently related to differences in diet, which depend on both income and style of life.[20]

People in the lowest-income strata spend nearly three-fourths of their total income for food, while those in the higher strata spend less than one-fourth for food. Obviously, this leaves lower-class families with not only less money but a lower *proportion* of their total incomes available for education and other expenditures that might improve their class position. The smaller amount of money available for purposes other than groceries is reflected in the fact that a sample of lower-class people exceeded those in wealthier classes both in symptoms of illness and in the proportion of those symptoms which were not being treated by a physician. The class structure tends to perpetuate itself. People having high incomes and college educations are more likely to be in favor of having their children get college educations.[21] And those who receive a college education are considerably more likely than those who do not to be able to afford to send their children to college.

Poverty in America

Amidst all the wealth of contemporary America, poverty persists, a stubborn backwash that resists the leavening influence of industrial development. Unlike the poverty of yesterday, the poverty of today seems needless. We do not now believe with Arthur Young that "the lower classes must be kept poor or they will never be industrious." The growth of income has made poverty expendable and its persistence, therefore, all the more aggravating.

---

[18]Hans Gerth and C. Wright Mills, *Character and Social Structure* (New York: Harcourt, Brace & Co., 1954), p. 313.
[19]Albert J. Mayer and Philip Hauser, "Class Differentials in Expectation of Life at Birth," in Reinhard Bendix and Seymour M. Lipset, eds., *Class, Status and Power* (Glencoe, Ill.: The Free Press, 1953), pp. 281–284.
[20]See Raymond W. Mack, "Housing as an Index of Social Class," *Social Forces*, 1951, 29: 391–400.
[21]Herbert Hyman, "The Value Systems of Different Classes," in Bendix and Lipset, pp. 426–442.

The quantitative scope of poverty in the United States today depends on how one defines it. The Social Security Administration has established a poverty-income standard which takes into account family size, composition, age of family head, and place of residence. The 1970 poverty-income line for nonfarm, four-person families was $3,950; for farm families of this size, the poverty-income line was $3,350. If we apply criteria like these to the structure of incomes in the United States in 1970, we find there were 25 million poor persons, representing 13 per cent of the population. The poverty-income standard is hardly munificient, as anyone must realize who contemplates the urban family of four trying to survive on an annual income of $3,950. The observation that in 1970 close to one-eighth of the American population was poverty-stricken is, therefore, a minimal estimate.

Moreover, the aggregated data on poverty conceal the extent to which it is concentrated on particular subsets of the population. It is the aged, the nonwhite, and women and children that bear the burden of poverty—"The Other America" in Michael Harrington's phrase or "The Invisible Poor" in Dwight MacDonald's—whose separation, indeed alienation, from the mainstream of American life seems to perpetuate the condition. Two-thirds of all the poor are either under 22 years of age or over 64 years old.

Table 11-7   Incidence of Poverty in the United States

All persons	1 in 8	White female-headed	
All white persons	1 in 10	families	1 in 3
All nonwhite persons	1 in 3	Nonwhite female-headed	
Nonfarm white		families	2 in 3
households	1 in 10	White male laborer	1 in 6
Farm white households	1 in 6	Nonwhite male laborer	1 in 3
Nonfarm nonwhite		White male skilled	
households	1 in 3	laborer	1 in 20
Farm nonwhite		Nonwhite male skilled	
households	2 in 3	laborer	1 in 5
White male employed	1 in 20	White male professional	1 in 50
Nonwhite male employed	1 in 3	Nonwhite male	
White elderly persons	1 in 3	professional	1 in 10
Nonwhite elderly persons	2 in 3	White children	1 in 8
		Nonwhite children	1 in 3

SOURCE: U.S. Bureau of the Census, *Statistical Abstract of the United States: 1969* (Washington, D.C., 1969), p. 329; and Mollie Orshansky, "Consumption, Work and Poverty," in Ben B. Seligman, ed., *Poverty as a Public Issue* (New York: The Free Press, 1965), pp. 72–80; and Herman P. Miller, "The Dimensions of Poverty," in Seligman, *Poverty as a Public Issue*, pp. 20–51.

SOCIAL MOBILITY

By social mobility we mean movement within the social structure. When a person leaves a job paying $5,000 a year to accept one paying $80,000 that person alters his or her class position. That person has become socially mobile. Since one's class is determined originally by the class of his or her parents, when one acquires a fundamentally different amount of education from that of one's parents and moves into a different occupation, with a different life style and different life chances, he or she has been socially mobile.

Individual Mobility

An alteration in status can be either upward or downward in the stratification structure. A truck driver's son who wins a college scholarship, joins a law firm as an accountant upon graduation, and is later elected chair of the board of a large corporation, has achieved upward mobility from the status into which he was born. If his children become waiters in a restaurant, they are downwardly mobile. Individual mobility, however, is always relative; one can be upwardly mobile only if someone else is downwardly mobile.

Structural Mobility— *forced mobility.*

Most mobility is structural mobility, not individual mobility. Many persons have occupations different from those of their parents because of technological changes and shifts in the division of labor. As farming occupations have decreased, many farm children have been "forced" into other occupations and thus do not "inherit" the occupations of their parents. As machines do more and more tasks in the factory, the number of "unskilled" workers decreases and the children of former "unskilled" workers are "forced" into service occupations and white-collar clerical jobs. These kinds of changes in the social structure tend to benefit the entire society. Since the social structure, rather than individual persons, is directly responsible for improvements in the situation of individuals in relation to others, we refer to these changes as structural mobility.

Sometimes a person experiences mobility simply by being a member of some social category if a change takes place in the prestige accorded that category. In time of war, for example, career military men, without any alteration in their education, income, or occupation, are suddenly more sought after as party guests, luncheon club speakers, and subjects of feature articles. The occupational status of soldier understandably holds more prestige for many people during a time of war than in peacetime; hence incumbents of the status are automatically upwardly mobile.[22] Similarly, after the stock market crash of 1929 and during the depression of the 1930s, the prestige of bankers and brokers suffered. It was not necessary for an individual banker to alter his occupation or income or style of life to experience vertical mobility; the occupational status itself was downwardly mobile.

Immigration

Another source of structural social mobility in the United States has been immigration. The millions of immigrants who entered the United States in the late nineteenth and early twentieth centuries made a certain amount of upward mobility virtually automatic for the people already here. Mass immigration increased the size of the population dramatically, and thus contributed to a growth of the economy. Such growth meant that there was an increase in the number of occupational statuses to be filled at all levels in the stratification structure. The filling of the statuses at the bottom of the structure by immigrants working as low-paid unskilled laborers allowed "native" Americans and their sons to move up and fill some of the higher statuses in the social structure.

As a factor in the rate of vertical mobility in the United States, immigration is less important now than it once was. Yet, even with legislation which has slowed greatly the rate of immigration, there is still a steady stream of people entering the United States from other countries. Furthermore, the internal migration from rural areas to urban centers, particularly the movement of blacks from the South to the North, has much the same effect on the total stratification structure that immigration used to have.

---

[22]This is in keeping with the idea that social stratification is essentially a function of the division of labor, and that statuses are therefore differentially evaluated according to the scarcity of personnel qualified to fill them and the degree of importance assigned to the statuses by the normative structure of the society. For the classic statement of this position, see Kingsley Davis and Wilbert E. Moore, "Some Principles of Stratification," *American Sociological Review*, 1945, 10: 242–249. For a discussion of this approach to stratification, see Melvin M. Tumin, "Some Principles of Stratification: A Critical Analysis," *American Sociological Review*, 1953, 18: 387–394; Davis, "Reply," *American Sociological Review*, 1953, 18: 672–673; Tumin, "Rewards and Task Orientations," *American Sociological Review*, 1955, 20: 419–423; Richard D. Schwartz, "Functional Alternatives to Inequality," *American Sociological Review*, 1955, 20: 424–430. For a critique of an extension to economic theory of the idea of functional importance as a criterion in the stratification of statuses, see Richard L. Simpson, "A Modification of the Functional Theory of Social Stratification," *Social Forces*, 1956, 35: 132–137.

Mechanization

Some of this internal migration is symptomatic of another factor that has contributed to a high rate of upward mobility in American society: technological change. The constant trend toward replacing human energy with machinery, culminating in automation, has reduced the proportion of occupational statuses that call for un-skilled labor and increased the number of semiskilled jobs. With this have come the growth of bureaucratic industrial organizations and the expansion of government services, both of which require more white-collar personnel. Mechanization of larger and larger proportions of the labor force has allowed the expansion of service industries.

The creation of new occupational statuses in the middle part of the stratification structure and the reduction in the number of occupations at the lower end of the structure necessitate some upward mobility. There is an historical tendency for the division of labor to change as the economy becomes more mechanized and more bureaucratic. That is, there is a contraction at the bottom of the occupational structure as fewer and fewer people are engaged in unskilled work and an expansion in the middle as more and more people enter semiskilled and lower white-collar statuses. This means that if every family had just enough children to assume the jobs the parents had occupied in the stratification structure, there would still be some upward mobility, since there would not be enough lower occupations for the children of the poor, and there would be more middle occupations than middle-class children to fill them.

Differential Fertility

Actually, people in each class do not have exactly the same number of children. There are marked differences in the birth rates in the various income classes, with the reproduction rate of the lower income classes being higher than that of the top strata. Professionals and other managerial people typically do not have enough children to replace themselves in the labor force. Farmers and farm laborers, on the other hand, have as much as 50 per cent more than enough children to take their places. This would be true even if there were no changes in the number of people needed to fill each occupational category from generation to generation. Actually, we know that clerical and professional personnel have been an increasing proportion of the labor force, while unskilled laborers and farm laborers have become a smaller proportion of the total number of workers. The openings created in the stratification structure by the relatively low birth rates of the professionals are filled by the children of farmers and manual workers. Thus differential fertility, like mechanization and immigration, induces a certain amount of vertical mobility.

By far the most frequently used indicator of mobility in sociological research is change in occupation; the next most common indicator is change in income.[23] As we have seen, occupational status is closely correlated with educational status, income, style of life, and the other aspects of social class.[24] Occupational mobility may be measured in either of two ways: (1) career mobility may be studied by charting a person's work history in order to see whether he or she has been upwardly mobile, stable, or downwardly mobile since he or she entered the labor force; or (2) a person's occupation may be compared with that of one's parents to determine the direction and degree of intergenerational mobility.

Social Mobility and Social Structure

Sociologists study social mobility in order to ascertain the relative "openness" of a social structure. In other words, they are interested in the relative difficulty which different persons, groups, or categories experience in acquiring the goods and services that are valued in the culture and are objects of unequal distribution.

In slave and caste societies, the stratification system is closed to individual mobility. There is relatively no mobility because statuses are ascribed at birth. The occupational status one will enter, the amount of education one will receive, one's income, and one's whole style of life are known at birth. In an open-class society, these statuses are initially ascribed but opportunities are available for some individuals to change their initial position. The life chances of a street sweeper's son born in the slums differ considerably from those of a broker's son born in the suburbs, but the culture does not exclude the former from achievements equal to or greater than those of his contemporaries. On the contrary, the ethos of an open-class society will encourage him to try to achieve statuses carrying higher prestige than those into which he is born.

---

[23]Raymond W. Mack, Linton Freeman, and Seymour Yellin, *Social Mobility: Thirty Years of Research and Theory* (Syracuse: Syracuse University Press, 1957), p. 2.
[24]As Chinoy points out, occupational data are relevant to all theories of stratification utilized by contemporary sociologists, whether they define the class structure in Marxian, Weberian, or "class-consciousness" categories. See Ely Chinoy, "Social Mobility Trends in the United States," *American Sociological Review*, 1955, 20: 180–186. This is not to deny that mobility is multidimensional. For evidence that what we call mobility has a number of components, see Charles F. Westoff, Marvin Bressler, and Philip C. Sagi, "The Concept of Social Mobility: An Empirical Inquiry," *American Sociological Review*, 1960, 25: 375–385.

Table 11-8   Social Mobility in Industralized Societies

Society	Per Cent Moving from Manual to Nonmanual Occupations
United States	34
Sweden	32
Great Britain	31
Denmark	30
Norway	30
France	29
West Germany	25
Japan	25
Italy	22

SOURCE: Gerhard E. Lenski, *Power and Privilege* (New York: McGraw-Hill Book Company, Inc., 1966), p. 411. Reprinted by permission.

Just as there is some mobility, even though very little, in India, so that it cannot be referred to as a perfect example of immobility, so there is some ascription in open-class societies. Our own structure is only relatively open; race, for example, is an ascribed status, and members of racial and gender minorities are often blocked in their attempts to achieve certain statuses. In general, however, United States society emphasizes the open-class ideal, and people are socialized into a belief system which encourages them to try to be upwardly mobile.

THE MOBILITY ETHIC

The emphasis on vertical social mobility in the American social structure is one of the most striking features of our class system. Mayer points out that

> . . . the United States has placed greater emphasis on social mobility than any other large nation in modern times. Americans have firmly proclaimed the idea of equality and freedom of achievement and have acclaimed the large numbers of individuals who have risen from humble origins to positions of prominence and affluence. Indeed, the belief in opportunity is so strongly entrenched in the culture that most Americans feel not only that each individual has the "right to succeed" but that it is his duty to do so. Thus we are apt to look with disapproval upon those who fail or make no attempt to "better themselves."[25]

---

[25]Kurt B. Mayer, *Class and Society* (New York: Random House, 1955), p. 69. By permission.

This mobility ethic, or cultural value attached to improving one's position, has roots both in a normative structure growing out of political revolution and frontier economics and in a religious heritage from the Protestant Reformation in Europe. The relative importance of achieved status so characteristic of the open-class system has permeated the ethos of the United States for several reasons. First of all, this country afforded economic opportunities for the ordinary person—free land for settlement, other natural resources for easy exploitation, and a rapidly expanding economy. Second, political freedom was an essential tenet almost from the beginning of our country, and it became increasingly significant as the population expanded under favorable material conditions. Third, religious tolerance and freedom not only furnished an outlet for individual choice but gave democracy a strong supporting non-economic, nonpolitical ideology and practice. And fourth, freedom of research and invention, of personal migration, and other associated features of individualism and liberalism became deeply and firmly embedded in the value system of American culture.

The Protestant Ethic

The religious institutions of a society both influence and justify its social structure. The values associated with the Protestant Reformation and the rise of capitalism in Europe were most compatible with an open-class structure.[26] The moral system of the Roman Catholic Church stressed otherworldliness; its emphasis was on rewards in the hereafter. The culturally established Catholic ethic of medieval times urged one to accept his lot—that is, to do the best possible job in the status in which he found himself. If a person were a serf, it was because God had intended him to be a serf, and he was as surely engaged in the Lord's work digging potatoes as he would have been ruling an empire. The rationale for the perfor-

---

[26]For a more detailed discussion of the relationship between Protestantism and capitalism, see Max Weber, *The Protestant Ethic and the Spirit of Capitalism*, trans. Talcott Parsons (New York: Charles Scribner's Sons, 1930); and R. H. Tawney, *Religion and the Rise of Capitalism* (New York: Harcourt, Brace & Co., 1936). The most damning indictment of the whole thesis of Weber, Tawney, Sombart, and others is Kurt Samuelsson, *Religion and Economic Action: The Protestant Ethic, the Rise of Capitalism, and the Abuses of Scholarship* (New York: Basic Books, 1961). An excellent general summary of the literature on the functions of religious structure is Elizabeth K. Nottingham, *Religion and Society* (New York: Random House, 1954). Two careful case studies of the relationship between religion and other social institutions are Herman Israel, "Some Influence of Hebraic Culture on Modern Social Organization," *American Journal of Sociology*, 1966, 71: 384–394; and Herman Israel, "Some Religious Factors in the Emergence of Industrial Society in England," *American Sociological Review*, 1966, 31: 589–599.

mance of worldly tasks was otherworldly: reparation for sins and purification through humility. Like the Hindus, medieval Christians were encouraged to make the best of the ascribed statuses into which they were born, with the promise that they would be rewarded for the acceptance of their worldly lot when they were reborn into an afterlife.

The Protestant Reformation changed all this by emphasizing the importance of good works. Protestantism was a morality of individualism, and the individual was to be judged not on his humility but on the basis of what he accomplished. Luther and Calvin sanctified work; they made virtues of industry, thrift, and self-denial. Wesley preached that the fruits of one's labor were the signs of salvation.[27] Favor with God no longer depended on trying, but on doing; a person was saved not for accepting his lot but for proving that he could better it. The culmination of the Protestant Reformation, then, according to Weber, was to give divine sanction to the drive to excel.

It should not be thought that the expression "Protestant Ethic" implies that people in contemporary American society who are reared in Protestant faiths are socialized to accept the mobility ethic, while American Roman Catholics and those of other religions are not. "Protestant Ethic" is simply a phrase applied to a cultural value associated historically with the Reformation and the rise of capitalism; the concept has become part of the American ethos, and research indicates that people of all faiths internalize it.[28] The point is that, in the words of Nottingham,

> In the same manner that religion has aided the Hindus to interpret the rigidities of their caste system, religion has provided moral justification to Americans for certain aspects of the American competitive class system–particularly the high premium placed on success and the consequent penalization of failure. Without this interpretation the successful might feel guilty about their success and the unsuccessful discouraged and resentful about their failures. Futhermore, given positive attitudes to the material world, it is not enough to claim that all moral imbalances will be rectified in heaven: it is crucial to interpret success as morally right—and failure as implying moral lack—here and now.[29]

Political, economic, and religious institutions—all buttress the idea in the United States that upward mobility is a good thing.

---

[27] A detailed analysis of the material here summarized can be found in Adriano Tilger, *Work: What It Has Meant to Man Through the Ages* (New York: Harcourt, Brace & Co., 1930).

[28] See Raymond W. Mack, Raymond J. Murphy, and Seymour Yellin, "The Protestant Ethic, Level of Aspiration, and Social Mobility: An Empirical Test," *American Sociological Review*, 1956, 21: 295–300.

[29] Nottingham, *Religion and Society*, p. 74. By permission.

But believing in mobility and personally experiencing it are two different things.

SOCIAL MOBILITY IN THE UNITED STATES

The mobility ethic, the belief that upward mobility is both possible and desirable in our society, has probably led to an exaggerated general notion of the number of cases in which the poor laborer's son becomes president of a corporation. A study comparing more than 8,000 top executives in the largest firms in the United States in 1952 with the top business leaders in 1928 shows that, in both periods, more than 50 per cent of the business leaders were sons of owners or executives.[30]

Intergenerational Mobility

Most of the research on occupational mobility indicates that while many sons experience *some* mobility, very few experience *much*.[31]

Table 11-9   Social Mobility in the United States, 1962

| Son's Occupation | Per Cent Who Have: | | |
| | Moved Up | Moved Down | Not Changed |
	From Father's Occupation		
Professionals	88	0	12
Managers	85	6	9
Clerks	78	18	4
Factory Laborers	40	54	6
Farmers	3	15	82
Farm Laborers	0	86	14

SOURCE: Peter M. Blau and Otis Dudley Duncan, The *American Occupational Structure* (John Wiley and Sons, Inc., 1967), p. 39.

[30]W. Lloyd Warner and James C. Abegglen, *Occupational Mobility in American Business and Industry 1928–1952* (Minneapolis: University of Minnesota Press, 1955), p. 45. See also F. W. Taussing and C. S. Joslyn, *American Business Leaders* (New York: The Macmillan Co.. 1932j.
[31]See Floyd Hunter, *Community Power Structure: A Study of Decision Makers* (Chapel Hill: University of North Carolina Press, 1953); P. E. Davidson and H. D. Anderson, *Occupational Mobility in an American Community* (Stanford, California: Stanford University Press, 1937); Richard Centers, "Occupational Mobility of Urban Occupational Strata," *American Sociological Review*, 1948, 13: 197–203; Seymour M. Lipset and Reinhard Bendix, "Social Mobility and Occupational Career Patterns," *American Journal of Sociology*, 1952, 57: 366–374, 494–504; Natalie Rogoff, *Recent Trends in Occupational Mobility* (Glencoe, Ill.: Free Press, 1953); Cecil G. North and Paul K. Hatt, "Jobs and Occupations: A Popular Evaluation," *Opinion News*, 1947, 9: 3–13.

ILLUSTRATIVE DATA 11-1   THE SON ALSO RISES

Mr. Parks has one son, Mark, Jr., who is now the more active member of the team he and his father represent. He is an alert and capable man, as active in a variety of civic affairs as his father is said to have been some years ago. His rise in the company was from the bottom up. Several of the leaders in Regional City who have inherited businesses have followed the pattern of beginning at the bottom of the ladder in the company. The rise of these men has been meteoric, in many instances, but the newspapers in biographical accounts of the lives of such persons solemnly report that they have "worked their way to the top." The occupational ascent of Mark Parks, Jr., illustrates the rapidity of such a rise up the ladder of success. The pattern is in the American tradition, but most men find the ascent a longer process than did Mark, Jr.

Young Mark, upon graduation from college, came into his father's business as a shipping clerk. He became successively a stockroom clerk, a stock foreman, and an office manager for one of the branch warehouses. Two years after he started as a shipping clerk, he was elected a director of the corporation and placed in charge of one of the major subsidiaries of the company. Three years later he was named treasurer of the company, and in three years more he became operations vice-president. After two years in this position he was made president. His father then became chairman of the board and has since gradually relinquished active control of the business in favor of his son. He still retains a firm control in matters of general policy, however. Mark, Jr., is the authority on administrative matters. So we see that within ten years this young man rose from stock clerk to company president. It is claimed, and rightly so, perhaps, that by dint of hard work he made good. Certainly it cannot be denied that so young a person as he was in the earlier years of his service in the business shouldered considerable responsibility and has continued to do so increasingly. It may be surmised, nevertheless, that his father's position in the company was extremely helpful in his business success.

Source: Floyd Hunter, *Community Power Structure: A Study of Decision Makers* (Chapel Hill: University of North Carolina Press, 1953), pp. 27—28. By permission.

They move, but not far. If one is not in the same occupational category as his father, the next most likely place for him is in the occupational category either immediately above or immediately below that of his father. If a semiskilled worker in a mass-production factory has a son who is mobile, that son is most likely to move one step down to unskilled work or one step up to skilled labor; it is unlikely that he will become an executive or a professional man. In summary, we can say that more sons are mobile than are not, but that most sons work at either the same occupational level or one immediately adjacent to that of their fathers.

In the light of the effects of immigration, mechanization, and differential fertility on the openness of the class structure, it is not surprising that there is more upward than downward mobility. One study of the mobility of a representative sample of white urban males showed that nearly 30 per cent of the sons of manual laborers moved up into nonmanual occupational statuses, while fewer than 20 per cent of the sons of fathers in nonmanual work were downwardly mobile into manual occupations.[32] Nevertheless, a recent study reported that over two-fifths of the sons of self-employed professionals enter one of the professions and one-third enter some other white-collar job. On the other hand, only five per cent of the sons of laborers enter a profession and one-sixth enter other white collar jobs. The opportunity to attain the economic security of an upper white-collar professional or business occupation is inversely related to one's initial class position. Table 11-10 shows that the changes of a professional or managerial career are nearly five times better if one's father was a professional than if one's father was an unskilled laborer. The point that most mobility is into adjacent strata still holds: sons of manual laborers who move up into white-collar work are more likely to become salesmen or clerical workers than professional men or business executives.

   Despite the mobility between white-collar and the so-called "blue-collar" occupational statuses, the line between them remains a

Table 11-10 Father's Occupation and the Percentage of Sons in
Professional or Managerial Occupations

Father's Occupation	Percentage of Sons in Professional or Managerial Occupations
Professional	55
Managerial	49
Sales	46
Clerical	38
Skilled	28
Semiskilled	20
Service	21
Unskilled	12

SOURCE: Peter M. Blau, "The Flow of Occupational Supply and Recruitment," *American Sociological Review*, XXX (August, 1965), 475–490.

---

[32]Richard Centers, *The Psychology of Social Classes* (Princeton: Princeton University Press, 1949), p. 180.

major hurdle in the class structure. There is more mobility within the manual strata and within white-collar categories than there is between the two.

Career Mobility

Studies of the mobility experienced by individuals during the time they are in the labor force point in general to the same conclusions as intergenerational studies. They reveal more mobility than stability, but the bulk of the mobility is horizontal rather than vertical, occurring within occupational categories, not between them.[33] While it is not unusual for a person to change his occupation four or five times during his career, about half these moves are from one semi-skilled job to another, or from one managerial post to another, and so on. Those shifts which do involve vertical mobility are usually limited in extent, the most common pattern being a move to an immediately adjacent occupational category in the class structure. Career moves from the bottom to the top of the occupational hierarchy are as exceptional as intergenerational mobility of this type. Research on career mobility further confirms the studies of intergenerational movement in indicating that there is slightly more upward than downward mobility.

Trends in Social Mobility

Many social scientists have speculated that the mobility ethic might become a norm inconsistent with the facts of American class structure. They have said that the rate of upward mobility has been declining, that "the strata are becoming more rigid; the holes in the sieve are becoming smaller."[34] Certainly one can cite arguments which suggest that the chances to work one's way up in American society are diminishing: the passing of the frontier days of free homesteading, the decline in immigration, the fact that the fertility rates of the different classes are not as disparate as they used to be. As early as 1948, however, Edward Shils pointed out that "In spite of the oft-asserted claim that opportunities for ascent into the upper

---

[33]Lipset and Bendix, "Social Mobility"; Davidson and Anderson, *Occupational Mobility.*
[34]The quotation is from J. O. Hertzler, "Some Tendencies Toward a Closed Class System in the United States," *Social Forces,* 1952, 30: 313–323. For other arguments that the amount of upward mobility in the United States is decreasing, see Elbridge Sibley, "Some Demographic Clues to Stratification," *American Sociological Review,* 1942, 7: 322–330; C. Wright Mills, *White Collar* (New York: Oxford University Press, 1951), p. 259; and W. Lloyd Warner, *Structure of American Life* (Edinburgh: The University Press, 1952), p. 76.

strata are diminishing in the United States, no conclusive evidence has been presented on either side of the issue by social research."[35]

Since that time, a considerable amount of research has been published on trends in rates of social mobility in the United States. These studies certainly offer no evidence that the American class structure is becoming more rigid. Rogoff has concluded that the rate of upward mobility was about the same in 1940 as in 1910.[36] If the mobility rate was about the same in 1940 as in 1910, even if one does *not* count the mobility which is an automatic result of changes in the occupational structure, then the actual mobility rate would seem to be higher now that it used to be. The conclusions reached in the research comparing the social origins of American business leaders in 1928 and 1952 confirm this fact:

> American society is not becoming more caste-like; the recruitment of business leaders from the bottom is taking place now and seems to be increasing. Mobility to the top is not decreasing; in fact, for the last quarter century it has been slowly increasing.[37]

The study of social mobility by Jackson and Crockett showed that ". . . no striking changes have occurred in mobility patterns and [in the decade following] World War II. . . . what movement has occurred, however, is in the direction of increasing rates of movement."[38] In the most recent and perhaps the most definitive study of the trend of occupational mobility in the United States, the author concluded that there is ". . . little immediate cause for anxiety about whether the American occupational structure is providing more restricted opportunities."[39] However, the author goes on to caution that the data used in his study refer to an ". . . historial experience in which the transition to complete industrialization was rapidly nearing its end. If the movement off farms has been a major factor inducing upward mobility from nonfarm origins in the past, it is not clear what its counterpart may be in an era when few persons originate on farms.[40] Undoubtedly a significant proportion of this mobility is traceable to the changes in the distribution of occupations growing out of mechanization.

---

[35]Edward Shils, *The Present State of American Sociology* (Glencoe, Ill.: The Free Press, 1948).
[36]Rogoff, *Recent Trends*, p. 106.
[37]Warner and Abegglen, *Occupational Mobility*, p. 36.
[38]Otis Dudley Duncan, "The Trend of Occupational Mobility in the United States," *American Sociological Review*, XXX (August, 1965), 498.
[39]*Ibid.*
[40]Elton F. Jackson and Harry J. Crockett, Jr., "Occupational Mobility in the United States: A Point Estimate and Trend Comparison," *American Sociological Review*, XXIX (February, 1964), 25.

Class Consciousness

How do most people perceive the class structure? How conscious are ordinary citizens of the differential prestige accorded to various statuses?

The fact that there is a high degree of consensus on such things as occupational rankings indicates that people have been socialized into the stratification structure. Research showing that children between the ages of 4 and 6 years have already learned to respond to racial differences as a criterion for evaluating people demonstrates that socialization concerning this part of the stratification structure is powerful and effective.[41] Yet, despite the evidence that Americans are aware of the stratification system, many polls indicate that the overwhelming majority of Americans consider themselves to be "middle class."[42] Part of the explanation for the fact that people polled in these studies identify themselves as middle class probably rests in the mobility ethic itself, the norm which says that everyone is supposed to want to move up and which makes it self-derogatory to identify oneself as lower class. On the other hand, the American distaste for aristocracy makes it snobbish for one to claim that he or she is upper class. In a nationwide poll Centers found that Americans saw themselves as follows: upper class—3 per cent; middle class—43 per cent; working class—51 per cent; and lower class—1 per cent.[43]

The significance of class consciousness for social mobility lies in the fact that attitudes and values have consequences in behavior patterns. If one believes he or she can be mobile, one will try to be. One's level of aspiration depends on what he has been socialized to believe about his present status and the chances and desirability of altering it. Research has shown that manual workers are aware that most of them are not going to rise to managerial positions and that, reconciled to the status in which they find themselves, they do not plan upward mobility for themselves but project their ambitions onto their children.[44] Of course, the ones most likely to be upwardly mobile are those who actively seek to achieve upward mobility.[45]

---

[41]Mary Ellen Goodman, *Race Awareness in Young People* (Reading, Mass.: Addison-Wesley Co., 1952).

[42]See, for example, *Fortune* Survey, "The People of the United States—A Self-Portrait," *Fortune*, 1940, 21: 21; George Gallup and S. F. Rae, *The Pulse of Democracy* (New York: Simon and Schuster, 1940); Hadley Cantril, "Identification with Social and Economic Class," *Journal of Abnormal and Social Psychology*, 1943, 38: 74–80.

[43]Centers, *Psychology of Social Classes*, p. 180.

[44]Ely Chinoy, "The Tradition of Opportunity and the Aspirations of Automobile Workers," *American Journal of Sociology*, 1952, 57: 453–459.

[45]Richard Scudder and C. Arnold Anderson, "Migration and Vertical Occupational Mobility," *American Sociological Review*, 1954, 19: 329–334.

One reason for the high degree of occupational inheritance in business leadership statuses is that businessmen's sons are taught to expect to fill these occupational statuses and manual workers' sons are socialized to believe that there is little chance of their attaining such positions. The higher the prestige of the father in the hierarchy of occupational statuses, the more likely the son is to aspire to high occupational status himself.

Thus, just as race can become an ascribed status through the social definition imposed by the culture, so can class subcultures make education and occupation, and hence income, tend to be ascribed. Coates and Pellegrin, after comparing top-level executives with lower-level supervisors, conclude as follows:

> The social origins and socio-cultural backgrounds of executives and supervisors are significantly different. These variations are basic factors in differential occupational opportunities and placement. Occupational placement and early career experiences lead individuals to adopt attitudes, values and behavior patterns which function as important positive or negative influences in subsequent career progress and occupational mobility.
> . . . Subjective factors, such as attitudes and values which affect occupational behavior patterns, are extremely important influences in determining comparative levels of occupational aspiration.
> Levels of aspiration, as they result from attitudes and values, not only affect occupational behavior, but also determine occupational plans and goals and condition mobility drives.[46]

INTERPRETIVE SUMMARY

Some tribal societies, particularly nomadic ones, have no complicated class structure; but most societies have either a rigid system called a *caste* system, or a more flexible system called a *class* structure. Broad changes occurring toward the end of the Middle Ages brought an increase in social mobility in European societies. These changes—the rise of capitalism in the economic realm and, in the realm of thought, the emergence of scientific method, religious tolerance, nationalism—had in common the assumption that individuals and their achievements are supremely important.

The United States has a flexible class system, with the exception of its treatment of minorities. Important indicators of class position in our society are income, wealth, and occupation. It is frequently difficult, however, to determine the social class of a particular individual, since in a given situation one factor may outweigh other usually important ones. Then, too, regional differences in class structure exist, some communities placing em-

---

[46]Charles H. Coates and Roland J. Pellegrin, "Executives and Supervisors: A Situational Theory of Differential Occupational Mobility," *Social Forces*, 1956, 35: 121–126. Quotation from p. 125. By permission.

phasis on statuses which other communities minimize or do not even recognize.

Though a given individual's position in the hierarchy may be difficult to pinpoint, that position is not likely to change much in his or his children's lifetime. This is true because, first, his position will determine his style of life; and the behavior patterns he learns from others who share his style of life will in turn indicate his position and pinion him to it. Second, he will teach his children his own way of life, since it will be the only way he knows. Third, if he is poor, he will find it difficult to help his children find a better way of life even if he wants to.

In American society, people have had highly favorable, even unique conditions for upward social movement. Political freedom and democracy were held sacred from the beginning of the nation. The country afforded unprecedented opportunities for agricultural and industrial pioneering. The Protestant Ethic, embraced by most Americans, taught that achievement in this world is not only justifiable but morally obligatory. As the country developed, immigration and mechanization led to increasingly skilled and "important" jobs for people already here, while the tendency of the upper classes to have fewer children than others also provided for some mobility. Even though many of these factors have become less important in our century, factors such as increasing mechanization continued to provide some opportunity for mobility.

Vertical mobility is generally not dramatic, however. Many sons succeed in reaching the occupational category immediately above that of their father; few go higher, and some go lower. The most difficult gap to bridge in one generation is that between blue-collar and white-collar jobs. One reason for the lack of great intergenerational mobility is class consciousness. While class consciousness, combined with a good dose of the Protestant Ethic, may lead to a longing for a better life, it may also lead to a sound recognition of what is possible, based on what has generally been possible for members of one's class. Then too, class consciousness may lead to pride in one's class, and thus a father may socialize his child to want to put on a white or a blue collar.

SUGGESTIONS FOR FURTHER READING

Blau, Peter H., and Duncan, Otis Dudley. *The American Occupational Structure.* New York: John Wiley, 1967. This is a major research study that details the patterns and determinants of occupational mobility in the United States.

Bottomore, T. B. *Classes in Modern Society.* New York: Pantheon Books, 1966. This is an excellent discussion of capitalism, socialism, and social class, with predictions of the emergence of a less stratified social structure.

Caplovitz, David. *The Poor Pay More: Consumer Practices of Low-Income Families.* New York: The Free Press of Glencoe, 1963. This is a carefully documented research study of low-income families in New York showing the inflated cost of living for the poor.

Kahl, Joseph A. *The American Class Structure.* New York: Rinehart and Company, 1957. A highly literate discussion of class structure in the United States, this volume has an especially good chapter on income, wealth, and style of life.

Keller, Suzanne. *Beyond the Ruling Class: Strategic Elites in Modern Society.* New York: Random House, 1963. This is a theory of elites that draws upon data from many institutional realms including business, the military, science, and the arts.

Kolko, Gabriel. *Wealth and Power in America: An Analysis of Social Class and Income Distribution.* New York: Frederick A. Praeger, 1964. This book deals primarily with the patterns of economic inequality in American society.

Lenski, Gerhard. *Power and Privilege: A Theory of Social Stratification.* New York: McGraw-Hill, 1966. A major statement on social stratification, this book uses a comparative approach and deals more with historical causes than with contemporary correlates.

Lipset, Seymour M., and Bendix, Reinhard. *Social Mobility in Industrial Society.* Berkeley and Los Angeles: University of California Press, 1960. This volume is a comprehensive, well-documented analysis of the rates of mobility in industrial society.

Mayer, Kurt B., and Buckley, Walter. *Class and Society.* 3rd ed. New York: Random House, 1955. This is a sound introduction to the topic of social stratification and has good illustrative data.

Reissman, Leonard. *Class in American Society.* Glencoe, Ill.: The Free Press, 1959. This useful book for the student interested in the various theories of class structure includes a chapter on several methods for stratification study.

Turner, Ralph H. *The Social Context of Ambition: A Study of High School Seniors in Los Angeles.* Chicago: Chandler, 1964. This is a study of the various settings in which mobility occurs and their consequences.

Warner, W. Lloyd, and Abegglen, James C. *Occupational Mobility in American Business and Industry, 1928-1952.* Minneapolis: University of Minnesota Press, 1955. This book studies social mobility among business executives.

EVER SINCE HE WAS KNEE HIGH TO A GRASS HOPPER I'D SAY TO LITTLE BEN, "LITTLE BEN, YOU'RE SHIFTLESS AN' LAZY," AN' LITTLE BEN WOULD SHUFFLE A STEP OR TWO AN' SAY "GUESS I IS, MR. TOM." WE GOT ALONG FINE THAT WAY, LITTLE BEN AN' ME.

I'D KEEP TELLIN' HIM WHAT HE WAS AN' SURE ENOUGH HE COME T'BE THAT WAY.

AN' HE WAS GROWIN' UP JES' FINE TILL THEM OUTSIDERS COME ALONG AN' TOLD LITTLE BEN JES' BECAUSE I TOLD HIM HE WAS SHIFT-LESS AN' LAZY DIDN'T MAKE IT SO.

WELL, AFTER THAT LITTLE BEN DIDN'T LISTEN TO ME THE WAY HE USE' TO. I'D SAY, "LITTLE BEN, NO MATTER WHAT ANYBODY SAYS, YOU'RE SHIFTLESS AN' LAZY AN' TOTALLY DEVOTED T'ME."

AN' HE'D SASS RIGHT BACK WITH, "MR. TOM, NO MATTER WHAT ANYBODY SAYS, YOU'RE A RACIST, YOU'RE A KILLER AN' YOUR TIME IS COMIN'."

WELL, I BEAT HIM UP PRETTY GOOD FOR THAT AN' ANYTIME I'D SEE MORE AGITATORS AROUND I TOOK A GUN TO THEM. BUT IT DIDN'T DO NO GOOD.

I BEGUN T'WORRY IF I WASN'T LIKE WHAT LITTLE BEN SAID.

SO I KILLED LITTLE BEN.

THAT'S WHAT HE GETS FOR MAK-IN' ME BELIEVE HIS DREAM INSTEAD O' HIS BELIEVIN' MINE.

12
Minority
Status

There are few issues that have occupied the minds of people more than the issue of equality. The two great revolutions of the eighteenth century, one in France and the other in the United States, were directed toward extending equality. The two major revolutions of the twentieth century, one in Russia and the other in China, were aimed at establishing "complete equality." For more than a decade, the central political question in the United States has been the question of equality for persons of minority status. In recent years the discrimination and prejudice directed against women, blacks, Chicanos, Indians, Puerto Ricans, and others have become increasingly prominent in the national consciousness. Concern about racism and sexism are commonplace. Indeed, one of the defining characteristics of our time is that masses of people no longer concede their "exclusion" from society. This situation is being dramatically expressed by black Americans and increasingly echoed by women, Chicanos, Indians, and others.

A black may be a college graduate and an experienced pilot in the United States Air Force and yet be rejected as a job applicant by a commercial airline needing pilots. A woman may have graduated from college with high honors and a degree in chemistry only to be offered a typing job when she applies for work.

A private club with a membership composed exclusively of wealthy businessmen who are graduates of New England universities may refuse to admit a wealthy businessman with whom some of its members attended college because he is Jewish. A political party caucus may refuse to run an intelligent, willing young attorney for the legislature because his name is Colucci. Obviously, other factors may override income, occupation, and education in determining one's position in the class structure. It is not true that two people occupy equal statuses merely because they have the same income and education and occupy similar occupational statuses—not true, that is, if one is Protestant and the other Jewish, or if one is white and the other black. Two persons with the same qualifications and the same educational backgrounds who are of the same religion, race, and age have very different chances for a high paying executive position if one is a man and the other a woman. Opportunities in society are not the same for all people. The discrimination which people of minority status receive varies from time to time and from group to group, but it is always reflected in their life chances and life styles.

The term "minority status" is used to designate those members of society who are prevented from participating fully and equally in all phases of social life, who are subordinate to the majority, who can be distinguished on the basis of physical or cultural characteristics, and who therefore have poorer life chances and fewer rights and privileges than the majority. Persons who are discriminated against, who are accorded unequal treatment on the basis of their religion, sex, race, or national origins, occupy a minority status.[1] The sociological meaning of the concept "minority" is sometimes misunderstood because the term minority also has a quantitative meaning. Many people are likely to speak of white Americans as a majority because they constitute more than one half of the population. The sociological meaning of minority status, however, is a matter of social status and social power, not of numbers. The Bantu Negroes of the Union of South Africa have minority status even though they are more numerous than the whites in that country. The whites are in power; they control the institutions of society; and they subordinate the black Africans to a minority status. The aristocracy, the rich and powerful, the royalty, and the ruling elite always

---

[1]Our definitions of "dominant" and "minority" follow closely those of R. A. Schermerhorn, *These Our People* (Boston: D. C. Health, 1949), pp. 5–6. We use the terms majority group and dominant group interchangeably.

constitute a numerical minority of a society, but they never occupy minority status.

MINORITIES AS SOCIAL CATEGORIES

If the members of a society are to exclude some people from full participation in the culture and define them as a minority, the members of the majority and minority groups must be readily identifiable to one another. The Negroes of the Ituri Forest can treat the pygmies as a minority because they can tell by a man's stature that he is a pygmy.[2] New England Yankees can treat local French-Canadians as a minority because the latter's speech and family names set them off from the majority group. A minority identification may result from speaking a different language, having a different skin color, possessing different eye color, or attending a different church from the people in the majority group. In other words, minorities can either be physically or culturally different, but one or the other is necessary to be discriminated against as a minority. The Nazis forced German Jews to wear arm bands so that they could be more easily identified.

If it is cultural behavior that makes people identifiable, they can become socialized into the dominant culture and be assimilated. But physical differences are more permanent; if it is skin color or sex that identifies the minority status, no amount of socialization into the culture of the dominant category removes minority status. If physical differences such as skin color or hair type make a person identifiable, the only thing that will remove one from minority status is a change in the beliefs and practices of the dominant group.

The most frequently used term for labelling identifiability of a minority is race. Race is a confusing word, however, because it means different things to different people. Mongoloids share certain physical characteristics, and we speak of the Mongoloid race. Some Jews are blond and blue-eyed, others dark-haired and brown-eyed; all of them share a cultural heritage centered around a religion, and many people speak of the Jewish race. The English have a melting-pot history which includes Celts, Vikings, Angles, Saxons, Norman, Jutes, Hungarians, Turks, and even some African Negro genes via Mediterranean peoples; they share a language and political boundary, and one can read of the characteristics of the English as a race. Aryan is a term referring to the Indo-European languages (Latin,

---

[2]Carleton S. Coon and Patrick Putnam, "The Pygmies of the Ituri Forest," A Reader in General Anthropology, ed. Carleton S. Coon (New York: Henry Holt & Co., 1948), pp. 323–325.

Germanic, Celtic, Slavonic, etc.), yet people discuss the differences between Aryan and non-Aryan *races*. Actually, the word *race* has one meaning to scientists and many other meanings in popular usage.

Race as a Biological Concept

A race, as the concept is used by geneticists and physical anthropologists, is a number of people who share a set of innate physical characteristics. Non-scientists often assume that members of a race share an unchangeable set of physical characteristics that set them apart permanently from other races. This is not so; races are subject to the same processes of genetic change as all other living organisms.

All human beings belong to a single species. The races of people, that today inhabit the earth probably developed through a combination of mutations (some of which permitted survival more easily in one environment than in another), long periods of relative isolation which facilitated inbreeding, and a selection resulting from various cultural standards of what were and were not desirable physical traits.[3] The major groups of races formed through mutation, islotion, adaptation, and selection have not remained unchanged, because the peoples have not remained absolutely isolated. Since the earliest period of human history, individuals, armies, traders, and whole tribes have migrated and have intermarried with other physical types, thus breaking up the distinctive hereditary patterns.

As a result, there are no pure races within the human species. It is therefore impossible to devise a system of classification on the basis of inherited physical traits. Physical anthropologists have been trying for years to develop such a classification. The magnitude of their difficulties can be seen by noting the vagueness of the categories in Table 12-1. Loose as this three-way classification is, it does not cover all the races of people. African Bushmen-Hottentots, for example, have "Mongoloid" eyes. Australian aborigines have "Negroid" skin and "Caucasoid" hair. Some Polynesians have white skin and some dark brown skin; most of them have wavy hair, but there are many with straight or kinky hair. Some have broad and short faces, others long and narrow features. Since there is no such thing as pure race among human beings, one obviously cannot set up a classification scheme for pure races and expect the data to correspond to the theory.

[3]For an excellent, readable discussion of genetics and the development of the races of man, see the Department of Mass Communication, UNESCO, *What Is Race? Evidence from Scientists* (Paris: United Nations Educational, Scientific and Cultural Organization, 1952).

Table 12-1   Physical Characteristics of the Three Main Races of Mankind

Trait	Caucasoid	Mongoloid	Negroid
Skin color	Pale reddish white to olive brown; some dark brown.	Pale yellow to yellow-brown; some reddish brown.	Brown to brown-black; some yellow-brown.
Stature	Medium to tall.	Medium tall to medium short.	Tall to very short.
Head form	Long to broad and short; medium high to very high.	Predominantly broad; height medium.	Predominantly long; height low to medium.
Face	Narrow to medium broad; no projecting jaw.	Medium broad to very broad; cheekbones high and flat.	Medium broad to narrow; frequent projecting jaws.
Hair	Head hair; color light blond to dark brown; texture fine to medium, form straight to wavy. Body hair; moderate to profuse.	Head hair: color brown to brown-black; texture coarse; form straight. Body hair: sparse.	Head hair; color brown-black; texture, coarse; form light curl to woolly or frizzly. Body hair: slight.
Eye	Color: light blue to dark brown; occasional side eye-fold.	Color: brown to dark brown; fold of flesh in inner corner very common.	Color: brown to brown-black; vertical eye-fold common.
Nose	Bridge usually high; form narrow to medium broad.	Bridge usually low to medium; form medium broad.	Bridge usually low; form medium broad to very broad.
Body build	Slim to broad; slender to rugged.	Tends to be broad; occasional slimness.	Tends to be broad and muscular, but occasional slimness.

SOURCE: Adapted from Wilton M. Krogman, "The Concept of Race," *The Science of Man in the World Crisis*, ed. Ralph Linton (New York: Columbia University Press, 1945), p. 50. By permission.

The most important thing to realize about racial classifications is that they do not correlate with either social structures or culture patterns. High cheekbones show some relationship to reddish-brown skin, and brown-black hair is associated with brown-black skin, but none of these characteristics is associated with intelligence, or a caste structure, or musical ability, or inventiveness, or a belief in one God, or the practice of polygamy, or anything else except other physical characteristics. Such an expression as "It's Arnold's Negro blood that makes him dance so well" is simply a holdover from the era before scientists discovered genes, when people believed that traits were transmitted through the blood.

Berry summarizes nicely the biological concept of race:

The term "race," as used by most biological scientists, refers to a set of categories rather than to discrete, invariable entities. Races are not so much real things which man has discovered as they are pigeon-holes which man has constructed. These categories, to be sure, are based upon clusters of hereditary, physical characteristics. . . . The criteria upon which racial classification is based are non-adaptive, physical, secondary, and have little survival value. Certain societies, however, have come to attach great social significance to these biological trivia.[4]

Race and Culture

Culture is one of the basic determinants of personality. What one has an opportunity to learn shapes one's responses to situations and sets limits on one's performance as a member of society. This has been illustrated in studies of identical twins who had varying interests and attitudes and even different I.Q.'s because they were socialized in different environments.

The results of cultural environments have often been interpreted as innate racial differences. An example is the old widespread belief that there are inherited differences between races in intelligence. People used to take the fact that blacks were more often unskilled laborers than whites or that whites were more often found in high economic or educational statuses than were blacks as evidence of racial inferiority. We now know that these differences between the races were consequences of social stratification, not biology.

Table 12-2 seems to indicate that whites are more intelligent than blacks. But the fact that the differences between Northern and Southern blacks are even greater than those between Northern blacks and whites raises a question: how much of the differences in intelligence test scores is attributable to differences in cultural experience? There is no evidence to support the theory that the more intelligent blacks move North. How much of the Southern black's inferiority, then, is traceable to inferior schools, less well-educated teachers and parents, fewer years of formal education, and so on? The answer is apparent from Table 12-3, which contrasts blacks from the three highest-scoring states with whites from the lowest-scoring states. Several other studies made at different times in various parts of the country indicate that differences in performance on intelligence tests by race, as well as differences by region, are attributable to environmental factors.[5] It should be stressed that differences in cul-

---

[4]Brewton Berry, *Race and Ethnic Relations*, 2nd ed. (Boston: Houghton Mifflin Co., 1958), p. 49. By permission.
[5]For an exhaustive review of such studies, see Robert D. North, pp. 2–8.

Table 12-2   Average Scores on Two Army Intelligence Tests of
1,750,000 Men During World War I

Category	Alpha Test (for literates)	Beta Test (for illiterates)
White	59	43
Northern Negro	39	32
Southern Negro	12	20

SOURCE: Robert D. North, "The Intelligence of American Negroes," *Research Reports*, 1955, 3:2–8. Tables from p. 4. By permission.

Table 12-3   Contrasts of Whites from Three Lowest Scoring States
with Negroes from Three Highest Scoring States on Army
Alpha Test of Intelligence During World War I

State	Whites Number of Cases	Median Score	State	Negroes Number of Cases	Median Score
Arkansas	618	41.0	New York	850	44.5
Kentucky	832	41.0	Ohio	152	48.8
Mississippi	665	40.8	Illinois	578	46.9

SOURCE: North, "The Intelligence of American Negroes," p. 4.

tural experience make it just as difficult to prove that there are *not* inherited differences between races as to prove that there *are*. But there is no scientific evidence to support the belief that such inherited differences exist. A group of distinguished social scientists has summarized the situation in a statement on race issued from a meeting in UNESCO House in Paris:

> Whatever classification the anthropologist makes of man, he never includes mental characteristics as part of those classifications. It is now generally recognized that intelligence tests do not in themselves enable us to differentiate safely between what is due to innate capacity and what is the result of environmental influences, training, and education. Wherever it has been possible to make allowances for differences in environmental opportunities, the tests have shown essential similarity in mental characters among all human groups. In short, given similar degrees of cultural opportunity to realize their potentialities, the average achievement of the members of each ethnic group is about the same.[6]

---

[6]Department of Mass Communication, UNESCO, *What Is Race?* p. 62.

ILLUSTRATIVE DATA 12-1   RACE AND CULTURE

School children brought up in a Western heritage do not know about the Zulu conqueror, Chaka, or about his heroic opponent, Moshesh, or about Shamba Bolongogo, king of the Bakuba, who after three centuries is still remembered for his great reforms and inventions and for his love of peace. Few people have heard of the Liberian prophet Harris or of Kamehameha, King of Hawaii, or of the Mandingo Emperor, Gongo Musa, who is said to have embellished his cities with buildings of a style still used in the mosques of the Western Sudan. These, and a score of others, may well have been prevented merely by their isolated environment from achieving recognition as "great" men in the Western sense of the term. . . .

Cultures have flourished and waned in the past, undoubtedly they will continue to have their ups and downs in the future. . . . All that science can say is that no connection has been found between the biological constitution of the peoples and the level of their past or present culture; nor is there any hereditary or other biological reason for supposing that, just because White civilization is leading in the development of the present highly technical age, some races have less aptitude for learning technological skills. There is no reason, for example, why an African, because he is a Negro, cannot learn to drive a tractor or be a soil chemist, or any other of the tasks necessary for underdeveloped countries to help themselves. Such abilities cannot be considered racial ones.

Of course, children of a highly technical civilization have an enormous advantage over those who live in . . . isolated cultures. At an early age they learn the logic that two and two make four, they unconsciously learn the principle of cause and effect, they tinker with machines to see how they work. A . . . child born in the . . . Congo is brought up in a world with a different image of nature and its forces. If he is to adopt Western culture he has to learn, not only how a machine works, but also to interpret natural phenomena according to rigid laws which no longer permit the intervention of spirits or magic. But these are cultural, not racial, differences.

Source: Department of Mass Communication, UNESCO, *What Is Race?* pp. 62–63.

It is possible to marshal evidence that one race has produced a culture superior to that of the others, *if you ignore human history.* For example, one can argue that, on the basis of industrialization and the present world balance of powers, Caucasoids are obviously superior to Mongoloids. But this does not explain where this superiority was when Mongoloids under Attila or Genghis Khan were overrunning Europe, or why the Chinese invented printing four centuries before Europeans did, or why Africans were smelting iron ore while Europeans were still living in caves.

ILLUSTRATIVE DATA 12-2 SOCIAL DISTANCE ON THE CAMPUS: PERCENT-
AGE OF STUDENTS IN 40 AMERICAN COLLEGES WHO WOULD ACCEPT OR
REJECT PERSONAL CONTACTS WITH OTHER GROUP MEMBERS

Other groups	Work beside on job	Live on same block	Have as inti- mate friend	Date or allow child to date	Marry	Bar from social club	Bar from block
Italians	92%	84%	84%	76%	65%	4%	4%
Negroes	89	58	63	24	29	24	26
Jews	93	84	85	60	37	12	6
Japanese	90	74	72	46	24	11	8
Catholics	95	83	92	73	56	3	1
Filipinos	89	73	69	42	24	12	11
Protestants	95	96	92	83	74	1	1
Mexicans	88	66	68	45	31	15	14
Greeks	93	82	80	64	50	6	4
Irish	95	88	87	77	64	3	2
Polish	93	83	83	72	61	4	3

Source: Adapted from Albert I. Gordon, *Intermarriage,* Beacon Press, Boston, 1964.
Copyright © 1964 by Albert I. Gordon. Reprinted by permission of Beacon Press.

The Social Definition of Race

What we call "races" in the United States depends on social belief, not on biology. Whether or not one is a white, Indian, or black,
depends on whether or not people think he or she is, not on any
specific hair color, hair type, head form, or degree of darkness of
skin color. It is obvious that the criteria of classification used are
not biological, since the biological characteristics show overlap between the races—for instance, some people considered white have
darker skins than some people considered black. What ultimately
determines whether or not an American is an Indian American is
a matter of social definition. Social definition also decides whether
or not one is a member of an ethnic minority. Suppose a woman is
the daughter of a family known in their community as Jews. Even
if their name is Smith and they do not attend a synagogue, their
parents were Jewish and they are considered Jews. But what happens
if the woman moves to a new community and does not tell anyone
that she is a Jew? She is no longer Jewish! She is the same person,
but the social definition of her status has been altered. When we
say that the descendants of nineteenth-century German-Americans
are almost completely assimilated, we mean that most of them are

identified by the members of American society not as Germans or as German-Americans but as Americans.

Minority status, then, is as changeable as the characteristic that is used to define and identify the minority. If the only thing that confers minority status on a person is her or his surname, one can change the name and no longer be identifiable as a member of the category. If, however, it is her sex or skin color that is the basis for discrimination, she is more permanently consigned to minority status because she is visibly different.

Self-Fulfilling Prophecy

In either case, the definition of the status is social, and the members of the minority are a social category—that is, the characteristics associated with the minority are present because people *believe* they are present. Statuses are, after all, simply sets of rights and duties assigned to people by other people. A role is a set of expected behaviors, and this is as true of a minority role as of any other. By expecting certain social behaviors from members of a minority, therefore, the people in the dominant category tend to make their own beliefs come true.[7] "The majority group asserts that the minority group is inferior and incapable of achievement, then acts in a discriminatory fashion to ensure that such inferior performance will be the outcome."[8] As Merton has pointed out, "the self-fulfilling prophecy is, in the beginning, a *false* definition of the situation evoking a new behavior which makes the originally false conception come true."[9]

For example, white Americans believed for years that black Americans were less capable of learning than whites, that they were innately less intelligent. What, given this belief, was the course of action for the dominant whites? Provide inferior schools and inferior teachers for blacks. Then compare the scores of whites and blacks on intelligence tests and blacks will average lower than whites. By the very fact of believing that blacks cannot perform as well as whites, whites have made this true. Similarly, part of the stereotype of the Jew is that he is aggressive or "pushy." Because the members of the dominant category believe this, they set up extra hurdles for the Jew, such as quotas for admission to medical schools. Thus, if a Jewish person wants to become a doctor, he has to be not

---

[7]An extremely interesting discussion of the process by which "social beliefs father social reality" can be found in Robert K. Merton, *Social Theory and Social Structure,* rev. ed., "The Self-fulfilling Prophecy" (New York: The Free Press of Glencoe, 1957), pp. 421–438.
[8]James B. McKee, *Introduction to Sociology* (New York: Holt, Rinehart and Winston, 1969), p. 295.
[9]Merton, *Social Theory and Social Structure,* p. 423.

only as good as his non-Jewish competitors, but better. He has to work hard enough and perform well enough to overcome discrimination. In other words, he *has* to be aggressive and "pushy."

The same tendency holds for women who apply for a "man's" job, for blacks who seek occupations traditionally held by whites, and so on. As Robert Merton has noted, "the systematic condemnation of the [minority status person] continues largely irrespective of what he [or she] does."[10]

> [O]bserve how the very same behavior undergoes a complete change of evaluation in its transition from the in-group Abe Lincoln to the out-group Abe Cohen or Abe Kurokawa. We proceed systematically. Did Lincoln work far into the night? This testifies that he was industrious, resolute, perserverant, and eager to realize his capacities to the full. Do the out-group Jews or Japanese keep these same hours? This only bears witness to their sweatshop mentality, their ruthless undercutting of American standards, their unfair competitive practices. Is the in-group hero frugal, thrifty, and sparing? Then the out-group villain is stingy, miserly and penny-pinching. All honor is due the in-group Abe for his having been smart, shrewd, and intelligent and, by the same token, all contempt is owing the out-group Abes for their being sharp, cunning, crafty, and too clever by far. Did the indomitable Lincoln refuse to remain content with a life of work with the hands? Did he prefer to make use of his brain? Then, all praise for his plucky climb up the shaky ladder of opportunity. But, of course, the eschewing of manual work for brain work among the merchants and lawyers of the out-group deserves nothing but censure for a parasitic way of life. Was Abe Lincoln eager to learn the accumulated wisdom of the ages by unending study? The trouble with the Jew is that he's a greasy grind, with his head always in a book, while decent people are going to a show or a ball game. Was the resolute Lincoln unwilling to limit his standards to those of his provincial community? That is what we should expect of a man of vision. And if the out-groupers criticize the vulnerable areas in our society, then send 'em back where they came from.[11]

The sociological principle involved is described by Merton as: "the moral virtues remain virtues only so long as they are jealously confined to the proper in-group. The right activity by the wrong people becomes a thing of contempt, not of honor. For clearly, only in this way, by holding these virtues exclusively to themselves, can the men of power retain their distinction, their prestige, and their power. No wiser procedure could be devised to hold intact a system of social stratification and social power."[12]

---

[10]Merton, *Social Theory and Social Structure*, p. 428.
[11]Merton, *Social Theory and Social Structure*, pp. 428–429.
[12]*Ibid*, p. 429.

It should be clear that self-fulfilling prophecies and majority status require the exercise of social power.

The pattern of majority-minority relations in any society is not to be explained primarily in terms of some set of prevailing prejudices; rather, minority status can be understood only as one kind of social inequality, and this is a structural arrangement that is sustained by more than just attitudes. Indeed, the domination of a minority group by a majority group cannot occur except through the exercise of *social power*. To be a majority group and to confine a minority group to a subordinate position within the social structure requires the majority group to have the instruments and mechanisms of power necessary to sustain its dominant position. To discriminate in employment requires that the majority group have control over the distribution of jobs. To discriminate in education requires that the majority group control the educational process. *social power*

It is this process of discrimination that creates a minority group. The very act of discriminating—in jobs, housing, income, social services, and education—constitutes the social process by which a racial or ethnic group is converted into a minority group. The mere holding of prejudicial attitudes by one group toward another does not make of the recipient group a minority; such a situation merely indicates the existence of group hostility. Thus, Negroes develop attitudes of resentment and hostility toward whites, but whites do not become a minority because of this.

Given such a pattern of relationships as acts of discrimination bring about, it is understandable that the majority group will possess . . . a set of beliefs that will validate its own majority status as well as the minority status of the other group.[13]

Discrimination and Prejudice

The crux of minority status is the capacity of one category of people to impose discrimination upon another. Many people think of prejudice and discrimination as one and the same process; many more believe that whenever prejudice exists, there must be discrimination and vice versa or that an absence of discrimination necessarily means an absence of prejudice. However, there are times when people who are not prejudiced persons are unable to act upon their beliefs and attitudes. For many of us, law, custom, and organizational policy intervene between our individual attitudes and our capacity to act accordingly. Indeed, persons usually do not behave on the basis of their own personal prejudices and individual whims but are constrained in their behavior by law, custom, and the social situation. Most individuals do not act according to their attitudes in any sphere of life; and behavior—whether it is discriminatory or

---

[13]James B. McKee, *Introduction to Sociology*, p. 294.

not—is more likely an organizational or social decision than a personal one. Most people function in situations in which prevailing situational requirements control and constrain their behavior; and the structure of the situation is more important than an isolated attitude. People in the army, on the job, in school, in a traffic jam, and at a social function generally find that they cannot do what they want but must acquiesce to the social requirements of the situation they are in. Social scientists have found that once the social structure is changed, attitudes and beliefs reform themselves in the crucible of the new conditions. Thus, Ruth Benedict argues that racial beliefs and prejudices came *after* the onset of slavery to justify existing behavior.[14]

MINORITIES IN THE SOCIAL STRUCTURE

Minorities, then, are social categories of people who have poorer life chances than members of the majority group. In this sense, minorities are similar to classes in the stratification structure. A businessman has higher prestige than a laborer, but a Protestant businessman has higher prestige than a Jewish businessman. Any citizen who meets the age and certain other Constitutional requirements may be President of the United States of America, but the chances of realizing that goal are significantly lower for persons of minority status. Indeed, there is considerable evidence that the chances to achieve the positions which offer the most prestige and power and the highest rewards are relatively low for women, blacks, Mexican Americans, Indian Americans, Jews, Puerto Ricans, and other minority-status persons.

In 1970, there were more than 22 million black Americans; more than 9 million foreign-born white Americans; more than 5 million Jewish Americans; more than 5 million Mexican Americans; more than one million Puerto Rican Americans; more than a million Japanese Americans, Chinese Americans, Filipino Americans and Korean Americans; and at least 85 million women not included in other minority groups. Clearly, more than three-fifths of the American population occupy minority status and experience some amount of social discrimination.

To be sure, not all life chances are exactly the same for all persons of minority status, for there are important variations both between and within the many minority statuses. For example, black Americans have been disproportionately burdened with very low incomes, but some blacks are quite wealthy. Similarly, the opportunity for a white collar job is higher for Jews than for Indian Americans and

---

[14]Ruth Benedict, *Race: Science and Politics* (New York: Viking, 1940), Chapter VIII, "A Natural History of Racism."

ILLUSTRATIVE DATA 12–3 ESTIMATED JEWISH POPULATION BY
COUNTRIES, 1968

Country	Jewish Population
United States	5,870,000
Soviet Union	2,594,000
Israel	2,436,000
France	535,000
Argentina	500,000
England	410,000
Canada	280,000
Brazil	140,800
Republic of South Africa	114,000
Rumania	100,000
Hungary	80,000
Iran	80,000
Morocco	50,000
All other countries	596,200
Total	13,786,000

Source: The American Jewish Year Book, Vol. 70, 1969. © 1969 the Jewish Publication Society of America. Reprinted by permission.

the chance for quality medical care is higher for Japanese Americans than it is for Puerto Rican Americans. The amount of occupational segregation is higher for women than it is for blacks, and so on. Nonetheless, *all* persons of minority status are denied full and equal participation in all phases of the society.

As recently as 1910, racial and ethnic minorities accounted for more than one-fourth of the population of the United States, as can be seen from Tables 12-4 and 12-5. In this century the black population has remained a fairly constant ten to eleven per cent of the total while the foreign-born population has diminished markedly. How do people become minorities? What places some people in a society in racial or ethnic social categories? Ordinarily, a racial or ethnic population becomes defined as different and placed in a social category in one of four ways.

Patterns of Minority Emergence[15]

A number of people may become a minority through annexation, colonialism, or migration, either involuntary or voluntary. Most European minorities, such as the Poles in Russia or the Greeks in

---

[15]For a more detailed discussion of these patterns, see Charles F. Marden and Gladys Meyer, *Minorities in American Society*, 4th ed. (New York: D. Van Nostrand Company, 1973), Ch. 3.

Table 12-4   Size and Proportion of Negro Population
in the United States, 1850–1970

Year	Population (millions)	Percentage
1850	3.6	15.5
1870	4.9	12.3
1890	7.5	11.9
1910	9.8	10.7
1930	11.9	11.4
1950	15.0	10.0
1960	18.9	10.5
1970	22.7	11.2

SOURCE: *Statistical Abstract of the United States*, 1953 and 1971, U.S. Bureau of the Census, Tables 2, 101, 102; *Historical Statistics of the United States, 1789–1945*, 1949, p. 25; *Seventeenth Census of Population* (1950), *Characteristics of the Population*, Table 35 (Washington, D.C.: U.S. Government Printing Office). 1960 data from preliminary census reports.

Table 12-5   Size and Proportion of the Foreign-born
Population in the United States, 1850–1960

Year	Foreign-born (White) (millions)	U.S. Population (Census) (millions)	Percentage of Foreign-born
1850	2.2	23.2	9.5
1870	5.5	39.8	13.8
1890	9.1	62.9	14.5
1910	13.3	92.0	14.5
1930	14.0	122.8	11.4
1950	10.2	150.7	6.8
1960	9.3	179.3	5.4

SOURCE: *Statistical Abstract of the United States*, 1953, U.S. Bureau of the Census, Tables 2, 101, 102; *Historical Statistics of the United States, 1789–1945*, 1949, p. 25; *Seventeenth Census of Population* (1950), Vol. II, *Characteristics of the Population*, Table 35 (Washington, D.C.: U.S. Government Printing Office); 1960 *Census of Population*, Volume 1, Characteristics of the Population, Part 1, United States Summary.

Turkey, have acquired minority status because of political annexation. The only time a sizable minority was created in the United States through annexation was after the Mexican War, when the Mexicans in Texas, California, and the Southwest were taken into the United States.

The colonial pattern became common in Asia and Africa as European nations succeeded in dominating the political and economic

ILLUSTRATIVE DATA 12-4   THE GOLDEN DOOR

Give me your tired, your poor,
Your huddled masses yearning to breathe free,
The wretched refuse of your teeming shore,
Send these, the homeless, tempest-tossed, to me,
I lift my lamp beside the golden door.
                    Emma Lazarus, Inscription on the
                                Statue of Liberty

lives of the natives in those regions. Relations between the dominant people in the United States and Indian Americans have in
general followed the colonial pattern of political and economic sub-
ordination of the native population, the maintenance of a color line,
and minimal development of social services for the natives. U.S.
relations in the past with the native populations of Cuba, Alaska,
Puerto Rico, the Hawaiian Islands, and the Philippines have tended
toward the creation of colonial minorities.

A third pattern for creating a minority is migration. The method
by which black Africans were forced into slavery in the United
States is a case of involuntary migration. Taking slaves obviously
creates a social minority, since the slave lacks the rights of citizens
of the society, and a pattern of dominance and submission comes
into being.

The vast bulk of the people who have occupied minority status in
the United States came through voluntary migration. Over 36 million immigrants entered the United States during the past century.
Fewer than one million of these came from Asia and Africa. More
than three-fourths of them emigrated from Germany, Italy, Ireland,
Poland, Great Britain, Austria, Hungary, and Russia.[16] Analyses of
this immigration usually divide it into the "old" immigration, from
northern Europe, most of which occurred before 1890; and the "new"
immigration, from southern and eastern Europe after that time. In
the decades around the turn of the century, immigration was nearly
as great a factor as the birth rate in increasing the nation's population. Since the Immigration Act of 1924, the number of people entering minority status in our society through voluntary immigration
has decreased.

All immigrants enter a society as minorities. The reasons for this
are stated well by Kahl:

---

[16]The figures in this paragraph are from the United States Immigration and Naturalization Service, *Annual Report*, 1948, Tables 1, 4 (Washington: U.S. Government
Printing Office).

It has been emphasized that men evaluate one another in terms of group values; individuals are considered worthy of deference if their behavior exemplifies the ideals of their culture. In ordinary circumstances a man cannot be a model citizen if he is not thoroughly familiar with the culture, and this is not possible if he has not grown up in it. Most groups distrust outsiders and even before they have observed them sufficiently, assume that they will not behave as well as group members. Consequently, outsiders are devalued and granted low prestige.

The outsider has other disadvantages. Not being familiar with all the intricacies of the local culture, he is less likely to have occupational skills that will earn him a high income. He will not have friends and relatives in high places who can assist his career. He will not have a family name that bestows prestige through the halo effect of noteworthy ancestors.

Each of those disadvantages can be great or small, depending upon the circumstances. If the outsider is a well-trained physician who comes to a backward community that desperately needs medical service, he is likely to be honored. If he is an ambitious farm boy who moves to a city in his own nation, and shows great ability in business and complete respectability in his personal behavior, he can, through time, earn high prestige among the city's successful people. But if he is an uneducated peasant, who comes to an advanced industrial nation and walks the streets behind a pushcart selling apples, and fails to master the language and the urban habits of the host culture, then he is relegated to a low position and may well be regarded as "that stupid, dirty foreigner."[17]

Patterns of Dominant-Minority Relations

A minority can cease to exist as a minority in one of two ways: it can be exterminated, or its members can be totally amalgamated and assimilated into the dominant category. As long as the minority exists, some kind of accommodation between these two extremes must operate. The accommodation may range from the acceptance of slavery by the minority to the acceptance by the dominant category of the minority's attempt to become assimilated, and even the offer by the dominant category of active assistance toward assimilation. Government schools to help immigrants learn the language and the ways of American culture exemplify dominant encouragement of assimilation.

In general, European immigrants have been encouraged to assimilate. Many Americans have been critical, indeed, of ethnic minorities that segregate themselves and retain their "foreign" institu-

---

[17]Joseph A. Kahl, *The American Class Structure* (New York: Rinehart & Company, 1957), pp. 221–222. By permission.

ILLUSTRATIVE DATA 12–5   NATIONAL OPINION ON MARRIAGE BETWEEN
WHITES AND NONWHITES

Nation	Approve	Disapprove	No opinion
Sweden	67	21	12
France	62	25	13
Finland	58	34	8
Netherlands	51	23	26
Greece	50	36	14
Switzerland	50	35	15
Austria	39	53	8
Canada	36	53	11
West Germany	35	47	18
Norway	35	44	21
Uruguay	30	44	26
Great Britain	29	57	14
United States	20	72	8
United States: non-South	25	70	5

Source: The San Francisco Chronicle, November 11, 1968.

tions. The immigrant considered most desirable has been the one who socializes his children into his adopted culture patterns and becomes "Americanized." Racial minorities, on the other hand, have been discouraged from assimilating. Many states had laws against intermarriage between whites and blacks or Mongoloids. All the culture patterns that keep racial minorities separate from the dominant category—segregated housing, schools, churches, and so on—are a deterrent to total assimilation.

Identifiability is one key to the rate and degree of assimilation of a minority. How recently the members of a minority have arrived in a society is usually indicated by how well assimilated they are. The reason for this is that the more recently they have arrived, the less time they have had to learn new culture patterns; and the less they act like dominant people, the more identifiable they are. The similarity of the culture in which they were socialized to the one where they have immigrated is a factor in the rate of their assimilation for the same reason: the more different they are, the more identifiable they are. An English factory laborer recently arrived in the United States is much less identifiable than a recently arrived Sicilian peasant; the Englishman speaks, dresses, and acts more "American." And because he is less identifiable, he can be assimilated more rapidly.

A basic difference between European ethnic minorities and Asiatic and African racial minorities is the degree to which their identifiability is readily changeable. The options to change majority-minority relations which are available to sexual and racial minorities are more limited than those available to "cultural" minorities. The Greek immigrant who learns English and changes his name will rear children who not only will not be identifiable as Greeks, but will indeed not *be* Greeks. Their identifiability is reduced to the vanishing point. But no matter how completely American a black is in his thoughts, language, and behavior patterns, he is identifiable as a member of a minority because his visibility depends on his physical features, not on his cultural behavior.

Minority Status and Life Chances

By definition, minorities occupy a distinctive position in the stratification system and they experience the life chances that accompany that position (see Table 12-6). At the turn of the century, for example, the maternal mortality rate among nonwhites was nearly twice as high as it was among whites. The maternal mortality rate has been reduced in this century and the relative advantage of whites has increased to the point where the maternal mortality rate is nearly four times as high for nonwhites as it is for whites. (Black Americans constitute 94 per cent of the nonwhite population of the United States).

Such variations in life chances extend throughout the stratification system: "only 13 per cent of the black men are professional or managerial workers compared to 30 per cent among whites; 17 per cent of blacks, in contrast to 6 per cent of whites, work as laborers."[18]

Table 12-6   Maternal Mortality Rate, by Race (Per 10,000 Live Births), 1900–1968

Year	White	Nonwhite
1900	60.1	105.6
1936	51.2	97.2
1950	6.1	22.2
1960	2.6	9.7
1968	1.7	6.4

SOURCE: *Maternal Mortality Statistics, United States, 1950*, National Office of Vital Statistics, U.S. Public Health Service, December 3, 1953 (Washington, D.C.: U.S. Government Printing Office), p. 368, and *Statistical Abstract of the United States, 1971*, p. 55.

---

[18]Reynolds Farley and Albert Hermalin, "The 1960s: A Decade of Progress for Blacks?" *Demography*, IX (August, 1972), 353.

Table 12-7 Education and Income of White and Black Females, 1959 and 1969*

Education	Income in 1959 Median Income			Income in 1969 Median Income		
	White Females	Nonwhite Females	Ratio of Nonwhite to White	White Females	Black Females	Ratio of Black to White
Elementary						
Less than 8 years	$1081	$ 914	.85	$1303	$1195	.92
8 years	1435	1222	.85	1688	1320	.78
High School						
1–3 years	2131	1506	.71	2355	2268	.96
4 years	2809	2182	.78	3234	3257	1.01
College						
1–3 years	3060	2729	.89	3427	4247	1.24
4 years	4745	4625	.97	5707	6747	1.18

*Data for women 25 years of age and older.
SOURCE: Reynolds Farley and Albert Hermalin, "The 1960's: A Decade of Progress for Blacks?" *Demography*, IX (August, 1972), Table 6, p. 361.

In 1969, black men with a college degree had a lower median income than white men with only a high school diploma.[19] The income of nonwhite families was only 63 per cent of the income of white families in 1960.[20]

The conflict between the cultural values of political equality and opportunity for economic advancement as opposed to the ascribed status of blacks constitutes what Myrdal has called the "American dilemma."[21] Attempts to solve it have changed the class status of the black in the United States radically in the past few decades.[22] Many Americans, mostly blacks, have made major attempts in recent years to solve the dilemma, and although racial equality is not yet a reality in America, the efforts of the last few years have helped to close the gap between the races.

Table 12-8   Occupation of Employed Persons by Race and Sex, 1950–1970

Occupation	Nonwhites			Whites		
	1950	1960	1970	1950	1960	1970
Males						
Total per cent	100	100	100	100	100	100
Professional, managerial	4	5	13	20	23	30
Clerical, sales	4	7	9	14	15	13
Craftsmen	8	11	14	20	22	21
Operatives, service	36	43	41	25	26	25
Laborers	24	22	17	7	6	6
Farmers, farm labor	24	12	6	14	8	5
Females						
Total per cent	100	100	100	100	100	100
Professional, managerial	7	9	13	18	19	20
Clerical, sales	5	10	22	40	44	44
Craftsmen	1	1	1	2	1	1
Operatives, service	34	36	44	32	30	29
Private household	42	39	18	4	4	4
Laborers	2	1	1	1	—	—
Farmers, farm labor	9	4	1	3	2	2

SOURCE: Reynolds Farley and Albert Hermalin, "The 1960s: A Decade of Progress for Blacks?" Demography, IX (August, 1972), Table 7, p. 363.

---

[19]Ibid., p. 360.
[20]Ibid., p. 355.
[21]Gunnar Myrdal, An American Dilemma (New York: Harper & Brothers, 1944).
[22]Five volumes documenting the status of the Negro in relation to housing were published in 1960 by the University of California Press, Berkeley and Los Angeles: Nathan Glazer and Davis McEntire, Studies in Housing and Minority Groups; Eunice and George Grier, Privately Developed Interracial Housing; Luigi Laurenti, Property Values and Race; Davis McEntire, Residence and Race; and Chester Rapkin and William G. Grigsby, The Demand for Housing in Racially Mixed Areas.

SOCIAL CHANGE IN AMERICAN RACE RELATIONS[23]

As recently as 1950, only eighteen states prohibited segregation in transportation and recreation facilities. Now the Interstate Commerce Commission has outlawed all racial barriers on trains and buses and in terminals. In 1956, the time of the famous bus boycott in Montgomery, Alabama, only 25 per cent of Southern whites and 60 per cent of all whites in the United States favored integrated public transit.[24] In 1970, 88 per cent of all whites and 67 per cent of Southern whites favored integrated public transportation.[25]

In 1950 there were still more states in which segregation in the public schools was mandatory than there were states in which school segregation was prohibited. The Supreme Court outlawed public school segregation in 1954. Seven years later, there were only three states that had not begun to comply with the order. (One of them was the locus of the original lawsuit that resulted in the Court's decision.) In 1942 only 30 per cent of whites favored integrated schools, but in 1970, 75 per cent did.

Twenty-five years ago the white primary kept most blacks out of the elections in the South. The Supreme Court struck at white primaries in 1954, and in 1957 Congress passed the first civil rights act in eighty years, empowering the Justice Department to bring suit to win the ballot for blacks. Literacy tests and other devices used to exclude the black from the voting booth have been under heavy attack; voting cases are pending in the courts, and the Justice Department is involved in a number of other investigations. The apportionment decision of March 1962 by the Supreme Court reduced the rural dominance in a number of Southern state legislatures. In 1960, only 29 per cent of eligible blacks in the Southern states were registered to vote; in 1970, 62 per cent were registered.

The Presidential Committee on Equal Employment Opportunity is pressuring government contractors to employ blacks in skilled jobs. The median income of black families is more than six times higher than it was twenty years ago.

In 1952 one-tenth of all black Americans could neither read nor write. That illiteracy rate had been reduced to under four per cent by 1970, and among blacks between the ages of 14 and 24, less than one-half of one per cent are illiterate. The proportion of college graduates among young black adults has nearly tripled in the past

---

[23]Much of the material in this section is from Raymond W. Mack, "Desegregation and the Frustrated White Rats," *New Society*, 1963, 37: 6–9.
[24]Andrew M. Greeley and Paul B. Sheatsley, "Attitudes toward Racial Integration," *The Scientific American*, CCXXV (1971), 14.
[25]*Ibid.*

twenty years. In 1970, 7.3 per cent of all blacks between the ages of 25 and 29 had completed college.

Besides these changes in the status of black Americans there is an emerging body of public opinion that is intolerant of intolerance. The National Opinion Research Center asked a national sample of white Americans in 1942 whether they believed that "Negroes are as intelligent as white people—that is, can they learn just as well if they are given the same education?" Only 42 per cent of the whites said "Yes". But by 1956, the proportion answering "Yes" to the same question had risen to 77 per cent. Another NORC survey asked white adults, "If a Negro with just as much income and education as you had moved into your block, would it make any difference to you?" In 1942, only a little over a third of the respondents said "No"; by 1962, 44 per cent of all whites favored integrated neighborhoods, and 50 per cent favored them in 1970.

Most striking for projecting what the future holds are research studies that tabulate responses according to amount of education and age. The American Institute of Public Opinion asked a national sample of Americans, "If your party nominated a generally well-qualified man for President, and he happened to be a Negro, would you vote for him?" Of those who had only a grade school education, 49 per cent said "No." The percentage dropped to 39 per cent for those who had completed high school, and among those with a college education, only 21 per cent said they would reject a well-qualified candidate because of his race. A similar pattern emerges with age. Thirty-four per cent of the voters 21 through 29 years of age said "No." The percentage rose to 37 among those aged 39 to 49. The highest negative response was among people 50 years of age and and over—48 per cent. Four out of five American youths now graduate from high school, and one-half of these go on to college. The youthful and the educated constitute a growing pressure group.

Research on the desegregation by Melvin M. Tumin suggests that "the hard core" of Southern resistance to desegregation lies among the poor and uneducated.[26] The outstanding characteristic of those most willing to resort to violence to defy the law of the land is a below-average amount of schooling. The violence-prone, hard-core people are as stable in residence patterns as their neighbors; they belong to churches in about the same proportion and attend about as frequently. But their earning power is significantly lower than that of their neighbors, partly because few of them have completed

---

[26]Melvin M. Tumin, "Readiness and Resistance to Desegregation: A Social Portrait of the Hard Core," *Social Forces,* 1958, 36: 256–263.

nine or more years of school. The wider society impinges much less directly upon them. They are less influenced by newspapers and magazines. They are less well prepared than their fellow citizens to adjust to rapid social change.

Desegregation of the South is of course especially difficult, since the South is characterized by the very factors that make resistance to change part of its way of life. The South remains largely agrarian, with a high birth rate and a low level of formal education. It is the most rural section of urban America, the least schooled region in a highly educated society, the unindustrialized portion of a technologically oriented nation.

But it is short-sighted to think of desegregation as a problem belonging only to the South. Fifty years ago 90 per cent of all black Americans lived in the states of the old Confederacy. One measure of the swiftness of the change in the black's status is the fact that nearly half of all blacks now live in the cities of the North and West. The central city population of New York City is 21 per cent black; Chicago is 33 per cent; Philadelphia, 34 per cent; Detroit, 44 per cent; and Washington, D. C., 71 per cent black. Those most likely to migrate are the young people with better than average education. And every year these people are packing into already overcrowded ghettoes in Northern and Western cities with residential segregation which tends to facilitate segregation in schools and other facilities.

The problem of desegregation is a national problem. The Southern states which depended for segregation on laws that have been declared unconstitutional have been partially vulnerable to rapid change, while the North has not experienced the same pressures because its segregation is accomplished informally through residential patterns and is harder to strike at through the courts. But race relations is not just a Southern problem; it is what Gunnar Myrdal called it—an American dilemma.

The upheaval of desegregation imposes strains on our social system far beyond the immediate results of human inertia and resistance to change. Within the span of a generation, we have projected into urban life the majority of one-tenth of our population, many of whom were brought up to live in feudal serfdom. While enormous strides are being made in education and other endeavors, an enormous price is also being paid for the suddenness of the change. As Philip M. Hauser points out, "Tossing an empty bottle on an asphalt pavement in the city has quite different consequences from tossing it into a cotton field. Using physical force, including a knife or gun, in the resolution of personal conflict receives much more attention and has a much greater impact on the community in the city than it has in the rural South. The patterns of family and sexual behavior that the Negro inherited as a product of his history and his share in the American way of life have created . . . many complications . . . in the urban setting."[27]

Other immigrant groups have reacted to urbanization with personal and social disorganization. But it is a foolish disservice to the minority and to the society to state that, or act as if, no special problem exists. There is a black problem. But it is a problem born of rapid social change, not of biology. And at the very moment when responsible black and white Americans are trying valiantly to cope with it, there is pressure for more and more rapid change.

Inequalities remain, and while they remain there will be continuing agitation for change. When a national sample of Americans was asked, "Do you think most Negroes in the United States are being treated fairly or unfairly?" one-third of the whites and two-thirds of the blacks answered "Unfairly." Together, these people constitute a sizable group of dissatisfied citizens.

They are dissatisfied because equality of opportunity is basic to the American ethic of self-realization and achievement, and the blacks are denied equality of opportunity. Black Americans learn the rules of the American way of life from the same textbooks as white Americans, but they find that many of the economic trails are blocked for them. Black youths learn from books and movies and television that an American should work to get a better job and improve himself by study, but they are excluded from apprentice training by many craft unions. Black median family income is only 63 per cent of that of whites.

The South has no monopoly on racial discrimination. Americans are taught to work and earn recognition and the social rewards of success, but United Nations Under-Secretary Ralph Bunche's son was denied membership in a tennis club. Judge James C. Flanigan of Denver was turned away from the local golf course. The citizens of Deerfield, Illinois, voted to increase their taxes, and purchase as a park the land on which a builder had begun to construct 51 houses to cost about $30,000, twelve of them earmarked for black families.

What does the black American want? To answer that question, one need only strike out the word "black." He and she want what other Americans want: equal treatment, an end to injustice and discrimination, economic security, and a friendly community. As American citizens, he and she want a fair chance to compete for a share in the American way of life. "All we want," says Congressman Conyers, "is for America to be what it says it is."

---

[27]Philip M. Hauser, *Population Perspectives* (New Brunswick, N.J.: Rutgers University Press, 1960).

INTERPRETIVE SUMMARY

Minority status persons are people who are discriminated against because they have physical features and/or behavioral patterns which differ from those of the dominant culture. Minorities enter a society through colonialism, in which case the minority may well be numerically superior; through voluntary or forced migration; or through annexation. Treatment of a minority may range from attempts to exterminate the group to extreme persecution to some form of accommodation. If the minority is distinguished by its behavior rather than by some physical characteristic, members of the group may become assimilated in the new culture. Such assimilation will be accomplished more quickly if the dominant culture is willing to help and if the minority shows willingness to break away from its old ways and learn new. Of course, minorities whose old and new cultures are similar will generally have the easiest time in becoming assimilated.

Minority status that is defined in terms of sex and race is less amenable to assimilation since people identify racial minorities by physical characteristics. Though there is no pure race and no correlation between any physical trait and any innate ability, majorities continue to discriminate against individuals having imagined racial characteristics. Indeed, a majority may even place members of a minority in positions where they have no choice but to develop the imagined behavior patterns; the majority then considers its original opinion confirmed, and the minority is kept from assimilation indefinitely. Such a situation has long existed between blacks and whites and between men and women in American society.

Though the blacks in American society have historically been treated as a virtual caste, they have recently brought about changes in their relative social position. The Supreme Court, Congress, and Presidential committees have acted on the national level to desegregate schools, transportation and recreational facilities, jobs, and elections. Studies show that attitudes of whites toward blacks are changing, especially among young and educated whites from the South as well as the North.

SUGGESTIONS FOR FURTHER READING

Brink, William, and Harris, Louis. *The Negro Revolution in America.* New York: Simon and Shuster, 1964. A nationwide sample of American blacks tell what they want and how they intend to obtain what they want. Also included are data gathered from 100 black leaders and a section on what whites think of blacks.

Broom, Leonard, and Glenn, Norval D. *Transformation of the Negro American.* New York: Harper and Row, 1965. This is a careful study of the trends in the American black population—education, occupations, income, values, and attitudes.

Burma, John. *Spanish-Speaking Groups in the United States.* Durham, N. C.: Duke University Press, 1954. The author chronicles the adjustments of Spanish-speaking people to the dominant culture of this country.

Clark, Kenneth B. *Dark Ghetto: Dilemmas of Social Power.* New York: Harper and Row, 1965. This is a sensitive description of the social structure and consequences of ghettos that is largely based on the author's work in Harlem.

De Beauvoir, Simone. *The Second Sex.* Translated by H. M. Parshley. New York: Bantam Books, 1952. This is the classic statement of the status of women in Western society.

Dodge, Norton. *Women in the Soviet Economy.* Baltimore: The John Hopkins Press, 1966. This volume is the result of an exhaustive study of the roles of women in the Soviet Union.

Frazier, E. Franklin. *The Negro in the United States*, rev. ed. New York: Macmillan, 1957. This is the most complete analysis available of the historial backgrounds of the black minority, racial conflict and its accommodation in the United States, and the institutional structure of the black community.

Hughes, Everett C., and Hughes, Helen M. *Where Peoples Meet: Racial and Ethnic Frontiers.* Glencoe, Ill.: The Free Press, 1952. This is a collection of essays on ethnic subcultures and the process of assimilation.

Killian, Lewis M. *The Impossible Revolution?* New York: Random House, 1968. This is a bleak and pessimistic account of the future of the black movement in American society.

Mack, Raymond W., ed. *Our Children's Burden: Desegration in Ten American Communities.* New York: Random House, 1968. This book presents original case studies of varying definitions of the situation concerning public school desegregation in large and small towns in the North and the South.

Marden, Charles F., and Meyer, Gladys. *Minorities In American Society*, 4th ed. New York: D. Van Nostrand, 1973. This is a good textbook on racial and ethnic relations in the United States.

van den Berghe, Pierre L. *Race and Racism: A Comparative Perspective.* New York: John Wiley and Sons, 1967. The author presents case studies of the historical development of racial and ethnic relations in the four societies of Brazil, Mexico, South Africa, and the United States and compares colonialism and slavery as instances of stratification within an excellent theoretical framework.

3/Social Institutions

13
Economy
and
Society

In folk societies there typically is no formal organization of economic endeavor. That is, there are no secondary groups, such as labor unions or manufacturing corporations, whose chief reason for being is related to the production and distribution of goods and services. In a folk society, it is more likely that the economic function will be performed by a group already in existence than by one created especially for that purpose. Ordinarily, the economic institution is just one of the many sets of norms which define the familial roles. A father fishes because one of a father's duties is to provide food for his family, not because he is an employee of the Apex Seafood Corporation.

The form of property ownership varies from society to society. In some societies it may be divided among members according to some ranking system by age, sex, and social position. In other societies, individuals considered responsible for creating an item may be recognized as entitled to own it. The development of Western capitalism has gone through certain phases which reflect the shift from a primary-group organization of society to an industrialized, impersonal mass society and culture. Capital is wealth devoted to the production of commodities or services. The accumulation of capital depends on some form of abstinence, some restraint of the impulse to consume goods at once. Long ago people learned to forego immediate consumption so that they might secure more goods at a later time. Even in nonindustrial economies, people save meat they might otherwise eat in order to use it for bait to trap more meat.

Whether or not an item is capital is determined by the use to which it is put. Coal burned in a grate to heat a living room is a consumers' good; used in a blast furnace in making steel, it is a capital good. Capital or producers' goods are easily distinguishable in machines, plants, railroad equipment, and the like. A box of breakfast cereal and a dress are obviously consumers' goods when they are in the hands of those who actually will make use of them.

ECONOMIC STRUCTURES

One of the most important changes in the transition from folk to urban society is the change from status to contract. In medieval times the serfs had the land because of their status, because of who they were. A baron was a baron for the same reason: his grandfather had been a baron, and it was his right. The serfs owed him certain obligations and he owed them certain obligations, not because of some peculiar training they had had, not because of achievement, but because each man was born into his status. The whole society was structured on ascribed statuses.

From Status to Contract

By the time the cottagers were moved into town to work in factories, this structure was crumbling. No longer did people owe these kinds of obligations simply because of the positions they occupied. The nearest thing to the old system in an industrial situation is the small one company town that survives for generations. Here the owner is the grandson of the original owner; the odds are that the foreman is the grandson of the original foreman and that many of the laborers are grandchildren of the original laborers. Everybody knows everybody else; people speak to one another on the street; and everybody knows what church everybody goes to and whose daughter is being courted by whose son. Suppose a worker in this kind of situation falls ill. There is no unemployment compensation. But none is needed, because a system of mutual obligations exists. When a man is ill, the owner's wife comes by with a basket of groceries and asks if there is anything she can do to help, and a couple of people who work with him will have their wives or daughters over helping nurse him. When he has recovered, he returns to his job. This is a system of mutual obligations. In a

ILLUSTRATIVE DATA 13-1   FROM STATUS TO CONTRACT

[In] the so-called "putting out" system [which preceded the "Industrial Revolution"] a merchant or group of merchants undertook to organize and finance certain production. The actual techniques of production were unchanged; craftsmen worked at their traditional tasks in a familiar shop environment, or farm families plied their household crafts, without any direct or regular supervision from the merchant-employer who hired their services and supplied materials. In craft manufacture, relations between masters and servants were personal and close. Though the master was senior, he too must conform to the custom and opinion of his peers: he worked with his journeymen and apprentices in an avuncular if not paternal fashion. The latter were protected in their ascribed status by craft tradition and local usage. Unmarried dependents lived in domestic quarters, taking their meals at the place of work. The journeyman could aspire to his own premises and elevation to a master's rank. He might cherish designs on his master's daughter and thereby inherit the shop and its good will. The pace of work and the job routine accorded with this intimate round of everyday life. But as the master withdraws from the shop, as the numbers of journeymen increase and their labor is casualized, so the establishment is more of a factory. Work discipline is less habitual and more contrived; rules and regulations become impersonal and objective. The master departs from the center of the scene, one eye is fixed on the employees, the other on competitors. The position of the journeyman is correspondingly reduced, his status lowered. . . .

It is easy to romanticize a golden age of the crafts before the hectic pace of the machine or the factory's insistent whistle. There is a familiar image of the benign master guiding his trusty servants through their daily tasks with youthful novices romping at their feet. It was never like this. But, leaving aside the tyrannical masters, sullen journeymen, and cringing apprentices, craft and merchant-employer organizations functioned within the accepted custom and domesticity of their less hurried age. The factory brought a furious pace and shaped a relentless discipline, broken only when the crude machines fell apart or the waters ceased to flow. As more processes were integrated under one roof and when, during the industrial revolution, the factory moved into town, men found themselves living in a stark and unfamiliar world. The essential but elusive quality of the factory seems to reside in the relations of employer and employed and in the style of job routine. . . .

Source: Eric E. Lampard, *Industrial Revolution: Interpretations and Perspectives* (Washington, D.C.: American Historical Association, 1957), pp. 24–5.

larger economy, in which most people work for big organizations, contracts are substituted for this kind of status system. Wherever there is a social need which the baron would have met for the serfs or the serfs would have filled for one another, the trend is toward contracting an obligation.

We are no longer a society of rural villages and independent entrepreneurs. The economic and political institutions of an urban-industrial society are inextricably interwoven because, in the shift from status to contract as a principle of social organization, a wage contract alone replaces only a small part of the total system of mutual obligations. The history of our learning to live with urbanization and industrialization is a history of the process of negotiating supplementary contracts. We start with a wage contract, but we supplement it with a Social Security contract, an unemployment insurance contract, and so on. This is the method which industrial societies—democratic or totalitarian, capitalist or socialist—have devised as a substitute for the mutual-obligation system found where institutions tend to be coterminous—where familial, economic, and political functions derive from the same group.

The economic institutions of modern states are generally labeled "capitalist" or "socialist" according to whether or not the state controls the capital goods. A society in which most of the capital goods are owned and controlled by individuals is called capitalist; when the state takes over ownership and control of capital goods, the economic structure is said to be socialist. The two may be (and usually are) some combination.

Formal Structures

One highly important form of ownership and control is *individual (or sole) proprietorship.* As capitalist enterprises expanded, one person joined with another and systems of partnership arose. This enabled two or more individuals to pool their resources, capital, and labor with a view toward making a profit. Sociologically, a partnership represents a particular form of cooperation.

In time, a third kind of ownership, the economic *corporation,* emerged. As a kind of secondary group, the corporation enables individuals to act under a common name in order to own, hold, and manage property or an enterprise. The benefits of such an operation are distributed among the associated stockholders. The corporation operates under a charter from the state which defines its rights, duties, and obligations. The individual stockholder ordinarily is not liable for the debts of the corporation, and the life of the corporation is usually independent of the lives of those who own the stock.

There is perhaps no other phenomenon of our time that typifies mass society more adequately than the corporation. Although recognized in law as a legal unit with many of the rights and duties of an individual, it operates in complete anonymity and impersonality.

While it may enter into a contract, the controls which may be exercised over it are not exactly those which society may exercise over an individual. A corporation may be fined or enjoined by the courts, but it cannot be put in jail, nor can it suffer from a sense of guilt and conscience. Yet corporations are the property of multiple individuals, and particular persons run them. (As seen in 1961, though a corporation cannot be put in jail, the individuals who run it can, and several officials of General Electric were so punished for price-fixing.) They make decisions on policy and practice and hence affect the lives of workers, consumers, and many others. In fact, present-day corporate organization influences productive capacity, the financial system, the employment of labor, and the buying habits of consumers.

The corporation is not confined to capitalistic economies; it is found also under socialism. For example, the nationalization of banking and coal mining in Britain modified only slightly the essential corporate forms of organization and control of these enterprises. The Soviet Union has developed most of its state-controlled and state-managed economy along corporate lines.

The Dominance of the Corporation

In the United States, 95 per cent of the business firms have fewer than 20 employees. A glance at this statistic might lead one to the conclusion that small businesses dominate the economy, but this is not true. The firms with fewer than 20 employees account for less than one-fourth of the wage and salaried workers in the economy. The other three-fourths are employed by the corporate giants which comprise only 5 per cent of the total number of firms. More than one-third of the workers are in firms which have 1,000 or more employees.[1]

The extent of corporate concentration varies greatly among industries. It is greatest in manufacturing, transportation, and public utilities. In utilities, for example, more than two-thirds of the employees work for firms hiring 1,000 or more. On the other hand, in construction, service industries, and retail trade, from 40 to 50 per cent of the workers are in firms employing fewer than 20 persons.

One classic study of corporations reported that as of January 1, 1930, the 200 largest corporations (each with assets of 90 million dollars or more) other than banks controlled nearly one-half the total corporate wealth, two-fifths of total business wealth (other

---

[1] U.S. Department of Labor, Bureau of Labor Statistics, *Economic Forces in the U.S.A. in Facts and Figures* (Washington, D.C.: U.S. Government Printing Office, June, 1955), pp. 62–63.

Table 13-1   Share of Assets held by the Largest Manufacturing
Corporations: 1948 to 1968

Corporation Rank Group	1948	1955	1968
100 largest	40.3%	44.3%	49.1%
200 largest	48.3	53.1	60.8

SOURCE: U.S. Bureau of the Census, *Statistical Abstract of the United States,
1971* (Washington, D.C.: U.S. Government Printing Office, 1971), p. 467.

than banking), and somewhat more than one-fifth of all the national
wealth. Even today if we define as "small" those companies with
assets of less than a million dollars, the small companies have less
than 13 per cent of the market. Small companies operate on a
smaller profit margin than large companies. Furthermore, companies
with fewer than 500 employees (and that includes over 99 per cent
of the firms) receive less than 20 per cent of the military contracts
from the federal government. Finally, one should note that, in all
three of these areas—per cent of market, margin of profit, and share
of military contracts from the Department of Defense—the trend
seems to be running against the small firm.[2] Economic concentration in manufacturing has increased substantially during the past
twenty years. (See Table 13-1.)

Corporate Control

Corporate concentration has been accompanied by a separation
of ownership from control in American industry. Most of the functions which used to be performed by an entrepreneur—an owner-
proprietor—are now performed by a salaried manager. The large
individual business is owned, not by one man who can run it but,
as some of the institutional advertising tells us, by millions of
people. The stockholders among whom this diversified ownership
is spread do control their companies. But they delegate control of
the corporation to salaried management. The *owners* of the corporation do not dominate it as individuals. As a matter of fact, we have
here a sort of collectivization of ownership. It is voluntary and so
is extremely different from state collectivization; but it is collectivization nonetheless. In some respects, the differences in the occupational role of the manager of a Soviet factory and of an American
factory are not as extreme as they seem at first glance. Modern

---

[2]See the *New York Times,* January 15, 1956, p. E5. See A. A. Berle, Jr., and G. C.
Means, *The Modern Corporation and Private Property* (New York: The Mac-
millan Co., 1933), p. 32. See also A. A. Berle, Jr., *Power Without Property* (New
York: Harcourt, Brace & Co., 1959).

industrial systems, no matter what their economic norms and political goals, are staffed and run by salaried managers.

Economic Interdependence

The economic interdependence of modern nations has been greatly increased by the rise and spread of industry, which requires raw materials from widely scattered sources. In the century preceding World War I a sort of economic world order arose despite the persistence in some nations of tariffs and other limitations on free trade. The restrictive nature of much of the world's trade is related to shifts in the balance of political power which have been under way for some time. Nonetheless, economic interdependence is clear. People purchase and use articles of food, clothes, implements, tools, machines, and recreational objects that are made of raw materials from all over the world. One's breakfast coffee, tea, or cocoa is imported, as are the tin and bauxite which go into kitchen utensils used in preparing the meal. People ride to work in motor vehicles that could not be made without imported tin, bauxite, chromium, and rubber.

The United States, for example, exports great quantities of coal, copper, gypsum, lead, petroleum, phosphate, rock, silver, and zinc. So too, meats, dairy products, apples, tobacco, wheat, and lumber are shipped abroad in large quantities. Of manufactured articles the most important exports are automobiles, electrical machinery, engines, hardware, farm equipment, sewing machines, firearms, cotton goods, motion pictures, and rubber products.

One instance of the extent of economic interdependence is the heavy United States investment in Latin America. In one sense, it is a fiction to speak of "the" economy of "a" society when the economies of many societies are intertwined. What happens to production or to the market in one society is bound to have repercussions in other societies.

In order to move the needed goods and services from region to region and from country to country, the world is covered with a network of land, sea, and air transport and communication lines. From the turn of the present century to the outbreak of World War II, the marine tonnage in the world increased 136 per cent. To facilitate transportation, common navigation rules have been worked out by international agreements. Similarly, uniform freight rates on shipping lines operating in the same regions or between the same ports have been generally agreed upon. Long before the coming of the railroad, many of the larger rivers of the world were "internationalized" for traffic, and all sorts of provisions for the use of port facilities were made. In Europe particularly, international

Table 13-2   United States Direct Investment in Latin America, 1963

Country	Millions of Dollars
Venezuela	$3,017
Brazil	1,000
Mexico	822
Chile	725
Argentina	635
Panama	468
Peru	437
Colombia	425
Guatemala	126
Dominican Republic	105
Honduras	95
Costa Rica	62
Uruguay	49
Ecuador	48
Bolivia	43
Haiti	41
El Salvador	34
Nicaragua	19
Paraguay	15
Total Direct Investment	8,166,000

SOURCE: The *New York Times,* April 14, 1963, p. 4E. Direct investment is the value of U.S. funds in companies with at least 25 per cent U.S. control.

arrangements were developed to facilitate railway transport across the thousands of miles of political boundaries. Uniform bills of lading, reciprocal use of rolling stock, agreements fixing responsibility for damages, coordinated timetables, and many other common practices were set up. There were also agreements among European nations to aid in motor transport services.

The story of air transport is even more striking. In the two decades separating the two world wars, airplane lines reached into every part of the globe. Almost overnight remote regions came within relatively easy flying distance. In 1947 an aviation treaty established the International Civil Aviation Organization, with 26 nations participating. This institution set up basic standards for global air traffic.

The international postal service, known as the Universal Postal Union, was established in 1874 and, except during wartime, embraces practically the entire habitable globe in a single worldwide postal area. The development of radio communication followed a somewhat similar course. After early monopolistic trends, international agreements were made regarding commercial radio and the use of radio in shipping. Since World War I, radio broadcasting has become not only commercially but politically one of the most important media of communication to the masses.

The telephone and, later, the radio-telephone have made possible worldwide conversation. The Americas have taken the lead in the international use of the telephone. As early as 1938, through a combination of radio, cables, and land transmission lines, the United States could reach every continent and the major islands of the sea by means of 74 different telephone circuits.

It is evident from all this that, in transportation of raw materials and manufactured goods and in communications, the world has moved toward an international order. In fact, we find a rather paradoxical situation in which we have international traffic and communication rules but national ownership and national control determining the final decisions. The isolationism which has become linked to nationalism stands in sharp contrast with the interdependence of economic structures and functions.

THE INDUSTRIAL GROUP AS A COMMUNITY

Large organizations, whether they are voluntary associations, business firms, or whole societies, eventually reach a critical point of complexity where they assume formally organized hierarchical structures. Such structures, of course, make for more rigidly specified roles. Adolph Berle, Jr.[3] called attention to a problem that occurs when a conflict in values leads to friction between the economic institution and the maintenance of a sense of purpose. Ownership and proprietorship, which have traditionally been parallel, are becoming separate occupational specialties. This trend is probably the source of much of the complaining about "the organization man"—when a complex organization has socialized replacements to perform its specialized roles, it is not likely to be tolerant of deviance. While such a man has the prestige that goes along with wearing a white collar, there are plenty of white collars above him.

Situs

However, individuals have a way of "building in" compensations. Such a bureaucratic division of labor through a whole society leads to what some sociologists have called *situses*—sets of related occupational specialties arranged hierarchically and separated from other sets of related roles, which also are arranged in hierarchies. Each situs or family of related occupations builds up a set of norms

---

[3]See *Power Without Property: A New Development in American Political Economy* (New York: Harcourt, Brace & Co., 1959).

peculiar to it. These occupational subcultures insulate their participants from the members of another situs. Doctors and nurses hold values not shared by railroaders and truck drivers; the occupational norms of longshoremen are not those of laboratory workers.

Societies with elaborate occupational differentiation, therefore, while bound together by a common culture, are at the same time fragmented by occupational subcultures. People who share an occupational history develop norms, enforce an in-group ideology, and come to serve as a reference group for one another. We see this at its extreme when physicists from the Soviet Union and from the United States have more to talk about with one another than either group has with the farmers from its own country.

But role segmentalization is not synonymous with a fragmented social structure. The stuff of occupational subcultures can serve as the specialized urban-industrial worker's social substitute for community. Occupational codes can contribute to what Durkheim called organic solidarity; they can help replace the mechanical solidarity of the rural village. Occupational groups, with their shared values, can contribute to the sense of purpose which formerly was a function of the small community. Certainly the Industrial Revolution has brought drastic changes in economic institutions.

In economic organization as in other areas of social life, it is not always easy to separate formal from informal structures. In industrial groups, as elsewhere, the people who come to fill roles in the formal organization soon develop informal social relationships and groups that emerge within the industrial plant. A factory, department or other retail store, business office, or any other aggregate of individuals concerned with economic production or distribution develops many features of a community, though not all of them. Since the aim of the plant is narrower and more specialized than that of the community, and since its population consists only of members of the labor force, it necessarily lacks the breadth and scope of the community as usually defined. Yet in many of its features the resemblance is close. The factory, like the community, is characterized by a given locus, and certain functions are carried on by individuals in particular roles and statuses. In both cases—factory and community—some of the relations of individuals and groups are formal and institutionalized; others, of an informal sort, develop naturally from the very circumstance of people living or working together in close proximity.

The personnel have certain contractual relations to one another. The most obvious division is that between management and labor. The former may be the owner but under corporate organization is usually an agent of the owners. The relations of management to workers are those of graded authority and responsibility. Within this large framework there is a ranked status system. In management it ranges from the chief executive downward through subordinate management personnel to the foreman. Among the workers there are gradations in skill, seniority, and other accepted criteria of differentiation of role. These gradations are measurable not only in wages, working conditions, and various work privileges but in patterns of social interaction and socially shared definitions of the situation. For example, among railroaders, engineers and conductors are at the top of the prestige pyramid, section hands and repair workers are at the bottom.

Spatial arrangements are made in accordance with management's decisions as to what makes for highest industrial efficiency. Thus a plant has a certain ecology related to the roles of the various workers. To keep the plant operating successfully, all sorts of rules are laid down as to where to do one's job, skills expected, use of materials, avoidance of wastage and spoilage, compliance with safety measures, provision of light, ventilation, rest periods, devices for handling grievances and suggestions for improvement of product or working conditions, and so on.

Primary Relationships

On the informal side, workers tend to develop cliques or groupings among themselves depending largely on spatial proximity, similarity of work, and level of skill, especially as related to the status factor, commonality of outside interests, and other situations which serve to bring about associations not recognized in the formal organization of the plant as an economic unit. Such groupings may and often do result in certain informal status systems that may influence the morale of the workers.

For example, in spite of the rapid development of mechanization and even automation in industry, there are certain sections in which hard physical work is performed today under almost the same conditions as a century ago. One of these sections is dock work. H. J. Helle worked among longshoremen in five major European seaports in order to study hiring practices and the formation of groups in relation to the danger of accidents on the job. He used multiple-choice questionnaires to collect comparable data on "organization," "attitudes" and "accident rates" in the five ports. Where hiring procedures disregarded both friendship and antipathy among longshoremen by assigning workers to gangs according to their registration number, attitudes toward the work environment were comparatively negative and accident frequencies were high. Conversely, where longshoremen themselves had the opportunity to choose gang members and foremen and where association with able and popular foremen was related to good work performance, work attitudes were comparatively positive and accident rates were lower.[4]

Thus failure of management to take informal associations into account by using them or breaking them up in the interest of efficiency may result in loss of efficiency. These informal groupings are often powerful factors in influencing the level and amount of production. There are norms of plant performance involving how much work to do for a day's pay, avoidance of speed-up which may affect other workers' wages, protection of one another from foremen in matters involving wastage and spoilage of machines or materials, and many other features of work activity. Failure to conform to these norms usually leads to various forms of punishment: ridicule, ostracism, and at times even bodily injury.

While such patterns, formal and informal, arise and continue in most plants, they are further influenced when labor unions are organized and collective bargaining comes into operation. Union contracts frequently not only act to modify the formal features of the plant in such matters as wage rates, hours, conditions of work, insurance benefits, amount of product to be turned out per worker per day, and so on, but also may influence the informal features of life in the plant by affecting status relations. And in plants not completely unionized, divisions of workers along lines of membership or nonmembership may make for conflict.

ECONOMIC FUNCTIONS

The essential function of the economic system is, of course, the production and distribution of goods and services. In even a very simple economy, such as one which requires only picking coconuts or catching fish, there is usually some organization in which roles are assigned. There is some normative order governing who gathers coconuts, who is responsible for dividing the catch of fish, at what age one is obligated or expected to enter the labor force and support oneself, what is to become of persons who are too old to gather their own food, and so on. This is simply another way of saying that one function of the economic system is division of labor.

---

[4]Horst Jurgen Helle, *Die unstetig beschäftigen Hafenarbeiter in den nordwesteuropäischen Hafen: eine industriesoziologische Untersuchung in Antwerpen, Bremen, Bremerhaven, Hamburg and Rotterdam* [The unsteadily employed longshoremen in the ports of northwestern Europe: an industrial sociological investigation in Antwerp, Bremen, Bremerhaven, Hamburg and Rotterdam] (Stuttgart: G. Fischer, 1960).

The Division of Labor

The restriction or expansion of role differentiation depends on the complexity of the economic structure. A society which depends solely on hunting for its sustenance will have a relatively small number of economic roles. Not much economic differentiation can take place in a community where every able-bodied person must devote most of his waking hours to throwing spears at rabbits in order to keep from starving. A sedentary agrarian culture frees more people from full-time food production, allows some members the leisure to become priests or craftsmen, and generally implements differentiation of roles. In an urban, industrial society, the economy requires so many specialists and provides so many different roles that it becomes a major criterion for social stratification. One consequence of the economic structure is social stratification. While a small agricultural community is likely to rank its members on the basis of family lineage in industrialized societies position in the division of labor is a major basis of social rank.

The Distribution of Power

Like other social structures, the economic order has many consequences in addition to its manifest function of producing and distributing goods and services. Important among these is the effect which economic organization has on the distribution of political power.[5] One example of the potential of economic position as a political factor may be seen in the fact that more than 20 million Americans belong to labor unions (see Table 13-3). There is a high correlation between a state's having a low percentage of union members in its electorate and the likelihood that the state has a tradition both of conservative state administration and of sending conservative legislators to Congress. Another example of association between economic position and politics is shown in the expenditures in national election campaigns. People with corporate interests, as well as those with labor interests, seem to have definite ideas as to which party best represents those interests. The Republican Party receives donations largely from persons with big business investments, while financial aid from organized labor goes usually in large part to the Democrats.

The fact that radio and television costs have constituted the largest single item of expenditure for both parties in recent Presi-

---

[5]For two sociological discussions of this phenomenon, the first on the local level and the second on the national, see Floyd Hunter, *Community Power Structure* (Chapel Hill: University of North Carolina Press, 1953); and C. Wright Mills, *The Power Elite* (New York: Oxford University Press, 1956).

Table 13-3   Union Membership in the United States

Year	Union Membership (in millions)	Union Membership as Per Cent of the Nonagricultural Labor Force
1930	3.4	11.7
1950	15.0	31.5
1968	20.3	27.9

SOURCE: U.S. Bureau of the Census, *Statistical Abstract of the United States, 1971* (Washington, D.C.: U.S. Government Printing Office, 1971), and U.S. Bureau of the Census, *Historical Statistics of the United States, Colonial Times to 1957* (Washington, D.C.: U.S. Government Printing Office, 1960).

dential election campaigns means that greater wealth gives greater opportunity to plead one's case before the electorate. In 1968, over 58 million dollars was spent for radio and television broadcasts in the primary and general elections. To the extent that the mass media are molders of public opinion, wealth is power.

Table 13-4   Characteristics of the United States Labor Force, 1969

Characteristics	Total Labor Force (millions)	Participation Rates (per cent)
Male	53.7	79.4
16–19 years	4.3	57.6
20–24 years	7.1	85.3
25–34 years	11.7	95.4
35–44 years	10.9	95.7
45–54 years	10.4	93.2
55–64 years	7.1	81.8
65 years and over	2.2	26.2
Female	30.6	42.2
16–19 years	3.1	43.1
20–24 years	4.6	56.5
25–34 years	5.4	43.5
35–44 years	5.9	49.7
45–54 years	6.4	53.3
55–64 years	4.1	42.5
65 years and over	1.1	9.4
Labor force, total	84.2	60.2
White	74.9	58.6
Black and other	9.3	61.5

SOURCE: U.S. Bureau of the Census, *Pocket Data Book, USA, 1971* (Washington, D.C.: U.S. Government Printing Office, 1971).

ECONOMIC PATTERNS IN THE UNITED STATES

The labor supply of any society consists of all its potential workers, male and female. At what age an individual is counted as a potential worker is a matter of cultural definition. For example, adolescents under 14 years of age are not considered to be in the labor force of the United States. Earlier, and still in some societies, younger children were considered part of the labor force. The actual *labor force* may be defined as that fraction of a population which is engaged in producing or distributing goods or services. Those persons temporarily unemployed are also included.

Composition of the Labor Force

The labor force in 1900 consisted of 29 million persons, 38 per cent of the total population. In 1950 it was 60 million (40 per cent of the population), and by 1969 it was nearly 76 million or 37 per cent of all Americans. Not all people who are in the labor force are employed, however. In 1970 five per cent of the total labor force was out of work and among female, black, and young workers, unemployment ranged from 6 to 15 per cent (see Table 13-5).

One important feature of the U.S. labor force is the increasing number and proportion of workers who are women. In 1870 slightly

Table 13-5   Unemployment in the United States, 1970

Social Group	Per Cent
Male	4.4
Female	5.9
White	4.5
Negro and other nonwhites	8.2
Blue-collar workers	4.5
White-collar workers	2.7
16–19 years	15.3
20–24 years	8.2
25–44 years	2.6
45–64 years	2.3
65 years and older	3.2
Total labor force	4.9
Average duration of unemployment	8.8 (weeks)

SOURCE: U.S. Bureau of the Census, *Pocket Data Book, USA, 1971* (Washington, D.C.: U.S. Government Printing Office, 1971), p. 136.

Table 13-6   Labor Force Participation of Women, 1890–1970

| | Per Cent of Women in Labor Force | | | | |
| | | | Year | | |
Marital Status	*1890*	*1940*	*1950*	*1960*	*1970**
Single	37	48	51	44	53
Married	5	17	25	32	41
No children under 18					41
Children aged 6–17					49
Children under age 6					29
Widowed or divorced	29	32	36	37	36
All women	18	27	31	35	43

*Women age 16 years and older. Percents for 1890–1960 are based on data for persons 14 years and older.
SOURCE: U.S. Bureau of the Census, *Statistical Abstract of the United States, 1971* (Washington, D.C.: U.S. Government Printing Office, 1971); and U.S. Bureau of the Census, *Historical Statistics of the United States, Colonial Times to 1957* (Washington, D.C.: U.S. Government Printing Office, 1960).

less than 15 per cent of the work force was female; in 1970 there were 31 million women workers, 43 per cent of all women over the age of 15 and 37 per cent of the total work force. In 1890 just 18 per cent of women (over the age of 13) were part of the paid labor force. Most of the increase in the number of working women has been the increase in the proportion of married women who work for pay (in addition to housework). Five per cent of all married women were in the labor force in 1890 while one-fourth of all married women worked in 1950. In 1970, 41 per cent of all married women were employed in paid jobs.

The increase in the number of gainfully employed women—married, divorced, widowed, and single—is, of course, a major aspect of the changing status of women in American society. It should be noted, however, that women are generally discriminated against in employment and promotions, and women who are equally qualified generally receive less pay for their work than do men. Moreover, women contribute an enormous amount to the society in the form of unpaid (house)work, child care, and volunteer work for the community.

Age and the Labor Force

In many societies, particularly the agricultural, productive work begins fairly early in life: the child and the youth are part of the labor force. In urban industrialized America, the work period tends to be confined to a rather limited part of the life cycle. With the extension of life expectancy, of course, the working period is much longer for the average person than it was in the past. But the age at which one enters the labor force is also later than heretofore. In fact, viewed historically, the most striking changes in the age composition of the labor force have been in the youngest and the oldest age groups. Both male and female child labor increased steadily from 1870 to 1900, when the peak of children gainfully employed was 1,250,000. In 1900 in the United States, 26 per cent of all boys 10 to 15 years old and 10 per cent of all girls in this age bracket were in the working force. By 1940 the gainful employment of young children had practically ceased, and it remains rare today.

At the other end of the age scale, there has been a marked decrease —though less than in the case of children—in the percentage of men aged 65 and over in the labor force. The proportion of men 65 and older who are in the labor force has declined from more than two-thirds in 1890 to about 26 per cent in 1969. This long-term trend is correlated with the changing nature and declining importance of farming, an occupation adapted to the capabilities of both young and old; with the decrease in self-employment; and with the substitution of semiskilled for skilled labor. Moreover, the private pension programs and old-age security programs have made earlier retirement possible and many employers have made it compulsory.

One of the most significant features of the labor force in this country is the high number of persons in the 16–24 age group who are kept out of the working cohort because they remain in school. At no time in the history of mankind and in no other country has there been such a high proportion of individuals in this age bracket still engaged in getting an education. The situation reflects both our high prosperity and our great faith in the value of an education. Associated with the progressive aging of the population is the fact that our labor force has come to consist more largely of individuals from 35 to 64 years old.

The total amount of time expended in work in the United States society has also decreased for most workers. Not only are many workers limited to part-time work, but the length of the work week itself has been reduced over the years. The most reliable estimates are that the standard work week was 70 hours in 1850, 55 hours in 1900, and slightly less than 40 hours per week in 1970. A person steadily employed in a manufacturing plant in 1900 worked 3,000 hours a year. Today such a worker averages about 2,000 work hours a year.

Distribution of the Labor Force

In the last century there has been a major industrial shift from the production of goods to the production of services. In 1870 about three-fourths of the people in the labor force were engaged in producing tangible goods; by 1950 the proportion was less than half. The figures include employers and the self-employed, as well as wage and salary workers. This shift in the distribution of the labor force has been brought about largely by technological improvements. Heavy manual labor has given way to machine production, which has freed a larger portion of the labor force to run laundromats, rent out evening clothes, provide package delivery services, give pedicures to French poodles, be tree surgeons or public stenographers—in short, to enter service industries.

Of course, agriculture too has become more mechanized. At the time the United States was founded, farming was the most important income-producing activity, and as recently as 1870 more than half the labor force was engaged in agriculture. Today farmers comprise only 4 per cent of the labor force. The trend in agriculture is toward fewer farmers and larger farms.[6] Individuals who under

Table 13-7   The Changing Occupational Structure of the United States

Total Labor Force (in 1000's)	1900 29,030	1920 42,206	1940 51,742	1960 66,681	1969 76,520
White-collar workers	17.6	24.9	31.1	43.1	47.6
Professional & technical workers	4.2	5.4	7.4	11.2	14.3
Managers, officials, & proprietors	5.8	6.6	7.3	10.5	10.3
Clerical workers	3.0	8.0	9.6	14.7	17.1
Sales workers	4.5	4.9	6.7	6.6	6.0
Blue-collar workers	35.8	40.2	39.8	36.3	35.7
Craftsmen & foremen	10.5	13.0	12.0	12.8	12.9
Operatives	12.0	15.6	18.4	18.0	18.5
Non-farm laborers	12.5	11.6	9.4	5.5	4.3
Service workers	9.0	7.8	11.7	12.5	12.6
Private household workers	5.4	3.3	4.7	3.3	2.2
Other service workers	3.6	4.5	7.1	9.2	10.4
Farmworkers	37.5	27.0	7.4	8.1	4.0

SOURCE: Bureau of the Census, *Historical Statistics of the United States, Colonial Times to 1957*, p. 74 (for data before 1950); *Statistical Abstract of the United States, 1969*, p. 222. Data beginning 1950 not strictly comparable with earlier years.

---

[6]"Fewer and Larger Farms Shown in Latest Summary of Census," *Agricultural Situation*, 1956, 40: 12. (Agricultural Marketing Service, U.S. Department of Agriculture, Washington, D.C.: U.S. Government Printing Office.)

other conditions might have been farmers are entering the urban labor force, particularly the service industries. (See Table 13-7.)

Since 1900 clerical workers in the labor force have increased nearly sixfold, professional and technical workers threefold, proprietors and managers twofold, and sales workers by almost one-half. Household workers declined 60 per cent, but other service workers, such as barbers, beauticians, cooks, firemen, janitors, policemen, and waitresses, have nearly tripled.

The nation's economy is less and less dependent on muscle power and more and more dependent on professional, technical, and clerical skills. The shift from brawn and manpower to education and brain power reflects a basic trend in American economic life.

Automation

Another economic trend with implications for the labor force is automation, which may be defined as mechanization to the point where machines run other machines. Most of our engineering technology in the last century and a half has been put to inventing and perfecting machines that produce a product—that is, production machines. It is only recently that machines have been developed that will do such formerly expensive and time-consuming tasks as quality testing and readjustment of the production line machine. With a whole factory automated, fixed capital will take on new meaning.

By the standards of an automated economy, the present fixed capital of the United States is inadequate. The Industrial Revolution is just beginning. The concept of fixed capital brings to mind huge factories, with big steel machines that cannot be picked up and moved. Think of the meaning of fixed capital when one machine is running another machine, so that the greatest expense is not turning out the product but stopping the machine. Here fixed capital reaches the point where the costliest thing one can do is cease production. A stable market, a steady demand, become essential.

ECONOMIC INSTITUTIONS

Competition is a basic value in American culture; there are norms structured around the value of competition in each basic institution. In courtship, young people compete for dates with the members of the opposite sex considered to be the most desirable. Through missionaries and revivals, churches compete for members. Major political offices are filled by the process of competition: office-seekers compete for popularity with the voters. In the area of socialization, we motivate children to learn by having them compete for grades.

Economic Competition

Economic competition is rivalry and struggle to get possession of those things which a given culture considers wealth. It is one phase of the larger universal struggle for goods, tangible and intangible. There exists, on the one hand, a limited resource, and, on the other, a population with a seemingly ever-increasing number of wants, both basic and culturally defined. The traditional view of economic competition assumes complete self-interest on the part of buyers and sellers. It takes for granted a rational judgment of wants and of the means of satisfying them. It postulates the principle that each person acts to get the most he or she can from others while giving as little of oneself as possible.

This view of competition clearly reflects the whole social-cultural period in which modern capitalism developed. Capitalism assumed a self-regulating interrelation of price, demand, and supply. This, in turn, rested on the simple notion of rational motivation directed "to *economizing* or *utility-maximizing* behavior" believed to flow directly "from the fact that human wants are comparatively unlimited in relation to the resources avaiable for the satisfaction of such wants."[7]

It was the contention of laissez-faire economists of the eighteenth and nineteenth centuries that the free flow of goods and services through rational and unhampered competition would result in the most efficient production and distribution of goods, capital, and labor supply—all to the ultimate benefit of the consumers. They fully believed in the competitive practice of their time—that the institutions of private property, contract, profit-making, and laissez-faire freedom of action were a true and objective operation of universal forces in nature and society.

Modern social psychology does not support this view of human behavior. People have impulses and interests that do not completely correspond to their rational needs. Political and religious views, class, and life style also influence economic behavior. Love, sympathy, hatred, anxiety, and indifference, tied to irrational attitudes and values, enter into the economic choices people make.

Consumer Activity

Modern technology and complex business enterprise have profoundly altered the market situation in which the ordinary con-

---

[7]See J. J. Spengler, "Sociological Presuppositions in Economic Theory," *Southern Economic Journal*, 1940, 7: 131–157, quotation from p. 132, italics in the original. This is a thoughtful and stimulating paper on the limitations of classical theory.

sumer finds oneself. Such changes are due to mass production, to the disappearance of the earlier competitive pattern with the rise of many near-monopolies, to the shift from an agricultural to an industrial economy, to the high degree of division of labor, and to urban life. The consumer has become more and more dependent on the institutions of the market place. At an earlier date, say 1900, the ordinary person in a small town or rural trading center purchased goods that were usually of a quality not very difficult to determine. On the basis of what he could see, touch, or taste, he could decide whether or not to buy. Today in modern retailing the quality, durability, and utility of goods are not well standardized in relation to price. The research of consumers' testing agencies indicates that the less expensive of two competing products frequently is the one of higher quality. The more expensive product may capture a sizable share of the market, however, by skillful advertising and packaging. Advertising profoundly influences consumer preferences and habits of buying. Some advertising is useful in informing prospective buyers about available materials or services, but much of it is emotional and status-appealing. "Keeping up with the Joneses" is an old motive, and all sorts of advertisements stimulate people to buy so that they may have a product popular with the "best people."

The nature of retailing has changed greatly over the years. The department store, the mail-order house, and the chain store all give witness to the growing complexity of the market, to alterations in the earlier competitive patterns, and to changes in the role of the ultimate consumer. The chain store is a good reflection of business enterprise in mass society. It is efficient—it eliminates the middleman and handles standardized goods—but its merchandising tends to be impersonal.

Finally, alterations have been made in the use of credit. Many consumers no longer pay cash or use an open charge account. Rather, they pay on some sort of fixed installment plan. Installment buying has become, indeed, a culture pattern for large sections of the American population, and the charges for this service are passed on, in one form or another, to the consumer.

The difficulties for the consumer can be traced to the transition from an old to a new method of distributing consumption goods. While many critics decry advertising, chain-store, and other aspects of contemporary selling, all these activities are intimately interwoven with the whole fabric of modern business enterprise.

The government of the United States, acting as an agency for the consuming public, has taken some interest in consumer protection. There are laws providing for pure food and drugs, for standard methods of packaging and labeling, and for licensing and inspection

---

ILLUSTRATIVE DATA 13-2   SOME MAJOR VALUE-ORIENTATIONS IN
AMERICA

Achievement and Success: American culture has long been marked
   by an emphasis upon personal achievement—"making good"—
   especially secular occupational achievement.

Activity and Work: "Active" people are held in high esteem and people encourage each other to "get busy." It has been said that few
   Americans "find it easy to be happy unless they are doing something." To a large degree, work is regarded as an end in itself.

Moral Orientation: Americans tend to see the world in moral terms,
   to think in terms of right or wrong, good or bad, etc.

Efficiency and Practicality: "Efficient" is a word of high praise in a
   society that has long emphasized economic expansion, mass production, up-to-dateness, practicality, expediency, and "getting
   things done." Similarly, "impractical" has long been one of the
   strongest pejorative words in America.

Progress: The rich vocabulary of epithets ("backward," "outmoded,"
   "old-fashioned," "stagnant," etc.) in America can be understood
   as epithets only against the unquestioning assumption that the
   new is better—that "forward" is better than "backward" and that
   progress is "just around the corner."

Material Comfort: "Americans," a French observer once remarked,
   "consider it only natural that their slightest whim should be
   gratified."

Source: Robin M. Williams, Jr., *American Society,* 2nd ed. (New York: Alfred A.
Knopf, 1961), pp. 414–468. The descriptive comments borrow generously from
Williams' text.

—control over the conditions surrounding the production of a good
or a service rather than over the nature of the product itself. Such
regulations are found in public transportation systems, in restaurants, packing houses, and so on. So too, governments attempt to
set up standards regarding such matters as weight, freshness, chemical composition, and quality. In addition, various private consumer
organizations have been set up to inform prospective buyers about
quality and price. Such organizations often publish buyers' guides.

The Social Meaning of Work

People are socialized to participate in economic activity. People
are motivated to work for reasons in addition to supporting themselves. If not, why would the person who earns fifty thousand
dollars a year put in extra hours striving for a promotion and a raise,
or why would the person who inherited enough wealth to live

comfortably do the work necessary to get through professional school and then show up at an office every day? Why do sociologists who study industrial organization find it not unusual for a member of a small work group in a factory to turn down a chance for a job as foreman, accompanied by a pay raise?

Both the wealthy man who continues to work and the worker who rejects a promotion illustrate the fact that there are incentives governing work which are not exclusively economic. People pursue economic activity not only to make money but to gain power and prestige, to cultivate and maintain primary group relations, to contribute to a sense of purpose, and to fulfill the expectations of other social roles, such as parent and citizen. The worker who would rather stay with his production gang than be promoted is willing, perhaps, to forego economic gain for the feeling of "belonging" which he enjoys as a member of the primary group. Many people who have enough wealth to permit them to enjoy full-time leisure continue to work because they have been socialized in American society, where the norms of the culture have convinced them that healthy adults ought to be engaged in some productive activity. It is common for people who have retired to complain of feeling useless; they have lost a sense of purpose which their work gave them.

INTERPRETIVE SUMMARY

The Industrial Revolution has had a profound effect on the economic structure. It influenced the production and distribution of services as domestic industry gave way to the entrepeneur and finally the corporate system, in which ownership and management separated, productivity per person and employee income increased and general working conditions improved, while hours in the work week gradually decreased. Automation, the industrial system in which machines run machines, is already demanding increased amounts of fixed capital and bringing further changes in the way this basic function is carried out.

Although workers are free to leave a job and employers free to make dismissals, for the term of employment the two interests are required to make contracts for every obligation which in earlier times would have been fulfilled by each as a matter of status.

In an industrial-urban economy, where the person works away from home, individual sense of purpose or lack of it is greatly dependent on how one views oneself as worker. The hierarchical structure of large corporations, especially the management structures, would seem at first glance to stifle creativity, freedom, and thus dignity. However, stratification has also led to the development of situses, occupational "in-groups."

In mass societies, the production and distribution of goods and services tend to be handled by a few large corporate structures, state or private. These structures resemble community structure in several ways: individuals have roles and statuses, in this case related to the division of labor; informal groups supplement the formal structure; and both tacit and stated norms govern behavior.

Besides being a sort of community unto itself, the corporation has profoundly affected the larger community. For one thing, an individual's job status is likely to be the determining factor in his ultimate status in the community. Moreover, one will identify oneself so strongly with members of similar occupational strata that he may vote for and help finance political figures and parties who seem sympathetic to that stratum; thus the economic institution influences the political institutions of a culture. Under systems of free enterprise, the existence of highly mechanized corporate giants has led to many minor culture patterns affecting consumers: the emergence of big retailing combines, the extension of advertising and credit, and even the extension of protective government control, an action that was not contemplated in the days of widespread trust in laissez-faire economics.

In the United States, both the composition and the distribution of the labor force have changed over the years, largely as a result of technological advances which were in turn made possible by the existence of large amounts of corporate capital. The labor force presently has more women than ever before, fewer very old people, many more people performing white-collar jobs, and more occupied in performing services. On the world scale there is increased economic interdependence. Though concern for the political balance of power has dictated caution, the general trend is toward increased cooperation, a cooperation which has been implemented by vast international communication and transportation networks.

SUGGESTIONS FOR FURTHER READING

Berle, Adolf A., and Means, Gardner. *The Modern Corporation and Private Property*. New York: Macmillan, 1932. This was the first study to systematically investigate the impact of the widespread distribution of corporate ownership upon property institutions in the United States.

Durkheim, Emile. *The Division of Labor in Society*. Translated by George Simpson. Glencoe, Ill.: The Free Press, 1947. This is the classic essay on the division of labor in society.

Form, William H., and Miller, Delbert C. *Industry, Labor, and Community*. New York: Harper and Brothers, 1970. The authors discuss the relations between the economic institution and other institutions in an industrial society within the framework of community power structure.

Friedman, Milton. *An Economist's Protest: Columns in Political Economy*. Glen Ridge, N. J.: Thomas Horton and Company, 1972. This is a collection of short essays by one of America's most prominent economists on contemporary economic issues.

Galbraith, John Kenneth. *The Affluent Society*. Boston: Houghton Mifflin Company, 1958. The question of whether an economic theory based on an economy of scarcity is relevant to the problems of a society of plenty is posed.

Gouldner, Alvin W. *Patterns of Industrial Bureaucracy*. Glencoe, Ill.: The Free Press, 1954. A fascinating case study of the norms governing behavior in a mine and a factory, this book contributes to sociological theory a typology of bureaucratic rules.

Greer, Scott. *Last Man In: Racial Access to Union Power*. Glencoe, Ill.: The Free Press, 1959. This book reports research on the power structure of labor unions and its consequences for racial relations and the role of the leader.

Meadows, Paul. *The Culture of Industrial Man*. Lincoln: The University of Nebraska Press, 1950. An excellent analysis of the culture patterns peculiar to an industrial society and their implications for the individual is presented.

Miller, Delbert C., and Form, William H. *Industrial Sociology*. 2nd ed. New York: Harper and Row, 1964. This is a first-rate basic textbook on the sociology of work and economy.

Moore, Wilbert E. *The Conduct of the Corporation*. New York: Random House, 1963. This is a well-written sociological discussion of the inside workings of a large-scale modern business bureaucracies.

Veblen, Thorstein. *The Theory of the Business Enterprise*. Introduction by C. Wright Mills. Mentor Books. The New American Library, 1958. Veblen discusses industry, the impact of technology, and other aspects of the business enterprise.

Wilensky, Harold L. *Intellectuals in Labor Unions: Organizational Pressures on Professional Roles*. Glencoe, Ill.: The Free Press, 1956. This is essentially a study of decision-making as it is determined by the varied norms shaping the role of the staff expert.

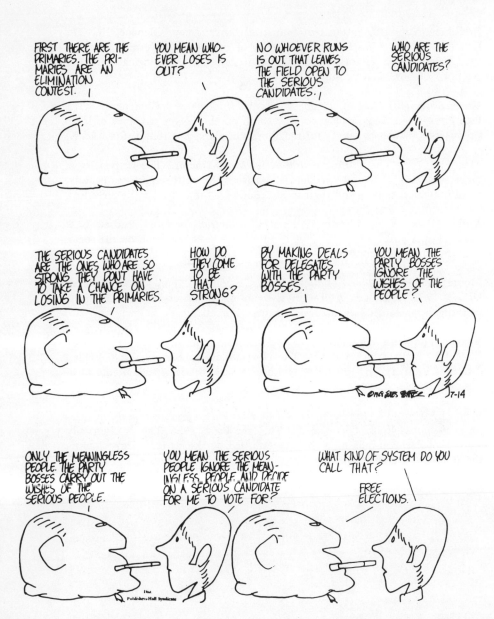

14
Polity
and
Society

All societies have some sort of larger, overall regulations dealing with the general welfare of the tribe or the community. Usually there are designated groups or persons who set up the rules and act to see that they are enforced. In its broadest sense, this wider regulatory force may be called the government. In more rudimentary societies such controls are largely informal. In more complex societies they are both informal and formal. Generally, the more complex the community, the more formalized the controls. More definite organization is reflected in special personnel—legislative, administrative, and judicial—whose roles are to operate the various control agencies. In the strict sense, the concept of political order or government refers to these special regulations and the operating personnel.

Political scientists specialize in the study of the structure and processes of government. Yet some political data have considerable interest to sociologists. These include the relationship of the society to the nation-state, the way in which the mores and public opinion influence political interaction, the place of political revolution in social change, and the functions of political structures for other institutions.

POLITICAL STRUCTURES

In ancient Greece a citizen was a full member of the city-state, with a certain role and status in public life. These stood in contrast with his culturally deep-rooted relations with his family, kin, and occupational or other associations. The distinction between public and private matters is historically important because it indicates the shift from a kinship to a territorial basis of control, from private vengeance to public punishment, from small, primary-group obligations to larger obligations based on secondary contacts.

In modern times the political order is centered in the sovereign state. As a social myth and as a set of practices, the state is the core of contemporary nationalism. The sovereign state has become the principal instrument of public order and reflects, in fact, the continuing need for some overall agency of control in an industrialized mass society.

One may look on the *state* as an organized power structure the functions of which are the management and control of the society. This involves such things as external and internal security, justice, and welfare, and varying provisions for individual freedom, depending on the nature of the state and the national society. The state also has sole power to levy taxes to pay for these services.

In nonliterate societies a separate political structure may be barely discernible. In such a society, where the social structure is practically coterminous with a few families or clans, most matters of social control are handled within the family structure. In such a situation, there is usually a chief or council of elders in whom ultimate authority for major decisions resides. But regardless of how elaborate the machinery of government may become, some of the norms are always enforced through informal structures. Behind the formal organization of the state there are always follways and mores supported by informal sanctions.

Formal Structures

The state is, of course, a historical product. As populations grew, increasing differentiation of roles led to a breakdown of controls and the need for extension of regulations to new areas of conduct. This meant a shift from a family or kinship basis of social control to one founded on the larger community, with particular individuals, groups, or classes setting down the rules and putting them into effect. More integrated forms of government tended to arise as groups or societies were threatened by, or fell into conflict with, other societies. This tendency was most important in the rise of

Table 14-1   Units of Government in the United States,
1930–1933 and 1967

Type of Government	1930–1933	1967
The Nation	1	1
States	48	50
Counties	3,053	3,049
Municipalities	16,366	18,048
Townships	20,262	17,105
School Districts	127,108	21,782
Special Districts	8,580	21,264
Total	175,418	81,299

SOURCE: U.S. Bureau of the Census, *Statistical Abstract of the United States, 1971* (Washington, D.C.: U.S. Government Printing Office, 1971), p. 397; and U.S. Bureau of the Census, *Historical Statistics of the United States, Colonial Times to 1957* (Washington, D.C.: U.S. Government Printing Office, 1960), p. 694.

more complex states: warfare between groups makes for strong in-group solidarity.

It seems a far cry from the simple tribal or village council of older men to the elaborate operations of modern government, and yet these institutions have much in common. Both revolve around a power structure and its functions. Someone or some group makes the rules and laws or at least standardizes those at hand, without which there could be no social order. This is the legislative structure. Second, somebody or some group enforces the regulations. This is the executive or administrative structure. Third, some group is responsible for settling controversies where the meaning and application of the laws or codes are in question. This is the judicial structure.

In the United States there are over 80,000 governments, each with the power to tax and otherwise influence the lives of people (see Table 14-1). And although the number of governments has been reduced substantially in the past four decades due mostly to the reduction of the number of school districts, there is an increasing number of social analysts who are convinced that the number and character of formal government structures in the United States will have to be drastically changed before the society will be able to effectively deal with such major social problems as pollution, transportation, and education. Problems such as these are increasingly regional rather than state and local problems. The complexity of the problem can be seen from the fact that the Chicago metropolitan area includes some 250 local governments, small villages, and school districts each with its own administrative powers. In the

New York metropolitan area, there are over 1,500 such local governments. Thus, it is argued, local and state government boundaries are inadequate to present-day social needs and some form of regional government is increasingly required.

Regional Planning

Yet even a regional form of government is a problematic solution. The meaning of "region" varies with different functions: a water region, a transportation region, and even an economic region have very different overlays. It is no surprise then that there has been continuous and at times bitter debate about the criteria to be used in setting up "regions." Some experts have advocated that such regions be delimited around the major metropolitan areas. Others suggest that regions be delineated according to administrative convenience, such as transportation facilities or proximity to state institutions and federal administrative offices. This does not always create realistic regions.

Still another plan calls for combining groups of states. Actually, the earliest recognition of regional differences grew out of the traditional division of the country into such geographic divisions as the Northeast, Southeast, and North Central. While recent proposals would not follow the traditional combination of states, such a scheme would still be open to the criticism that states and combinations of states cut across too many regional differences in climate, soil, industry, and ways of life. As one commentator puts it, "States or groups of states are not particularly suited to function as planning regions."[1]

Another proposal is to base regions on single functions and then combine single-function areas when it is administratively feasible to do so. The division of the United States into drainage basins is one illustration of this approach. But here again, overlapping obviously would be increased. One practical plan, though not the easiest to draw up, was suggested in the 1930s. The suggestion was to develop regions around a composite of physiographic and cultural data. Physiographic data include such things as climate, soil, topography, flora and fauna, and mineral resources. Cultural data include population density, metropolitan influence, major types of productive operations, commerce, farm income, and the like. It is evident that the boundaries of such composite regions are not sharp, and certainly would not follow state lines (see Figure 14-1).

Setting up a specific regional area is clearly bound up not only

---

[1]National Resources Committee, *Regional Factors in National Planning and Development* (Washington, D.C.: U.S. Government Printing Office, 1935), p. 163.

Figure 14-1   Regions of the Continental United States*

*Possible planning regions based upon composite planning problems. Possible regional headquarters are indicated on the map by dots.
Source: U.S. National Resources Committee, Regional Factors in National Planning and Development (Washington, D.C.: U.S. Government Printing Office, 1935), p. 166, figure 20.

with physiographic, economic, and political factors, but with the whole subculture of the area. If a region is to become a vital unit in social organization, it must be supported by a consciousness of shared subcultural patterns among its inhabitants. Unless regions develop the supporting attitudes and values of group solidarity and common action, the economic or political aspects will be largely superficial. A viable social structure requires the participation that stems from commitment.

POLITICAL FUNCTIONS

We have mentioned three major types of formal political structures: legislative, executive, and judicial. These need not, of course, be operated by separate or distinct groups. In a totalitarian society, one man and a handful of subordinates can make the laws, enforce them, and arbitrate disputes about them. In American society, there is usually insistence that roles in the three structures be mutually exclusive. One cannot at the same time fill the status of a Senator who makes laws and that of a Supreme Court Justice who adjudicates disputes about those laws, nor can one assume the role of a Representative who makes laws and simultaneously be the Attorney General charged with enforcing them. What is called a system of checks and balances in the government of the United States is an arrangement whereby the three major functions of government are the responsibility of three separate groups, each of which exercises some limitation on the powers of the others.

The three principal internal functions of government (as opposed to its external function, the protection of the society against other societies) are (1) the institutionalization of norms, or decreeing the rules under which the society shall operate; (2) the adjudication of conflicts, or settling disputes between groups within the society about the application of institutionalized norms and their sanction; and (3) the planning of the state's operation and the enforcement of its institutionalized norms.

Institutionalization of Norms

The central role of legislative bodies is to make the laws which become the governmental controls of the society. Other chief functions are taxation and investigation of administrative personnel to see that they carry out the mandates of the legislature. In some systems legislators may act, on occasion, as a judicial body, as in the impeachment of public officials. The legislative group—parliament, assembly, congress—set up to make the laws usually does so in accordance with some written or unwritten constitution. Lawmaking, however, need not be confined to the legislative structure. In the United States, law is also made by judges in rendering court decisions, by administrative action, and by a machinery of initiative and referendum which permits direct legislation by the voters.

In democratic countries, legislators are elected by various systems of voting, sometimes directly and sometimes, as when one legislative body chooses the members of another, indirectly. Representation is usually on the basis of territory, such as the precinct, county, or other geographic district. And in this country at least, prospective legislators must live in the local residential area where they stand for office, for it is traditionally held that persons who live in a neighborhood, city, or region will serve its interests best. The British hold a different view and nominate and elect men to the House of Commons regardless of their home address. Despite practice in the United States, there is little doubt that the older theory of geographic locus breaks down under modern conditions. It reflects the primary-group culture from which it sprang. Today individuals and groups believe they should also be represented in accordance with the secondary-group interests of their professions, businesses, labor unions, and the like. The lobby and the pressure group show the extent to which modern legislatures must deal with problems other than those which are confined to primary groups living in limited localities.

The Soviet system of representation on the basis of one's being a worker in a plant, or in a railroad system, or a member of a labor union, or a farmer illustrates a shift from a strictly territorial to a more functional basis of representation. And indeed, the American pressure group or lobby is a kind of unofficial functional representation.

The Adjudication of Conflicts

While the law—constitutional, statute, or judge-made—fixes the rules of human conduct, conflicts of interest constantly require some adjudication. Hence courts are set up, usually at two levels: those of original jurisdiction and those for appeal, the latter culminate in American society in the United States Supreme Court.

The selection and qualifications of individuals to operate the courts vary with the culture. In Anglo-American practice, judicial functions have been divided between those of jury and those of judge. The jury system goes back to the primary-group theory of democracy, that an individual accused of crime has the right to be tried by his equals—his "peers," as the legal language puts it. Though the jury system of the United States has been much criticized and though there has been a trend to abandon trial by jury except in more serious criminal cases, it still represents an important link between citizenry and government.

The Enforcement of Norms

A third basic function of government is to put into effect the "will" or laws of the state. Where government is at all complex there are usually several levels of administrative power and function. First, there is the *head of state*. He may be elected by popular vote, or he may derive his role and status from being a member of a ruling family or from his headship of a dictatorial clique or party. He is charged with the responsibility of enforcing the power of the state. The dictator-head may be both law-maker and law-enforcer, though this situation exists less often than popular notion imagines.

The head of the state usually has some kind of council or cabinet to advise him. Sometimes the council itself is the head of the state in the sense that its decisions are binding, as in Britain. Sometimes it is only advisory, as in the United States. In Soviet Russia the real head of the country is the Politburo of the Communist Party, although it is not even mentioned in the published constitution. This is a case of single-party dominance of the executive and legislative functions. The various congresses and presidia are largely window-dressing for the real control exercised by the Communist Party.

The second-level administrators are the heads of major governmental departments or bureaus. They are charged with carrying out the executive policies determined by the head of the state and his advisors. Below this second level are several other layers of administrators: division and bureau chiefs, and a mass of specialists of various qualification, duties, and responsibilities.

In democracies it was once common to draw practically all administrative personnel from the membership of the political party in office. (The "spoils" system, as it is called, has also existed under authoritarian and dictatorial forms of government.) But as the duties of administrators became more complex and required special skills and experience, and as the abuses of patronage mushroomed, devices such as the civil service were set up to limit the spoils system. The function of the civil service is to take much public administration out of the hands of politicans and set up professional standards for the selection, continuity, and promotion of most governmental personnel.

Protection from External Forces

The first three functions of government are necessary to the preservation of order within the society. But it is also essential that the society defend itself against outside attack. The two principal means for accomplishing this end are war and diplomacy. The accommodation of conflicts with other societies can be implemented by bargaining, compromise, or threats, or the societies can attempt to subjugate or destroy each other through warfare.

Despite modern communication, the spread of technology, and the exchange of goods and ideas from country to country and region to region, the world is marked by a high degree of cultural diversity. Consider the matter of language, the principal carrier of cultural diversity. Including all the local and regional variations, there are several hundred languages. There are 284 million people who speak English, 161 million who speak Russian, 598 million who speak Chinese, and more than 200 million who speak Hindustani. These make up about half the world's population. Moreover, the first three of these languages are the core of rather distinctive cultural systems. In the rest of the world are other nations not far removed from the cultural systems of, say, the English- or the Russian-speaking peoples. Yet there are still other linguistic groups with rather sharp cultural differences. Facile solutions of the problems of war and peace too frequently neglect the fact of peoples' intolerance of those who are different.

People are not only intolerant but inconsistent. Many may desire a world order based on law or rule of reason; but countering this, as always, is the play of nationalist myths and legends which may serve to block movements to establish a global legal system with one central structure for enforcing norms. It is very doubtful that the masses of people in the countries with a high standard of living will voluntarily submit to plans which would take from them what they now hold. Given what we know about the distribution of population and resources in the world, we can expect competition and conflict among states to continue. Each society, therefore, will have some structure with the function of protecting it from external threats.

POLITICAL PATTERNS IN THE UNITED STATES

In highly dynamic periods such as the present, political patterns do not remain static. They are influenced by technological inventions, the relative decrease of primary-group forms of living, and the related extension of secondary and mass-society patterns of action. These changes have been associated particularly with an extension of governmental controls, especially in the area of the planning function of the executive structure.

The Growth of Government

One of the most striking changes in modern life is the expansion of the government into areas of action long considered outside the direct scope of the state. This is particularly true with reference to economic institutions, but it is evident in almost all other important phases of our society. The manner in which a state tends to become the all-embracing, controlling agent depends on the cultural values and practices of the time and place. In most democratic countries the trend has been chiefly in the direction of administrative regulation of capitalistic enterprises and of furnishing certain public services. On the whole, such trends have influenced the familial, religious, and economic institutions. In some societies the state has taken over property and economic enterprise almost entirely, with more and more regimentation and planning of nearly every aspect of both public (and private) life.

There are various ways of measuring the expansion of functions in the political order. The most obvious are increases in the cost of government and in number of public personnel. Others are the growth in services and regulations. The extension of the political structure in the U.S. is easily seen in the increasing proportion of the labor force employed by the government. In 1970 there were nearly 13 million persons employed by various branches of government. Contrary to popular opinion, however, there are three times as many state and local employees as there are federal employees. (See Table 14-2.) Moreover, the rate of employment among the state and local governments is increasing more rapidly than it is in the federal government.

Another indication of the trend toward government's increasing responsibility for many aspects of social life is revealed in the fact that United States citizens pay an average of 31 per cent of their income for local, state, and federal taxes.

It is true that American society is much larger in population and in geographic area than it used to be, but the major share of governmental expansion in personnel and budget is attributable to increases in services provided by the government. The state now takes at least some of the responsibility for caring for the aged, the mentally ill, and the unemployed, as well as providing all of the citizenry with postal service, highways, schools, parks, and many other services. It also regulates the currency, the mass media of communication, interstate transportation, the quality of foods and drugs, and numerous other enterprises regarded as needing supervision in the public interest.

The single largest expenditure of government in the United States is for the preservation of external order through the diplomatic and military structures. In addition to financing our own military forces, we spend billions of dollars annually helping support the military forces and economies of other societies. The economic aid which we furnish to other countries accounts for considerably less than half our foreign expenditures, the bulk of which goes to military aid.

The Party System

Those who want direct political power have two simple but basic aims. The first is to get into office—legislative, administrative, or judicial. The other is to stay in office. In democratic societies these purposes are institutionalized in the multiple-party system. In some societies either a ruling class or a single party, which soon takes on the features of a stabilized ruling class, retains this power by various devices, such as physical force and propaganda.

Under the democratic system, parties seek election by a plurality of the citizens under certain rules laid down in the law and the mores. As a means of securing the general support or popular "will," political parties become organized in a hierarchical fashion and develop codes, leadership, tactics, and strategy for capturing elections,

ILLUSTRATIVE DATA 14–1   SELECTED CHARACTERISTICS OF THE
MEMBERS OF CONGRESS, 1971

Characteristic	Repre- sentatives*	Senators	Total
Male	421	99	520
Female	12	1	13
White	421	99	520
Black	12	1	13
Protestant	295	83	378
Roman Catholic	91	10	101
Jewish	12	2	14
Other	35	5	40

*There were two vacancies in the House of Representatives at the time of the survey.
Source: U.S. Bureau of the Census, Statistical Abstract of the United States, 1971 (Washington, D.C.: U.S. Government Printing Office, 1971), p. 355.

Table 14-2   Government Employment in the United States, 1816–1970

Year	Federal Government Employment	State and Local Government Employment
1816	4,800	NA
1851	26,300	NA
1901	239,500	2,532,000
1929	579,600	NA
1950	1,960,700	4,285,000
1970	2,881,000	10,147,000

NA = data not available.
SOURCE: U.S. Bureau of the Census, Statistical Abstract of the United States, 1971 (Washington, D.C.: U.S. Government Printing Office, 1971), pp. 388–389; and U.S. Bureau of the Census, Historical Statistics of the United States (Washington, D.C.: U.S. Government Printing Office, 1960), pp. 710–711.

including membership drives, propaganda, and "getting out the vote."

While parties struggle in the larger public arena in an effort to best their opponents through elections, there is also frequent competition and factional conflict within the party organization itself, aiming at domination of policy. Inner cliques develop, which furnish continuity between one campaign and the next. These political factions are usually more thoroughly organized than the party itself. It is generally believed that the most successful parliamentary gov-

Political Pluralism

Sociologist Seymour Martin Lipset commented that "...multiple and politically inconsistent affiliations, loyalties, and stimuli reduce the emotion and aggressiveness involved in political choice." While in the past decade there has been some marked "aggressiveness" in the American political arena, the United States has a tradition of political pluralism. In such a system, power is divided among a number of groups and factions representing different interests and values. In spite of the fact that only 54.5 per cent of Americans eighteen and over voted in the 1972 presidential election, political pluralism provides for the airing of majority and minority views, opinions, and interests.

ILLUSTRATIVE DATA 14–2   POLITICAL AFFILIATION OF AMERICANS, 1970

1970	Republican	Democrat	Independent
Nationwide	33%	48%	9%
East	31	45	24
Midwest	36	43	21
Southwest	22	64	14
West	38	44	18
Cities	24	52	24
Suburbs	34	43	23
Towns	39	47	14
Rural	37	47	16
White	36	43	21
Black	17	76	7
21–29 yrs. old	33	45	22
30–49	33	49	18
50 and over	35	50	15
Income under $5,000	27	52	21
$5,000–9,999	28	55	17
$10,000 and over	40	39	21
8th grade or less	30	60	10
High school educated	27	50	23
College educated	44	35	21
WASP	44	38	18
Catholic	??	6?	06
Jewish	16	60	24

Source: Harris Survey, by Louis Harris. San Francisco Examiner, Feb. 20, 1970.

ernments have operated through the two-party system. In countries of many political parties, the conflicts for power are often hard to resolve by compromise and other accommodations. This is particularly true in periods of grave crisis, such as prolonged economic depressions or war. Table 14-3 shows the executive instability which, in France, was a consequence of a multiplicity of political parties, no one of which was able to attain a majority. From January, 1946, when DeGaulle left office until June, 1958, when he again became the Premier of France, the premiership of France changed

23 times. DeGaulle's ascendancy in the late 1950s was partly influenced by the fact that only two French premiers lasted more than a year in the troubled years following World War II.

Under ordinary conditions of stable society, election of a party to manage the government does not mean that the party defeated at the polls has no influence. Rather, it represents an important minority for the period—"His Majesty's loyal opposition," as the British phrase it. It influences public opinion in favor of its countersuggestions to proposed legislation. It acts as a balance to and an alert critic of the party in power. Both parties operate under mutually accepted rules of the political code. In time the parties have to face the national community again to seek election for a new term of office. In American society, the citizenry typically awards control of the government first to one party, then to the other. Never has one party kept control of the national government for more than twenty consecutive years.

The political institutions of the United States are unlike those of the French and British, as well as most other representative systems, in that they do not guarantee a legislature with a majority from the same party which elects the executive. A president from one party may stay in office even when the other party wins control of the legislative branch or branches.

Politics and Stratification

One might expect that, under the American system, parties would tend to represent the interests of certain secondary groups and, indeed, the voters apparently feel that they do. There is a direct relationship between the status one occupies in the stratification structure and the party which he or she feels best serves his or her interests. In general, the lower one's position in the stratification system, the more likely he or she is to believe that his or her interests are best represented by the Democratic Party. This set of beliefs is carried into the polling booth. Table 14-4 indicates that professionals, white-collar workers, and businessmen, including farmers, are more likely to vote Republican while manual laborers more often vote Democratic.

In the United States as well as in other industrialized societies, political affiliation, political participation, and political choice are all very much related to one's position in the stratification order. Although there are notable exceptions, the poor and the minority groups tend to identify themselves with, and vote for, "liberal" politics, and they tend to vote less often than other members of the society. Generally speaking, men vote more often than women in American society; people who live outside of the South vote more

Table 14-3 Lifespan of French Premierships, 1946–1958

Premier	Term of Office
Gouin	January, 1946 to June, 1946
Bidault	June, 1946 to December, 1946
Blum	December, 1946 to January, 1947
Ramadier	January, 1947 to November, 1947
Schuman	November, 1947 to July, 1948
Marie	July, 1948 to August, 1948
Schuman	September, 1948 to September, 1948
Queuille	September, 1948 to October, 1949
Bidault	October, 1949 to June, 1950
Queuille	July, 1950 to July, 1950
Pleven	July, 1950 to February, 1951
Queuille	March, 1951 to July, 1951
Pleven	August, 1951 to January, 1952
Faure	January, 1952 to February, 1952
Pinay	March, 1952 to December, 1952
Mayer	January, 1953 to May, 1953
Laniel	June, 1953 to June, 1954
Mendes-France	June, 1954 to February, 1955
Faure	February, 1955 to January, 1956
Mollet	February, 1956 to May, 1957
Bourges-Maunoury	June, 1957 to October, 1957
Gaillard	November, 1957 to April, 1958
Pflimlin	May, 1958 to June, 1958

SOURCE: The New York Times, February 10, 1957, E6. By permission.

often than Southerners; the middle-aged vote more often than the young; the rich and affluent vote more often than the unemployed; the college educated more than those with only a grammar school education; the whites more often than blacks and Indians; and the urban more than the rural. The rate of voting is always higher in presidential elections than it is in "off-year" elections, indicating perhaps that people see the executive branch of government as more important than the legislative branch of government. In the presidential election of 1968, nearly 68 per cent of the eligible voters went to the polls whereas only 55 per cent voted in the "off-year" election of 1970. (See Table 14-5.)

POLITICAL INSTITUTIONS

The relation of the national community or public to the party system and government—at least under a democracy as we know it—is characterized by a number of important theories and practices. The core of these is stated in the "Bill of Rights," including

Table 14-4   Pattern of Voting in Presidential Elections, 1956–1964

| | 1956 | | 1960 | | 1964 | |
	Dem. %	Rep. %	Dem. %	Rep. %	Dem. %	Rep. %
NATIONAL	42.2	57.8	50.1	49.9	61.3	38.7
Men	45	55	52	48	60	40
Women	39	61	49	51	62	38
White	41	59	49	51	59	41
Nonwhite	61	39	68	32	94	6
College	31	69	39	61	52	48
High school	42	58	52	48	62	38
Grade school	50	50	55	45	66	34
Professional and business	32	68	42	58	54	46
White collar	37	63	48	52	57	43
Manual	50	50	60	40	71	29
Farmers	46	54	48	52	53	47
21–29 years	43	57	54	46	64	36
30–49 years	45	55	54	46	63	37
50 years and older	39	61	46	54	59	41
Protestant	37	63	38	62	55	45
Catholic	51	49	78	22	76	24
Republicans	4	96	5	95	20	80
Democrats	85	15	84	16	87	13
Independents	30	70	43	57	56	44
East	40	60	53	47	68	32
Midwest	41	59	48	52	61	39
South	49	51	51	49	52	48
West	43	57	49	51	60	40

such items as the rights of free speech, free assembly, petition, trial by jury, the writ of habeas corpus, and a number of others.

Mores and Law

The mere fact that the Bill of Rights is the law of the United States does not mean, of course, that its provisions are known and accepted by all citizens. As a matter of fact, research indicates that even most college students are not familiar with its provisions.

Table 14-5   Voter Participation in the United States, 1968 and 1970

Social Category	Per Cent Reporting They Voted	
	1968	1970
Male	69.8	56.8
Female	66.0	52.7
White	69.1	56.0
Black	57.6	43.5
Age:		
18–20 years	33.3	25.7
21–24 years	51.1	30.4
25–34 years	62.5	46.2
35-44 years	70.8	58.1
45–64 years	74.9	64.2
65 years and over	65.8	57.0
Residence:		
Metropolitan	68.0	55.3
Nonmetropolitan	67.3	53.2
North and West	71.0	59.0
South	60.1	44.7
Education:		
8 years or less	54.5	43.4
9–11 years	61.3	47.1
12 years	72.5	58.4
More than 12 years	81.2	65.7
Employed	71.1	57.2
Unemployed	52.1	41.1
Family Income:		
Under $3,000	53.7	42.0
$3,000–$4,999	58.2	45.0
$5,000–$7,499	65.8	48.0
$7,500–$9,999	73.1	55.3
$10,000 and over	80.4	66.2
Total	67.8	54.6

SOURCE: U.S. Bureau of the Census, *Statistical Abstract of the United States, 1971* (Washington, D.C.: U.S. Government Printing Office, 1971), p. 365.

Table 14-6 Extent of Agreement with Bill of Rights Among
560 University Students

Amendment	Provision	Per Cent Indicating Agree	Dis-agree	No opinion
I	Freedom of speech, press	82.5	14.3	3.2
I	Freedom of religion	77.1	13.6	9.3
I	Peaceable assembly	56.8	35.7	7.5
II, III	Bear arms, quartering of troops	63.6	20.3	16.1
IV	Search and seizure	81.8	14.6	3.6
V	Self-incrimination	56.1	33.2	10.7
V	Due process	70.0	25.7	4.3
V	Double jeopardy	23.6	71.8	4.6
VI	Public trial	54.3	34.3	11.4
VI	Confront accuser	23.9	67.5	8.6
VI	Informed of accusation	94.8	2.3	2.9
VI, VII	Trial by jury	89.6	9.3	1.1
VIII	Excessive bail and punishment	61.4	32.2	6.4
IX, X	Reserved rights of people	44.3	51.1	4.6

SOURCE: Raymond W. Mack, "Do We Really Believe in the Bill of Rights?" *Social Problems*, 1956, 3:267. By permission. This research, originally done at Northwestern University, has since been replicated by J. Harold Ennis at Cornell College, Linton C. Freeman and Sherwin J. Feinhandler at Syracuse University, Robert McGinnis at the University of Wisconsin, and Paul Lasakow at the University of Alabama. See also Hanan C. Selvin and Warren O. Hagstrom, "Determinants of Support for Civil Liberties," *British Journal of Sociology*, 1960, 11:51–73.

Furthermore, when students were given an opinion questionnaire about the provisions of the first ten amendments to the Constitution without being told the source of the questionnaire items, most of them indicated disagreement with some of the provisions, and a majority disagreed with several of the amendments. (See Table 14-6.) Despite this demonstrated lack of information about the Constitution, when these people were asked whether or not they agreed with all of the provisions in the Bill of Rights, an overwhelming majority said yes.

What is the sociological significance of widespread ignorance of a statute basic to the governing of United States society? The traditional position of sociologists has been that the mores and community opinion precede law; and the classic illustration has been the Eighteenth Amendment—"You can't legislate morality." Many sociologists have moved to the position that, while morality cannot be legislated in a democracy through the enforcement of law to which the majority stands opposed, legislation *can* guide the development of community opinion on matters regarding which the bulk

Table 14-7   Black and White Voter Registration in Eleven
Southern States, 1960 and 1970

| States | Per Cent of Eligible Persons Registered to Vote | | | |
| | 1960 | | 1970 | |
	Blacks	Whites	Blacks	Whites
Alabama	14	64	66	85
Arkansas	38	61	82	74
Florida	39	69	55	66
Georgia	29	57	57	72
Louisiana	31	77	57	77
Mississippi	5	64	71	82
North Carolina	39	92	51	68
South Carolina	14	57	56	62
Tennessee	59	73	72	79
Texas	36	43	73	62
Virginia	23	46	57	65
All Eleven States	29	61	62	69

SOURCE: U.S. Bureau of the Census, *Statistical Abstract of the United States,
1971* (Washington, D.C.: U.S. Government Printing Office, 1971), p. 365.

of the citizenry have not taken a strong stand one way or the other.
An act outlawing reading cannot be enforced and will not be
obeyed, because most people believe that they have a right to read.
Most Americans indicate that they are unwilling to vote for members of the Communist Party (93 per cent), the Ku Klux Klan
(84 per cent), or the John Birch Society (61 per cent) and would
probably not react negatively to government action designed to
curtail the activities of these groups.[2] On the other hand, a law
forbidding the manufacture, sale, or use of sulphur matches could
probably be enforced simply because of the indifference of public
feeling in the matter of sulphur matches. In other words, most
people tend to obey the law if it does not run counter to some
strongly held value. Table 14-7 shows, for example, the dramatic
increase in black voter registration in the South under the im-
petus of federal civil rights legislation, especially the comprehensive
law adopted in 1965. In 1960 only 29 per cent of voting age blacks
in the South were registered to vote. In Mississippi only five per
cent were registered; only in Tennessee were more than half of
those eligible registered. By 1970 black voter registration in these
same 11 states had increased to 62 per cent and in no state was it
less than 50 per cent. In two states, Arkansas and Texas, the pro-

[2]These data are from a Harris Survey as reported in *The Washington Post*, February 21, 1966, p. A2.

portion of eligible blacks who are registered exceeds the registration among whites. The majesty of the law can be employed to create and strengthen community mores and is, for that reason, of sociological significance.

The End of Colonialism

The diffusion of Western European patterns of culture around the world has had political consequences. The colonial patterns of the eighteenth and nineteenth centuries brought more than technology to Africa, Asia, and Latin America; they also brought colonialism. Intentionally or unintentionally, the colonial administrators, the missionaries, the traders, and the settlers taught the natives of these continents many of the values of European cultures. We know enough about the integration of institutions not to expect Asians or Africans to learn our economic institutions, adopt Western notions of education, and so on, without changing some of their political norms.

Africa especially has been a continent of extreme change. Since 1950, when there were only four independent states in Africa, it has developed into a complex of independent countries and countries moving rapidly toward self-rule. Change has been effected through referendums, war, U.N. intervention, and realignment.

Society and Government

The norms of representative democracy prescribe that the state shall not be identical or coterminous with the society in which it is embedded. Under this theory, in the words of the usual Fourth of July oration, "The state is the servant, not the master, of the people." The theory means, in brief, that ultimate power in a democratic society rests with the citizens, not with the state.[3] When we call a democracy "representative," we mean just that. Individuals "represent" the members of the national society and, in the last analysis, are responsible to them. The party system is only a convenient device to implement this basic relationship.

The theory of representative government is not, of course, uniformly and universally accepted. But that is not to say that even dictatorships neglect the matter of support from the wider national society. Certainly modern dictators attempt to win popular support and conformity by education and propaganda, as well as by coercion. Stable society and governmental order rest on human accept-

[3]See Kimball Young, "Society and the State: Some Neglected Areas of Research and Theory," *American Sociological Review*, 1946, 11: 137–146.

ance and expectations; and skillful masters of people realize that to get this in revolutionary times, changes in values and patterns of social interaction must occur. Although concentration camps, machine guns, and the secret police are effective as controls, nothing but minimum participation in government can be expected unless people share the political norms and are a viable part of the institutional structure of the society. As Mosca once wrote:

> . . . ruling classes do not justify their power exclusively by *de facto* possession of it, but try to find a moral and legal basis for it, representing it as the logical and necessary consequence of doctrines and beliefs that are generally recognized and accepted. . . .[4]

INTERPRETIVE SUMMARY

Most societies have some structure which is responsible for maintaining internal order. Historically, the same structure or groups of structures has been responsible for protecting the society from outside attack; and this function will undoubtedly be necessary as long as people remain nationalistic and mistrustful of cultural differences, and as long as the needs of certain societies outstrip their resources.

In modern times, the political order is typically centered in the sovereign state. There are two main types of states: the dictatorship, in which a dominant minority imposes its will on the people; and the democratic state, in which elected officials serve the people. Both types of government have gradually become more complex and bureaucratic in administration.

While dictatorships tend to centralize all functions in the hands of a small group, modern democracies have generally divided the three main internal functions of government—the creation of law, administration of law, and judging of disputes involving law—among three structures, though functions of the three structures may overlap somewhat. The legislative branch codifies existing mores into law and, less frequently, may initiate legislation for the purpose of changing mores. It usually acts under some sort of constitution. The executive branch consists of an elected chief executive, various advisers, the extent of whose influence varies among countries, and various administrative sub-heads. It is this branch of democratic governments that is generally criticized for being bureaucratic. Judicial systems show variations in number of authority levels, as well as in provisions concerning who shall be judges.

Democratic officials are elected by plurality, after first being nominated by parties. The two-party system, in which the minority retains considerable influence, has generally been the most stable form of parliamentary government.

The United States has a three-branch government with some overlap of

---

[4]Gaetano Mosca, *The Ruling Class* (New York: McGraw-Hill Book Company, 1939), p. 70.

functions among the branches. The system contains some checks against bureaucracy and "spoils" appointments. One unique feature of the system is that the election of a chief executive from one of the two major parties does not guarantee a majority of that party in the legislature. Another pattern involves the extension of government control to new areas, especially the areas of economics and welfare. A final feature is the American emphasis on defense spending. Defense is the United States' biggest single expenditure, enormous sums going for economic and military aid to allies as well.

A world trend toward self-government is now in progress; note especially the patterns in former colonies of the huge European empires. Even in authoritarian countries, dictators who would remain in power generally cannot rely on coercion, but must give some attention to indoctrinating people into at least *thinking* they are getting what they want.

SUGGESTIONS FOR FURTHER READING

Alford, Robert R. *Party and Society.* New York: Rand McNally, 1963. This is an excellent study of the class and regional factors in voting in the United States since the 1930s.

Bendix, Reinhard. *Nation Building and Citizenship: Studies in a Changing Social Order.* New York: John Wiley and Sons, 1964. The author examines the emerging non-Western nations against the backdrop of the Western experience.

Greer, Scott. *Governing the Metropolis.* New York: John Wiley and Sons, 1962. This book inquires into the functions of metropolitan social structures for political systems.

Greer, Scott. *Metropolitics: A Study of Political Culture.* New York: John Wiley and Sons, 1963. This is an empirical description and comparison of metropolitan political reform campaigns in St. Louis, Miami, and Cleveland.

Hunter, Floyd. *Community Power Structure.* Chapel Hill: University of North Carolina Press, 1953. This is a classic study of the structure of power in an American city.

Kornhauser, Arthur; Sheppard, Harold L.; and Mayer, Albert J. *When Labor Votes: A Study of Auto Workers.* New York: University Books, 1956. This is a study of the voting behavior of union members and of the factors that affect their vote. Included is discussion of the union's role in politics from the union members' point of view.

Lipset, Seymour Martin. *Political Man.* Garden City, N.Y.: Doubleday and Company, Inc., 1959. This is a useful summary of a wealth of data on the social basis of politics in Western societies.

MacRae, Duncan, Jr. *Parliament, Parties, and Society in France, 1946–1958.* New York: St. Martin's Press, 1967. This careful statistical analysis of the votes of the electorate and of the Assembly treats the failure of the Fourth Republic as a case study in political sociology.

Mills, C. Wright. *The Power Elite.* New York: Oxford University Press, 1956. This is an important and provocative study of the structure and distribution of power in American society.

Rose, Arnold. *The Power Structure.* New York: Oxford University Press, 1967. Rose presents a strong argument for power in American society being distributed among a number of different social units.

Truman, David B. *The Governmental Process: Political Interests and Public Opinion.* New York: Alfred A. Knopf, 1951. An incisive analysis, this book deals with groups and group organization in the political process, leadership, and the tactics of influence with regard to political parties and to the legislative, administrative, and judicial operations of government.

Woods, Robert C. *Suburbia: Its People and Their Politics.* Boston: Houghton Mifflin, 1963. This book is a study of the political views and political practices of the American suburban population.

15
Family
and
Society

The family is the basic primary group and the natural matrix of personality. "The family is a social group characterized by common residence, economic cooperation, and reproduction. It includes adults of both sexes, at least two of whom maintain a socially approved sexual relationship, and one or more children, own or adopted, of the sexually cohabiting adults."[1] The precise facts about how the human family originated are unknown. Certain theorists contend that the original human grouping consisted of "group marriage," or a number of males and females living indiscriminately together, with the children of these unions considered the offspring of the whole group. Others have held that the original family was made up of only mother and children, the father, aside from his sexual function, playing a very insignificant role. Actually, no such condition as these theorists assume has ever been found, though in some societies male relatives in the mother's line have played a more important role than the biological father.

---

[1]George Peter Murdock, *Social Structure* (New York: The Free Press, 1965), p. 1.

FAMILIAL STRUCTURES

In every society there is some form of regulation of family relations, fixing—within certain limits—not only the roles and statuses
of the father and the mother but also making the child a legitimate
member of the group. The father or his surrogate normally has a
family function, and the children have an approved role and status.
This status carries over into the child's relations with the wider
community.

Systems of Descent

While biologically each individual is the product of two streams
of genes—one from each parent—in many societies, social lineage is
counted in only one family line. When descent is traced in the
father's line, or is *patrilineal,* the child takes the father's family
name, becomes associated formally with the paternal family and
clan, and has little or no relation with the mother's relatives. When
descent is *matrilineal,* the child takes the mother's family name and
is customarily more closely associated with her blood relatives than
with the father's.

The *bilateral* family system, which we practice, seldom permits
the solidarity and continuity possible in a unilateral scheme. Here
the adults come together without the restrictions and binding influences found in the unilateral cultures. Although in our own bilateral system the children take their father's family name, both the
mother's and father's relatives are considered kin of the child.

Structures of Authority

When the father or his family exercises control of the family, the
organization is called *patriarchal.* Matriarchal families are those
where control is exercised by the mother or her relatives. Matrilineal families tend to be matriarchal in control, patrilineal to be
patriarchal. Although in matriarchal families the mother has considerable power over the children, it is more often her family, rather
than she alone, that regulates family contacts, as in the case of
the Zuñi.

Types of Families

Particularly in folk societies, we find extended families, where the
household unit consists of grandparents, married children, and
grandchildren. (In patriarchal societies, such families are usually
patrilocal—that is, a daughter lives with the family of her husband.

In matriarchal societies, households tend to be *matrilocal;* the husband moves into the wife's home.) Such extended families are called *consanguine;* their boundaries are determined by blood relationship rather than by generations. In American society the families are conjugal or nuclear. An ordinary household consists of parents and their dependent children. When the children marry, they establish separate households.

Types of Marriage

Marriage is the institution or set of norms which determines the particular relation of parents to each other and to their children. The chief forms of marriage are monogamy, polygyny, and polyandry. (In popular usage *polygyny* is known as "polygamy.") Under any of these forms of marriage, the children's descent may be patrilineal, or bilateral, depending on the particular culture.

Monogamy, the marriage of one man to one woman, is the most widespread form of marriage. Since males and females are everywhere about equal in number—barring some special culture pattern such as infanticide—perhaps it is not surprising that monogamy is so universal. In an analysis of some 250 human societies, however, Murdock found that monogamy was the sole choice in only forty-three. Two societies practiced polyandry, in which two or more men are married to one woman, and the remaining societies recognized polygyny, a form of marriage in which two or more women are legitimately married to one man.[2] In most societies that recognize polygyny as a legitimate form of marriage, most men have one wife, largely because of the economics of supporting two or more.

The only extensive instance of polygyny in recent times in Western society was among the Utah Mormons, from about 1850 until 1890, when it was officially given up by the Mormon Church as a result of legal and moral pressures from the outside. It is estimated that about 5 per cent of the marriages in this group were polygynous.[3]

It is a mistake to assume that polygyny arises from any marked sexual urges of the male. In most societies there is ample opportunity for sexual gratification outside conventional mating. Polygyny is really a form of multiple, if interrupted, monogamy. In most instances, each household is separate, and the husband rotates his attention among his wives. In some societies, however, there are joint households, where two or more wives and their children live together.

---

[2] George Peter Murdock, *Social Structure* (New York: The Free Press, 1965).
[3] For sociological accounts of Mormon polygyny, see Nels Anderson, *Desert Saints* (Chicago: University of Chicago Press, 1942); Kimball Young, *Isn't One Wife Enough?* (New York: Henry Holt & Co., Inc., 1954); and Thomas F. O'Dea, *The Mormons* (Chicago: University of Chicago Press, 1957).

The most important motivations for polygyny are economic need and prestige. In certain parts of Africa, for instance, wives are added to a household as the husband demands more help in order to increase his wealth. In the Trobriand Islands of Melanesia, a chief's income consists of the annual endowments from the families of his various wives. Among the Tupis of South America, prominent men keep several wives for their prestige value, as well as for domestic service and labor in the fields. The same is true in Madagascar, in large sections of Africa, and among the Kai of New Guinea. Often the first wife urges the husband to take additional wives, each new one lightening the burden of the others, adding to the economic benefits, and improving the social status of the husband. The first wife frequently retains a certain position of favor and dominance over the other wives.

In polyandry several men are legally bound to one woman. This is the least common form of marriage, there being apparently but four or five localities in which it is found: in the Arctic among certain Eskimo tribes; in Central Asia, especially Tibet; in the Marquesas; occasionally among the Bahima of Africa; among the Nayars of southwest and the Todas of southern India.

FUNCTIONS OF THE FAMILY

Of all the many attempts to explain the importance and universality of the family, few have been as persuasive as the thesis that the family is functionally necessary.

> In the . . . family . . . we see assembled . . . functions fundamental to human social life—the sexual, the economic, the reproductive, and the educational. Without provision for the first and the third, society would become extinct; for the second, life itself would cease; for the fourth, culture would come to an end. The immense social utility of the . . . family and the basic reason for its universality thus begin to emerge in strong relief.[4]

In modern industrial societies the family shares some functions with other social structures. For example, socialization is a consequence of the familial structure but it is a function which is also fulfilled by religious structures through Sunday School classes, by formal educational organizations, by economic structures through on-the-job training programs, by informal neighborhood play groups, and so on. Conversely, the family participates in the maintenance of a sense of purpose, in the production and distribution of goods

[4]Quoted in Norman W. Bell and Ezra F. Vogel, The Family (New York: The Free Press, 1968), p. 43.

and services, and in other functions, even though it may not be the structure to which primary responsibility for these activities is assigned. We shall look first at reproduction, the one social function unique to the family in all societies, and then examine some of the other functions in which the family plays an important part.

Reproduction

The sexual life of people is not confined to the marriage situation, but all societies have norms attempting to guarantee that reproduction shall take place within a family framework. Everywhere there are variations in regard to premarital relations, and various extramarital patterns may be permitted along with more formalized family life.

In some tribes prenuptial intercouse is not only permitted but expected, though there is no evidence of complete promiscuity in any society. Everywhere incest taboos, kinship, age, and class rules limit the relations of the sexes both before and after marriage. While many peoples encourage, or at least tolerate, premarital relations, such relations are considered preparatory to marriage.

There is no uniformity in permissive premarital relations. In contiguous tribes, for instance, one group may put a high value on chastity, while their neighbors consider it of no consequence at all. Some folk societies, such as the Veddahs and other Negrito peoples, have as strong taboos against prenuptial sexual relations as our own Christian society, where chastity is a high virtue. In the Christian culture the sense of sin and guilt associated with sex affects not only premarital conduct but profoundly influences subsequent marital relations as well.

Among Christian peoples, however, rather striking differences often occur between ideal and practice. Kinsey's research indicates that a considerably greater amount of sexual activity takes place outside the marriage relationship than the ideal norms of our society would lead one to expect.[5] Since the patriarchal system, with all it implies for male dominance and female submission, was carried over into Christianity, it was very easy for the "double standard of morality" to arise. In many Christian communities the unmarried male is permitted prenuptial sexual freedom, but only with women whom he would not marry. The marriageable women of the community, in contrast, are held to strict taboos on premarital sexual relations. In such a society virginity is rated high, but male con-

---

[5]Alfred C. Kinsey, W. B. Pomeroy, and C. E. Martin, *Sexual Behavior in the Human Male* (Philadelphia: W. B. Saunders Co., 1948); and Alfred C. Kinsey, W. B. Pomeroy, C. E. Martin, and P. H. Beghard, *Sexual Behavior in the Human Female* (Philadelphia: W. B. Saunders Co., 1953).

tinence is neither expected nor often valued, in spite of theological taboos.

A study of 110 nonliterate societies around the world revealed that the least frequently and most lightly punished of deviations from the sexual mores is that of having premarital sexual relations. This is especially true when the partners are betrothed. The sexual offenses most frequently and severally punished are "incest, abduction, and rape." Moreover, the punishment increases with the likelihood of the offender's causing a child to be born outside the familial structure. Since a pregnancy arising from premarital sexual relations is likely to be followed by marriage, such relations are less severely punished than rape. In Western societies, the mother of an "illegitmate" child is scorned, and the child is often denied the right of inheritance. In all societies, some set of sanctions encourages the confining of reproduction to the family.

Socialization

The basic socialization of the child takes place in the family. All the fundamental ideas, muscular skills, and norms are acquired in the home. Some of the things thus learned are deliberately and consciously taught the child by the parents, older siblings, and other close relatives. The child also learns a great deal nondeliberately—that is, unconsciously. This is especially true of basic attitudes and values.

The religious and moral training of children has always been bound up with the home; and though in much of Western society formal religious education has reached into the earliest years, the family still furnishes basic notions of God, of salvation, and of morality.

The home also provides the first recreational patterns for the child, though play groups furnish important connections with the wider world. In earlier times the family as a unit frequently participated in recreation together: games, picnics, family reunions. Today the commercialized and individualized nature of recreation has increasingly removed this function almost entirely from the home, though radio, television, and the automobile provide some basis for the family in recreation.

As to education, the family provides the bases of all the child's later formal learning. In earlier societies the home furnished much of what is now in the hands of formal education; in spite of great changes, the family still gives the children their basic training in the social attitudes and social behavior important to adult participation in social life.

Habits of bodily care, of social relations, and of seeing the material world are learned in interaction with one's parents. Mother and father symbolize to the child forms of personal power. The child's own wishes must give way in the face of demands for obedience and conformity to these powers external to him or her. The manner in which the child learns how to get along with his or her family will be carried over to interactions with school authorities, religious leaders, the police, and other agents of social control. So too, the way the child learns to look at the material forces around him will influence his future interests and attitudes toward science, religion, and art.

Normally, as the child grows up, he learns to manage situations outside the home and family; he extends his interests to other groups; his intelligence, his emotions, and his social habits develop until he weans himself from the original dependence on the mother, father, and other family members, who have served as his principal source of socialization.

Another important function of the family is to provide a sense of self for the child. Since the child is born helpless and incapable of managing his or her own behavior, it is highly important that he develop a sense of security out of his earliest social contacts in the family. The foundations of the sense of safety are laid as the child is shown love, care, and protection, and trained in regular habits of eating, sleeping, bodily care, and play. Consistency of training accompanied by love is of first importance; it provides the stability needed for further learning. It is basic to making the child's world friendly, understandable, and predcitable. He must learn that his contacts with mother, with father, with brothers and sisters, and with others fall into more or less comprehensible and regular patterns—patterns marked by both affection and authority.

The sense of security is related to the child's definition of his own role. His assessment of his position in the family is fundamental to all his future relations in groups outside the home. Very often feelings of rejection, of difference, and of inferiority arise in the family and may carry over to later life. The self- or ego-ideal of the child will be affected at every point by his contacts with his parents. Parents may talk about honesty, truthfulness, perseverance, and other virtues of our culture, but it is their overt conduct more than their words, that provide the model.

The Economic Function

Present-day American family life reveals changes in the relations of parents and children which grow out of current economic conditions. In urban communities particularly, the absence of the father from the home for long hours has often left to the mother nearly

ILLUSTRATIVE DATA 15-1   CHANGING FUNCTIONS OF THE FAMILY

What is a man? A man is nothing. Without his family he is of less importance than that bug crossing the trail, of less importance than the sputum or exuviae. At least they can be used to help poison [sorcery—black magic] a man. A man must be with his family to amount to anything with us. If he had nobody else to help him, the first trouble he got into he would be killed by his enemies because there would be no relatives to help him fight the poison of the other group. No woman would marry him because her family would not let her marry a man with no family. He would be poorer than a new-born child; he would be poorer than a worm, and the family would not consider him worth anything. He would not bring renown or glory with him. He would not bring support of other relatives either. The family is important. If a man has a large family and a profession and upbringing by a family that is known to produce good children, then he is somebody and every family is willing to have him marry a woman of their group. It is the family that is important. In the white ways of doing things the family is not so important. The police and soldiers take care of protecting you, the courts give you justice, the post office carries messages for you, the school teaches you. Everything is taken care of, even your children, if you die; but with us the family must do all that.   A Pomo Indian

Source: B. W. Aginsky, "An Indian's Soliloquy," *The American Journal of Sociology,* XLVI (July, 1940), 43–44. © 1940 by The University of Chicago.

all duties of child training and discipline, a condition not true of the earlier American family nor even now so true in rural America, where the father and children—at least those old enough to work—are often together for long hours daily.

The contrasts in the early and recent economy of the household are striking. In pioneer and early rural America, the husband and wife shared most economic activities. The household was the center of many work activities in which the wife played a definite role. Spinning, weaving, and making clothes continued for a long time to be her duty, and even when machine industry replaced a great deal of home manufacture, she made the clothes for the family. Then too, she took charge of curing meat, of preserving vegetables and fruit for winter use, and usually of the milk, eggs, and garden produce. The household members were concerned with making a living rather than with *earning* wages. The money economy had but slight place in the scheme of things.

Today the family is less and less an economic unit, especially in urban localities. In rural-farm families some of the older patterns remain. But the commercialization and mechanization of agriculture are dissolving the older rural home-centered economy.

Historically, the child has often been considered an economic asset. Among peasant peoples everywhere children are put to work at early ages in the fields and in the household. Even in some pre-agricultural societies boys are initiated early into fishing and hunting activities and girls into household duties. Today in the more industrialized societies child labor is nearly nonexistent and children are noted for consuming rather than producing.

Status Ascription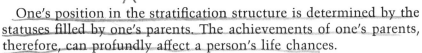

One's position in the stratification structure is determined by the statuses filled by one's parents. The achievements of one's parents, therefore, can profoundly affect a person's life chances.

> At birth one acquires a variety of initial statuses, and most of these are determined by the family and kinship organization into which he is born. As the individual passes through childhood into adulthood, he continues to possess some statuses which flow from his membership in a family group. Both child and adult, then, receive certain statuses because of their membership in a family. . . . Statuses conferred by the family consist of: (1) those which orient one in his relations with other members of the family (as designated by such kinship terms as brother, father, niece, etc.) and (2) those shared with the other members of the family which orient one with members of the society outside the family (urban, Protestant, middle-class, etc.).[6]

The Affectional Function

It is easy to overemphasize the reproductive and socializing functions and to overlook the fact that the familial structure has functions as well for the many married couples who are childless. Some couples never have children; others live together for years before having children; in a society which has conjugal families, many couples live together for years after their children have left to form households of their own. What, then, is the function of the institutionalized set of social relations between husband and wife?

A strong need for dependency and security is present in every human being. This is built up in the child within the structure of the family. Adults carry over into later life this same need for confidence, reassurance, and emotional support from others. Today, with fewer children per family and with the increasing disappearance of economic and educational activities from the home, husbands and wives are more and more dependent on companionship and sexual attraction to keep them together.

---

[6]Robert F. Winch, *The Modern Family* (New York: Henry Holt & Co., 1952), pp. 83–84. By permission.

There is an especially important interaction centering in the sexual life. At the purely biological level this relationship among human beings is not far removed from that of the anthropoids. Actually, however, human sexual activity is profoundly influenced by culture. While in some societies relatively little emphasis is put on the emotional aspects of sex, among many groups the act is bound up with mutual admiration, respect, and the desire of each mate to please the other in every way. As society removes from the family other functions, including much of the former heavy burdens in connection with child training, these more intimate relations are becoming more important.

FAMILIAL PATTERNS IN THE UNITED STATES

Our basic familial organization has its roots in the folk culture of western Europe, where family control was patriarchal in form. In adddition to the major functions of childbearing and child rearing, the family was the important economic unit of the community. It also performed other important functions in education, religion, recreation, and the development of proper values about the community and other aspects of culture.

The Christian Church arose within the older primary-group organization of Europe. The church's position regarding family life was expressed in the doctrine of other-worldly asceticism, the doctrine of sexual sin, and ascription of low status to women. Christian taboos against sex were supported by all sorts of notions about its being sinful, lewd, nasty, and debasing. Women were thought chiefly responsible for man's downfall with the first instance. Marriage, while by no means man's highest state, was encouraged for the average person; and the church made marriage one of the sacraments in order to keep family life under its rule. This view continued for centuries, until disrupted by romanticism, individualism, and economic changes.

Romanticism fostered the idea of free choice of mates on the basis of love. The Renaissance, with its general enlightenments and criticism of tradition, influenced both theory and practice in regard to sex. Though the Protestant Reformation, especially its Calvinistic branch, laid heavy taboos on sexual freedom, its emphasis on individualism in other areas had the long-term effect of loosening the taboos. The Commercial Revolution furthered the trend, which expressed itself in business enterprise, in freedom of thought and expression, in the growth of the idea of the right of the individual to take part in the affairs of government, and in a general loosening of the older rigid class system. As individualism developed, as eighteenth-century rationalism began to have its effects, and as certain romantic notions persisted, the position of women was somewhat improved.

Changes in familial patterns came slowly. Besides her major role of bearing and training children, the woman was obedient to her husband and a heavy contributor to the economic activities of the household, at least in all but the highest social class. She had no property rights of her own, and in law she was treated as a minor. She could not enter into a contract to do work or perform other services, and wages paid her went to her husband. She had no political rights or duties, such as voting or jury service.[7]

With the Industrial Revolution came the gradual emancipation of women from complete dominance by father or husband; the attainment, finally, of political rights such as the vote; the gradual relaxation of the more severe Christian taboos on sex for both men and women; and the urbanization of population, with its effects on the economics of the household and on the decline of the importance of the home in education, religious training, and recreation.

In short, then, role expectations and familial functions have changed in relative importance. Sexual relations, childbearing, and child rearing have proportionately a much larger place in total family life than they once had. In contrast, the economic function of the family and the home has become steadily less important. Comparable changes have occurred in other familial functions: religion and occupational training, for example.

Mate Selection

Research indicates a strong tendency for people to select as spouses persons similar to themselves. That is, like marries like. (This is technically known as *homogamy*.) "Like" refers to such sociological variables as age, education, social class, race, religion, previous marital status, and area of residence.[8]

---

[7]Gunnar Myrdal, "A Parallel to the Negro Problem," *An American Dilemma* (New York: Harper & Row, 1944), pp. 1073–1078.

[8]For evidence of homogamy in each of these areas, see: AGE: Paul C. Glick and Emanuel Landau, "Age as a Factor in Marriage," *American Sociological Review,* 1950, 15: 517–29; August B. Hollingshead, "Age Relationships and Marriage," *American Sociological Review,* 1951, 16: 492–499; A. Philip Sundal and Thomas C. McCormick, "Age at Marriage and Mate Selection: Madison, Wisconsin, 1937–43," *American Sociological Review,* 1951, 16: 37-48; EDUCATION: Paul H. Landis and Katherine H. Day, "Education as a Factor in Mate Selection," *American Sociological Review,* 1945, 10: 558–560; SOCIAL CLASS: Richard Centers, "Marital Selection and Occupational Strata," *American Journal of Sociology,* 1949, 54: 530–535; August B. Hollingshead, "Cultural Factors in the Selection of Marriage Mates," *American Sociological Review,* 1950, 15: 619-627; RACE: John H. Burma, "Research Note on the Measurement of Interracial Marriage," *American Journal*

How mate selection is affected by residential propinquity, for example, is shown by a number of studies. When J. H. S. Bossard examined 5,000 consecutive marriage licenses issued in Philadelphia, he found that more than 17 per cent of the couples gave residential addresses within one block of each other, 23 per cent within two blocks, and over one-third within five blocks. More than half (52 per cent) lived within 20 blocks of each other. Only 17 per cent resided in different cities. Moreover, there is some evidence that the tendency of people to marry those in the same vicinity has actually increased, at least in certain cities. Ray H. Abrams found this to be true for Philadelphia, as did Ruby Jo Reeves Kennedy for New Haven.[9]

Apparently not only distance but also density of population influences the relative rates of selection of those nearby. On the basis of his studies in New England, John S. Ellsworth concludes tentatively, "Other things being equal, the possibility of marriage between persons living in different population groupings decreases as the distance between them increases but tends to increase with the number of persons available at given distances."[10]

It is not mere propinquity or density, however, which determines the selection of a mate. Rather, it is that people of similar race, nationality, occupation, religion, and social class tend to live in the same neighborhoods. In short, the ecological factors of segregation have a place in this process.

While homogamy prevails in mate selection so far as social char-

---

of Sociology, 1952, 57: 587–589; R. Risdon, "A Study of Interracial Marriages Based on Data for Los Angeles County," *Sociology and Social Research*, 1954, 39: 92–95; RELIGION: August B. Hollingshead, "Cultural Factors in the Selection of Marriage Mates," *American Sociological Review*, 1950, 15: 517–529; Ruby Jo Reeves Kennedy, "Single or Triple Melting Pot? Intermarriage in New Haven, 1870–1940," *American Journal of Sociology*, 1944, 49: 331–339; Kennedy, "Single or Triple Melting Pot? Intermarriage in New Haven, 1870–1950," *American Journal of Sociology*, 1952, 58: 56–59, PREVIOUS MARITAL STATUS: Paul C. Glick, "First Marriages and Remarriages," *American Sociological Review*, 1949, 14: 726–734.

[9]See J. H. S. Bossard, "Residential Propinquity as a Factor in Marriage Selection," *American Journal of Sociology*, 1932, 38: 219–224; Ray H. Abrams, "Residential Propinquity as a Factor in Marriage Selection: Fifty-year Trends in Philadelphia," *American Sociological Review*, 1943, 8: 288–294; Ruby Jo Reeves Kennedy, "Premarital Residential Propinquity and Ethnic Endogamy," *American Journal of Sociology*, 1943, 48: 580–584. See also M. R. Koller, "Residential Propinquity of White Mates at Marriage in Relation to Age and Occupation of Males, Columbus, Ohio," *American Sociological Review*, 1948, 13: 613–616; and J. R. Marches and G. Turbeville, "The Effect of Residential Propinquity on Marriage Selection," *American Journal of Sociology*, 1953, 58: 592–595.

[10]From John S. Ellsworth, "The Relationship of Population Density to Residential Propinquity as a Factor in Marriage Selection," *American Sociological Review*, 1948, 13: 444–448. Quotation from p. 448. By permission. Ellsworth's findings may be tied in with S. A. Stouffer's theory of "intervening opportunities." See the latter's "Intervening Opportunities: A Theory Relating Mobility and Distance," *American Sociological Review*, 1940, 5: 845–867.

Table 15-1   Marital Status of the U.S. Population*

Marital Status	Males	Females
Single	28.2%	22.1%
Married	66.6	61.9
Widowed	3.0	12.5
Divorced	2.2	3.5
Total	100.0	100.0

*Persons 14 years of age and older only.
SOURCE: U.S. Bureau of the Census, *Statistical Abstract of the United States, 1971* (Washington, D.C.: U.S. Government Printing Office, 1971), p. 32.

acteristics are concerned, it does not necessarily follow that like marries like in so far as psychological variables are concerned. For example, while a young person is likely to marry another young person of the same social class, same religion, and comparable education, he or she may marry a person whose personality tends to be opposite to rather than similar in make-up. If a submissive man marries a dominant woman or a deferent woman marries a hostile man, we may say that their motivations or needs are complementary.[11]

Marital Adjustment

Various attempts have been made to determine the specific elements which make marriage a success or failure in American society. These studies deal chiefly with middle-class urban families.[12] They throw light on the possibility of predicting marital satisfaction on the basis of premarital experiences and situations, since they indicate some of the factors making for success or failure in wedded life.

The researchers report that a high degree of marital happiness between one's parents, absence of conflict with parents, adequate sex information in childhood, approval of the marriage by parents and other significant persons, personal happiness in childhood, and strong attachments to mother or father are predictive of success in one's own marriage. They find that having had firm but not violent discipline and parental instruction in sexual matters is important. It must be stressed that no one of these factors is crucially important

[11]For a fuller explication of this theory, with illustrative cases, see Robert F. Winch, *Mate-Selection: A Study of Complementary Needs* (New York: Harper & Row, 1958).
[12]See E. W. Burgess and L. S. Cottrell, Jr., *Predicting Success or Failure in Marriage* (Englewood Cliffs, N.J.: Prentice-Hall, 1939); and E. W. Burgess and Paul Wallin, *Engagement and Marriage* (Philadelphia: J. B. Lippincott Co., 1953).

in itself, but that combinations of them may be highly significant. Of all the factors, probably happy home life and likeness in socialization are the most important.

Marriage and Family in America

In spite of some popular notions about the ill effects of divorce and the emancipation of women on the American family generally, more than 90 per cent of the population will marry at some time during their lives. The median age at marriage, which had dropped slowly but steadily at least since 1890, has gone up slightly in the past decade. (See Table 15-2.) The median age at first marriage for men declined from 26.1 years in 1890 to 22.8 in 1950 and after a decade of stability, increased slightly to 23.2 in 1970. The corresponding figures for women reveal the same trend: a change from 22.0 years in 1890 to 20.3 years in 1950, and then after a decade of stability a slight increase to 20.8 years in 1970. One trend that has remained unchanged in the past 80 years is that the age difference at marriage between men and women has been decreasing. In 1890 the male was typically 4.1 years older than the female at the time of marriage, but in 1970 the difference was only 2.4 years.

The relatively early marriage age in the United States results in a high proportion of married persons in the total population. The situation is quite different in most other industrialized countries where an aging population, less national wealth, and lower standards of living probably play a part in delaying entrance into matrimony. To cite a few comparative figures from the late 1940s: For males aged 20–24 and 25–29 who had ever married, the United States percentages were 28 and 64 respectively. In England and Wales the percentages for these two ages groups were 53 per cent; in France, 21 and 64 per cent—much nearer our own. For females aged 15–19 years and 20–24 years, the United States percentages were 12 and 55 respectively; for England and Wales, 2 and 26; for France, 6 and 49.[13]

Although the marriage rate has been high, the average size of the American family has been shrinking. At the time of the first census in 1790, the average number of persons per family was 5.7. A hundred years later it was 4.9. By 1940 it had fallen to 3.8, and by 1960 to 3.62.

The changes in family size are correlated, of course, with (1) childless marriages—the extent of which is indicated by the fact that 15 per cent of American women who marry bear no children; (2) an aging population, which means that more families with no minor

---

[13]"Americans Marry Young," *Statistical Bulletin*, 1947, 28, No. 2, p. 9.

Table 15-2 Median Age at First Marriage by Sex for the
United States: 1890 to 1970

Year	Males	Females	Difference
1890	26.1	22.0	4.1
1900	25.9	21.9	4.0
1910	25.1	21.6	3.5
1920	24.6	21.2	3.4
1930	24.3	21.3	3.0
1940	24.3	21.5	2.8
1950	22.8	20.3	2.5
1960	22.8	20.3	2.5
1970	23.2	20.8	2.4

SOURCE: U.S. Bureau of the Census, *Current Population Reports,* Population Characteristics, Series P-20, No. 72 (Washington, D.C.: U.S. Government Printing Office, December 21, 1956), p. 3; "U.S.A. Population Changes: 1950–1960," *Population Bulletin,* XIX (1963), 32; and U.S. Bureau of the Census, *Statistical Abstract of the United States, 1971* (Washington, D.C.: U.S. Government Printing Office, 1971), p. 60.

children survive than formerly; (3) an increase in the average span of time between marriage and birth of the first child; (4) the general decline in the rate of population growth; and (5) "a growing tendency for old people to live in independent households instead of as dependents with their married children."[14]

FAMILIAL INSTITUTIONS

Sexual relations and marriage must not be confused. Marriage is a group-sanctioned bond establishing the family relations, especially with reference to offspring. Sexual relations do not necessarily lead to marriage. Indeed, marriage in most societies is not generally encouraged for sexual or romantic reasons. It is not sexual gratification that is the primary purpose of marriage but rather the legitimacy of the offspring and their care and training through the early years. In the words of Malinowski, "Marriage on the whole is rather a contract for the production and maintenance of children than an authorization of sexual intercourse."[15] In our own culture, however, the sexual and affectional phases of marriage may become more important with the decline of economic and related functions in the family.

In most societies, marriage is a secular, not a religious, contract.

---

[14]J. E. Goldthorpe, *An Introduction to Sociology* (Cambridge, England, 1968), p. 84.
[15]Bronislaw Malinowski, "Marriage," *Encyclopaedia Britannica,* 14th ed., 14: 940–950 (Chicago: Encyclopaedia Britannica, 1929).

Religious sanctions, true enough, are often added, but marriage is not universally supported by religion. When religion has a part, as in Judeo-Christianity, it may serve to increase the emotional bonds and to put more weight behind the community controls over the family.

Marriage implies a welding of two lives together in reference to certain obligations and duties. Since people think concretely, this union is usually expressed by a symbol. In various parts of the world one finds such rites as the bride and groom eating out of a common bowl, drinking from the same vessel, mixing clay or earth together from two separate lots, performed as symbolic of the union. Marriage symbolism is illustrated in our own society by, among other things, the use of engagement and wedding rings.

Marriage Sanctions

No society permits absolutely free selection of mates. As we have seen, close degrees of blood relationship, age differences, class differences, and wider kinship relations limit this choice. The *incest taboo* is without doubt the most nearly universal restriction on mating. It prohibits marriage chiefly between parent and child and between brother and sister. Yet it often reaches out to more remote blood relatives. The few historical instances of sanctioned incest, as among the ruling families of ancient Egypt, Peru, and Ireland, were not the result of primitive conditions but of a belief in divine powers that would be dissipated by marriage outside the royal line. And in the case of ancient Egypt, brother-sister marriages had the consequence of preserving the economic advantage of the family.[16] Daughters usually inherited a substantial part of the family estate and marriage to their brothers prevented splintering the estate into small and economically unproductive units. The intensity of the incest taboo is some indication that the rules are sometimes broken. Social workers, psychiatrists, lawyers, clergymen, and others dealing with more intimate family problems report that incest is not unknown in present-day society; nor is it confined to any one social class.

Exogamy is the type of union in which a person marries someone outside his or her own group, whether the group be family, clan, village, or other social unit. The opposite type of union, in which a person mates within his or her own group, is called *endogamy*.

Tribal endogamy is almost universal. In the more rudimentary societies it is a natural outcome of isolation and strong in-group

---

[16]Russell Middleton, "A Deviant Case: Brother-Sister and Father-Daughter Marriage in Ancient Egypt," *American Sociological Review*, XXVII (October, 1962), 603–611.

Table 15-3   Control of Premarital Mating in 250 Societies

Control	Number	Per Cent
Fully permitted (except incest)	65	26
Permitted under specified conditions	43	17
Mildly disapproved	6	2
Forbidden	44	18
Inadequate data	92	37
Total	250	100

SOURCE: Compiled from data reported in George Peter Murdock, *Social Structure* (New York: The Macmillan Company, 1949), p. 265.

solidarity. Within the tribe or larger society, where a clan system develops or where professional or aristocratic ranking or economic status or a caste system arises, endogamy is generally required or at least strongly encouraged.

Exogamy arises wherever groups of persons are believed sufficiently related to be forbidden to marry, with a consequent insistence on their mating in other groups within the wider community. It is usually found in association with wider kinship and clan relations. In the American bilateral system, formal exogamy is in little evidence, marriages between distant relations usually not being considered incestuous.

Two factors that govern the selection of a spouse are (1) the degree to which the normative structure of the society allows one a free choice, on the one hand, or, on the other, allows his or her parents, priest, employer, or someone else to decide whom he or she should marry; and (2) the degree to which the norms rule ineligible some persons whom one might marry. Linton Freeman has cited four extreme situations which can arise from variations of these two factors.[17]

When a man from the Yaruro Indian tribe of Venezuela is of marriageable age, his mother's brother picks one of his daughters for the young man, and the bridegroom moves into his uncle's household. The only females who are eligible brides are his mother's brother's daughters, and he does not even select the one he will marry. The Hottentots also marry within a small field of eligibles determined by kinship, but within the field one is allowed free choice of mates. In feudal Japan the field of eligibles was wide, but the participant had his spouse selected by his family. In the United States a situation opposite to that of the Yaruro prevails: an open

---

[17]This discussion is adapted from Linton C. Freeman, "Marriage Without Love: Mate Selection in Non-Western Societies," Chapter 2, in Robert F. Winch, *Mate Selection: A Study of Complementary Needs* (New York: Harper & Row, 1958).

field of eligible mates and the individual free to select his own spouse. Aside from the incest taboos concerning sexual relationships within the immediate family or between close cousins, which are enforced by custom and by law, people in the United States are not required to select their mates within determined limits.

Marital Dissolution

In very few societies is marriage a contract terminated only by death; nearly everywhere there is provision for the dissolution of marriage under special conditions. Moreover, the rate of marital dissolution is greater among many preindustrial societies than it is in many industrial societies, including the United States. (See Table 15-4.) In a survey of marital stability in some forty societies, Murdock found that

> In . . . twenty-four societies, constituting 60 per cent of the total, the divorce rate manifestly exceeds that among ourselves. Despite the widespread alarm about increasing "family disorganization" in our own society, the comparative evidence makes it clear that we still remain well within the limits which human experience has shown that societies can tolerate with safety.[18]

When marriage is a religious rite or sacrament, however, divorce is often forbidden or extremely difficult to obtain. In many societies, when the family is an economic unit and offspring are economically valuable, a sterile wife may be returned to her family. If a bride-price has been paid, this may be—often must be—repaid to the husband or to his father or family representative. Impotence in the husband is often recognized as a cause for marriage dissolution. Adultery is a widespread reason for divorce, though in societies dominated by patriarchal and masculine authority, adultery on the part of the husband is often condoned. Other grounds for divorce in some societies are economic insufficiency, emotional incompatibility, and insanity.

There has been a marked increase in the divorce rate in Western countries during the past century and the United States is no exception. (See Table 15-5.) Of all the major nations of the world, the United States currently has the highest rate of divorce. The divorce rate in 1890 was 0.5 per thousand population and by 1970 it had risen more than sixfold to 3.2. Such an increase is clear evidence that the right to dissolve marriage by divorce has become more widely recognized and accepted both in the mores and in the law.

---

[18]George P. Murdock, "Family Stability in Non-European Cultures," *The Annals of the American Academy of Political and Social Science*, CCLXXII (November, 1950), 43.

Table 15-4   Divorce Rates in Selected Industrial and
Industrializing Societies, 1965

Nation	Divorce Rate*
Industrial societies:	
United States	2.5
Hungary	2.0
Union of Soviet Socialist Republics	1.6
Austria	1.2
England (1964)	0.7
Canada	0.5
Italy	0.0
Industrializing (agrarian) societies:	
Morocco (1955)	2.9
United Arab Republic	2.2
Iran	1.0
Syria	0.6
Iraq (1962)	0.2
Ceylon (1962)	0.2
Thailand (1962)	0.1

*Number of divorces per 1,000 population.
SOURCE: Statistical Office of the United Nations, *Demographic Yearbook, 1963*
(New York: United Nations, 1964), Table 29; Statistical Office of the United
Nations, *Demographic Yearbook, 1966* (New York: United Nations, 1967), Table
26; and U.S. Bureau of the Census, *Statistical Abstract of the United States, 1967*
(Washington, D.C.: U.S. Government Printing Office, 1967), Table 48.

Table 15-5   Divorce Rates in Selected Western Countries,
1910 and 1956

Country	Divorce Rate*	
	1910	*1956*
United States	87.4	246.2
Germany	30.2	89.2
England and Wales	2.2†	74.4
Australia	12.9	90.4
France	46.3	100.5
Sweden	18.4	175.4

*Number of divorces per 1,000 marriages.
†This rate is for 1911.
SOURCE: William J. Goode, *The Family* © 1964. Reprinted by permission of
Prentice-Hall, Inc., Englewood Cliffs, New Jersey.

Almost everywhere, the presence of children acts as a deterrent
to divorce, even though the customary or legal code permits dissolution. The tribe or state generally takes the view that the care of
children is a primary obligation of the family, a fact which we have

emphasized as basic to the whole historical function of the family. The economic value of children, as well as the difficulties involved in settling inheritance and financial questions when a family is dissolved, have also been important factors in keeping the family intact.

The Future of the Family

In the midst of the many and varied changes which the family has undergone during the past century, much has been written and spoken about its future. Exactly what the future of the family is and how it will be organized is a matter of considerable speculation and there are those who write of "The Death of the Family."[19] But most others expect at least some form of the family to endure. As Ralph Linton once wrote:

> The ancient trinity of father, mother, and child has survived more vicissitudes than any other human relationship. It is the bedrock underlying all other family structures. Although more elaborate family patterns can be broken from without or may even collapse of their own weight, the rock remains. In the Götterdammerung which over-wise science and over-foolish statesmanship are preparing for us, the last man will spend his last hours searching for his wife and child.[20]

INTERPRETIVE SUMMARY

The familial structure normally consists of a mother, a father, their children, and, in some societies, certain members of one parent's extended kinship group. Where the system is patrilineal, control is likely to be patriarchal, and the wife may live with her husband's extended kinship group. In matrilineal societies, the reverse tends to be the norm. Bilateral structures have historically been patriarchal, though the household itself has tended to include all but the two parents and their children. Monogamy is the most common type of marriage. Polygyny and polyandry exist in some societies, an individual taking multiple spouses for purposes of prestige and/ or economic aid. All societies have some prohibitions involving mate selection. One almost universal prohibition is that against incest, within or without marriage; however, the definition of incest varies. Many societies further restrict eligibility along class or other in-group lines. Finally, a society may require that an individual's parents or some extended kinship group select his mate. Most societies have some provision for dissolution of marriage, though what constitutes justification for dissolution varies.

Reproduction is the one social function unique to the family in all soci-

---

[19]David Cooper, *The Death of the Family* (New York: Random House, Inc., 1970).
[20]Ralph Linton, "The Natural History of the Family," *The Family: Its Function and Destiny*, ed. by Ruth Nada Anshen (New York: Harper and Row, Publishers, 1949), p. 38.

eties, and all societies have more or less severe sanctions to ensure that reproduction does not occur outside marriage. Probably the next most important function is socialization of offspring. From early social experiences within the family, the child learns what his statuses and probable life chances are, and he develops a self-image. Historically, the family has been the basic economic unit, though this function has diminished in urban societies. As this and other functions have been removed from the family, the function of satisfying the basic human need for affection has become especially important.

The family in the United States is conjugal in nature. Descent is traced patrilineally, though the husband's and wife's kinship groups are both important, and the control of the father over the family is partial and by no means absolute.

Most of the characteristics of the contemporary American family can be traced to economic upheavals such as the Industrial Revolution and to related ideational forces, particularly romanticism, the Renaissance, and the Protestant Reformation. For example, the emphasis on individualism has increased individual choice in mate selection, except for certain incest taboos. The belief in individual value has also led gradually, and so far incompletely, to increased freedom and privileges for women. High standards of living, medical advances, and other factors have caused the marriage age to drop and the size of the family to decline.

Researchers have found that the factors most responsible for happy marriages in our country are similarity of social background, previous happy family life, and healthy attitudes toward sex. Though individuals in the United States tend to marry people with socially similar backgrounds, the divorce rate in this century is relatively high.

SUGGESTIONS FOR FURTHER READING

Bell, Robert R. *Premarital Sex in a Changing Society.* Englewood Cliffs, N. J.: Prentice-Hall, Inc., 1966. This book is an analysis of changing sexual mores in American society.

Bernard, Jessie. *Remarriage: A Study of Marriage.* New York: Holt, Rinehart, and Winston, Inc., 1956. This competent research study uses census data, case materials, and data on 2,009 marriages collected through interviews. Among other topics discussed are success and failure of remarriages, personality types of spouses in remarriages, intrafamily relationships, status of stepchildren, and the problems of aging.

Billingsley, Andrew. *Black Families in White America.* Englewood Cliffs, N. J.: Prentice Hall, Inc., 1968. The problems of black families in America, particularly in the move from the ghetto to the larger community, are examined.

Burgess, E. W.; Locke, Harvey J.; and Thomes, Mary Margaret. *The Family: From Institution to Companionship.* 3rd ed. New York: American Book Company, 1963. The book provides broad social psychological coverage.

Frazier, E. Franklin. *The Negro Family in the United States*. Rev. ed. New York: The Dryden Press, 1951. This is an historical and sociological account of the Negro family in the United States.

Glick, Paul C. *American Families*. New York: John Wiley and Sons, 1957. Based on census data, this is a very good description of the demographic and structural charactersitics of the American family.

Goode, William J. *After Divorce*. Glencoe, Ill.: The Free Press, 1956. Various cultural and personal background facts are analyzed; the conflict process leading to divorce is examined; and post-divorce problems are discussed at some length in an empirical study of 425 urban mothers aged 20 to 38 at the time of divorce.

Gordon, Albert I. *Intermarriage*. Boston, Mass.: Beacon Press, 1964. This is a comprehensive survey of interfaith, interracial, and interethnic intermarriages.

Scanzoni, John H. *Opportunity and the Family*. New York: The Free Press, 1970. The thesis that the main structural tie of the modern nuclear family is to the economic system of the society is effectively presented.

Winch, Robert F. *The Modern Family*. Rev. ed. New York: Holt, Rinehart, and Winston, Inc., 1963. This volume contains a nice contrast between the traditional Chinese peasant family and the family in an Israeli kibbutz as well as an excellent analysis of the structure of the American family and its basic and derived functions.

Winter, Gibson. *Love and Conflict: New Patterns in Family Life*. Garden City, N.Y.: Doubleday and Company, 1958. Cleavage between the demands for impersonal competition in the commercial world and the need for intimacy and love in the family is discussed.

Young, Michael, and Willmott, Peter. *Family and Kinship in East London*. New York: The Free Press, 1957. This is an empirical study of working class families in London.

SO ONE DAY DADDY AND MOMMY ASKED ME – "WHAT DO YOU WANT TO BE WHEN YOU GROW UP, JOEY?" AND I SAID "A **COWBOY**."

SO DADDY SAID TO MOMMY "HE'S A LITTLE OLD TO BEGIN, SO WE'LL HAVE TO APPLY RIGHT AWAY" AND HE TOOK ME TO THIS FUNNY KIND OF SCHOOL THAT GAVE ME A WHOLE LOT OF TESTS.

AND AFTER THE TESTS THE TEACHER TOLD DADDY, "THE TESTS PROVE THAT JOEY HAS THE **APTITUDE** TO BE A COWBOY, THE **MENTAL ALERTNESS** TO BE A COWBOY AND THE **CAREER INTEREST** TO BE A COWBOY. OF COURSE, HE'LL HAVE TO TAKE AN **EMOTIONAL QUALIFICATION EXAM**."

SO THEY GAVE ME ONE. AND AFTER THE TEST THE DOCTOR SAID TO DADDY, "THE TEST PROVES THAT JOEY WOULD MAKE AN EXCELLENT ADJUSTMENT TO THE WEST."

SO DADDY TOOK ME HOME AND SAID TO MOMMY – "WE'LL GET HIM INTO EXETER AND THEN INTO HARVARD AND THEN HE CAN TAKE HIS GRADUATE WORK IN COWBOY AT EITHER STANFORD OR U.C.L.A. DOESN'T THAT MAKE YOU HAPPY, JOEY?" AND I BEGAN TO CRY. AND MOMMY SAID, "WHAT'S THE MATTER, JOEY?"

9-23

AND I SAID, "I CHANGED MY MIND. I WANT TO BE A NURSE."

16
Education
and
Society

There is considerable variation in the social structure of societies. Some are small in numbers, some relatively large; some permit polygyny, some are strictly monogamous; some have a rigid stratification system, in others the class system is relatively loose and flexible; and so on. But regardless of size and the combination of choices from the cultural spectrum that prevails in any society, some structures to provide the function of socialization will be present. Each individual must learn the lore accumulated by his ancestors, must practice certain skills, must be indoctrinated with the values of his group, and must learn the expectations associated with the roles he will play.

EDUCATIONAL STRUCTURES

The transmission of culture can be only partially delegated to formal organizations, such as school sysems or religious organizations. Much education always takes place in informal structures, such as play groups, where thc person learns by imitating his older playmates. Even in structures specifically set up to perform the function of socialization, there is, in addition to conscious and formal transmission of culture, a great deal of nondeliberate and informal passing-on of knowledge, skills, and values. In American schools, for instance, both competition and cooperation are stressed. The former is found in strong rivalry for rewards, such as grades for academic work or success in athletics. Cooperation is taught through stress on group spirit and teamwork.

Informal Groups

All nonliterate peoples have some form of transmission of culture, but the functions we think of as "educational" fall to the family, clan, or vocational or magico-religious guild. While there are many variations, the fundamental content of folk education is not unlike that of urban societies: folklore, mythology, history, manual skills, appropriate manners, and instruction and practice in the folkways and mores.

The differences in education among nonliterate people rest, as they do with other peoples, on their views of the child. Some, like the Plains Indians, regard the child as a miniature adult, with much the same motives as an adult. Such tribes give much time to deliberate instruction in legends, moral tales, and religion. The Bantu-speaking Negroes of South Africa view the child as an irritating creature who is unaccountable in his conduct and subject, as are adults, to deception, threats, and intimidation. The Arapesh, in contrast, look on the child as one to be carefully guarded and gently instructed, since his function will be to take over the care and protection of his elders.

Sometimes the work of teaching is done by the parents, with one or the other taking the main responsibility; sometimes it is in the hands of uncles or aunts or grandparents. Though formal schools as we know them are entirely lacking, some differentiation of specialists is present. Such are the craftsmen of certain guilds who teach the crafts, shamans or priests who instruct in magical or religious rituals, and war leaders who train youth in skills of warfare.

Formal Organizations

Education as a special function of a particular group or agency did not arise until the invention of writing and arithmetic and advances in agriculture, metallurgy, and commerce. All the ancient civilizations — Egypt, Babylonia, Assyria, Persia, India, China, Greece, and Rome— had systems of formal education. In all these, however, it was confined to the privileged and leisure classes and much of what has now become a part of formal schooling, such as vocational and civic training, was left to other groups: familial, religious, political, and economic. The upper classes tended to stress philosophy and ethics, art and music, rhetoric, mathematics, and gymnastics and military arts—studies considered proper interests of the ruling classes.

In Europe, education in the Middle Ages was in the hands of the Roman Catholic Church. At first it was rather meager, consisting of simple instruction of the illiterate masses in church regulations and intellectual and moral initiation of individuals into the priesthood and orders of the church.

The serious beginnings of modern education, both elementary and higher, had to await the Renaissance, the Reformation, and important economic changes. Protestantism, with its emphasis on individualism in religion, the rise of trade and city life, and the Industrial Revolution, which freed the individual from serfdom and feudalism, began to break the upper class and the theological holds on education. It became increasingly apparent that neither a sound representative government nor an efficient business or industry could be managed without literate and technically trained individuals.

Today all urban societies have extensive educational facilities: the school plant, a wide variety of curricula and methods of teaching, a specially trained personnel for management and instruction, and a rationale or philosophy of the aims, methods, and values of education.

Supplements to Formal Structures

The existence of schools, formal organizations which have as their principal function the education of the population, does not mean that all or even most socialization is provided by them. Both in folk and urban societies, most individuals receive their essential early training from their families and others. From parents and brothers and sisters people learn to walk and talk, and to distinguish the basic concepts of right and wrong which prevail in their societies. Even those who live in societies having elaborate formal educational systems get a large proportion of their knowledge and ideas of good and evil outside the school—from friends, elders, and from observing people in everyday situations.

In addition to learning in primary groups and in school, the individual in a literate society is exposed to an enormous amount of facts and opinions through the mass media. It makes good sense to consider newspapers, radio corporations, book publishers, and similar organizations as supplementary educational structures.

The Press

Books are pouring from American presses at the rate of about 15,000 titles a year. Nearly one-third of them are of a more or less technical character. These books furnish material for formal education, and the reading habits set up in school carry over to provide a means of further acquisition of skills, knowledge, and entertainment. Perhaps even more important than books are magazines and newspapers, which have been increasing in circulation in recent decades.

Books, magazines, and newspapers flood us with a stream of words that cannot fail to leave their impression. This material is constantly providing not only facts but myths, legends, and stereotypes that are reflected sooner or later in political, economic, religious, and moral attitudes and behavior. Reverence for the printed word is one of the reasons propaganda and advertising are very effective.

Movies, Radio and Television

In addition, the motion picture, radio, and television have become powerful media of mass communication. On the evening of March 7, 1955, for example, one out of every two Americans was watching Mary Martin perform Peter Pan before the television cameras. Never before in history had a single person been seen and heard by so many people at the same time. But it is not in entertainment alone that such a gigantic visual impact has influence on people. The death of President Kennedy brought an estimated 90 per cent of the nation together in a common beholding of the funeral and a common mourning of the late President by way of television. The close-ups of police in Selma, Alabama, chasing black people with gas, clubs, pistols, and riot guns made that city an instantaneous symbol of moral indignation for many Americans. Within a week thousands of people poured into that small city from all over the county to demonstrate their sense of outrage. Clearly, the mass media has a substantial impact on the beliefs and behavior of people. In addition to their functions of newscasting and entertainment, both radio and television have been increasingly used in schools and universities to supplement formal instruction.

Never before has the world had such an array of agencies for mass impression. Oratory, formal teaching, religious exhortation, and all other methods of arousing groups of people with the same stimuli at the same time pale into insignificance beside these mighty forces. Whoever controls these media determines in large measure the mentality of people. In the United States, while formal education is predominantly state-controlled, these other means of stimulation are, with few execptions, in the hands of private enterprise. But to an increasing extent, other nation-states are taking over control of the newer devices, combining them with the traditional educational system, sometimes in order to bend them to the ends of their particular political and economic systems. This raises the profound question of the effect of propaganda, as well as of education, on thought and conduct.

Since the consequences of educational structures depend directly on the values embodied in the other institutions of a society, let us examine the contrast between two principal kinds of educational socialization found in contemporary societies: those that are politically closed such as rigid dictatorships and those that are politically open and egalitarian such as representative democracies.

EDUCATIONAL FUNCTIONS

While the modern world has seen the emergence of a variety of educational systems, the two modal patterns are those which center around the values and practices of representative democracy and those which are oriented toward authoritarian values and practices. The aim of education, both formal and informal, in all societies is to socialize the young and old alike into the fundamental values, norms, and practices of the society. Each society justifies its kind of education as being "good" for its members. The crux of the difference, of course, lies in what is considered good—that is, in what is defined as good by the culture.

Politics and Education

Since the contrasts in values have bearing on both domestic and international affairs, it is important to know just what these differences mean, not only for political and economic institutions, but for such a powerful agency of cultural training as the school. Some of the important differences in the two social systems are reflected in the aims of education as related to the classes which manage the social controls and sanctions, and especially to the larger purposes of the state.

The aim and content of education are bound up with the theory of the interrelation of the society, the state, and the individual. Under a rigid dictatorship, the state is considered to be coterminous and identical with the society. In the words of Benito Mussolini, "Everything for the state, nothing outside the state, and nothing against the state."[1] Such a philosophy leaves no place for the rights and liberties of the individual as recognized under democracy.

---

[1]Quoted in I. L. Kandel, "The End of an Era," *Educational Yearbook of the International Institute of Teachers College,* Columbia University (New York: Teachers College, Bureau of Publications, 1941), p. 71.

Authoritarian states have a ruling elite which determines the basic philosophy of the state, its goals, and the methods of attaining those goals. Such a ruling group believes it has a mission. And the leaders provide the symbols of identification which help unite the masses to their rulers, all in the name of the total society.

In all dictatorial countries it is considered important to indoctrinate the young, through the schools and otherwise, with deference for and loyalty to the purposes of the ruling class. The methods of accomplishing such conformity and control often take the form of regimentation of practically every aspect of the lives of the people. The stress on group solidarity is repeated in drama, song, literature, and in state-controlled organizations for all ages. Under such rule, the control of the ruling class over the school is complete. The teachers are chosen in part because of their party loyalty, and are closely supervised; deviations from the "party line" are severely punished. The course of study is laid down by central authorities, and little or no modification at the local level is tolerated. Students of all ages must be given nothing but the "truth" prescribed by the ruling elite.

During the Stalin period there was a bitter controversy among Soviet scientists over the Mendelian principles of heredity. Marxist philosophers looked askance at genetics, since it does not appear to give sufficient weight to the role of the environment in making and remaking the individual. Periodically the debates of Russian biologists came to the attention of the Communist Party leaders. Lest such controversies undermine faith in the official Party views, pressure was exerted to enforce conformity. Thus in September, 1948, *Pravda*, the official newspaper of the Communist Party, published an open letter, addressed to Stalin and signed by the head of the national Academy of Medical Sciences of the Soviet Union, which said, in part, "We promise you, our dear leader, to remove the errors committed by us in the shortest time, and to reconstruct all our scientific work in the spirit shown us by the great party of Lenin and Stalin."[2] In such authoritarian countries the idea of a free science and a free literature is no more to be tolerated than are conceptions and practices of free speech and free elections, if they run counter to the views of the ruling elite. The controls are always rationalized, of course, as measures based on the sound views of the rulers.

Democratic Socialization

In contrast to the patterns of authoritarianism under dictatorship are those associated with representative democracy. The ideal of a

---

[2]Quoted in the *New York Times*, September 23, 1948, C8.

free person in a free society is so much taken for granted by individuals socialized to the dominant values of democracy that it is often difficult for them to comprehend any other scheme.

Democracy is more than a set of political institutions and processes. Under its philosophy the society is not considered to be co-equal and coterminous with the political order. As an old maxim has it, "The State is for man, not man for the State." The basic philosophy rests on beliefs in natural rights to "life, liberty, and the pursuit of happiness." This implies, further, not only a jealous regard for one's own rights but a duty to provide and guard similar rights for others.

An examination of the American Bill of Rights reveals a good foundation for the basic democratic philosophy that the state is the servant rather than the master of the citizen. The Bill of Rights is a heritage from those who opposed the monarchy, with its concept of divine right to rule, setting forth—rather explicitly—what is regarded as democratic rights. The chief items are to be found in the first ten amendments to the Constitution of the United States. Among the most important today are the provisions for free worship, for freedom of speech and writing, and for the rights of petition, private property, and trial by jury.[3]

The Control of Education

It would be a mistake, of course, to assume that there are no class and other group controls in a representative democracy. There are. In some European countries the class structure is more rigid than it is in the United States. In Britain, for example, both the Anglican Church and the upper class have, in the past, largely determined policy and practice in education. While the Industrial Revolution brought an increasing extension of school opportunities for the middle and lower classes, the system itself changed slowly toward a pattern more democratic in aim, content, and procedure.

In the United States, education was at first largely in the hands of the church and the local community; and it tended to be restricted to the rich and affluent. Free public education was not considered essential until it became clear to leaders and masses alike that universal literacy goes hand in hand with universal suffrage, participation in civil life, and complex technology. In most democratic countries the abolition of property qualifications for voting and office-holding is correlated with the demand for compulsory publicly financed elementary education.

While the classroom subject matter has changed through the

---

[3]Among college students, at least, there is great ignorance of the meaning of the Bill of Rights. See Raymond W. Mack, "Do We Really Believe in the Bill of Rights?," *Social Problems*, 1956, 3: 264–269.

decades, American education has revolved around the concepts of sound knowledge, public welfare, training in basic skills, and indoctrination in the fundamental values of democracy. An educated citizenry in a democracy means persons with not only sound knowledge and skill but also the ability to combine individual choice and freedom with a sense of personal and public responsibility for their judgments and actions. This does not imply that everyone will finish the same grade with the same education. Rather, it indicates that every means possible should be used to provide equality of opportunity in education for all the children of all the people, with due regard for individual differences. It is presumed that out of such a system will come intelligent citizens who will be capable of managing their own affairs and who at the same time will be voluntary participants in the larger concerns of the community and the nation. While the U. S. has not always been entirely clear as to the central theme of public education, for the most part it has been successful in the diffusion of mass education.

Despite the many sharp and striking contrasts between education under representative democracy and under dictatorial systems, the aim of mass education is always to prepare the young for later participation in adult society. Hence the school will carry society's values to its charges. The aims and values may seem bizarre or dangerous to outsiders. For example, some nations, which stress cooperation might be aghast at the degree to which Americans emphasize rivalry and competition in schools; while most Americans would certainly oppose the even greater degree to which competition is stressed in a country like, say, Japan, where suicides because of college failure are common. But so long as a cultural system persists, the school will be its servant. Moreover, the moral principles of loyalty, obedience, patriotism, and a whole host of codes of good manners and mutual participation in group life have much in common in both systems. For example, many of the "Rules for School Children" adopted in 1943 by the Soviet leaders could fit, with slight modification, the democratic schools. The stress on diligence, obedience, personal cleanliness, good posture, use of proper language, and like matters is pretty much the same general tradition as our own.[4]

Illiteracy

The availability of education, especially basic education, in various countries is very much related to the economy of the society.

---

[4]See *I Want to Be Like Stalin* (New York: John Day Company, 1947), pp. 149–150. This book, from the Russian text on pedagogy by B. P. Yesipov and N. K.

Literacy and industrialization, for instance, go hand in hand. (See Table 16-1.) In 1969, one per cent (1,433,000 persons) of all Americans 14 years of age and older were illiterate. (The figure for the United States given in Table 16-1 is for the year 1959 to make it comparable to the other data in the table.) Cultural and structural variations are seldom completely distinctive and unique. So it is with matters of education.

Table 16-1   Illiteracy in Selected Countries

Country	Per Cent Illiterate*	Year
Argentina[1]	8.6	1960
Brazil	39.3	1960
Bulgaria	14.7	1956
Chile	16.4	1960
Dominican Republic	35.5	1960
Ecuador	32.7	1962
France[1]	3.6	1946
Greece	19.6	1961
Hungary	2.6	1963
India	72.2	1961
Indonesia	57.1	1961
Iran	77.0	1966
Iraq	85.5	1957
Israel[1]	15.8	1961
Italy[2]	8.4	1961
Japan	2.2	1960
Liberia	91.1	1962
Mexico	34.6	1960
Morocco	86.2	1960
Nicaragua	50.4	1963
Niger	99.1	1960
Pakistan	81.2	1961
Panama	26.7	1960
Paraguay	25.7	1962
Peru[3]	39.4	1961
Philippines	28.1	1960
Poland[1]	4.7	1960
Portugal	38.1	1960
Romania	11.4	1956
Senegal[1]	94.4	1961
South Africa[4]	68.5	1960

Goncharov, translated by George S. Counts and Nucia P. Lodge, is a mine of information about the content and method of teaching children in the Soviet Union under Stalin.

Table 16-1   Illiteracy in Selected Countries *(Cont.)*

Country	Per Cent Illiterate*	Year
South West Africa	61.6	1960
Spain	13.3	1960
Sudan	88.0	1956
Syria[4]	70.5	1960
Taiwan	46.1	1956
Thailand	32.3	1960
Turkey	61.9	1960
U.S.S.R.[5]	1.5	1959
United Arab Republic	80.5	1960
United States[1]	2.2	1959
Uruguay	9.7	1963
Venezuela	34.2	1961
Yugoslavia	23.5	1961

*Per cent illiterate refers to the per cent of the total population 15 years of age and older (except as noted) unable to read and write.
[1]Population aged 14 and older.
[2]Population aged 6 and older.
[3]Population aged 17 and older.
[4]Population aged 10 and older.
[5]Population aged 9–49.
SOURCE: U.S. Bureau of the Census, *Pocket Data Book, USA 1971* (Washington, D.C.: U.S. Government Printing Office, 1971), p. 162.

Like social institutions, the educational institution performs functions other than those for which it was manifestly created and intended. Formal school systems ordinarily have several latent functions. For one thing, beyond the elementary grades, schools serve as a marriage market. People tend to select spouses of a class and educational status approximately equal to their own, and there is no more likely place to find them than at school. Both high schools and colleges afford opportunities to meet and get to know persons of the opposite sex in one's age category and educational status.

A related latent function of educational structures is to provide an opportunity to widen the student's circle of acquaintances. One usually leaves college, for example, with a set of friends different from and broader than the set with which he left high school. Related to this consequence is, for many, the function of forming relationships with people who will become business or professional contacts in the future.

One latent function of the educational system of the United States is that schools keep a sizable and fairly predictable proportion of young people out of the labor force. Imagine the unemployment problem if more than fourteen million young people fourteen to eighteen years of age who are now attending school were part of the labor force.

Education and Status

Other than socialization, probably the most important function of educational structures is conferring status. The amount of formal education one has is highly correlated with his class position. Research indicates that this is true not only in the United States but in Japan, Germany, the Soviet Union, and other industrial societies.[5] Actually, education is related to one's position in the stratification structure in two ways: (1) a portion of people's evaluation of one's status derives directly from how much and what kind of education he or she has received, and (2) many of the other important criteria of class position, such as occupation, income, and style of life, are partially consequences of the type and amount of education one has had.

A majority of male college graduates, for example, have professional jobs while less than one-tenth of those with a high school education attain such prestigious occupations. Similarly, men who finish college earn more than twice as much as men who have only a grammar school education. (See Table 16-2.) The cash value of

Table 16-2   Relationship of Education to Income for Persons
Aged 25 and Over, 1968

	Mean Annual Income		
Highest Level of Education Completed	*Males*	*Females*	*Year-round, Full-time, Female Workers*
Elementary School			
Less than 8 years	$3,333	$1,664	$3,222
8 years	5,096	2,153	3,744
High School			
1–3 years	6,569	2,616	4,067
4 years	7,731	3,321	4,904
College			
1–3 years	8,618	3,717	5,699
4 or more years	11,257	5,349	7.416

SOURCE: Herman P. Miller, *Rich Man, Poor Man* (New York: Thomas Y. Crowell Company, 1971), pp. 169–174.

---

[5] Alex Inkeles and Peter H. Rossi, "National Comparison of Occupational Prestige," *American Journal of Sociology*, 1956, 61: 329–339.

education, however, is not the same for everyone. At every educational level, the annual income for women is less than half of what it is for men. Moreover, this income difference is not solely due to the lack of full-time employment opportunities for women. As Table 16-2 indicates, the annual income for year-round, full-time women workers is lower than the annual income for men (including those who do not have year-round, full-time employment) at every educational level. Women with a high school education earn less than men who have only a grade school education and female college graduates with full-time employment have lower incomes than men with only a high school education.

Perhaps the surest indicator of the importance of education in the stratification system is the eagerness with which newly wealthy but relatively uneducated people surround themselves with the trappings of learning: a library, paintings, a symphony subscription, and so on. Nor is this deference to education confined to the wealthy. Fathers of moderate means who never graduated from high school see to it that their children attend college. Education, then, not only helps one acquire income and occupational prestige; the education itself confers status, as illustrated in the concept "educated person."

EDUCATION IN THE UNITED STATES

Formal education in the United States has developed through three major phases. During colonial times and even during the first fifty years of our history as a nation, the support and control of education was almost entirely local. Between 1830 and 1880 the foundations of the modern school system were laid down, paralleling in development the nation's expanding industrial life. During this period the states more and more assumed control over their educational systems.

After about 1880 there was growing recognition of the central importance of schooling. Child labor was gradually abolished, girls and women were afforded more—but not equal—educational opportunities, and the curriculum was broadened to include health and vocational education. There was a great increase in the total amount of time spent in school. There was even greater attention to high school training; and there has come, since World War II, a great increase in enrollments in colleges and universities. Recently the belief has spread that education should be a continuous process from infancy throughout life, and there has been a tremendous growth in programs of formal adult education.

Table 16-3   Per Cent of All 17 Year Olds Completing
High School, 1870–1970

Year	Per Cent
1870	2.0
1880	2.5
1890	3.5
1900	6.4
1910	8.8
1920	16.8
1930	29.0
1940	50.8
1950	59.0
1960	65.1
1970	76.5

SOURCE: U.S. Bureau of the Census, *Statistical Abstract of the United States,
1971* (Washington, D.C.: U.S. Government Printing Office, 1971), p. 124; and U.S.
Bureau of the Census, *Historical Statistics of the United States* (Washington,
D.C.: U.S. Government Printing Office, 1960), p. 207.

The Increase of Formal Education

One indication of the emphasis that people in the United States
put on education is the fact that in 1970 more than 58 million
persons were enrolled in schools and colleges. Nearly three-fifths
(58.9 per cent) of all Americans between the ages of 5 and 34 were
enrolled in some program of formal education. College enrollment
in the U.S. more than doubled between 1960 and 1970 and the
enrollment of women during this time increased one and one-half
times while the college enrollment of black Americans nearly
trebled. Of all American children between the ages of 7 and 14
more than 99 per cent are enrolled in school. In 1920, 18 per cent
of all 18 and 19 year old Americans were enrolled in school and
fifty years later nearly one-half (48 per cent) were enrolled. In no
other country in the world and at no other time in history has such
a large proportion of a population been in school. This reflects an
amazing faith in the value of formal education.

School opportunities have been expanding for the past hundred
years. In 1870, 57 per cent of all persons in the United States between the ages of 5 and 17 were enrolled in school; by the end of
World War I two-thirds of these young people were in school. By
the end of World War II the number had risen to 80 per cent; in
1970 more than 95 per cent were enrolled in school. In 1870, 2 per
cent of all 17 year olds were high school graduates and 100 years
later 77 per cent of all 17 year olds had completed high school.

Table 16-4   Educational Attainment of U.S. Adult
Population, 1970*

Year of School Completed	Per Cent Completing Each Educational Level				
	All Persons	White Males	White Females	Black Males	Black Females
Elementary					
Less than 5 years	100.0	100.0	100.0	100.0	100.0
5–7 years	94.8	94.0	96.2	81.5	87.9
8 years	85.7	85.2	88.4	65.5	70.6
High School					
1–3 years	72.3	71.3	75.0	54.4	59.3
4 years	55.2	57.2	57.7	32.5	34.8
College					
1–3 years	21.2	26.3	18.7	10.0	10.4
4 or more years	11.0	15.0	8.6	4.6	4.4
Median School					
Years Completed	12.2	12.2	12.2	9.6	10.2

*Persons 25 years of age and older.
SOURCE: U.S. Bureau of the Census, *Statistical Abstract of the United States,
1971* (Washington, D.C.: U.S. Government Printing Office, 1971), p. 108.

Elementary education had become firmly established in the
United States by the turn of the nineteenth century and secondary enrollments had been going up slowly since 1880. In 1890
there were about 400,000 high-school students; in 1910 about
900,000. In 1940 there were 6.6 million; by 1970 there were more
than 14 million. The growth of college and university enrollments
has also been impressive. In 1900 there were only about 200,000
students in this category. The next 40 years saw a million added to
this number. In 1950 there were more than 2.2 million students in
American colleges and universities; and in 1970 college and university enrollments reached a record high of over 7 million.

Changes in Curriculum

Since what is taught in school is largely a reflection of the norms
of the larger society, changes in the curriculum are indicators of
the total institutional structure of our society. The main shifts in
elementary-secondary education have been from curricula oriented
around subject matter to those focused on the child as a growing
personality. The former stressed content and capacity to reproduce
what had been read or heard. Today the school is more child-cen-
tered, with stress on the self and on social development. In methods,
the shift has been from a rather severe authoritarian to a more permissive practice, in which the child has a larger degree of partici-

pation. "Progressive education," though now largely discarded as a formal technique, has influenced even the more conservative public and parochial schools. Motivation, cooperative learning, and mental hygiene are given much attention.

The rapid rise in high-school population, especially after 1910, led to a proliferation of separate courses and various groupings of courses of study, such as liberal or college-preparatory, commercial, vocational, and fine arts. There has been a drift away from courses designed to prepare the pupil for higher education to those which have a more practical usefulness in jobs or in the home and which give the future citizen some preparation for his public and political rights and duties. The ancient languages, algebra, geometry, trigonometry, and formal political history have tended to give way to modern languages, "modern" mathematics (with emphasis on understanding rather than mere mastery of operations), and social studies with emphasis on current problems. Intense competition with the Soviet Union has led to re-examination of the desirability of a stronger curriculum in science and mathematics. After Sputnik, it was contended in many high quarters of government and education that the Soviet "superiority" or "success" was due to the fact that students in the USSR were far more thoroughly trained in the natural sciences, mathematics, and technology than those in the United States.

Along with these trends has gone considerable reorganization of the institutional framework. The secondary school is being extended downward to include the last two years of the traditional elementary program, and upward to cover the first two years of college. The former we know as the junior high school; the latter, the junior college. American junior colleges have grown rapidly. In 1928 they had an enrollment of about 50,000; four decades later their enrollment was 1,300,000. Under the growing pressure for college education, many communities have established a two-year college course, sometimes in connection with their high schools. It may well be that these "community colleges" and the junior colleges will come to be the typical terminus of formal education for most of the population.

While development of high schools has been, to some extent, a hit-or-miss affair, and while there has been some confusion of purpose, the leaders of American education have come more and more to take the position that virtually every person should have at least a high-school education, and an ever-growing portion of our young people at least two years of college. The trends in secondary education look largely to occupational preparation, but it is assumed that citizens must have some general education as well. Programs to meet this need include literature, history, and science and try to stress also social values that make for a "well-rounded" personality.

Like the secondary schools, colleges have witnessed considerable changes in the course of study, though these have been less drastic than in the high schools. There has been a shift from classical courses to those of a more applied or "practical" sort. There has been a considerable increase in preprofessional and professional courses in medicine, engineering, journalism, art, agriculture, social work, and teaching. As new specialized vocations arise—for example, in personnel and other administrative work, in public relations for business and government, and in radio and television—the colleges and universities provide training for these new occupations.

Adult Education

A public opinion poll reports that "more than two out of every five adults in the voting population expressed the desire to engage in some kind of study." The survey also showed that more women than men wanted adult education; that the 21–29 age group expressed the greatest demand; and that the more schooling a person has, the more additional education he or she wants. In subject matter, social science stood first, with professional fields second.[6]

There are various reasons for this interest in adult education. Desire to improve one's knowledge and skill with respect to job or profession is one. Wide public interest in domestic and foreign affairs, coupled with the growing belief that only through an informed citizenry can the country solve its problems, is another. Then too, people have much more leisure than formerly and want to take up reading, crafts, arts, or other activities to enrich their lives. The press, the radio, television, and the motion picture provide some of the needed information, but not enough. More formal school facilities are also required.

In the early days there were lecture series and chautauqua, educational-recreational assemblies of several days' duration. Then came public forums and more formal adult education under both private and public sponsorship. Various universities set up extension and correspondence courses. Every state now has some facilities for extension work. While many students work for credit in these courses, many others enroll for the satisfaction of getting additional knowledge.

---

[6]See "A Report of the President's Commission on Higher Education," *Higher Education for American Democracy, Vol. II* (Washington, D.C.: U.S. Government Printing Office, 1947), p. 61. See also Howard Y. McClusky, "Adult Education," *Social Work Year Book*, 1957, ed. Russell H. Kurtz (New York: National Association of Social Workers, 1957), pp. 88–93.

Table 16-5 School Retention Rates—Fifth Grade Through College Entrance

Year of Entrance Into 5th Grade	Retention Per 1,000 Pupils Who Entered 5th Grade								High School Graduates	Year of High School Graduation	First-time College Students
	5th grade	6th grade	7th grade	8th grade	9th grade	10th grade	11th grade	12th grade			
1926	1,000	919	824	754	677	552	453	400	333	1934	129
1936	1,000	954	895	849	839	704	554	425	393	1944	121
1946	1,000	954	945	919	872	775	641	583	553	1954	283
1956	1,000	985	984	948	930	871	790	728	676	1964	362
1962	1,000	990	983	976	963	931	863	793	752*	1970	465*

*Preliminary.
SOURCE: U.S. Bureau of the Census, Statistical Abstract of the United States, 1971 (Washington, D.C.: U.S. Government Printing Office, 1971), p. 125.

Another adult education effort has been the Americanization pro-gram, especially during the decades when this country was receiving thousands of European immigrants each year. More recently, various plans to combat discrimination against minority groups and to foster good will have been attempted under such titles as "Intercultural Education."

There is a wide variety of technical institutes, both public and pri-vate, which as yet have not been integrated into the formal educa-tional system. In addition, many industrial and business firms have programs of apprentice and in-service training for specialized voca-tions.

EDUCATION AND STRATIFICATION

One of the consequences of formal education has been the con-ferral of status. An examination of the system of formal education in American society reveals that the amount and quality of educa-tion one receives varies with income, occupation, sex, race, and region. Each of these variables has consequences for the stratifica-tion system, not only in its own right but to the degree that it influences educational opportunity and hence life chances.

Income

It can generally be said that the lower the income the higher the fertility rate. This makes for a relative concentration of school-age children in low-income families. Thus the families which can least afford to send even one child through school are those most likely to have a number of children. Not only is the family hard put to

Table 16-6   Percentage of Families with Children Attending College and Family Income, 1960

Annual Family Income	Percentage of Children Attending College	Per Cent of All Families in This Income Category
less than $5,000	9	52
between $5,000 and $7,500	17	NA
between $7,500 and $10,000	32	NA
$10,000 and more	44	14

NA = not available.
SOURCE: Adapted from U.S. Bureau of the Census, *Statistical Abstract of the United States, 1971* (Washington, D.C.: U.S. Government Printing Office, 1971), p. 316 and U.S. Bureau of the Census, *Current Population Reports—Population Characteristics*, Series P-20, No. 110, Table 10.

finance a college education for any of its members, but their children have higher probabilities of terminating their educations prior to college.

The family income is related not only to the amount but to the kind of education one is likely to receive. Students from higher-income families can afford more education and are hence more likely to aspire to the professions, which require more years of preparation and more expensive schooling. Students from families with lower incomes usually have little choice but to enroll in commercial and industrial courses.[7]

Occupation

Income and occupational prestige are positively correlated and there is a direct relationship between the occupational status of the parents and the amount of education children receive. The lower the occupational level of the parents, the less the educational attainment of their children. Research at Indiana University shortly after World War II revealed that 14 per cent of the student body was composed of sons of professional men, although professionals constituted only 4 per cent of the state's population. On the other hand, only 13 per cent of the students were sons of semiskilled and un-

Table 16-7   Father's Education and Son's Education

Son's Educational Attainment	Educational Status of Father			
	Not High-school Graduate	High-school Graduate But No College	Some College	College Graduate
No high-school diploma	42.6	10.3	6.5	4.0
High-school diploma but no college	34.1	36.1	23.8	8.2
At least some college attendance	23.3	43.7	69.7	87.9

SOURCE: Murray Gendell and Hans L. Zetterberg, eds., *A Sociological Almanac for the United States*, 2nd ed. (New York: Charles Scribner's Sons, 1964), p. 80; based upon men twenty to twenty-four years of age, October 1960.

---

[7]See W. Lloyd Warner, Robert J. Havighurst, and Martin B. Loeb, *Who Shall Be Educated?* (New York: Harper & Brothers, 1944).

skilled laborers, although such workers constituted 44 per cent of the population. This situation existed despite the fact that government aid had greatly increased the number of students from lower-class homes attending college: the G.I. Bill of Rights had nearly doubled the proportion of students from the lower occupational strata attending the university.[8]

These occupational and income data indicate, of course, that the class structure has functions for the educational institutions themselves. Studies have shown that most public-school teachers in the United States come from middle-class families. It is not surprising, then, that the schools are oriented to middle-class norms.[9]

Race

Black Americans have long been discriminated against in education as in most other areas of American life. Although the situation has changed in recent years, discrimination persists. One indication of the relative educational situation of black and white Americans is shown in Table 16-8. In 1950, black Americans in their late twenties had an average of three and one-half years less education than other Americans of the same age. By 1960 the difference had been reduced to a year and a half and by 1970, the difference was 0.4 years.

Under a system which forced blacks to attend segregated schools, the quality as well as the quantity of education was lower than that for the whites. Since the ruling of the United States Supreme Court on May 17, 1954, which held racial segregation in the schools to be unconstitutional, there has been a steady—though still re-

Table 16-8   Median School Years Completed by Race for Persons 25–29 Years of Age, 1940–1970

| Year | Median School Years Completed | | |
	All Persons	Blacks Only	Difference
1940	10.3	7.0	−3.3
1950	12.1	8.6	−3.5
1960	12.3	10.8	−1.5
1970	12.6	12.2	−0.4

SOURCE: U.S. Bureau of the Census, Statistical Abstract of the United States, 1971 (Washington, D.C.: U.S. Government Printing Office, 1971), p. 109.

[8]Raymond A. Mulligan, "Socio-economic Background and College Enrollment," American Sociological Review, 1951, 16: 188–196.
[9]Probably the best sociological research on the functions of the stratification structure for the adolescent in school is August B. Hollingshead's Elmtown's Youth (New York: John Wiley & Sons, 1949).

sisted—advance in integrating the schools. This should mean a gradual improvement in the education given the black pupils.

Region

Even desegregation will not alone wipe out inequalities in opportunity according to race. Nearly one-half of all black Americans still live in the Southern region, and in terms of the ranking of the regions according to the quality of formal education, the South stands at the bottom. The Southern states, for the most part spend less for schools and invest less per pupil than most states in other sections.

This situation exists in the South partly as a reflection of rural-urban differences. The South is heavily rural and, throughout the United States, the proportion of individuals enrolled in school for each age category is highest in urban and lowest in rural-farm areas.

Clearly, a sizable proportion of the population is capable of acquiring more formal education than it is now given opportunity to secure. The stratification system operates to remove some of these people from school before they have an opportunity to realize their educational potential.

EDUCATIONAL INSTITUTIONS

Teaching is a matter of social contact of students and teachers. While skills and the materials in books must be mastered, these do not exist without the interaction of teacher and student. Unfortunately, much of our earlier educational psychology failed to recognize that *all learning is essentially social.* If the social climate of learning is not conducive to efficient work, if the teacher sets up emotional resistances in the students or fails to present the material in such a way that they can comprehend it, learning is retarded or actually made impossible.

Contemporary teacher-training courses have stressed the social nature of learning, and the result has been a trend toward the "student-oriented" classroom, where healthy personality development is considered as important as the acquisition of knowledge. Particular attention has been paid to individual differences in learning, both by provision of separate classes for fast, medium, and slow learners and by means of day-to-day realization of such differences on the part of the teacher.[10] The prevalent, though by no means unchal-

---

[10]For a discussion of this problem, especially as it concerns high-school students, see "Education of the Academically Talented," *Annual Report, 1958–59,* of the Carnegie Foundation for the Advancement of Teaching.

lenged, educational theory is that homogeneous ability groups not only expedite learning but foster security.

Student-to-Student Relations

Students themselves build up distinctive patterns of action. They assist one another in the learning process. It is unfortunate that little use has been made of the natural social interaction of students in the teaching process. Formal provision might easily be made in many instances for the students to teach one another.

Just as the teachers acquire from the students such social designations as "easy mark," "square," "cool," "old grouch," or "groovy," so do the students. There is the "teacher's pet," the athletic "hero," the "sissy," the "grind," the "grade-getter," and the "clown." Teachers as well as students are responsible for the development of these stereotypes.

The primary, spontaneous groups of students, exemplified in play activities, are not long left to carry on by themselves: the school provides formal control through athletics and clubs. In our increasingly complex society these more specialized secondary groups serve an invaluable function in helping direct play activities along lines which prepare the boy or girl for later participation in other groups in the community.

The Family and the School

The teacher assumes the role of a substitute parent in administering discipline and in exercising authority. Parents expect the teacher to assume such responsibility and frequently object if they imagine that the school is failing to carry over this pattern of authority. Parents are often really more concerned with the moral and social effects of education than with formal instruction, even though they hold dearly to the fetish of book learning.

The school affects the daily routine of the family in many ways and the family culture itself is affected. Instruction very often reaches back into the home, perhaps challenging parental ideas and habits and sometimes creating conflict between the children and the parents, especially when the parents have a cultural background different from the American culture which the child gets from the school.

The Community and the School

In spite of our faith in education, the function of teachers is limited largely to formal instruction of the children. In general, teachers are treated casually, are seldom brought into close contact with the families of their students, and are often looked on as "social" nonentities.

Certain phases of our American educational system make for this condition. For a long time nearly all elementary-school teachers were women, and even today the ratio of women to men teachers in elementary schools is about 3 to 1. Doubtless the lower social status of women generally reflects upon teachers. Although in recent years there has been a movement toward unionization of teachers, in many instances there is still a lack of formal organization of teachers. Without the advantages of group solidarity which would provide bargaining power, the teacher is nearly always dealt with as an individual. When there is any difficulty, the teacher usually has to fight a battle with the community and the school board almost single-handed.

In moral conduct the teacher must conform to the code of the most conservative groups in the community. Even parents who themselves indulge in less traditional forms of conduct demand that the teachers of their children exemplify the highest virtue.

In instructional materials also, conservative beliefs predominate. No textbook is likely to be selected which contains material that will offend the prejudices of any group in the community sufficiently well organized to protest. When the American Legion, the Daughters of the American Revolution, chambers of commerce, political cliques, labor unions, religious organizations, and like groups object to a book or disapprove of a teacher, their protests are likely to be heeded. There is an orthodoxy in the schools not unlike that demanded by theology. Nor is it only in the lower grades that restrictions operate. Some colleges endowed by conservative churches restrict the teaching of science. Economic and political radicalism are also taboo. In spite of their potential leadership, educational institutions tend to conform to conservative standards, and generally do not direct communities in new thought and action.

INSTITUTIONAL CONFLICTS

There are numerous conflicts in educational ideology that continue to be topics of public discussion.

Specialization vs. Liberal Arts

What should be the optimum amount of specialization in the curriculum? At what point should highly specialized subjects be introduced, and how much should they be emphasized? Only a course of study focused on subject matter readily lends itself to specialization.

As outside vocational demands have more and more influence on secondary and advanced education alike, it is easy to emphasize technical courses on the grounds that they fit individuals more adequately for their future occupations.

The bits-and-pieces character of much of liberal-arts education is well-recognized, and various attempts have been made to develop some kind of "core of general education" for both high school and college. This core, which represents those parts of the total course of study that are considered basic for all students, consists of materials organized without regard to traditional subject-matter divisions. Various general orientation and survey courses in the sciences and humanities make up this approach at the college level. So too, the trend in some quarters to reduce the number of free electives and the number of different courses in the college curriculum is a reaction to what is seen as diffuseness and compartmentalization.

Social Action vs. Conformity

In examining the place of the school in the community, there is the perennial question of the treatment of public issues in the classroom. The problem of academic freedom usually arises whenever special-interest groups in the community object to teachers' discussing topics which such groups consider either "dangerous" or none of the school's business.

In the matter of social action the taboo is even more severe. Direct participation in reform on the part of teachers usually meets with strong opposition from those who control the schools at every level. High-school or college students seldom take part in conflicts between labor unions and employers or become active in political campaigns. This is not true, of course, in some countries, where the institutions of higher learning especially are often the seedbeds of progressive and even radical movements.

Federal Aid and Local Control

Another problem has to do with the nature and kind of federal aid which public education may or should receive. In the past, the major support of education has come largely from local and state sources. While most states have tried to equalize educational opportunities within their own boundaries, marked differences between states and regions continue, as we have seen. Out of an awareness of this differential and out of general concern about further extension of schooling has come a growing pressure for more federal funds for the schools.

There has been much opposition to such proposals from business interests that object to further federal taxation and from many educators who believe that, if such aid were given, the federal government would play an ever larger part in the direct control of the schools. There is, in other words, some anxiety that further governmental control of the school might be a threat to traditional freedom of education. Nonetheless, the enormous growth in number of public school students, exerts pressure for federal aid.

Public vs. Private Schools

What is the relation of private to public education in a democracy? The courts have more or less consistently contended that education is a function of the nonpolitical groups of our national society, as well as of the government.[11] There can be no doubt that privately endowed institutions of higher learning have played an important part in our national life. Yet mounting costs of schooling have led some to argue in favor of government aid to such institutions. Again, the fear of direct control makes many people connected with privately supported schools hesitate to press for government help. Since a good deal of the private schooling in this country is in the hands of religious denominations, there is the further complication of government support for church activities.

Indeed, there has been a good deal of sharp public debate, as well as a number of court cases, dealing with tax aid to private schools. Such matters as teachers' salaries, provision of school buses, free textbooks, and free lunches are controversial. Many parents believe that since they pay taxes to support the public schools even though they send their children to private schools for which they must pay fees, it is only just and proper that aid be given to the private schools.[12]

In 1960, for the first time in American history, a Roman Catholic was elected President. This event may well have symbolized changes in some of our old beliefs regarding the relations of church and state.[13]

INTERPRETIVE SUMMARY

All societies have some provisions, formal or informal or both, for socialization of individuals. In dictatorial societies, a central purpose of education

---

[11]See Kimball Young, *Social Psychology*, 3rd ed. (New York: Appleton-Century-Crofts, 1956), pp. 554–555.

[12]Regarding this discussion, see these editorials: "Christian and State in America," *The Christian Century*, 1959, 76: 891–893; and "A Regrettable Revival," *The Christian Century*, 1961, 78: 131–132. The latter discusses the views of Cardinal Francis Joseph Spellman in defense of public tax support for parochial schools.

[13]The following articles reflect various views on this matter: Winthrop S. Hudson, "The Religious Issues in the Campaign"; Charles A. Andrews, "A Catholic President: Pro"; and Harold A. Bosley, "A Catholic President: Con," *The Christian Century*, 1960, 77: 1239–1247.

is to develop loyalty and subservience to the state. In democracies, the purpose of education is to develop individuals who are both self-sufficient and capable of making the democratic system work.

The American emphasis on individual worth has led to increased education for all classes. However, the situation even today, with a larger proportion of the United States population in school or part-time school than at any other place at any time, is still not ideal. Accessibility of education is still limited by one's race, sex, region, and the occupation and income of one's family. The fact is particularly sobering when the latent functions of education are considered.

Increased school enrollment is only one of the changes that have occurred in the American educational system. Many of these changes are related to the American belief in universal education. For example, the recognition that for many people high school education is terminal education has led to emphasis on useful subjects, particularly vocational subjects, and on new methods which will help the average child understand his schoolwork more easily. Traditional liberal arts subjects have been revamped, and sometimes combined, with the average student in mind. The number of junior colleges and relatively inexpensive two-year community colleges is increasing. Other changes, such as the proliferation of ability-grouped classrooms, have been a result of current psychological emphasis on a secure, student-oriented atmosphere. Still other changes, such as increased specialization in curriculums and emphasis on mathematics and science, may be traced to specialization in all areas of American culture and to competition with the Soviet Union.

One aspect of American education that has not changed substantially is its source of control, which has always been local and state. In fact, both teacher behavior and curriculum have historically been controlled by the more conservative elements in the community, and needed federal aid has been resisted on the grounds that it would lead to federal control. Certain sub-groups have set up private schools in order to increase control over their children; for them the dilemma posed by federal aid has been an especially difficult one.

SUGGESTIONS FOR FURTHER READING

Barzun, Jacques. *Teacher in America*. Boston: Little, Brown, and Company, 1944. This is a delightfully written and incisive analysis of the role of the teacher in the United States.

Cicourel, Aaron V., and Kitsuse, John I. *The Educational Decision-Makers*. Indianapolis: The Bobbs-Merrill Company, 1963. The results of a research study on the processes of differentiation and mobility as they operate through parental guidance, peer-group pressures, and educational counseling in a suburban high school are reported.

Clark, Burton. *Educating the Expert Society*. San Francisco: Chandler Publishing Company, 1962. The dominant characteristics of modern industrial societies such as technological change and the resultant educational complex are investigated.

Crain, Robert. *The Politics of School Desegregation.* Anchor Books. Garden City, N.Y.: Doubleday and Company, Inc., 1969. The political aspects of desegregation in both northern and southern cities are empirically analyzed.

Freedman, Mervin B. *The College Experience.* San Francisco: Jossey-Bass, 1967. This book examines what happens to students during the college years in terms of personality development, sexuality, and the roots of student discontent.

Gross, Neal. *Who Runs Our Schools?* New York: John Wiley and Sons, 1958. This is a study of teachers' beliefs about educational administration, educational goals, and the conflict of values over organizational objectives.

Jencks, Christopher, and Riesman, David. *The Academic Revolution.* Garden City, N. Y.: Doubleday and Company, Inc., 1968. The authors present an excellent historical and sociological account of higher education in America.

Sanford, Nevitt. *Where Colleges Fail.* San Francisco: Jossey-Bass, 1967. This book examines educational goals and the educational environment and attempts to link them to the present generation of students and the larger society.

Stinchcombe, Arthur. *Rebellion in a High School.* Chicago: Quadrangle Books, 1969. Stinchcombe sees the difference between what students know about society and what they are taught in the schools as one of the main sources of "rebellion."

Thomas, Lawrence G. *The Occupational Structure and Education.* Englewood Cliffs, N. J.: Prentice-Hall, Inc., 1956. The socioeconomic significance of socialization is examined with particular reference to its effect on the labor force.

Ulich, Robert. *Philosophy of Education.* New York: American Book Company, 1961. A masterly textbook by one of the twentieth century's great educators, this volume treats basic philosophical issues and their practical results in education.

Young, Michael. *The Rise of the Meritocracy, 1870–2033: An Essay on Education and Equality.* Pelican Books. Baltimore: Penguin Books, 1958. This is a sociological novel of a society in which I.Q. + effort = merit and thus the good things in life.

DO YOU
BELIEVE
IN LIFE
AFTER
DEATH?

WHAT DO
YOU CALL
THIS?

17
Religion
and Society

In the course of trying to satisfy the more immediate needs of sustenance, shelter, reproduction, and group and personal safety, prehistoric people found themselves confronted with many forces in nature which they did not understand. They speculated, and that was the beginning of philosophy. They put forth a finger to investigate, and that was the beginning of science. They experienced awe and fear, and these were the beginnings of religion.

In his classic study of religious behavior first published in 1912, Durkheim defined religion as "... a unified system of beliefs and practices relative to sacred things, uniting into a single moral community all those who adhere to those beliefs and practices."[1] Religion concerns belief in supernatural forces which influence human events. Many societies have a wide range of organizations associated with religion, including special officials, forms of worship, ceremonies, sacred objects, tithes, pilgrimages, and the like. In literate societies, religious leaders have developed elaborate theories or theologies to explain humankind's place in the universe. Further-

---
[1]Emile Durkheim, *The Elementary Forms of Religious Life* (New York: The Free Press, 1947), p. 47.

443

more, the world religions—Hinduism, Buddhism, Confucianism, Judaism, Christianity, and Mohammedanism—are cores of elaborate cultural systems that have dominated whole societies for centuries.

RELIGIOUS STRUCTURES

Religion in nonliterate societies rests on a belief in personal and impersonal powers which play a part in human life. Belief in personal powers is called animism and it is illustrated by belief in spirits, ghosts, and demons which bring good or bad luck. Impersonal power, called *mana* (Melanesian), *orenda* (Iroquois), *manitou* (Algonquian), and other names, manifests itself in natural objects, and not necessarily through people, spirits, or ghosts. In Polynesia and Melanesia, for example, mana refers to an extraordinary force yielding extraordinary results and may be located in any object— person, plant, rock, music, or animal.

> If a man's pigs multiply and his gardens are productive, it is not because he is industrious and looks after his property, but because of the stones full of mana for pigs and yams that he possesses. Of course a yam naturally grows when planted, that is well known, but it will not be very large unless mana comes into play: a canoe will not be swift unless mana be brought to bear upon it, a net will not catch many fish, nor an arrow inflict a mortal wound.[2]

Among nonliterate peoples, the various phases of life are not sharply divided, as they typically are in industrial societies. Work and art, play and religion, magic and toolmaking are all closely interwoven. Economic activities are often surrounded by noneconomic rituals. Recurrent events in the life of the group, such as birth, death, illness, marriage, and seasonal changes, have special emotional significance. Ceremonies connected with these events become part of the folkways.

Magic

Surrounded as they were by forces of nature and of other people, forces which they did not fully understand, early people probably did not distinguish in any logical way between natural and supernatural elements. In fact, it is difficult to sort out the religion of nonliterate people from the other phases of their rudimentary

---

[2]R. H. Codrington, "Man," *Reader in Comparative Religion,* 2nd ed., edited by W. A. Lessa and E. Z. Vogt (New York: Harper and Row, 1965), p. 257.

culture. In particular, what we call magic permeates both religion on the one hand and practical behavior on the other.

Magic is invented or discovered in the same way other techniques are invented or discovered. An act is performed, either accidentally or because imagination suggests that it might be successful. If it seems to work, it is adopted as a rule of action. If, for example, it is discovered that friction produces heat, this may suggest fire. The imagination furnishes a clue which proves valid in overt action. But imagination suggests also that if one were to burn a wax effigy of an enemy, he or she would be doing that enemy harm and that if a barren woman has a wooden image of a child placed in her lap, she will bear a child (as the Batak of Sumatra believe). If the intended victim actually does fall ill or if the woman does conceive, the practice is regarded as successful. We call fire-making naturalistic or realistic because its action is fully explained by present-day physical science. We call effigy-making magic because any success it may seem to have is outside the cause-and-effect relations known to science.

Because members of nonliterate societies do not ordinarily organize secondary groups as a setting for religious interaction, there is seldom any sense of the separation of religious norms from other norms, of religious groups from other groups, or of religious activities from other activities. One would never hear in such a society the sentiment, often voiced in ours, that "we should bring business and religion closer together." In folk society they have never been separated.

Religious Organization

In the United States, religious belief and expression have become institutionalized into secondary organizations called churches. The term "church" has different meanings for different people. Some consider a church to be (1) a body of devotees (2) organized for a religious purpose and developing as an agency for this with (3) a hierarchy of officials and leaders and (4) a body of doctrine and philosophy which ties the whole together into a systematic unit. In popular speech, too, the term *church* is sometimes used to mean a unit of common religious beliefs and practices, as when we speak of the Christian Church. At other times, *church* refers to a more limited body of believers within this larger grouping, such as the Presbyterian or the Methodist Church. (These, properly speaking, are denominations.) In a fourth sense, *church* refers to a congregation or locally organized body of worshipers—and, of course, to the building where these people gather for religious services.

The most basic distinction in the forms of religious organization is that of church and sect, which comes from the work of the German scholar Ernst Troeltsch.[3] Many scholars also subclassify churches into two main types, the ecclesia and the denomination. The ecclesia, in principle, is universal, has complete unity with the rest of society (including the state), and possesses universal membership. The Roman Catholic Church of the Middle Ages is the closest actual approximation of an ecclesia. The denomination is positioned between the ecclesia and the sect. It seeks neither to control the world nor to withdraw from it. Instead, it attempts to co-exist with other churches and openly approves of the separation of church and state. The major religious bodies of the United States are examples of denominations.

The sect is at odds with the institutionalized church on almost every count: it is a primary group whose institutions refuse integration with the institutionalized church's social order and reject cultural values which are at variance with its religious ideology. Today's sect is likely to be tomorrow's church. The whole history of the development of the Protestant denominations, as indicated by their name, is a story of groups objecting to certain ways of a church and breaking away to start sects. In time, a sect makes its peace with the wider society and becomes a church itself; later, a new generation of people may break away from it and form another sect. Indeed, Christianity itself was first a sect that emerged in a time of social discontent as the religion of the poor, the dispossessed, and the outcast.

A *sect* is a body of believers that grows up within the larger church.[4] Certain persons, often few in number at first, begin to disagree about points in the main ceremonials and doctrine of the parent organization. At the outset they do not think of themselves as outside their denomination: only as they come into conflict with the ecclesiastical officials of the principal body does the idea of separation arise. Often it is only after they have been expelled from the organized church that they formulate their own creed, their

---

[3]Ernst Troeltsch, *The Social Teaching of the Christian Churches*, translated by Olive Wyon (New York: The Macmillan Company, 1931). See also: H. Richard Niebuhr, *The Social Sources of Denominationalism* (New York: Henry Holt and Company, Inc., 1929), and S. D. Clark, *Church and Sect in Canada* (Toronto, Canada: University of Toronto Press, 1948). For a critique of the typology, see: Harold W. Pfautz, "The Sociology of Secularization," *The American Journal of Sociology*, LXI (September, 1955), 121–128, and Benton Johnson, "A Critical Appraisal of the Church-Sect Typology," *American Sociological Review*, XXII (February, 1957), 88–92.
[4]Bryan R. Wilson, "An Analysis of Sect Development," *American Sociological Review*, XXIV (February, 1959), 3–15.

ILLUSTRATIVE DATA 17-1   FROM SECT TO CHURCH

Sect	Church
From: Membership composed chiefly of the propertyless	*To:* Membership composed of property owners
From: Economic poverty	*To:* Economic wealth, as disclosed especially in the value of church property and the salary paid to ministers
From: The cultural periphery	*To:* The cultural center of the community
From: Renunciation of prevailing culture and social organization, or indifference to it	*To:* Affirmation of prevailing culture and social organization
From: Self-centered (or personal) religion	*To:* Culture-centered religion
From: "Experience"	*To:* A social institution
From: Noncoöperation, or positive ridicule, toward established religious institutions	*To:* Coöperation with the established churches of the community
From: Suspicion of rival sects	*To:* Disdain or pity for all sects
From: A moral community excluding unworthy members	*To:* A social institution embracing all who are socially compatible within it
From: An unspecialized, unprofessionalized, part-time ministry	*To:* A specialized, professional, full-time ministry
From: A psychology of persecution	*To:* A psychology of success and dominance
From: Voluntary, confessional bases of membership	*To:* Ritual or social prerequisites only (such as a certificate of previous membership in another respected denomination, or training in an educational process established by the denomination itself)
From: Principal concern with adult membership	*To:* Equal concern for children of members
From: Emphasis on evangelism and conversion	*To:* Emphasis on religious education
From: Stress on a future in the next world	*To:* Primary interest in a future in this world—a future for the institution, for its members, and for their children
From: Emphasis on death	*To:* Emphasis on successful earthly life

From: Adherence to strict Biblical standards, such as tithing or nonresistance	*To: Acceptance of general cultural standards as a practical definition of religious obligation*
From: A high degree of congregational participation in the services and administration of the religious group	*To: Delegation of responsibility to a comparatively small percentage of the membership*
From: Fervor in worship services	*To: Restraint*
From: Positive action— a comparatively large number of special religious services	*To: Passive listening— a program of regular services at stated intervals*
From: Reliance on spontaneous "leadings of the spirit" in religious services and administration	*To: A fixed order of worship and of administrative procedure*
From: The use of hymns resembling contemporary folk music	*To: The use of slower, more stately hymns coming out of more remote liturgical tradition*
From: Emphasis on religion in the home	*To: Delegation of responsibility for religion to church officials and organizations*

Source: Liston Pope, *Millhands and Preachers.* Copyright © 1942 by Yale University Press. Reprinted by permission.

own official hierarchy, and take on a distinctive name and become a new "denomination."

Religious Roles

Religious norms and practices give rise to distinctive social roles. As an elderly Maori once remarked to a white man, "Gods die if there are no priests to keep them alive."[5] Social roles in religion fall into two general categories: the religious thinkers and mystics, found in both formal and informal religious structures, and executives or operators, who are by definition more prevalent in formal structures. The former category includes the mystics proper, the prophets, and the messiahs. The latter category includes the priests,

---

[5]Quoted in W. I. Thomas, *Primitive Behavior* (New York: McGraw-Hill Book Co., 1937), p. 329.

pastors, formal teachers, missionaries, and various administrators. Mystics are likely to be innovators and disturbers of the established order. Religious executives are generally conservative, preferring the old and tried to the new. There is, in fact, something of a continuing struggle in religious organizations between these two kinds of social roles. Some would confine religious expression within rather definite limits set by symbols, rites, traditions, and established theology. Others would not unduly hamper religious experience by such established patterns of thought and action but would leave much room for the individual's unique experience.

The *priest, rabbi,* or *pastor* fills the role expectations of carrying on the religious rituals and expounding theology. He or she is the special person who officiates at the church ceremonies and cares for both spiritual and temporal affairs.

Religious *teachers* or *philosophers* have played a central part in the rise of the great world religions. Jesus, St. Paul, Mohammed, and Buddha are all familiar instances. The *missionary* is a special teacher whose business it is to carry the message, rituals, and symbolism of an established religion to nonbelievers.

The *religious executive* may be, like St. Paul, both missionary and organizer. In many Protestant churches where a priestly hierarchy is not developed or is practically nonexistent, the affairs of the church organization are carried on by executives whose work combines that of priest or pastor with social-service activities and management.

The *mystic* plays a special part in the growth of religion. He identifies himself or comes into union with the god, or with the world-spirit, or with the Absolute—however the culture phrases the idea of supernatural forces. The mystic illustrates the place in a society of the divergent person who may initiate changes in culture. Mystics believe that, through their dreams, visions, and other unique mental experiences, they come into direct personal communication with divine powers.

The *prophet* is an important religious leader. While he may be a priest, often he is a mystic. He serves as spokesman for some divine power, issuing warnings, giving commands, and revealing the course of future events. Obviously, the prophet's role is set by the culture. When there is a strong priestly hierarchy, as among the Ekoi of West Africa or in the Roman Catholic Church, there is little opportunity for such persons to appear.

The *messiah* is the divine leader or prophet who is recognized as having supernatural attributes, who foretells some catastrophic end of the world and often assumes the role of final judge. The messiah ordinarily comes from among the people themselves, who in a time of crisis look to him to save the society from disaster. Mohammed,

for example, was the messiah of the people who came to call themselves, after him, Mohammedans. Christ, of course, is the messiah
of Christians.

Basic Religious Patterns

The institutional practices and formal theories which have grown
up about religion are many. The most important are ceremonials,
symbolism, sacred objects and buildings, and creed and theology.

Ceremony or *ritual* is a standardized and accepted action directed
toward some specific end. (Rituals and ceremonies are not confined,
of course, to religion.) In religion, ritual is a settled manner of
entreating or controlling the supernatural powers in regard to some
particular situation. Ordination, the sacraments, various forms of
sacrifice, and penance call for special rituals. In some churches,
such as the Greek Orthodox or Roman Catholic, the ceremonials
are elaborate. In other churches, like those of the Quakers or Calvinists, the forms play only a slight part in religious life.

Throughout religion, *symbolism* is important. Symbols are substitutes for or representations of objects or situations. They may be
verbal or tangible. A commonly recognized religious symbol helps
the person identify himself with his fellows and so promotes a
sense of solidarity. Often it comes to stand not alone for the particular object or situation to which it was originally attached but
for the whole group and its culture: the cross stands for Christianity,
the crescent for Mohammedanism. The symbol in the mind of the
user may serve either an intellectual or an emotional purpose. For
the religious worshiper, the object and its symbol are combined into
an indivisible emotional experience, which asserts itself whenever
the symbol is brought forth. The Eucharist, for example, symbolizes
for the Christian the supreme sacrifice of Jesus, and in this ritual
the worshiper identifies himself intellectually and emotionally with
one of the main tenets of his theology.

Sacred objects associated with the various religions have symbolic
power insofar as they evoke memories of a religion's history and
traditions. The Hebrew ark of the covenant and the phylactery, the
Christian candles, altar, and especially the cross play important
parts in many religious ceremonials. For their religious exercises
people often repair to special sacred localities: mountaintops, mineral springs, groves of trees, river banks, seashores. Special *buildings*
are erected, such as the tabernacle of the ancient Hebrews; the
temples of ancient Babylonia, Egypt, Greece, and Rome; the syna-
gogues of the Jews; and the cathedrals and churches of Christians.

Theology is the systemic explanation which religious leaders work
out to show man's relation to his god and to the universe. Often

Illustrative Data 17–2 Religious Beliefs in America

Religious Belief

1. I know God really exists and I have no doubts about it
2. Jesus is the Divine Son of God and I have no doubts about it
3. Jesus was born of a virgin*
4. Jesus walked on water*
5. I believe that Jesus will actually return to the earth some day*
6. There is a life beyond death*
7. The Devil actually exists*
8. A child is born into the world already guilty of sin*
9. Belief in Jesus Christ as saviour is absolutely necessary for salvation
10. Being of the Jewish religion definitely prevents salvation
11. Being anti-Semitic definitely prevents salvation
12. Practicing artificial birth control definitely prevents salvation
13. Discriminating against other races definitely prevents salvation

Religious Organization	Per Cent Holding Religious Belief												
	1	2	3	4	5	6	7	8	9	10	11	12	13
Congregationalists	41	40	21	19	13	36	6	2	38	1	23	0	27
Methodists	60	54	34	26	21	49	13	7	45	3	23	0	25
Episcopalians	63	59	39	30	24	53	17	18	47	3	26	2	27
Presbyterians	75	72	57	51	43	69	31	21	66	7	20	1	22
American Baptists	78	76	69	62	57	72	49	23	78	7	13	1	17
Southern Baptists	99	99	99	99	94	97	92	43	97	25	10	5	16
Sects**	96	97	96	94	89	94	90	47	96	23	26	4	29
Catholics	81	86	81	71	47	75	66	68	51	1	20	23	24

*Per cent who said "completely true."   †Per cent who said "definitely."
**Sects include The Assemblies of Gods, The Church of God, The Church of Christ, The Church of the Nazarene, The Foursquare Gospel Church, and one independent Tabernacle.
Source: Charles Y. Glock and Rodney Stark, Religion and Society in Tension (Chicago: Rand McNally, 1965).

this includes some account of the origin of the world and of man, such as the stories of creation in the Bible. It represents the *creed*, or body of beliefs and doctrines of the church. The written words become the sacred scriptures.

RELIGIOUS FUNCTIONS

Religious structures exist in every society, and they function for the continuity of the society. The supernatural laws and beings around which such structures are oriented supply an ultimate idea of reality to which the cultural values and social norms can be related. Religion provides a higher court of appeal when a person feels his or her fellows have treated him or her unjustly and promises better things in the future. It provides the individual with an institutionalized crystallization of hopes and an outlet for fears in ways that almost predetermine his or her choice of immed- iate goals.

> Throughout most of the world religious education, broadly con- ceived, helps the individual make sense of much instruction which might otherwise appear to him as a meaningless and arbitrary assort- ment of directions and prohibitions. If, for instance, a child learns (as in some Christian denominations) that the attainment of salvation is the main goal of life and that to that end he is to attend church regularly, read the Bible and pray daily, honor and love his parents, work hard, live frugally, refrain from dishonest conduct, unchastity and riotous behavior, avoid dancing, drinking and card-playing, his social development is not only given a very definite direction but a certain internal consistency.[6]

Sanctions for the Mores

Religion has frequently been a powerful factor in lending emo- tional support to the moral code. In all the great religions there is an intermingling of religion and morals. There is little doubt that the belief in a god influences moral conduct. Among the Ekoi of West Africa, where magic is considered very powerful and where spirits are used for malevolent ends, people believe in benign spirits who counteract the evil ones and aid humankind in more humane ways. So too, some nonliterates of relatively simple culture, such as the Australian Bushmen and the Andaman Islanders, believe in spirits that are considered guardians of morality.

As the concept of an ethical god develops, the relation of religion

---

[6]Elizabeth K. Nottingham, *Religion and Society* (New York: Random House, Inc., 1954), p. 17.

to morality becomes more important. By identifying himself with such a god, an individual may modify his conduct. Among the Hebrews, Jehovah, at first a tribal god of vengeance, gradually emerged as a universalistic god of high moral qualities.

In Christian theology the struggle between the forces of God and the forces of Satan symbolizes the conflict within the individual between the moral and the immoral, between the spirit and the flesh, between good and evil. Throughout Christian history the role of God and the saints as standards of virtue has been highly important. A personal deity becomes an ideal with which one may compare his own conduct.

Any scheme of otherworldly reward or punishment for conduct becomes a powerful aid to morality. But although the idea of continuity of life after death is rather widespread, not all groups have the notion of retribution or divine judgment. Indeed, this idea came rather late in cultural development.

In many religions the belief in a final judgment, with its terrible punishments for the evil and glorious rewards for the virtuous, is pictured in bold and striking manners. Without doubt, the fear of hell fire and damnation has been a powerful factor in the control of conduct. Associated with fear, systems of penance and absolution have been developed to remove or at least lighten the burden of future punishment.

The virtues of honesty, fair-dealing, conformity to sexual codes—in short, all the accepted details of moral conduct of the community or society—may become integrated with religious beliefs and practices. Today there is a tendency to integrate principles of social welfare, the morality of fairer distribution of wealth, of sound and honest politics, of high community standards of health and conduct into the religious ideals of the church.

Religion and Economy

In nonliterate societies nearly every feature of life is intermixed with religion. This is clearly evident in the economy: food-gathering, hunting, fishing, herding, agriculture, trade, and barter—each is directly related to the gods. It is not always so apparent that religion also plays a part in our more complex capitalistic economy, but Max Weber, a German sociologist, R. H. Tawney, a British economist, and others have argued that there is a parallel between the development of Protestant ideas and practices and the rise of modern capitalism in Western Europe and America.[7] The individualism of

---

[7]See Max Weber, *The Protestant Ethic and the Spirit of Capitalism*, trans. Talcott Parsons (New York: Charles Scribner's Sons, 1930); and R. H. Tawney, *Religion*

Protestantism goes hand in hand with the rise of nationalism and the change from the relatively rigid class structure of the Middle Ages to the open-class system of the Industrial Revolution. The otherworldly asceticism of Catholicism, in which emphasis was put on confession of sins and absolution as preparation for the hereafter, gave way to what Weber aptly calls "worldly asceticism," in which, while the moral virtues of hard work, honestly, truthfulness, and steadfastness of purpose are retained, activity is directed toward the affairs of this world as preparation for the hereafter. Assuming a method of salvation such as the Calvinist doctrine of predestination or the Lutheran doctrine of grace, the individual must fulfill his role in the world of everyday affairs in order to demonstrate his worthiness for membership in the Kingdom of God.

During the Middle Ages, money-making was considered distinctly secondary to godly pursuits. By the sixteenth century, material gain had assumed greater importance, and the profit system was well established by the time of the Reformation. The dogmas of the Protestant religious movement were, in part, an outcome of a more materialistic philosophy which was influencing business and state-craft, and these dogma, in turn, gave further support to capitalistic endeavor. Hard work, sacrifice of present pleasures for future profits in a business, honesty in business dealings, and other homely virtues became the daily morality of the pious Protestants, especially the Calvinists, the Quakers, and the Separatists. The individual, having religious assurance of salvation, practiced these virtues as evidence of his godliness. While these new ideas and practices had to fight their way step by step against religious tradition, in time they won wide acceptance.

Capitalism, Protestantism, and political democracy, bound together by certain accidents of history and certain similar ideologies, came to full bloom in America. The emphasis on religious piety, individualism, liberty and activity, and the worship of material success, coupled with almost unlimited natural resources, made early America a living example of this combination of the repression of pleasure-seeking and the direction of energy into hard work, success, and religious satisfaction. Nowadays, however, one cannot assume the existence of any direct cause-and-effect relationship between the Protestant and Catholic faiths and role behavior in contemporary American society. Research indicates that whatever influence these two religious subcultures have on their adherents in

and the Rise of Capitalism (New York: Harcourt, Brace & Co., 1926). The whole notion of such a relationship is called into serious question by the work of Kurt Samuelsson, Religion and Economic Action: The Protestant Ethic, The Rise of Capitalism, and the Abuses of Scholarship (New York: Basic Books, Inc., 1961).

our society is overriden by the general ethos.[8] There is no evidence that the so-called Protestant ethic is participated in any less by Catholics than by Protestants or Jews in the contemporary United States.

Yet institutions are interrelated, and there remains in our normative structure not only some connection between economic and religious institutions, but a belief on the part of many that such a relationship ought to exist. Yet there are many who believe that capitalism has been injurious to the true aim of religion. The inequalities of wealth and the exploitation of people, both as workers and as consumers, by business interests have led some church leaders and others to give thought to reforms in the economic order. In the early twentieth century there arose among certain American Protestant groups what was known as the "social gospel" movement, which contended that human rights should come before those of property; that mutual service, not profit, should be the chief economic motive; and that cooperation, not competition, should be the mode of economic production and distribution.

Yet so long as the church gets its chief support from the dominant capitalist class, it is not easy for it to go far in economic views from those who pay its bills. If the church, like the traditional school, continues to reflect the dominant economic and political views of those in power, it will consume much of its time and energy defending the prevailing economic and political order.

Religion and Education

Formal teaching has long been a prerogative of organized religion. In Christian history, the church has played a decisive part in education. The cathedral schools of the Middle Ages were used for religious and moral training, and early Protestantism fostered elementary learning so that members might read the Bible. The Sunday School was established in 1780 by an Englishman, Robert Raikes, with a view to more formal religious and moral education. The movement soon spread to America and in the last religious census in the United States (1936), about four-fifths of the congregations had Sunday Schools.[9]

Even more influential than the Sunday School has been the parochial school, organized to fulfill the legal demands for formal

[8]Raymond W. Mack, Raymond J. Murphy, and Seymour Yellin, "The Protestant Ethic, Level of Aspiration, and Social Mobility: An Empirical Test," *American Sociological Review,* XXI (June, 1956), 295–300, and W. Lloyd Warner and Leo Srole, *The Social Systems of American Ethnic Groups* (New Haven, Connecticut: Yale University Press, 1945).
[9]*Summary and Detailed Tables, Religious Bodies, 1936,* vol. 1 (Washington, D.C.: U.S. Government Printing Office, 1941).

schooling but offering children of various churches religious and moral instruction not available in public schools. The philosophy underlying this form of education was set forth in the "Encyclical on Education" (1930) by Pope Pius XI:

> It is necessary that all the teaching and whole organization of the school, and its teachers, syllabus and textbooks in every branch, be regulated by the Christian spirit, under the direction and maternal supervision of the Church; so that Religion may be in very truth the foundation and the crown of youth's entire training; and this in every grade of school, not only in the elementary but in the intermediate and the higher institutions of learning as well.[10]

Closely related to more formal religious education has been the development of such organizations as the Young Men's Christian Association, the Catholic Youth Organization, and the Young Men's Hebrew Association. There are, in addition, vacation schools, clubs, and forums, and the churches sponsor other activities in which more formal education is supplemented with opportunities for discussion of current moral, religious, and economic problems.

The Boy Scouts, Girl Scouts, and Camp Fire Girls, though not strictly religious organizations, have much in common with these other agencies. These groups carry on chiefly leisure-time activities but relate these activities rather explicitly to the ethical and religious principles taught in the church. The Boy Scouts, for instance, are taught to respect their parents, to have reverence for God, and to play fairly.

It is significant that religious organizations are taking over some of the functions formerly located in the home, in the neighborhood, and even in the school. For many Americans, religious activity serves as a focus for the integration of a host of other activities.

RELIGIOUS PATTERNS IN THE UNITED STATES

Community and Church

In the primary community of medieval Europe the Church was the focus of much of the people's lives. In Protestant countries it continued to serve important functions, although where rival denominations and sects arose, the integrating benefits of religion and church organization were often lost in theological conflicts. In spite of the continuation of these divisive tendencies, churches in the United States have served the community as the center not only of

---

[10]See "The Pope's Encyclical on Education," *Current History*, 1930, 31: 1101.

religious thought and action but also of moral standards. Today the primary-community church reflects the changes which have gone on in the wider world outside. Open-country churches, for example, are declining, while village and town churches are becoming the center of both farm and village religious activity. The rural and village church has added educational, recreational, and social-service activities to its functions.

Formerly the church was the focus of much of the neighborhood life. The Catholic churches have continued to be particularly effective as neighborhood centers, since the membership is divided geographically into parishes, in the same manner as voting precincts or school districts are laid out. This gives the pastor an opportunity to serve the people who are themselves neighbors and who already have attitudes of solidarity growing out of common life. The urban Protestant parishes, for the most part, are now divided on geographic lines, with the result that members are often drawn from widespread areas. So long as the population remained fairly stationary, this handicap was overcome by the fact that the church buildings were located in the residential sections in which most of the members lived. In rapidly growing American cities the situation is quite different. Many church edifices are left stranded in the midst of retail or wholesale districts or in cheap rooming-house or emerging slum areas just beyond the retail business section. The members often live so far from the home church that they drift away to other parishes nearer by or give up their church affiliation entirely.

In many other ways the city church is also affected by changes in the society, especially in the growing emphasis on secondary-group organization. Many sophisticated urban people are skeptical of what organized religion has to offer. There is frequently a conflict within the church body itself as to whether it should liberalize its dogma, taking up social-service and educational and recreational programs, or stick by the old and tried at the cost of younger membership and at the risk of slow decay and perhaps final disappearance.

Religious Participation

For several reasons, statistics on church membership are not a very dependable measure of the extent of participation in organized religious groups. First, there is no adequate census of church members throughout the world—nor, for that matter, in the United States. There has been strong opposition in the United States to a scientifically conducted census of religious membership. Religion is regarded as a form of individual and group activity which has no relationship to the government, except insofar as the state protects

Table 17-1 Estimated Religious Composition of the Adult
Population of the United States

Religious Group	Per Cent of the Adult Population*
Protestants	72
Baptists	21
Methodists	17
Lutherans	7
Presbyterians	6
Episcopalians	3
Other Protestants	18
Roman Catholics	22
Jews	3
Other Religions	1
No Religion or Religion not reported	2
Sample Size	5,827
U.S. Adult Population	108,051,172

*Persons 21 years or older as reported by the 1960 Census of Population.
SOURCE: Bernard Lazerwitz, "Religion and Social Structure in the United States," *Religion, Culture, and Society*, ed. Louis Schneider (New York: John Wiley and Sons, Inc., 1964), p. 427. Based on data obtained by the University of Michigan Research Center in 1957 and 1958, from a sample of the civilian population twenty-one years old and over. Reprinted by permission.

churches, like any other accepted institution, from interference in their activities. As a result, members of many denominations, as well as a number of citizens concerned with civil liberties, view an objective census of church membership as none of the state's affair.

Second, there is little agreement among denominations as to what constitutes membership. Some groups count anyone born or baptized into their fold as a member, even if that person denies membership and/or has not participated in church activities for years. Some churches count infants and children as members, while others count only adolescents and adults.

Finally, there is the question of a satisfactory measure of participation. Is the indifferent member to be equated with the ardent one? Just how real this question is becomes apparent when we realize that, though the most reliable estimates posit that well over half the people in the United States are church members, a public-opinion poll conducted by an independent commercial research firm indicates that slightly less than one-third of the people in the United States attend church regularly.[11]

Nevertheless, an approximate description of the extent and dis-

---

[11]Reported in "Do Americans Go to Church?" *Catholic Digest*, VII (1952), 1–7.

Table 17-2 Principal Religions of the World*

Religion	Estimated Membership
Total Christian	924,274,000
Roman Catholic	580,470,000
Eastern Orthodox	125,684,000
Protestant	218,120,000
Jewish	13,537,000
Moselm	493,012,000
Zoroastrian	138,000
Shinto	69,662,000
Taoist	54,324,000
Confucian	371,587,000
Buddhist	176,920,000
Hindu	436,745,000
Others†	829,221,000
Total	3,369,420,000

*Statistics of the world's religions are only rough approximations. Aside from Christianity, few religions attempt to keep statistical records; and even Protestants and Catholics employ different methods of counting members. All persons of whatever age who have received baptism in the Catholic Church are counted as members, while in most Protestant Churches only those who "join" the church are numbered. The compiling of statistics is further complicated by the fact that in China one may be at the same time a Confucian, a Taoist, and a Buddhist. In Japan, one may be both a Buddhist and a Shintoist.
†Includes "primitive" religions and none.
SOURCE: Reprinted with permission from *1969 Britannica Book of the Year.* © 1969 The Encyclopedia Britannica, Inc., Chicago.

tribution of church membership in the United States is shown in Table 17-1. Uncertain as these figures are, they are better estimates than are available for world religions. An educated guess as to the membership of the principal religions of the world is reported in Table 17-2. There are more Christians in the world than there are believers in any other religion. The Roman Catholic Church is the single largest unified religious organization in the world. Christians comprise the largest single category, although they constitute only about 30 per cent of the total.

About three-fourths of the church members in the United States belong to the six largest organizations. But it is worth noting that there are about 250 other denominations in the United States, many with fewer than 1,000 members.

Religion and Stratification

A considerable body of research offers evidence that religious beliefs, as well as religious participation, vary from stratum to

Table 17-3   Income, Education and Religious Affiliation
in the United States

Religious Group	Family Income	Education*	Number
Jewish	$9,830	13.3	242
Episcopalian	9,173	13.5	199
Congregationalist	9,067	12.9	127
Presbyterian	8,013	12.5	435
Mormon	7,488	12.0	101
Methodist	7,485	11.6	1,031
Catholic	7,432	11.1	1,936
Lutheran	7,120	11.1	680
Baptist	5,612	10.1	1,713
Total	6,941	11.2	7,518

*Education of the male head of the family.
SOURCE: Galen L. Gpekel, "Income and Religious Affiliation: A Regression Analysis," The American Journal of Sociology, LXXIV (May, 1969), 637. © 1969 by The University of Chicago. Reprinted by permission.

stratum in the class structure.[12] Research has shown, for example, that acceptance of the sect type of organization is associated with low socioeconomic status, while acceptance of the church type of structure is more frequently found among those with more formal education who fill occupational statuses of higher prestige.[13] Research also indicates a direct relationship between incidence of church membership and economic status or prestige.[14] Church attendance is highest among the middle class. One careful and detailed research project found that religious interest was related to social mobility—upwardly mobile people were more interested, downwardly mobile people less interested.[15] Certainly the denomination to which one belongs is a salient factor of his social status. (See Table 17-3.)

---

[12]For a summary of this literature, see Will Herberg, Protestant—Catholic—Jew: An Essay in American Religious Sociology (Garden City, New York: Doubleday & Co., Inc., 1956).
[13]Russell R. Dynes, "Church-Sect Typology and Socio-Economic Status," American Sociological Review, 1955, 20: 555-560. For a critique of the church-sect typology, see Peter L. Berger, "Sectarianism and Religious Sociation," The American Journal of Sociology, 1958, 54: 41-44.
[14]See Hadley Cantril, "Education and Economic Composition of Religious Groups: An Analysis of Poll Data," American Journal of Sociology, 1943, 48: 574-579; Louis Bultena, "Church Membership and Church Attendance in Madison, Wisconsin," American Sociological Review, 1949, 14: 384-389; August B. Hollingshead, Elmtown's Youth (New York: John Wiley & Sons, Inc., 1949), pp. 243-266.
[15]Gerhard E. Lenski, "Social Correlates of Religious Interest," American Sociological Review, 1953, 18: 533-544. Lenski also found an association between degree of religious interest and amount of income, but did not find interest significantly related to occupational status or educational level attained.

RELIGIOUS CONFLICT

Like all social institutions, religion is both a source of social integration and a source of social division within society. Indeed, James S. Coleman has argued that cleavage and conflict are inherent in the existence of religious groups, and there is much evidence to support his thesis.[16] Religious bodies are usually no different from others in their jealous regard for power and control. Frequently, when a church group is threatened, it responds, as do other groups, by avoidance, escape, or some kind of aggressive counteraction. How violent religious conflict may become is witnessed in Western history by the Crusades of the Middle Ages against the infidel, by the bloody and violent Thirty Years' War between Catholic and Protestant monarchs following the publication of Martin Luther's famous *Theses* in 1517, and by the cruelty of sectarian strife in the British Isles during the seventeenth century. More recently the bitter conflicts between Moslems and Hindus in India, between Arabs and Jews in the Near East, and between Catholics and Protestants in Northern Ireland show that religion, when linked with economic and political aims and institutions, may be a powerful element in open conflict.

Given the numerous religious subcultures in the United States, the norms governing behavior in the religious realm are anything but universal. Sets of values have clashed in several areas, including the role of religion in socialization, the denominational differences in dogma, and the competition of religion and science as structures meeting the necessary function of providing a sense of purpose.

Separation of Church and State

Historically, Christianity has frequently been involved in a conflict between church and state. The controversy over the claims of the Roman Catholic Church to temporal power—that is, political control—went on all through the Middle Ages. Protestantism arose, in part, out of this struggle. Today the separation of church and state is a basic tenet of all democratic countries. Yet difficulties arise from time to time regarding the place of the church in education. Many believe that all basic education in a democratic country should take the form of public schooling. But various churches have long contended that the home and the church are the essential and proper agencies of education. Efforts to close parochial schools by legislation have met with failure. For example, an Oregon law

---

[16]James S. Coleman, "Social Cleavage and Religious Conflict," *Journal of Social Issues*, XII (1956), 44–56.

of 1922 provided that after 1926 all parents must send their children to public schools. Yet the Supreme Court held as follows:

> As often heretofore pointed out, rights guaranteed by the Constitution may not be abridged by legislation which has no reasonable relation to some purpose within the competency of the state. The fundamental theory of liberty upon which all governments in this Union repose excludes any general power of the state to standardize its children by forcing them to accept instruction from public teachers only. The child is not the mere creature of the state; those who nurture him and direct his destiny have the right, coupled with the high duty, to recognize and prepare him for additional obligations.[17]

It is clear that education continues to be regarded in this country as a family and religious prerogative, in spite of the theory of public schooling for all. But the matter has not rested there. Since the Oregon case was settled, many problems regarding religion and education have arisen.

One of these has to do with provision for religious instruction. The system of "released time," as it is called, is an arrangement under which time is allowed from the regular school hours for children to attend classes in religion taught by people from their respective denominations. In most states such instruction is not permitted in public-school buildings but must be elsewhere, in places determined by the churches concerned. Children are required either to attend or do their regular schoolwork in this period. In Illinois such instruction was permitted, for a time, in the school building. But in a test case, the Illinois enabling law was declared unconstitutional by an 8 to 1 decision of the United States Supreme Court.[18] The decision held that the Illinois law contravened the First Amendment to the Constitution, which had "erected a wall between church and state," as Justice Hugo Black put it in the majority opinion.

Aside from the legal aspects, there has been considerable controversy over the value of the released time plan of religious instruction. While there is much support for it from some leaders of all

---

[17]See *Society of the Sisters of the Holy Names of Jesus and Mary* v. *Pierce, Governor of Oregon. 296 Federal Reporter 929.* Case affirmed in *268 US Reporter 510.*

[18]See *Illinois ex rel. McCollum* v. *Board of Education, School District No. 71, Champaign County, Illinois, et al.* Appeal from the Supreme Court of Illinois No. 90, argued December 8, 1947; decided March 8, 1948, *333 US Official Reporter No. 2,* pp. 203–256. For discussions of this problem, including reviews of similar cases, see Donald McDonald, ed., *Religion and Freedom* (New York: The Fund for the Republic, 1958, pamphlet); William Lee Miller *et al., Religion and the Free Society* (New York: The Fund for the Republic, 1958, pamphlet); and Robert Gordis *et al., Religion and the Schools* (New York: The Fund for the Republic, 1959, pamphlet).

three major faiths, there is growing criticism from many educators who believe that such a program actually stimulates a sense of religious difference among children and thereby fosters prejudice.

More recently, in 1964, a case protesting the saying of prayers in public schools was brought before the Supreme Court and won. The decision is significant not only in that it upholds the fundamental separation of church and state, but in that it recognizes the rights of nonbelievers in American society: most prayers in the public schools had been short and nonsectarian, and only nonbelievers and those opposed on philosophical grounds had objected in the first place.

Yet the courts have approved legislation which provides for free textbooks and free bus transportation for children who attend parochial schools. Moreover, there is growing pressure from some Catholic leaders for federal and other tax aid for parochial schools, on the grounds that such schools deserve public aid, since they provide education for a large number of young people. To counteract this trend, many Protestant groups take a firm stand against any plan to permit the use of public funds for parochial schools.

The whole conflict reveals many of the basic difficulties in a highly diverse culture. The plea for cultural diversity must always face the counterargument that, to survive, a culture system must also have a large degree of uniformity and agreement within its institutional systems.

Denominations and Dogma

While conflict has marked the relations between many religious bodies, cooperation is by no means lacking. In American Protestantism there has been a trend toward consolidation and cooperation. Indeed, there has been considerable support for consolidation for some time. For instance, more than 40 per cent of those asked in a 1948 poll of Protestant churchgoers favored a combination of all Protestants in the United States into one church. Denominations have frequently federated for various purposes and for longer and shorter periods of time. For example, the National Council of Churches of Christ, established in 1950, consists of 29 Protestant and certain Eastern Orthodox denominations. This organization represents about three-fifths of all Protestant church members. It has four divisions: Christian Education, Christian Life and Works, Home Missions, and Foreign Missions.[19]

Another instance of cooperation is the "community church" that

[19]*The World Almanac, 1961* (New York: New York World-Telegram and Sun, 1961), p. 700. See also Purnell H. Benson, *Religion in Contemporary Culture* (New York: Harper & Brothers, 1960), pp. 656–667.

emerges with the union of separate Protestant groups. Such action sometimes takes place, of course, when the separate denominations become too weak to keep going by themselves. But sometimes the union is born of a strong public view that a community-wide church will serve the religious needs of people more effectively than separate denominations. The community church often stimulates public forums, offers recreational facilities to the young people of the entire city, and undertakes preventive programs in health and delinquency. This is a far cry from the church which functioned only as the dispenser of dogma, moral advice, and unregulated charity.

Cooperation across the traditional barriers between Catholic and Protestant or between Christian and Jew has been much less frequent. Recent decades have seen a tendency toward certain joint action among these churches. The organization of local ministerial associations is a step in this direction. The National Conference of Christians and Jews, founded in 1928, has tried to develop tolerance and cooperation. In the late 1930s the Methodist Episcopal Church, the Methodist Episcopal Church South, and the Methodist Protestant Church merged after a long split over slavery. One of the largest mergers of the 1940s occurred between the Evangelical Church and the United Brethren, resulting in the Evangelical United Brethren. During the 1950s another religious merger resulted in the United Presbyterian Church of North America. In the 1950s and the early 1960s there were a number of mergers within various Lutheran bodies culminating in 1962 with the formation of the Lutheran Church of America. Since the papacy of John XXIII there has also been a significant diminution of Catholic-Protestant church conflicts, and delegate-observers from numerous Protestant organizations attended the first Ecumenical Council in 100 years in Vatican City. Nonetheless, most such efforts have been limited by strong interfaith rivalry.

The distinctive features of the major religions reflect the larger cultures of which they are a part. Yet, as some of the barriers of prejudice and isolation have disappeared, certain tendencies toward worldwide cooperation have arisen. Such gatherings as world religious conferences, in which representatives of all the major religions have participated, are evidence of a growing awareness of common problems in religion in spite of differences of creed. But such efforts must of necessity remain largely verbal so long as political conflict continues on the international scene.

Religion and Science

There is still a widespread belief that religion and science are in fundamental conflict. Many feel that, as science is more and more applied to solving modern problems—both technological and social —there is less need for religion. When people talk about religion and science being in conflict, they usually refer to the fact that church officials have at various times opposed the findings of scientists which the church officials regard as contravening the long-established creed or dogma of their respective organizations. In this sense history is indeed full of conflicts between theology and scientific findings. For example, when Galileo was taken before the Court of Inquisition for his scientific work, he was indicted

> ... for holding as true the false doctrine taught by many—namely, that the sun is immovable in the center of the world and that the earth moves and also with a diurnal motion;... following the hypothesis of Copernicus, you include several propositions contrary to the true sense and authority of the Holy Scripture.... The proposition that the sun is the center of the world and immovable from its place is absurd philosophically, false and formally heretical because it is expressly contrary to the Holy Scriptures....

Galileo recanted and renounced his alleged heresy. But Bruno, who refused to renounce Copernican cosmology, was burned at the stake in Rome, and as late as 1819 the books of Galileo, Copernicus, and Kepler were on the Catholic *Index* of forbidden books. However, neither Martin Luther, whose break with Catholicism started the Protestant Reformation, nor the Orthodox Jews of the time were any more sympathetic toward the discoveries of science.

Because science depends on maximum freedom of thought and because its findings run counter to many church dogmas, perhaps it was inevitable that conflict should arise. The Copernican system, which replaced the older view of the cosmos, reduced the earth to a mere speck in the total universe and robbed man of much of his former importance in his own eyes. Later, in the nineteenth century, the Darwinian theory of evolution placed human beings in the animal kingdom. And during the past seventy-five years, psychology and the social sciences have shown that the mental life and behavior of humans can be studied and understood in large part through the method of science.

Religion and science do not always conflict, however. For instance, Merton has argued that the Puritan religion of seventeenth-century England was one important element in the rise and spread of modern science. According to Merton, "the deep-rooted religious *interests* of the day demanded in their forceful implications the systematic, rational, and empirical study of Nature for the glorification of God in His works and for the control of the corrupt world."[20] On a more personal level, consider the following observation of Albert Einstein.

> Whoever has undergone the intense experience of successful advances in this domain of scientific thought is moved by profound reverence for the rationality made manifest in existence. By way of the understanding, he achieves a far-reaching emancipation from the shackles of personal hope and desires, and thereby attains that humble attitude of mind toward the grandeur of reason incarnate in existence, which, in its profoundest depths is inaccessible to man. This attitude, however, appears to me to be religion in the highest sense of the word.[21]

There is no doubt that education and practical technology have altered many views about God, sin, immortality, and other features of traditional theology. In 1948 a public opinion poll made in ten countries reported the answers to a question about personal belief in God. "Yes" answers ranged from 96 per cent in Brazil and 94 per cent in the United States to 66 per cent in France. That skepticism is related to various political and other views is apparent. For example, in France the Communist part of the sample reported nearly two-thirds "No" answers.[22]

It is somewhat difficult to evaluate such findings, since people may be loath to tell exactly what they believe in matters they consider personal. Nevertheless, there are other evidences of loss of belief. James H. Leuba's studies show that between 1914 and 1933 there was a decline in the percentage of scientists who declared a belief in God and immortality. Furthermore, scientists who dealt with the inorganic world reported a higher percentage of believers than did biologists, psychologists, and sociologists. The higher the eminence in science, the lower the proportion who reported such beliefs. In a companion study of student opinions, it was found that the proportion of believers decreased sharply in the move from college freshman to college senior.[23] While later studies have shown that students still felt the need for some kind of belief, it was also clear that their views on specific doctrines were hazy and often nonexistent.[24] One relatively recent national survey of college students reported that although eighty per cent of the students

---

[20]Robert K. Merton, *Social Theory and Social Structure*, rev. ed. (Glencoe, Ililnois: The Free Press, 1957), pp. 574–575.
[21]Albert Einstein, "Science and Religion," *Science Newsletter* (September 21, 1940), p. 182.
[22]See *Public Opinion Quarterly*, 1948, 12: 173–174.
[23]For a convenient summary of this work, see James H. Leuba, "Religious Beliefs of American Scientists," *Harper's Magazine*, 1934, 169: 291–300.
[24]See Paul C. Glick and Kimball Young, "Justification for Religious Attitudes and Habits," *Journal of Social Psychology*, 1943, 17: 45–68, and Gordon W. Allport, James M. Gillespie, and Jacqueline Young, "The Religion of the Postwar College Student," *Journal of Psychology*, 1948, 25: 3–33.

ILLUSTRATIVE DATA 17-3   THE ROLE OF RELIGION IN SOCIETY

Two extreme positions emerge in the debate over the role of religion in society. The first is represented by the volatile combination of Karl Marx and Sigmund Freud. Both argued—for different reasons—that religion is an illusion that distracts its adherents from their real selves and situations. For Marx, it was an "opiate" that converted economic oppression into a "false consciousness" of well-being. For Freud, it was a sexual sublimation that merely tightened constraints on the natural impulses.

The contrasting second position is more firmly sociological. Although neither Emile Durkheim nor Max Weber were religious themselves, each described religion's importance to society. For Durkheim, religion supported basic values; indeed, it was society itself that was being worshipped. For Weber, religion gave the stamp of legitimacy which an activity required for full development. If religion was a "moon for the misbegotten" in the eyes of Marx and Freud, it could be a source of light for society as a whole in the judgment of Durkheim and Weber.

Now one rapprochement for this divergence inheres in the classic church-sect distinction. The distinction suggests that Western societies at least confirm both views. On the one hand, the church caters to those who are firmly integrated into society by providing justifications for secular values and pursuits. On the other hand, the sect serves the disenfranchised by providing an escape to a community that is set apart from the secular world. If the church is evidence for Durkheim and Weber, the sect is a buttress for Marx and Freud.

Source: N.J. Demerath III, *Social Class in American Protestantism* (Chicago: Rand McNally and Company, 1965), p. 178. Reprinted by permission.

expressed a felt "need for religious faith," nearly half indicated that religion to them did not necessarily include a belief in God. Only 47 per cent felt that "acceptance of the Deity is a highly important component of a religious or ethical system."[25]

Belief as a Universal Function

The mystic identification with power outside oneself may offset or balance the disappointments, heartaches, and pain of daily living, in which half-measures, compromises, and self-denials are common. It is easy for the critic of religion to point out that this sort of thing is "an escape from reality," a mass neurosis or, as Freud argued, a mere "illusion."[26] But cultural reality is not something material or

---

[25]Rose K. Goldsen, *et al., What College Students Think* (New York: Van Nostrand Company, 1960), p. 153.

[26]See Sigmund Freud, *The Future of an Illusion,* trans. W. D. Robson-Scott (New York: Liveright Publishing Corp., 1928); and *Civilization and Its Discontents,* trans. J. Riviere (New York: Random House, 1930).

made up of biological reactions to food, drink, and sexual objects. It is a matter of socially learned beliefs, attitudes, ideas, meanings. It exists in the minds of men. One cannot, therefore, blandly dismiss religious experience as an unfortunate illusion without at the same time raising the question as to whether art, philosophy, and most of the other fundamentals of social organization and family life are not illusions also. Faithfulness to a mate, loyalty to a country, or belief in a bank note can be shown by this logic to be illusions too.

One need not affiliate oneself with a religious organization in order to survive. But everywhere people believe in something which imbues them with a sense of purpose, be it science, religion, or philosophy. An explanation of reality is a part of every culture, and the student of society must take that explanation into account if he or she is to understand social structure.

Secularization

Like all social institutions religion has undergone important changes in the great transition from communal to associational forms of social organization. Increasingly, people question the relevance of religion in the modern world and conclude that religion is no longer a central institution in the secular societies of the twentieth century. Religion has become highly secularized in America; the heavy church participation in such secular matters as civil rights, education, welfare, recreation, drug rehabilitation, and other social issues of the day and the de-emphasis of purely sectarian matters underscore this fact. For many Americans religion has become separated from a large area of their life. But reported church membership in the United States has been increasing for a century and it is now higher than it has been at any time since at least 1850.[27] It is difficult to know how to evaluate these statistics because, as Herberg pointed out, "church membership does not mean the same today as it meant in the eighteenth or early nineteenth century, when something of the older sense of personal conversion and commitment still remained."[28] Nevertheless, Herberg goes on to report that 95 per cent of all Americans identify themselves as a member of some religious group.

Robin Williams is probably correct in his estimation that "neither mass religiosity nor complete secularism appear to be permanent

---

[27]W. Seward Salisbury, *Religion in American Culture* (Homewood, Ill.: The Dorsey Press, 1964), p. 84.
[28]Will Herberg, *Protestant, Catholic, Jew* (Garden City, New York: Doubleday and Company, Inc.), pp. 46–49.

Table 17-4   Reported Church Membership in the United States

Year	Per Cent of the Adult Population
1850	16
1900	36
1920	43
1930	47
1940	49
1950	57
1961	63
1966	64

historical possibilities."[29] It also seems clear that religious activity in the United States today is manifestly secular. Religion in the secular societies of the mid-twentieth century is no longer a faith that permeates every aspect of life. But people who expect the secularization of religious life to continue unabated might well consider Kingsley Davis' answer to the question of how far this secularization can go.

> The answer, I think, is that it can go a long way but that there is ultimately a limit. If the population becomes too matter-of-fact in its attitudes, too calculating in its behavior, too sophisticated in its values, it is likely not to stick together sufficiently to maintain order and protection. The resulting social disorder may give rise to new religious sects that preach a return to the pristine values and promise salvation if the people will listen to the message of the supernatural. The rise of Christianity in Rome was at the start just such an emergence of an obscure sect preaching its doctrine to a sophisticated civilization. Within a remarkably short time it was the state religion of the Empire.[30]

INTERPRETIVE SUMMARY

Throughout history, religions have served the functions of explaining the unknown and making it less terrifying, of defining man's place in the universe and giving him a sense of purpose. Religions have provided people with standards of morality and, conversely, have frequently lent sanctions for already existing political, economic, and other mores of a society. Finally, in order to preserve their more general functions, religious organizations have increasingly entered the areas of recreation and social work.

Religions differ in theology. Many religions have tried to answer such

[29]Robin Williams, *American Society* (New York: Random House, 1960), p. 383.
[30]Kingsley Davis, *Human Society* (New York: The Macmillan Company, 1949), p. 543.

questions as: Is there one god, or more than one? If so, is God good or bad, carnate or incarnate, etc.? Is there an afterlife? What is it like? Upon what is admission based? To what extent should I work now to gain entrance?

In folk societies, worship of intangible divinities tends to go along with belief in animism and magic. As might be expected, formal religious structures do not exist, although religion itself may pervade all areas of life. Religious leaders may be mystics or priests; in more complex societies, the former are generally outside the pale of the established churches, which tend to be conservative. All religions, folk and urban, rely on ceremonies, with their attendant symbols, sacred objects, special locales or buildings, for perpetuation.

Historically, religious conflict is more common than cooperation; in fact, the history of religion involves a series of bitter conflicts within established organizations, gradual splits, and emergence of sects into new denominations. More recently there has been a trend toward consolidation of similar groups and there has even been limited cooperation among dissimilar national and international organizations for specific purposes.

In the United States, the influence of religion on human behavior is especially difficult to assess, since the "Protestant ethic" is by now firmly a part of the American ethos. Figures concerning the number of individuals participating in each church are also inexact, since individuals are reluctant to give "private" information about their religious habits, and since churches differ on the question of what constitutes membership. However, available statistics indicate that the United States has hundreds of denominations, that Christianity is the largest single category, and that middle-class individuals and upwardly mobile individuals tend to be the most avid participants. As for the social location of churches, Protestants have largely discarded the "community church" of earlier times in favor of denominational churches, although recently there has been a slight reversal. Catholics have retained the community church, as well as church-run community schools. The Supreme Court has banned prayer in public schools and the use of public-school facilities for sectarian religious training, but the right of private groups to build private schools which include religious training has been considered basic, and heated and sometimes bitter arguments have arisen concerning financial responsibility of the federal and state governments for these parochial schools.

SUGGESTIONS FOR FURTHER READING

Berger, Peter L. *A Rumor of Angels: Modern Society and the Rediscovery of the Supernatural.* Garden City, N. Y.: Doubleday and Company, Inc., 1969. Berger argues that people can adequately grasp the significance of many of their experiences only through a belief in the supernatural. This is a persuasive argument of the significance of religion, even in this secular age.

Demerath N. J., III. *Social Class in American Protestantism.* Chicago: Rand McNally and Company, 1965. This is a first-rate analysis of the web of social class and religious involvement which makes critical use of the church sect typology.

Glock, Charles Y., and Stark, Rodney. *Christian Beliefs and Anti-Semitism.* New York: Harper and Row, 1966. This is a sample survey linking Christian Sunday School teachings to the rhetoric of anti-Semitism.

Lenski, Gerhard. *The Religious Factor.* Garden City, N. Y.: Doubleday and Company, Inc., 1961. This is the report of an empirical study regarding differences in political and economic values and practices among white Protestants, Negro Protestants, Catholics, and Jews.

Lofland, John. *Doomsday Cult: A Study of Conversion, Proselytization, and Maintenance of Faith.* Englewood Cliffs, N. J.: Prentice-Hall, Inc., 1966. This research study interprets conversion as a social and situational rather than a psychological process.

O'Dea, Thomas F. *The Sociology of Religion.* Englewood Cliffs, N. J.: Prentice-Hall, Inc., 1966. The association between religion and other elements of social structure as well as the processes of institutionalization and conflict are explored.

Pope, Liston. *Millhands and Preachers: A Study of Gastona.* New Haven, Conn.: Yale University Press, 1942. A fine study of religion in a southern mill town, this volume contributes to an explanation of relationship of religious sects and economics.

Russell, Bertrand. *Religion and Science.* New York: Oxford University Press, 1935. The author discusses, among other topics, the grounds for the conflict of religion and science and many of the phenomena, such as the Copernican revolution, biological evolution, modern psychology, and the doctrine of the soul that have been connected with this conflict. There is a stimulating chapter on science and ethics.

Schneider, Louis, and Dornbusch, Sanford M. *Popular Religion: Inspirational Books in America.* Chicago: University of Chicago Press, 1958. This is a sociological analysis of 46 books characterized as "inspirational religious literature," among them the works of Bruce Barton, Russell H. Conway, Harry E. Fosdick, Emmet Fox, E. Stanley Jones, Norman Vincent Peale, Fulton J. Sheen, and Ralph Waldo Trine.

Wach, Joachim. *Types of Religious Experience, Christian and Non-Christian.* Chicago: University of Chicago Press, 1951. This is a collection of the author's previously published papers written with appreciative insight.

Weber, Max. *The Protestant Ethic and the Spirit of Capitalism.* Translated by Talcott Parsons. New York: Scribners', 1930. Weber's most famous work, this book pursues the thesis that the widespread acceptance of Protestant values encouraged and facilitated the growth of (European) capitalism.

Yinger, J. Milton. *Religion, Society, and the Individual: An Introduction to the Sociology of Religion.* New York: The Macmillan Company, 1957. The first half of this book discusses various sociological facets of religion. The second half consists of a wide selection of material from various publications on religion.

4/Social Change and Social Problems

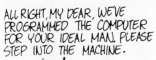

18
Social and Cultural Change

While social life contains many elements of permanency and stability, it is also characterized by aspects of social change. Every society is characterized by an interplay of those forces that make for cultural stability and those that make for change. Culture is never wholly static. Yet, for purposes of indicating broad differences, we say a culture is *stable* when a condition of equilibrium of patterns and processes is its basic feature. In contrast, a culture marked by rather extensive alteration of its patterns and resulting disequilibrium is said to be *dynamic*. Many nonliterate peoples, especially those living under conditions of isolation, have remained relatively unchanged for long periods of time. Such were the Australian aborigines before the arrival of the white people. Certain relatively complex cultures continued a long time without any striking changes. This was the situation in Egypt during long periods of its ancient history. Yet it would be a mistake to assume that the culture of any society, large or small, is ever completely stable and static.

Two major ways in which cultures are changed are diffusion— that is, borrowing traits or patterns from other cultures—and the invention or discovery of new cultural elements within the society.

In either case, social change will be the result: the addition of traits or patterns to the culture will produce modifications in the social structure.

DISCOVERY AND INVENTION

It is not always easy to draw a distinction between discovery and invention. The former represents perception of relationships between elements not previously recognized or understood. The relationship may have been deliberately sought or it may have been found accidentally. On the other hand, invention is a combination of known elements or devices into some new form. In a sense, discovery is fundamental to invention, since people must have certain knowledge and skill regarding things, people, and situations before one can put knowledge and skill to work to produce something novel. Yet the discovery of new facts or relations may depend on the invention of new methods of thinking or acting. For our purpose, the term *invention* will serve both for the discovery of some fact or principle and for the creation of a new device or pattern.

Since technology has made a striking impression on daily life in our time, people sometimes get the notion that invention involves only mechanical devices. But inventions occur in both material and nonmaterial phases of culture. The automobile and the telephone seem—and are—highly significant inventions. But so, too, are the Australian ballot, intelligence testing, and chainstore merchandising.

Basic Features of Invention

Inventions may be classified into two sorts: empirical and planned. Until the rise of modern science, most inventions were of the former type. Empirical invention generally grows out of trial-and-error attempts to improve some device or institution already at hand, or out of accidental discovery of a technique. Science has now provided us with the means of planning or directing and even predicting many of our inventions.

We may well ask what stimulates inventiveness. The old saying that "necessity is the mother of invention" requires qualification. Recurrent need may or may not induce inventiveness. The long-continued use of old and ineffective ways of doing things is ample evidence that sheer necessity does not always give birth to efficient invention. The truth is that very often, in the words of Thorstein Veblen, "Invention is the mother of necessity." That is to say, once an invention has become accepted as a new element in a culture, it may set up wants and motives not previously present in the society. The whole expansion of human needs under conditions of modern industry and merchandising is evidence enough of this fact.

It is the cultural and social situation that makes invention possible. The existence of sufficient leisure for calm and deliberate examination of various possibilities is important. An element of curiosity must be present. Without doubt, "just monkeying around" with mechanical devices or ideas has brought about valuable new combinations. In trial-and-error invention, as in all hit-or-miss learning, accidental combinations are often significant. False combinations may even suggest correct solutions later. Musing or daydreaming is also important. Getting "hunches" or making guesses is as necessary, especially in the early phases, as actual manipulation of physical objects or of social situations.

Yet neither pressing necessity nor mental reverie alone, nor the two together, fully account for invention. Such advances depend on two major factors: culture and the individual. These are closely interrelated, but for purposes of discussion we shall deal with (1) the general cultural base; (2) the culture's values and attitudes toward invention—that is, the interest or run of attention; and (3) the place of special and high intellectual abilities.

The Cultural Base

With reference to the effect on culture and society, inventions may be classed as primary or basic, and as secondary—that is, derived, or "improving," as Ralph Linton calls them.[1] Primary inventions are illustrated by such things as the discovery of the use of fire, the discovery of ultraviolet rays, and the invention of the phonetic alphabet; the wheel; the means of smelting iron ore; and the zero, negative numbers, and calculus. Secondary inventions are those which have to do with improving or modifying other inventions, such as air conditioning or the introduction of the automatic transmission in the automobile.

An invention, if it is to survive, must have relevance to the existing culture. There is, in fact, a selective process going on at all times with reference to inventions in any society. If there is strong intellectual or emotional resistance to change, an invention may be dropped before being tried out. If, on the other hand, a society is receptive, the invention may effect profound changes. So too, the use of an invention in the total culture is important.

---

[1]Ralph Linton, *The Study of Man* (New York: Appleton-Century-Crofts, Inc., 1936), pp. 316–317.

The Greeks, for example, invented a steam engine but limited its use to religious rituals. Their culture was not ready for its application to modes of transportation or machine production.

Both basic and improving inventions depend on the state of knowledge and skill in a given society. The effect of the lack of scientific knowledge and techniques is illustrated in the work of Leonardo da Vinci. Certainly he was intellectually capable of inventing a successful flying machine—in fact, he did constuct some interesting models of airplanes. But they were not workable, because he lacked the necessary tools of modern mathematics and mechanics. As a painter, however, Da Vinci was one of the greatest masters of all time, and his contributions to the study of human anatomy and to military techniques were outstanding. For these attainments there was an adequate cultural foundation.

Not only do potential inventors sometimes lack the mechanical principles or methods, but the essential materials may not be at hand. The lack of essential materials usually reflects cultural retardation in some related skill or knowledge. Thus hard steel could not be produced until certain alloys were developed.

In our society, extensions of inventions depend on the ever-larger cultural base from which they emerge, on cultural acceptance of inventions in general, and on the stimulation of capitalistic enterprise which seeks to apply inventions in order to make greater profits. Capitalism has been a stimulant to both science and technology. In all societies inventions have resulted from efforts to improve public welfare. The Soviet successes in rocketry and space technology are dramatic examples of great strides in science and engineering under a noncapitalistic system.

Planned Invention and Science

Until the rise of modern science, most inventions were empirical. Science now provides us with a means of directing and even predicting many inventions. Of course, one discovery or invention often has to wait for another. The photoelectric cell, for example, long known to physics, was not perfected for practical use until the invention of a vacuum-tube amplifier.

The planning of inventions for the larger needs of society has only begun. An early example was the designing and testing of the Liberty motor during World War I. Under a governmental directive, a number of engineers and other experts cooperated to develop a more satisfactory airplane engine. The development of the submarine detector during the same war was another case of necessity followed by planned and cooperative research. During World War II there was much more of this sort of thing. The outstanding example was the Manhattan Project, out of which came the atomic bomb.

Such planned invention is not the product of wartime needs only. In agriculture, too, there are a considerable number of planned inventions. One of the most striking is the development of hybrid corn, which has made possible an increase in yield of nearly 30 per cent. This new corn was developed by controlling the process of pollination so as to secure vigor, uniformity, and other desired characteristics. So far, most of our planned inventions have had to do with mechanical and biological problems.

Values and Run of Attention

Along with the necessary cultural base in knowledge and skill, the social values regarding invention are important. From our standpoint, nonliterate people had a real need for public health measures to prevent disease, reduce the death rate, and improve their physical well-being. That they did not obtain these measures was partly because they lacked information and techniques but partly also because their ideas and values regarding birth, death, and disease were vastly different from our own. What a culture demands and what it values will help direct its inventors. Among the Crow Indians, for example, there was considerable stress on individual visionary experience, which encouraged the introduction of a new religious cult. In Samoa there is some allowance for innovation in ritual and decorative arts, yet "in the decorative arts, the freedom given to the individuals is rendered nugatory by the absence of cultural recognition of the innovator and by the strong prejudice against active imitation so the gifted individual receives but passing praise for his work."[2]

The Samoan attitude grows out of the general cultural patterning which stresses individual conformity to tradition and cooperative relations. Americans, in contrast, put much emphasis on interpersonal competition for attainment, especially in mechanical invention and business enterprise. However, there is no reward of either money or honor for those who suggest sharply different institutional norms.

It is evident, then, that what W. I. Thomas calls "the run of attention" in a society has much to do with the particular direction that inventions will take. The entire matrix of technology and money-making sets the framework within which potential innovators growing up in American society will operate. Were we to

[2]Margaret Mead, "The Role of the Individual in Samoan Culture," *Journal of the Royal Anthropological Institute of Great Britain and Ireland*, 1928, 58: 481–495.

fix our present material culture at about its present level and turn our inventive attention elsewhere, we might experience greater and more numerous changes in patterns of political, religious, artistic, or recreational activities.

Intellectual Ability and Inventiveness

To recognize that the particular run of attention will be determined by culture does not deny the importance of persons of superior mental endowment in producing new inventions. One may well ask what place special ability or so-called inventive genius has in invention. It is very easy to assume that inventions are the result of the innate ability of a few chosen persons. There is no doubt that, given the proper cultural encouragement, intellectually gifted persons become inventors. Yet who these people are and what they do with their capacity depends on the society. It is hardly conceivable that the genius of the jungle would become a great physician, though he might well become a military leader or the inventor of a new religious ritual. Due to the lack of social opportunities, it is no surprise that there are proportionately fewer women inventors in twentieth century America than there are male inventors. Men, of course, are not proportionately more intelligent than women.

The relation of culture to individual ability raises the question of the "great-man theory" of history—that is, does history make great men or do great men make history? Confining ourselves only to the matter of invention, the particular direction of inventions and their nature are determined by culture. Often we forget the slow accumulation of basic knowledge by less well-known men who made possible the more spectacular work which we hear about. The inventions of Thomas A. Edison in electricity, for instance, would have been impossible without hundreds of researches in the century before him.

Clearly, inventions and discoveries do not depend on one particular exceptional person but on the nature of the culture out of which the new elements in the invention arise. Advances in invention depend so much on minor accretions to the total body of knowledge, it is indeed doubtful that any one particular inventor is essential at a given time. "Great men" alone do not make inventions. As Ralph Linton once wrote:

> Unpleasant as the realization may be to egotists, very few individuals can be considered as more than incidents in the life histories of the societies to which they belong. Our species long ago reached the point

where organized groups rather than their individual members became
the functional units in its struggle for survival.[3]

DIFFUSION

Social and cultural change occurs not only by invention or discovery but also by diffusion. *Diffusion* is the borrowing and adopting of cultural traits or patterns from other social units. Ordinarily, diffusion is thought of as a movement of traits through *space*. In this sense it is not to be confused with *transmission* of culture, which has to do with passing traits and patterns through *time*— that is, from generation to generation. Thus, formal education is not diffusion but transmission.

The Spread of Culture

The elements of culture may diffuse between nations and regions, from class to class, from community to community, and between any other association of people. For example, Christianity and, later, industrialism spread from Europe and the United States to Japan and China. Much of the American system of education was borrowed from nineteenth-century Germany. As a rule, social fashions spread from the upper to the working classes. Urban ways are diffused to rural localities.

Diffusion can be either direct or indirect. Direct diffusion occurs when groups have physical contact. Indirect diffusion is the spread of traits without group contact. The first is illustrated by migration and colonization, by contact through war and trade, and by the work of religious missionaries. The second is witnessed in the spread of printed materials, by radio and television, and by the infiltration of ideas and goods in commerce carried on without direct personal contact. Indirect diffusion accompanies the development of secondary-group organization.

The spread of culture is not always just from Western societies to nonliterate societies. It is often reciprocal. While Western people have diffused their culture, especially the material phases, over most of the earth, nonliterate peoples have contributed heavily to literate societies. The contribution of this kind most obvious to Americans is, of course, the large number of cultural items received from native Indians. These include, among many others, maize or Indian corn and many methods of its cultivation, the potato, beans,

[3]Ralph Linton, *The Cultural Background of Personality* (New York: Appleton, 1945), p. 12.

ILLUSTRATIVE DATA 18-1   TEACHING IN THE 1870s

The following rules for teachers were posted in 1872 by a principal in the city of New York.

1. *Teachers each day will fill lamps, clean chimneys and trim wicks.*
2. *Each teacher will bring a bucket of water and a scuttle of coal for the day's session.*
3. *Make your pens carefully. You may whittle nibs to the individual taste of the pupil.*
4. *Men teachers may take one evening each week for courting purposes or two evenings each week if they attend church regularly.*
5. *After ten hours in school, the teacher should spend the remaining time reading the Bible or other good books.*
6. *Women teachers who marry or engage in unseemly conduct will be dismissed.*
7. *Every teacher should lay aside from each payday a goodly sum of his earnings for his benefit during his declining years so that he will not become a burden on society.*
8. *Any teacher who smokes, uses liquor in any form, frequents pool or public, or gets shaved in a barber shop will give good reason to suspect his worth, intentions, integrity, and honesty.*
9. *The teacher who performs his labor faithfully and without fault for five years will be given an increase of twenty-five cents per week in his pay, providing the Board of Education approves.*

---

tomatoes, and tobacco. The Indians also gave us the game of lacrosse, and taught colonists new methods of stalking game and the enemy in dense woods.

In turn, the white man brought the Indian the horse and saddle and firearms. These items produced great changes in the culture of the tribes on the Great Plains, giving them mobility, adding to their efficiency in game hunting, and stimulating their interest in warfare. On the other hand, these very alterations probably retarded any incipient tendencies toward more settled community life and agriculture. The whites also brought Christianity to the Indians but, as elsewhere, it tended in many instances to be fused with the native religion, an indication that the items which are diffused sooner or later merge with the indigenous culture patterns if they do not replace them.

War and conquest have been important factors in diffusion. The Roman legions spread Latin culture around the Mediterranean and beyond. Not only new political systems but also new economic organization and religion have followed in the wake of war.

Diffusion is generally more important than invention in the total building of any culture: of all the items in any given culture, more are borrowed from other peoples than are invented. Very often culture traits which are thought to have arisen from geographical conditions or from crises actually have come from other culture groups. Some anthropologists go so far as to lay down a kind of rule that, other things being equal, it is easier to borrow than to invent. Perhaps because of the inertia of habit and man's lack of originality, it seems more common to look around and find some method already in use than to think up an entirely new device to meet the situation.

Rates of Diffusion

Culture traits and patterns diffuse at different rates. As a rule, material traits spread much more quickly than those which have to do with forms of the family, political organization, art, religion, or recreation. Native peoples, for example, often readily accept firearms, utensils, tools, and cloth, but at the same time retain their own language, kinship organization, religion, and art. The diffusion nearly always involves some modification. Rarely is any trait, unless it is of a material nature, borrowed by people without some modification at their hands.

Diffusion may go on in an informal and almost unconscious way, or it may be the result of a conscious attempt to foist an alien culture on another society. Spreading by trade and migration is often of the first sort; that fostered by organized religion or by a conquering state usually is more deliberate.

There are also certain hindrances to diffusion, such as inadequate transportation and communication, complete isolation, taboos on change, and resistance to foreign ideas and techniques. So too, displacement of one pattern by another prevents the further spread of the pattern displaced. The practice of drinking coffee is not likely to spread rapidly in a country such as China, long addicted to tea.

The factors affecting rate of diffusion may be summarized as follows: (1) availability of transportation and communication, including distance and barriers to travel such as mountains or sea; (2) resistance to culture changes, such as taboo, sense of superiority, and general cultural inertia; (3) prestige of the lending culture and its people; (4) conquest of one people by another; (5) migration, especially when *en masse*, as in the Teutonic invasions of the Roman Empire, in modern immigration, or in enforced moving of large populations from one region to another; (6) the need for some new element to meet a critical situation; and (7) adaptability of the recipients of the new culture, as in the ready adoption of Western industrialism by Japan.

As a matter of fact, the cultural elements operating in diffusion are not unlike those which more or less determine invention. That is, the broad cultural base of prior skill and knowledge must be taken into account. So too, the basic values of potential recipients are important. Persons of high status, scholars, political and industrial leaders, war chiefs, and religious functionaries will usually be in the vanguard of reception. Finally, since nearly all borrowed traits are subject to some modification in their new setting, special ability will play a part in adapting the item to the new situation.

FACTORS INFLUENCING INNOVATIONS

The acceptance of innovations is qualified by the nature and extent of the changes, by the rate at which they are introduced, and by the degree of readiness of groups. We have already indicated that societies differ in their receptiveness to change. In a society oriented to modern technology, new cultural elements that contribute to further technology are more acceptable, on the whole, than radical innovations in institutions that support the moral system of the society. So too, changes of wide scope will tend to induce more reaction than will minor changes. One factor contributing to present-day anxieties is the fact that people cannot readjust themselves fast enough to the large number of innovations to which they are exposed. In personal terms this means that individuals cannot do the "unlearning" necessary to the acquisition of the many new thoughts and patterns of social interaction without becoming confused and distressed in the process.

Cultural Lag

Whether induced by political revolution or by slower methods, changes in one field often induce dislocations in another area of behavior. For example, the last 150 years have seen a tremendous burst of material inventions in western Europe and America which have altered the nature of technological culture the world over. In sharp contrast, corresponding modifications in the nonmaterial culture have been slow, halting, and ineffective. Often new needs arising from rather sudden material changes have not been adequately satisfied. In other words, the previous integration of the major parts of a total culture has been disturbed by these changes.

This differential in the rate of change W. F. Ogburn termed *cultural lag*, which he defined in these words:

> The thesis is that the various parts of modern culture are not changing at the same rate, some parts are changing much more rapidly than

others; and that since there is a correlation and interdependence of parts, a rapid change in one part of our culture requires adjustments through other changes in the various correlated parts. . . . Where one part of culture changes first, through some discovery or invention, and occasions changes in some part of culture dependent upon it, there frequently is a delay in the changes occasioned in the dependent part of the culture.[4]

Many of the contemporary problems of society can be viewed in terms of "cultural lag." There is today a wide range of new patterns of social interaction and new ideas fostered by material alterations which were not anticipated and for which there has been no preparation. This dislocation is largely a result of differentials in rates of change. In fact, *social disorganization* is often characterized as the breakdown of societal order to such an extent that the former social controls are dissipated and social disorder arises.

Few people would deny that advantages have accrued from technological innovations: lessening of the severity of work and hours of labor, increase in leisure, widespread education, mobility and travel, increased "animation" of life, extension of contacts, and a higher standard of living for millions. But it is also true that many dislocations have arisen from the failure of the nonmaterial culture —especially that connected with societal organization—to keep pace with these new material culture patterns. Social mobility has decreased the significance of the neighborhood and community for many people, weakened social controls, and fostered certain types of crime. Changes in industrial production have caused technological unemployment, pollution, and alienation.

The political order, too, is marked by many dislocations: the continuance of outworn political units of voting, the restriction of residence for office-holders, and the persistence of many governmental forms that belonged to the horse-and-buggy era. The lag in laws and administration of justice and in the correction and care of dependents, delinquents, and criminals is compounded by the lack of personnel adequately trained for work in a complex society.

When new patterns are believed to threaten old values and long-accepted ways of doing things, resistance is bound to arise. The receptivity to social change is a function of the existing social situation. In American society change has at times been resisted by business, labor, class and community interests, as well as by government bodies and by scientific experts.

---

[4]*Social Change*, pp. 200–201. By permission.

Changes in Technology

There are hundreds of instances of opposition to technological change in the history of modern industry. The major aim of profits often blinds entrepreneurs to new opportunities to make money and to serve the public more efficiently at the same time. The major consideration is often not "Will it work?" but "Will it pay?" Various factors enter into this inertia. Among others may be mentioned these: the large capital investments in going concerns already providing goods and services; the cost of putting new plants into operation and of selling the product or service; the desire to maintain a dominant position over existing or potential competitors; the somewhat unwieldy ways and means; and the trouble smaller businesses have securing capital to start new enterprises. There are almost endless illustrations of such resistance; we shall select but a few from the history of transportation.

The introduction of the railroad into the United States met with great opposition. In 1812 John Stevens' proposal to introduce railway lines into New York State was flatly turned down by such leaders as DeWitt Clinton, Gouverneur Morris, and Robert R. Livingston. When later—1815 in New Jersey and 1823 in Pennsylvania—Stevens obtained charters, he had difficulty persuading capitalists to invest in his enterprises. The owners of canal barges and of stagecoach lines were particularly bitter about the railroads. The rationalizations of potential investors who objected to the railway were many and ingenious: fear of speed, of setting fire to towns, of disrupting the local life, and so on.

Once the railroads had become fairly well established, moreover, a process of crystallization set in. Owners and investors opposed further advances. Commodore Cornelius Vanderbilt, one of the early railroad magnates, dismissed George Westinghouse and his air-brake invention with the remark that he had no time to waste on fools. Eli J. Janney, the inventor of the car-coupler, had to wait ten years before he could get a foundry to manufacture it for him. Until very recently, the design of the Pullman sleeper was pretty much the same as it was in 1859. Electric locomotives, streamlined trains, and other improvements were adopted very slowly. When the autobus came into use, railway executives and employee unions alike opposed the extension of bus lines because it was felt that their competition would ruin the railroads.

The automobile presents another story of long, slow development. As early as 1769, Nicholas Joseph Cugnot invented a three-wheeled vehicle powered by two steam cylinders. But he got no popular support for his device. Other steam-propelled carriages were tried out with only limited acceptance. When the internal-combustion engine, in combination with other inventions, made the automobile practicable, years went by before the new vehicle was accepted. The automobile was "a rich man's toy" which would never have any practical use. The first American automobile manufacturers got a cool reception from the Wall Street bankers. In 1908, John Pierpont Morgan and his partners refused to buy a block of securities priced at $5,000,000 in a concern that was later consolidated into General Motors.

As with the railroads, improvements in the automobile were opposed by corporate owners, although the lag in accepting what people called "refinements" was less than with many other mechanical devices. Yet the self-starter, six- and eight-cylinder engines, four-wheel brakes, balloon tires, and automatic transmission were slow to be adopted.

The story of the airplane parallels these others. This radical departure in the means of transportation and communication seemed fantastic even to a generation already attuned to rapid technological changes, and all the early airplane manufacturers had difficulty financing their inventions.

Laborers, like investors, have often been slow to accept new technologies. The factory system in England and elsewhere met with much opposition from the workers. The most recurrent opposition to modifications in industrial processes has come from labor unions. In the 1870s, the introduction of labor-saving devices in the boot-and-shoe industry was bitterly opposed by the workers' unions. Silk workers went on strike against the three- or four-loom system. Building and construction workers have fought a steady battle against the introduction of machine processing into their work. Agreements with union painters have dictated the width of brushes so that workers would not be able to cover more surface than the unions considered fair. Union painters have long opposed the introduction of spray guns. The history of trade unionism is filled with such cases.

The introduction of the Diesel locomotive was opposed by the railroad unions because it threatened the fireman's job. Indeed, it was only after the railroads agreed to keep firemen on the engine crews that Diesels were put into wide use.

Political Resistance

Political factors have also played a part in retarding industrial advancement. Public officials have felt pressures of two sorts: from the people in general, and from such vested interests as those of business or labor. Public opposition to the railroad as dangerous and disruptive of custom and tradition delayed legislation that would have facilitated the railroad's development. Some states even passed laws against this new form of transportation. For example, since the state of New York had gone into heavy public debt to subsidize the Erie canal, it wrote into early railroad charters and franchises restrictions that made it practically impossible for the railroads to compete with the canal barges. A tonnage tax so high as to make it impossible for railroads to carry freight was one of these restrictions. When the railroad unions became strong, they agitated in Congress to limit the length of trains and to determine the size of train crews—at the very time when improved roadbeds, more powerful locomotives, and safety devices made possible longer trains and smaller crews. This is a kind of socially induced cultural lag.

United States naval officials were highly skeptical of John Ericcson's screw propeller, and at first they flatly rejected his plans for the famous *Monitor*. The submarine was considered an insane invention; and though the first successful undersea craft was built for the United States in 1898, it was not until World War I that submarines came into general use. During the time between the two world wars, the French General Staff consistently refused to take seriously the airplane, the armored tank, and other mechanical means of military offense and defense—this despite the fact that the Germans not only were making great strides in these mechanized instruments of warfare but were in many instances making no secret of their progress. The French military leaders developed what has been called "the Maginot Line psychosis"—they considered their major preparation for war the Maginot defense system.

Through patent laws, the government gives legal protection to patentees. A patent is regarded as private property by the law, and there is nothing to force a person or corporation holding a patent to make use of it. Thus, by developing new products and processes themselves and then storing them away, corporations have been able to prevent technological advances in the interests of their prior investments, a frequent pretext being that the novel product is not worth what it would cost to make.

Inertia Among the Experts

A most interesting aspect of this entire subject is the frequent resistance of experts themselves. Scientific training is highly specialized; and people who for years have done work in one particular line, especially if they have obtained high prestige, often oppose changes if these run counter to their professional or other beliefs.

In 1826 an engineer said of the railroad that "a rate of speed of more than six miles an hour would exceed the bounds of providence," and the suggestion of John Stevens that trains might travel 20 miles an hour was met with derision. A notable instance of scientific authority invoked against an invention was the astronomer Simon Newcomb's criticism of the airplane. In 1906 Newcomb publicly declared that neither the laws of physics nor the state of the industrial arts made it practicable for man to "fly long distances through the air."

The history of modern medicine is replete with illustrations of hostility to innovations. Opposition greeted the pioneer work of Louis Pasteur in the field of bacteriology and immunology. In the study of mental diseases an interesting instance is the ridicule which greeted Dr. Sigmuud Freud when, before a distinguished group of neurologists in Vienna, he reported a case of male hysteria. He was informed in no uncertain terms by the most eminent neurologists of the day that this was impossible, since hysteria was associated only with female physical functions. Freud lived long enough to see complete verification of his contention and recognition of his competence in the field of mental disease.

Class and Community Resistance

Not only do vested economic interests, political organizations, and experts often resist cultural change, but the general population also frequently does so, often taking its justification for opposition from these other groups.

Class factors enter very thoroughly into resistance. An amusing and revealing class attitude was expressed in the English Parliament by Craven Fitzhardinge Berkeley in these words: "Nothing is more distasteful to me than to hear the echo of our hills reverberating with the hissing of railroad engines running through the heart of our hunting country, and destroying that noble sport, fox hunting, to which I have been accustomed from my childhood."[5] The royalty of Europe long opposed the substitution of automobiles for horse-drawn carriages on state occasions.

Class resistance to institutional modifications is well-known. Attempts to modify the system of private enterprise have met with recurrent criticism from the propertied classes, and agitation to abolish the capitalistic system has led to legal and violent extralegal means to silence such ideas.

The opposition of the general public at times is no less vigorous than that of the privileged classes. When the railroads first came

---

[5]Quoted by B. J. Stern in "Resistances to the Adoption of Technological Innovations," Part I, sec. 4, *Technological Trends and National Policy* (Washington, D.C.: U.S. Government Printing Office, 1937), p. 40.

ILLUSTRATIVE DATA 18-2   TWO VIEWS OF HUMAN SOCIETY AND
SOCIAL CHANGE

The Consensus View of Society	The Conflict View of Society
1. *Every society is a relatively persistent, stable structure of elements.*	1. *Every society is subject at every moment to processes of social change: social change is ubiquitous.*
2. *Every society is a well-integrated structure of elements.*	2. *Every society experiences at every moment social conflict: social conflict is ubiquitous.*
3. *Every element in a society has a function, i.e., contributes to the maintenance of the society.*	3. *Every element in a society contributes to its disintegration and change.*
4. *Every society is based on the consensus of values among its members.*	4. *Every society rests on the coercion of some of its members by others.*

Source: Adapted from Ralf Dahrendorf, "Towards a Theory of Social Conflict," *Social Change,* edited by A. Etzioni and Eva Etzioni (New York: Basic Books, Inc., 1964), p. 103.

into rather general use, preachers, merchants, and the man in the street often denounced them as instruments likely to destroy their way of life. There are numerous examples in the history of education of negative reactions to new pedagogical practices. In one community the system of staggering the time for recess so as to allow more play space for the children had to be abandoned because some parents who saw children on the playground all though the day spread the word that this "new-fangled" plan meant all play and no work. The introduction of a course of study which would lessen the emphasis on such subjects as Latin and incorporate vocational subjects, art music, and the like had to overcome opposition in community after community before being accepted.

Not every innovation is met by strong resistance, however. Many changes are facilitated by the pressure of grave economic-political crises. The establishment of the Securities and Exchange Commission, following the stock market crash of 1929, is a case in point. But on the whole, the more drastic the change, the more intense the emotional opposition is likely to be. In spite of the American belief in progress and the stress progress gets in both formal and informal education, alterations which touch our more basic values arouse anxiety, hostility, and negative feelings. The most acceptable changes are those which are in line with principles already taken for granted. The knowledge of science remains far in advance of application.

TECHNOLOGY AND INSTITUTIONS

New technological or other devices, whether originating within a society or borrowed from outside, obviously set up a network of effects. Innovations influence one another and constantly alter the culture and social structure.

Culture and Technology

The influences of innovations are both direct (primary) and indirect (secondary). Direct or primary influences are evident in such an invention as the cotton gin, which almost completely replaced former production techniques. So too, if a state changes from a representative democracy to a dictatorship, many former institutions will be liquidated and others replaced, although some old ways of doing things will continue alongside the new.

The secondary or derivative influences are even more striking. These have to do with extension of effects to other technologies and institutions or associations. For example, the cotton gin stimulated cotton raising and the large plantation system; it influenced slavery and so had a great effect on political and everyday life, not only of the South but of the North as well.

In recent decades we have witnessed profound modifications in life as a result of the introduction of motor vehicles. The automobile, at first considered a luxury, soon became a routine necessity. To mention only a few of its more obvious effects: It led to the building of hard-surfaced, all-weather roads, which permitted higher speeds. This in turn led to further improvement of highways: the elimination of sharp turns, the construction of super-highways, the production of more automobiles, and, of course, increased air pollution. Robert L. Heilbroner has described some of the effects of the automobile on the American economy this way:

> By 1905 there were 121 establishments making automobiles, and 10,000 wage earners were employed in the industry. By 1923 the number of plants had risen to 2,471, making the industry the largest in the country. In 1960 its annual payroll was as large as the national income of the United States in 1890. Not only that, but the automobile industry had become the single greatest customer for sheet steel, zinc, rubber, leather. It was the buyer of one out of every three radios produced in the nation. It absorbed twenty-five billion pounds of chemicals a year. It was the second largest user of engineering talent in the country, bowing only to national defense. It was the source of one-sixth of all consumer spending in the country. In fact, it has been estimated that no less than one job out of every seven and one business out of every six owed their existence directly or indirectly to the car.

Even this impressive array of figures by no means exhausts the impact of the internal combustion engine and its vehicular mounting. Because of the existence of the car, some fifty thousand towns managed to flourish without rail or water connections, an erstwhile impossibility. Seven out of ten workers no longer lived within walking distance of their places of employment but drove to work. Of the nation's freight tonnage, 76 per cent no longer moved by rail but by truck.[6]

New elements in a culture often have far-reaching effects. The automobile may reduce the revenue of the railroads and hence influence the consumption of coal. On the other hand, the automobile "causes" an extension of pipelines for oil, increases the consumption of gasoline, and creates a need for experts to control pollution. The introduction of two items serving the same end, such as gas and electricity for household use, sets up a struggle for dominance. Such competition serves a selective function.

The motor vehicle also influenced the displacement of draft animals on the farm and in our cities altered the importance of forage crops and pasturage in the rural economy. The automobile has increased the mobility of people—daily, seasonally, yearly. Because it increased congestion in urban centers, it aided the decentralization of population and so affected the growth of suburbs. It has influenced home life, made union school districts possible, and so on and on.

Or take the changes brought about by the radio. As early as 1933, W. F. Ogburn and S. C. Gilfillan indicated at least 150 definite effects of the radio in such categories as uniformity of programs—especially those originating in urban centers—recreation and entertainment, transportation, education, the spread of information, religion, industry and business, occupations, medicine, government and politics, and other new inventions.[7] Radio waves are used in guiding ships to port, in flying airplanes, as danger signals when navigators are in distress, and in exterminating parasites. Radio and television have also brought in new words: broadcast, newscaster, shortwave, frequency modulation, televise, high fidelity, Telstar, and Comsat.

With regard to advances in communication and transportation, modern man has not yet fully understood what increased speed through space may mean for future economic and political organization or for human personality itself. Certainly the contraction of space as measured by time may bring about great changes in many

[6]Robert L. Heilbroner, The Making of Economic Society (Englewood Cliffs, N. J.: Prentice-Hall, Inc., 1962), p. 104. Reprinted by permission.
[7]W. F. Ogburn and S. C. Gilfillan, "The Influence of Invention and Discovery," in Recent Social Trends in the United States (New York: McGraw-Hill Book Co., 1933), pp. 153–157.

of our institutions. One can only imagine the political and social changes that simultaneous worldwide telecasting may bring.

Advances in the biological sciences have also been striking. Medical research, coupled with public health programs, has eliminated contagious and infectious diseases to a degree literally undreamed of a century ago. The changes influence the age distribution of the population and hence affect the entire social structure.

Nonmaterial changes are also important, because institutional inventions have widespread effects. For example, the juvenile court system, set up in this country about 1899, has had far-reaching influence not only on the care of young delinquents but also on public attitudes toward the delinquent boy or girl. As a result, too, schools are learning to recognize misconduct among their pupils with a view to prevention of delinquency, and parents are changing their attitudes toward control of children. The juvenile court has also broadened the field of social work and instilled new ideas regarding the causes of crime in the minds of many judges and attorneys.

Material and nonmaterial changes influence one another. The nonmaterial effects of mechanical inventions are of varying degrees and kinds. The introduction of the typewriter first changed the habits of clerks, who had formerly used pen and ink. Later, it gave rise to a class of special operatives, mostly women.

Lag in Application

These examples are striking but one must not assume that invention necessarily means use. New devices often fail to become part of the technology or institutions. For example, the recall of judges, which once attracted great public interest, did not persist. So too, as noted above, resistance may long delay otherwise useful changes. With regard to technology, there are other factors to be taken into account. A new instrument or machine must be durable, simple, safe, and economical to install, operate, and repair. Then also, there must be the materials needed for its manufacture, and it generally must be capable of mass production.

The application of knowledge of nuclear physics is an interesting case in point. Its first use in war was not followed by any rapid application to peacetime industry, partly because of its possible use in future wars and partly because of the high cost of building plants and of switching over to this form of power.

INTERPRETIVE SUMMARY

No society is completely static. A culture never accepts all potential innovations, and those that are used enter at varying rates. Social need is not the only factor affecting acceptance. Material innovations are accepted more readily than concomitant changes in basic values and beliefs, regardless of need. Both material and ideological innovations may be resisted because the "run of attention" of the society lies elsewhere. Vested interests, such as business, labor, scientific groups, social classes, or communities, may resist change because of the fear of losing an investment, prestige, or other security, or inability to see that a "far-fetched" idea might work. A society's political structures, also having investments to protect or not wishing to alienate the public for other reasons, may resist change. Of course, an innovation may also be rejected because it really is not practical or relevant to a culture.

Cultures are modified in two general ways: by invention and by diffusion, wholesale or modified adoption of elements from outside cultures and from subcultures within the society. Invention is stimulated or discouraged by the factors above, as well as by the "cultural" base, which includes the cumulative knowledge, skills, and materials present in a culture at a given time. The scientific method is now an invaluable part of the cultural base of many societies. Diffusion, which is responsible for most cultural changes, is affected by the basic factors influencing all innovation and by certain other factors, notably prestige of the lending culture and immigration.

Innovations are likely to have more widespread effects than those that were specifically intended. For example, one material change may cause far-reaching changes in a culture's basic institutions and structures. Conversely, when a material innovation is accepted but necessary changes in institutions are resisted or people are unable to carry out institutional changes quickly enough, a society may undergo a long period of deleterious cultural lag or even become disorganized.

SUGGESTIONS FOR FURTHER READING

De Vries, Egbert. *Man in Rapid Social Change*. Garden City, N. Y.: Doubleday and Company, 1961. This is a brief, well-organized treatment of a wide range of changes that focuses upon economic modernization.

Dobzhansky, Theodosius. *Mankind Evolving*. New Haven: Yale University Press, 1962. This is a sophisticated discussion of the relationship between biological and social evolution.

Etzioni, Amitai, and Etzioni, Eva, eds. *Social Change: Sources, Patterns, Consequences*. New York: Basic Books, 1964. Set in an historical perspective, this collection of readings includes a stimulating introduction by the editors.

Goldschmidt, Walter. *As You Sow*. Glencoe, Ill.: The Free Press, 1947. This is a fine study of the consequences of industrialization for the character and organization of rural life in the United States.

Hoselitz, Bert F., and Moore, Wilbert E., eds. *Industrialization and Society*. Paris: UNESCO, 1963. This is a volume of papers prepared for the UNESCO Conference in 1963.

Maher, Robert F. *The New Men of Papua: A Study of Culture Change.* Madison: The University of Wisconsin Press, 1961. This book is a brilliant study of cultural change in a nonliterate society.

Mead, Margaret, ed. *Cultural Patterns and Technical Change.* New York: The New American Library of World Literature, 1955. Prepared by The World Federation for Mental Health for UNESCO, this manual deals with problems of mental health as related to the impact of modern technology on peoples who have been living in nonindustrialized societies.

Moore, Wilbert E. *Social Change.* Englewood Cliffs, N. J.: Prentice-Hall, 1963. A concise, scholarly discussion of the normality and quality of change, this book gives some attention to the extent of change and to the process of modernization. Also included is an excellent analysis of the long-standing problem of social evolution.

Ogburn, William F. *Social Change.* New York: The Viking Press, 1922. This is the classic study of social change.

Ogburn, W. F., and Nimkoff, M. F. *Technology and the Changing Family.* Boston: Houghton Mifflin Company, 1955. This is a descriptive analysis of the impact of technology on familial institutions.

Sahlins, M. B., and Service, E. R. *Evolution and Culture.* Ann Arbor: University of Michigan Press, 1960. The authors see the long-range view of social evolution as useful background material for the study of economic modernization.

Thomas, W. L., Jr., ed. *Man's Role in Changing the Face of the Earth.* Chicago: University of Chicago Press, 1956. This is an extensive symposium that covers a wide range of topics, from the biological and physiographic aspects of humanity's role in changing the face of the earth to the social and cultural.

19
Collective Behavior

People live most of their lives within the confines of normative social structure and within the routines that yield form and stability to social life. Social behavior is usually, but not always, institutionalized. Smelser reports that "in all civilizations men have thrown themselves into episodes of dramatic behavior, such as the craze, the riot, and the revolution."[1] The clash of striking workers and police that results in shouting, the destruction of property, the use of tear gas and night sticks, and personal injury is an example of behavior which is violent and not routinized by the social norms that govern more institutionalized behavior. Other less dramatic examples of collective behavior include the movie audience, the crowd leaving a football game, the skillful manipulation of public opinion by the propagandist, and the movements of minorities for equal rights and social status. The major areas of collective behavior include crowds, publics and public opinion, and social movements.

---

[1]Neil J. Smelser, *Theory of Collective Behavior* (New York: The Free Press, 1963), p. 1.

CROWD BEHAVIOR

Relatively impermanent and unstructured forms of human association are usually classified according to the intensity, frequency, duration, and focus of the interaction occurring among the people involved.

Audiences

An audience is a number of persons in physical contiguity (that is, in the same place at the same time) all of whom are subject to the same stimulus. It is therefore proper to speak of a theater audience, a football audience, or, during a sermon, a minister's audience. It is not correct, in sociological language, to refer to everyone in the United States who is watching a play on Saturday night as a television audience, because the viewers are not in physical contiguity. And even though one member of the group attending a football game is gazing into his girl friend's eyes instead of focusing on the stimulus being shared by the others, this group is still a football audience.

The intensity of interaction among the members of an audience is, in general, fairly low. On occasion, the wild screaming of others in a stadium may stimulate someone to a like response. But most of the time the members of an audience interact only at the level of being aware that others are there, and hence modifying their behavior to the extent, say, of not removing their shoes at a concert, as they might if they were not in interaction with the rest of the audience.

The focus of an audience is the common stimulus of the play, concert, baseball game, or whatever its members came to see. Because of this focus, the duration is usually relatively brief. Ordinarily, the members of an audience interact as such on only one occasion, an obvious exception being the audience with concert series tickets or season passes to sports events.

Crowds

A crowd is a number of persons interacting on only one occasion, and at a very low level of intensity. A crowd is of brief duration. The members of the group are in physical contiguity, but they seldom have a shared and definite focus; hence they are characterized by relatively random activity, or milling. After the common stimulus has been withdrawn, a group which has been an audience becomes a crowd. The people leaving a football stadium or a theater are a crowd. People standing on a street corner waiting for a bus are a crowd. A number of persons pushing past one another in a department store constitutes a crowd. They are aware of one another's presence, but their level of interaction is not at all intense. They certainly are not organized with relation to one another in a manner comparable to a club. They do not have a focus, as an audience does. Each member of the crowd may have a purpose, as in the case of a shopping crowd, but the members are not subject to a common stimulus in the same sense as are people attending a concert.

Mobs

Like crowds, mobs usually interact on only one occasion, and ordinarily for a brief time. Unlike crowds, however, mobs pitch their interaction at a high level of intensity; they are characterized by a display of emotion, usually accompanied by violent behavior. Mobs usually have a leader or leaders who help them focus their emotions and violence on a goal or target.

On a typical night in a college town, you can find an audience at the movie theater. Here is a group of persons in physical contiguity, together temporarily to focus on a common stimulus, the movie. Their interaction is not very intense; each person there is scarcely aware of the others. Yet this awareness will inhibit each person in some of his behavior: if the music on the sound track were on the radio at home, a couple might get up and dance to it; they will not do so here. On the other hand, being a group member encourages some behavior: one is more likely to laugh if the rest of the audience laughs than if he were alone.

Suppose the film breaks. Some members of the audience will whistle; others will shout. A few will throw their empty popcorn boxes at others' heads. Most people will turn to chat with their companions. Some will leave to get a drink of water or buy more popcorn. The common focus for the group is gone; people mill around. The audience has been transformed into a chattering and very loosely structured crowd.

Suppose at this point the lights go on, and the theater manager appears and says, "We can't repair the film, so there will be no movie tonight. We're sorry, but we can't give you your money back." Someone jumps up on his seat and shouts, "Let's fix him!" and with a roar the movie goers surge toward the stage to revenge themselves on the theater manager. The crowd has become a mob.

Any relatively impermanent group, such as an audience, crowd, or mob, is composed of individuals who are also members of more permanent social structures, such as families, friendship groups, and organizations. This seems obvious enough, but we sometimes forget it when emotion dims rationality. It is easy to hate a lynch mob by thinking of it as composed of bestial persons who are full-time lynch mob members. It is more difficult to understand such a mob, since its participants spend the greatest portion of their social lives as members of families and other primary groups.

The interaction which converts a crowd into a mob often seems trivial: an argument over who will dance with whom, rough treatment of a traffic violator by a policeman, the shutting off of fire hydrants around which slum children are frolicking on a hot day, an exchange of verbal insults between adolescent gang members. In recent years interracial mob behavior erupted in Rochester, Jersey City, Elizabeth, Paterson, the Dixmoor suburb of Chicago, North Philadelphia, the Bedford-Stuyvesant section of Brooklyn, and Harlem. Violence ranged from Danbury, Connecticut, to the Watts area of Los Angeles, again in east Brooklyn, Chicago, and in Cleveland, Des Moines, Omaha, and Troy, Newark, and Detroit.

A good deal is known about the social structure of slum tenements, economic discrimination, and educational deprivation that provide a basis and context for such consequences. What patterns can we identify as associated with the process of mob formation, rioting, and its aftermath?

A look at the race riots widespread in the United States in 1919 is instructive. The number of violent racial confrontations one counts in the United States that year depends on one's definition of a riot. The author of *From Race Riot to Sit-in, 1919 and the 1960's: A Study in the Connections between Conflict and Violence*[2] presents brief descriptions of sixteen others in an appendix to his book, but focuses on the seven cases where blacks and whites actively fought one another in groups: Charleston, Knoxville, Omaha, Chicago, Washington, D.C., Longview, Texas, and Elaine, Arkansas. A number of patterns emerge.

(1) Violence usually erupted during a period of stiflingly hot weather.

(2) Gangs of black and white adolescents were involved.

(3) Communists were frequently blamed for inciting the violence.

(4) Local police were rarely neutral and vigorous in enforcing the law, and were often replaced by troops.

(5) The standard post-riot public response was a demand for more repressive police action.

One of the major manifestations of mob behavior has been the lynch mob. Although many people associate lynching only with

---

[2]Arthur I. Waskow, *From Race Riot to Sit-In, 1919 and the 1960's: A Study in the Connections between Conflict and Violence* (Garden City, N. Y.: Doubleday and Co., Inc., 1966).

ILLUSTRATIVE DATA 19–1   KKK: NIGHTGOWN CRUSADERS

From 1955 through 1958 the Ku Klux Klan was revived in the South. In the wake of the revival came an outbreak of bombings, cross burnings, torchlight rallies, whippings, and beatings. For example, Judge Aaron, a mentally retarded Negro handyman, was abducted and castrated on Labor Day, 1957. Testimony at a subsequent trial revealed that the klansmen had been out to find just any Negro as their victim. Ten men, members of the Ku Klux Klan of the Confederacy, had held a special Labor Day meeting where, agitated by "integration talk" about Birmingham, they designated six of their number to find "some damn Negro to scare the hell out of." Stopping at a drugstore, the six secured razor blades and turpentine and then drove about in search of a Negro. When Aaron was sighted walking with a girl companion, the klansmen forced him into the car and drove to a Klan-built, concrete-block shelter. Here one of the klansmen, Bart A. Floyd, performed the castration as part of a test to prove himself "worthy of becoming assistant exalted cyclops." The klansmen were subsequently convicted of mayhem and given the maximum sentence of twenty years imprisonment.

In another case in 1958, in Charlotte, North Carolina, klansmen, under cover of darkness, undertook to plant a two-stick dynamite bomb at a Negro elementary school. Authorities, tipped off by an undercover agent, laid in wait at the school and apprehended the conspirators. The klansmen had planned the retaliatory venture after Lumbee Indians subjected the Klan to national ridicule—the nation's press depicted the klansmen as scampering in disarray before Lumbee war whoops and gun shots. The embarrassed Klan was out to make headlines because, according to one of the conspirators, "the Klan was dying on the vine." Authorities also implicated klansmen in church bombings in Montgomery and Atlanta, although acquittals were returned in these cases. Similarly, at least three floggings were linked with the Klan.

Source: James W. Vander Zanden, *Race Relations in Transition* (New York: Random House, 1965), pp. 37–38. Reprinted by permission of Random House, Inc.

hanging, lynching includes a broader range of violent behavior. The Tuskegee Institute, which probably has the most complete data on the subject, classifies as lynching all those events in which (1) there is legal evidence that a person was killed; (2) the victim met his death through illegal means; (3) a group participated in the killing; and (4) the group acted under the pretext of service to justice, race, or tradition.[3] The social character of lynching in the United States from 1882 (the first year for which reliable statistics are available) to 1951 are shown in Table 19-1.

---

[3]Tuskegee Institute, *1952 Negro Year Book* (Tuskegee, Alabama: The Negro Year Book Publishing Company, 1952), p. 303.

Table 19-1 Lynching in the United States, 1882–1951

	Total Number Lynched	Average Annual Number Lynched	Number Negroes Lynched	Negroes as a Percentage of those Lynched %	Number Whites Lynched	Whites as a Percentage of those Lynched %
1882–1890	1299	144.3	619	47.7	680	52.3
1891–1900	1599	155.9	1132	72.6	427	27.4
1901–1910	846	84.6	752	88.9	94	11.1
1911–1920	606	60.6	554	91.4	52	8.6
1921–1930	275	27.5	248	90.2	27	9.8
1931–1940	114	11.4	103	90.4	11	9.6
1941–1951	31	2.8	29	93.5	2	6.5
TOTAL	4730		3437	72.7	1293	27.3

SOURCE: Tuskegee Institute, 1952 *Negro Year Book* (Tuskegee, Alabama: The Negro Year Book Publishing Company, 1952), p. 278.

Crowd Behavior Control

The maintenance of social control in crowd situations is usually the responsibility of law enforcement agencies. The actions of police have sometimes contributed to crowd action, as they did with striking crowds during the period from 1890 to 1940. The police have spurred crowd behavior by demonstrating hostility to the crowd, thus making themselves a target of hostility and focus of action, by not being present in time to provide protection, or by doing little when they were on hand. The sentiment of the authorities has much to do with the action of a crowd. Many a lynching occurred because the sheriff arrived too late to protect the victims from attack.

One set of procedures for controlling and/or terminating mobs was developed by Joseph Lohman for use by police departments:

(1) Removal or isolation of the individuals involved in the precipitating incident before the crowd has begun to achieve substantial unity.

(2) Interruption of communication during the milling process by dividing the crowd into small units.

(3) Removal of the crowd leaders, if it can be done without the use of force.

(4) Distracting the attention of the crowd from its focal point by creating diversions at other points.

(5) Preventing the spread and reinforcement of the crowd by isolating it.[4]

PUBLICS AND PUBLIC OPINION

Sociologists use the concept of public in two essential ways: first, to refer to a physically dispersed number of people who share an interest in a given topic. In this sense a public is composed of a number of persons who are subject to a common stimulus but are not in physical contiguity. A public, then, is an aggregate rather than a group, because its members do not interact with one another. A speaker in an auditorium addresses an audience; a speaker on a radio broadcast addresses a public. Not all of the readers of a newspaper interact with one another; a newspaper public is therefore not a group. Accordingly, one speaks of a concert *audience,* a lecture *audience,* a movie *audience,* but of a newspaper *public,* a radio *public,* and a television *public.*

Secondly, the term public is used to refer to a collection of people

[1]Cited in Ralph H. Turner and Lewis M. Killian, *Collective Behavior* (Englewood Cliffs, N. J.: Prentice-Hall, 1957), p. 144.

who are concerned about, divided upon, and engaged in direct and indirect communication and discussion about an issue. Publics arise through spontaneous reaction to debatable issues. There is no "public" in the sense of one all-encompassing public—there are publics. Each issue has a public and there are as many publics as there are issues. Typically, different (public) issues are of concern to different segments of the society; gun control, personal property taxes, foreign trade regulations, and equal rights for women are all issues which do not concern the same people.

As the members of a public consider, discuss, and form opinions about the issue, a public opinion is developed. Although the objective of a public is to arrive at a prevailing collective opinion concerning an issue, decisions are not unanimous. When such a composite point of view is reached as the result of discussion, it is called a public opinion.

Propaganda

The formation of public opinion is never a spontaneous process left only to chance. Instead, it is shaped and influenced by propaganda. Propaganda is the deliberate use of communication to persuade people to favor one predetermined line of thought or action over another. The essence of propaganda is intent. Propagandists use an extensive repertoire of techniques to influence and control public opinion, all of which "involve either the control of fact or the control of interpretation."[5] (See Figure 19-1.)

SOCIAL MOVEMENTS

Crowds, audiences, and publics do not exhaust the major forms of collective behavior. Another major form is the social movement. Social movements refer to "a collectivity acting with some continuity to promote or resist a change in the society or group of which it it is a part."[6] Social movements "have their inception in a condition of unrest and derive their motive power on one hand from dissatisfaction with the current form of life, and on the other hand, from wishes and hopes for a new scheme or system of living."[7] Social movements include the civil rights movement, the peace movement, the ecology movement, and the feminist movement.

Like the mob, the social movement begins as a response to a

---

[5]Kingsley Davis, *Human Society* (New York: The Macmillan Company, 1949), p. 160.
[6]Turner and Killian, *Collective Behavior*, p. 308.
[7]Herbert Blumer, "Collective Behavior," in Alfred McClung Lee, ed., *Principles of Sociology*, rev. ed. (New York: Barnes and Noble, Inc., 1951), p. 199.

Figure 19-1 Propaganda: The Tricks of the Trade

 Name-calling—giving an idea a bad label—is used to make us reject and condemn the idea without examining the evidence. Symbolized by the ancient sign of condemnation used by the Vestal Virgins in the Roman Coliseum, a thumb turned down.

 Glittering generality—associating an idea with a "virtue" word—is used to make us accept and approve the idea without examining the evidence. Symbolized by a glittering gem that may or may not have much intrinsic value.

 Transfer—associating an idea with a person, image, or symbol which is respected and revered making us accept or reject the idea not on its own merit, but on the basis of the authority and prestige that has been transferred to it. Symbolized by the theatrical mask.

 Testimonial—having some loved or hated person approve or condemn a given idea. Symbolized by a seal and ribbons, the "stamp of authority."

 Plain folks—attempting to convince one's public that one's ideas are good because they are those "of the people." Symbolized by the traditional analogue for an old friend, an old shoe.

 Card-stacking—the use of only such highly selected material, whether true or false, as supports one's case. Symbolized by the ace of spades, the card traditionally used to signify treachery.

 Band wagon—"Everybody's doing it," with the implication that we must therefore "jump on the band wagon." Symbolized by a bandmaster's hat and baton, used on old-fashioned band wagons.

Source: Alfred McClung Lee and Elizabeth Briant Lee, *The Fine Art of Propaganda* (New York: Octagon Books, copyright 1939, renewed 1967). Reprinted by permission.

collectively perceived problem, something in the prevailing social order which appears unjust. But the aims and the method of the mob are more short-lived, more specific, and more intense than those of the social movement. The mob lacks the sustaining ideology, official rationale, and long-term objectives of the social movement as well as its structure and social organization.

A social movement tends to arise in response to some sort of perceived oppressive condition that members of the movement wish to overthrow or ameliorate. Social movements are unified and relatively long-lasting manifestations of collective behavior which have (1) a distinctive perspective and ideology, (2) a strong sense of solidarity and idealism, and (3) an orientation toward action. The ideology of a movement gives it direction, cohesion, and self-justification, and it offers hope and inspiration. Members of a social movement are typically persons who have a strong sense of commitment to the "cause." Social movements are a "group venture extending beyond a local community or a single event and involving a systematic effort to inaugurate changes in thought, behavior, and social relationships."[8]

LEADERSHIP AND COLLECTIVE BEHAVIOR

All in all, leadership is a combination of ability and opportunity. When class structure is rigid, dominance tends to be associated with a particular class or caste, and followership and submissiveness with membership in the lower ranks. In a democratic system, where class lines are somewhat vague and loose, leaders may and do arise from any class provided they follow the accepted patterns of the culture. Leaders in American society, however, are much more likely to be recruited from the upper and middle classes than from the lower classes.[9]

Types of Leaders

There have been many attempts to classify leaders.[10] An early effort using social role categories was E. B. Gowin's distinction between the "intellectual" and the "executive." In the former he included scientists, authors, philosophers, and artists; in the latter, corporation presidents, governors of states, high religious officials, and top trade-union officials.[11] O. L. Schwarz distinguished between "men of thought" and "men of action;"[12] and Sir Martin M. Conway, an English popularizer of social psychology, in discussing crowd behavior used a three-fold classification: "crowd representative," or group organizer; "crowd compeller," one who persuades or forces a group to follow him; and "crowd exponent," one who, perceiving the motives and frustrations of the masses, becomes their leader because he verbalizes and crystallizes their desires and shows them how to act.[13]

---

[8]C. Wendell King, *Social Movements in the United States* (New York: Random House, 1956), p. 27.
[9]See W. Lloyd Warner and James Abegglen, *Big Business Leaders in America* (New York: Harper & Brothers, 1955).
[10]Bernard M. Bass, *Leadership, Psychology, and Organizational Behavior* (New York: Harper & Brothers, 1960), pp. 86–87. Bass drew the list from L. F. Fisher, *Philosophy of Social Leadership According to Thomistic Principles* (Washington, D.C.: Catholic University Press, 1948).
[11]E. B. Gowin, *The Executive and His Control of Men* (New York: The Macmillan Co., 1915), pp. 6–7.
[12]O. L. Schwarz; *General Types of Superior Men* (Boston: Richard G. Badger, 1916).
[13]Sir Martin M. Conway, *The Crowd in Peace and War* (New York: Longmans, Green & Co., Inc., 1915).

A contemporary writer has come up with a three-way typology of "Princes," "Heroes," and "Supermen." The first are men motivated to dominate others; the second are dedicated to great and noble causes; and the third are iconoclasts who break down old norms and values.[14]

Still another typology has been proposed by Charles M. Bonjean on the basis of an empirical study of community leaders in a medium-sized city. The data consisted of ratings by known leaders and non-leaders of a specified number of local "leaders." The author found that leaders fall into three categories: (1) *"Visible leaders,"* who are playing widely perceived and accepted roles in the community. (2) *"Concealed leaders,"* who have more power or leadership function "within the leadership circle or power elite" than is commonly realized. And (3) *"symbolic leaders,"* who do not wield "as much influence in the community as the community at large thinks they do."[15]

From studies of small groups, ranging in size from three-man to six-man groups, Robert F. Bales and his co-workers found that participants differentiate between "idea specialists" and "best-liked men." While the former are highly regarded for their aid in solving problems presented to the group, they are not, on the whole, the best-liked.[16]

In his discussion of political leadership, H. D. Lasswell developed a five-fold typology: (1) The *bureaucrat*, or *administrator*, operates an institution or agency along precise, orderly, and fixed lines. (2) The *boss* is a hard-headed opportunist concerned with the manipulation of political power by direct or indirect means. (3) The *diplomat* is concerned with the manipulation of political power through suave manner, calmness, patience, and clever and sometimes insincere use of conversation and social graces. (4) The *agitator* strives for reform or revolution. He is adept in the use of programs, catchwords, and suggestive slogans. He paints the *status quo* as completely evil and decadent, the future as a new heaven on earth. And (5) the *theorist* makes a systemic analysis of his environment from which he formulates a logical and consistent picture of his world of men and events.[17]

None of these classifications of leadership is completely satisfac-

---

[14]Eugene E. Jennings, *An Anatomy of Leadership* (New York: Harper & Brothers, 1960).

[15]Charles M. Bonjean, "Community Leadership: A Case Study and Conceptual Refinement," *American Journal of Sociology*, 1963, 68: 672–81. Quotations are from page 678.

[16]See Robert F. Bales and Philip E. Slater, "Role Differentiation in Small Decision-making Groups," Chapter 5 in Talcott Parsons and Robert F. Bales, *Family, Socialization, and Interaction Process* (New York: The Free Press of Glencoe, 1955).

[17]See H. D. Lasswell, *Psychopathology and Politics* (Chicago: University of Chicago Press, 1930).

tory. Far too little is known about the causal sequences in the life course of leaders, the criteria for determining types, and the divergent historical situations in which leaders operate. Moreover, it is evident that the various classificatory schemes reflect both the culture and the personal experience of those who construct them.

Thus, whether there are general traits of leadership remains a moot question. There is one generalization we *can* make. Followers may *ascribe* to those in positions of dominance over them personality traits and powers that the latter may not possess. This is a familiar phenomenon: a distinguished natural scientist or engineer is expected by the masses to be expert also in international relations, labor-management problems, or the effect of comic books on children's conduct.

Once traits and powers are attributed to leaders, they may capitalize on these projections from their followers and assume knowledge, skill, and leadership in fields where they have no actual competence. Sometimes, too, individuals who are the beneficiaries of such projection of potency attain at least a modicum of capability in the areas in which wisdom has been attributed to them.[18]

Leadership in Mass Society

While Lasswell's classification of leaders is by no means to be regarded as final, a modification of it seems applicable to modern mass societies, both democratic and authoritarian. The three most significant types of leaders today seem to be the administrator, the expert, and the agitator. The unprecedented expansion of large-scale industry and business has placed managerial personnel in a highly strategic position in the power structure of economic enterprise. So too, the extension of political controls over new areas of social life has resulted in an increase in administrative functionaries, with all this implies as to further power of the governmental bureaucracy.[19]

Complicated industrial, political, and military systems cannot operate without the expert. His role as a specialist requires that he be completely objective, dispassionate, and unconcerned, in that role, with the moral implications of his function. While he occupies a position of control absolutely vital to the operation of a complex culture, as an expert he is set apart from the moral order. He sym-

---

[18]See Robert K. Merton, *Social Theory and Social Structure*, rev. ed. (New York: The Free Press of Glencoe, 1957), pp. 421–436.

[19]For an analysis of the growing importance of the administrative role in our military establishment, see Morris Janowitz, *The Professional Soldier, A Social and Political Portrait* (New York: The Free Press of Glencoe, 1960).

bolizes the highest degree of impersonality and segmentalization in a mass society.

On occasion the agitator will assume an important role in mass society, particularly in time of grave economic and political insecurity. In such situations the agitator easily changes into a would-be dictator and, with his appealing slogans and fine promises, may capture the support of the masses in his drive for power. If the agitator combines his talents with those of an organized revolutionary minority, he may become the agent for producing great changes, both political and economic. Often the mass of followers do not understand the changes that are brought about once the demagogue gets in power.

Relationship Between Leaders and Followers

The distribution of power among leaders and heads of organizations in a mass society suggests the whole problem of the relationship of those in positions of power to their followers. In societies where there is wide participation of the masses in politics, economic life, and religion, the role of the persuasive and responsible leader is especially vital. Such a leader crystallizes the vague feelings and attitudes of the masses when they are confronted with situations they cannot handle.

The followers find in the leader and his program an image which they can follow. So too, in setting his role and giving him prestige, they project upon the leader many qualities they believe a leader should have. Then, by identification, the followers seem to themselves to share these qualities. Their projection affects the leader, of course, who to be successful must assume these roles and accept the attendant status. As George C. Homans puts it, "The leader is the man who, on the whole, best lives up to the standard of behavior that the group values."[20] Such a leader as a *symbol* provides a focus for feeling and acting conjointly. Around him followers build up patterns of response which yield results and give much satisfaction as well.

Of course, in every society the leader is separated from his followers only in degree. He shares with them their participation in society and culture. Nevertheless, he embodies distinctiveness and variability in thought and action which the followers like and admire. The leader's behavior becomes a focus for the identification of the followers and hence makes for effective group activity and solidarity.

---

[20]George C. Homans, *The Human Group* (New York: Harcourt, Brace & Co., 1950), p. 169.

INTERPRETIVE SUMMARY

The character of collective behavior is suggested by consideration of such topics as crowds, audiences, mobs, publics, and social movements. Collective behavior refers to the relatively impermanent and unstructured activities wherein the norms and expectations that ordinarily define and limit human conduct are not operative.

An audience is a collectivity of persons in physical continuity with a common focus of attention, such as spectators at a baseball game who are in the stadium. A crowd refers to a number of persons, also in physical contiguity, but without a specific and shared focus of attention—such as a crowd leaving the baseball stadium. Mobs are collectivities where there is a high level of intense interaction and are typically characterized by violent behavior. The term "public" refers to a collection of people with the same interest who are not in physical contiguity, such as a radio public. A social movement is defined as "a collectivity acting with some continuity to promote or resist a change in the society or group of which it is a part." Social movements are the most structured and permanent forms of collective behavior.

Leadership everywhere is a combination of opportunity and ability. Followers tend to care less how their leader was chosen than how he treats them. They want above all to feel secure, which means that they want their leader to be fair, supportive, understanding, and interested in them. They will be more effective as a group if they have such a leader. This is particularly true in a highly specialized society where work is noncreative and relations impersonal; in fact, in such task-oriented groups workers will frequently band together defensively, informally choosing a leader who can fulfill needs their formal leader does not recognize. Followers feel secure with a leader who is like themselves, yet more knowledgeable and bolder.

SUGGESTIONS FOR FURTHER READING

Abel, Theodore. *The Nazi Movement.* New York: Atherton Press, 1966. This volume analyzes the rise of the Nazi movement, its history, and the social characteristics of those who participated in the movement.

Cantril, Hadley. *The Invasion from Mars.* New York: Harper and Row, 1966. Originally published in 1940, this book analyzes the effects of Orson Welles' famous Halloween broadcast, "The War of the Worlds."

Canot, Robert. *Rivers of Blood, Years of Darkness.* New York: Bantam Books, 1967. This is a study of the riot which occurred in the Watts section of Los Angeles in the mid-1960s.

Festinger, Leon; Riecken, Henry, W.; and Schachter, Stanley. *When Prophecy Fails.* Minneapolis: The University of Minnesota Press, 1956. This is a study of what happened when the prediction of a world disaster by the leaders of a marginal religious movement failed to materialize.

Gerlach, Luther P., and Hine, Virginia H. *People, Power, Change: Movements of Social Transformation.* Indianapolis: The Bobbs-Merrill Company, Inc., 1970. This is a study comparing and contrasting the Pentecostal revivalist movement with the black power movement.

Herberle, Rudolf. *Social Movements.* New York: Appleton-Century-Crofts, Inc., 1951. This is an excellent book on social movements with a historical perspective.

LeBon, Gustave. *The Crowd: A Study of the Popular Mind.* Introduction by Robert K. Merton. New York: Viking Press, 1960. This is an early classic work in the area of collective behavior.

Lee, Alfred McClung, and Lee, Elizabeth Briant. *The Fine Art of Propaganda.* New York: Octagon Books, 1972. Originally published in 1939, this small book remains one of the finest analyses of propaganda.

Smelser, Neil J. *Theory of Collective Behavior.* Glencoe, Ill.: The Free Press, 1963. This is a comprehensive and thoroughly sociological analysis of collective behavior.

Stouffer, Samuel A. *Communism, Conformity, and Civil Liberties.* New York: Doubleday and Company, 1955. This is a study of McCarthyism in the early 1950s.

Toch, Hans. *The Social Psychology of Social Movements.* Indianapolis: The Bobbs-Merrill Company, 1965. The book treats social movements of both the past and the present in a generalized manner.

Turner, Ralph, and Killian, Lewis M. *Collective Behavior.* Englewood Cliffs, N.J.: Prentice-Hall, Inc., 1957. This is an excellent textbook treatment of collective behavior.

20
Social
Deviance
and Social
Problems

Most of us live in a world of order most of the time. We live in a normative world of group-shared expectations. Yet the fact that a social group expects certain behaviors from an individual or from another group does not always mean that its expectations are met. No norm is *always* obeyed; individuals do not *always* conform to every set of expectations.

There are several reasons why the behavior of some people never conforms perfectly to the norms of the society in which they live. For one thing, norms are general, while an individual's behavior in any situation is specific. An expectation, if it is to apply to different people in varying situations over a period of time, must be conceived in quite general dimensions. Each of us learns the rules of his society as a set of broad (and usually "flat") generalizations: "You should eat meat with a fork, not with your fingers," or "Honor thy father and thy mother." But there are situations in which deviation from the norms is tolerated. One can eat meat with his fingers at a picnic, and no one would expect a starving man to eschew food because he did not have a fork. Indeed, there are situations where violation of the norm becomes itself an expectation: in many societies, the son whose father commits treason is expected to reject, not honor, his father.

THE DEFINITION OF DEVIANCE

The generalized nature of norms is only one factor which can help us explain deviation. Another is variation among individuals and groups in their perception of what the norms are and their interpretation of what they mean. It is possible, for reasons ranging from mental incompetence to geographic (and hence social) isolation, for a person to be unaware of some of the societal norms. In American society, for example, an illiterate is cut off from an important source of information about what is expected of a citizen. Many Americans are aware of the norm "Keep the sabbath day to sanctify it, as the Lord thy God hath commanded thee," but there is widespread variation in the interpretation of this rule.

Then too, norms differ in the degree to which they are considered obligatory. Considerably weaker sanctions are imposed on a person who deviates from a folkway, such as a clothing fashion, than on one who violates one of the mores. As one moves down a scale of tolerance toward the point where a custom passes from a folkway to a cultural alternative, deviance becomes more and more likely.

Cheating on examinations or term papers is not an unusual phenomenon on American college campuses. One 1966 nationwide study concluded that nearly half of all college students cheat.[1] Research reports show the following incidence of cheating by seniors: Columbia—26 per cent, Cornell—30 per cent, Fordham—52 per cent, Notre Dame—54 per cent.

When a norm is this widely violated, does it mean that it is not really a norm at all? No, because there is agreement, even among the cheaters, that cheating is wrong. Research covering a number of universities concludes that the majority of students believe that students are normally obligated not to cheat. What, then, is the difference between those who cheat and those who do not? One difference is a clearly sociological one; i.e., rates of cheating vary according to the different groups with which a student is affilated. Recent research at three colleges in an Ivy League university reveals marked differences in rates of cheating on term papers by the students' major. Following the freshman year, 42 per cent of the students in Agriculture reported cheating; 50 per cent of those in Engineering did so; but only 26 per cent of those in Arts and Sciences did. Other studies have also shown that students in vocational or career-ori-

---

[1]John Harp and Philip Taietz, "Academic Integrity and Social Structure: A Study of Cheating Among College Students," *Social Problems*, 1966, 13: 365–373.

ILLUSTRATIVE DATA 20-1   PUBLIC STEREOTYPES OF DEVIANTS

Marijuana smokers	%	Beatniks	%	Homosexuals	%	Political radicals	%
Looking for		Sloppy	57	Sexually		Ambitious	61
kicks	59	Noncon-		abnormal	72	Aggressive	47
Escapist	52	formist	46	Perverted	52	Stubborn	32
Insecure	49	Escapist	32	Mentally ill	40	Noncon-	
Lacking self-		Immature	28	Maladjusted	40	formist	32
control	41	Individ-		Effeminate	29	Impulsive	28
Frustrated	34	ualistic	27	Lonely	22	Dangerous	28
Excitement-		Lazy	27	Insecure	21	Individ-	
seeking	29	Insecure	26	Immoral	16	ualistic	26
Nervous	26	Irresponsible	20	Repulsive	14	Self-	
Maladjusted	24	Self-		Frustrated	14	interested	23
Lonely	22	interested	18	Weak-		Intelligent	22
Immature	21	False lives	16	minded	12	Irresponsible	21
Weak-		Artistic	16	Lacking-self-		Conceited	15
minded	17	Maladjusted	14	control	12	Imaginative	14
Irresponsible	15	Harmless	13	Sensual	11	Excitement-	
Mentally ill	13	Imaginative	12	Secretive	11	seeking	9
Pleasure-		Lonely	11	Over-sexed	10		
loving	11	Imitative	10	Dangerous	10		
Dangerous	11	Frustrated	10	Sinful	10		
		Happy-go-		Sensitive	10		
		lucky	9				

Source: J. L. Simmons, "Public Stereotypes of Deviants," Social Problems, XIII (Fall, 1965), p. 227. Reprinted by permission of The Society for the Study of Social Problems.

ented fields are more likely to cheat than students majoring in the humanities and that fraternity members report a higher incidence of cheating than non-fraternity members. This is true in all three colleges, but the fraternity members with the highest incidence of cheating are in Agriculture and Engineering.

One cannot understand the amount of deviance in a mass society without noting the extent to which it is the product of differing subcultures. Normative standards vary by social class, by ethnic group, by degree of urbanization, by region, by age group, by sex, and by occupation. A group-shared expectation in a company store patronized by sharecroppers in rural Arkansas may be a violation of the norms in a Park Avenue gift shop catering to wealthy New Yorkers. Taking a hubcap from an automobile in a lower-class area is stealing; taking a piece of the goal posts (much more expensive than hubcaps) after a football victory at a college stadium is only a high-spirited prank. In this case, what is or is not criminal is influenced by class position. In a multi-group society such as that of contemporary United States, with racial, ethnic, class, occupational, and regional subcultures, deviance is more than a little in the eye of the beholder.

Albert Cohen insists that "much—probably most—deviant behavior is produced by clinically normal people."[2] According to Cohen:

> ...we must always keep as our point of reference deviant behavior, not kinds of people. A major task before us is to get rid of the notion ...that the deviant, the abnormal, the pathological, and, in general, the deplorable always come wrapped in a single package.[3]

One of the most important studies in the area of deviant behavior in recent years is a provocative work by Howard Becker entitled *Outsiders: Studies in the Sociology of Deviance*. Becker does not accept society's definition that people are deviant, but he recognizes the fact that society does *label* people as deviants and that this labeling is consequential for the people who are labeled deviant. As Becker wrote:

> ...*social groups create deviance by making the rules whose infraction constitutes deviance*, and by applying those rules to particular people and labeling them as outsiders. From this point of view, deviance is *not* a quality of the act the person commits, but rather the consequence of the application by others of rules and sanctions to an "offender."[4]

Deviants are those who have been so labeled. Much, therefore, depends upon the rules of labeling and who applies the rules. Norms are not universally accepted in a large and heterogeneous society. The definition of deviance becomes a matter of social power. Older citizens set down the rules for the young; males enforce rules upon women; the middle classes define what is deviant for the poor; and white Anglo-Saxon Protestants establish rules for Indian Americans, blacks, and other minorities.

From the sociologist's point of view, it is useful to analyze deviant behavior as a function of the social structure. Rather than assuming that rural areas have a different proportion of innately deviant personalities than urban centers, or that lower-class people are more pathologically inclined than middle-class, sociologists ask what it is

---

[2]Albert K. Cohen, "The Study of Social Disorganization and Deviant Behavior," *Sociology Today*, edited by R. K. Merton, L. Broom, and L. S. Cottrell, Jr. (New York: Basic Books, Inc., 1959), p. 463.
[3]*Ibid*.
[4]Howard S. Becker, *Outsiders: Studies in the Sociology of Deviance* (New York: The Free Press, 1963), p. 9.

Table 20-1   Cultural Variation in Punishment
of Sexual Behavior

Number of Societies Measured	Percentage Punishing Given Behavior	Type of Behavior and Person Punished
54	100	Incest
82	100	Abduction of a married woman
84	99	Rape of a married woman
55	95	Rape of an unmarried woman
43	95	Sexual relations during the postpartum period
15	93	Bestiality by an adult
73	92	Sexual relations during menstruation
88	89	Adultery (the paramour punished)
93	87	Adultery (the wife punished)
22	86	Sexual relations during the lactation period
57	86	Infidelity of the fiancée
52	85	Seduction of another man's fiancée
74	85	Illegitimate impregnation (the woman punished)
62	84	Illegitimate impregnation (the man punished)
30	77	Seduction of a prenubile girl (the man punished)
44	68	Male homosexuality
49	67	Sexual relations during pregnancy
16	44	Masturbation
97	44	Premarital relations (the woman punished)
93	41	Premarital relations (the man punished)
12	33	Female homosexuality
67	10	Sexual relations with own betrothed

SOURCE: Julia S. Brown, "A Comparative Study of Deviations from Sexual Mores," *American Sociological Review,* 17 (1952), 138.

about the social structure that produced different consequences in, say, rates of drug use for laborers and professionals. In a society which honored the capacity to remove oneself from the reality known to others and to experience supernatural visions, the person we call schizophrenic might be highly esteemed as a mystic. One indication of the cultural variability regarding the definition of deviance is available from a comparative study conducted some years ago on the types of sexual behavior punished in various societies. (See Table 20-1.) All societies punish incest; two-thirds punish male homosexuality; one-third punish female homosexuality.

MODES OF ADAPTATION

Robert K. Merton has formulated a general typology of conformity and deviation. Merton contends that anomie is likely to be most severe when the culture, while prescribing certain ends or goals, leaves many individuals in positions where they do not have access to legitimate means for achieving these ends. For instance, a poor youth may turn to illegitimate means to obtain a part of the American dream when legitimate means are not available to him. Or a society may dictate that members must be literate while denying the schools, books, and teachers to large numbers of people. The consequence is severe stress for impoverished persons trying to reach the goal of literacy while having to spend most of their waking hours working to stay alive.

Merton mentions that while the society of the United States encourages everyone to aspire to wealth and social position, the culturally legitimate means are so restricted that many people —the poor, women, minorities—are denied opportunities for achieving them. In this sense, the problem is not one of people being unwilling to accept the values of the society but the inequality that prevents people from following the norms they willingly accept. According to Merton,

> It is only when a system of cultural values extols, virtually above all else, certain common success-goals for the population at large while the social structure rigorously restricts or completely closes access to approved modes of reaching these goals for a considerable part of the same population, that deviant behavior ensues on a large scale. . . .
>
> The moral mandate to achieve success thus exerts pressure to succeed, by fair means if possible and by foul means if necessary.[5]

Merton suggests five ways in which an individual can deal with the goals of his culture and the institutionalized ways of reaching them. (See Table 20-2.) A person can accept both the ends and the means for reaching them, *conformity;* one can accept the goals but reject the accepted ways of achieving them and invent methods of his own, *innovation;* one can cling to the institutionalized means as ends in themselves while forgetting the goals for which they were originally intended, *ritualism;* he can reject both his cultural goals and the forms appropriate to them, *retreatism;* or he can abandon both the cultural goals and means but take the position of a revolutionary and try to introduce new ones, *rebellion.*

While the first type is the true conformist, the third usually passes for one. Many people looked on in their society as deviants—the racketeer seeking upward mobility, for instance—constitute the second type. Retreatists include tramps, hermits, "drop-outs," and

---

[5]Robert K. Merton, "Social Structure and Anomie," in his *Social Theory and Social Structure* (The Free Press, New York, 1957), chap. 3, pp. 146, 169.

Table 20-2 A Typology of Modes of Individual Adaptation

Modes of Adaptation	Culture Goals	Institutionalized Means
I. Conformity	+	+
II. Innovation	+	−
III. Ritualism	−	+
IV. Retreatism	−	−
V. Rebellion	±	±

SOURCE: Robert K. Merton, *Social Theory and Social Structure*, rev. ed. (Glencoe, Ill.: The Free Press, 1957), p. 40.

bohemians, and the fifth type is characterized by the rebel with a cause.

Deviant behavior has impact on the social structure far beyond the deviant act itself. The process of dealing with deviants has its own consequences; jobs are created for policemen; undercover agents serve as role models for children; reformers meet their own emotional needs by ministering to others. The social structures created for the control of deviance evolve their own norms and ultimately leave their mark upon the culture in which they originate.

CRIMINAL BEHAVIOR

If sociologists are to explain the consequences of social structure, they must understand patterns of deviation from society's norms as well as patterns of adherence. A theory which accounts for conformity to the folkways and mores as a function of the way society is put together ought also to treat violation of norms as a consequence of the social structure.

Crime

To maintain internal social order, modern societies have developed written codes specifying what must or must not be done by an individual to another individual or to the state. Rules regarding wrongs committed against another individual are called torts. Taken together, they are known as civil law. Legal rules dealing with wrongs committed against the society as a whole are called criminal law; violation of one of these is a crime. Obviously, there is considerable overlap here. Some crimes are acts committed against an individual—for example, rape—but, because such crimes are considered threats to the social order, they are treated in criminal law. In the United States, crimes are divided into relatively serious violations, called felonies, and less grave offenses, known as misdemeanors.

Violation of a criminal law does not in itself constitute a crime. With few exceptions, the perpetrator of an act in violation of the criminal code must have *intended* to violate the law for his act to be considered a crime. It is this provision concerning criminal intent that is important in the definition of juvenile delinquency. In many states it is assumed that a person under a certain age (usually sixteen) is incapable of having criminal intent, and hence cannot commit a crime.

Patterns of Criminal Behavior

Statistics on crimes are not complete indicators of criminal activity. A number of crimes committed never come to the attention of law enforcement authorities. Considerably fewer than half the crimes reported to the police result in arrests. Many persons who are arrested are dismissed without ever being prosecuted in court. Of those prosecuted, many are acquitted. Given the steady filtering process between the commission of a crime and the conviction of a criminal, studying people in prison in order to learn about criminal behavior is like studying people at bankruptcy proceedings to learn about business. One can learn something about the world of business by observing the failures, but the picture will be incomplete. Similarly, one can learn something about crime by studying convicts but it should be borne in mind that the picture will be distorted and incomplete.

A study recently completed for the President's Crime Commission attempted to determine the accuracy of official crime statistics by conducting a house-to-house survey and asking people if they had been victims of certain major crimes. This "victimization rate" was then compared with the official "crime rate." The comparison showed that the official rates for murder and auto theft appeared to be quite accurate, but about half again as many robberies, twice as many serious thefts and serious assaults, three times as many burglaries, and four times as many rapes occur as FBI reports indicate. The study also found that in some central cities, the reported victimization rate was as much as ten times greater than the reported crime rate.[6]

Although the existing records are clearly inadequate, they are the only systematic data available. The best estimate of the disposition of the nearly three million crimes reported annually to police officials is as follows:

[6]James Q. Wilson, "A Reader's Guide to the Crime Commission Reports," *The Public Interest* (Fall, 1967), p. 67.

727,000 arrests made (remainder unapprehended)
440,000 cases formally presented to juvenile and adult courts (260,000 juveniles)
168,000 adults tried or plead guilty
154,000 adults sentenced:
   63,000 committed to institutions for felons
   56,000 placed on probation
   35,000 sentenced to jails or other local facilities[7]

Types of Crime

Crimes involving physical violence, while the backbone of the mystery novel trade, are relatively rare. In the United States, assault is the most frequent of those crimes committed against the person. Rape is second (counting both forcible and statutory), and the least common is felonious homicide. The Federal Bureau of Investigation lists as "major" crimes aggravated assault, auto theft, burglary, larceny, manslaughter by negligence, murder and non-negligent manslaughter, rape, and robbery. Of these, crimes against the person constitute a very small proportion, usually only about 5 per cent.

Far more numerous than assaults, rapes, or murders are crimes against property, of which the most frequent are auto theft, burglary, and larceny. Note that these crimes, unlike offenses against the person, do not necessitate face-to-face interaction between the criminal and the victim. One strong pressure to conform, internalized through the process of socialization, is the guilt an individual may feel at violating a norm in the presence of another. Thus it is not only safer but probably easier psychologically for most people to violate a social expectation when the victim is absent and anonymous.

A type of crime somewhat different from crimes against the person or against property is the crime against public safety and morals. It is in this realm that we find organized, or corporate, crime. Organized crime includes such offenses as gambling, selling narcotics, and prostitution. The peculiar features of these crimes is that the victim and the criminal often cooperate against the police and courts. For organized crime to exist, large numbers of people must patronize the criminals, and people charged with finding, arresting, prosecuting, and convicting must be failing to carry out their responsibilities.

Not all the crimes against public safety and morals occur as organized criminal activity, but probably most such offenses are in

---

[7]The President's Commission on Law Enforcement and the Administration of Justice, *The Challenge of Crime in a Free Society* (Washington, D.C.: U.S. Government Printing Office, 1967).

this pattern. It is easy to see a similarity between criminal activity and other economic activity: organized crime imitates in its organization the legitimate means of producing and distributing goods and services. The top executives in an illegal gambling operation engage in occupational role behavior not unlike that of the managers of a legitimate corporation.

Differential Rates of Crime

Sanctions, or rewards and punishments, exist to inhibit the commission of crimes. When such social controls are relatively weak, we can expect more violations of the law. As we have noted, differences among subcultures may account for variations in how seriously people view the norms. There is some evidence that crimes of violence, for example, differ by social class: middle-class people may abuse one another verbally in situations where lower-class people would use blows. There are also regional variations in the United States in crimes against the person: the South has significantly higher rates of felonious homicide, rape, and aggravated assault than the rest of the counrty. The South has also been traditionally more tolerant than the rest of the society of the expression of physical violence.[8]

It is widely believed that young people are more likely to be criminal than old people, but this is another generalization that requires cautious evaluation. In the first place, amateur or inexperienced criminals are more likely to be arrested, and hence influence crime statistics, than are older, professional criminals. Second, it is true that most persons arrested in the United States are under thirty-five years of age, but then, most people in the United States are under thirty-five years of age.

Too, nearly 90 per cent of the persons arrested in the United States are men. This sexual difference in criminality is clearly a social and cultural phenomenon. Sykes notes:

[I]t would follow that as the social status of men and women became more nearly alike, their crime rates would become more nearly alike. And, indeed, a number of comparisons bear out this line of reasoning. During the years of the Second World War women in the United States came to hold a social position more nearly like that of men, and the difference between their crime rates decreased accordingly. There is good evidence to indicate that in certain ethnic subgroups, such as

---

[8]Earl R. Moses, "Differentials in Crime Rates Between Negroes and Whites, Based on Comparisons of Four Socioeconomically Equated Areas," *American Sociological Review*, 1947, 12: 411–420.

Negroes in the United States, equality between the sexes is much increased; and among Negroes the difference between the crime rates of males and females is less than in the case of whites. It has long been argued that in large cities women play a less subordinate role than they do in small towns; and it is true that the crime rates of men and women are more alike in the former than in the latter.[9]

Probably the best predictor of criminal behavior is position in the stratification system. Occupation, race, education, income, and other indicators of one's position in the stratification structure are closely correlated with life chances. Among the consequences of low status is, for example, more frequent and direct contact with criminality.[10] It is perhaps not the years of schooling, the amount of money, or the standing of the job itself which is so important here as the intervening variables: the social factors which are themselves a consequence of low socioeconomic economic status, such as overcrowded housing in blighted neighborhoods; loss of self-respect; the squelching of ambition in a bright child attending a badly equipped and poorly staffed school; or the differential and unequal treatment which the poor and minorities receive from law enforcement officers. Police typically overestimate the arrest rates of minority groups.

SUICIDE

The frequency and meaning of suicide vary from society to society. The rate of suicides in the United States has generally declined since the turn of the century, but with some fluctuations. For example, in 1900 it was 11.5 per 100,000 population; it rose to 17.8 in 1908, dropped to little more than 10 during and after World War I, but rose to 17.4 in 1932. Since 1940 it has remained at about 10 or 11 per 100,000 (1950: 11.4; 1961: 10.4).

Suicide, at least in our Western world, is popularly thought to reflect the stress of urban living. Certainly for decades the urban rate was higher than the rural, though in recent times there is some evidence of a reversal.[11]

---

[9]Gresham M. Sykes, *Crime and Society* (New York: Random House, 1956), p. 65. By permission.
[10]This is the point of Sutherland's theory of differential association. See Edwin H. Sutherland and Donald R. Cressey, *Principles of Criminology*, 6th ed. (Philadelphia: J. B. Lippincott Co., 1960).
[11]See W. Widich Schroeder and J. Allan Beegle, "Suicide: An Instance of High Rural Rates," in *Mental Health and Mental Disorder*, Arnold M. Rose, ed. (New York: W. W. Norton Company, 1955), pp. 408–419.

Types of Suicide

The classic study of suicide was made by Émile Durkheim, the French sociologist.[12] Durkheim classified suicide into three types: anomic, egoistic, and, altruistic. The first occurs among individuals who are not closely integrated into group life, who experience a sense of what Durkheim called *anomie*—that is, a feeling of living in a world where the norms and values have broken down, a world lacking the cohesiveness and solidarity associated with an integrated society. The second type occurs among individuals who are not bound or integrated into a group. This is what Ruth Cavan calls "secret, personal suicide."[13] In sharp contrast, the altruistic suicide is a high expression of group membership, solidarity, and identification with the expected norms and values. This was amply illustrated in Ancient Rome, where it was regarded as honorable for a defeated general to fall upon his sword; in medieval Japan, where hara-kiri was both approved and expected; and in India where, until fairly recently, a widow was supposed to throw herself on her husband's funeral pyre (the suttee).

For years there was a difference of opinion about the occurrence of suicide among nonliterate peoples. Some anthropologists contended there was little suicide; others believed it to be very common and widesperad. Today most anthropologists agree with Paul Bohannan that "primitive societies vary as widely in matters of suicide as do record-keeping societies."[14]

Some writers believe that most suicide among nonliterate peoples is altruistic. This they conclude from noting practices in tribes where it is expected that the old and infirm will take their own lives. In other tribes wives kill themselves on the death of their husbands. In warring tribes the fighters may commit suicide to avoid capture or as a face-saving device. Then too, suicide may take place as expiation for the violation of some taboo or other prohibition in the mores.[15]

The Jews, Moslems, and Christians have long been conditioned to regard suicide as a sin, as a form of murder. The sacredness of human life and the doctrine that only God can give life or take it

[12]Emile Durkheim, *Suicide*. trans. John A. Spaulding and George Simpson (Glencoe, Ill.: The Free Press, 1951. Original French edition, 1897).
[13]See Ruth Cavan, *Suicide* (Chicago: University of Chicago Press, 1928), pp. 3ff.
[14]Paul J. Bohannan, ed., *African Homicide and Suicide* (Princeton: Princeton University Press, 1960), p. 23. The editor's review of the theories of homicide and suicide provides an excellent foundation for the specific discussion of these two closely related behaviors in seven African tribes.
[15]For a convenient summary of the relation of suicide to type of society, see Marshall B. Clinard, *Sociology of Deviant Behavior*, rev. ed. (New York: Rinehart & Company, Inc., 1963), pp. 408–412.

away are strongly held beliefs in these religions. When some of the teachings of the Catholic church were legalized in Europe, suicide became a crime as well as a sin. The first civil laws against suicide in England, which date from the eleventh century, provided that the offender's property be confiscated and the body denied a Christian burial.

The variation in cultural patterns, values, and norms of different countries is reflected in their suicide rates. Suicide is high in Denmark, Austria, Switzerland, Japan, and West Germany. It is very low in Northern Ireland, Scotland, Spain, Italy, the Netherlands, and Norway. The United States, England and Wales, France, and Finland fall in the middle range.

Differential Rates of Suicide

Suicide rates differ considerably according to age, sex, race, marital status, social class, and religion. Older people have a higher incidence of suicide than younger. Although people over 45 years make up only one-fifth of the population, 60 per cent of the suicides come from this group. For those 65 years or more the rate is three times as high as for those under 45. Taking one's life in later years may well be the result of weariness, ill-health, and disillusionment. When an adolescent or a lovesick young man destroys himself, it often gets great public attention, but actually the rate for young people is very low.

In our Western society suicide is much more frequent among men than among women: the ratio in the United States is approximately four to one. In older age groups the ratio of male to female incidence is even greater. It is interesting to note, however, that the rate of attempted suicide is higher for women than for men.

In the United States the rate for whites is about three times that for nonwhites. This difference is somewhat complicated by the fact that a high proportion of the Negro population has lived in the rural South, and rurality is probably a hidden variable.[16] With further increase in the number of Negroes in urban centers and with mobility pressures for status, we may witness an increase in the suicide rates for nonwhites.

Among people 20 years of age and over, the rate for married persons is much lower than that for either the single, widowed, or divorced. Furthermore, the suicide rate among childless couples is higher than among those who have children.

The rates of suicide also vary with religious affiliation, at least in

[16]See Jack P. Gibbs, "Suicide," in Robert K. Merton and Robert A. Nisbet, eds., *Contemporary Social Problems* (New York: Harcourt, Brace & Co., 1961), p. 244.

the Western world. In both Europe and America the rate for Roman Catholics is much lower than for Protestants. This may reflect the higher degree of group integration among Catholics. But for both groups the rates have tended to increase somewhat in recent decades.

Social-Psychological Factors

As a behavioral manifestation, suicide has much in common with homicide. Karl Menninger says that psychologically the act reveals three elements: a desire to kill, a desire to be killed, and a desire to die.[17] The Freudian interpretation links suicide to the "death instinct." Other social-psychological approaches have related suicide and homicide to the frustration-aggression hypothesis. A sense of blockage, stress, and tension arising from the frustration of some motive, drive, or wish may lead to an outlet through aggression. The most severe forms of this are obviously homicide and suicide.

There are many specific social-psychological factors which develop from various patterns of social interaction and lead a person to take his or her own life. Among others, ill-health, deep-seated anxieties, humiliation, feelings of inferiority, unrequited love, hostility, and guilt may contribute to the decision. Yet, as Bohannan remarked, ordinarily suicide is "not an act which occurs on the spur of the moment, but rather one which has a long explanatory history."[18]

The efforts to understand suicide have usually met with numerous obstacles. For one thing, it is difficult to get valid first-hand information: suicide notes are generally not much help. For another, survivors' explanations may be inaccurate and therefore useless. However, the cause assigned by the survivors may be a useful clue to what is considered worth living or dying for.[19] That is, it provides us insight into the values and norms of a given group or society.

DRUG ADDICTION

The federal statutes define a drug addict as any person who "habitually uses any habit-forming narcotic drug as defined . . . so as to endanger the public morals, health, safety, or welfare, or who is or has been so far addicted to the use of such habit-forming drugs as to have lost the power of self-control with reference to his addiction."[20] The chief drugs used are morphine and heroin, derived

---

[17]Karl Menninger, *Man Against Himself* (New York: Harcourt, Brace & Company, 1938), p. 71.
[18]Bohannan, p. 25.
[19]Bohannan, p. 26.
[20]Quoted by Clinard, p. 293.

from opium, and cocaine, which comes from the coca plant. From the physiological and psychological standpoint, these drugs fall into two categories: depressants and stimulants. The former decrease mental and physical activity; the latter facilitate and excite responses and reduce symptoms of fatigue. The chief depressants are morphine and heroin; the best-known stimulant is cocaine.

Judging by medical information found on Assyrian tablets, opium was widely used for therapeutic purposes as early as 4000 B.C. Its use spread throughout the Near East and later into the Classical World (Greece and Rome). During the Middle Ages, Arab physicians made extensive use of opium, and Arab traders of the time of Mohammed carried it to India. By the seventh century it had reached China.

In Europe opium was widely used in various disguised forms in medicine and confections from at least the fifteenth century. At the beginning of the nineteenth century, various European chemists succeeded in extracting certain alkaloids from the crude opium. The first was morphine, then narcotine, and finally codeine. In 1898 heroin, which is approximately three times as potent as morphine, was produced. Throughout the nineteenth century in both Europe and America opium was used for almost every known malady. The invention of the hypodermic needle in 1845 facilitated its use in both medicine and addiction.

Nonmedical Use of Opium

The personal and social problems associated with the nonmedical use of opium first appeared in those countries which cultivated the poppy: Persia, Turkey, and Arabia. Later the growing of poppies spread to India and China. The first forms of opium were the seeds of the capsule of the poppy. These were eaten or used to make a paste. Later, juice of the capsule was extracted. Smoking opium began with the Dutch in Formosa about 1800. From there it spread to China; later, Chinese laborers carried it with them wherever they migrated as a labor force.

It is not always easy to tell just when a person becomes a drug addict. Certainly the habit grows apace, but there are probably both physiological and psychological factors which make for differences in tolerance. There are physicians known to have used opiates for years without its ostensibly affecting their health or practice. Surely this too must be true of many other users. However, stress, tension, inner conflict, and other personality disturbances may facilitate more and more involvement in addiction until the personality disintegrates.[21]

---

[21]A telling description of the process of drug addiction is to be found in Alexander King, *Mine Enemy Grows Older* (New York: Simon and Schuster, Inc., 1958).

When the individual attempts to give up the habit or does cease its use altogether, there follow what are known as withdrawal symptoms. Their nature and the order of development have been stated as follows: "restlessness and depression, followed by yawning, sneezing, excessive mucous secretion, sweating, nausea, uncontrolled vomiting and purging, twitching and jerking, intense muscular cramps and pain, abdominal distress, marked circulatory and cardiac insufficiency and irregularity, face drawn and haggard, pallor deepening to grayness, exhaustion, collapse and in some cases death."[22]

Morphine and heroin account for about two-thirds of all the drug addiction in the United States. The number of addicts, according to the Federal Bureau of Narcotics, was 46,798 as of January 1, 1962. Public health doctors estimate a much higher incidence. It is said that the number of drug addicts has increased in recent times. Various government agencies and committees report that much of the increase is related to the war in Indo-China where drugs are both very available and relatively inexpensive. Drug use appears to be more prevalent in urban areas than in rural areas, more prevalent among men than women, and more prevalent among persons between the ages of 15 and 30 than any other age group.[23]

ALCOHOLISM

As noted above, alcoholism is a form of toxic psychosis. Because it has become such a serious worldwide problem, it is discussed in this separate section.

Someone has argued that alcoholic beverages probably came into use soon after prehistoric man invented a cup, beaker, bowl, or other vessel. Be that as it may, the antiquity and wide dispersion of the consumption of alcohol, in one form or another, is generally recognized although the cultural significance of this kind of drinking varies from society to society. Whether alcoholism in our modern sense is found among primitive peoples is not certain. Certainly many tribes periodically indulged in heavy drinking on various festive occasions.[24] Among literate societies there is a wide range, as illustrated by the sobriety of the Orthodox European Jews and the high incidence of drinking among the Irish. Shifts in the cultural

---

[22]From E. C. Terry, "Drug Addiction," *Encyclopedia of the Social Sciences*, 1931, 5: 246 (New York: The Macmillan Co., 1931). A literary but accurate picture of withdrawal symptoms is found in Nelson Algren, *The Man with the Golden Arm* (New York: Doubleday & Co., Inc., 1949).

[23]Much of the factual material cited in the last two paragraphs is from Clinard, pp. 295–297.

[24]See Donald Horton, "The Functions of Alcohol in Primitive Societies," in *Alcohol, Science, and Society* (New Haven: Quarterly Journal of Studies on Alcohol, 1945).

climate and definition, such as those that accompany immigration to the United States, may result in changes in drinking patterns.[25] The World Health Organization of the United Nations defines alcoholics as those "whose dependence upon alcohol has attained such a degree that it shows a noticeable mental disturbance, or an interference with their bodily or mental health, their interpersonal relations and their smooth social and economic functioning; or who show . . . signs of such development."[26] The riddle of why some heavy drinkers become alcoholics while others do not has not been fully solved, but it is now generally recognized that alcoholism is a physical disease.

There is some evidence that the incidence of alcoholism has declined in the past century. Certainly there is evidence in this country that the consumption of distilled liquors has decreased, while the drinking of beer and wine has increased. For example, in 1850 the annual per capita consumption of distilled spirits was 2.24 gallons; of malt liquors, 1.58 gallons; and of wines, 0.27 gallons. The corresponding figures for 1962 were 1.23, 15.29, and 0.91.[27] For the population over 21 years of age, estimates of those who drink range from 57 to 65 per cent. And of these the ratio of men to women is 3 to 2.

The Alcoholic Process

As with other forms of addiction, it takes time to become an alcoholic, sometimes as long as 20 years. Clinard states that what he terms "the alcoholic process" goes through four stages: (1) Early moderate drinking, usually in the company of other people. (2) Excessive drinking, in which the drinker begins to lose control of his consumption. Sometimes this begins with heavy drinking on weekends or vacations. (3) The relatively uncomplicated alcoholic stage. The individual now seems incapable of daily functioning without liquor. While he may promise over and over again to give up the habit, he is unable to do so. He resorts to lying, staying away from home at taverns and other places which dispense liquor, and spends more of his income to satisfy his craving. He begins to be a "lone drinker," to avoid his former friends. (4) The chronic stage, marked by intensive craving for liquor. As Clinard aptly puts it, "The alcoholic now drinks to live and lives to drink." He eats very little. He

---

[25]For a review of some of the literature on this topic, see Clinard, pp. 357–359.

[26]Expert Committee on Mental Health, Alcoholism Subcommittee, "Second Report," Technical Report Series, No. 48 (Geneva, Switzerland: World Health Organization, August, 1952), p. 16.

[27]Data from *Statistical Abstract of the United States*, 1963 (Washington, D.C.: U.S. Government Printing Office, 1963), p. 796.

develops a real anxiety neurosis that he will "run short" of a supply of drink. His body must have a quota of alcohol at all times. He is a sick man.[28]

Efforts to cure alcoholism have been going on for decades. Today, Alcoholics Anonymous is the best-known organization making a serious attempt to help alcoholics give up drink. The increasing recognition that alcoholism is a disease and not an indication of moral weakness should improve the attempts to deal with the problem.

MENTAL AND EMOTIONAL DISORDERS

As he matures, the individual is provided with a host of patterns or "copies" of thought and action that are defined for him as proper and good by parents, friends, teachers, employers, and others. Even mood, temperament, or disposition—whatever term one uses to describe fundamental and persistent patterns of feeling-emotional responses—must be considered, like other behavior, in the light of societal or cultural conditioning. Temperamental qualities fully accepted in one society may be considered pathological in another.

Norms are always relative, so far as the individual is concerned, first to those of the larger community, and second to those of subgroups to which he owes allegiance or with which he has a feeling of solidarity. The "normal" act or thought rests on general consensus in some particular group. This does not mean absolute conformity. All societies take cognizance of individual variations. Moreover, deviations in thought and words are often permitted so long as overt conduct conforms fairly well to the accepted and proper patterns. Usually it is only when the number of divergent features in behavior is believed excessive or when some unaccepted activity is so intense or violent as to be considered detrimental to others that it is dealt with as abnormal.

Neurosis

A *psychoneurosis*, or *neurosis*, is a form of mental and behavioral divergence from the normal which tends to make the individual less efficient socially and personally but which does not completely incapacitate him for social participation in everyday group life. Neurotic persons may express undue worries, obsessive fears, or extreme fatigue, or show hysteric responses which keep them from effective, emotionally and intellectually satisfying lives. With neu-

---

[28]Some of the data here are drawn from Clinard, pp. 341–346. See also Jessie Bernard, *Social Problems in Midcentury*, Chapter 11 (New York: The Dryden Press, 1957).

rotics there is usually no need for special hospital care; many of them, however, seek help from clinical psychologists or psychiatrists. They represent a borderline type of behavior and mentality between the normal and the psychotic.

There are various subcategories of neuroses. The three most common types are anxiety neurosis, obsessional-compulsive neurosis, and hysteria. The first may be characterized by a sense of fatigue, by fears, irritability, imaginary ailments, pessimism, and hypochondria. The second shows such symptoms as obsessive thoughts, suicidal and other compulsions, manias such as pyromania, or the impulse to set fires, and extreme fears such as claustrophobia, or fear of closed places. The third includes forms of dissociation of thought and action, of which the dual or multiple personality is the classic model.

Psychosomatic Disorders

In addition to the long-accepted classification of neuroses, there are a number of visceral and other bodily maladjustments of psychological rather than organic origin. These are known as psychosomatic disorders.[29]

The close interplay between fear, anger, and other emotions and certain bodily disturbances has long been recognized. But it is only in recent decades that specific psychogenic factors, such as frustration, anxiety, hosility, and dependency, have been positively correlated with various visceral and other bodily disorders. Obviously, not all visceral and other bodily ailments are psychosomatically induced, but it is becoming increasingly clear that a great many such disorders have a distinctly psychological foundation. For example, Miller and Baruch compared the hostility feelings of a group of allergic children with those of a nonallergic group. The latter children showed much more direct and indirect hostility to others and to themselves, and less "blocking" of restraint of overt hostility than did the allergic children.[29]

From data collected in Great Britain, J. L. Halliday has reported some interesting facts about age, sex, and class differentials and changes in the incidence of certain psychosomatic disorders. For example, during the latter part of the nineteenth century peptic ulcers and essential hypertension were predominantly female disorders. At the midpoint of the twentieth century these had become increasingly more evident in males. It is interesting also to note that exophthalmic goiter and hysteria, both of which have emotional components, have shifted to higher incidence among men. More-

---

[29]Hyman Miller and Dorothy W. Baruch, "A Study of Hostility in Allergic Children," *American Journal of Orthopsychiatry*, 1950, 20: 506–519.

over, the age incidence of gastritis, peptic ulcers, cardiovascular disorders, and anxiety states has dropped. Halliday has further shown that gastrointestinal disorders, essential hypertension, exophthalmic goiter, and rheumatism occur more frequently in urban than in rural areas. The rate of deaths from peptic ulcers is higher for both sexes in the lower occupational groups than in the professional and well-to-do classes. In hypertensive cardiovascular disorders, the death rate for males is highest in well-to-do classes but is highest for females in the poorest classes.[30] Halliday believes that these changes indicate a neutralization of former and culturally determined sex differences, but more particularly that they typify an increased complexity in modern urban living.

Indeed, it is generally thought that urbanization may well be at the root of many personal troubles and social problems. The results of a meticulous investigation which compared the rates of mental illness in Massachusetts in the mid-nineteenth century with those in the mid-twentieth century, however, found that the widespread belief that there is much more mental illness today than "in the good old days" was not supported by the data.

> When appropriate comparisons are made ... specific first admission rates for ages under 50 are revealed to be just as high during the last half of the 19th century as they are today. ... In the 19th century there was relatively a much higher concentration of admissions in the age group 20–50; and today there is relatively a high concentration in ages over 50 and more particularly over 60.[31]

Psychosis

Psychosis is a severe mental and behavioral disorder, involving so much divergence from normal conduct as to require medical and even institutional care, and often marked by disorders of mind and conduct which involve the entire makeup of the personality.[32] The psychotic frequently loses his orientation to the world around him.

[30]J. L. Halliday, *Psychosomatic Medicine: A Study of a Sick Society* (New York, W. W. Norton & Company, 1948).

[31]Herbert Goldhamer and Andrew W. Marshall, *Psychosis and Civilization* (Glencoe, Ill.: The Free Press, 1953), p. 91.

[32]For attempts to get at correlates and causes of mental breakdowns, see H. Warren Dunham, "Social Structure and Mental Disorder: Competing Hypotheses of Explanation," *Milbank Memorial Fund Quarterly*, 1961, 39: 259–311; Dorothy S. Thomas and Ben Z. Locke, "Marital Status, Education, and Occupational Differentials in Mental Disease: State Patterns in First Admissions to Mental Hospitals for All Disorders and for Schizophrenia, New York and Ohio as of 1950," *Milbank Memorial Fund Quarterly*, 1963, 41: 145–160; and Alexander H. Leighton and Jane M. Hughes, "Culture as a Causative of Mental Disorder," *Milbank Memorial Fund Quarterly*, 1961, 39: 446–488.

His acts become dangerous to others or are so divergent as to demand severe control by others. The psychotic person typically lacks insight into his conduct. In short, the psychotic individual becomes so unlike those around him that he loses practically all the socially accepted forms of interaction. The word *insane* is applied properly to those psychotics who are considered by legal definition to need institutional care. There are many psychotics, of course, who never reach the courts and who are not sent to public or private establishments for treatment.

Psychoses are traditionally divided into two large categories: the functional and the organic. Functional psychoses are those for which no obvious and easily detectable constitutional condition can be found responsible. The inception and development of this type of psychosis are considered to be largely psychological—that is, related to some inability to meet the adaptive demands of the social environment. Organic psychoses, in contrast, are those which have a detectable neurological lesion or some other physical condition as the foundation.

Functional Psychoses

The functional psychoses have been traditionally divided into schizophrenia, paranoia, and manic-depressive disorders. The first is characterized by extreme dissociation of components of the personality. (The word *schizophrenia* comes from the Greek and means a split mind.) The most distinctive feature of this disorder is gradual and insidious development of inattention and emotional indifference to the world outside the individual and growing incoherence of ideas, ending in deterioration of normal mental life. Fantasy often blossoms into most bizarre forms. Hallucinations of sight and hearing are common; delusions often appear.

The second type, *paranoia*, is marked by conceit, extreme suspiciousness, feelings of persecution, egocentricity, and projection of false ideas and intentions on other persons. The delusional system may become very elaborate, and persons and events in the paranoiac's world become misconstrued, twisted, changed, and falsified to fit into his delusions.

The third type of functional psychosis is sometimes called the cyclic or *manic-depressive*. Unlike schizophrenia and paranoia, there is no fundamental change in the personality but rather an exaggeration of tendencies already at hand. Sense of selfhood is retained, but there is marked extension of mood and emotion. There are two phases, the maniac and the depressed. The former is characterized by distractibility of ideas, flightiness, and a great pressure to be doing things. In this stage the patient seems to have boundless energy; at times there are delusions of grandeur and momentarily great rage. In contrast, the depressive phase is marked by inattention or conflict of attention and a gloomy and anxious outlook on life. The patient may attempt suicide to escape his anxiety and sense of guilt. Melancholy may be so extreme as to be marked by delusions that are sometimes paranoid in character.

Organic Psychoses

Those mental disorders in which there is some detectable brain or other neurological defect or in which there is some toxic or other physiological basis are called organic psychoses. We shall take note of the three most common: paresis, toxic psychoses, and senile dementia.

Paresis is the result of brain tissue injury caused by syphilitic infection. It is marked by gradual deterioration: loss of sound judgment, loss of insight, and development of delusions. The paretic may make foolhardy business deals, show no regard for the canons of conventional morality, and even commit serious offenses against persons and property quite out of keeping with his previous behavior. In the later stages of paresis there may be definite clouding of consciousness and a dreamlike disorientation to time and place. Reports indicate that only 4 or 5 per cent of those known to be infected with syphilis become paretic. Moreover, it is said that one-fifth of those diagnosed as paretic show no sign of syphilitic infection. The immediate background of this mental breakdown may be any one or a combination of the following: emotional stress, overwork, alcoholism, sexual excess, and other highly deviant behavior manifestations. Here, as in other organic disorders, we must reckon with both constitutional and social-psychological factors.

The *toxic psychoses* cover a wide range of mental disturbances derived from fever, nutritional deficiences, lead poisoning and carbon-monoxide poisoning. The symptoms differ with the particular cause. For example, those arising from fever often show severe delirium, with which are associated nightmares, restlessness, and excitement. *Senile dementia* is by definition the psychosis of old age. It may be marked by loss of memory, of ability to concentrate, and by egocentricity, insomnia, often hostility, and occasionally some paranoidal reactions.

INTERPRETIVE SUMMARY

No society expects all members to conform to all of its norms all of the time. Norms do not apply to all situations; they vary in importance and often conflict with subcultural norms. Deviance, then, is behavior that violates the norms of a given group or society in a given situation. The types of behavior labeled deviant are largely functions of the definition and interpretation of norms by various groups in various situations.

Merton has developed a typology of deviant behavior which seems applicable to those situations in which an individual is mentally and intellectually capable of recognizing society's goals. He says that while conformists work for accepted goals in accepted ways, deviants either use unacceptable tactics or actively attempt to change the goals.

Crimes which are considered serious in the United States are those involving violence against individuals, crimes against property, and crimes threatening the public safety and morals. However, criminal behavior as defined by a wider society may be accepted behavior in a subculture. In the United States, for example, there are class and regional differences in rates and kinds of crimes. Statistics concerning age differentials are necessarily inaccurate, but men seem to engage in this type of behavior more frequently than women.

Widespread patterns of deviant behavior include suicide, alcoholism, and drug addiction. Emile Durkheim has noted two extremes in suicide patterns: suicide by individuals who feel alone or confused and suicide by individuals who feel so closely integrated in their society that they are willing to kill themselves if the norms so dictate. Suicide rates and motivations vary among and within societies. In the United States, there are age, racial, religious, and other differentials.

Drug addiction and alcoholism are similar in several ways. Neither is of recent origin; both are widespread. In each case addiction is gradual. In each, tolerance varies among individuals. In the United States, more men than women are addicts or alcoholics and more young people than old people are addicted to drugs and alcohol.

An individual may for some reason be unaware of a norm or all norms. Similarly, people with mental disorders may deviate. Neurotic individuals are those who are disturbed to the point of crippling their own effectiveness. Such persons are still able to participate in society. Psychotics are those who are so severely disturbed, whether for organic or socio-psychological reasons, that they cannot carry on everyday interaction.

SUGGESTIONS FOR FURTHER READING

Becker, Howard S. *Outsiders: Studies in the Sociology of Deviance*. New York: Free Press, 1963. This is an excellent and well-written volume on deviance.

Bell, Daniel. *The End of Ideology*. Glencoe, Ill.: The Free Press, 1960. This volume contains three excellent chapters on crime in the United States: "Crime as an American Way of Life," on organized crime as a route to social mobility for immigrant minorities; "The Myth of Crime Waves;" and "The Racketridden Longshoremen," on the symbiotic relationship between legitimate businessmen and labor racketeers.

Cressey, Donald R. *Theft of a Nation*. New York: Harper and Row, 1969. This is a comprehensive examination of organized crime in the United States.

Douglas, Jack D. *The Social Meaning of Suicide.* Princeton, N. J.: Princeton University Press, 1967. The volume summarizes much of the theory and research on suicide.

Durkheim, Émile. *Suicide.* Glencoe, Ill.: Free Press, 1947. First published in 1897, this classic would be rated by most sociologists as one of the most influential sociological studies ever written.

Erikson, Kai T. *Wayward Puritans: A Study in the Sociology of Deviance.* New York: John Wiley and Sons, 1966. In this sociological-historical study, Erikson assesses the idea that the function of deviance is to define the normative boundaries of the group.

Goffman, Erving. *Stigma: Notes on the Management of Spoiled Identity.* Englewood Cliffs, N. J.: Prentice-Hall, 1963. This is an essay on the process of stigmatization.

Hollingshead, August B., and Redlich, Frederick C. *Social Class and Mental Illness: A Community Study.* New York: John Wiley and Sons, 1958. This is the report of one part of a large research project conducted by a team of social scientists and psychiatrists on the interrelationships between social stratification and mental illness in New Haven, Connecticut.

Matza, David. *Delinquency and Drift.* New York: John Wiley and Sons, 1964. This book is a fascinating and controversial theoretical contribution to the understanding of juvenile delinquency.

Short, James F., and Strodtbeck, Fred L. *Group Process and Gang Delinquency.* Chicago: University of Chicago Press, 1965. A detailed multivariate analysis of the structure and functions of sixteen Chicago gangs ranging from sixteen to sixty-eight members, this study presents data on home background of gang members and their everyday activities and attitudes.

Sutherland, Edwin H. *White Collar Crime.* New York: Dryden Press, 1949. This is the most famous work of one of the leading criminologists in the United States.

Yablonsky, Lewis. *The Violent Gang.* New York: Macmillan, 1962. Based on a four year study of youth killer gangs in New York City's upper West Side, this book focuses on two particular gangs.

Glossary

Accommodation   Used in two senses: As a condition, a state of equilibrium between individuals or groups in which certain working arrangements have been agreed upon or accepted. As a process, the social adjustment between individuals or groups, aimed at the temporary suspension of conflict. Also called "antagonistic cooperation." Some common forms of accommodation are tolerant participation, compromise, arbitration, and conciliation.

Acculturation   The merging of two or more cultures, ranging from accommodative arrangements to full assimilation or synthesis of cultures. The entire sequence of processes involved in the contact and subsequent intermixture of the traits and patterns of two or more cultures.

Aggregate   A number of persons who are classified together because they share some characteristic, but who do not necessarily interact with one another.

Amalgamation   The biological union of previously distinct racial or subracial groups.

537

Animism   The belief that all things, animate and inanimate, are endowed with personal power or souls.

Anomie   A condition of society marked by normlessness or lack of values and goals; characteristic of some members of mass society.

Assimilation   The fusion of divergent habits, attitudes, and ideas of two or more groups or societies into a common set of habits, attitudes, and ideas.

Association   A general term to describe a group of interacting persons; sometimes used to mean a consciously formed group, usually of a secondary sort. Also used to designate a special-interest group—for example, a trade association.

Attitude   The predisposition or tendency to react typically towards an object, situation, or value; usually accompanied by feelings and emotions.

Audience   A number of persons in physical contiguity all of whom are subject to the same stimulus.

Bureaucracy   A formal, rationally organized social structure involving clearly defined patterns of activity, characterized by rules, a hierarchy of offices, and centralized authority.

Capital goods   Those economic goods or forms of wealth used in the production of consumer goods.

Caste   A closed, endogamous category resulting from stratification in which status in a hierarchy of power relations is defined and permanently fixed by ancestry.

Class   A category resulting from stratification in which the status, while often determined at birth or during early life, is not so completely or irrevocably fixed as in caste.

Community   A group living in a given locality or region under the same culture and having a distinctive geographical focus for their major activities.

Competition   The act of striving for some object that is sought for by others at the same time; a contention of two or more persons or groups for the same object or goal.

Conflict   Direct and open antagonistic struggle of persons or groups for the same object or end. The aim of the conflict is the annihilation, defeat, or subjection of the other person or group as a way of obtaining the goal.

Congeniality group   A group which is formed and persists simply because friendships arise out of repeated association and shared interests or experiences.

Conjugal family A form of family organization in which the typical household consists only of parents and their dependent children.

Consanguine family A form of family organization in which several generations make up a single household.

Consensus General accord or agreement in matters of opinion, belief, values, and attitudes.

Consumer goods Economic goods or wealth produced for direct consumption, not for the production of other goods.

Cooperation Joint action or working or playing together for an object or end which may be shared; mutual aid.

Crowd A number of persons whose interaction is of brief duration and low intensity. The members are in physical contiguity but seldom share the specific focus typical of an audience.

Cultural alternatives Various possibilities of action with reference to the same object, situation, or problem, all of which are approved by the society in question. In other words, the group or the individual has a choice among a number of permitted courses of action.

Cultural lag A condition of disequilibrium arising out of an unequal or uneven rate of change in two or more cultural elements which are functionally interrelated.

Cultural learning Learning which is predetermined by the culture patterns of a group or society.

Culture The shared and learned recurrent patterns of behavior which people acquire as members of society.

Culture pattern Two or more separate units or traits of culture organized into some more or less constant form of configuration.

Culture system The large and more or less integrated patterns of culture which characterize a given society or civilization—for example, Oriental as contrasted with Occidental, or Classical as compared with Medieval.

Definition of the situation An individual's perception of an object or feature of the environment which influences his attitudes, ideas, and actions. It is related to anticipatory reactions or expectancies. Such a prior definition is usually culturally determined.

Demography The sociological and statistical study of human populations with particular reference to births, deaths, and migration.

Deviant behavior   Behavior which is defined as departing from or running counter to the norm and the accepted and expected ways of a group or society.

Differentiation   The process of developing different sets of rights and duties associated with various statuses.

Diffusion   The spread in space of culture patterns from one society to another.

Discovery   The perception of relations among elements not previously recognized or understood.

Division of labor   A concept used in the discussion of social organization to refer to the differentiation of roles.

Elite   The dominant and powerful prestige-bearing and prestige-receiving class within society.

Endogamy   Marriage within the tribe, class, or group.

Esteem   The evaluation of an individual's role behavior in a given status; the community judgment of how well one fulfills the expectations of his or her role.

Ethnic category   A number of people originally associated with a particular geographic area and sharing a common cultural heritage.

Ethnocentrism   Belief that one's race, society, culture, etc. is superior to all others; the tendency to judge other cultures by the standards prevalent in one's own.

Ethos   Those predominant characteristics of a whole culture system which distinguish it from other culture systems.

Exogamy   Marriage outside the tribe, class, or group.

Fecundity   The potential capacity for reproduction.

Fertility   Indication of the actual use of powers of fecundity; measured by the rate of reproduction.

Folk society   A social structure characterized by a small number of people living in relative social isolation; the entire society tends toward being a primary group, with such cultural features as familism, a strong sense of unity, and informal sanctions.

Folkways   Norms which can be violated without stringent punishment; minor rules of behavior.

Function   The activity or consequence associated with a structure.

Group   A plurality of persons involved in a pattern of social interaction (and shared understandings), conscious of sharing common membership and accepting the rights and obligations that accrue only to members.

Ideal-type   An analytical construct of a "pure" form of some social phenomena.

In-group   Any group toward which a person has a strong sense of belonging and of common ends; developed by identification. The opposite of out-group.

Invention   A combination of known elements or devices into some new form.

Labor force   That fraction of a society's population which is engaged in producing and distributing goods and services for remuneration.

Laissez faire   Literally, to let people do as they please or choose. In economics, a theory that economic behavior should not be regulated by governmental or other community controls or interferences.

Legend   A form of social myth based, in part, on historical fact, dealing chiefly with heroes and events related to the successes and failures of a group or society.

Life chances   The probability of an individual's having any given experience, as they are influenced by his or her class.

Magic   A practice believed to produce effects by the assistance of supernatural beings or by a mastery of secret forces in nature.

Marginal man   A person who participates in two different cultures without being totally accepted in either.

Mass society   Modern populations which are characterized chiefly by secondary-group contacts, by high specialization of role and status, by anonymity, high mobility, and impersonal relationships generally.

Matrilineal   The family form in which descent is traced through the mother's lineage.

Migration   The movement of individuals or groups in space.

Minority   A number of persons defined as a social category and excluded from full participation in the culture.

Mob   An emotionally aroused crowd with some purpose such as attack on a person, a group, or property; or such as escape from danger—for example, a panic crowd.

Monogamy The marriage form in which the norms require the union of one man and one woman.

Mores Norms which have strong moral meaning and whose violation results in severe sanctions.

Mortality The death rate; usually computed as the number of persons per thousand who die in a given year.

Myths Stories and descriptions, largely of an imaginative nature, which provide a group with the meaning of their life and culture. Myths represent the fundamental beliefs, convictions, and values of a group.

Neurosis A mild mental disorder which interferes with effective and normally expected behaviors. It is illustrated by compulsive habits, undue anxieties, and dissociative responses.

Norms Group-shared expectations, beliefs, etc.

Out-group Any group toward which a person feels a strong sense of avoidance or opposition. Opposite of in-group.

Patrilineal The family form in which descent is traced through the father's lineage.

Personality Totality of habits, attitudes, ideas, and characteristics of an individual which grow out of the interplay between one's constitutional make-up and one's role and status in the various groups of which one is a member and which determine one's sense of self.

Polyandry The marriage form in which the norms permit the union of one woman with two or more men.

Polygyny The marriage form in which the norms permit the union of one man with two or more women. Popularly known as "polygamy."

Positive checks Anything which increases the death rate.

Power The ability of a group or person to control the activities of others, even against their own will.

Prejudice Culturally predetermined biased attitude toward or conception of a person or group.

Prestige The evaluation of a status; the judgment within a society's norms of the desirability of a given status.

Preventive checks   Anything which decreases the birth rate.

Primary group   Basic social group operating through intimate, face-to-face contacts. The source of the early personal-social and cultural training which the individual receives from others; for example, the family, neighborhood, and play group.

Process   A series of changes taking place through time in a definite manner; the dynamics which occur in a structure, function, or pattern.

Propaganda   Open or veiled suggestions and other means of inducing modification or acceptance of certain beliefs, attitudes, and practices.

Psychosis   A severe and usually specific mental disorder which so seriously interferes with normal behaviors as to warrant nursing or medical care, either enforced or voluntary.

Public   An aggregation of individuals, not necessarily contiguous in space or time, held together through some more or less common interest or common stimulus.

Race   A main biological division of the human species the members of which have several physical traits in common. There are usually a number of "composite" and subraces with somewhat distinctive physical characteristics within the larger categories. Race is often confused with society and culture.

Region   A large area possessing considerable geographic and cultural unity.

Regionalism   A theory of, as well as a program regarding, the place of the region within the larger society of which it is a part.

Resource   A potential good or service, determined largely by the state of the culture and the social expectancies.

Role   The function of a status; the expectations which are a consequence of occupying a given position in a social structure.

Sanctions   The rewards or punishments used to enforce the norms in a society.

Secondary group   Group founded on conscious common interest, not necessarily dependent on face-to-face relations. Many secondary groups are related to institutions—for example, state, church, and education.

Self   The sense of individuality built up from drives and cycles of activity as they become associated with role-taking, with getting status, and with learning to view one's habits, attitudes, and ideas as other people do.

Sibling   One of two or more children of the same parents; not necessarily of the same birth or sex.

Situs   A set of related occupational specialties arranged hierarchically.

Social control   Power over members of a group through group-accepted codes, or power over a smaller group by a larger, more inclusive group.

Social distance   A term to express the idea of gradation of one's own group and its values with respect to those of another group; measured by the degree of acceptance and intimacy of contact.

Social expectancy   The belief or expectation that another or others will perform a certain act or take a particular attitude; developed from anticipatory responses built up in social interaction.

Social institution   A set of related norms integrated around a principal function of the society.

Social interaction   Action and/or communication between individuals involving reciprocal stimulation and response. Relationships set up between two or more people in regard to each other or in regard to some object or situation.

Social mobility   Movement from status to status within the social structure.

Social organization   More or less standardized or conventionalized form or structure of group life.

Social process   Mode of action, operation, or interaction among individuals or groups.

Social stratification   The unequal distribution of the valued things in society which persists over time.

Socialization   The interactional process by which the individual learns the social-cultural qualities (habits, ideas, attitudes, and so on) that make him or her a member of society and hence a human being.

Society   The general term for people living in social interaction. More specifically, the largest social group or aggregate in which more or less common culture patterns are found, covering the fundamental institutions.

Sociology   The scientific study of the social aspects of human life; the analysis of the structure of social life—the way in which groups are put together—and the way in which they function.

Specialization   A differentiated role based on special knowledge and skill.

Status A position in a social structure.

Stereotype A group-accepted but logically false or empirically inaccurate image or concept, usually expressed as a cliché, with which is associated a strong feeling-emotional tone.

Structure The way the parts of a whole are put together; the relationship of the parts to one another.

Subculture Shared, learned patterns of behavior common to a specific group or category within the larger society.

Symbol Any object, picture, gesture, sign, mark, printed or written matter, or sound which stands for another or serves to recall another, and which directs mental and actional associations.

Urban society A social structure characterized by large size and great density of population, heterogeneity, a complex division of labor, much relatively impersonal interaction, formal sanctions, and a proliferation of secondary groups.

Urbanism Culture patterns associated with urban society.

Urbanization The process of becoming urban.

Values The quality of desirability (or undesirability) believed to inhere in an idea, object, or action. Values are accepted, in time, by the group in certain orders of priority.

Author Index

Crozier, Michel, 199

Dahrendorf, Ralf, 490
Dallin, David, 277
Darwin, Charles, 92
Davidson, P. E., 298, 301
Davie, Maurice R., 258
Davis, Allison, 286
Davis, Kingsley, 50, 109, 137, 138, 205, 208, 242, 243, 247, 292, 469, 504
Day, Katherine H., 401
De Beauvoir, Simone, 335
Demerath, N. J. III, 467, 470
Denny, Reul, 152
De Vries, Egbert, 494
Dewey, Richard, 262
Dewhurst, J. Frederic, 229
Dickson, William, 194, 199
Dobzhansky, Theodosius, 105, 494
Dodge, Norton, 335
Doob, L. W., 56, 61
Dorn, Harold F., 202
Dornbusch, Sanford M., 471
Douglas, Jack D., 536
Drake, Joseph T., 126
Drucker, Peter, 195
Dubin, Louis I., 113
Dubin, Robert, 76
Duncan, Beverly, 268
Duncan, Hugh Dalziel, 151
Duncan, Otis Dudley, 231, 232, 268, 298, 302, 305
Dunham, H. Warren, 532
Dunn, E. S., Jr., 269
Durkheim, Emile, 113, 163, 177, 362, 443, 524, 536
Dynes, Russell R., 460

Edwards, Allen D., 238, 241
Eells, Kenneth, 282
Ehrlich, Anne H., 231
Ehrlich, Paul, 231
Eliot, George, 4
Ellsworth, John S., 402
Ennis, J. Harold, 383
Erikson, Kai T., 536
Etzioni, Amitai, 199, 490, 494
Etzioni, Eva, 490, 494
Evans, Bergen, 23, 137

Faris, Robert E. L., 23
Farley, Reynolds, 327, 328, 329
Fava, Sylvia Fleis, 261, 268
Fei, Hsaio-Tung, 124, 125
Feinhandler, Sherwin J., 383
Festinger, Leon, 510
Firey, Walter, 258
Fisher, L. F., 506
Form, William H., 91, 121, 362
Frazier, E. Franklin, 75, 335, 412

Freedman, Mervin B., 441
Freeman, Linton C., 294, 383, 407
Freud, Sigmund, 467
Fried, M. H., 124
Friedenberg, Edgar Z., 126
Friedman, Milton, 362
Friedrichs, Robert W., 23

Gabain, Majorie, 151
Galbraith, John Kenneth, 181, 362
Gallup, George, 303
Gardner, B. B., 286
Gardner, M. R., 286
Geertz, Clifford, 178
Gendell, Murray, 433
George, Charles H., 13
George, Katherine, 13
Gerlach, Luther P., 511
Gerth, Hans H., 184, 289
Gibbs, Jack P., 97, 247, 525
Giddings, Franklin Henry, 44
Gilfillan, S. C., 492
Gillespie, James M., 466
Gist, Noel P., 261, 268
Glazer, Nathan, 152, 329
Glenn, Norval D., 334
Glick, Paul C., 401, 402, 412, 466
Glock, Charles Y., 451, 471
Goffman, Erving, 151, 536
Goldhamer, Herbert, 532
Goldman, Irving, 64
Goldschmidt, Walter, 494
Goldsen, Rose K., 467
Goldthorpe, J. E., 405
Goncharov, N. K., 423
Goode, William J., 178, 412
Goodman, Mary Ellen, 303
Gordon, Albert I., 317, 412
Gordon, John E., 209
Gordon, Margaret S., 279
Gordon, Milton M., 75
Gordis, Robert, 462
Gould, Julius, 115
Gouldner, Alvin W., 23, 199
Gowin, E. B., 506
Greeley, Andrew M., 330
Greene, Fred, 276
Greenwood, Ernest, 10
Greer, Scott, 50, 254, 268, 363, 387
Grier, George, 329
Grigsby, William G., 329
Gross, Neal, 126, 441
Grutzner, Charles, 260, 264

Haas, Robert, 113
Habenstein, Robert W., 126
Hagstrom, Warren O., 383
Hall, Edward, T., 151
Halliday, J. L., 532
Handlin, Oscar, 231

Subject Index

Accommodation, 69
  forms of, 69–72

Acculturation, 73–74

Achieved status, 39–41
  in class structure, 278
  and mobility ethic, 296

Age
  and marriage patterns, 404
  median, of population, 224
  role in mate selection, 401–403
  role of various groups, 31–35

Aged
  in labor force, 355
  social status of, 34–35
  role in family, 35

Agriculture
  as type of community, 239–241
  labor force in, 356

Alcoholism, 528–530

Ascribed status, 30–31, 35–39

Assimilation
  cultural problems in, 252
  definition of, 72
  of minority groups, 325–327
  in urban centers, 252

Audiences, 498

Automation
  effect on labor force, 357

Behavior
  of audiences, 498
  as controlled by sanctions, 102
  criminal, 519–523
  of crowds, 498–503
  cultural uniformity, 92
  as determined by culture, 80–81
  of mobs, 499–502

Birth rates
  in Europe, 215
  and social class, 293–294

Bureaucracy, 181–198
  consequences of, 194–198
  personality of, 197–198
  rules and regulations in, 189
  and social control, 184
  social sources of, 184–186
  social structure of, 184, 191–192
  Weber's "ideal type," 186–190

Capital
  definition, 339

Careers
  in bureaucracy, 190
  and social mobility, 301

Caste
  in Mediterranean societies, 276
  and social stratification, 273–276

Censorship, 104

Census
  of cities, 259–260
  in urban analysis, 254–255

Ceremony
  in religion, 450

Change
  cultural and social, 475–494
  discovery and, 476
  emotional reaction to, 15–16
  and invention, 476
  race relations and, 330–333
  and science, 478–479

Children
  and divorce, 409
  feral, 137
  institutional effects on, 141–145

Church, 445–457
  and community, 456–457
  classification of, 446
  definition of, 445
  sect differences in, 446–447
  see also Religion

Cities, see Urban Society

552